IRIS MURDOCH

IRIS MURDOCH

A Life

PETER J. CONRADI

W. W. NORTON & COMPANY

New York • London

For information about permission to reproduce
selections from this book, write to Permissions,
W. W. Norton & Company, Inc., 500 Fifth Avenue,
New York, NY 10110

The text of this book is composed in
PostScript Linotype Baskerville
Manufacturing by The Haddon Craftsmen, Inc.
Production manager: Leelo Märjamaa-Reintal

Library of Congress Cataloging-in-Publication Data

Conradi, Peter J., 1945–
Iris Murdoch : a life / Peter J. Conradi.—1st American ed.
p. cm.
Originally published: London : HarperCollins Publishers, 2001.
Includes bibliographical references and index.
ISBN 0-393-04875-6
1. Murdoch, Iris. 2. Novelists, English—20th century—
Biography. 3. Philosophers—Great Britain—Biography. I. Title.

PR6063.U7 Z629 2001
823'.914—dc21
[B]   2001032972

W. W. Norton & Company, Inc.
500 Fifth Avenue, New York, N.Y. 10110
www.wwnorton.com

W. W. Norton & Company Ltd., Castle House
75/76 Wells Street, London W1T 3QT

1 2 3 4 5 6 7 8 9 0

For John Bayley and for Philippa Foot

CONTENTS

PART III: Wise Child: 1956–1999

ILLUSTRATIONS

Unless otherwise indicated, all photographs are from Iris Murdoch's albums.

IM's mother, Irene ('Rene') Alice Cooper Murdoch, *née* Richardson.

IM's father, Wills John Hughes Murdoch, 1918.

Rene and Hughes in Ireland, *c.*1930.

Rene, Hughes and baby Iris.

Rene and Iris, aged two, Dalkey, August 1921.

Family seaside picnic on Portstewart strand, mid-1930s. *(Sybil Livingston)*

Cousin Victor Bell, Rene, IM, *c.*1933.

4 Eastbourne Road, Chiswick.

In the back garden at Eastbourne Road, *c.*1927.

'The Powers' at Badminton School: 'Ski' Webb-Johnson, music mistress; housemistress Lucy Rendall ('LJR'); headmistress Beatrice May Baker ('BMB'). *(Leila Eveleigh)*

Badminton, summer 1937: Anne Leech, Marion Finch, IM. *(Leila Eveleigh)*

BMB in later years. *(Janet Stone)*

Group portrait, Somerville College, Oxford, 1938. *(By kind permission of Somerville College, Oxford)*

The Magpie Players, Bucklebury, 22 August 1939. *(Hulton Getty)*

The Magpie Players, 'Play of the Weather'. *(Hulton Getty)*

IM and Joanne Yexley on the Magpies tour. *(Hulton Getty)*

A postcard home on the brink of war, 30 August 1939.

IM in the grounds of Somerville. *(Margaret Stanier)*

'Gentle lioness' look, 1939.

Eduard Fraenkel. *(The British Academy)*

Donald MacKinnon. *(The British Academy/Laird Parker)*

Philippa Bosanquet, 1942.

Michael (M.R.D.) Foot, summer 1943.

Seaforth Place.
Noel Eldridge. *(Lilian Eldridge)*
'Tommy' Balogh.
Frank Thompson with his parents and younger brother Edward
  (Palmer), 1939. *(Dorothy Thompson)*
Second Lieutenant Thompson in the Libyan desert, spring 1942.
  (Dorothy Thompson)
Captain Thompson, SOE, Cairo, late 1943. *(Dorothy Thompson)*

Hochsteingasse displaced persons student camp, 21 July 1946. *(John
  Corsellis)*
Officer Murdoch, UNRRA Grade 7, at Hochsteingasse, summer
  1946.
Marija and Jože Jančar, 1948.*(John Corsellis)*
David Hicks. *(Tom Hicks)*
'Nadir'. IM in Oxford Street, winter 1946–47.
Wallace Robson. *(Mrs Anne Robson)*
IM with Hal Lidderdale in London, *c.*1947.
With Arnoldo Momigliano in Italy.
Three snapshots taken by Franz Steiner in June 1952. *(Franz Steiner.
  Second and third photographs provided by Jeremy Adler)*
Conversation in the Library, 1950, by Marie-Louise von Motesiczky.
  (Schiller Nationalmuseum, Marbach-am-Neckar, and *Marie-Louise von
  Motesiczky Trust)*
Elias Canetti, 1963. *(Marie-Louise von Motesiczky Trust)*
John Bayley and IM, St Antony's, July 1954.
IM, *c.*1954.
Eddy Sackville-West, Elizabeth Bowen and IM at Bowen's Court,
  July 1956. *(Finlay Colley)*
Dinner at Bowen's Court. *(Finlay Colley)*

Cedar Lodge, Steeple Aston. *(Janet Stone)*
Bayley and IM at Cedar Lodge. *(Reggie Livingston)*
Bayley and IM in the grounds of Cedar Lodge. *(Janet Stone)*
'Report reading at St Anne's, 1958'. *(By kind permission of St Anne's
  College, Oxford)*
Yorick Smythies. *(Peg Smythies)*
Peter Ady.
Lucy Klatschko/Sister Marian.
David Morgan. *(David Morgan)*

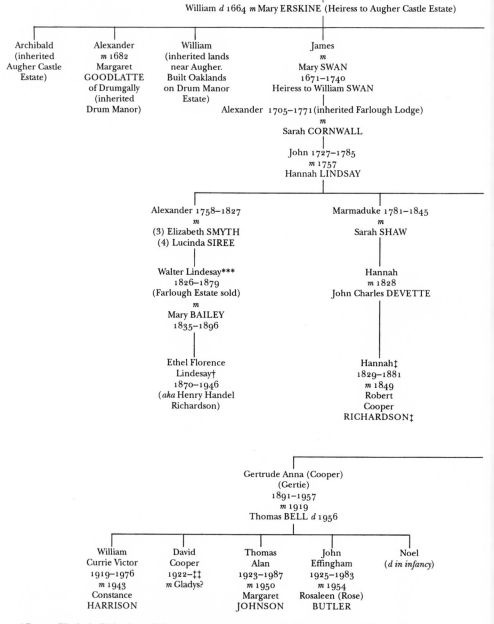

Alexander RICHARDSON
Living in Crayhalloch
Granted Drum Manor by James I

William *d* 1664 *m* Mary ERSKINE (Heiress to Augher Castle Estate)

Archibald
(inherited
Augher Castle
Estate)

Alexander
m 1682
Margaret
GOODLATTE
of Drumgally
(inherited
Drum Manor)

William
(inherited lands
near Augher.
Built Oaklands
on Drum Manor
Estate)

James
m
Mary SWAN
1671–1740
Heiress to William SWAN

Alexander 1705–1771 (inherited Farlough Lodge)
m
Sarah CORNWALL

John 1727–1785
m 1757
Hannah LINDSAY

Alexander 1758–1827
m
(3) Elizabeth SMYTH
(4) Lucinda SIREE

Walter Lindesay***
1826–1879
(Farlough Estate sold)
m
Mary BAILEY
1835–1896

Ethel Florence
Lindesay†
1870–1946
(*aka* Henry Handel
Richardson)

Marmaduke 1781–1845
m
Sarah SHAW

Hannah
m 1828
John Charles DEVETTE

Hannah‡
1829–1881
m 1849
Robert
Cooper
RICHARDSON‡

Gertrude Anna (Cooper)
(Gertie)
1891–1957
m 1919
Thomas BELL *d* 1956

William
Currie Victor
1919–1976
m 1943
Constance
HARRISON

David
Cooper
1922–‡‡
m Gladys?

Thomas
Alan
1923–1987
m 1950
Margaret
JOHNSON

John
Effingham
1925–1983
m 1954
Rosaleen (Rose)
BUTLER

Noel
(*d in infancy*)

* Frances Elizabeth (Richardson) Fisher wrote volumes of verse, and, *inter alia*, the novel *Love and Hatred*

† Ethel Florence Lindesay Richardson was the well-known Australian writer Henry Handel Richardson, the hero of whose *The Fortunes of Richard Mahony* was modelled upon her father, Walter Lindesay Richardson

‡Robert Cooper Richardson married his cousin once removed, Hannah Devette

§ Robert Lindsay Richardson married his second cousin Sarah Richardson, granddaughter of Alexander Richardson and his third wife Elizabeth Smyth

**Effingham Lindsay Richardson married his cousin Harriett Richardson, granddaughter of Alexander Richardson and his third wife, Elizabeth Smyth and sister to Sarah Richardson, above. There are at least three more incidences of intermarriage within the Richardson clan (shown only on an extended family tree)

IRIS MURDOCH'S DESCENT THROUGH
THE RICHARDSON FAMILY TREE

'Planted' in Co. Tyrone, Ireland in 1616

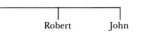

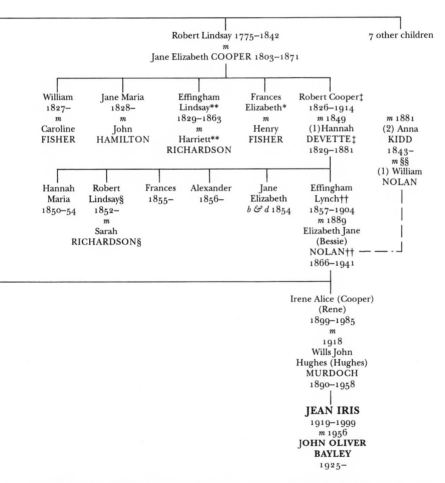

††Effingham Lynch Richardson, whose first marriage, to Winnifred Browne (not shown on the chart above), occurred in 1881, then appears in 1889 to have married his stepsister, Elizabeth Jane (Bessie) Nolan, as his second wife, eight years after his father married her mother

‡‡Moved to London

§§Eva Lee (*née* Robinson) believed her mother, who died in childbirth, to be a daughter of the marriage of Anna Kidd and William Nolan; father unknown

**Only this branch of the family uses the spelling LINDESAY

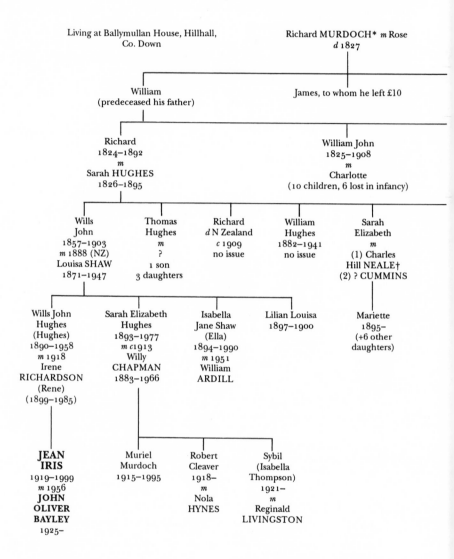

Living at Ballymullan House, Hillhall,
Co. Down

Richard MURDOCH* *m* Rose
d 1827

William
(predeceased his father)

James, to whom he left £10

Richard
1824–1892
m
Sarah HUGHES
1826–1895

William John
1825–1908
m
Charlotte
(10 children, 6 lost in infancy)

Wills
John
1857–1903
m 1888 (NZ)
Louisa SHAW
1871–1947

Thomas
Hughes
m
?
1 son
3 daughters

Richard
d N Zealand
c 1909
no issue

William
Hughes
1882–1941
no issue

Sarah
Elizabeth
m
(1) Charles
Hill NEALE†
(2) ? CUMMINS

Wills John
Hughes
(Hughes)
1890–1958
m 1918
Irene
RICHARDSON
(Rene)
(1899–1985)

Sarah Elizabeth
Hughes
1893–1977
*m c*1913
Willy
CHAPMAN
1883–1966

Isabella
Jane Shaw
(Ella)
1894–1990
m 1951
William
ARDILL

Lilian Louisa
1897–1900

Mariette
1895–
(+6 other
daughters)

**JEAN
IRIS**
1919–1999
m 1956
**JOHN
OLIVER
BAYLEY**
1925–

Muriel
Murdoch
1915–1995

Robert
Cleaver
1918–
m
Nola
HYNES

Sybil
(Isabella
Thompson)
1921–
m
Reginald
LIVINGSTON

THE MURDOCH FAMILY TREE

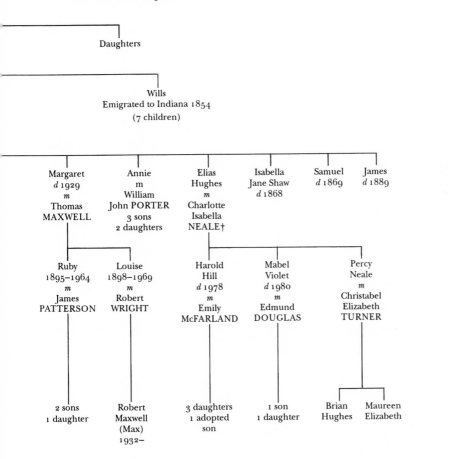

The farm was left jointly to his grandsons
Richard and William John

Daughters

Wills
Emigrated to Indiana 1854
(7 children)

Margaret	Annie	Elias	Isabella	Samuel	James
d 1929	*m*	Hughes	Jane Shaw	*d* 1869	*d* 1889
m	William	*m*	*d* 1868		
Thomas	John PORTER	Charlotte			
MAXWELL	3 sons	Isabella			
	2 daughters	NEALE†			

Ruby	Louise	Harold	Mabel	Percy
1895–1964	1898–1969	Hill	Violet	Neale
m	*m*	*d* 1978	*d* 1980	*m*
James	Robert	*m*	*m*	Christabel
PATTERSON	WRIGHT	Emily	Edmund	Elizabeth
		McFARLAND	DOUGLAS	TURNER

2 sons	Robert	3 daughters	1 son	Brian	Maureen
1 daughter	Maxwell	1 adopted	1 daughter	Hughes	Elizabeth
	(Max)	son			
	1932–				

* A letter (undated) from Annie Jane Murdoch (known as Lillie), one of three daughters of
Thomas Hughes Murdoch, to her nephew, Professor Brian Murdoch, states that before her grandfather Richard Murdoch (*d.* 1892) there had been eight previous generations of Murdochs living
at Ballymullan House, Hillhall; and this is a commonly accepted view.

† Charles Hill Neale and Charlotte Isabella Neale were siblings.

This family tree stops at Iris Murdoch's own generation and does not show later issue on either the
Murdoch side (where two first cousins have surviving issue) or on the Richardson side (where her
Bell first cousins also have issue).

'What follows is in its essence as in its contour a love story . . . Man's creative struggle, his search for wisdom and truth, is a love story.'

The Black Prince, p. 9

'Like Socrates, perhaps, love is the only subject on which I am really expert?'

Iris Murdoch, journal entry, 9 July 1976

INTRODUCTION

Iris Murdoch wrote to her friend the painter Harry Weinberger in October 1985, when he was contemplating writing his memoirs, 'how precious the past is, how soon forgotten', regretting how little she had researched her own family. She told her old refugee-camp friend Jože Jančar in about the same year to expect a call one day from her biographer. When 'feeling mortal' in 1963 she had sent some poems to her publisher at Chatto & Windus, Norah Smallwood, explaining, 'I would like one or two of these poems to have a chance of surviving.'[1] She lodged a story, her family tree and her husband John Bayley's Newdigate Prize poem with her literary agent Ed Victor in the 1980s. How she was remembered mattered: she once startled a Jesuit student who had quoted St Augustine by asking, 'Have you any evidence that he was *a good man?*' She kept in London a copy of H. House's *Sketches for a Portrait of Rimbaud,* and a well-thumbed *Life of Shakespeare* by A.L. Rowse. She encouraged Stephen Gardiner in his biographies of Jacob Epstein and Elisabeth Frink.

The idea of a biography of her was first mooted by the publisher Richard Cohen.[2] At first appalled, she later consented to her friend A.N. Wilson writing it, and Chatto showed interest in commissioning the book as a Socratic dialogue. At some point in their researches, after 1990, both she and Wilson cooled to the idea. Probably Dame Iris wanted only intellectual biography, at least during her lifetime, though she was resigned, as she told the American biographer Jeffrey Meyers, to the matter being resolved after she had 'departed this scene'. I raised the issue at the end of 1996, the year when Iris and John Bayley and my partner Jim O'Neill and I had started to spend weeks together in Radnorshire. It did not seem right that the life of so remarkable a person should go unrecorded, and I hoped that it would be written by someone sympathetic.

I had loved her work since finding *The Bell* in Oundle school library around 1960, and thought, like tens of thousands, 'These books are *about me.*' I wrote my Ph.D. on her Platonism (later published as *The Saint and the Artist: A Study of the Fiction of Iris Murdoch*), and we met at a lunch party in 1981 to celebrate her honorary doctorate from the University of East Anglia. Eighteen months later, listening to her give the ten Gifford lectures in natural theology over a fortnight in Edinburgh, and argue that the good man *literally* sees a different world from the mediocre or bad man, I was shocked into a new way of thinking. We met again, and I discovered I was a Buddhist. (Talking to her old Oxford contemporary M.R.D. Foot about Iris's converting Frank Thompson to Communism in March 1939, we decided she was always a collector of souls.) This interested her. John Bayley's *Iris: A Memoir of Iris Murdoch* (US title *Elegy for Iris*) suggests I taught her about Buddhism; at first she taught me.* We met for lunch, once or twice a year, often at Dino's in South Kensington. She liked the first-floor restaurant, where there were sometimes no other diners: despite her partial deafness, she could hear there. On one such occasion, having just learnt to stand on my head in a Hatha-Yoga class, I offered to demonstrate. She declined, but put the incident into *The Good Apprentice*, when Meredith stands on his head for Stuart. She was appalled to learn that there were Tibetan teachers who had love affairs with their students. She said fiercely, 'I have committed many sins, but never that one,' referred to it in *The Message to the Planet*, and introduced me to her friend Andrew Harvey, who had recently written the Buddhist-inspired *A Journey in Ladakh*, whom I think she hoped might wean me from my teachers. In 1988 she invited me to join her and John for Christmas lunch, but this invitation came unworkably late (Christmas morning). She attended a seminar on her work in 1989 at Kingston University, where I taught, and Kingston awarded her an honorary doctorate at the Barbican in 1993, where she gave away degrees. She sent me as a gift a typescript

---

* She profited more from Andrew Harvey's understanding of Buddhism (see Chapter 20).

liberally annotated in her hand of her radio opera *The One Alone*,[3] and after I had completed a three-month Rocky Mountain group meditation retreat came to dinner, to witness, perhaps, any effects. One was that, though no one has influenced me more, she alarmed me less. I lent her Heidegger's volumes on Nietzsche for her work-in-progress; discussed her work with her at symposia: in 1987 at the Free University of Amsterdam, in 1992 in Alcala de Henares in Spain, in 1994 at the Cheltenham Literary Festival. Around 1992 she put my and Jim O'Neill's blue-eyed collie into *The Green Knight* as Anax, which involved meeting and much conferring about detail. That we lifted the dog up interested her and made its way into the text. When I read the proofs, I wrote to her as if from the dog, suggesting emendations I was not sure a non-canine critic might effect. She replied (to the dog, whose influence exceeded that of Chatto editors) implementing the changes. In 1997 I collected her essays, which Chatto published as *Existentialists and Mystics*. Although the four of us became from 1996 until her death like 'family', I had the not uncommon sense of not knowing her, and was astonished to learn that in her will she had left me a Gandharva Buddha and a bequest and, although an inveterate destroyer of letters, had kept a number from me about Buddhist matters.

The matter of a biography rested until the summer of 1997, when I asked Iris how she felt about it, and she replied, 'You're a good friend.' We made cassettes together. She enjoyed helping, gave affirmative character references – 'A tip-top person', 'A splendid woman'; advised reticence on one (unimportant) matter. She was thrilled when introducing her old friend Philippa Foot and hastened a meeting with her brother-in-law Michael Bayley. As late as 1998 she identified her grandmother and first cousin Cleaver from photographs, and her response to three beloved names – Franz, Frank, Canetti – endured. Of the third she remarked in May 1997 with poetic ungrammatical-ness, 'His name shudders me with happiness.' As she gradually forgot her past, I rediscovered it. It sometimes seemed as if I were becoming her memory. There was something magical, and humbling, about revivifying someone so richly and intensely endowed with life. To her Oxford contemporary Leo Pliatzky she wrote in 1946, 'I'm glad I was born when I was, [aren't] you? I'm sorry to have missed pre-war Paris, but Lord, this is an interesting age.'[4]

2

A major artist is a contested site, and, rather as the Queen has an official birthday, is bound to acquire official friends. Iris, instantly memorable,* also made each friend feel uniquely befriended. Only the vainest believed that this was literally true, and she, who befriended so many, was known to few. This biography is a quest for the living flesh-and-blood creature hidden beneath the personae in which many invested: the blue-stocking, the icon, the mentor and John the Baptist to other writers who, that work satisfactorily fulfilled, could vacate the scene to others uncommemorated. The Indian writer Ved Mehta optimistically believed she had 'no enemies'. She was sometimes portrayed as a bourgeois grandee living an unworldly detached intellectual life, a stained-glass 'Abbess of North Oxford' cut off from reality, inventing a fantastical alternative world for compensation. 'Real life is so much odder than any book,' she wrote to Philippa Foot:[5] her life was as exciting and improbable as her fiction. Much in her fiction thought to be 'romance' turned out to be realism. Her novels are not just stylised comedies of manners with artificial complications, but reflect lived experience, albeit wonderfully transmuted. If, like Yeats, she was 'silly, like us', her gifts, as Auden put it, survived it all.

She has been claimed by many: as an example, magus or mentor both to younger writers and to seekers; by Stirling University,

---

* Sydney Afriat saw her outside the Collège Franco-Brittanique in Paris in 1949. She was strikingly not as others are, with a straw-coloured fringe, not beautiful, immobile, having a quality of stillness. Three years later at St Anne's he told her he'd seen her, with an older woman, and when and where. 'Yes, that was my mother,' IM replied without surprise. Such stories of strangers being struck by one sighting and remembering it are common.

where the Scottish Assembly voted the astonishing figure of £500,000 to help fund an Alzheimer's Centre in her name; by St Anne's College, Oxford, where a graduate scholarship may be called after her. She is to be acted by Dame Judi Dench in a film. There will surely be further memoirs. One task of the biographer must be to give the artist's '*mana*', power or prestige, back to herself. Another, to return the reader to her best work

The critic P.N. Furbank in *Encounter* once gallantly blamed his disappointment with *The Italian Girl* on the unrealities of Oxford life, on which he thought the book based. The Iris who wrote to Raymond Queneau of her love of 'this precious enclosed community . . . with all its pedantry & its intellectual jokes',[6] who lived at number 43 Park Town in North Oxford in 1940, at number 16 in 1948, and at number 58 in 1950, is not the whole story. This biography is a quest for other Irises: the Irishwoman; the Communist-bohemian; the Treasury civil servant; the worker in Austrian refugee camps; the Anglo-Catholic retreatant; the Royal College of Art lecturer; the lifelong devotee of friendship conducted at a distance and by letter – what Nietzsche in *The Gay Science* called 'star friendship'; the Buddhist-Christian mystic. The recent past is too close for objectivity, and this book might have been entitled 'Young Iris'. The period 1919 to 1956 is least known, and least discussed in John Bayley's memoirs of Iris. In 1997 no fewer than three Badminton schoolmistresses, who knew Iris from 1932, were still with us. That period was soonest likely to disappear from view. I would focus on the so-called formative years: the time before the creative confusion of youth gave way to a greater stability.

How extraordinary her life proved to be: nothing was as I expected, yet it was real as well as fantastical. She played two opposite and heroic parts: a Colette *de nos jours*, hard-headed, hard-working, ardent and sometimes humiliated, presiding over her own emotional life and so a role-model for other women;[7] the second other-centred to the degree that she lost much sense, in the service of her 'conjecture' about the Good, of who she was. How does one write about someone who thought she had 'no memory, no continuity, no identity'? Periodically rediscovering her own journals, Iris kept surprising herself: 'What an Ass I was!' Yet, as a novelist, she had digested and reworked her experience: it might be that she had finished with and shed the earlier persona. She certainly agreed with T.S. Eliot that 'the more perfect the artist, the more completely separate in him will be the man who suffers and the mind which creates.' Suffering interested her.

I believed, as Dorothy Thompson – sister-in-law to Frank Thompson, who loved Iris during the war – put it, that 'The articulate members of a generation speak for many others besides themselves,'[8] and planned a book in two parts, one leading up to Iris's marriage in 1956, recording her imaginative indebtedness to her Oxford generation, the second concentrating on her work. After I had drafted seven chapters, however, Tom Hicks made Iris's letters to his father David available to me; these were soon purchased by the Bodleian Library, and considerably complicated my view. The three-part structure which now seemed apt necessitated deciding what to leave out. As a non-philosopher, I had to leave authoritative 'placing' of her thought to others. It became apparent that those looking for in-depth literary criticism would have to find it in my earlier book *The Saint and the Artist*, itself in part intellectual biography, whose third edition comes out simultaneously with this biography. There was little space to describe foreign trips (seven in one year alone). Many who knew her loved her and wanted to claim her for their own. Despite this gift of becoming instantly important to others and the many and great debts I owe to later friends, there was little space to explore recent friendships, which in contrast with those negotiated before the age of thirty are 'apt to be burdened with reservations, constraints, inhibitions'.[9]

Michael (M.R.D.) Foot wrote after Iris died: 'Her light was once marvellously bright; and you are lucky to bathe in so much of it.' I felt that luck. Closeness to one's subject is simultaneously a strength and a liability, and I wanted to write the first biography of Iris, but not the last: to start the job of setting her work in the context of the cultural/intellectual life of the mid-twentieth century, of the generation who struggled to come to terms philosophically and emotionally and artistically with Stalin and Hitler, with existentialism, and with the slow collapse of organised religion. She left behind edited journals (1939–1996) which constituted an invaluable resource, carrying her unique 'voice'.

'How can one describe another human being justly?' the narrator of *The Black Prince* asks. Iris was, as many of her friends put it, more passionate for truth (generally the faintest of all human passions, A.E. Housman observed) than anyone they had known. Trying to tell the truth in the right way was challenging, and if this is anywhere achieved, I owe much to the hundreds who helped: to the generosity of the British Academy for their 1998 award of a small grant, to Magdalen College, Oxford, where I was happily Visiting Fellow in Hilary term 1999, and to Professor John Sutherland for inviting me to be Honorary Research Fellow at University College, London. Chapter 1 plunders, with their permission, the scrupulous genealogical researches both of Mr Arthur Green and of Iris's second cousin Canon Crawford. Professor Roy Foster kindly vetted what I had written on Iris's 'Irishness', and Chapters 1 and 16 benefited greatly from his kindly and authoritative guidance. Professor Miriam Allott read Chapter 2; John Corsellis Chapters 8 and 9; Marija Jančar Chapter 9; Mrs Anne Robson Chapter 11: all made helpful suggestions. Professor Dorothy Thompson generously allowed access to the closed collection of Thompson papers, and she and Frank Thompson's biographer Simon Kusseff helped with limitless patience; Simon read Chapters 4 to 7, and fine-tuned many points therein. Michael Holroyd commented on a number of passages. Professor Dennis Nineham shared his theological expertise. I'm deeply indebted to very many librarians and archivists: among them Christopher Bailey at Viking New York; Eugene Rae at the Royal College of Art; Pauline Adams at Somerville College, Oxford; Jane Read at Froebel College; Diane Elderton, Librarian of Ibstock Place School; Dr David Smith at St Anne's College; the British Library; all the staff of the Modern Papers room at the Bodleian Library; and Michael Bott at the University of Reading Library, where Dame Iris's Chatto archives live. My gratitude to Alison Samuel of Chatto for facilitating access, and to Daphne Turner for having researched that huge archive, amongst much else. Although Fletcher and Bove's *Iris Murdoch: A Primary and Secondary Annotated Bibliography* (London and New York, 1995, new edition forthcoming) shows that there are many of her letters in public collections in libraries scattered worldwide, I have relied much more heavily (except where indicated) on privately held letter-runs, and am deeply grateful that so many were made available to me.

I should like particularly to thank Mrs Olive Scott for allowing me access to James Scott's journals, Professor Jeremy Adler for access to Franz Steiner's papers and Johanna Canetti for her father's. I met with great kindness on many journeys: from Sybil Livingston and Cleaver Chapman in Belfast; from Billy Lee in Dublin; from Susie Ovadia and Jean-Marie Queneau on two trips to Paris; from Allan Forbes in Boston and on Naushon island; from Maria Panteleev in Bulgaria; from Lois MacKinnon in Aberdeen. This biography is the culmination of twenty-one years of research, teaching and publishing on Iris Murdoch.

I owe to my other great teachers, Sakyong Mipham Rinpoche and Chögyam Trungpa Rinpoche, their having taught me the courage to look closely.

I owe much to the following: Janet Adam Smith, Pauline Adams, Professor Jeremy Adler, Peter Ady, Sir Lawrence Airey, Professor Miriam Allott, Mulk Raj Anand, Lord Annan, Professor Elizabeth Anscombe, Jennifer Ashcroft, John Ashton, Reggie Askew, Lord Baker, Sir Peter Baldwin, Lady Catherine Balogh, Stephen Balogh, Jonathan Barker, Betsy Barnard, Wilhelmina Barnes-Graham, Margaret Bastock, Brigadier Michael Bayley, Denys Becher, Paul Binding, Hylan Booker, Dr Marjorie Boulton, Cheryl Bove, Lord Briggs, Michael Brock, Anne Brumfitt, Dame Antonia Byatt, Carmen Callil, Clare Campbell, Johanna Canetti, Sir Raymond Carr, Hugh Cecil, Jonathan Cecil, Cleaver Chapman, Professor Eric Christiansen, George Clive, Alex Colville, Robert Conquest, John Corsellis, Milein Cosman, Jean Coutts (later Austin), Barbara Craig, Rosemary Cramp, Vera and Donald Crane, Julian Chrysostomides, Don Cupitt, Marion Daniel, Peter Daniels, Gwenda David, Barbara Davies (later Mitchell), Jennifer Dawson, Rt Hon. Edmund Dell, Patrick Denby, Barbara Denny,

Kay Dick, Professor Mary Douglas, Professor Sir Kenneth Dover, Professor Sir Michael Dummett, Moira Dunbar, Katherine Duncan-Jones, Lilian Eldridge, Anne Elliott, Professor Dorothy Emmet, Leila Eveleigh, Professor Richard Fardon, Rachel Fenner, Professor John Fletcher, Professor Jean Floud, Professor M.R.D. Foot, Allan Forbes, Anthony Forster, Professor Christopher Frayling, Honor Frost, Lady Fulton, Reg Gadney, Margaret Gardiner, Stephen Gardiner, Susan Gardiner, Tony Garrett, Professor Peter Geach, Antonia Gianetti (later Robinson), Phillida Gili, Victoria Glendinning, Sir Ernst Gombrich, Carol and Francis Graham-Harrison, Sister Grant, Marjorie Grene, John and Patsie Grigg, Dominic de Grunne, Michael and Anne Hamburger, Sir Stuart Hampshire, Tiril Harris, Jennifer Hart, Andrew Harvey, Lord Healey, Katherine Hicks, Tom Hicks, Wasfi Hijab, Professor Christopher Hill, Professor Eric Hobsbawm, Michael Holroyd, Laura Hornack, Elizabeth Jane Howard, Maurice Howard, Gerry Hughes, Priscilla Hughes, Psiche Hughes, Professor Sally Humphreys, Rosalind Hursthouse, Julian Jackson, Dan Jacobson, Mervyn James, Jože and Marija Jančar, Lord Jenkins, John Jones, Madeleine Jones, Sandra Keenan, Professor Sir Anthony Kenny, Sir Frank Kermode, Charles Kidd, Francis King, Ruth Kingsbury (later Mills), Ken Kirk, Todorka Kotseva, Professor Georg Kreisel, Michael Krüger, Nicholas Lash, Michel Lécureur, Billy Lee, David Lee, Dr Ann Leech, Professor Graham and Alastine Lehmann, Sir Michael Levey, Paul and Penny Levi, Peter and Deirdre Levi, Deirdre Levinson, Mary Lidderdale, Professor Ian Little, Penelope Lively, Sybil Livingston, Professor Hugh Lloyd-Jones, Professor David Luke, Richard Lyne, Katherine McDonald, Professor John McDowell, Ben Macintyre, Shena Mackay, Dulcibel MacKenzie, Lois MacKinnon, Michael Mack, Holga Mackie, Aubrey Manning, Sister Marian (Lucy Klatschko), Noel and Barbara Martin, Derwent May, Stephen Medcalf, Mary Midgley, Professor Basil Mitchell, Julian Mitchell, Juliet Mitchell, Gina Moore, David Morgan, Professor Brian Murdoch, Professor Bernard and Pamela Myers, Professor A.D. Nuttall, John O'Regan, Margaret Orpen (later Lady Lintott), Susie Ovadia, Valerie Pakenham, Lynda Patterson (later Lynch), Denis Paul, Kate Paul,

Professor David Pears, Sister Perpetua, Professor D.Z. Phillips, Barry Pink, Julian Pitt-Rivers, Sir Leo Pliatzky, Frances Podmore, Elfrieda Powell, Joseph Prelis, Jean-Marie Queneau, Lord Quinton, Kathleen Raine, Professor David Raphael, Professor Marjorie Reeves, Professor Herbert Reiss, Frances Richardson, Gloria Richardson, John Richardson, Pierre Riches, Peter Rickman, Barbara Robbins, Professor Kenneth Robinson, Anne Robson, Professor Stanley Rosen, Dr Anne Rowe, Bernice Rubens, Chitra Rudingerova, Gabriele Rümelin (later Taylor), Geoffrey de Sainte-Croix, Inez Schlenker, Olive Scott, Elizabeth Sewell, Jenny Sharp, Patricia Shaw (later Lady Trend), John Simopoulos, Jan Skinner, Jewel Smith, Prudence Smith, Peg Smythies, Polly Smythies, Professor Susan Sontag, Natasha, Lady Spender, Naku Staminov, Peggy Stebbing (later Pyke-Lees), Professor Frances Stewart, Professor Anthony Storr, Professor Sir Peter Strawson, Professor Paul Streeten, Irene Sychrava, Richard Symonds, Professor Charles Taylor, Professor Dorothy Thompson, Olivier Todd, Professor Richard Todd, Svetlana Toderova, Ann Toulmin, Professor Stephen Toulmin, Jeremy Trafford, Nancy Trenamen, Professor Rachel Trickett, General Slavcho Trunski, Jane Turner, Garth Underwood, Anne Valery, Anne Venables, Nicholas Veto, Ed Victor, Audi Villers, Sir John Vinelott, Margaret Vintner (later Rake), Janice Wainwright, Rosemary Warhurst, Baroness Warnock, Harry Weinberger, Lord Weidenfeld, Dee Wells, Anne-Louise Wilkinson (later Luthi), John and Anne Willett, Professor Sir Bernard Williams, Charlotte Williams-Ellis (later Wallace), Susie Williams-Ellis (later Cooper-Willis), A.N. Wilson, Colin Wilson, Anne Wollheim, Professor Richard Wollheim, Professor David Worswick, Max Wright, Werner Wunsche, Pat Zealand (later Trenaman).

My agent Bill Hamilton gave unstinting support and excellent advice; I'm grateful to Phillida Gili, Emma Beck and Humphrey Stone for helping me find, and allowing me to use, the photos taken by their mother Janet Stone; and to the Schiller Nationalmuseum, Marbach-am-Neckar, for the transparency of *Conversation in the Library, 1950*. While every effort has been made to trace and acknowledge copyright-holders of photographs, in some cases this has proved impossible. I would be grateful for any information which would enable me to rectify such omissions in future editions.

Michael Fishwick and Robert Lacey's scrupulous editing has improved the text. Sarah Lee and Anne Roberts gave invaluable assistance. Douglas Matthews compiled the index and helped me correct a number of mistakes. Jane Jantet produced the family trees, and she and Daphne Turner worked with heroic ingenuity, energy and patience to find answers to myriad questions. Without their extraordinarily hard work, the task of writing would have taken at least twice as long. Any and all mistakes are my responsibility, and no one else's. My partner Jim O'Neill kept me sane. Without his love and support I could not have begun. I amassed so much material that an archive will accommodate the overflow.

3

In November 1999 in Bulgaria, Philippa Foot, who had brought Iris the news of Frank Thompson's murder in 1944, and I met Frank's partisan General Trunski, fourteen days before his death. We also listened to Naku Staminov's eye-witness account of Frank's execution, and stood in silence by his grave. Philippa handed me a red carnation to leave there, as from Iris. I owe more than I can convey to John Bayley and Philippa Foot, whose roles in Iris's story what follows makes clear. Each read the book in draft and saved me from errors. To both this book is dedicated.

I

Fairy-Tale Princess
1919–1944

'I get a frisson of joy to think that I am of *this* age, *this* Europe – saved or damned with it.'

Letter to Marjorie Boulton from Brussels,
6 November 1945

1

'You ask how Irish she is?'
1616–1925

One day in 1888, on the North Island of New Zealand, a runaway horse with an alarmed and excited girl on its back galloped into Wills Hughes Murdoch's view. He was twenty-seven years old,[1] and had been quietly tending his sheep. He managed to race after the horse, to jump out and grab the reins, calm and finally stop it. The girl, Louisa Shaw, who was on her way to school, was that November to be his bride. She was only seventeen when they married.[2]

This mode of meeting and instantly falling in love sounds like something invented by his future granddaughter. Her novels test to the point of self-parody the literary convention of the *coup de foudre*, or love at first sight: the chance meeting between kindred souls that changes lives for ever. It was as much a family tradition. Wills and Louisa's eldest child Hughes was to meet and fall for his nineteen-year-old future bride on a Dublin tram in 1918, towards the end of the First World War. And John Bayley was first to sight Wills's granddaughter Iris bicycling past his Oxford college window in 1953. In three successive generations the girl at least is on the move, while the man – and twice also the girl – is love-struck, and nothing again is quite as it was.

2

The Murdochs are a staunchly Protestant Scots-Irish family who crossed the Irish Sea to Ulster from their native Galloway in Scotland in the seventeenth century. The name 'Murdoch' is essentially Scots Gaelic – from Mhuirchaidh, though an Irish Gaelic version, O'Muircheartaigh, meaning navigator, sometimes written Murtagh, is also common. They farmed modestly in County Down, where they prided themselves on having been for seven generations. In the 1880s Wills John Murdoch left the family farm for his spell in New Zealand, to learn about sheep-rearing, and probably also to make good on his own. It was a period of agricultural unrest and depression, and of Irish emigration generally.[3] Family tradition suggests that Wills's uncle had left for Indiana twenty-five years earlier, while his elder brother Richard was also in New Zealand, working as a teacher, and died there, unmarried, not long before the First World War.

Wills and Louisa's first baby, Wills John Hughes Murdoch, was born in Thames, seventy miles south-east of Auckland, on 26 April 1890. When Hughes was a year and a half old, on 9 January 1892, Wills's father died, and Wills came back to help run the family farm in County Down. Legend has it that on the journey home baby Hughes was nearly washed overboard in a storm, but was saved by a vigilant sailor.

The farm was Ballymullan House, Hillhall, in County Down, eight miles outside Belfast, and at that time 'real country'. Even today it has not become suburban, but away from the old main road to Lisburn that cuts through it, it is a quiet country hamlet. Ballymullan House had been left by Wills's great-grandfather, another Richard, described in his will as 'merchant and farmer',[4] to Wills's father Richard (1824–92) and uncle William John (1825–1908). The five-bay, two-storeyed, shallow-roofed eighteenth-century house – 'Georgian' suggests something too English, insufficiently atmospheric and provincial – has dressed-stone corners, some old panelled windows, a large kitchen with a small-windowed 'gam' wall, a grey marble fireplace in the drawing-room, two fine old oak-panelled doors, an orchard and an old yard with a pump that produced 'the most beautiful well water'.[5] There were at least sixty acres of mixed farmland.

Louisa, whom Iris knew well – she died aged seventy-five, living at 8 Adelaide Avenue in Belfast, in 1947[6] – is remembered by her grandchildren as a cheerful, always youthful person. She was happy and had the gift of making others so. At twenty-one she had to leave her entire family and known world, to sail across the seas to a wholly strange place, and to live in a house with unknown in-laws. She was to share – contentedly – Ballymullan with her mother-in-law and three sisters-in-law – Margaret, Sarah and Annie.[7] There is an echo of her journey in Chloe, also a New Zealander, 'the girl from far-away' in *The Good Apprentice*.

Two aspects of the household Louisa bravely travelled to join are striking. Iris's father Hughes was brought up on a farm which had been inherited by the brothers Richard and William from their grandfather. Wills, son of the elder brother Richard, chose to leave for the southern hemisphere. Strife or tension between brothers is the main driving force behind the plots of many of Iris's novels, from *A Severed Head* to *The Green Knight*. Shakespeare's plots provide one model for this; life, another.

The second aspect, even allowing for the shorter life expectancy of that epoch, is the family's high death-rate. Richard had, it is true, seven surviving siblings, but Wills's sister Isabella died in 1868 aged fourteen, his brother Samuel in 1869 aged four, and his brother James in 1889 aged nineteen. As for Uncle William, the other heir to Hillhall, he had lost six children in infancy, and his wife Charlotte died in 1876. William had another four surviving children, three of them girls, one of whom, Charlotte Clark, was married. She and her elder sister Margaret died within a fortnight of each other in March 1893, aged twenty-seven and thirty-two respectively. Wills's mother Sarah died in 1895, three years after his father. His youngest child Lilian died, aged three, in 1900.

What might such reminders of mortality do to the Murdoch family's religious sense? Wills and Louisa's eldest daughter Sarah, born in 1893, was washed to the wilder shores of Irish

Protestantism. Her sister Ella (1894–1990) became a missionary. And Hughes, their only son – perhaps in reaction – probably turned free-thinker. In the following generation Hughes's only child Iris was to contrive to be both passionately religious by nature and by blood-instinct, yet devoutly sceptical about most traditions in practice. Dominic de Grunne, a tutor at Wadham College in the 1950s, observing her over many decades and working, when they first met, on a doctorate on lay religious feeling among seventeenth-century Britons, soon saw in her the extreme 'idealistic puritanism' of her planter-Ulster forebears.[8] Iris was, especially before her marriage, prone to humourless outrage about social and political issues – the wickedness of apartheid being one theme. Friends would later recount how, eyes flaming and flashing, she 'took up the cudgels' and 'stood on her dignity'. She also inherited from her father's side an intense radical individualism.

The Murdoch family burial plot is in the Church of Ireland graveyard at Deriaghy, County Down, not far from Hillhall. The church itself is an ugly Victorian confection. Two family graves, one for each brother – Richard, William – and his descendants, stand side by side like rival siblings within their low railing, opposite the south-facing door. A sum bequeathed around 1868 to keep the gravestones clean had dwindled by the 1920s, so that the grandchildren – who, most summers, included young Iris over from England – had to clean the headstones, scrape the railings, apply paint and keep the weeds in check.

There are many Richards and Williams in the Murdoch family tree. 'Hughes' was one common or standard middle name, 'Wills' another – probably emphasising a connexion with the family name of the Marquesses of Downshire, from whom the Murdochs in the nineteenth century rented eleven and a half acres of land. It is one curiosity of these graves that, as in the kind of doubling novelists delight in, two people buried here bear the same name – Wills's sister Isabella Jane Shaw Murdoch, who was Iris's great aunt and who died in 1868; and Iris's formidable aunt Ella Ardill, also born Isabella Jane Shaw Murdoch, who died in 1990. The 'Shaw' in Aunt Ella's name came from her mother Louisa Shaw from New Zealand, who – presumably – also came of Irish stock, and may indeed have been a distant cousin.

3

Louisa loved her first-born, Hughes. She used to carry him, at the age of three and a half, to the small National School in Hillhall, and then cry all the way back home because she could so little bear to leave him. Hughes went on to Brookfield, a Quaker boarding school in Moira, outside Belfast. It was a good school, and Wills's mother and his Dublin cousins alike were Quakers.[9] Hughes would send his washing home each week for Louisa to launder, and this became the stuff of family legend: she would cut off all the buttons from the garments before the wash, and sew them all on again afterwards before sending them back, week after week. Probably this was to avoid the buttons being chewed up in an old-fashioned mangle. That the story was handed down suggests that there were other ways of proceeding. 'Did you ever hear of anything so stupid?' asked Louisa's granddaughter Sybil.

The year before her death in 1895, Louisa's mother-in-law Sarah wrote to her about the well-being of the next baby, confusingly another Sarah, aunt to-be of Iris. Great-grandmother Sarah writes affectionately to her daughter-in-law in an educated cursive but unpunctuated script. Some words are misspelt.

> Ballymullan House,
> Lisburn, Sep 1st 94
>
> My dear Lousia
> I can imagine how you will be thinking of Sara it will seem wonderfull to you to hear she never murmured all yesterday nor going to bed nor going asleep and I kept out of the way so Rose got her ready and all was warm she had a lot of little things to amuse her and took her up Annie was here at the time as I did not wish her

to begin to fret I sent them early and we stood and lisined
not a word Rose told me this morning she went over and
over her to she tired and then lay down I called Rose at
5 she went out to milk at once and had milked before
she awoke I left my door open that she could come in
but she called out MaMa and I called Rose that was the
only time she cried not the only time she has said MaMa
but that was the only cry she had all the time I hope
you are enjoying yourself ever your Afft Mother Sarah
Murdoch.

I will be glad to see Wills home he is very soon missed
here

Wills had taken Louisa, and probably the four-year-old Hughes,
to the smart Dublin Horse Show, a key event in the Irish – and
especially the Anglo-Irish – social calendar well into the twentieth
century. Hughes was to inherit his father's love both of horses
and of betting on them. Both Sarah and Louisa were clearly
anxious about Louisa's absence from her second baby, yet the
fact of her absence might suggest that Hughes had more of her
love than did either of his two sisters Sarah and Ella. Ballymullan
House was not a large establishment: as Sarah's letter makes clear,
Rose doubled as nursemaid and milkmaid. The family were not
well enough off to employ a wet-nurse.

In the event, Ballymullan House did not pass to Hughes. There
were several years of mounting debts, and probably the farm
failed. Wills went to a funeral in the rain, developed pneumonia
and died, intestate and aged only forty-six, on 1 December 1903.
The family address at the time was 3 Craig Fernie Terrace, Lisburn
Road, Belfast. The Certificate of Probate on Wills's estate
describes him as a 'retired farmer' and tells us that he left £1,274.
The farm had been sold the year before.

4

Louisa was left on her own to bring up Hughes, Sarah and Ella. So bereft was she without Wills that she would often say her children alone kept her going. It is not clear how they lived, in those days before widows' benefits. She was poor, but uncomplaining, and somehow made do. Despite the family burial plot at Deriaghy being in a Church of Ireland graveyard, the family belonged mainly to Hillhall Presbyterian congregation, and partly to Malone Presbyterian Church. After a split in the latter some breakaways, such as Grandmother Louisa and Aunts Ella and Sarah, counted themselves Irish Evangelical, though the two aunts, on marrying, took the faiths of their husbands: Baptist for Ella when she married the carrier Willy Ardill, Brethren for Sarah when she married the quiet, easy-going self-taught dentist Willy Chapman.

Sectarianism in Ireland is of course not a two-cornered but a three-cornered fight, with Catholic, Church of Ireland (i.e. Anglican) and the various powerful competing Non-Conformist traditions all vying with each other.[10] Moreover the Protestant Non-Conformist traditions in Northern Ireland are intensely individualistic, quarrelsome and fissiparous. Brethren, Baptists and Elamites were at the cutting edge of turn-of-the-century Northern Irish Protestantism, much subject to internal splits. By 1911 there were no fewer than six sects with less than ten members.[11] Iris, direct heir to exactly such a tradition of stubborn, radical Ulster dissent, developed a 'faith' that emphasised the urgency and loneliness of the individual pilgrimage.

Iris's formidable Aunt Ella spent many years as a missionary with the Egypt General Mission, in which it did not much matter what denomination you belonged to. She learnt and spoke good Arabic and 'used to teach the young Egyptians to love God'.[12] Her older sister Sarah spent many of her holidays on a farm near Carryduff, five miles south-east of Belfast, belonging to an uncle who was 'saved', Thomas Maxwell. At around nineteen she was, together with her cousins, 'saved' too, and on her marriage she became a member of what on the mainland are sometimes known as Plymouth Brethren, in Ulster simply as 'Brethren'. Willy, her husband-to-be, was Treasurer to the Apsley Hall Brethren at Donegall Pass. Even today Ulster 'Brethren' – unlike their Scots cousins – have no women elders.

Both the Yeats and the Parnell families, like Iris's, had Brethren connexions.* The Brethren originated in Aungier Street, Dublin in 1827–28 when a group of men including a doctor, a lawyer, a minister and a peer started meeting together without any ritual, set prayers, forms of service or ordained ministry: they wished to return to the simplicity of the early apostolic Church. They believed in a 'timetable' of Last Things and taught that the saved can be caught up in the 'Rapture' before Christ's return, and so spared hellfire.

Willy and Sarah Chapman belonged to the Open Brethren, who split off in 1848, and who differ significantly from Exclusive Brethren. Open Brethren both fraternise and worship freely with other evangelistic Christians, and practise believers' (not infants') baptism. Although to leave the Church was still a momentous and alarming thing to do, your family might not necessarily refuse to break bread with you afterwards. Iris was pleased when her second cousin Max Wright, who taught philosophy at Queen's University, Belfast, wrote a book, a painfully humorous account of just such a departure.† Wright's family home contained thirty-seven Bibles. At fifteen he had shouted a gospel message at an unresponsive terrace of red-brick houses. There was constant pressure on Brethren to go all out for salvation, which led, one commentator believed, to a resulting impoverishment of outlook. Sarah and Willy Chapman's three children, Iris's closest living relatives, were bought up as Open Brethren, and Iris and her

---

* 'The strict faith of the Plymouth Brethren appealed to many mid-nineteenth-century Irish Protestant families, including that of Parnell.' Roy Foster, *W.B. Yeats: A Life, Vol. 1, The Apprentice Mage* (Oxford, 1997), p.543, n12.

† *Told in Gath* (Belfast, 1990), reviewed in *The Times Literary Supplement*, 21 June 1991, p.10, 'A Peculiar People' by Pat Raine, and by Patricia Beer in the *London Review of Books*, 23 May 1991, p.12. Iris and Wright met only once, when she received her honorary doctorate at Queen's University in 1977, although they corresponded thereafter.

parents spent the second part – after Dublin – of many of their summer holidays before the Second World War with these cousins. Muriel, the eldest, was Iris's particular ally.

The years before the First World War were the era of Edward Carson's inflammatory Unionist speeches against Home Rule, of 'not-an-inch-Jimmie', of 'Ulster will fight and Ulster will be right', of a developing siege mentality among many Ulster Protestants. While the Murdochs and Maxwells who were Brethren were unquestionably Unionist, they also – even if male and so eligible – did not dream of voting, *'For we have here no continuing city, but we look for one that is to come.'*

When Hughes went to London at the age of sixteen in June 1906 to train for his civil service exam, first as a boy clerk at Scotland Yard then, later that year, with the Charity Commission, he, who is remembered as gentle, liberal, and free-thinking, was escaping from what his daughter Iris was to term the puritanism of his 'black Protestant' forebears.[13] A letter from Hughes to his mother shortly after his arrival still evinces some fundamentalist piety, but perhaps the fleshpots of London helped wean him from it. This was a puritanism from which Iris claimed to have inherited something of value. Hughes would stay on friendly terms with both his sisters, and perhaps achieved this the more effectively by rationing their time together.

In 1908 he took his civil service exams, and in 1910 is shown certified as a 'second Division Clerk' with, in turn, the Local Government Board, the Home Office and the Treasury. In the four years running up to the outbreak of the First World War he worked at the 'General Valuation Department (Ireland)' in Dublin, staying with his Uncle Elias and his son Harold in Kingstown (later Dun Laoghaire), just outside the city, where they ran two ironmongers' shops.[14] From there it would have been a two-and-a-half-hour train journey to spend a weekend with his mother and sisters, 110 miles away in Belfast. Hughes swam in the so-called 'Forty-Foot', the natural pool 'for gentlemen only' by the Kingstown Martello Tower, both immortalised early on in Joyce's *Ulysses*. Swimming there was his idea of bliss, and he always referred to it reverentially.

Photographs show him as a tall and attractive fair-haired man, with a self-contained air and a mild blue-eyed gaze that seems both retiring and contemplative, yet also 'present'. The quality of quiet inwardness for which he is recalled, and which must have won him admirers, is visible too. The Murdoch family photograph album begins with cards from two girls, one strikingly beautiful, signed 'With love from Daisy, October 1916' and 'To Hughes with love from Lillie, October 1917.'*

In January 1916, when mainland conscription started, there was none in Ireland, for fear of its political unpopularity. Hughes enlisted on 19 November 1915;[15] the first photographs of him in his regimentals date from 1916. He was accustomed to farm life – 'He was very horsey,' Iris remarked[16] – which was why he entered a yeoman cavalry regiment, the First King Edward's Horse, 'The King's Oversea [*sic*] Dominions Regiment'. Whether, like Andrew in *The Red and the Green*, also an officer in King Edward's Horse, he did 'bombing from horse-back' – galloping in single file past German gun-emplacements and hurling Mills bombs into them – is not recorded. Generally, cavalry regiments were kept some distance from the front, and Iris later thought that this saved her father's life.

Six months of Hughes's war diary survive, starting at the end of 1916. The writing is spare and, even allowing for the fact that it is written 'on the move', the tone is notably impassive, without subjectivity. On New Year's Eve 1916 he is laying four hundred yards of telephone wire, in full view of the German trenches at Miraumont, to connect the artillery observation post to that of his regiment. He and his fellows were soon under shellfire. All afternoon they heard the shells coming, and they would throw themselves flat on the ground until after each set of explosions. Shrapnel fell round them for some hours. When they had finished they 'beat it back along the Hessian trench' and rejoined their horses. The line they had laid that day was cut by shellfire almost at once, and had to be relaid in heavy rain five days later. Again

---

* Probably his cousins Isabella and Annie Jane, always known as Daisy and Lillie, daughters of Thomas Hughes Murdoch.

Hughes's party was spotted. A 'whiz-bang' dropped overhead about ten yards away, followed by a 'perfect storm of shells round about'. They got safely away, but only just.

Hughes's diary notes not merely the death of companions – on 22 March 1917 he writes: 'Four B Sqn men were killed, and about 15 wounded' – but also the casualties among horses, which he loved, and is remembered as having taken care of. Even at the front, his mother would proudly and wonderingly relate, he kept half his food for his horse.[17] On 23 March 1917 he takes dispatches through the lines and is stopped 'about four times by the French and ten times by the English patrols, each way'. On 8 April his Lieutenant-Colonel – one Lionel or 'Jimmie' James, author-to-be of a regimental history which Hughes purchased – wrote to Louisa that her son was 'a most excellent and trustworthy British soldier' of whom she should, like him, be proud.

After the post-Easter Rising executions in April 1916 Irish opinion turned against the British government,[18] and King Edward's Horse found difficulty recruiting subalterns in Dublin. On 11 May 1917 – during the Arras offensive, when 159,000 lives were lost in thirty-nine days – Corporal Murdoch was interviewed for a commission by Brigadier-General Darell at Nesle, and two weeks later left Peronne, on the Somme, for Dublin and then Lisburn. The journey home took one full week. He was gazetted Second Lieutenant[19] on 22 February 1918.[20]

Musing about these diaries after they came to light in 1987,[21] Iris pondered various matters. One was that 'when (31.12.1916) my father wrote in his notebook, "All the afternoon shrapnel was dropping all around . . ." ', Wittgenstein, perhaps in similar circumstances, but fighting on the other side, might well have been making notes for the *Tractatus*. Even their ages – one born April 1889, the other April 1890 – were 'practically the same'. She sadly notes that after the war Hughes 'never saw a horse again, except the milkman's horse'.[22] He enjoyed betting on them, however, like his father, and 'surprisingly, being Irish, did it quite well'.[23]

5

In the last months of the war Hughes was on leave from his regiment, which was stationed at the Curragh. One Sunday in Dublin, probably in uniform,[24] he met Irene Richardson in a tram, *en route* for the Black Church on the corner of Mountjoy Street and St Mary's Place, where she sang in the choir.[25] They fell in love. Irene was dark, petite, very beautiful and spirited. Dublin is a great singing city, and 'Rene'[26] (rhyming with 'teeny') as she was always known had a beautiful voice. She was training as a singer, and had already started performing at amateur concerts. She sang the standard operatic arias, and was particularly fond of 'One Fine Day' from *Madama Butterfly*. Its story of an innocent girl made pregnant then abandoned by the sailor she loves perhaps distantly echoes her own, happier story.

Hughes and Rene were married in Dublin on 7 December 1918 – a photo shows Hughes in full-dress uniform. Rene's sister Gertie (later Bell) was a witness. On the wedding certificate Hughes gives his army rank, second lieutenant, under 'profession', and his address as 'Marlborough Barracks'. Jean Iris Murdoch was born on 15 July, St Swithin's Day, the following year, just over seven months later. The marriage was probably therefore hasty.[27] Even in October 1918, when Iris would have been conceived, an early end to the war was not certain. Her character Andrew Chase-White in *The Red and the Green*, born, like Hughes, in a colony and serving, like Hughes, as a young officer in King Edward's Horse, feels some pressure from relatives to marry and make his wife pregnant before he has to go to the front and a likely death. Arthur Green's hypothesis that Hughes might have felt he had a comparable duty to perform *before* his marriage seems unlikely. Iris was probably a happy accident.

6

The extended Murdoch family comes out as a very intelligent, middle-class organism, stuffed with independent minds, a model example of Protestant and British Ireland. One group stems from the Brethren and has strong dental and medical associations; the son of one of Iris's first cousins was a Unionist politician, while a second cousin was Professor of Philosophy at Queen's University.[28] Uncle Elias, a Presbyterian married to a Quaker,* and Harold, a Quaker, ran the two well-known ironmongers' stores at Dun Laoghaire; another cousin, Brian Murdoch, also a Quaker, became Professor of Mathematics at Trinity College, Dublin.[29] Cousin Sybil also married a Quaker in Reggie Livingston; and some Richardsons are Quakers. There are today a mere 1,500 Quakers in the whole of Ireland, and if the frequency with which Quakerism turns up in Iris's fiction invites comment,[†] it is also disproportionately reflected in Irish history, being particularly prominent in famine relief, big business and education.[30] If Iris was herself touched by Quakerism's emphasis on integrity, quietness and peace, its belief in the availability of Inner Light to all, that all are capable of growing in wisdom and understanding, it is as likely to be from her headmistress at Badminton School as from her Irish relations that the influence came.

Rene's family represents another strain in the history of Protestant middle-class Ireland: Church of Ireland rather than Presbyterian, Dublin-based rather than from Belfast, former 'plantation squires' rather than 'plantation farmers'.[31] Not yeoman farmers and merchants like the Murdochs, the Richardsons, a complex and highly inter-related family, began as major land-owners in the

---

* Elias married Charlotte Isabella Neale, a Quaker. His sister Sarah married firstly Charles Neale, who was Charlotte's brother and also a Quaker. One child of this marriage, Mariette Neale, an active Quaker, was step-aunt to Reggie Livingston, also a Quaker, who married Iris's first cousin Sybil.

† Quakers figure in *An Accidental Man, A Word Child, Henry and Cato, The Message to the Planet, The Philosopher's Pupil* and *Jackson's Dilemma*. See Arthur Green, 'The Worlds of Iris Murdoch', *Iris Murdoch Newsletter*, no. 10, 1996.

seventeenth century and became minor gentry in the eighteenth, when Catholics were debarred from sitting in Parliament and holding government office, as well as suffering many petty restrictions, and Protestants had a virtual monopoly of power and privilege. Thereafter, the family's status declines. It mattered to Iris that she was grandly descended from Alexander Richardson, 'planted in Ireland in 1616 to control the wild Irish',[32] as she put it, and living at Crayhalloch in 1619. Readers of *An Unofficial Rose* will recognise the similar name of the house 'Grayhallock', with its links to the wealthy linen merchants of County Tyrone. Alexander Richardson's family motto *'Virtuti paret robur'*, is proudly quoted in *The Green Knight*, and translated as either 'strength obeys virtue' or 'virtue overcometh strength'.

In the 1990s an amateur genealogist from Ulster, Arthur Green, wrote up his patient investigations into Iris's family history. He showed, amongst much else, that she was *'una bambina di sette mesi'*, painted her parents' marriage as a hasty register office affair, and tried to show that her claims to be descended from the Richardsons of Drum Manor, and her identification with an Anglo-Irish background, were, in his word, 'romanticism'. He also queried whether her father's civil service status on his retirement in 1950 was as exalted as she believed. Green, at the suggestion of A.S. Byatt, sent these findings to Iris's publishers, Chatto & Windus.[33] Iris defended her pedigree with (at first) some stiffness, later lamenting that she had not asked more questions of her parents, and so been better-informed. She referred Green to O'Hart's *History of Old Irish Families*,[34] telling him she had lodged copies of relevant pages with her agent Ed Victor for safekeeping. Both Rene's father Effingham Lynch Richardson and her grandfather Robert Cooper Richardson merit a mention in O'Hart, which is noted for being, before 1800, notoriously untrustworthy, a source of myth, not fact. Given the burning of papers during the Troubles of 1921–22, the chances of establishing the truth seemed remote.

Fortunately, and unbeknownst to Iris, at the start of the twentieth century the Rev. Henry G.W. Scott, Rector of Tullinisken in County Armagh, had documented these Richardsons well.[35] James

I indeed granted the original Alexander Richardson Drum Manor, or Manor Richardson, in County Tyrone. Alexander's son William married Mary Erskine, heiress to the Augher Castle estate, County Tyrone, which in turn descended to their son Archibald. William left Drum Manor to his second son Alexander, who in 1682 married Margaret Goodlatte of Drumgally. His third son William, as well as inheriting lands near Augher, also obtained a lease of lands from his brother Alexander in the townland of Tullyreavy on the Drum Manor estate, where he built a house by the lake known as Oaklands, Woodmount or Lisdhu. O'Hart[36] erroneously identified Crayhalloch with Drum Manor Forest Park and also with Oaklands, as if all were different names for one house, instead of separate Richardson estates, from each of which Rene could claim descent.

William (d.1664) and Mary Erskine had three further sons. The eldest, James, married Mary Swan (1671–1740), heiress of William Swan, and their son Alexander (1705–71) succeeded to the estate of over a thousand acres at Farlough Lodge, strikingly situated above the Torrent river: a small five-bay, two-storey Georgian house with a dressed sandstone front and a square central porch[37] near Newmills, County Tyrone, not far from Cookstown. Through the eighteenth century the head of the family was churchwarden and member of the vestry of Drumglass and Tullinisken parishes, overseer of the roads and an officer in the militia. Iris's great-great-great-grandfather, for example, was Alexander's eldest son John Richardson of Farlough (1727–85), who married Hannah Lindsay in 1757 and was a JP, High Sheriff of Tyrone in 1778, and Captain of the Dungannon Volunteers in 1782. Owning more than a thousand acres, successive heads of the family lived, it can be assumed, in some comfort as modest country gentlemen.

The Richardsons also produced serious artistic talent and had continuing artistic tastes, well before Iris emerged to give them retrospective interest. They formed a large extended family which included two women writers, one of them distinguished. Iris's great-great-aunt Frances Elizabeth Fisher (*née* Richardson) published well-received volumes of verse such as *Love or Hatred* (three volumes) and *The Secret of Two Houses* (two volumes), also a book about Killarney. The better-known is Ethel Florence Lindesay Richardson (1870–1946), who wrote under the name of Henry Handel Richardson. She was the daughter of Walter Lindesay Richardson MD, model for Richard Mahony in her trilogy *The Fortunes of Richard Mahony* (1917–21). Henry Handel Richardson was second cousin to Rene's father Effingham Lynch Richard-son.[38] Like Rene she was musically talented, going to Leipzig to study music before turning to writing. She spent her early life in Australia and then Germany, belonging, like her cousin Iris, to a broad British and European and not merely an Irish world.[39] In her unfinished autobiography *Myself When Young* (1948) she refers to her strongly Protestant Irish Richardson relations, and their penchant for odd names 'such as Henry Handel and a Duke, more than one Snow and *several Effinghams*'. In *The Unicorn* Iris was to award her foolish character Effingham Cooper a key moment of insight.

7

The nineteenth century saw a downturn in Richardson fortunes, with the sons of yet another Alexander Richardson (1758–1827) squandering part of the £8,000 realised from sale of the Farlough estate. The phenomenon of downstart Anglo-Irish gentry was so familiar as to earn its own ingenious characterisation. Sir Jonah Barrington, whose racy memories of Irish history both Yeats and Joyce plundered, defines as 'half-mounted gentlemen' the small grantees of Queen Elizabeth or Cromwell living off two hundred acres. The Richardsons had been grander, somewhere between 'gentlemen every inch of them', whose finances were 'not in good order', and 'gentlemen to the backbone', from the oldest settler-families, generally also 'a little out at elbows'.[40] Most of Iris's immediate maternal forebears were minor men-of-law – Dublin was a litigious city with many attorneys – belonging to the Protestant Irish lower-middle class. Rene's paternal grandfather Robert Cooper Richardson, grandson to Tyrone's High Sheriff, born in 1827, and son of Robert Lindesay Richardson, a revenue officer, was a clerk in the Dublin Probate Court. Robert Cooper's son by his first wife Hannah, Effingham Lynch Richardson, a 'law assistant' born in 1857, after a first marriage without issue made a second to Elizabeth Jane Nolan, daughter of William Nolan Esquire.[41] Effingham and Jane had two daughters, Gertrude Anna (born 1891)[42] and Irene Alice (born 29 March 1899), mother-to-be of Iris.

Rene's father Effingham Lynch Richardson died on 6 July 1904, not long after *Ulysses*' 'Bloomsday', one tradition making his death, officially from 'erphelsocora of the groin', drink-related.[43] The fact that the Rev. A.W. Barton, Rector of St George's, rather than one of his three curates, took the funeral service, suggests that the family were actively involved in the life of the Church of Ireland at parish level. Iris also claimed Catholic ancestors.[44] Curiously, a second Effingham L. Richardson was shown living at 40 Iona Road, Glasnevin, Dublin, until 1947, and working until 1934 at the Dublin Ministry of Labour. This second E.L. Richardson, a first cousin of the first, was re-baptised as a Catholic before marrying in 1883.[45] Rene and her elder sister Gertie took 'Cooper', not among the baptismal names of either, as their middle name; they lived thereafter in the house of their grandfather Robert Cooper Richardson, and the twice-adopted name suggests gratitude to him for his generosity in fostering them after their father's death. The only story Rene would tell of her grandfather was that, though a man of industrious habits who at first kept his family well, when the 6 p.m. mail van arrived he would be facetious about this, in his Dublin manner. It was a signal for his first drink of the evening.

From 1906 the girls lived with their grandfather at 59 Blessington Street, a 'wide, sad, dirty street', Iris wrote, with 'its own quiet air of dereliction, a street leading nowhere, always full of idling dogs and open doorways'.[46] It runs parallel to Leopold Bloom's Eccles Street close by, and is halfway between St Joseph's Carmelite Church and the Anglican 'Black' Church, at the heart of that cheerless north inner city to which the Joyces retreated across the Liffey, with all their baggage in two large yellow caravans, when their fortunes took a downturn. Within a twilit world there are degrees of gloom and seediness. It is not hard to see why the 1906 move that Rene's grandfather made, away from the address given as 34 'Upper' Rutland Street,[47] where Rene and Gertie were growing up, was propitious. A street of ill-repute, Joyce placed Nighttown and its brothels at the end of it at that time.

The northern inner city[48] had been defeated first by the Duke of Leinster choosing in the 1740s to build on the South Side – 'Where I build, Fashion will follow' – and next by the exodus of gentry to England from around Luke Gardiner's Mountjoy Square after the 1801 Act of Union. But, above all, by the massive immigration into the area of starving country people during and after the Famine, resulting in the division of whole terraces into tenements. In their novel *The Real Charlotte* Somerville and Ross's down-at-heel, petit-bourgeois, essentially vulgar Protestant heroine Francie lives, in 1895, around Mountjoy Square, very near Blessington Street – like the Richardsons.[49] Today number 59 is divided into seven flats, the ground floor having been around 1990 a betting-shop.

8

A marriage brings two worlds, as well as two people, into collision. Hughes's cousin Don Douglas, grandson of Elias and so a 'solid' Murdoch by birth, regarded the Richardsons as rackety, and recalled Hughes's marriage as a serious social blunder.[50] If Rene had, by the hypocritical standards of the day, 'got herself into trouble', such odium would be explained. Her sister Gertie must also have been pregnant when she married, on 26 February 1919: Gertie gave birth at 59 Blessington Street to her eldest child Victor four months later, only three weeks before Iris was born at the identical address, probably in the same room. Gertie's Scottish husband Thomas Bell, like Hughes, was a Second Lieutenant in King Edward's Horse. There must have been a double courtship. It is striking that there is no Murdoch witness to Iris's parents' marriage certificate, especially as Hughes's uncle lived close by in Kingstown, and his mother and sisters in Belfast.* Rene's father is moreover shown, erroneously, as a solicitor (deceased). The Law Society in Dublin has no record of a solicitor called Effingham Richardson. In fact he worked in a solicitor's office, 'law assistant' probably signifying a clerk. Perhaps Rene and Gertie enhanced his status to compensate for any loss of caste on Hughes's part, or perhaps their mother had misremembered and misinformed them.

Iris's birth at 59 Blessington Street was probably difficult, perhaps, John Bayley believed, with the umbilical cord wrapped around the baby's neck. Rene had also had a rough time from Hughes's sisters and mother. She 'didn't fit in with the Protestant ethic', thought Iris's first cousin Cleaver Chapman.[51] As an Elder in the Apsley Hall Brethren assembly, his words come with some authority. Rene was beautifully made-up, cheerful and bright; she loved the coffee-shop, Cardews, in Kildare Street, where she went as a 'flapper'. Her new sister-in-law, 'wonderful'[52] Aunt Ella, was bossy and critical and on occasion ungenerous, smiling but lacking charity. Rene handled the disapproval very well, with tact, patience and good grace.

Rene liked to joke about North and South Dublin, and to be ironical at her own expense, socially speaking. When Iris's husband John Bayley in later life complimented her gallantly by saying that he was sure Rene must have been 'the toast of Dublin' when she was a girl, she would jokingly reply, 'Only of *North* Dublin.'[53] While Dublin north of the River Liffey was seedy and poor, the rich, smart suburbs stretched out to the south, from Rathmines to Dalkey. None the less, Rene had started to make her mark as a singer, and as a charming and modest personality.

---

* Nor did Rene's mother, Elizabeth Jane Richardson, witness the marriage. Dean's Grange Cemetery shows that she died, aged seventy-five, on 10 February 1941 at 34 Monkstown Road, where she was living, together with Mrs Walton, with the newly-wed Eva and Billy Lee. The two witnesses are Rene's sister Gertie and one 'Annie Hammond', whose son Richard Frederick Hammond went, often hand-in-hand, to primary school with Rene. Annie Hammond (*née* Gould) worked as housekeeper first to her husband's brother Harry Hammond, later to Dr Bobby Jackson of Merrion Square. (Letter from R.F. Hammond's son Rae Hammond to Iris Murdoch, 4 February 1987.)

Like her mother-in-law, she had a happy temperament. There was a great deal of amateur opera about in Dublin, 'that great singing city', as Joyce's own life, and his story 'The Dead', display. After her marriage Rene gave up professional performance, although choir-singing continued, and her beautiful voice was most often heard privately. She never said she minded abandoning her training, had 'no great agony about it', and appeared indifferent to fame and ambition. She knew she was talented, but did not take her gift too seriously. Iris, on the other hand, minded for her, and grieved for her mother's loss of career.[54] In her fiction she depicted wife after wife who has abandoned career for her husband.[55]

9

The fine comic writer Honor Tracy[56] first met Iris and John in Dalkey around 1958. A big jolly woman with rubicund and endearingly porcine features, Honor wore her flaming Anglo-Norman red hair somewhere between *en brosse* and beehive, had an occasionally combative manner, and appeared to be one (mainly) for the ladies.[57] Thus began a close friendship that survived until Tracy's death in 1989. Over the following thirty years her graphic letters provide an extravagant, loving, tough-minded and unreliable chorus to Iris's developing self-invention and what Tracy termed her 'weird extravagant fancies':

> You ask how Irish she is – the answer is, strictly not at all. Her father was of Ulster Protestant stock, but that is really a Scottish race, and Murdoch is a Scottish name. Mr Murdoch was a Civil Servant and happened to be posted to Dublin (pre-Republic) for a short time, during which Iris was born. She makes the most of it, as people are very apt to do: the number of English people who claim 'Irish grandmothers' is a famous joke in Ireland.[58]

The 'Jean' of Jean Iris Murdoch must indeed be Scots-Irish, from the Murdoch side, albeit never used. From the first she was known as 'Iris', complementing her mother's 'Irene'.[59] One charm of her name is that 'Iris' does not quite belong to 'Murdoch': 'Jean' or 'Jeannie' Murdoch might be some tough lady from Glasgow; Iris Murdoch confounds two sets of expectations. An accidental charm is that another 'Iris' was goddess of rainbows, many-coloured, protean, hard to pin down.

'Irish when it suits them, English when it does not,' was what Honor Tracy's erstwhile friend and neighbour Elizabeth Bowen said the 'true' Irish claimed of the Anglo-Irish – both the Protestant Anglo-Irish like the Bowens, and also 'castle Catholics'[60] like the original Tracys. Tracy, for example, spoke aggressively County English when in England, yet with a brogue when the Bayleys visited her house on Achill Island in County Mayo. Is Tracy's wit at Iris's expense partly tribal? It is certainly an irony at the expense of someone who – to an extraordinary degree – was to become the darling of the English, far more than of the Irish, intellectual and cultural establishments.[61] She loved to tease Iris about her Irishness in a way that was envious, admiring, combative, ignorant (as in her letter above) and flirtatious. Iris took this in good part – in *The Red and the Green* she was to create an Anglo-Irish character for whom calling himself Irish was 'more of an act than a description, an assumption of a crest or a picturesque cockade'.[62] Both Iris's parents showed their Irishness in their voices. Rene had a Dublin voice, a 'refined' voice, with that Dublin habit of pronouncing 'th' as 't', especially at the start of a word – for example, 't'ings like that'. Hughes had a very mild Ulster intonation and idiom: 'Wait while I tell you!' he would advise. Young Iris had a slight brogue, acquired from her parents. Well into adult life she would sometimes pronounce 'I think' as 'I t'ink'. On 1 April 1954, on a trip to Glengarriff on the Beara peninsula, most westerly of all the peninsulas of Cork, she noted, 'I have an only partly faked-up impression of being *at home* here.'

The last of Tracy's Catholic Anglo-Norman ancestors to have lived in Ireland was Beau Tracy, who left in 1775, when Iris's great-great-great-grandfather was High Sheriff of Tyrone. Tracy, born in Bury St Edmunds, Suffolk, educated in Dresden and at the Sorbonne, first lived in Ireland at the age of thirty-seven, when the *Sunday Times* sent her there as a special correspondent in 1950, and she set six of her thirteen books there. But no one ever agrees about who is entitled to lay claim to Irishness. Iris's Belfast cousins today call themselves British, not Irish, while Hughes's humorous comment on a photograph of Paddy O'Regan, Iris's boyfriend of Irish descent around 1940, was, 'Typically Irish – he looks as if he wants to fight something.'[63] With both parents brought up in Ireland, and an ancestry within Ireland both North and South going back three centuries, Iris had as valid a claim to call herself Irish as most North Americans have to call themselves American, generally after a shorter time on that continent.[64]

Iris recorded on an early dust-jacket that 'although most of her life has been spent in England, she still calls herself an Irish writer'. From 1961, with the Anglo-Irish narrator of *A Severed Head*, and following her father's death, this changes permanently to 'she comes of Anglo-Irish parentage', a doubtful claim if meant to refer to an Ascendancy, land-owning, horse-riding background. Iris never claimed to belong to the Ascendancy as such, and it is doubtful that Rene used the word. Yet Rene certainly knew that her once grand family had, in her own phrase, 'gone to pot'. Iris's interest in this pedigree dates from August 1934, when she discovered on holiday in Dun Laoghaire that the Richardsons had a family motto, and a 'jolly good one'. She noted that, as well as 'virtue', '*virtus*' in '*Virtuti paret robur*' could also mean 'courage . . . But never mind, away with Latin. We shall be climbing the Mourne mountains next week, the Wicklow mountains the week after.'[65] Pious about distant glories the family may have been.[66] Snobs they were not. Hughes got on very well with Rene's brother-in-law Thomas Bell, who had been commissioned with him in the same regiment and now worked as a car-mechanic at Walton's, a Talbot Street Ford showroom;[67] one of Thomas's four sons, Victor, later a long-distance lorry-driver for Cadbury's, appears with Iris in holiday snaps; a further two, Alan (also known as Tom) and John Effingham Bell, also worked for Cadbury's in Dublin, as fitter and storeman respectively. They lived on Bishop Street.[68] If by Anglo-Irish is meant 'a Protestant on a horse', a big house, the world of Molly Keane or of Elizabeth Bowen's Bowen's Court, this is not it.

In her first year at Oxford, in an article in *Cherwell* entitled 'The Irish, are they Human?', Iris was to refer to the Anglo-Irish as 'a special breed'. In her second, after the IRA had declared war on Britain in January 1939, which was to cause over three hundred explosions, seven deaths and ninety-six casualties,[69] and at the start of what in Ireland is called the 'Emergency',[70] she was treasurer of the Irish Club, listened to Frank Pakenham (later Lord Longford) talk of 'chatting with De Valera' and herself gave a paper on James Connolly, Communist hero of the 1916 Rising.[71] To Frank Thompson in 1941 she wrote of Ireland as 'an awful pitiful mess of a country', full, like herself, of 'pretences and attitudes . . . but Ireland at least has had its baptism of blood and fire'. The Richardson family motto '*Virtuti paret robur*' is often repeated in her later journals, like a talisman or mantra. Iris saw herself, like her friend from 1956 Elizabeth Bowen, as caught between two worlds and at home in neither.[72]

To be of a once distinguished Protestant family in Ireland at the beginning of the twentieth century still conferred a sense of caste.[73] As recently as 1991 Iris defined her mother's family as Anglo-Irish gentry whose 'estate in County Tyrone . . . had vanished some time ago'.[74] Insistence that one's family was still 'gentry', no matter how impoverished, was partly tribal Protestantism. Even those Irish Protestants in the early Irish Free State who came of humble stock felt that they emphatically belonged, none the less, to a '*corps d'élite*':

> Ex-Unionists – including those who were not very book-ish – were proud of the Anglo-Irish literary heritage. They prided themselves . . . on possessing what were regarded as Protestant virtues, a stern sense of duty, industry and integrity together with the ability to enjoy gracefully and whole-heartedly the good things of life. [This] *esprit de corps* . . . was voiced with vibrant force by Yeats in his famous and thunderous intervention in a Senate debate in 1925. Speaking for the minority, he declaimed, 'we are no petty people. We are one of the

great stocks of Europe. We are the people of Berkeley; we are the people of Swift; we are the people of Parnell.'[75]

Iris's willingness to mythologise her own origins, and to lament a long-lost demesne (in her case, a real ancestry), both mark her out as a kinswoman of Yeats.* The 'Butler' appended to the Yeats family name proposed a not entirely fictitious connexion to that grandest of clans, the Anglo-Irish Dukes of Ormonde. Family pride runs through much of Iris's rhetoric about her background, both in interviews and also in Chapter 2 of *The Red and the Green*, with its authorial identification with the old Protestant ruling order, as well as its claim for that order to speak for the whole of Ireland, Catholic and Protestant alike.

The relation between Iris and her cousins was complex. Another Richardson relative she claimed,[76] who had presumably not suffered from the general Richardson decline, was a Major-General Alexander Arthur Richardson, serving with the Royal Ulster Rifles in the Second World War. The Belfast family phrase 'the Ladies' bathing-place' amused Iris. So did the Belfast cousins calling a 'slop-basin' – for tea-slops – a 'refuse-vase', which the Murdochs considered a genteelism.[77] If Iris's family found the Belfast cousinry genteel, Belfast cousin Sybil Livingston conversely thought the cigarette-holder Iris sported for a while 'posh'; and she was amazed in 1998 to learn that Rene had a sister of any kind, let alone one with four sons, giving Iris first cousins in Dublin as well as Belfast. 'You are my only family,' Sybil recalls Iris saying – mysteriously as it might appear: perhaps there was a remarkable depth of reserve on both sides.[78] Sybil around 1930 had passed on to her a 'wonderful' party frock of Iris's, pale blue satin, with a braid of little pink and blue and white rosebuds sewn round the neck and sleeves. For Iris, a much-loved only child, as for Elizabeth Bowen, Ireland represented company.

---

* See Roy Foster, *Paddy and Mr Punch* (London, 1993), Chapter 11, 'Protestant Magic', pp.215ff. The Richardson version of the 'Butler' worn by Yeats may be the frequently recurring middle name of 'Lindsay', associating them with the Earls of that name. *The Australian Dictionary of National Biography*, under 'Richardson (Henry Handel)', notes that Richardsons claimed descent from the Earls of Lindesay. O'Hart gives four different Lindesay Richardsons among IM's immediate ancestors.

Iris believed that, after her birth in Dublin, her parents lived with her there for one or two years,[79] until the inauguration of the Irish Free State at the very end of 1921. These Dublin years, often mentioned in interviews – again, like Elizabeth Bowen – confirmed her Irish identity. Around 1921 all Irish civil servants were offered the choice of moving to Belfast or London. It is easy to see why, in the political turmoil of those years, with the Troubles, the introduction of martial law, and then the civil war looming, Hughes, who was after all not merely a Protestant and an Ulsterman but also an ex-officer, might have opted for London, a city he had known on and off since 1906. Iris said he came to England to find his fortune[80] but saw this as a radical move, a kind of exile. In fact, if Iris as a baby spent even as much as one year in Dublin, it was only with her mother. On Iris's birth certificate Hughes gives 51 Summerlands Avenue, Acton, London W3 as his address, and his civil service position was second division clerk in the National Health Insurance Committee, working in Buckingham Gate, London (apart from his three years' active service) from 15 June 1914 until 24 November 1919, when he joined the Ministry of Health. Cards from fellow-conscripts during the war give his working address as 'Printing, Insurance Commission, Buckingham Gate, London, S.W.'. The move to London – in reaction against the madnesses of Ulster in 1914, just as much as against those of Dublin in 1921 – had already begun. Presumably Iris was born in Dublin because Rene could rely there on kin and womenfolk to help with the birth. And perhaps Rene and Iris had to wait for Hughes to find the flat in Brook Green where they first all lived together.

Honor Tracy was certainly right that the value to Iris of her Irishness was great: '. . . my Irishness is Anglo-Irishness in a very strict sense . . . People sometimes say to me rudely, "Oh! You're not Irish at all!" But of course I'm Irish. I'm profoundly Irish and I've been conscious of this all my life, and in a mode of being Irish which has produced a lot of very distinguished thinkers and writers'[81] – Bowen, Congreve, Sheridan, Wilde, Goldsmith and Yeats all epitomised Irish modes of expression while living in England and 'regretting Ireland'.[82] The term 'Anglo-Irish' is less unhelpful if it means, as Arthur Green argued and the *OED* allows, some broad confluence of English, Irish and indeed Scots-Irish – a product, in fact, of both islands. It is from this point of view interesting that Iris believed she had Catholic Irish connexions,[83] as well as Quaker, Church of Ireland and Presbyterian ones. The pattern of English life, she wrote in 1963, can be dull, making little appeal to the imagination.[84] Ireland, by contrast, was romantic. Moreover she identified, until 1968, with Ireland-as-underdog.[85] England had destroyed Ireland, one of her characters argued in *The Red and the Green*, 'slowly and casually, without malice, without mercy, practically without thought, like someone who treads upon an insect, forgets it, then sees it quivering and treads upon it a second time'.[86]

Iris's Irish identification was more than romanticism. Her family, Irish on both sides for three hundred years, never assimilated into English life, staying a small enclosed unit on its own, never gaining many – if any – English friends. When Hughes died in 1958, having lived for forty-three of his sixty-eight years in England, there were only, to Rene's distress, six people at the funeral: Iris and John, Rene, cousin Sybil's husband Reggie, Hughes's solicitor, and a single kindly neighbour, Mr Cohen, who owned the 'semi' with which the Murdoch house was twinned. Not one civil service mourner materialised. Iris's first act that year of bereavement was to take Rene and John to Dublin, to find a suitable house for Rene to move back to. The following year Rene took Iris and John to see Drum Manor. There was a dilapidated gatehouse, and some sense of a gloomy and run-down demesne.[87] Rene and Iris were reverential.

As Roy Foster has shown, the cult in Ireland of a lost house was a central component of that 'Protestant Magic' that both Yeats and Elizabeth Bowen shared:[88] Irish Protestantism, Foster argues, even in its non-Ulster mode, is a social and cultural identity as much as a religious one. Some of its elements – a preoccupation with good manners together with a love of drama and occasional flamboyant emotionalism, a superstitious bent towards occultism and magic,* an inability to grow up, an obsession with

* For Iris Murdoch's interest in these matters see pp. 277, 451, 525–6.

the hauntings of history and a disturbed love-hate relation with Ireland itself – can be found in Iris as in Bowen and Yeats. Bowen's Protestant Irishness made of her a 'naturally separated person': so did Iris's. Yeats, coming from 'an insecure middle-class with a race memory of elitism',[89] conquered the inhabitants of great houses such as Coole Park through unique 'charm and the social power of art',[90] rather as Iris later visited Clandeboye and Bowen's Court. Both Yeats and Iris elevated themselves socially 'by a sort of moral effort and a historical sleight-of-hand'.[91] Each was, differently, an audacious fabulator, in life as in art.

In the confusion of her latter years when much was to be forgotten, the words 'Irish' and 'Ireland' were unfailing reminders of Iris's own otherness. Both struck deep chords, and she would perk up and show particular interest. In Provence in June 1997 she remarked emphatically, 'I'm *nothing* if not Irish.' The following winter, sitting at the small deal kitchen table after a bracing walk on the Radnorshire hills, she disconcerted her hearers by asking, 'Who am I?', to which she almost at once soothed herself by musing, 'Well I'm Irish anyway, *that's something.*' A lifetime's investment in Irishness, visible in every decade of her life, was then, as it had always been, a source of reassurance, a reference-point, a credential, somewhere to start out from and return to.

10

Iris's early memories were of swimming, singing and being sung to, of animals, and of wonderment at the workings of the adult world. She sat at the age of about seven under the table while her parents played bridge – either reading a favourite childhood book or, as she put it, 'simply sitting in quietness'[92] and listening in astonishment to the altercations and mutual reproaches of the adults at the end of each rubber. Wonderment, imaginative identification with a fantastic range of creature-kind, capacity to feel strong emotions, secretiveness, and also Irishness: these are recurrent and related themes within her story.

Early photographs show her a blonde, plump, exceedingly pretty baby, flirting in a straw Kate Greenaway bonnet with her mother, and even more with her photographer-father, in Dalkey in August 1921. If the family was by then already based in London, neither this nor the Black and Tans, who had that year raided 'rebel' houses in Blessington Street itself,[93] prevented the annual Irish summer holiday. The truce of 11 July that year would have offered holidaymakers, among others, reassurance.

Hughes, Rene and baby Iris lived first of all in a flat at 12 Caithness Road, Brook Green, Hammersmith. Hughes was fairly low down on the civil service ladder but had a permanent position as a second class clerk in the Ministry of Health, a ministry he was to stay at until 1942. He kept a pocketbook in which he noted the day's expenditures, no matter how minor.[94] This same meticulousness shows itself in the young Iris's carefully managed stamp collection. She tucked away in the back both a small 'duplicate book', in case of losses, and an envelope marked emphatically '*valuable* stamps: King Edward', referring, of course, to stamps pertaining to the short reign of Edward VIII.

What exactly constitutes a '*first*' memory? Surely later imaginative significance as much as strict chronological primacy. Iris gave as her 'first' memory not 'My mother flying up above me like a white bird',[95] but herself swimming in the salt-water baths near Dun Laoghaire when she was three or four years old.[96] Her father got quickly to the further side, where he sat and called out encouragement. In 1997 she could still enact the excitement, fear, sense of challenge, and deep love entailed in her infant efforts slowly to swim to the other side and regain her father's protection – a powerful enough proto-image in itself of her continuing life-quest for the authority of the Father. Another version has Hughes first of all persuading her to jump in, and into his arms.

Swimming was the secret family religion. It is not merely that Hughes liked to swim in the Forty-Foot: swimming is mentioned on postcard after postcard, in letter after letter, from and to Iris over many decades, and the word order of one particular card from Sandycove, Dun Laoghaire, from her mother to Iris makes clear which activity carried the greater weight: 'Had a bathe this morning – after church.'[97] Churchgoing is likely to have occurred mainly because Rene was still singing in the choir.

In her journals Iris would recollect, especially latterly, many songs her mother taught her. In January 1990 she records:

> Recalling Rene. A prayer she must have taught me when I was a small child. I remember it as phrased –
>
>> Jesus teacher: shepherd hear me:
>> bless thy little: lamb tonight:
>> in the darkness: be thou near me:
>
> keep me safe till: morning light.
> She must have taught it to me word for word as soon as I could talk.[98]

Rene also sang to Iris 'Tell me the old, old story of Jesus and His Love'. But who exactly *was* Jesus's love? The infant Iris, misconstruing this sentence as small children are apt to, used to wonder . . .

Grown-up Iris knew the words of the combative 'Old Orange Flute', probably from her father, who could also recite Percy French's 'Abdul the Bulbul Ameer'. Rene sang, as well as works such as Handel's *Messiah* in a choir, light ballads, French's among others. Percy French songs suggest the comfortable synthetic Irishness Tracy later made fun of in her books. Rene took pride, too, in singing Nationalist or 'rebel' songs:

> Here's to De Valera,
> The hero of the right,
> We'll follow him to battle,
> With orange green and white.
> We'll fight against old England
> And we'll give her hell's delight.
> And we'll make De Valera King of Ireland.

After the shootings that followed the Easter Rising, when Rene was seventeen, some Protestant Richardsons were pro-rebel;[99] Rene was pro-Michael Collins and against De Valera in 1922, when the two found themselves on opposing sides in the civil war. She took delight, when she learnt it later, in the song 'Johnson's

Motor-Car'. The Nationalist 'rebels' borrow Constable Johnson's car for urgent use, and promise to return it in this fashion:

> We'll give you a receipt for it, all signed by Captain Barr.
> And when Ireland gets her freedom, boy, ye'll get your
>   motor-car.

Grandma Louisa, after a visit to London in the twenties, would often recount Iris sitting on the pavement and weeping inconsolably about a dog which had been hit by a car. Iris was to give the death of a pet dog as a first memory, and first trauma, to characters in successive books.* The dog might have been hers: a photograph of Hughes with a mongrel (possibly containing some smooth-haired terrier) survives, and a smaller third hand must belong to the child Iris, otherwise wholly hidden behind the animal. Another shows Iris proudly stroking the same beast on her own.

There were cats also, Tabby and Danny-Boy. Danny-Boy uttered memorable growling noises on sighting birds from the windowsill. Seventy years later Iris recalled her father wishing the cats goodnight before putting out the lights.[100] They attracted friends: Cousin Cleaver recalls Hughes putting out fish and chicken for the neighbourhood strays.[101] There seems never to have been a time when Iris was not capable of identifying with and being moved by the predicament of animals – dogs especially. When the *Mail on Sunday* invited her in 1996 to contribute to a series on 'My First Love',[102] her husband John, writing on her behalf, told of her first falling in love as a small girl with a slug. It is not wholly implausible. Cousin Sybil remembers Iris and Hughes carefully collecting slugs from the garden, and then tipping them gently onto waste land beyond. In the autumn of 1963, seeing John's colleague John Buxton look sadly at his old dog Sammy during dinner, Iris was moved to tears and could hardly stop weeping. The dog died a few weeks later.

---

* Eugene in *The Time of the Angels*; Willy in *The Nice and the Good.*

2

No Mean City
1925–1932

Happy childhoods are rare. Iris was both a happy and a 'docile'[1] child. She led an idyllic life at home. When she wrote about her pre-war life, especially at her two intensely high-minded and eccentric schools, all was, despite a rocky start at the second, golden, grateful and rhapsodic, a cross between late Henry James and Winnie in Beckett's *Happy Days*. These reminiscences were requested by the schools in question – 'Why did I agree?' Iris wrote in vexation.[2] Moreover, though three friends had already sent their daughters to Iris's old school Badminton on the strength of her example,[3] when the critic Frank Kermode in 1968 wished to send his daughter there, Iris advised against it: 'she had not been altogether happy there'. Presumably the tone of her written recollections – decorous, nostalgic, pious, suppressing the uncomfortable – owed something to Iris's desire to please former mentors. With such provisos, and especially by contrast with what was to come, this period was broadly happy, and she was lucky in both her schooling and her family life. She once said to Philippa Foot, 'I don't understand this thing about "two's company, three's none". My mother and father and I were always three, and we were always happy.' She pictured her parents and herself as 'a perfect trinity of love'.[4] They were a self-sufficient family unit, contented to be doing things together.

Hughes was interested in reading and study. He loved second-hand bookshops, frequenting one during his lunch-hour in Southampton Row,[5] where classics such as Dickens and Thackeray could be picked up for, say, sixpence.[6] He bought first editions of Jane Austen,[7] and read Ernst Jünger's First World War fiction.[8] Both her parents loved reading to Iris, and Hughes would discuss the stories they read together. Her 'earliest absolutely favourite books' were *Alice in Wonderland* and *Through the Looking Glass, Treasure Island, Kidnapped* and *Kim,*[9] which she had a great feeling of living 'inside'.[10] *Treasure Island* was the perfect adventure story, and she and Hughes would both enjoy being frightened by Blind Pew's stick tapping along the road, and the exciting moment when Jim goes up the mast – 'And another step Mr Hands and I'll blow your brains out.' This passage later became part of her and her husband John's private mythology, with its brilliantly observed detail of the fish or two which 'whip past' the shot and drowned Hands.

The childlike, visceral excitements of these works travelled with Iris through adulthood. Intellectual though she was, she never despised the old-fashioned, primitive satisfactions of storytelling. She gave Hands's surname to a favoured character, Georgie, in *A Severed Head.* Among the first passages to move her was a quarrel between the swashbuckling Alan Breck and David Balfour, the quiet abducted Lowlander in Stevenson's *Kidnapped,*[11] and a quarrel between two men later fuelled many of her novels. *Kim* is cited in *Nuns and Soldiers* when Gertrude and the ex-nun Anne imagine travelling through life 'like Kim and the lama'. And in her most difficult and intimate novel, *The Black Prince,* she gave her semi-autobiographical hero the dying words 'I wish I'd written *Treasure Island.*' 'Stories are art, too,' he had earlier explained. Perhaps good writers retain their childlike interest in and wonder at the world. Iris's Belfast cousins were much struck that Iris, though so intelligent and academic, was simultaneously so simple. When cousin Sybil lost her husband and Iris at the Festival of Britain in 1951, she discovered them riding together on the merry-go-round, *en route* to see the 'amazing motor-cyclists' on the Wall of Death. 'I do *like* your Reggie,' Iris pronounced, with the only child's unconscious egoism.

When the family came to England, their absolute friendlessness there somehow did not matter, since the three of them were such a 'tight little entity'. Hughes probably did not introduce his office acquaintance into the family circle. Nor did he and Irene miss social life, Hughes being, like many men of his class and time, a home-body. Yet the compactness and intimacy of this family unit is remarkable. Iris had her own names for her parents, unusual for a child in those inter-war days. 'Rene' and 'Doodle' was how she normally addressed them – 'Doodle' being Iris's coinage, and perhaps a baby's mispronunciation of 'Daddy'.

When Iris created the aptly named (since innocent) 'Adam' Arrowby in *The Sea, The Sea*, it was of her own father that she was thinking.

> My father was a quiet bookish man and somehow the gentlest being I have ever encountered. I do not mean he was timid, though I suppose he *was* timid. He had a positive moral quality of gentleness. I can picture him now so clearly, bending down with his perpetual nervous smile to pick up a spider on a piece of paper and put it carefully out of the window or into some corner where it would not be disturbed. I was his comrade, his reading companion, *possibly the only person with whom he ever had a serious conversation* ... We read the same books and discussed them: children's books, adventure stories, then novels, history, biography, poetry, Shakespeare. We enjoyed and craved for each other's company ... I remember feeling in later life that no one else ever knew how *good* my father was.[12]

Perhaps the family's Irishness contributed to their self-containment. Landladies, after all, put up notices advertising rooms with the proviso 'No blacks, no dogs, no Irish' as late as the 1950s. In the 1920s, at the height of the Troubles, when the Murdochs first settled in London, an Irish accent could not have been an asset. Iris's future mother-in-law Olivia Bayley, *née* Heanan and half-Irish by descent, was determinedly English, '*plus royaliste que le roi*'. Rene by contrast had a brogue which deepened in some situations. And, as cousin Sybil was to discover on a visit to Birmingham coinciding with the terrible IRA bombings of the 1970s,[13] the English are not always skilled in making nice distinctions between varieties of Irish voice and identity.

2

Around Iris's sixth birthday memorable things started to happen. Rene got her a little wind-up man on a tricycle – 'I see him so clearly, and her.'[14] She went to her first school. And, not long after, the family moved from Brook Green to Chiswick. Hughes must have had an adventurous streak as well as being a homebody, since around 1926 he bought a small, newly built, semi-detached gabled house in Chiswick. His annual salary was well under £400 per year, so he took out a mortgage. There was a newly planted chestnut tree outside, and the house, at 4 Eastbourne Road, was tucked away off what was soon to become the Great West Road. The family took walks in the grounds of nearby Chiswick House.

On 15 January 1925, aged five and a half, Iris had entered the Froebel Demonstration School at Colet Gardens, a very good, quite expensive day-school, a fifteen-minute walk across Brook Green from the Caithness Road flat, presumably chosen partly because of proximity. It was the 'demonstration school' for Froebel College at Grove House in Roehampton, and had just over a hundred pupils. Iris flourished there. The new house must also have been bought with proximity in mind. Eastbourne Road was five short stops from Froebel on the District Line, close enough to be walkable in summer.

At first Iris's mother took her to school – a contemporary recalled Rene as very pretty and smart, intimidatingly attractive and stylish.[15] Later, after the move, Hughes would sometimes accompany her on the Tube on his way to work, Iris getting out and walking the last two minutes from Barons Court station by herself. She used to buy sweets on the way. Another contemporary recalls the general taste for 'sudden-death boiled sweets', the Wall's ice cream man who would drive along the road in front of the school with his van marked 'Stop Me and Buy One', the excitement of the children clustering round and buying a cold, hard, sharpish-flavoured triangular water-ice on a stick, good value at about a penny, roast chestnuts in winter, when Hammersmith was enlivened by barrows lit up with paraffin flares.[16] Some little schoolfriend, to tease Iris, suggested as a joke that she go into the sweet-shop and order 'one quarter of a pound of Gleedale Munchums'. Gleedale toffees existed, but not Gleedale Munchums. ('Gleedale Munchums' became a lifelong Bayley family joke.)

Iris's first day at school was 'momentous and gratifying'. She had been placed in the kindergarten in the one-storeyed building which had been the original school in 1893, under either Miss Ilse Williams or the capable and imaginative Miss Gladys Short, who died from a bee sting twenty years later. Both the term 'kindergarten' and the concept of learning through creative play and adventures had been coined by the German educationalist Friedrich Froebel (1782–1852). Hughes's excellent tuition of Iris 'told', and she was promptly moved up to the Transition group. She exchanged the simple shantung 'overall' – kindergarten uniform – for the green serge pinafore dress – gingham in summer – worn over a cream shantung blouse by the older girls, and a leaf-green jacket bearing the Froebel badge of that time, a reversed swastika within a circle, embroidered with a black outline and filled in with white embroidery thread. Called a Greek cross symbol or '*fylfot*', the full version bore the legends 'Outworld – Facts and Acts' on the upper plane, and on the lower 'Inworld – Memories and Plans'. After 1939, for reasons not hard to discern, this quaint school symbol was changed to a Michaelis daisy. The school motto – '*Vincit qui se vincit*' – suggests the humanism which the adult Iris would passionately defend: 'He conquers who conquers himself.'

There were boys up to the age of eleven – another symptom of the school's progressivism – dressed in grey shirts, shorts and blazers. Some daring girl taught Iris, almost at once, to slide across the parquet floor. And she learnt to write, with a relief nib with a hard square tip, what was termed 'script'. It replaced the old copperplate with a larger font. The first sentence she copied, in noble plain 'script' letters, was: 'The snowdrop hangs its head down. Why?' 'Why indeed!' she later wrote. 'A thought-provoking question, a good introduction to a world which is full of mysteries.' Recalling Froebel evoked reverence and gratitude: 'A spirit of courtesy, of dignity, of standards, of care for others, was painlessly induced. Relations between boys and girls . . . were happy and orderly and innocent. We were all remarkably good children.' Learning was 'both rigorous and painless'. Her images of those schooldays were 'of *light*, of freedom and happiness, the great greedy pleasures of learning, the calm kindly authority of teachers, the mutual amiability of children'.[17]

Competition, 'essential to education', existed in variety. Of teachers she singled out Miss Burdett, who taught the girls Latin from the age of eleven, thereby opening the way to Greek later; and 'magisterial and warm-hearted' Miss Bain, the headmistress. There was cricket too, taught by Mr Keegan, wont to call out 'Stop picking a daisy, *sir*,' to some little girl who found the wild-flowers more interesting than the cricket ball. Not Iris; she, like her father,[18] loved cricket all her life.

The school had been pacifist during the Great War, when instead of the standard version of 'God Save the King', this verse was bravely sung:

> God bless our native land
> May Heaven's protective hand
> Still guard her shore.
> May peace her power extend,
> Foe be transformed to friend
> And Britain's might depend
> On war no more.[19]

This suggests republicanism as well as pacifism.

Froebel was certainly a highly original and an engagingly dotty place, 'modern' for its time, with a friendly and relaxed discipline and no strong religious bias. Two exact contemporaries remembered Iris vividly. The father of Barbara Denny (*née* Roberts, and later to write a fictionalised life of Friedrich Froebel[20]) had heard that this was the school 'where the children did nothing but play'. His meeting with the headmistress, Ethel M. Bain, changed his mind. She was a small, frail-looking Scotswoman with considerable strength of character, with neat, spry, sparrowish features, thin but equally neatly moulded lips, greying hair drawn back in properly prim fashion, and a quiet way of talking which was attended to respectfully. Miss Bain would appear to have been both imaginative and sympathetic: a carefully scripted card from her to Iris showing the bunsen burners in the school science room, dated 24 January 1930, reads: 'I am so sorry that you have got such a horrid cough. Get well as quickly as you can and come back to school. *The Irish girl is here.* Love from E.M. Bain.'

3

Many aspects of the school that then seemed 'modern' have since become standard: the garden area where each form tended its own flowerbed, the two ponds providing instruction and delight in the form of frogs, newts and tadpoles. Play areas, well stocked with trees and shrubs, contained an ancient wooden summer-house and hutches for rabbits and guinea pigs.

Other aspects now look quaint. A child could choose on his or her birthday a story to be read by Miss Bain – often, in that decade, by A.A. Milne. The first form introduced the children to the strange glories of 'Knights and Ladies', entailing remarkable dressings-up and an 'omnipresent form of chivalry that was more than a game', probably Miss Bain's inspiration, since it departed with her in 1933. It was an imaginative version of the house and prefect system used in more conventional schools. The boys and girls in the top form – known as Squires and Dames – each had a household of about ten younger children down the school to whom they acted as mother- or father-figure in both work and play. A Dame sewed her banner – becoming a Dame preceded being dubbed a 'Lady' – with an appropriate device; her Squire built himself a shield in the woodwork class.* At least once a term

---

* Miriam Allott's Squire was Garth Underwood, whose sculptor-father Leon provided inspiration for A.P. Herbert in *The Water-Gypsies* (1930). His names being Garth Lionel, his emblem was a golden lion rampant cut out of a yellow duster, with an embroidered flame issuing from its mouth. Miriam's Egyptian maiden name, Farris, meant 'knight', so surrounding the lion they had two silver knight's spurs made

the whole school would assemble at the 'King's Court' in the larger College Hall, the Dames and Squires in two lines, their households lined up behind them in order of age. King Bain would enter, walking down the aisle in a velvet cloak and cardboard crown, the boys bowing and the girls curtseying. The *Old Froebelian's News Letter* of 1934 recalled the scene: 'Oyez! Oyez!! Know ye that this day ... the King holds high revel and would welcome all his Court, Knights and Ladies, Squires and Dames, Pages (&tc ...) to a joust and a feast. Thus ran the message and right merrily did the Lands assent thereto.'* King Bain would first address the assembly on some important matter. Courtesy was a strong point:

> Of Courtesy ... it is much less
> Than courage of heart, or holiness
> But in my walks, it seems to me
> That the grace of God is in courtesy
> *(Hilaire Belloc)*

At this point jousting with King Bain, that tiny, frail and grey-haired little lady, began. Barbara Denny remembered her challenging her squires to battle with quarterstaffs of rolled-up brown paper. Miriam Allott recalls a wooden sword. Might the wooden sword have belonged to King Bain, while the squires jousted with mere rolled-up brown paper? A discourteous thought.[†] In any case, King Bain would fight with one or other of the squires or knights in turn, jousting with him up and down the hall between the ranks of the households, and signifying when a bout was to end. For this she wore, besides a copper-coloured crown, a knee-length blue tunic and grey stockings, not wool but the fine lisle or faux-silk common at that time.

---

from balloon cloth, plus seven stars, for 'Miriam' (= Mary). They were known as the household of the Silver Knight and the Golden Lion.

* 'Thereafter all the Court all joined with merriment in the strange game of "Ye Knight he chased ye dragon up ye hickoree tree!" Truly terrible was the advance of the nobel Baron Dane ...' etc., etc. Account of the final Knights and Ladies, *Old Froebelian's News Letter*, 1934, pp.3-4.

† Miriam Allott, however, is sure that the wooden sword was at Miss Bain's belt, and that when jousting it was either wooden swords for all, or rolled-up paper for all.

Once a year at Christmas there was a special occasion described by Miss Bain as a 'coloured picture'. The children dressed up in party clothes with veils for the girls, paper helmets and silver-painted dishcloth or possibly papier-mâché armour for the boys. Staff wore tights and tunics, velvet hats or wimples and medieval gowns, with various badge devices for the few male teachers. Miss Short, wearing a wimple, one year sang 'I'm off with the raggle-taggle gypsies, oh'.

As well as special dressing-up, this was also a time for special recognition. It was a rare honour on such a day to be 'dubbed' a knight or lady. The chosen person would kneel before King Bain, a boy to be dubbed with the sword, a girl to receive a tall wimple with a muslin veil, and the gift of a roll of bread (for sustenance) and a bunch of violets (for beauty and gentleness). Barbara Denny found the occasion one of the most moving of her young life, and Miss Bain would address her in letters for the next fifty or so years (she lived well into her nineties) as 'My Lady Barbara'. Denny recalled Iris being made a lady and receiving her bouquet. Highlight of the banquet was a Boar's Head made by the local bakery – Hamilton's – chocolate-iced sponge with a lemon in its mouth, and banana tusks. This was borne in on a tray held high by four members of staff dressed as 'pages', to the singing of the medieval carol:

> The Boar's Head in hand bear I,
> Bedecked with mace and rosemary.
> I pray ye my masters be merrie . . .
> *Caput apri defero ridens Laudis Domino.**

On one such splendid Christmas occasion, with King Bain presiding in androgynous style, young Miriam Allott overheard her father murmur *sotto voce* to her mother, '*We shall have to take that girl away . . .* '

Around 1927 two inspired teachers, Miss Dorothy Coates and Miss Joan Armitage (rather handsome, dark straight hair drawn back into the customary plaited bun, no make-up, simple

---

* 'Laughing I bear the boar's head in to the Lord of Praise.'

straight Liberty dresses, a 'cared-for Pond's cold cream look, *et c'est tout*[21]), introduced the school to Hiawatha and Red Indians. Chief Oskenonton, star of the *Hiawatha* performances then acted by large casts at the Albert Hall, was heralded by Miss Armitage, standing with folded arms and impassive expression, a squaw's headband with its tall feather at the back of her hopsack tunic. The Chief had come to visit his young brother- and sister-braves at Froebel. Miss Armitage joined in the Indian chant he taught, one hand rising and falling with the rhythm: 'Wah kon dah di doo/Wah kon din ah tonnee'.[22] Pupils made beaded and feathered head-dresses, mothers sewed up cotton tunics and trousers, wampum, moccasins and peace-pipes were improvised. A pow-wow took place in the long grass in Kew Gardens, the girls following Miss Armitage's tunic-covered rear as they tracked her through the long grass on hands and knees. Miriam Allott does not think her father would have been reassured.

4

French was taught by Mme Barbier, a mild little elderly French-woman with her hair in a 'bird's nest' bun on top of her head, wearing the purple ribbon of the Legion d'Honneur. History began as stories, starting with Blakie's *Britain and her Neigbours*, and moving on to Marten and Carter's (1930).[23] Greek and Roman history were taught with a merging of history and litera-ture. There were also lessons on the Greek myths and Nordic folklore. Grammar lessons were formal, so was spelling. Miss Bur-dett would read poetry soulfully – 'O filigree petal!'[24] Miss Bain's lessons to older pupils, known as 'Affairs', brought them into contact with the League of Nations Union, with at least one (bor-ing) lecture by a founder, Dr Gooch. Iris's next school, Badmin-ton, was to deepen this connexion, and her first trip abroad, in 1935, would be to the League's Summer School in Geneva. Economics involved making 'cheque-books', running a 'bank', buying and selling 'shares'. In September 1931 there was a talk about going off the Gold Standard. The pupils also joined 'The

Men of the Trees', founded by Richard St Barbe Baker, the earliest 'green movement'.

There were imaginative visits. The children were taken to the Surrey Docks to visit the SS *Alaunia,* a P&O ship on the Australia line. When it sailed they followed its progress through the 'Shipping News' which then appeared daily in the newspapers, receiving a lesson on each port of call, then inventing a letter home as if they had been passengers calling at Gibraltar, Port Said, Colombo. They visited the Bryant & May match factory at Silvertown in the East End, saw fir trees reduced to matchwood by huge screaming saws, were awed by the vats of bubbling chemicals. They visited Walter de la Mare, in Bayswater, and met the tiny poet, who told them a story about a fly.[25]

A girl who did well amassed a cluster of red stars, each denoting an 'excellent' mark. Some stuck these on the timetable pinned to the inside lid of their desk.[26] By 1931–32 Iris was doing so well as to be head girl – 'a Botticelli angel' with straight bobbed blonde hair.[27] Barbara Denny was in awe of Iris: she was 'so good, so beautiful, and so intelligent and so nice' that Barbara, who was to succeed her as head girl, did not dare speak to her. Iris had the job of ringing the bell in the corridor for everyone to calm down and progress into the Main Hall for prayers.[28]

'Prayers' were idiosyncratic. 'Jesus: my first (and last?) Jewish boy,' Iris was to note later,[29] but it is not clear how much Froebel was responsible for introducing her to that first Jewish boy. The children took their places not in conventional class rows but in concentric circles, referred to by Miss Bain as 'a symbol of our one-ness',[30] the oldest against the walls on fixed benches, the others sitting cross-legged in diminishing circles to the babies in the centre who were supposed to be holding hands, though some waved to watching Mamas in the gallery above. There was a hymn, perhaps a psalm, finally a doxology such as 'God be in my Head', 'Glad that I live am I', 'Lord God in Paradise look upon our Sowing', 'Lead me' and 'The Year's at the Spring'. Entering and leaving the hall was accompanied by the music mistress Miss Catherine Tosh to tunes such as Grieg's Homage March. The choice of hymns, probably from a hymnal called *Laudate,* may have reflected

Miss Bain's Unitarianism, with hymns orientated towards God the Father rather than the Son.

The English teacher Miss Burdett – rather formal: tailored silk blouses, hair drawn back, careful manner – enjoined pupils to become members of the Bible Club and to read a portion of the Holy Book, printed off onto cards, each day. But the religious mood was non-doctrinal and non-dogmatic, uncontroversial if not indeed 'virtually secular'. Iris recalled, 'When I was 5 or 6 years old I remember a girl at school saying: "God can do that. He can do anything because he's magic." A teacher said "No, he is not magic. He is wonderful." The odd thing is that, I think, I understood the point at once!'[31]

The school library saw much quiet work and study. Projects began early, and research involved cutting up old copies – unsupervised – of the *Illustrated London News* to make 'books' on ancient Greece, medieval England or Egypt. Punishment was almost non-existent,[32] and so were serious misdemeanours.

There were theatricals. Among Iris's first writings was a fairy play with a chorus for rabbits, probably put on during a school concert. Barbara Denny remembered her mother around 1926 making her a rabbit's bonnet from white velvet, with ears with pale pink lining, which stayed in her dressing-up box for many years. In 1930, inspired by Miss Tosh who, clad in a green Grecian tunic, taught the newly fashionable Dalcroze eurhythmics on the lawn, the pupils mimed a version of *Eros and Psyche* which Iris, later to explore Plato's *Eros* in her own philosophy, recalled in 1982.[33] When Psyche said goodbye to her parents, the children had to look very sad. Photographs survive, and include a sweet-faced June Duprez, who in 1942 would impress Iris's future husband John Bayley when she starred in the early Technicolor *Thief of Baghdad*. They also dressed up in black sack-like garments, learning dull blank verse to impersonate the chorus of mourning women for a well-received production of Euripedes' *Alcestis* at Grove House.

5

After her arrival at Froebel in 1927, Miriam Allott (*née* Farris), sat next to Iris.

> The prime image: Iris in profile on my right – sitting together on the same bench? Or two desks close together? This strong image is a kind of close-up: head bent forward but not far enough to hide outline of the features – slightly snub nose, slightly retroussé, high cheek bones, high colour there . . . I can hear the strong Irish brogue, firm clear voice, forceful, authoritative enunciation (possibly countering shyness) . . . Round her neck a thin cord suspending a money purse which disappeared under the protective tunic – I didn't wear such a purse but many did.

It was this image which darted into Allott's head when, thirty years later and a literary critic, she saw an *Observer* profile on Iris and realised for the first time that the novelist whose works she had begun to teach at university, and to publish on, was her fellow Old Froebelian.[34] Miriam's mother may have been uneasy about Iris, possibly in case she were a bit of a tomboy, possibly because she was Irish. Miriam had two imaginary and genderless friends, known as Chelsea and Battersea, while Iris for her part invented a brother, her references to whom always 'express[ed] some special feeling for him'. He was a rounded character who developed over time. Miriam Allott wrote to Iris in the 1960s that she wondered 'whether the character of Toby in *The Bell* had been inspired by Iris's brother'.[35] Iris's reply could not have touched on this subject, since Allott was stunned to learn only in 1998 that he never existed.* It is hard to know how much to make of this. The invention of an imaginary or magical friend or sibling is not uncommon among children. It can assuage loneliness by providing fantasy company, but in another sense increase it because of

---

* Iris invited Allott, if she ever had time, to visit Rene in Barons Court; partly, Allott now (2001) believes, to get straight her understanding of the Murdoch family.

the complications involved in inviting friends home, leading to possible discovery. Living within a fictional world can replace the satisfactions of real friendship. It can also augment the intimacy of the family unit.

Iris herself said that she began writing stories at nine in order to provide herself with imaginary siblings. So writing was an extension of inventing companions. She 'loved words, sentences, paragraphs'; learning Latin at Froebel made a deep impression also.[36] All this suggests some qualification of the purely 'idyllic' picture of her childhood, and a compensatory process that started early. There are few clues. One comes in a 1945 letter in which Iris described her childhood as a time when she sometimes felt 'weak at the knees', and, presumably remembering her anxieties as a child, goes on, 'What a fantastic frightening irrational world one lives in.'[37] Writing as a strategy for assuaging anxiety or loneliness is certainly common: witness, for example, Beatrix Potter or Elizabeth Bowen.

6

'The child is innocent, the man is not,' an Iris character was to proclaim.[38] Did Iris idealise Froebel? Miriam Allott thinks this possible, since her own memories of Miss Bain are of a figure less than 'magisterial' (Iris's word). 'Innocence' among the children was probably not as widespread as Iris recorded in 1992. Allott recalls that there was competitiveness among the squires and knights when jockeying for their dames and ladies, and some pronounced pre-adolescent passion, occasionally even some odd and tentative, if innocuous, pre-sexual behaviour. Allott thinks Froebel's insistence on script writing for everyday use, which Iris admired, led to difficulties when pupils began 'joined-up' fast writing, which often descended into a scrawl. '[Iris's] own grown-up handwriting was appalling [a judgement at which others demur] and so generally was mine.'

What was the reason for the winter and summer games, the medieval and the Native American Indian? Presumably they were thought of as inculcating a certain spiritual and moral nobility, and respect for the shared nobility of different cultures. Might the general system reflected in the 'Knights and Ladies' game have unwittingly encouraged a certain kind of moral snobbery – and possibly on reflection some social distinctions too?[39] Titles came into Iris's life, she remarked, easily and early.

> The rituals associated with being Knighted and Lady-ed (kneeling before the King, accolades, the violets &tc), together with the accompanying kudos and sense of being somehow specially endowed with grace, have something in common with less edifying aspects of the Honours system . . . It was never clear whether the elevations were based on being clever and good, or being somehow 'elect', and if so, how determined and by whom?

Both Allott and Iris are reminiscing 'through' the Second World War. One exercise touches Allott deeply to remember. Selected children were invited to come to the front of the form and speak about how they would like things to turn out in life, what they would like to do when they grew up, what they planned for themselves, and what they would like to achieve. Edward Meyer, small, fair-haired, the son of a doctor or dentist, perhaps partly central European, stood at the front and gestured to indicate some kind of physical activity – travel, or was it sport? Whatever it was he wished to do with his life, he had little more than ten years ahead of him. He was to be killed in the war, like the red-haired and freckled John Clements.

Barbara Denny wept copiously when she had to leave Froebel for Putney High School in 1934. Miriam Allott also 'grieved' to have to leave, in her case for Egypt in the spring of 1932. She missed the bizarre pageant of Froebel life, bright days in Kensington Gardens, Peter Pan and the Serpentine, so wretchedly that she wrote to Miss Bain. Miss Bain replied kindly and conventionally, but 'happened by' Cairo later with Miss Armitage, a friend of Miriam's mother, and tried to cheer her up on the tram between Heliopolis and Cairo. And Iris? 'Dame is such a nice concept, so old-fashioned and romantic,' she commented after becoming DBE in 1987. 'Knights and Ladies' casts a fresh light on *The Unicorn* and *The Green Knight*, on her taste for Gothic, her explorations of courtly love, her invention of a fictional universe simultaneously contemporary and yet mythical and timeless, where the young wear 'tunics and tabards' and the boys have a 'raffish Renaissance look'.[40]

Around 1933 it seems there was a palace coup at Froebel. Miss Bain left, and since Mr Dane, Miss Bosley and Miss Short left too, parental protest or controversy were probably involved. The touchingly absurd, idealistic school ethos was conscripted into the humdrum twentieth century. When Quaker Miss Barbara Priestman became headmistress in 1934, 'Knights and Ladies' (too martial?) was replaced by 'Guilds', more appropriate for the socially engaged 1930s, but less enthusiastically received by the children. After wartime evacuation in Buckinghamshire, the Demonstration School moved to its current position in Roehampton; and soon the buildings in Colet Gardens were taken over by the Royal Ballet School and extensively altered. In the hall where the strange concentric prayer-meetings had been held, young girls in tutus now exercised.

7

Iris once told her friend from Somerville College, Oxford, Vera Crane that she had been 'brought up on love'. 'She was a denizen of no mean city,' says Crane. If Froebel was not entirely idyllic, how was life at home in Eastbourne Road? Because Iris was an only child, of very loving parents, and she a loving child, they got on together as if they were all equals.

Iris's grandmother Louisa once asked Rene whether Iris was going to have any children: 'I jolly well hope NOT!' Rene at once returned vehemently, to her mother-in-law's surprise.[41] This exchange, long before Louisa Murdoch's death in 1947, may be taken as evidence for John Bayley's theory that Iris's birth had been a traumatic experience. Rene had been only nineteen, it was a difficult birth, and Rene decided that 'she wasn't going to go through *that* again', which is why Iris never had a real as opposed to imaginary little brother. Some, John Bayley among them, think that Hughes and Rene's marriage was a *mariage blanc*, with abstinence the normal form of contraception, a view Billy Lee, widower of Iris's quasi-cousin Eva Robinson,* did not find implausible. Perhaps this was not uncommon at the time, despite Marie Stopes, and despite Hughes's having married Rene in haste when she was pregnant.

If so, various things follow. When *The Green Knight* came out in 1993 Iris remarked that she might well, like Lucas in that book, have felt murderous towards a real sibling. She would have had to sacrifice herself to a younger brother who, being male, would seriously have embarrassed her education by taking priority. Her father was then a junior civil servant, earning very little. Rene had no money, there was a mortgage and Hughes, determined to give Iris a good education, borrowed from the bank to do so. John Bayley's hypothesis helps throw light elsewhere. When in *The Sea, The Sea* Iris has her hero-narrator boast about *not* being highly sexed, she pointedly subverts contemporary pieties. We do not wish to imagine a hero as less than highly sexed, or a happy marriage as less than 'fully' sexual. It does not accord with these

---

* Eva Robinson (later, Lee) was always close to Iris, while her exact relationship remained unclear. A 1984 letter from Eva to Iris suggests that Eva believed her mother to be sister to Iris's grandmother Bessie (Elizabeth Jane), making her first cousin to Rene, and first cousin once removed to Iris. She possessed a birth certificate showing that the woman she referred to as 'Mummie', who had died in 1912 when Eva was born, was one Annie Nolan, child to Anna Kidd and William Nolan. The 1911 census for 59 Blessington Street suggests that she may have been the nurse Annie Nolan, single, born in Leopardstown, County Dublin, living in 1911 in a household that included Gertie and Rene, their mother Bessie, widow to Effingham Lynch Richardson; Effingham's father Robert Cooper Richardson and his second wife Anna, *née* Kidd, previously Nolan. It appears that eight years after his father married Anna, Effingham Cooper married Anna's daughter Bessie, by now his step-sister (Anna Kidd, who is seventy-three in 1911 and was born in Tullamore, Kings County, Ireland, appears mysteriously as fifty-eight on the 1901 census, with a birth-place in Scotland). Eva's father is unknown, and thus her relationship to the Richardsons was never clearly spelt out. Billy Lee, whom Eva married in 1941, believed her father to have been a prosperous Colonel Berry, from a big house near Newcastle in County Down, who looked after Eva's finances.

pieties, either, to imagine that Rene's happiness in her self and her body, clear in photographs and reminiscence alike, could have been wholly unrelated to the marriage bed, as the hypothesis would require.

Iris's adult philosophy, both written and lived, was to give to non-sexual love an absolutely central place. She advocated what she once called to her friend Brigid Brophy 'a sufficiently diffused eroticism'. It is a striking feature of her fictional universe, too, that love and sexual emotion are ubiquitous and ill-distinguished. Yet chaste love, for her as for Plato, is the highest form of love. A family in which sexual love is sublimated might be one in which – ideally – the currents of love flow even more strongly towards the child, and awaken what Wordsworth termed 'a co-respondent breeze'. Sublimated love, Bayley remarked, resembles Shakespeare's mercy, 'It blesses him that gives, and him that takes', and was Iris's natural state. How might this connect with the fact that the adult Iris frequently fell in love with men considerably older than herself? A father adept at sublimating all such impulses – Iris's cousin Sybil, for example, could not recall Hughes cross, or even imagine it easily – could be, as Hughes was, a source of 'anxieties',[42] as well as of reverential love. Anxiety and reverence could indeed be two faces of the same emotion. Iris was to comment on this obliquely, and transmuted into high art, in *The Black Prince.*

8

The bond between Iris and Hughes was very great. He played both father and, to some degree, mother. It was said to be Hughes who bought her elaborate school outfits at Bourne & Hollingsworth on Oxford Street, when she went away to Badminton in 1932, and he shared the task of taking her to Froebel in the mornings. Redeeming himself after his schooldays, it was he who often did the laundry. Rene was no more a housekeeper than Iris turned out to be. She was 'not a housekeeper at all', much to grandmother Louisa's distress. Louisa was certainly, says Sybil, horrified that her son should have to do so many of the things women were then expected to do. Cleaver, more directly, says that Aunt Ella thought of Rene as having 'sluttish ways', a wife who could not even cook for her husband or keep a tidy house. Sybil also remembers Hughes doing the gardening, housekeeping, laundry, much of the shopping and organising, for example, the travel arrangements for the annual Irish trip. He cooked and washed up while Rene sat back and looked pretty. No one did *much* cleaning. Once Cleaver was staying in Chiswick and he and Hughes came in late. 'Have you had anything to eat?' asked Rene, and on learning that they had not, went off to the kitchen to cook, 'with an expression on her face' at having to do so. Bayley takes another view. The Belfast ethos, from which Hughes was in lifelong flight, militated against Rene's domestic virtues being fairly appraised.[43] He remembers Irene cooking and washing up, smoking a cigarette, and believes she was competent without being house-proud, taking her housekeeping duties lightly. Cleaver does not recall Chiswick being *very* untidy. There was no home-help, no car, and no wine at home: the family could not afford it.

Hughes is remembered by John Bayley as asking either Rene or Iris or both, in his mild Ulster brogue, 'Have you no sense *at all*, woman?' The question was good-humoured and rhetorical, and there is a danger of making Hughes sound like Nora's husband Torvald in Ibsen's *A Doll's House*. A biographer wishing to fuel such a comparison would make much of the only facial expression of her father's Iris recorded, a look of 'impatient nervous irritation' which she feared she inherited;[44] and of Rene's lost singing career, a loss that probably caused Iris more grief than it did easy-going Irene. Hughes did 'baby' Rene, who would simply say sweetly in her Dublin brogue, 'If that makes him happy . . . There's no point in fighting over a thing like that'; 'Well, if he wants to do that, let him get on with it.' Rene got her hair seen to, sang in a choir, joined a swimming club (a photo of young Iris and Irene there survives), played bridge.[45] There was a piano at Eastbourne Road. When Hughes died in 1958 the family were very concerned about how Rene would cope. But, as the Belfast cousins wryly put it, 'it's wonderful what you can do when you've got to'.[46] She turned out to be perfectly well able to look after herself, until old age and illness supervened.

Unlike Nora and Torvald, Rene and Hughes were clearly extremely happy together. Rene increasingly saw herself as a 'duckling that had hatched a swan' – she didn't know what Iris was doing, quite, but was all in favour of it anyway.[47] Cleaver remembers Rene's physical and inner beauty alike: 'welcoming, cheerful, charming . . . lovely'. She was very pretty and good fun, with a happy temperament, vivacious, often laughing or smiling, a jolly and welcoming and open-hearted person. In early photographs Irene is dark-haired. Later on she dyed it blonde. Once, when Louisa, Irene and Sybil were waiting for a bus, coming home from shopping, both Louisa and Irene burdened with parcels, a gallant young man sprang to Irene's rescue, taking her parcels for her. Poor elderly Louisa had to fend for herself. '*Now* you see what blonde hair can do for you,' Irene quipped: if capable of being a vamp, she could also be witty.

Hughes, formal, dignified, interested in everything that was going on in the world, was more serious than Irene but seemed contented, at peace with himself. Elias Canetti would later recall him as 'thoughtful, tremendously engaging'.[48] One of his fingernails was broken and grew in a horny, claw-like shape, in evidence when he counted his cigarettes. Probably he had injured it during the war. He would speak of the long Tube journey into work, where, at a later period, he was known as 'old Murdoch',[49] seeming self-contained to the point of isolation, an 'odd bird' working on the census with a personal grade of Assistant Registrar General at Somerset House in 1950 when he retired. He did not light any fires, but worked quietly, unassumingly, ably, treating everyone with great courtesy.[50] He had a sense of humour, told jokes against himself.[51]

9

Summer holidays were usually spent in Ireland, 'a very romantic land, a land I always wanted to get to ... and discover'.[52] Iris had seven first cousins, three in Ulster, four in Dublin, and doubtless sometimes felt, like Andrew in *The Red and the Green*, that these Irish cousins

> served [her] in those long hated and yet loved holidays of childhood as sibling-substitutes, temporary trial brothers and sisters, for whom [her] uncertain affection took the form of an irritated rivalry. [She] felt [herself] indubitably superior to this heterogeneous, and, it seemed ... uncultivated and provincial gang of young persons, always noisier, gayer and more athletic than [herself].[53]

They disembarked from the Holyhead boat-train in Dun Laoghaire harbour, and a two-minute walk got them to Mellifont Avenue, where at number 16 was the nursing home run and owned by Mrs Walton, Belfast-born foster-mother to Iris's cousin Eva Robinson, seven years Iris's senior, and closer to her than Rene's sister Gertie's four sons. Eva, who had polio as a child and wore a leg-brace, was protective and kind to the younger Iris. Mrs Walton's new address at Mellifont Avenue – she had previously had a stationery shop – was convenient, too, for the salt-water baths at the end of the road, where they all swam. Eva and Iris shared a love of 'stories', and as they sat on the rocks on Dun Laoghaire beach Eva would make up enthralling tales.[54] After marriage in 1941 Eva and her husband Billy Lee shared 34 Monkstown Road with Iris's grandmother Elizabeth Jane ('Bessie') Richardson and Mrs Walton, until the deaths of the two older women in 1941 and 1944 respectively. Iris used Eva as a model in her only published short story, 'Something Special'.[55] Mrs Walton and Eva worshipped at the neighbouring Anglican Mariner's Church (now closed), and Iris and her parents almost certainly attended Revivalist meetings run by the 'Crusaders' there.* After Dublin there would be a longer stay in the North, whose 'black Protestantism' Rene did not always look forward to, but met with good grace. Hughes's sister Sarah and her husband Willy from Belfast rented a different house for one month each summer for themselves and their three children, Cleaver, Muriel and Sybil, in the seaside town of Portrush. There the Murdochs joined them. William Chapman, from a farming community near Lisburn, had gone to the Boer War with the Medical Corps on the strength of knowing a little pharmacy, and won a stripe there. On his return he taught himself dentistry and, though without professional qualification, did very well. When he was about fifty he contracted multiple sclerosis.

Family prayers featured during these holidays. Swimming in the Atlantic breakers off Portstewart strand was one source of fun,[56] board games in the evening, which Iris enjoyed if she won, another. (Presumably, since the Chapmans were Brethren, games with 'court' playing cards were excluded.) Iris is not recalled as always a good loser, though she could be even-tempered too. On one occasion she was painting, which she loved. After she broke off cousin Sybil thought she would help by tidying up all her paints. When Iris came back to continue, the special colours she had prepared had been cleaned away. She calmly set about mixing similar ones. The Chapmans recall Iris's goodness, kind-heartedness, strangeness, strong will and shyness. Self-effacing cousin Muriel, to whom Iris was always closest, a closeness later strengthened when Muriel taught in Reigate during the war, pro-tected her. Saying goodbye, Iris would occasionally 'fill up' and be tearful: she cried without difficulty. Sybil never saw this emotionalism in Irene, who was far more happy-go-lucky.

Goethe said, in a little rhyme, that from his father, who was

---

* Before the war, and for a time at least after it, the Crusaders were 'an organisation designed to attract middle- and upper-class children – boys chiefly, I fancy – to evangelical Christianity. There was a badge, possibly some minimal uniforms relating to those of crusading orders, and meetings combined Bible study and religious instruction with activities of a more Boy Scout-ish kind' (Dennis Nineham, letter to author). Chapter 4 of *The Red and the Green* starts with such a meeting, and Iris's journals abound in memories of hymns, some evangelical.

from north Germany, he got his *gravitas*, his sense of reason, order and logic; from his mother, who came from the south, he got his '*Lust zum fabulieren*', his love of telling tales. Rene adored the cinema, adored reading novels, liked stories, had the sense of a story. Perhaps Iris distantly echoes Goethe's mixed inheritance. She had been writing since she was at least nine. An early confident talent for turning life into narrative drama shows in a letter written to a friend from 15 Mellifont Avenue, Dun Laoghaire, on 29 August 1934, when Iris was fifteen.[57] It is prefaced by a drawing of two mackintoshed girls walking in the Dublin rain.

Hello! A grey and relentless sky has been pouring rain on us for the last week, and the sun has forgotten how to shine . . . Great excitement here! Last Sunday week night (that sounds queer) a terrible storm got up, and on Monday morning about 8 a.m. the first maroon went for the lifeboat. I was in the bathroom at the time. I never got washed so quick as I did then. I was dressed & doing my hair when the second maroon went. Then I flew out of the house. Doors were banging all the way down the street, and the entire population of Dun Laoghaire seemed to be running to the harbour. Doodle (Daddy) & my cousin [Eva Robinson] had already left . . . The lifeboat was in the harbour mouth when I arrived. I asked a man what was up. A yacht had evidently broken its moorings and drifted out of the harbour or something, anyway we could just see it on the horizon. A high sea was running and I was glad to have my mackintosh with me. I dashed down the pier – which by the way is a mile long – and was drenched by the spray and the waves breaking over the pier. The sand whipped up by the wind, drove in clouds and I got some in my eye, which hurt like anything. The lifeboat had an awful job, it was pitching and tossing, and once we thought it was going down but it got to the yacht, which turned out to be empty, and towed it back amid the enthusiastic cheers of the populace. Three other yachts broke their moorings in the harbour, of these, two went down, and the other was saved and towed to calmer waters just as it was dashing itself to pieces against the pier. That was a great thrill. The next excitement was a huge German liner – three times as big as the mailboat – that anchored in the bay . . .

On the mail-boat to Dublin in summer 1936, the Hammond and Murdoch familiies met. Annie Hammond had been witness at Rene and Hughes's wedding, and her son Richard asked the seventeen-year-old Iris what she wished to do in life. 'Write,' she replied.[58]

3

The Clean-Cut Rational World
1932–1938

Early in 1932 Hughes and Iris travelled down to Badminton School[1] (motto: '*Pro omnibus quisque, pro Deo omnes*'*) in a suburb of Bristol to meet the head, the redoubtable Miss Beatrice May Baker, known as 'BMB'. In an article in *Queen* magazine in 1931, Miss Baker had emphasised the school's ideal of service, the duties of simplicity in dress and living, and the proper use of money. Above all, and admirably, 'a school can no longer be a self-contained little community . . . it should be related to the world outside'.

Badminton was not then necessarily the West Country school with the greatest social cachet, but it was likely to appeal to liberal and free-thinking parents such as Rene and Hughes, who did not object to religion in others, but happened not to go in for it much themselves, even at Christmas or Easter. The school was small – 163 girls, of whom ninety-six were boarders – internationally-minded, 'forward-looking', tolerant and liberal.[2] Though sporty, it was not inhospitable to the arts. The distinguished painter Mary Fedden (Trevelyan) was there, as were the daughters of the sculptor Bernard Leach, painter Stanley Spencer, publisher Victor Gollancz and writer Naomi Mitchison. Indira Gandhi (*née* Nehru) was briefly there in Iris's time,[3] complaining to her father, imprisoned by the British for many years,

---

* 'Each for all, all for God.'

about 'all the stupid rules and regulations',* and mourning her mother's recent death. Iris would recall her as 'very unhappy, very lonely, intensely worried about her father and her country and thoroughly uncertain about the future'.[4]

On this first visit Iris, only twelve, entered the Northcote drawing-room with Hughes and felt tongue-tied. She looked about and thought how beautiful and calm the room was. Pale sunshine was coming in through the tall windows. She was always to recall Miss Baker in that 'cool light'.[5] BMB was five foot six and lithe, dressed typically in pastel green with a white blouse, had an oval, very sunburnt, leathery and somehow ageless face with flat, centrally-parted silver hair over which she wore a black velvet band. Many a girl feared that BMB could read her innermost thoughts. She had the brightest of blue eyes, a sudden and quick-fading smile, a springy step in flat-heeled and polished shoes. She loved her dogs, probably at this time 'Major', a lean, short-haired, leggy Belgian hound, recalled neither as beautiful nor especially affectionate.

Happily, Hughes 'got on jolly well' with BMB, said Iris. 'They respected each other,' said John Bayley.[6] As for Iris, at first she feared BMB. Respect came later, followed by a strong and loyal affection. BMB was eventually to be the first of a long series of authoritative and influential surrogate parent-figures, giving thrust to each of Iris's tendencies towards other-centredness, puritanism, stoicism and idealism.

Iris was exactly the serious-minded, academic type of girl BMB most loved to bring on, with enough strength of character to resist her desire to dominate, yet enough malleability to undergo some moulding, and she would become BMB's favourite. BMB lived to be ninety-seven, and Iris stayed in touch.[7] When she fell in love with John, Iris sought her old headmistress's approval before marrying him. And Iris was to be, after Dame Sybil

---

* Regulations posted in the entrance hall began: '1. Stockings must always be worn with wellingtons for all walks. 2. During term time girls must never wear mufti unless they are in their own rooms. Mufti must never be worn in Bristol. 3. No girl is to bring talcum powder back to school...' See Katherine Frank, *Indira: The Life of Indira Gandhi* (London, 2001), p.117.

Thorndike and Lord Caradon, Badminton's official School Visitor from 1992, when she wrote an oratorio for the school choir. She had dreams of BMB in later life, and of her bee garden.[8] In 1981, following a formal dinner after she was awarded an honorary doctorate from Bristol University, she alarmed her companion by taking him on an unheralded and uncanny midnight walk inside the school, in term-time, to revisit old haunts.[9] It might have been of BMB that Iris was thinking when she wrote of brisk and bleakly sensible Norah Shaddox-Brown, tireless 1930s Fabian warhorse in *The Time of the Angels*: 'The clean-cut rational world for which she had campaigned had not materialized, and she had never come to terms with the more bewildering world that really existed.' Clean-cut rationalism and the League of Nations could not cope with Hitler: 'Nazism was incredible – that was a part of its strength.'[10]

It was later to be said of Iris that she was a 'poor girl who only just made it into a rich girls' school'.[11] She did indeed, with great brio and sparkle,[12] win one of the first two available open scholarships to Badminton – the other went to her friend Ann Leech, a doctor's daughter. It was happily one strength of the school that girls from prosperous homes never dared mention their ponies or foreign holidays – 'bad form ... absolutely *out*'.[13] The school secretary Miss Colebrook wrote to Hughes on 29 June 1932 that the announcement of Iris's scholarship was in *The Times*, the *Manchester Guardian* and the local press: 'It looks very well.'[14]

2

Iris arrived at the school on 22 September. She had first to take the 'never to be forgotten, and dreaded' Paddington to Badminton train, which always left at 1.15 sharp.[15] On her arrival she was put in a house called 'Badock', after Badminton's founder in 1858. She ran round and round the playground with her hair all over her face, weeping,[16] then found a cloakroom-basement to cry in.[17] She twitched, perhaps with shyness, and put her head down between her knees with her book during the reading hour.[18]

Margaret Rake, then a prefect, saw Iris looking very timid and washed out, her head on her desk in grief or concentration or both. Extreme cleverness can isolate a child as much as homesickness: neither made her immediately comprehensible to her fellows, and some girls may have been unkind – one friend, witnessing her homesick tears, formed a society called 'The Prevention of Cruelty to Iris'.[19] Iris wrote to Hughes asking him to take her away. He was very upset and probably came again to see BMB. It was Iris's belief in her father that got her through this misery: 'I trusted him.'[20]

BMB's therapy was garden-work under the care of the fair-haired, short head-gardener Miss Bond, in her mannish breeches. (A male head gardener had been sacked over a sexual indiscretion.) Stout, red-cheeked, blazered, fair and straight-haired Leila Eveleigh, who taught maths, would find Iris quietly and painstakingly pricking out seedlings in the greenhouse. Iris appreciated the less stimulating and calmer atmosphere there – the physical activity too, which took her out of herself – and slowly became less bewildered and homesick. BMB also asked another girl, Margaret Orpen, who was unhappy at Badminton because it was so sporty, to keep an eye on Iris; a skilful move, to allow two unhappy girls to comfort each other. Both hated early-morning drill. 'Orpen' (the school had too many Margarets), niece of the artist Sir William, kept all Iris's letters from 1932 on: Iris was her greatest friend, her letters 'special'.[21] They wept together during 'awful moments' on Paddington station, felt corresponding joy on the return journey, shared jokes. Fifty years later, Iris still recalled Orpen's gift of strawberries for her birthday.

Each morning began with a cold bath at 7.15. BMB had one herself, and if the bottom of the bath was warm to her feet, the last bather would be brought to justice. Then the girls had to turn their mattresses, and once a week run down the long drive (drill) carrying their laundry. Skipping was permitted as an alternative to running. Iris was cheered to learn that Dulcibel Broderick turned her mattress only once a week, and had made up a rhyme about it. The food – generally – was good, although

BMB, housemistress Miss Rendall ('LJR') and school secretary Miss Colebrook were all vegetarians, BMB probably subsisting on raw vegetables. Twice a week the girls' food was vegetarian. But twice a week also there were hot rolls for breakfast (spoiled for some by the raspberry jam from the Co-op with wooden 'pits' that got into your teeth) with fruit, and coffee on Sundays. Iris had a favourite chocolate blancmange pudding, known as 'Avon mud' in honour of the local river. The girls hid cake in their shoe baskets: kneeling for prayers, portions could be eaten clandestinely.[22] Iris kept a photograph of the very good school cook, Miss Valentine ('Val') – short, plain, very pale with black hair cut in a fringe, spectacled, an army cook in France during the Great War, who made a famous shepherd's pie.

In class Iris would ask clever questions that others might not have asked, eliciting interesting answers. This propitiated some of her contemporaries.[23] Not that all classes were taxing. Engagingly short, fat, brown-haired Ida Hinde taught singing lessons and elocution part-time. Her recitation of Browning's 'Home Thoughts from Abroad' joined the stock of well-worn Bayley family jokes. She would exhort them, 'Now girls, you must put *expression* into it,' and, starting very quietly, recite:

> Whoever wakes in England
> Sees, some morning, unaware
> That the lowest boughs, and the brushwood sheaf
> Round the elm-tree bole [*dramatic crescendo*]
> ARE IN TINY LEAF.

In summer they swam each day in the narrow open-air pool, played tennis, slept out in sleeping bags on the flat roof, had marvellous outings and picnics.[24]

Iris gradually settled in, and, it slowly became clear, was good at almost everything. At the end of her first term the school magazine contains her ballad 'The Fate of the Daisy Lee'.[25] She had cheered up enough to write a pleasant melodrama in which Sir John blows a lighthouse to pieces and years later is aptly killed, driven onto the rocks where the lighthouse might have saved him. Its slender interest lies in its location, the Irish Sea and its Oedipal drama: Sir John destroys the lighthouse because his daughter (who dies too) has married its keeper. 'Orpen' had also to read out her own ballad, which ran: 'A knight rode on his horse/A damsel to find./Together they went riding/Through the wind./The knight fell off his horse/Alas, poor maid/He broke his legs and arms/And was dead.' When Orpen was given only three out of ten for this, Iris defended her publicly and staunchly: 'It is full of action, short, and has a courtly subject.' All her life, Iris's literary criticism of her friends' work owed as much to enthusiasm as to accuracy. Fierce loyalty made her quixotic.

Badminton, both in its real virtues and its undoubted priggishness, left its mark upon her. In her adult world-view education takes an absolutely central place: 'Teaching children, teaching attention, accuracy, getting this right, respect, truth, a love of learning: those years are so profoundly important.'[26] Two of her novels feature first-person male narrators whose egomania has been tempered only by the patient goodness of one outstanding schoolteacher,[27] and the career she chose for the one non-allegorical 'saint' of her novels was schoolmastering.[28] Her shifts of adult political allegiance were mainly caused by revulsion at some aspect of the party in power's education policy.

Iris did not need the first part of BMB's officious advice for the holidays: 'Be kind to your mother and go for a walk every day.' She and her mother were like sisters, with Iris seeming increasingly to many observers the elder. 'How *did* I do it, will you tell me that now?' Rene would ask, amazed at having produced so brilliant a child. For a while Iris detested having to go back to school at the start of each term. As the holidays came to an end, every moment was the more passionately enjoyed because the more fraught with the anticipated shock of the changes that were to come: 'Two more meals, one more meal, then it's coming up.' Hughes would take her to the horror of the special school train, leaving from Paddington. Iris would shed tears, and her father was probably very gallant. Cleaver recalls a story of Hughes, Irene and Iris, at the start of Iris's second term, walking up the long drive to Badminton, each of them crying at the forthcoming separation.

Hughes's letters to his daughter were loving and pedantic, 'rather like a legal document, with many phrases like "having due regard to"'.[29] A journal entry of Iris's reads: 'My father visiting at half term at Badminton. We go to Avonmouth Docks – men are shooting down pigeons who tumble off the roofs near our feet – I am crying terribly, for the pigeons, and because I must soon part from my father. My father of course also very upset. After that I asked my parents not to come to visit me at school.'[30] She would put the Bristol pigeon-shooters into *The Black Prince*: 'the poor flopping bundle upon the ground, trying helplessly, desperately, vainly to rise again. Through tears I saw the stricken birds tumbling over and over down the sloping roofs of the warehouse.'

3

BMB had arrived at Badminton in 1911, aged thirty-five,[31] with her great friend Lucy Rendall who taught P.T. (physical training), both of them from Cardiff High School. 'Look at them – early Victorians!' BMB had said, watching the school tennis-players in their frilly petticoats. She herself wore the free-flowing clothes associated with advocates of female suffrage, and, to the horror of some 'early Victorian' mamas, soon abolished both 'Sunday hats' and 'stays' alike. Like Miss Buss and Miss Beale at Cheltenham Ladies' College, BMB was a pioneering and dedicated educationalist of great moral courage and probity who had to fight her corner in a man's world, and of course risked becoming crabbed in the process.[32]

She was a tough disciplinarian, a feminist, a Socialist and a fellow-travelling Quaker. In 1919 she appointed Mr Harris, newly released from prison as a conscientious objector, head of the Junior School, and imported, looked after and educated two small, starving Austrian boys. She admitted girls from India, Burma, West Africa and the West Indies, believed in teaching birth-control and hoped to make the school fully co-educational.[33] She set up a country holiday home for Bristol slum children, which the girls tended.

Over forty years later, Iris would recall in her journal: 'Evening prayers at school, on dark cold winter evenings, kneeling on the parquet floor in the rather ill-lit hall.'[34] BMB was a pioneer also in her insistence on freedom of expression in regard to religious matters. She did not rate the established Church highly, and in 1928 had dedicated a combined chapel and hall as a 'Peace Memorial'. Morning Assembly was non-denominational.[35] Every second Sunday, attendance was required at a church chosen by the child's parents. (Iris is remembered by one friend as first attending the Congregational church, by another as Anglican.[36] Around 1936 Iris and Orpen tried Quaker Meeting. It made them laugh that, though 'the spirit' moved the Friends at any time, it always stopped moving them punctually at midday, just in time for lunch.) The Sundays in between one could either visit a church of one's own choice or go on a walk, and that evening BMB would take an idiosyncratic fortnightly service during which she might, for example, discourse on the saintliness of Mahatma Gandhi or Sir Stafford Cripps.[37]

Inspiring mottoes, a new one every term, were printed and pinned up in each form-room: from the Epistles, Browning, Rabindranath Tagore, the *Rig Veda*. John Bayley does not believe that BMB, even after 1932, was a 'believing' Quaker (a question Iris addresses in her poem to BMB, see below). If this was so, she kept her rationalistic opinions to herself, being very much in the nineteenth-century tradition of free-thinking, rather like George Eliot, and believing passionately, for example, in goodness.

Orpen and Iris did not discuss religion, Iris then appearing not greatly interested. They did debate the difference between Right and Wrong. Which was worse: to run from Northcote Buildings to Schoolhouse, or to tell a lie? Probably in late November 1934 Iris was confirmed into the Anglican Church:[38] that year R.K. Pagett at St Peter's Henleaze, the Anglican church used by Badmintonians, gave her *The King's Daughters: A Book of Devotion for Girls*. She would speak of having had 'a religious experience of the kind that many people have at that age' although she never specified the experience.

Badminton's uniforms were modern for the time, even 'art

deco'.[39] On weekday mornings the girls wore a navy-blue serge gym tunic, with pleats only at the top, which had to touch the floor when they knelt down, and a white Viyella blouse. Their navy-blue blazers had 'BS' stitched in white on the pocket. After exercise each afternoon they changed – real little ladies – into sleeveless fawn corduroy 'sack' garments and fawn Shetland cardigans worn over tussore silk blouses. There were 'jolly' navy-blue Tam o'shanters for ordinary days, for Sundays round blue velour hats with a navy-blue-and-white band, again with 'BS' stitched on them. Seasonal variations dictated navy-blue serge overcoats in winter and blue gingham frocks in summer, not always warm enough in an English June – Bourne & Hollingworth came and measured you for these. On summer Sundays grand natural white tussore silk dresses and coats, with a panama hat. The strict dress-code was later relaxed, as the school photograph for 1937 demonstrates, with Iris in a print frock, a happy and beautiful free spirit. As for the mistresses, none dressed very becomingly. To worry too much about one's appearance might not have counted as what BMB called a 'worthwhile activity'. Yet the 'Powers' (BMB, LJR and the skilful music mistress 'Ski' Webb-Johnson) did dress in semi-evening wear, such as long skirts and velvet jackets, for dinner.

BMB's possible unbelief did not stop her from laying down the law about how others should live. She was not an easy woman, and Iris notes that she was too impatient and frightening to be a really good teacher: she could be a 'blunt instrument'. A 'powerful domineering brave woman', she could make mistakes, and there were casualties. Mary Fedden hated BMB and thought her wicked: BMB, she felt, despised her as a mere day-girl, and Mary would hide and weep with fear on seeing her approach. Others could not stand the unremitting idealism of this 'high-minded bully'. Iris would write: 'Nietzsche would have been interested in BMB: a case of a huge unselfconscious totally non-cynical will to power.' BMB so bullied the gifted Maud Wills that her friend Margaret Rake (later Vintner) recalled each algebra lesson as a nightmare. When Margaret found the courage to protest, BMB first took it on the chin, then summoned Maud and told her about the complaint, breaking the girls' friendship and isolating Margaret.

The quaint practice of all the girls walking the length of the room after eight o'clock evening prayers and shaking the head-mistress's hand (before the First World War, curtseying) while saying goodnight, provided an opportunity for BMB to tick off those who had talked in prep or run down the corridor. She liked to organise and control the staff as well as the pupils: 'Brace up!' she would say, and 'Fill your lives!' One vexed staff member was heard to murmur, 'If I fill my life any more I shall go mad.' BMB did not accept anything at face value but judged it by her own exacting, eccentric standards, often finding it wanting. She was critical, analytical and not to be put upon, sometimes perverse in her opinions. She believed she was using a Socratic method, trying to make the girls think for themselves, and was never more pleased than when told by an Old Girl how 'shaken up' she had been at Badminton by her. Behind her somewhat forbidding appearance was great *joie de vivre* and sardonic humour.

BMB would pounce on girls after lunch and ask what they were reading. A register was kept, four hours reading per week being thought exemplary.[40] (Most films, by contrast, as Indira Gandhi remembered, were seen as 'mental dope'.) BMB used repeatedly to ask: '*Are you engaged in worthwhile activities?*' One of Iris's school friends was once asked what she was reading, and replied, with a strong, distinctive lisp, '*Detection, Mystewy, and Howwor*, Miss Baker.' Though the reading of such an omnibus would scarcely have passed for a 'worthwhile activity', the answer was given in so prim a tone that BMB was floored, and passed on.

One Lent she gave a stirring sermon on the decadent wicked-ness of hot-water bottles. The dormitories were unheated – Iris noted, 'We were Athenians but we were Spartans too.' Girls were allowed exactly four sweets a week, and were not encouraged to sit next to their friends either in class or in the house.[41] BMB hated – and perhaps feared – illness. 'Weak fool!' one Old Girl imagined BMB, by then ninety-four, saying under her breath at the news that another of her contemporaries had succumbed and proven mortal. In Iris's time Hazel Earle was rusticated for washing her hair and then going to bed with it wet; and Orpen, when she caught a cold was falsely accused of 'going out without your galoshes'. Moreover the vegetarian food gave Orpen a headache. Headaches and colds did not count as 'worthwhile activities'.

BMB displayed a mixture of 'ruthless' practical idealism and an imagination with strict limits. On the one hand she would take pains to buy presents for the foreign children who would otherwise have received none. On the other, BMB was legal guardian to Inge, a Jewish refugee-child who had suffered the deportation and death in Poland of her parents and brother, and whenever she or any other '*foreign friend*' – they would far rather have been known as 'refugees' – failed to volunteer for some irksome task, like gardening in the bitter mid-winter, they were called to BMB's study and reminded that, 'being in receipt of charity', the least they could do was volunteer for unpopular chores. BMB, though wishing to inspire it, seemed to this girl 'totally incapable of affection'. When, on her last night at school, BMB leaned forward to kiss her for the first time ever, she drew back. 'Don't you love me, Inge?' asked BMB. Having been taught 'uprightness' by BMB, Inge truthfully replied, 'I respect and admire you, but I could never, never love you.' BMB was deeply hurt.

BMB lived in Iris's house with her housemistress LJR, in a close liaison. This, in the days of inter-war innocence, was not considered odd, even though the two shared a bedroom. Happily BMB's idealistic ruthlessness was tempered both by LJR's calmer pragmatism and by 'Ski' Webb-Johnson's kindness. 'She's right, of course, but you can't go straight *for* it, like that!' LJR would comment. Together they made an indivisible couple, mutually supporting, happy and immensely positive. LJR was the 'jolly and practical one' – the doer – while BMB had the visionary edge. Both were keen walkers and cyclists.

Around 1935 they built, on the site of a farm, a showpiece art deco house for themselves which they called Little Grange.[42] Iris was to be a lifelong visitor and guest. A very spacious lounge with french windows, designed for concerts and talks, gave onto the charming garden, where a paved courtyard had replaced a cow-byre. There was a grand piano, hundreds of books, and BMB's favourite paintings (Italian masters) on the walls. Iris saw this house, in which BMB was to stay for many years after her retirement – to the occasional discomfiture of her successors – effectively BMB's own dower-house, as 'a creation of her will ... a masterpiece of art deco ... BMB belongs in an art deco world, evidence that that mode could be guileless without being insipid'. Iris gave the name 'Little Grange' to one of the winning horses on which Jake gambles for high stakes in *Under the Net*.

4

At a Christmas fancy-dress party soon after the First World War, BMB arrived disguised as the League of Nations. This might suggest an unusual depth of identification. The League played a great part in the Badminton girls' lives, BMB arguing that it guaranteed both democracy and peace. Many girls delivered leaflets on disarmament and talked to local residents about such matters, collecting signatures for petitions. Membership of the Junior League cost one shilling a term. One girl, Annette Petter, was asked by BMB why she alone did *not* belong. 'Because, Miss Baker,' she replied with brave good humour, greatly encouraged by BMB's belief in free speech, 'my father manufactures aeroplane oil.'[43] This did not go down too well.

Each girl carried a copy of the article dealing with sanctions from the covenant of the League of Nations in her pocket; and bevies of students went to the annual League Summer School in Geneva. In August 1935 Iris went for ten days[44] with a party of seven. It was her first trip abroad. They had a calm Channel crossing, and Iris was too excited to sleep more than two hours on the subsequent train journey. She sent enthusiastic postcards home of the Mer-de-Glace on Mont Blanc, the monument to heroes of the Reformation, and – in colour – the Palace of Nations itself. The group was received by the acting Secretary-General, shown round old Geneva, climbed both the Mer-de-Glace and Mont Salève ('exhausting'), and bathed often in the lake, as 'blue-as-blue'. Ice-creams cost them 1/6*d* each. They stayed in a luxurious hotel – their room had a balcony, private bathroom and telephone – talking to the *femme de chambre* every night to improve their French.[45] There were high-minded lectures, and they were impressed by the Assembly's facilities for instantaneous translation. Iris sent home peremptory instructions: 'You needn't write again after answering this.' And Hughes and Rene were 'not to be late' in meeting her train back 'at 6.06 the following Monday'.

'Are your family interested in politics? Are they right or left wing?' BMB asked one teacher who was being interviewed for a post. 'We're all left wing here, you know.' Another teacher, asked by a first former, 'What are politics?', riposted, 'Why do you want to know?' 'I am going to sit by Miss Baker at lunch . . . Miss Baker is interested in politics, but I don't know what they are.' BMB, who liked to tell this story, talked to the girl about her favourite pudding instead – the intensity was sometimes relaxed. But some members of the staff were reluctant to sit next to BMB if they had not read the *Times* leader that day. BMB subscribed to the Left Book Club, took students on field trips to the local Wills' cigarette factory; there were weekly current-events discussions on the international situation; refugees from the Spanish Civil War were invited to speak.[46]

The political scene at the time was indeed dramatic. On 7 March 1936 Hitler invaded the Rhineland. Iris heard the newspaper-sellers on the main road calling out the ominous news in the late evening, and saw BMB, aged sixty, running down the drive to buy a paper. Those of left-wing tendencies commonly regarded the Soviet Union as a place of hope and wished for closer ties with it – Iris later wrote: 'Jesus, as teacher, shared the stage in morning prayers with a large variety of other mentors, including Lenin.' Indeed staff sometimes addressed each other as 'Com', for Comrade, to indicate friendliness. One observer even compared the school to the USSR: 'a democracy with a very strong leader'. This is doubly ironic. BMB was no Stalin. Nor was either institution precisely a democracy. This illuminates Iris's own later Communist Party membership. She once remarked that she was a Communist by the age of thirteen.[47]

BMB started by getting three refugee girls into the school, then rented a house nearby where she placed ten more refugees, from Germany, Austria and Czechoslovakia, mostly children of mixed marriages. Christians and Jews, she explained, were aided by their co-religionists, while children of mixed marriages had no such advocates. The Badminton girls were proud of their 'foreign friends', and treated them more kindly than they did their own compatriots. Soon the school bulged at every seam. BMB once asked the Jewish girls to organise a seder, which she attended, and was deeply moved. And she found a rest-home for the mother of Margot Slade (Friedland), one of the refugee girls, where she could recuperate from the trauma of her years under the Nazis. Iris commented: 'We knew about the concentration camps considerably before this idea was taken seriously by the general public.'

Indira Gandhi later recalled groups of senior girls sharing living quarters with a teacher, and having to help look after the housekeeping. On Sunday mornings the Jewish and Indian girls would go for walks in groups of four. Indira would lead one group. On 10 December 1936 a gym session was interrupted and the girls asked to hurry into the next room for some special news, without waiting to get dressed in their smart afternoon wear. Indira recalled their squatting on the floor in their navy-blue gym tunics to listen to Edward VIII's abdication broadcast. The atmosphere was charged with emotion. Many were in tears.

5

BMB and Iris developed a deep rapport; they 'got on famously'.[48] BMB was at her best with serious, studious girls, and Iris, at least from the sixth form, was quite outstanding. She had 'an obviously potentially great mind with a humility and a probing determination to know and understand other people and nationalities'.[49] Iris took from BMB a strong intuitive sense of – and a missionary zeal about – the distinctions between right and wrong. They would sit and discuss the Good,[50] a discussion that was to continue over many decades. At a soirée for sixth-form girls BMB remarked that Iris was not only remarkable but 'already had a philosophy of life'. Fellow student Pat Zealand, unsure what a philosophy of life was, was nonetheless impressed that Iris had one. The mottoes chosen by BMB for the school magazine presage the adult Iris's searching moral passion: 'As a man thinketh in his heart, so is he' (Proverbs, 23: 7); 'The essence of religion is that it should inform the whole of one's daily practical life' (J. Middleton Murry).

Margaret Rake, the prefect who had observed Iris's unhappiness in her first year, came back to teach history at Badminton in 1936–37, and she and BMB helped Iris prepare for the alarming General Paper for her Oxford entrance. Set by Iris's future tutor Isobel Henderson (with help that year from Iris's future colleague Jennifer Hart), it was notorious for eccentric questions – 'Describe the workings of a bicycle', and 'Here are fifteen rules of grammar for a new language ... Now translate the National Anthem into that language'.[51] Iris, it soon became clear, knew more history than Margaret; luckily they could laugh about this. Iris, Margaret remembered, looked like a white rabbit, and lowered her head in despair at the human race because it was so stupid, and so frivolous.

Margaret Rake believed that BMB was dedicated to too narrow a conception of Good, and did not see her own frailties. Iris, who saw BMB with considerable objectivity, describes her not merely as a bully but also as a 'great general'. The atmosphere she created 'outlawed malice and lying and vulgar snobbery'. BMB nurtured a 'strong positive innocence' and a 'lucid security which inspired faith and ... freedom'. One source of her strength may have been that, though thought by some to be an intellectual snob, she was not herself really an intellectual, and was therefore presumably neither a nihilist nor a cynic. Led by BMB the girls were athletes, craftswomen, scholars, practitioners of all the arts. They were introduced, Iris wrote, to 'the whole of history, the Assyrians, the Egyptians, the Romans were our familiar friends, and most of all the Greeks. The cool drawing-room light was soon transformed for me into the light of Hellas, the last gleam of a Victorian vision of those brilliant but terrible people.'

In 1983 Iris published a poem about her kind but formidable old headmistress, meditating on much of this, and entitled simply 'Miss Beatrice May Baker, Headmistress of Badminton School, Bristol, from 1911 to 1946'.

Your genius was a monumental confidence
To which even the word 'courage' seems untrue.
In your *art deco* pastel ambience
You sat, *knowing* what to do.
Pure idealism was what you had to give,
Like no one now *tells* people how to live.

With your thin silver hair and velvet band
And colourless enthusiastic eyes
You waved the passport to a purer land,
A sort of universal Ancient Greece,
Under whose cool and scrutinizing sun
Beauty and Truth and Good were *obviously* one.

Upon your Everest we were to climb,
At first together, later on alone,
To leave our footprints in the snows of time
And glimpse of Good the high and airless cone.
How could we have considered this ascent
Had not our cynic hearts adjudged *you* innocent?

Politics too seemed innocent at that time
When we believed there would be no more war.
How shocked we were to learn that a small one
Was actually *going on* somewhere!
We lived through the jazz age with golden eyes
Reflecting what we thought was the sunrise.

And yet we knew of Hitler and his hell
Before most people did, when all those bright
Jewish girls kept arriving; they were well
Aware of the beginning of the night,
The League of Nations fading in the gloom,
And burning lips of first love, cold so soon.

Restlessly you proclaimed the upward way,
Seeing with clarity the awful stairs,
While we laddered our lisle stockings on the splintery parquet
Kneeling to worship something at morning prayers.
But did you really believe in God,
Quakerish lady? The question is absurd.

This elegy, partly inspired by Auden's 'September 1, 1939', shares with that poem the jazzy collision between a rationalistic optimism and the coming of the night-time of civilisation. Both poems, too, by implication celebrate 'the just' who enliven the coming darkness. But Iris's poem shines with its own light of irony and of yearning, a light ignited, surely, by BMB herself. BMB here is not so much an algebra teacher as a sybil summoning humankind to pursue the mysteries of the path towards love and goodness, a new Diotima from Plato's *Symposium*.

6

Leila Eveleigh recalled Iris as good all round – a good hockey player, interested in and gifted at art (painting), not particularly musical, though she 'had a go', but excelling at classics and English. Enthusiastic and alive in all her many activities, she was quiet and inward also. It would not be surprising if Iris's omnicompetence aroused dislike or envy; none has stepped forward to say it did.[52]

Latin was taught first by rosy, large, countrified Miss Parkin. Then came Marjorie Bird: tall, thin, no make-up, very plainly dressed and a devout Quaker. Known as 'The Bird', she taught Iris Latin and Greek from 1934 to 1937. 'What a help The Bird was,' Iris later remembered. The only pupil mentioned by name in Miss Bird's diaries for the thirties is Iris.* In Iris's last year Miss

---

* e.g. 12 December 1934: 'Pleasant lesson with I. Murdoch – asked her what she wanted to do next year – vague, but wants to go on with Greek.' After Miss Bird had left the school in July 1937 and was settled in Cambridge, about to marry Maurice Howard, she noted, 'H.C. [Higher Certificate]. Iris didn't get distinction in Latin, though she did in English. So she hasn't got a State Scholarship' – no mention of

73

Jeffery replaced her, a good scholar who should have been a don. She loved esoteric jokes, gave a brilliant lecture to the whole school on medieval Latin poetry, held Roman supper-parties for the out-of-school Classics Club. Teaching a 'pearl' like Iris must have cheered her up. Together they read some of Xenophon's *Anabasis*, source of the title for Iris's Booker Prize-winning *The Sea, The Sea*, the Greeks' cry during the Persian wars when they finally sight salt-water; also 'those evergreen charmers' *Odyssey* Books VI and VII. Miss Jeffery remembered Iris as 'one of the kindest people [she] had ever met'.[53] Iris's excellent teacher of English, Miss Horsfall – known as 'The Horse' – tall, very thin and a little ungainly, wore *pince-nez* at the end of her nose, her hair in a bun, and was a devout Anglo-Catholic. She often read Iris's exemplary essays out to the class. An atmosphere of emotionality surrounded her.

Successive issues of the *Badminton School Magazine* point to Iris's impact on the school. In the autumn of 1933 she wrote up the new Architecture Club's expedition to Bradford-on-Avon, describing the Tithe Barn and the 'oldest existing' Saxon Church of Saint Aldhelm, which the girls sketched. The following term she contributes to 'Contrasting Views of Highbrows and Lowbrows', a subject then exercising Virginia Woolf.[54] Iris's lowbrows follow Arsenal and go to the music-hall. Her highbrows read Dickens and Shakespeare and follow 'the situation in Germany' – suggesting how politically aware Badmintonians were. How many other English fourteen-year-olds were then preoccupied by Hitler, who had risen to power only a year before? Iris proposed tolerant understanding through a mutual expansion of pleasure-sources. The lowbrows should read Walter Scott and try Horowitz on the wireless; the highbrows should listen to dance-tunes. She was later to call the songs of the thirties 'the best pop-tunes of the century',[55] and to regret that Badminton had so much Greek dancing, classical music, quickstep and Viennese waltz, and not enough jazz:[56] 'The most interesting kind of man is the one who knows

---

a Greek result, though in those days students normally offered three main subjects and a subsidiary.

something about everything.' This looks forward to the kind of novel she would later hope to write, with, as she expressed it later, 'something for everyone';[57] 'like Shakespeare', John Bayley observed.

In the magazine in 1934 Iris celebrated the value of 'Unimportant Persons', amongst whom she includes herself. In 1935, as well as taking her School Certificate, she wrote 'How I Would Govern the Country', defending constitutional monarchy, criticising imperialism and totalitarianism alike; and after her trip to Geneva attended the League of Nations Junior Branch, published a piece on 'Leonardo da Vinci as a Man of Science', telling of his drainage schemes, canal-making machines, devices for measuring distance and wind-force, and for flying; acted as First Citizen in Laurence Housman's *The Peace Makers*, played right half at hockey, won fifteen votes as Socialist candidate in a mock election for the Debating Society (Orpen for the National Conservatives won with twenty-two votes: the girls were less left-wing than their teachers*), and published a competent translation of Horace's ode '*Quis multa gracilis te puer in rosa*'.† 1936 sees Iris vice-captain of her house, involved in League activities, the Debating Society, the 2nd XI hockey team, and writing a poem entitled 'The Diver' which recalls the 1930s fashion for the aviator as culture-hero but, in true Murdoch fashion, substitutes water for air and celebrates swimming instead. She writes up the activities of the Literary and Architecture Clubs (*Lady Precious Stream*,‡ Francis Bacon, Chesterton, an exhibition of Everyday Things in Bristol); acts in a parody of Euripides' *Alcestis* ('Al's Sisters') where, arrayed as a butler bearing cocktails, she is noted as 'among the stars of the cast', and also plays Hank Eisenbaum in 'Hollywood Rehearses Shakespeare'. Her dramatic activities at Froebel and Badminton, and

---

* Indira Gandhi commented that 'despite a terribly anti-Fascist and pacifist' atmosphere, 'imperialism seems to be inherent in the bones of the girls' at Badminton, '... [though] they hate to hear you say so'. Frank, *Indira*, p.119.

† 'What slim youngster (soaked in perfumes) is hugging you now, Pyrrha, on a bed of roses?' (David West's translation). Iris's translation: 'What graceful boy in fragrant odours steeped,/'Mid crimson roses in a cavern dim,/Worships your smile ...'

‡ S.I. Hsiung's old Chinese play had been translated into English in 1935.

later at Oxford, are interesting. Although the adult and puritan Iris disliked theatre, young Iris enjoyed acting and was famous at Oxford for her talent.

7

In mid-January 1937 Iris won joint first prize (£2.12s.6d) for an essay on lectures organised at Regent Street Polytechnic by the Education Department of the League of Nations Union. She watched the German (and Nazi) lecturer fatuously explaining that persecution of the Jews was designed merely 'to make an independent people of them', and wrote of how the choice between democracy and dictatorship was made urgent by Spain. She is engaged with the Literary Club, and wins her hockey colours. She is now in her eighteenth year, and her political judgements must be thought of as those of an adult, albeit a very young one. She finds space in a piece praising community singing – 'Music was everywhere,' she was later to write – to commend 'that courageous and much maligned country, Soviet Russia'. On the verso page of this eulogy appears, with dramatic irony, one of Iris's lino-cuts, entitled 'The Prisoner', of a man evidently suffering in solitary confinement – but not, of course, in the USSR, which Iris believes 'is now becoming more and more democratic'. This was a view, horribly wrong-headed as it now appears, that Iris and BMB were scarcely alone in holding.

In 1936–37 alone, we now know, two million died in Stalin's purges.[58] Nor was such knowledge hidden at the time. Two years later George Orwell famously wrote that to English intellectuals 'such things as purges, secret police, summary executions, imprisonment without trial, &tc &tc are too remote to be terrifying. They can swallow totalitarianism because they have no experience of anything except liberalism.'[59] The appeal of the Communist Party – which Iris joined the following year – at the time of the Spanish Civil War is well attested, and not just by Orwell. Yet it is remarkable that Iris, who praised the Communist Party as late as spring 1943 to Ruth Kingsbury, a graduate of Lady Margaret

Hall, rarely expressed misgivings about the USSR. She thought Russia on the whole misunderstood over the non-aggression pact with Nazi Germany, and even after the Russian invasion of Finland in November 1939 she stayed 'on the Stalinist line'. Badminton, she later pointed out, had caused her, like many others, to 'live in a sort of dream world' politically: they really believed that politics was a much simpler matter than it later turned out to be, and that 'the Soviet Union was a good state, rather than a thoroughly bad state'.[60]

By 1945 her view of the USSR had shifted, and in the 1970s she would help campaign for the release of the Soviet dissident Vladimir Bukovsky, of course seeing Stalinism as a great evil. That she had no such understanding before 1943 may attest a political naïveté some friends[61] felt long accompanied her. Tender-heartedness, in politics as in love, may be accompanied by unsettling blindness.

8

By spring term 1937 Iris is head girl, mediating on at least one committee between staff and girls, reporting on the League of Nations Union, determined 'not to falter in our search for peace', recording a visit to the home of the millionaire marmalade manufacturer and amateur archaeologist Alexander Keiller, whose taste and Druidic megaliths alike leave her 'dazed', playing lacrosse, publishing an untitled poem in which her love of London is apparent: 'And I watch for the bended bow of the Milky Way/ Over London asleep'. In July she wins a distinction in English for her Higher School Certificate, plays a home cricket game against a neighbouring school – probably the match at which Rene made a rare appearance and a great impression. Iris seemed, to Dulcibel Broderick as she did to others, more like Rene's elder sister than her daughter.

She published an eighteen-line translation from Sophocles' *Oedipus at Colonos* – her Greek was coming on stream. W.H. Auden visited the school and read part of a new play he and Christopher

Isherwood were writing – presumably *On the Frontier*. Iris sat next to Auden, finding him 'young and beautiful with his golden hair'.[62] She soon enlisted his help in writing a foreword to *Poet Venturers*, her own brainchild, a collection of poems by Bristol schoolchildren published by Gollancz at a price of 'only one shilling' – the proceeds to be given to the Chinese Medical Aid Fund. Iris's poem, 'The Phoenix-Hearted', lyrically hymns China's powers of recuperation from the invading Japanese 'hosts of glittering dragon-flies'. She wins an Open Exhibition of £40 a year for three years at Somerville College, Oxford.

For the second year running she won a prize for a League of Nations essay competition, this time entitled 'If I were Foreign Secretary' (the second prize of one guinea went to the future critic Raymond Williams, of King Henry VII School, Abergavenny). Apart from advocating, among other measures, recognition of the legality of the Spanish government, her essay is of greatest interest for its pious belief that the Fascist countries can be brought to heel through sanctions alone, after which 'the world would be calmed and reassured and the menace of war would gradually disappear'. After she joined the Communist Party the following year, Iris's pacifism would strengthen. 'Looking back we see the thirties as a time of dangerously unrealistic political dreams,' she later commented, dreams embodied above all in the statutes of the League of Nations, based on the optimistic premise that all nations were already, or could by persuasion soon become, freedom-loving, peace-loving democracies. Iris renounced her own advocacy of peace at all costs only in 1941.

It could be said that all her fiction, and much of her moral philosophy, are acts of penance for, and attacks upon, the facile rationalistic optimism of her extreme youth, when she thought that setting people free was easy, that 'socialism (of which we had no very clear idea) would bring freedom and justice to all countries, and the world would get better'.[63] This optimism entailed a belief in the imminent birth of a 'clean-cut rational world' within the century dominated by Hitler and Stalin. Her work explores, among other matters, those 'irrational' psychic forces within the individual which make Hitlers possible, and freedom problematic.

Despite BMB's hostility to most films as 'mental dope', a school cinema was opened, and Iris gave a speech thanking the Governors. The first film shown was Robert Flaherty's *Man of Aran*. She published two promising poems.[64] In spring 1938 she was one of four soloists in Pergolesi's *Stabat Mater*,[65] and she records an expedition to see the Severn bore. She recalled both its strange noise, and the equally strange local pride in it, thirty years later.[66] The paper she read to the Literary Club on Modern Poetry is described as 'exceptionally interesting'. Iris kept her schoolmistress Ida Hinde's 1937 gift of a book of her own poems, *At the Edge of a Dream*, inscribed 'with love' from its author, with its *pièce-de-résistance*, 'Sapphics'. Yet exclusive friendships were closely monitored and frowned upon, and seating arrangements at meals periodically altered, which helped pre-empt them.

'One sound way of preventing complete forgetfulness of school . . . and its ideals is to become a Life Member of the O.B.A.' – the Old Badmintonians' Association – BMB advised the departing Iris and others, and Iris became a 'Life Member Without Magazine'. BMB's advice about choosing a husband had her usual gruff good sense: 'Try to remember that this is the person to whom you will have to pass the marmalade 365 days a year until one of you dies.' She gave pride of place to a picture by Iris of Lynmouth harbour painted when the school moved there in 1941, and there was an old-girl reunion.[67] BMB, who asked Ann Leech to 'keep an eye' on Iris at Oxford, may have feared, Leech later thought, that Iris might be 'wild' there.[68]

9

Iris began her first romance, by correspondence, around 1937. When a letter came to tell of his death in 1970, she noted, 'James is dead. First event of my adult life. Such a good man. And a good *influence* (on me, then),' and wrote to his widow that he had been a 'great awakener'. She gives no surname, but her

Belfast cousins remember James Henderson Scott, who would facetiously identify himself as 'Scott of Belfast', born in 1913, and a good friend of cousin Cleaver.[69] Scott finished his dentistry studies at Queen's in 1937, medicine in 1942. Born into Methodism, he converted to Catholicism, was gifted and literary, and an enthusiast for that earlier convert Cardinal Newman. When he later became Professor of Dental Anatomy at Queen's, he gave his inaugural lecture in blank verse.

Cleaver suggested that clever, bookish, 'romantic' James, who wrote and loved poetry, write to Cleaver's highly intelligent, book-ish cousin Iris, who also loved and wrote poetry. Both were Irish and loved Ireland. A correspondence started – 'an elusive some-thing drew [them] together'. Both had a feeling for Virgil's 'tears of things', something sad and deep that belonged to 'the very structure of the universe' – though Iris's apprehension was then more political, James's religious. He fell for Iris – at least the dream-Iris he encountered in her imaginative, responsive letters – and then for the being he first met, his journals suggest, at the Peter Pan statue in Kensington Gardens just after noon on Saturday, 2 April 1938. 'Something snapped' inside him, he noted a year later, 'which has never been repaired'. A romantic interest on Iris's side did not survive this meeting, and she was able slowly to get James to accept this. 'I want and I need your friendship over and above even that of the girl I marry,' James noted. They sailed to Belfast on the *Duke of Lancaster* together on 5 April 1939, and spent time with Iris's cousins and other friends. Iris and James climbed the tower of Queen's University, tying a friend's pyjamas to the flagpost. She witnessed her first operation at the Royal Victoria Hospital, James noting that she 'would have made a wonderful medical student', and had a fierce quarrel about Christianity and Communism. Friendship survived: Iris was good at this feat. She was later famous for a complicated private life in which she found it hard to disencumber herself of any of her many admirers. James then fell in unrequited love with cousin Sybil, and married Olive Marron in 1945.

Summer Irish holidays belong elsewhere in her story. Glimpses of London holidays are given by Margaret Orpen: she and Iris

visited each other. Once they were to give a joint lecture to the
school Architecture Club, for which they visited London's Wren
churches. On another occasion they went together to the Cale-
donian market in Islington, where Iris bought a necklace for
sixpence. On Wednesday, 28 September 1938, after both had left
school, Orpen and Iris found themselves standing in the gods at
Covent Garden – they could not afford seats – watching a ballet,
probably the de Basil company. It was exceptionally hot and stuffy.
It was also the eve of Chamberlain and Hitler's Munich agreement, the most critical moment of that 'strange year full of anxiety
and fear'.[70] The letter Iris wrote Orpen afterwards ended with,
'If we should meet again, why then we'll smile,' from *Julius Caesar*,
a quotation that would resonate with deeper meaning six years
later.

4

A Very Grand Finale
1938–1939

'My schooldays lacked colour and gaiety in a way that they needn't have done – and in a way which made the change from school to student life violent and positively intoxicating.'[1] Iris, who had read Angela Brazil's exciting boarding-school tales, found her own schooldays unnecessarily 'dreary' by comparison: she had had to 'spend my time making bloody dresses when I could have been learning languages'.[2] None the less, most Oxford peers noted that she arrived at the university with some assurance.[3] Her memory differed. A schoolchild before the war had no 'part' to play. Teenagers had not yet been invented. Being able to play-act the role of a student, by contrast, gave Iris confidence at a time when she 'needed it badly'.

Iris and her fellow new arrivals at Somerville were given a talking-to by the tall, gaunt French scholar Vera Farnell, speaking as Dean: 'You must seriously realise that you have to be careful how you behave. It isn't a joking-matter, the women are still very much on probation in this University. You may think that it doesn't matter if you do something a little wild, but I can tell you that it will.' This was the voice of hard experience: a second-year Somerville student to whose case Farnell was reported to be unsympathetic had, the previous year, been 'sent down', or permanently dismissed from Oxford, after being found *in flagrante* in her boyfriend's rooms by his landlady. The boyfriend's fate, by contrast, was merely to be 'rusticated', or banished for a term, after which he resumed his studies. Lucy Klatschko, quiet, fey and very beautiful, half-Latvian and Jewish senior scholar reading

Modern languages, who was later to be both a nun and lifelong friend of Iris, is the student referred to in John Bayley's *Iris: A Memoir of Iris Murdoch* (*Elegy for Iris* in the USA) as being helped by a boyfriend back over the college wall. There was an easy place, and she climbed back quite often.[4]

Despite Vera Farnell's caveats, and the fact that keeping Iris at Oxford was 'just ruining' Hughes,[5] life here was different, joyous and painful, full at last of Iris's intellectual equals. She positively threw herself into the stage-role of 'being-a-student', into a 'hurricane of essays and proses and campaigns and committees and sherry parties and political and aesthetic arguments'.[6] She had heard plenty of classical music at school, but no jazz, despite growing up during the best part of the jazz age. She had to wait until she was nineteen before she realised that dancing – as opposed to the Greek dancing practised at Badminton – 'can be something marvellous, something ecstatic'. There were further sources of bliss and pain, apart from the untoward number of men who fell in love with her.

Iris felt joyous when, having been called 'Iris' at school, her tutors called her 'Miss Murdoch'.[7] There was her very first alcoholic drink, consumed in the Royal Oak opposite Somerville in the company of Carol Stewart and another undergraduate.[8] Drinking was a forbidden pleasure. No students were officially allowed to keep drink in their rooms, or to enter a pub – a delightful adventure in itself because one might be 'progged' – caught by the rule-enforcing Proctors. Iris did not know the names of any drinks, so one of her companions ordered a gin and lime for her: 'The experience comes back to me surrounded by a halo of the purest and most intense joy.'[9] Carol Stewart saw something 'aboriginal' in Iris – 'simplicity, naiveté, power, and space'. She further noted how unusually watchful and observant Iris was. The joy of her first drink accompanied her joy at freedom. There were disappointments also. She thought she would get straight into the Bach Choir, but was turned down when she admitted she could not sight-read: 'They didn't even hear me sing. That caused me such rage.'[10]

Mary Scrutton (later Midgley, the philosopher), daughter of a canon who had been Chaplain at King's College, Cambridge, has a strong memory of Iris when both first came up. Iris's peers were timid, very afraid of making fools of themselves, doubtful about what was expected of them, anxious about opening their mouths. Iris was different. When she went to tea with the Principal, the painfully shy Helen Darbyshire, she reported herself disgusted by the claustrophobic and stilted conversation: 'What a waste, to go to tea with a really intelligent woman, & talk about Siamese cats.'[11] Iris's confidence, Mary Scrutton felt, was extraordinarily helpful to others in her year. She had a faculty which stayed with her: she *didn't care much what people thought*, was not self-conscious. She was there to get on with things and enjoy them. She at once arranged her room in East Quad, on the first floor above the archway, overlooking the quad and the Woodstock Road,[12] which she managed to make look like an art student's room, with posters and an art deco cushion which lived on for sixty years at her flat in Cornwall Gardens, aquamarine, stripy, with inset spheres. Mary and Iris took to each other right away – Mary sat on the floor, and they began a conversation that went on for decades, and which in 1998 Iris recalled with warmth.

Iris occupied a position simultaneously central, and yet also apart, at Somerville. The tables *across* the dining-room went third-year (by the windows), second-year, first-year (by the doors). But *down* the dining-room they went, unofficially, 'stodgy, middling, and wild'. Those who sat at the top table were nearest to the dons: 'some dull people from the history school' who trooped in punctually in a body from the library, then trooped back to the library immediately afterwards (or so, with the superciliousness of youth, it appeared to Iris and Mary). Nearest the door was the 'wild' table, comprising those who least wanted it to be noticed whether they arrived on time or not. There sat a Princess Natalya Galitzine, who eloped in her first term, beautiful, quiet, slim, composed Anne Cloake, and Leonie Marsh, a 'flamboyant Bolshevik' with a face like 'a slightly dissipated lion's'. Wildness here referred primarily to politics, meaning membership of the Oxford Labour Group and/or the Communist Party, also to frequent changes of partner, to attractiveness, dress and hairstyle. Leonie

dressed 'like a bolshevik . . . in her warm woollen jerkin, her blue
serge skirt, red belt, sandals and red mittens'.[13] Respectable hair
was short or up-and-back; 'wild' hair could be long or curled in
some exciting manner, possibly dyed. Iris's hair was long and
blonde; Leonie's a 'black defiant lion's mane'.

Then there was the bourgeois middle table where sat Mary,
Charlotte Williams-Ellis and Nancy Fisher. Philippa Bosanquet,
who came up in 1939, sat either at the middle table or, if in
trousers, at the 'end' table. Iris was liable to turn up anywhere,
at the wild or the middle tables, even at the top. What was distinctive about this, and unlike anyone else that Mary knew, was that
Iris always had important friendships of very varied kinds. Her
movement from table to table seemed a metaphor for her way of
appearing at home in different *milieux*, throughout her life, while
belonging essentially to herself.

Iris believed that university friendships lasted for life.[14] Hers
were to. Novel after Iris novel depends upon the convention that
a court of characters have been friends since college days. Did
she understand how uniquely true this was of her own generation
– more, arguably, than of any other? Friendships formed just
before the war partook of the same intensity as did politics and
love; no one, after all, knew who would survive the coming
onslaught. Casualties of war apart, Iris mislaid few friends notably
or dramatically, and when losses did happen she brooded over
them, accounting them significant. David Hicks, Hal Lidderdale,
Noel Martin, Mary Midgley, Leo Pliatzky, Frank Thompson,
Philippa and Michael (M.R.D.) Foot: their names resonate
through the nearly sixty years of her journals.

2

English is what Iris was accepted into Somerville to study, but
she ended by reading Classics. Possibly the English tutor Mary
Lascelles, remembered as hard to please, failed to take to Iris.
Happily Iris's brilliant General Paper had won her an Exhibition
for merit, and in it she had used a Greek word, in Greek script.

Isobel Henderson, who taught Iris the history of the ancient world from 1940 on, snapped her up. No record survives of when she changed to Classics, or 'Mods and Greats'.[15]

Mods and Greats, moreover, took four years rather than the normal three required for an undergraduate degree. In Mods (Honour Moderations), which took the first five terms, students read most of Classical Greek and Latin literature, and wrote prose and verse in both languages. Greats (*Literae Humaniores*) was divided into ancient history and ancient philosophy, with a smattering of later philosophers up to Kant. Designed by Benjamin Jowett in the nineteenth century for young gentlemen who were thus readied, for example, for the Colonial Civil Service, Mods and Greats trained analytic capacity, and placed its students firmly within the category of the civilised, as opposed to the barbarian, of belonging to that part of Europe which, unlike Germany, had been ruled by Rome, and had retained some degree of cultural coherence ever since:[16] an opposition fraught with critical significance in 1938–39, when Germany appeared to be returning to the Middle Ages, unillumined this time by the mercy of Christ. Male students who had been to the great public schools were best prepared for the rigours of the course; pre-war Classical training at girls' schools was not always equal to them.

Iris and Mary's Mods tutor, Mildred Hartley, was understandably keen to have everything done in such a way as to be a credit to Somerville, and indeed to her. She intensely wanted her students to be good scholars – which they were, carrying off many Classical prizes. She insisted that the girls do not only Latin and Greek prose translations, but also verse – particularly hard if you had not been trained. There was a sense of background nagging as she put them through their paces. Iris's training had been a bit better than Mary's; they suffered together. Both had extra tutorial coaching in Classics.[17]

Mildred Hartley had had a hard struggle to come up in the world, and could appear pedantic and fussy. Her hidden eccentricity – celebrating the end of term by donning trousers, taking down a thriller from the shelves and smoking a pipe – is a modest one.[18] Iris was furious when it was reported to her that Hartley had remarked that she was always in fancy-dress,[19] an observation also pointing towards identity itself as like 'dressing-up'. (Iris's Dublin 'cousins' Eva and Billy Lee always looked forward to meeting Iris off the Dun Laoghaire boat-train, never knowing in advance what she would this time come 'dressed *as*'.) Certainly Iris had her *own* dress-sense. Hartley would later refer to Iris as 'my shaggy little Shetland pony', suggesting no lack of affection,[20] and would comment accurately that Iris 'did not understand the meaning of idleness'.[21] Most undergraduates had to choose between evenings out and getting essays written. Iris somehow did both, coming in late and yet being first down to breakfast, looking rested and lively.[22]

The students got a lot out of their course. They went to the great and terrifying Eduard Fraenkel's lectures on Horace, and also studied some Plato, lectured on by the impressive, but very shy E.R. Dodds: a few dialogues – certainly *Phaedo*, probably *Symposium* and *Phaedrus*. Iris despised Plato, thinking him reactionary, dishonest, full of cheap dialectical tricks. Reading the *Republic* left her feeling aggressive, and she opposed Plato, in letters to a friend, directly to Marx. After denouncing Plato as 'the old reactionary', she wished she lived 'near enough to know how people live in mines & cotton mills . . . I feel very bitterly the second-handness of most of my knowledge of life' – a sense that a later Iris would use Plato to explain. As if to cure herself of the taste of Plato, she sold the *Daily Worker* to the 'thronging multitudes of Blackpool', where her parents were evacuated in 1939.[23] Dodds also lectured on the Greek dramatists.

Greek Vase Painting was Iris's special subject: Professor Sir John Beazley, an inspiring scholar and teacher, lectured on Classical archaeology at the Ashmolean Museum. He showed his classes beautiful Attic objects, taught ways of understanding them. Gifted students would be invited 'back-stage' to view the more 'frank' or salacious vases otherwise relegated to a top shelf.[24] Iris's careful, copious, string-bound, loose-leaf handwritten notes for the class, comprising some few hundred pages, are illustrated by her pen-and-ink drawings of decorative details and of statues of Greek youths.

3

To find out who someone is, Napoleon remarked, one must ask, 'How did the world look, around the time that they were twenty?' The twelve months before the outbreak of the Second World War were a time of intense hope and fear, anxiety and dread. The young were intensely stirred up. *Intensity* is the key-word in politics, in friendship and in love alike; a dramatic intensity that radically divided the lives of those who went up to Oxford a year before the war – like Iris, to 'serious-minded'[25] Somerville College in 1938 – from those who, like John Bayley, went up in the disenchanted post-war years. In 1938–39 a Manichean fight against the powers of darkness was imminent, the drumbeat of war unmistakable. There was constant talk of Nazism, the Moscow treason trials, marching and raising money for arms for Spain, the bestial pogrom against German Jews in November 1938, Hitler's annexation of the Sudetenland. At the same time student life for the first year after Iris came up in late September 1938 was still agreeably wild, irresponsible, aesthetic and cranky. There was still a sense of scope and completeness.[26] Charismatic figures abounded, among the students as among the dons. The sober diminishment of university life came later, with war and mobilisation.

The dominant international issue was the Spanish Civil War, which ended only in April 1939. No other cause ever stirred comparable passions in Oxford. The death in Spain of the poet John Cornford, whose brother Christopher was to play a significant role in Iris's life in the 1960s, had made him 'a martyr of mythic power'. The war in Spain was so real 'that it hurt'.[27] Iris denied having penned early in 1939[28] a bad poem about Barcelona, signed 'IM', which appeared in the progressive university magazine *Oxford Forward.* Entitled 'Vanguard', it began: 'Remember – they have ringed/Us England, roundabout with steel/Spain-tempered', and ends: 'Yes, gutters running red/In broken Barcelona bear/Witness to a debt. Look,/England, who fights for you.'

A lot of the English aristocracy, together with powerful financiers, were members of the sinister pro-Hitler 'Anglo-German Fellowship'. Might Britain even enter the war on the wrong side?[29] In October 1938 the sitting Conservative Member of Parliament for Oxford had died. Student pressure helped force Patrick Gordon-Walker, the Labour candidate, out of the running, so that tall, shambling Sandy Lindsay, Master of Balliol – the first confessed Socialist to head a college – could fight as the Popular Front candidate against the Conservatives' Quintin Hogg, the 'flamboyant and ill-mannered supporter of Chamberlain',[30] without a rival from the left. Lindsay's support stretched from the Communists through the Labour and Liberal parties, to dissident Conservatives. The international context, immediately after Neville Chamberlain's agreement with Hitler, made this 'Munich' by-election a fight of mythic proportions. 'Save Peace, Save Czechoslovakia' was one Lindsay slogan; 'A vote for Hogg is a vote for Hitler' another: the by-election was both a referendum on the Munich agreement and a vote of confidence in Chamberlain, who had proposed on 18 September to allow Hitler's annexation of the Sudetenland.

The substitution of Lindsay for Gordon-Walker affronted sections of middle-class Oxford. Iris canvassed, together with Raymond Carr, a clever, ambitious scholarship boy, down the left-hand side of the Woodstock Road, both of them ill-at-ease and both sympathetic to, and soon members of, the Communist Party. Iris was later to claim, 'The very first thing I did when I arrived at Oxford was to join the CP':[31] this went well with the ideals of Badminton.[32] They also worked stuffing envelopes in the Lindsay campaign room opposite St Peter's College. Carr was in awe of Iris because she was intellectually very impressive, did not care about her dishevelled appearance, and seemed to him to have been at Oxford a full year before him. In fact this was her first month there.[33] He was not the first or the last to be struck by Iris's extraordinary confidence. She also worked in this by-election with fellow-Somervillian Anne Cloake,[34] with whom Carr thought her in love. Certainly Anne Cloake, who had no lesbian proclivity, but did like to shock, later boasted of having helped teach Iris the 'facts of life'; in their second year they shared digs at 43 Park Town.

Hogg won by a small majority. In St Aldates the defeated Lindsay supporters with their tattered red-and-yellow rosettes confronted the Conservatives 'in their horsey check-coats, with their carnations and rolled umbrellas' who, they felt, rushed to sneer and crow at them 'as if after a day's beagling, or a night in London': 'What depressed us was that obscurantism had triumphed.' On the Lindsay side were 'the creative, the generous, the imaginative. In the other we saw only selfishness, stodginess and insincerity.' 'I hope North Oxford gets the first bombs, but it would be rough on the pekinese,' commented one supporter.[35]

4

In November 1938, on the afternoon when he had just become College Secretary of the Liberal Club, Frank Thompson went to Queen's College to listen to Rex Warner, who had recently published the left-wing allegorical novel *The Aerodrome,* and the poet Stephen Spender talk about Spain. Munich, he wrote, which had numbed them for a time, 'still filled us with a deep restless anger'. The hall, which Spender described 'foolishly' as a 'glorified railway station', was crowded. Students were sitting on the tables and floor, but Frank managed to squeeze onto a bench against a wall. While Spender was making a woolly speech about 'the poet in politics', Frank noticed a girl leaning on her elbow on the table in front of him. She wasn't pretty, and her figure was too thick to be good.

> But there was something about her warm green dress, her long yellow locks like a cavalier's, and her gentle profile, that gave a pleasing impression of harmony. My feeling of loneliness redoubled. 'Why didn't I know anyone like that?' I saw her again at a Labour Club Social, dancing, – perhaps 'waddling' is a better word, with some poisonous-looking bureaucrat. It wasn't until the middle of next term that I got a chance to speak to her.

Frank was brilliant, tall, slim, fair-haired, grey-blue-eyed, high-cheekboned, a gifted poet, an intense idealist dedicated to stopping Hitler, a Wykehamist who spoke six languages and later acquired three more. His was a *nature riche*. He was one year younger than Iris,[36] and was reading Mods at New College. He came from a liberal, anti-imperialist and well-connected bohemian family that was also hospitable, 'quick with ideas and poetry and international visitors';[37] his younger brother E.P. Thompson was to make his mark as the best-known left-wing historian and activist of his generation. A childhood friend of both, Anthony Carritt, had been blown up and killed while driving an ambulance with the International Brigade in Spain.[38] As a student Frank is remembered as charming, shambolic and unco-ordinated. 'Stop apologising,' friends would say to him. Wartime photographs show a face of some beauty, intelligence, and grace.[39] The first time Iris had seen him 'he was very drunk and lying flat on his back in the entrance hall of the Union with his head inside the telephone-box'.[40] ('He couldn't tell one drink from another,' Iris wrote to his mother in 1941.) It was almost certainly at that November meeting at Queen's that someone – probably Leonie Marsh, among the first to join the Communist Party – pointed Frank out to Iris: '"There's Frank Thompson. He's a most remarkable man. We must get him into the Party." And so,' Iris remembered, 'we did . . . He was, I think, the most remarkable person that I met as an undergraduate at Oxford.'[41] Their first meeting happened a term later.

There is a pleasing symmetry about the fact that Iris is remembered in her Oxford years, among other things, for her involvement in political life and in amateur theatricals, especially her memorable Leader of the 'Chorus' in the Christ Church production of T.S. Eliot's *Murder in the Cathedral* in June 1940.*[42] The two relate. Even if her play-acting was not always politicised, her politics were certainly dramatic, and it is fitting that the by-election

---

* Directed by Frances Podmore, it was the first play at Oxford in which male and female students were allowed to act together. Prior to that dons' wives acted the women's parts in college performances; West End actresses were called upon for the Oxford University Dramatic Society (OUDS).

in which she played a role was rapidly turned into part of a student play. A play, moreover, in which most of the leading players were, in real life, to be in love with each other, but not in the right order, and many of the men, sooner or later, were in love with Iris. In Auden's 'A Summer Night', a favourite poem,[43] where a bitter historical and political irony collides with an intense elegiac lyricism, Continental Europe is about to be convulsed in suffering, while the guilty English 'whom hunger cannot move,/In gardens where we feel secure,/Look up, and with a sigh endure,/The tyrannies of love'. Love intoxicated the players as well as politics.

The Lindsay/Hogg by-election continued to resonate in Iris's second term at Oxford. To show the dangers of Fascism in Britain, Frank and some friends, notably Leo Pliatzky and Leonie Marsh, wrote, produced and acted in *It Can Happen Here*, which imagined Britain as a Fascist police state.[44] Frank and Leo's friendship spanned the social spectrum, and the two constituencies from which the Labour Party drew its strength. Leo Pliatzky – 'the old cynic himself', Iris was to call him[45] – was at Corpus reading Honour Mods. Later to be Secretary of the Fabian Society and a distinguished, indeed knighted, Treasury civil servant, he was Jewish, Manchester-born and poor, with a St Petersburg-born father who gambled. He had been rescued by the Professor of Political Science at the London School of Economics, Harold Laski, from working for 17/6*d* a week in the Houndsditch Warehouse Company;[46] Laski paid to complete Leo's education, and Oxford was memorable in part for offering, for the first time in his life, three square meals a day. Mainly set in a concentration camp in Christ Church Meadow, with flashbacks to a sherry party and to a meeting of the Oxford Union, *It Can Happen Here* also portrayed the proctors and a works meeting. The Lindsay committee rooms during the by-election featured significantly. The play had one performance at 8.15 p.m. on 6 March 1939, admission price sixpence, in St Michael's Hall to a (largely) Labour Club audience, and was well received.

Frank (who played 'Dennis Fairlie') and Leo (who wrote but did not act) went on a pub-crawl afterwards, ending up with a bottle of whisky in the play's producer Doug Lowe's rooms in

Ruskin. Leonie had seen to it that Iris – 'the dream-girl to whom I'd never spoken', as Frank called her – was with them. Doug Lowe told Frank that Iris was 'a nice girl, and *pretty easy too*, from wot I 'ear' – wishful thinking on Lowe's part.[47] Lowe, on one side of the bed on which Iris reclined, started to 'paw' her. Frank, on the other, wanted to stroke her too: 'Anyone would want to stroke Iris,' Frank observed. Indeed a 'witty liberal' was trying to edge Frank out. But Frank could see that Iris did not wish to be pawed, and wanting to make a good first impression despite being pretty drunk, he grew solemn and started on politics. He had left the Liberal Club the week before because it was 'too frivolous'. He had no use for the Labour leaders either. Iris asked him provocatively, 'What about the Communist Party?'

> I was dumbstruck. I'd never thought of it before. Right then I couldn't see anything against it, but I felt it would be wise to wait till I'd sobered up before deciding. So I said, 'Come to tea in a couple of days and convert me'. Then I staggered home and lay on a sofa . . . announcing to the world that I had met a stunner of a girl and was joining the Communist party for love of her. But next morning it still seemed good. I read [Lenin's] *State and Revolution*, talked to several people, and soon made up my mind.

By the time Iris came to tea in Frank's very untidy room with, typically, 'Liddell and Scott always open on the table, and a large teddy-bear and a top hat on the mantelpiece and *Voi che Sapete* on the gramophone',[48] there was no need for a conversion: 'My meeting her was only the point at where quantitative change gave place to change in quality.' Frank pondered, 'maybe I needed to meet her, to realise how gentle and artistic communists can be. Or maybe I needed to be drunk, so I could consider the question with an open mind.' Leonie welcomed him into the Party with a 'dramatic gesture, saved by a wicked smile'. He wrote to a friend,[49] 'I've met my dream-girl – a poetic Irish Communist who's doing Honour Mods. I worship her.'

The group associated with *It Can Happen Here* took to 'knocking about together': Frank, Leonie Marsh, Leo, Iris, and also fellow-Wykehamist Michael (M.R.D.) Foot. 'That was a bad passage, the first fortnight of the summer term,' wrote Frank:

> Like something in rather poor taste by de Musset. I was pining green for Iris, who was gently sympathetic but not at all helpful. Michael was lashing himself into a frenzy for Leonie [Marsh] who would draw him on and then let him down with a thud. In the evenings we would swap sorrows and read bits of Verlaine to each other.

Frank spent three whole days that May walking round and round New College gardens, observing the chestnuts bearing their white candles, the pink tulips and blue forget-me-nots, in the intervals between writing letters to Iris and tearing them up. He wrote poems to her expressing 'calf-love'.[50] Iris, 'with her gentleness and her simplicity', was the person from whom he wanted to hear good news about himself, 'But Iris never told a lie yet, so I got worse and worse.' Michael hid Frank's cut-throat razor from him. Leo, more down-to-earth, invited him to dinner. When, one evening, Iris disappeared into Doug Lowe's rooms in Ruskin, Frank went back to his parents' house on Boar's Hill and, on his mother's sensible advice, dug up an entire bed of irises as a counter-charm.[51] He stopped sleeping, started talking to himself, was in such a bad way that he escaped to spend a week at home, gardening, going for walks, climbing trees. Other things cheered him. There was the 'big joyous world of his friends, not only political ones'.[52] He found comfort in the idylls of Theocritus, especially the tenth, and in two other Greek pastoral poets, Bion and Moschus, whom Iris recalled his quoting to her 'exuberantly'.

So Frank's old schoolfriend and rival from Winchester Michael (M.R.D.) Foot was crazy about Leonie, who adored Frank, who was hopelessly in love with Iris. If Iris had loved Michael, it would have made a perfect quartet of frustrated desire, like that of *A Midsummer Night's Dream*, Act III, and doubtless one blueprint – there would be others – for the love-vortices of her novels. On this unhappy love quartet, Frank was able to joke in a parody of

Marxist-Leninist Newspeak: 'It's not shortage of resources that's the problem, comrades. It's maldistribution of supplies.'[53]

5

Scarcity of resources, however, also played its part. The ratio of men to women at Oxford at that time exceeded six to one, and the Labour Club was reputed to have the best women. Some men joined the club merely to meet and get 'lined-up with', in the jargon of the period, a woman. Within that closed society-within-a-society, 'line-ups' were regarded as temporary, and might – equally might not – involve a sexual affair.* Leo Pliatzky's first 'line-up', for example, was with Leonie, his second with Iris, his third with Edna Edmonds (later Healey). Who Iris's first lover was, and what such affairs meant to her, will have to wait for a later chapter. A comment of Leonie Marsh gives the general impression of Iris at that time. Leonie left Oxford in June 1940, married in February 1941 and was surprised when Iris declared herself envious of the baby that followed: 'Funny, she was always so virginal.'[54]

It was probably on a punt journey to the arboured tables and chairs at the Victoria Arms, with Mary Scrutton and the two shy and unpretentious Williams-Ellis sisters, Charlotte and Susie, that Iris said, in the summer of 1939, 'I *long* to get married, I'd do *anything* to get married.' 'But you've had six proposals this term alone,' said one of the other girls. 'Oh, they don't count,' Iris retorted dismissively. Susie thought Iris incredibly beautiful, with great big round blue eyes, very blonde shoulder-length hair cut straight across in a fringe: 'beauty of character as well as of appearance'. Susie had come to Ruskin for one term from the Chelsea School of Art; Charlotte was at Somerville. It is interesting that Iris's apparent confidence so far exceeded that of the patrician

---

* Denis Healey recounts the fury caused in the OULC by Tom Harrisson, founder of Mass Observation and then at Cambridge, with his savage essay on what he called 'Oxsex', which Healey thought 'not unfair' (*The Time of my Life*).

'Char' and Susie, whose father was Clough Williams-Ellis, architect of Portmeirion, and whose mother Amabel Strachey, children's story-writer and cousin to Lytton. Charlotte recalled: 'Iris was kind and pleasant to the shy and socially inept as I was.'[55] Clare Campbell, granddaughter of a distinguished Professor of Classics at Liverpool, who gained a first in Honour Mods without apparent effort, was none the less 'amazed by Iris's social poise as well as fluency' at meetings of the Jowett Society – the undergraduate club where philosophical discussion took place. By comparison with Iris she felt like 'an over-age schoolgirl'.

M.R.D. Foot noted that 'practically everyone who was up with Iris fell for her. She had personality and that wonderful Irish voice.'[56] 'Pretty and buxom, with blonde hair and dirndl skirts,' is how Leo Pliatzky recalled her. Leo had turned his attentions towards Iris before Frank, Michael some time after. They were not alone. At times Iris at Oxford seems like a cross between Zuleika Dobson and Wendy in *Peter Pan*, looking after the 'lost boys'. Despite the 'thick' figure Frank accurately noted, and a walk which a fellow-student compared to the rolling gait of the oxen in Homer,[57] others outside the close-knit central group of Iris, Frank, Leonie, Leo and Michael felt her attractions. The interest of David Hicks, who had graduated in PPE at Worcester in 1938, and was taking a Dip. Ed., was aroused in November 1938.[58] Hicks was three years older than Iris, who resembled, he wrote to her, a 'fairy-tale princess' but one with a 'quaint virginity cult'. She visited his London home on Boxing Day 1938. His friend, kind, warm-hearted, undiplomatic Hal Lidderdale, a scholar at Magdalen reading Greats, also sympathetic to the Communist Party,[59] was another who fell for Iris. Iris liked his 'warmth & humanness, his lazy pleasure in life's good things, his lack of petty vanities & meannesses'.[60] She planned a camping holiday with Patrick O'Regan at Merton, who loaned her some cash which she repaid, and sent her, in July 1940, a book that seems positively emblematic. This was C.S. Lewis's *Allegory of Love*, with its history of the courtly cult, by many gentleman-admirers, of the *princesse lointaine*.[61] Nor is this an exhaustive list. Another (un-named) Irishman wrote her verse.[62] John Willett, stage designer for *It Can*

Happen Here, school-friend of Frank and Michael, and with the distinction of *not* being in love with Iris, thought – echoing others including Charlotte Williams-Ellis – that it was Iris's inner quality that attracted everyone: not a classic beauty, a beauty of soul.[63]

This would tally with the view of shy and gentle Noel Martin. Martin[64] was sitting in a friend's room on the first floor of Corpus quad one early evening in the autumn of 1938. Aged only eighteen and headed for a first in Mods, he saw a gowned and corn-haired Iris pass the pelican sundial with a Somerville girlfriend, probably Mary. She had a lively gait and looked, he thought, 'different'. Leonie Marsh, for example, whom he knew, was 'quite a girl' – one of those who get noticed. Iris, by contrast, was unassertive, grave,[65] reserved. But there was something about her, and he felt attracted. Iris and her companion were on their way to Eduard Fraenkel's brilliant, towering explication of the *Agamemnon* on the far left of the quad, on the ground floor.[66] Noel simply came down the stairs and followed her. He could not profit from the seminar, but spent his time gazing at Iris. Later, he and Iris talked. Frank Thompson observed that good-natured Noel's being 'sick for Iris' made him 'dopier than usual'. Twenty years later Iris wrote, '[Leo] loved me, in the days when Frank and Noel Martin loved me too. And indeed I loved them. My God, that was a golden time.'[67]

Philippa Bosanquet, who came up in 1939, recalls that the fascination with Iris then, as later, was general. Many were in love with her, could not get enough of her company. And she struck women, as well as men. Mary Douglas recalls her as 'dazzlingly pretty and tremendously dynamic in her personal style – with a formidable reputation as a debater'. Milein Cosman, at the Slade, which was evacuated to Oxford, saw Iris – ash-blonde, white blonde, high Slavic cheekbones – at a talk by 'splendid-looking' Graham Sutherland at New College: 'Look at that fantastic-looking girl, I'd like to draw her.' Milein's companion egged her on to talk to her, and an invitation from Iris to cocoa at Somerville ensued. Milein, a refugee from the Rhineland, had never heard of the exotic Oxford custom of inviting people for cocoa – but out of it came her first lithograph, of Iris's head, executed on the steps of the Ashmolean. Iris looks solemn, preoccupied, fey, melancholy, *jolie-laide.*

6

Iris sent an account of her first year at Oxford to her old school magazine.[68] She 'loves her work passionately, and . . . takes a zest-ful interest in the life of the University. She . . . finds a day of twenty-four hours quite insufficient for her needs. She represents the First Year on the Junior Common Room Committee, is a member of the College Debating and Dramatic Societies – is to play Polixenes in next term's *A Winter's Tale.*[69] The Classical Association, the Arts Club, the B.U.L.N.S [British Universities League of Nations Society] claim other parts of her day. She helps run Somerville Labour Club. For 4 terms she was advertising manager to *Oxford Forward*, progressive University weekly, has joined the staff of *Cherwell*, and hopes next term to sub-edit that paper.' In her first summer she contributed four reports about events at Somerville to *Oxford Magazine*,[70] and attended a one-week Communist Party summer school in Surrey, where the future historian Eric Hobsbawm, then studying at Cambridge, was deeply impressed by her looks, character and intelligence, noting that she associated there with the daughters of Ulster grandees.[71]

Franco won the war in Spain that April. In that love-fraught May Iris continued to publish poems. 'Lovely is earth now, splen-did/With year-youth' casts her in the role of world-watcher, and shows the imprint of Housman and Hopkins: 'to like,/To breathe, is pain and wonder'. 'Oxford Lament' begins:

> Deliver me from the usual thing,
> The clever inevitability of the conversation,
> The brilliant platitudes and second-hand
> Remarks about life.

She expresses both the self-conscious world-weariness behind which the averagely intelligent student in so many periods hides unconfident immaturity, but also a brave revulsion from the pose of having-seen-through-all-poses, and a longing for an intensity of expression that might strike the reader as unmediated and fresh. A frustrated longing, in a sense, for the powers of a 'grown-up' sensibility that might still evoke intensity:

> O for the tangent terror
> Of the metaphor no one has used –
> The keenness of cutting edges
> On fresh green ice of thought.

Gradually, the young men at Oxford were called up for the war. The summer of 1939 was the last of Oxford for Frank. One of his last nights was spent at Corpus with Leo and Noel.

> In Corpus everyone stands one drinks and I was pretty whistled . . . After I had eaten two tulips in the quad and bust a window, they dragged me into Leo's room and sat on me. I calmed down and they thought I was safe enough to take on the river. The red clouds round Magdalen tower were fading to grey, when we met two people we didn't like. We chased them and tried to upset their canoe. We got slowed up at the rollers, and then I dropped my paddle. With the excitement all the beer surged up in me. Shouting the historic slogan, 'All hands to the defence of the Soviet fatherland!' I plunged into the river. They fished me out but I plunged in again. By a series of forced marches they dragged me back and dumped me on the disgusted porter at the Holywell gate.

After Frank had burst into 'an important meeting of the college communist group' Comrade Foot, by a unanimous vote, was given 'the revolutionary task of putting [him] to bed'. Such jokey accounts make Frank sound like a rugger 'hearty'. His inclinations, in fact, were political, passionately humanistic and aesthetic, and he spent much of that year putting his idealism to the test. That Easter he had worked in a school for refugee Jewish boys at New Herrlingen in Kent: 'I like the Jews . . . They have a queer fascination for me. They're so alive, so intelligent and so generous.' (Iris shared this impassioned philo-Semitism, which belongs to its epoch: 'I find my pro-Semitism becoming more & more fanatical with the years.'[72])

Frank was understandably struck and unnerved by a request from two of the boys for help in getting their parents out of Germany. In July, as Secretary to New College Boys' Club in impoverished Hoxton, in London's East End, he spent ten days supervising activities in the boys' camp, then a fortnight working in a camp for the unemployed at Carmarthen in Wales ('thundering good value'), finally a week at the Communist Party summer school near Guildford, for political education.[73] Such experiences left him more than ever critical of the government's failure to address the issues of unemployment and Fascism.

On 31 July 1939, just before his nineteenth birthday, Frank completed a sonnet dedicated to Iris, entitled 'To Irushka at the Coming of War':

> If you should hear my name among those killed
> Say you have lost a friend, half man, half boy
> Who, if the years had spared him, might have built within
> Courage, strength and harmony.
> Uncouth and garrulous, with tangled mind
> Seething with warm ideas of truth and light,
> His help was worthless. Yet had fate been kind,
> He might have learned to steel himself and fight.
> He thought he loved you. By what right could he
> Claim such high praise, who only felt his frame
> Riddled with burning lead, and failed to see
> His own false pride behind the barrel's flame?
> Say you have lost a friend, and then forget.
> Stronger and truer ones are with you yet.

Rupert Brooke, more than the other soldier-poets Owen or Sassoon, lies behind this attempt to enlist sympathy and invite Iris to 'love what [she] must leave ere long', and it is hard to disentangle the myth of the poem from what was to happen to Frank. Yet, if the poetry does not only lie in the self-pity, the self-dramatisation is also less boldly absolute than in Frank's deservedly renowned poem 'Polliciti Meliora', written a year or so later, and more memorably poignant.

7

Iris spent the last two glorious August weeks of that final summer of peace with the strolling Magpie Players, exploring a different kind of poetry and a different mode of self-dramatisation. Scatty and likeable Tom Fletcher from Ruskin, who lived on Magpie Lane – 'a little king and . . . no constitutional monarch either' – organised a dozen or more students into a group reminiscent of J.B. Priestley's 'good companions' to tour the countryside around Oxford, performing mainly set-piece ballads and songs[74] ('It Ain't Gonna Rain no Mo'' for the company, and, among others, Samuel Daniel's 'Love is a Sickness' for Iris, which, she wrote, 'filled me with joy'), and short dramatic or comic interludes – 'Tam Lin', 'The Lay of the Heads', 'Auld Witch Wife', 'Binnorie', 'Green-sleeves', 'Clydewater', the medieval 'Play of the Weather', 'Donna Lombarda' . . . Since the group aimed to capitalise on 'the fascination Oxford holds for the general public',[75] they were enacting the roles of 'care-free students', as much as the parts within the sketches. Proceeds went to the Oxford University Refugee Appeal Fund.* They start on 16 August at the Blade Bone pub in Bucklebury, the first time Iris had lived 'on a genuine farm'. She is bemused to be woken early by roosters and cows, to whom she plays her recorder. Later, seven horses stop to listen. The takings in Bucklebury are £7. They make their own publicity, both stunts and posters, and proceed, with ten stops, to Winchcombe, by which time war has been declared. It is a lyrical, picaresque, hand-to-mouth progress, with daily uncertainty about scenery and props arriving in time for a performance at a new venue, uncertainty about where the next meal or hot bath will come from – 'wolfed dinner' is one *leitmotiv* – uncertainty about audiences, who vary from the parsons and 'intelligentsia', who pay two-and-six to five shillings, to the toughs of Northleach paying a few pennies. They sew their own costumes: 'Mother of God preserve me from

* This included the Earl Baldwin Refugee Fund, the China Relief Committee and the National Joint Spanish Relief Committee.

the simple sewing machine' precedes a comic rant in Iris's journal about defective tension, needles, bobbins. On Tuesday, 22 August, Fox Photos turn up and take two hundred snaps for *Picture Post.* One shows a notably attractive Iris prettily sewing, another wolfing food, a third as the emblematic 'Fairy-tale princess'.

Her hundred-page journal of those two weeks is her first surviving prose narrative. She archaically spells – and was for decades to spell – 'show' as 'shew'. The handwriting is firm and very confident, fluent about what she perceives. The troupe's antics are juvenile – she had only the previous month reached twenty, after all – but her eye is keen in discerning the painful jocularities of youth, and the agonising *fou rires* that are really signs of pre-first night nerves. Meeting a group of gypsies, the Magpies note a kinship, leading as both do a wandering existence cut off from the ordinary run of life. Iris expects daily arrest since 'the number of copyright songs we are singing without permission, & performances we are giving without licences, and cars we are driving without insurances, is really amazing'. She notes: 'Riding on running boards when the car is going a good forty is most exhilarating sport.'

She muses to herself of the company: 'They're a wonderful collection to be sure, & it's devilish fond I am of them': Irishness was her stock-in-trade. *Cherwell* had recently published her satirical 'The Irish – Are they Human?' – an answering polemic pointed out that she was obviously Scots-Irish[76] – and Denis Healey, part-Irish, two years older, and not knowing her well, believed for the following sixty years that Iris had come straight to Oxford from Dublin. Iris writes of Virginia Woolf as 'the darling, dangerous woman'[77] and is given to the imprecation 'Holy Mother of God'. After big, unshaven and, to Iris, very attractive Hugh Vaughan James finally arrives – a link with the Labour Club and the Communist Party – 'with all the dust of Kerry on him and the same old devil in his extraordinarily blue eyes', having hitch-hiked from the west of Ireland on cars and a tramp steamer, missing two nights' sleep, she soon notes that his brogue is 'better than mine', a phrase that suggests Irishness as a matter of identification and impersonation as well as inheritance. Hugh was mistaken for a member of the IRA in Valencia. Tom Fletcher's indifferent Irish accent, and worse jigs, by contrast, grate. It is no accident that Iris's writing persona, in her first published novel, was to have an Irish voice.

She talks about Communism and the international situation with Hugh, for whom she felt a *tendresse* to which they briefly give expression, Iris imagining him an old Bolshevik and amazed to find he has been 'in' (i.e. the Party) only a few months. He fills the scene-shifting intervals with 'brilliant' songs and patter, does Cossack dances on the running-board travelling at sixty. At fifteen stone and with a three-day growth of beard he resembles a Viking chieftain or some ancient Celtic hero. Indeed he pleases Iris by believing in the little people; he is, after all, himself a 'giant'.

Low points of the tour, for opposite reasons, were Buscot and Northleach. At glorious Buscot Park, seat of Lord Faringdon, Iris approves the rows and rows of Left Book Club covers, of Marx and of Engels in the library, and even frescos of the Socialist 'Lord Faringdon addressing the Labour Party'. Moreover there is a magnificent theatre with every conceivable gadget except the blackout facility needed for 'Tam Lin'. But the twenty noble lords and ladies who arrive in their Rolls-Royces are 'as dead as door-nails' and not to be pleased. Each turn misfires or falls flat. 'Well-bred. God! but they were well-bred,' comments Iris. 'The devil take them, they were neither flesh nor fowl nor good red herring – we didn't know where to have them. If they had been less genteel they'd have liked the broader things, & if they'd been more cultured they'd have liked the ballads – but they were merely gentry & so got no fun.' She has nice and democratic social instincts, and values them in others. In Faringdon's library the company behaved badly, talking loudly amongst themselves about the performance. Only she and Hugh took pains to speak to Faringdon's secretary Captain Bourne, whom both had noticed looking ill at ease.

Worse was to come two days later at Northleach, the town covered in 'recruiting bills and adjurations to young men to join the Territorials and defend their homes'. The place is 'scared

stiff & in an appalling state of nerves. Never having seen or heard
of gas masks before, they are now in a panic & imagining slaughter
& sudden death.' A great mob of toughs barracked, laughed and
cat-called. The intelligentsia shushed them, to no avail. Iris was
'mad with rage', nearly weeping with fury. Tom Fletcher lost his
head and offended the rest of the cast by guying the 'Play of the
Weather'. They were saved when all the lights failed: air raid
precautions? 'Northleach hospitality' received its final blow when
the company arrived at an immense Elizabethan manor and
found no food prepared.

By contrast, the high point on 29 August was Tusmore Park,
abode of Lady Bicester – not merely the 'wide tall tawnily-
weathered 18th C building with mile-long terraces & a most
beautiful lake to double it all in reflection', but also 'lamb both
hot and cold to eat, sauces and vegetables, veal, ham, apple pie
& cream & peaches, washed down with cider or beer and barley-
water, & apologies for an impromptu meal', off silver plate, to
boot. Iris's acting is admired by Irish Lady Bicester,[78] who likes
'Tam Lin' best. Iris records throughout an innocent hunger
for praise. She had been instantly enslaved to fellow-Magpie
Ruth Kingsbury (who recalled Iris's publicly declared willingness
to deploy her charm on Hugh Vaughan James) when Ruth
had praised her *Cherwell* poems. Iris notes happily that 'Joyce
[Taylor] said my arm movements reminded her of Peggy Ashcroft,' embraces the Magpie harpist Frances Podmore for
reporting one member of the audience whispering, 'Aren't her
movements perfectly beautiful?' and on 29 August 'shrieked with
joy inside' at being asked by a charming American girl which
drama school she had attended, as she had been such 'a delight
to look upon'. This was not necessarily sycophancy. Three fellow-
Magpies – Moira Dunbar, Denys Becher and Frances Podmore –
wrote unprompted sixty years later about Iris's 'marvellous way
with the old ballads'. Moira Dunbar could still hear Iris's low
mellow voice reciting lines from 'Tam Lin', and could recall many
verses verbatim. As could Iris; she declaimed from 'Tam Lin' for
years:

> Then up spake the Queen of the Fairies
> Out of a bush of Broom –
> She that has gotten the young Tam Lin
> Has gotten a stately groom.

Denys Becher, who had arrived 'looking more than ever like some unutterably wronged and tragic lad out of Housman',[79] played Tam Lin ('perfect – wild and intense and unearthly'), who falls tragically in love both with Janet, played by Iris, and with the Queen of the Fairies. (Only nineteen, he was in fact smitten with Iris, who never guessed.[80] He first sighted her standing in Bucklebury stream, rapt in silent contemplation, and thought her 'the most beautiful woman he had ever seen'.) When they gave a (successful) free matinee to a Basque refugee children's camp on 28 August, near Shipton-under-Wychwood, 'to crown our joy three real bushes of broom were in flower behind the "stage"'.

As well as enjoying her own proficiency, Iris takes delight in others too, notably Hugh fencing with Cecil Quentin (not the 'lofty conceited and utterly snobbish young swine' she first took him for); and quietly persuades Tom Fletcher to allow her to give up a coveted part in 'Clydewater' to a weeping fellow-actress,[81] whose career depends upon the tour as she wants a job as an actress with a repertory company.

8

'Is there any better way of spending the eve of war?' asked Tom Fletcher at Filkins early in the tour. The interest of the Magpies interlude lies in the confluence of the dramatic international events with a pastoral living-for-the-moment world so soon to be threatened and destroyed: acting out Auden's 'A Summer Night' itself. The Nazis were readying for their invasion of Poland, with their own wicked amateur-theatrical feint of dressing up German convicts in Polish uniforms at the wireless station at Gleiwitz (Gliwice) on 31 August – the convicts were then shot, so that German newspapers could claim a Polish 'invasion' of the Reich.

Uncertainty about the international situation fills Iris's journal, as do the problems of apprehending it as real without over-dramatising it. In Bucklebury on 23 August, the day the Ribben-trop–Molotov non-aggression pact is signed – 'over which,' she writes, 'much unnecessary fuss is being made', and 'Curious how many intelligent people are getting the Soviet Union wrong over this business' – she notes that 'the papers seem scared and I suppose a grave crisis is on but I cant seem to feel any emotion about it whatsoever. This is a such a strange, new, different, exist-ence I'm leading & so entirely cut-off from the world.' The follow-ing day at Buscot 'there is more trouble over Danzig.* But all the people we meet seem very upset, & it must be a great storm to ripple these placid waters.' That afternoon the performance is interrupted by a speech on the wireless by the Foreign Secretary Lord Halifax. On Friday, 25 August, on the way between Walling-ford and Brightwell, Iris tries to argue Tom out of doing Auden's 'Soldiers Coming': 'with things as they are' Auden's melodramatic ballad, with its haunting sense of imminent and anarchic male soldierly violence, 'comes far too close to the bone'.

On Sunday, 27 August Iris and Joyce Taylor, having lost their cases, stay with a hearty old couple, about whom Iris comments with brisk condescension, 'good working class stock, but unintelli-gent'. They are 'the sort of people who are nice to you when you come canvassing, but who will not buy a copy of the *Daily Worker*, as they "already get the *Herald*, thank you very much".' On Mon-day, 28 August 'a worried letter from home' and the *Daily Worker* sounding desperate both cause Iris to ponder, 'Maybe things are worse than I thought . . . I wonder if this is the end of everything at last? Anyhow, if it is, I am having a very grand finale.' Michael Foot is called up and writes to make Iris his literary executor 'with instructions what to publish should Anything Happen to him. But Michael always did take life melodramatically.' The fol-lowing day after lunch, the group 'walked down to the lake and admired the beauty of the place & wondered if we were to die

---

* Hitler agitated about the position of Germans in Danzig as a pretext for the invasion of Poland.

young & what it all meant anyway'. In the churchyard – 'God, but it's beautiful' – Iris lay across one of the graves and 'thought how quiet it would be to be dead'. On 30 August: 'The Territorials were called up, today.' Iris feels 'strangely unmoved' and sends a postcard home, self-consciously nonchalant: 'Bibury has unexpectedly cancelled our performance – Crisis I suppose. We are most wonderfully oblivious of the international situation.' On 31 August the horrible Gliwice farce was staged, and almost at once the brave, doomed Poles at Westerplatte on the North Sea were attacked by the German battleship *Schleswig-Holstein.* Since they were in civilian dress when they returned fire, they were subsequently shot without mercy after capture. In the small hours of 1 September the German invasion of Poland began, and by 6 a.m. Warsaw was being bombed. The first evacuation of women and children from London and other major centres began the same day.

The Magpies spent 1 September at an agricultural cooperative set up in Gloucestershire by a German refugee group, the Brüderhof, who in the circumstances preferred to skip the performance. The men sat on one side of the table, the women on the other, while their leader spoke emotionally to his followers of their precarious position in the event of war. The heavy atmosphere was almost too much for Moria Dunbar. She thought, 'God, if war is going to be like this I might as well slit my throat now.'[82] After the war, Tom Fletcher promised, the Magpies would tour again. But, he added sadly, 'our show will be frightfully pre-war, I'm afraid.'[83]

Much against the will of the company ('Do you realise there's a pretty good chance of London being bombed tonight? Don't be a little fool') Iris resolved, the day war was declared,[84] to return to London. She and Hugh travelled in the dicky of the Magpie business-manager Jack Trotman's grand, buff-yellow, Renault sports-car de luxe, as it roared over the Berkshire Downs to Oxford station. It was intensely exhilarating. Grey-blue clouds and streaks of green and pink sky wreathed the horizon. Hugh put his arm round Iris and they sighed at their luck. A long wait at Reading, the place deserted and troop trains packed with 'singing canon fodder' passing every ten minutes, and she chatted in the carriage to two half-drunk reservists who had just been called up. At Paddington she caught the last train, after 1 a.m, but at Hammersmith waited vainly for either Tube or trolley-bus. Somehow she got home.[85] The epoch she was later aptly to describe to Frank as 'the playtime of the '30s, when we were all conscience-ridden spectators',[86] was coming to an end.

5

Madonna Bolshevicka

1939–1942

Wartime Oxford was different. Iris later elegised to Frank the passing of

> the Oxford of our first year – utterly Bohemian & fantastic – when everyone was master of their fate and captain of their soul in a way that I have not met since. Those people just didn't care a damn – and they lived vividly, individually, wildly, beautifully. Now we are all more earnest and more timid and no more careless rapture.[1]

In October 1939 Frank came up from Larkhill Officer Cadet Training Unit on Salisbury Plain to take his Pass Mods (exam). He was in Oxford one week, and spent 'a very placid evening with a Bolshevicka of my acquaintance' – certainly Iris.[2] Though under-age, having just turned nineteen, he had already volunteered, on 2 September, one crucial symbolic day before the formal outbreak of hostilities. He 'simply wanted to fight'. Frank's act created a stir because it ignored government regulations safeguarding undergraduates from being called up before their twentieth birthday. His parents tried to have his enlistment rescinded on the grounds of his age, but that made him the more determined. There was also the question of the Party line. On the outbreak of war the Communist Party, after one week of supporting a war on two fronts – i.e. against Fascism *and* Imperialism – finally declared it an Imperialist war 'waged between

Hitlerite Fascism and British and French Imperialism for profit and domination', and thus to be opposed. Some *Spectator* readers wanted University Labour Federation scholarships withdrawn.[3] Leo Pliatzky quipped: 'Dulce et Decorum est/To die for Vested Interest', and 'Here dead we lie/For F.B.I'.[4] The Oxford CP, Iris told Mary, spent a week sorting out their line, and two unpublished poems suggest that Iris battled with her own doubts.* Two months before the outbreak of war Frank had probably participated with Michael Foot in a deputation to the House of Commons against conscription: a Prime Minister as bad as Chamberlain might use powers to conscript to break strikes instead of to fight Nazis.[5] This deputation paradoxically included many progressive and idealistic souls who were willing *voluntarily* to join up despite the statistic their fathers never let them forget – that the expectation of life of an infantry subaltern on the Western Front in the First World War had been three weeks.[6] In the intervening months Frank had been upset by the USSR–German non-aggression pact, and 'hit in the kidneys' by the Soviet aggression against Finland. On the outbreak of that 'Winter War', on 30 November 1939, Frank burst into Leo's rooms in Corpus, very distressed. Leo found some way of rationalising and justifying the conflict; Iris, too, despite her signs of hesitation, continued to support the USSR. Yet, if only momentarily, Frank's trust in the Russians was shaken.[7] He was well able to be independent-minded. Iris never had cause to doubt that in 1944, on trial for his life, Frank bravely and defiantly declared himself a Communist. Yet he also appears attractively indifferent to the heresies of 'democratic centralism' and 'factionalism' alike.[8] The 'placidity' of the evening suggests that his emotional turmoil of May and June may by now have lessened. Iris's could be a soothing as well as a stimulating presence. But he was still in love, and stayed so.

---

* 'A New Non Nobis, the War-Song of the British Public', August 1939, attacks the British for lazy pacifism. The USSR–German non-aggression pact was signed on 23 August, and she wrote 'Dangerous Thoughts inspired by Curious Conduct on the part of the USSR' on 1 October.

'MADONNA BOLSHEVICKA'[9]

Sure, lady, I know the party line is better.
I know what Marx would have said. I know you're right.
When this is over we'll fight for the things that matter.
Somehow, today, I simply want to fight.
That's heresy? Okay. But I'm past caring.
There's blood about my eyes, and mist and hate.
I know the things we're fighting now and loathe them.
Now's not the time you say? But I can't wait.

Maybe I'm not so wrong. Maybe tomorrow
We'll meet again. You'll smile and you'll agree.
And then we'll raise revolt and blast the heavens.
But now there's only one course left for me.

Across this autumn 1939 poem Frank wrote 'BILGE', rejecting the poor poetry more than the political line. Iris – like Frank, having spent a week in Surrey that June at a CP student summer school – had evidently questioned his having volunteered. She stayed pacifist until June 1941, three months after he sailed from England. He had elected her to be muse, soul-mate, keeper of his conscience, and she was often capable of the 'passionate intensity' Yeats feared. Small wonder Denis Healey identified Iris at that time with the epithet 'this latter-day Joan-of-Arc'.[10]

Frank's poem, if a gesture of independence, proposes a more equal relationship between them. He and Iris must have discussed the war and his motives in enlisting as they processed, near Magdalen Bridge, through the moonlit Oxford blackout. A whimsical writer had commented on the vision of Oxford lit only by moonlight as 'almost worth a war':[11] against such callow aestheticism, Frank wryly notes that 'somehow most of us could do without a war even so.'

Over the succeeding months other friends were called up, degrees interrupted or compressed. Noel Martin would leave Corpus in June 1940, with mounting debts and the certainty of being called up that August, to work at Holton Manor Farm, Wheatley, as a farm labourer for forty shillings a week.* Before leaving Oxford, he telephoned Iris from the kiosk near the Gothic martyrs' memorial, proposing marriage. She gently declined. Refugees, many of them learned, flooded the Oxford streets. Iris wrote: 'East London & East Europe jostle for Lebensraum on the pavements of the High & Corn ... A thousand people sleep & live in unimaginable conditions in the Majestic Cinema. The main stream seems to have been diverted into our backwater.'[12] Britain's internment of refugees who had been fighting Fascism, some suicidal, drove her 'frantic'. Undergraduates and dons alike who were left in Oxford included the aged, ordinands, the unfit, and those awaiting active service. 'Youthful dons & adult male undergraduates,' wrote Iris, 'are as rare as butterflies in March.'[13]

Part of Somerville having been requisitioned by the Radcliffe Infirmary, she was living in her second year in considerable freedom at 43 Park Town in North Oxford with Anne Cloake, Lindsay Patterson and Jean Coutts. The others soon married, Anne to the left-wing economist Teddy Jackson, Jean to the philosopher John Austin, of whose lectures Iris was appreciative.[14] Elderly refugees from the London Blitz on occasion joined the household; they all huddled together in the basement during the few air raids. Their landlady Miss Lepper kept a benign eye on them, and they were glad to get away from college cooking. Iris and Jean subsisted for a while on sardines, bread and as yet unrationed oranges.[15] Iris was painting a lot; many of her paintings of the time had ladders in them. One survives: of a copy of Joyce's *Ulysses* – the first unlimited edition came out in 1937 – lying by a blue pottery jar of coltsfoot.[16]

In November 1939 Iris published an untitled poem, 'You take life tiptoe':[17]

---

* Frank Thompson inaccurately recorded that Noel, 'like most sane people' depressed by the 'stupidity of Greats', had left Oxford for farming in the Berkshire hills, where he 'married a rich Jewess after only a fortnight's acquaintance'. The friends wagged their heads and said, 'We knew he had it in him.' The farm was in Oxfordshire; Ruth Basch, the Czech Jewess to whom Noel became semi-engaged there, was not rich; and nor did he marry her, or anyone else, until 17 February 1943, when he married Carol (also known as Grace) Nethersole. Such inaccuracies may be set down to the fact that Frank, only nineteen and a writer in the making, could have given himself 'poetic licence'. Wartime too made it harder to check one's facts.

. . . Cry
In salute of life – not in dread
Of dizzy cross-sections of being – relating
All things to all. The black soil
My fingers divide is death,
Yet it crumbles to life in a seed.
Horror is real; but real too
The unashamed certainties – knowledge
Of intricate events,
Of the past in the present fixing
The future's invincible waking-point.

T.S. Eliot's 'Burnt Norton', which had come out in 1936, six years before the other quartets, may lie behind the poem's visionary attempt to see all time as indivisible.[18] What were the 'unashamed certainties' whose reality she asserts? They were not always to be those of the left, though vehemence, later yoked to mildness and reserve, accompanied the different phases of Iris's beliefs. Only-children, she observed, 'are completely secure in our point of view'.[19] One of her ten 1982 Gifford lectures was entitled 'Certainty'. And to be named 'Bolshevicka', even in fun, suggests a recognition of Iris as possessing 'certainties'. Mary Midgley recalls that Iris (unlike Frank) always championed the USSR; a position easier to defend after 1941, when Russian courage in resisting Hitler saved Britain from being invaded itself.

Throughout the bitter winter of 1938–39, the coldest since 1895, Port Meadow, which had flooded, was frozen. All Somerville, it seemed, skated,[20] Mary breaking a leg in the process. And after five terms – in the spring of 1940 – they took 'Schools' in the fan-vaulted early-Tudor Divinity Schools, beautiful but, no doubt for wartime reasons, unheated. They brought hot-water bottles but still froze in the three-hour sessions. The Eldridges, Noel (involved, like Iris, with student journalism and politics), twin sister Lilian and their mother, visiting Iris for tea in Somerville, found her sitting cross-legged, keening and crying with alarm, sure she had failed. In the event she got a second, and wrote generously to Clare Campbell to congratulate her on her first, vindicating the honour of their sex:

O excellently done. I hope you're feeling very pleased
with life. I suspected I should get a second, but am none
the less annoyed at having my suspicions confirmed . . .
I am inebriating myself with French poetry and Malory
. . . Away with [Plato and Aristotle]! Just now I am for
Helicon. Before next term though there will probably
be a change of heart . . . Much love, Iris.[21]

2

Perhaps there was a streak of absolutism in both Iris and Frank: in
her, for sticking to the Party line; in him, for ignoring it. Headstrong as she always was, Iris was cross when she experienced the
'confusion and suspension of judgement', which she with scornful
humour associated only with '*New Statesman* liberals'.[22] The sources
of some 'unashamed certainties' lay in the exigencies of the period,
but received expression – very differently – in two immensely influential male tutors. One, Eduard Fraenkel, must have been known
to Frank. The other, Donald MacKinnon, she wrote to him about.
Their imaginative impact on her was lifelong: both helped mould
and form her. Both are 'larger than life', and it is hard to convey
their uniqueness and present them briefly as more than collections
of eccentricities. The relationships with both went awry.

In May 1940 Iris and Mary moved on to Greats. Isobel ('Iso')
Henderson was their tutor for ancient history. Lively and interesting, from a fortunate and distinguished background, widowed in
the first weeks of her marriage, she lived with her family in Lincoln
College, very different from the somewhat boarding-school existence of dons resident at Somerville. Her father J.A.R. Munro was
a distinguished historian and Rector of Lincoln. She was very
much a child of Oxford, worldly, good at power-broking.[23] Physically beautiful, fair, with a lovely voice, polyglot and passionate
about music, horse-racing, poetry, cricket, Spanish culture and sailing in the Mediterranean – 'One is always wrong not to like things,'
she used to say. If you did not like music or horse-racing, she felt,
you simply had not taken the trouble to find out enough to make

your enjoyment real. 'She had a basic certainty,' a colleague recalled after her death in 1967, 'about what had been best in ancient civilisation, and was still the best in the liberal European civilisation of which she felt herself a part.'[24] This certainty that a continuity existed between the 'brilliant but terrible people' of the ancient world,[25] and those of the modern world, Iris inherited. Frank's letters abound in it, and are forward-looking too.

Although Noel Martin simply followed Iris into Fraenkel's seminar on the *Agamemnon*, tutors normally recommended their better students for it. The seminar had no designed relevance to the syllabus. Iris recalled Isobel Henderson[26] saying briskly in the first year, 'Go to Fraenkel's classes – I expect he'll paw you a bit, but never mind.' Iris did not mind Fraenkel putting his arm about her, or stroking hers. This was before the days when such demonstrativeness was deemed gross moral turpitude. Fraenkel 'adored' Iris;[27] Iris 'loved' Fraenkel. She had private tuition from him, and he gave her Wilamowitz's *Pindar* in March 1940. Their relation was chaste. Not all undergraduates had Iris's confidence, or were so reverential.[28] A little later Mary Warnock was disturbed to find Fraenkel's mixture of superb pedagogy and indiscretion, the marriage in him of the intellectual and the erotic, exciting.[29] Preparing for a class was for Warnock like dressing for battle, to ensure that Fraenkel's 'pawings' stayed within the bounds of acceptability, and that tears were, if possible, avoided. Iris had no objection to 'difficult' men (or women). She was moreover later to make of the relations between eros and intelligence a whole philosophy.

The German tradition of the *Seminar* was new to Oxford. Between twelve and twenty people sat around a long table, in the ground-floor room in Corpus 'so visibly ancient that one had the impression of forming part of a timeless tradition of scholars'.[30] Fraenkel presided at the top, for two hours between five and seven, once a week. There was 'a lot of passion around, including Fraenkel's passion for dominance'.[31] Many distinguished scholars acknowledge these famous *Agamemnon* seminars, which went on for years, as their own first-beginnings. To Hugh Lloyd-Jones, later Regius Professor of Greek at Oxford, the remarkable impact of Fraenkel's teaching was due to them.[32] To the future scholar

Kenneth Dover they were simply 'what mattered most at Oxford'.[33] To Iris, Fraenkel gave

> ever since the days of the *Agamemnon* class, a vision of excellence . . . The tones of the Merton clock striking the quarters still brings back to me the tense atmosphere of that class – and how afraid I felt in case I was asked something I didn't know.[34]

The 'terrifying'[35] seminar has also been described as a circle of rabbits addressed by a stoat.[36] To try out an idea on Fraenkel was awesome – his head would begin to shake, his cheeks quivered with dissent. Iris's class-notes include Fraenkel's expostulations at variant readings from previous scholars: 'Nonsense' – 'Unspeakable!'[37] He could be persistent in following up a casual remark and liked to reprove error. Hugh Lloyd-Jones recalled, 'How terrifying it could be to see him bearing down on one.'[38] Yet a note next day might admit that his view needed qualification, and in the preface to his exhaustive and heavy-going three-volume study of the *Agamemnon*, published in 1950, he particularly acknowledged his indebtedness to the 'common-sense of the young'. Iris later noted, 'The best teachers are a trifle sadistic.'[39]

Dover was unfrightened, since the seminar was attended by dons – Wade-Gery from Corpus, Bryan-Brown of Worcester and the historian R.C.K. Ensor – as well as undergraduates: 'On occasion their ignorance stood as nakedly revealed as ours.'[40] To others the sight of a college head 'curtly commanded to fetch a book, a celebrated scholar berated for his poor "*Englisch*"', made the event the more terrifying. Many prayed they would not be picked on, some were scared off altogether. Those who stayed gained: Fraenkel had the imaginative sympathy that brings literature alive. Even apathetic students found themselves infected with 'the vitality of ideas that struck home because they were actually lived by the speaker'.[41] He read poetry with a moving expressiveness and in lectures would, to the delight of his young hearers, break into song, singing Horace's *Integer Vitae* to a tune presumably learnt in the Gymnasium, or rendering raucously the frog-chorus from Aristophanes' *Frogs*.

Iris and Mary Midgley had to prepare Clytemnestra's speech, lines 920–34. After a term of silent participation:

> One had to . . . try and understand both the poetry, and at the same time, why the language was what it was and what to do about the variant readings. In the hands of a pedant, this might have been less useful. But Fraenkel was really profoundly into the poetry, and we concentrated on the Cassandra scene . . . a don . . . prepared the same dozen lines. Discussion went to and fro, and you were expected to follow, and to see what humane scholarship was like for people whose life it was . . . [Fraenkel] really did take you into what Aeschylus was all about, which is about as deep as things get. There was a terrific insistence on getting the details [of the scholarship] right, and he did it in a way that really was creative and important and useful . . . he would tell you the history of the scholars, of what had happened in the Renaissance and in medieval times: . . . it was extremely hard work.

After one class Fraenkel started to invite Iris back to his rooms, but she was giggling with Mary and with Nick Crosbie, with whom Mary was in love, and he got the whole party instead. He showed them all the passage in Goethe's *Faust* where Mephistopheles says, '*ich bin der Geist der stets verneint*' – the spirit that continually negates, and spoke of its connexion with the nature of evil. Shortly after, they met him in Mildred Hartley's room, and on somebody's mentioning Nick, Fraenkel said, 'Ach, he is the Cherubino of my classes.' That implied that he saw himself as the Count.*

3

Reverencing her father, Iris thirsted for fatherly guidance for the intellectual she was becoming. Hence her need for gurus, for the same qualities on a more august and majestic scale. She found

---

* In Mozart's *Marriage of Figaro* Cherubino is page to Countess Almaviva, whose husband the Count has a wandering eye.

them in a series of learned exiles who famously influenced every aspect of British intellectual life,[42] of whom Fraenkel might be taken as a prototype. Czechs, Austrians and elderly German Jews – 'scholars with long hair and longer sentences'[43] – crowded the wartime Oxford pavements, and on the buses to North Oxford it used to be said that one needed to speak German.[44] The Central European refugees that Iris admired, pitied and collected had lost their culture, their language, their homes, sometimes their families, their money, their professions, their way of life. These were wounded patriarchs, deprived even, in many cases, of the ability to fight. The British attitude towards them was not uniformly generous:[45] 'What are they doing, taking jobs away from our boys who are away at the front?' was a common reaction. Small surprise if some could be difficult.

An immensely learned, formidable and astonishingly generous man – generous with his time, and with money – with a complex, intense and dominating personality, Fraenkel was without deviousness, but could be impetuous, hot-headed, easily hurt. He was born a Jew in Berlin in 1888, and came out of the greatest period of German Classical scholarship: on his desk stood a large photo of Leo (1851–1914), his stern taskmaster; on his library walls, Wilamowitz (1848–1931) and Mommsen (1817–1903). Such were his models. He had forced himself to learn to use an arm withered from osteomyelitis and a grossly deformed hand, in a gruelling daily routine that started at 8.30 a.m. and often continued through the small hours.[46]

During the summer of 1933, after the Nazis had come to power, books were burnt, university classes disrupted. Fraenkel was deprived of his professorship at Freiburg-im-Breisgau, forbidden to teach, subjected to insults – a senior Professor publicly denouncing him as a '*frecher Judenjunge*'.* Another colleague and 'close friend' wrote to explain why he could henceforth no longer have anything to do with him.† It was not until the Röhm purges

---

* Roughly, 'uppity Jewboy'.
† This colleague tried to make it up in the 1950s, sending Fraenkel a book in which he professed: '*memor*' (I remember). Fraenkel sent him back a two-word answer: '*et ego*' (I also).

of 1934 that he and his Lutheran wife Ruth[47] left Germany and, with help from Gilbert Murray,* settled first in Cambridge, before he took the Corpus Professorship of Latin at Oxford, which he held until his retirement in 1953. A disdainful letter to the *Sunday Times* asking whether there was no English person who could have done the job just as well was wittily answered by A.E. Housman: there was only one English person better qualified – himself – and 'he is not interested in the Chair'.[48]

There were coolnesses and misunderstandings. Fraenkel was capable at first of treating kindness with startling rudeness. He could be tactless with colleagues, severe towards pupils, dogmatic and single-minded. Originally the very type of the unassimilated foreigner, disdaining the superficiality of British scholarship, he later became part of the fabric of college life. Some felt that his 'inhuman' devotion to scholarship was at the expense of his wife and family.

> He was short, with a disproportionately large head, a magnificent forehead merging into a dome that was bald except for a fringe of hair, had fine eyes, large ears and nose, a most determined jaw ... Mobile eyebrows, and a face expressive of feelings to a comic degree so that anger was a terrifying mask, laughter a complete dissolution of the features, his smile a disarmingly conspiratorial surprise.
>
> Physically vigorous, walking fast with a shuffling pace, he wore a brown beret which he could dextrously scrape on and off.[49]

Fraenkel's admiration for Iris is clear. David Pears attended the seminar for one week only in 1941, and though he did not speak to or properly meet Iris for another decade, he found her the most riveting, noticeable person in the room, 'with her lioness's face, very square, very strong, but very gentle'. To Pears, Fraenkel called her the only truly educated person of her

---

* Murray, Regius Professor of Greek at Oxford, Chairman of the League of Nations Union and President of the Board of Governors at Badminton School, was also a neighbour and friend of the Thompsons on Boar's Hill.

generation, using the Greek word '*mousikee*', meaning inspired by the muses, hence genuinely cultivated. Fraenkel, whom Pears admired, recalled to him nonetheless the vain and dictatorial Professor Unrath in the film *Blue Angel.*

4

Fraenkel haunts Iris's novels. The dedicatee of *The Time of the Angels,* he lies behind the magisterial and dying Levquist in *The Book and the Brotherhood,* and behind Max Lejour in the earlier *The Unicorn,* who movingly sings to a 'plain-song lilt of his own' a chorus from Aeschylus' *Agamemnon,* while his old pupil listens to the 'healing familiar lines':

> Zeus, who leads men into the ways of understanding, has established the rule that we must learn by suffering. As sad care, with memories of pain, comes dropping upon the heart in sleep, so even against our wills does wisdom come upon us.[50]

Here Aeschylus' crucial Hymn to Zeus is a key to the novel's gainsaying of the liberal-humanist illusion that life can (or should) have to do only with the pursuits of happiness and 'freedom'. On the contrary, only those who are positively wounded[51] – if not corrupted by the experience – have the chance of learning wisdom ('suffering teaches,' Iris wrote in 1945[52]). Moreover, in her Platonic dialogue *Art and Eros* Callistos tries to recite a different translation of the same hymn throughout, succeeding in being heard only in the play's culminating moments. Here Callistos is putting on show a high-point of literary art, and disturbing, moving and infuriating Plato – who is 'anti-art' – with the 'terrible beauty' of the Hymn to Zeus.

In the commentary to the *Agamemnon* he finally published, the fruit of twenty-five years' labour disrupted by exile, the most detailed commentary ever devoted to a Greek classic, Fraenkel writes that in the Hymn to Zeus '[Aeschylus] *endeavours in a sublime effort to unriddle the ultimate cause of the fate and suffering of man.*[53] He identifies the views of the chorus with those of Aeschylus, being obsessed by the theology of Agamemnon's guilt. It is noteworthy that Iris wrote of the lines as 'healing'. Not all suffering was amenable to Socialist 'correction'. Much is built into the very conditions of life, and the Party offered 'too obtuse and partial an explanation of the world's evil and of human goodness'.[54]

Probably Fraenkel also found in the play a grand key to the general drama being acted out in Europe at that time, a magisterial exploration of the themes of evil and implacable divine justice, a commentary on the bitter roots of all suffering, including his own.* Perhaps he saw human affairs as simpler and more dramatic than they actually were – seeing his friends, for example, as endowed with vices or virtues,[55] seeing Agamemnon as a 'gentleman'. If Fraenkel gives, either here or in his work on Horace, a sentimental or false picture of the relationship between poetry and politics,[56] this was a simplicity Iris shared, to the enrichment of her own work.

Iris's later poem about Fraenkel's seminar, 'The Agamemnon Class, 1939' (1977), is remarkable for its deliberate conflation of different kinds of dread: of the war; of being unable correctly to identify the tenses of some familiar verb; and what might be termed *moral* dread, the deep fears that can accompany the awakening of an acute adult moral consciousness. She also conflates two kinds of heroism, ancient and modern, Greek and twentieth-century British. The long poem, dedicated to Frank Thompson's memory, starts thus:

> Do you remember Professor
> Eduard Fraenkel's endless
> Class on the *Agamemnon?*
> Between line eighty three and line a thousand
> It seemed to us our innocence
> Was lost, our youth laid waste,
> In that pellucid unforgiving air,

* Arnoldo Momigliano understood the Jewish aspects of Fraenkel's thought. See his *Quinto contributo all storia degli studi classici e mondo antico* (Rome, 1977), pp.1026–9.

The aftermath experienced before,
Focused by dread into a lurid flicker,
A most uncanny composite of sun and rain.
Did we expect the war? What did we fear?
First love's incinerating crippling flame,
Or that it would appear
In public that we could not name
The Aorist of some familiar verb.
The spirit's failure we knew nothing of,
Nothing really of sin and of pain,
The work of the knife and the axe,
How absolute death is,
Betrayal of lover and friend,
Of egotism the veiled crux,
Mistaking still for guilt
The anxiety of a child.
With exquisite dressage
We ruled a chaste soul.
They had not yet made an end
Of the returning hero.
The demons that travelled with us
Were still smiling in their sleep . . .

Mary Warnock, who joined Fraenkel's seminar in 1942, pleased Iris by commenting on the poem: 'that atmosphere of dread and apprehension brought it all back to me. One dread merging into another. How amazing.'[57] Frank, too, who may have attended the seminar in the summer of 1939,* believed *Agamemnon* the greatest drama yet written,[58] and wrote an Aeschylean chorus comparing the Trojan to the Second World War, in both of which 'boys died bravely, in a war of others' making'.[59] His father had written on Aeschylus and Athens. To his brother E.P. he refers, albeit within a joke, to 'suffering as stark and Aeschylean as any I have known in this war'.[60]

---

* It is likely from her dedicating the poem to him that Iris believed Frank had attended the class. His presence is not recalled by any survivors, most of whom had other matters on their minds: Noel Martin, Leo Pliatzky, Clare Campbell, Mary Midgley, Kenneth Dover. Of these Leo was closest by far to Frank – Frank visited Leo's parents' home in the East End – and was most likely to remember. Probably

5

In the third winter of the war Iris wrote twice to Frank about Donald MacKinnon, her and Mary's philosophy tutor for Greats.

> This man MacKinnon is a jewel, it's bucked me up a lot meeting him. He's a moral being as well as a good philosopher. I had almost given up thinking of people & actions in terms of value – meeting him has made it a significant way of thinking again.

One month later:

> I have this incredibly fine guy MacKinnon as a tutor, which makes things lucky. It's good to meet someone so extravagantly unselfish, so fantastically noble, as well as so extremely intelligent as this cove. He inspires a pure devotion. One feels vaguely one would go through fire for him, & so on. Sorry if this makes him sound like a superman. There are snags. He's perpetually on the brink of a nervous break-down ... He is perpetually making demands of one – there is a moral as well as an intellectual challenge – & there is no room for spiritual lassitude of any kind.[61]

Vera Hoar, who was tutored by MacKinnon at about the same time,[62] wrote: 'If I think of the two people who have most influenced me, they would be Donald MacKinnon and Iris – I think of them together.' He gave his tutorials in one of the towers of Victorian-Gothic Keble in a room utterly bare, save for a table – no desk – in the middle cluttered high with books and papers, and Iris and Vera sometimes exchanged greetings in the dark passage there. To Vera Iris said that MacKinnon inspired the sort of love one would have for Christ – quite unconditional. He was a passionate High Anglo-Catholic married to a Scots-Norwegian girl at odds with his High Church connexions. 'The vitality of ideas that struck home because they were actually lived by the

---

Frank came to a few sessions in Trinity 1939 when he was most disturbed about Iris. His letters abound in references to Aeschylus.

speaker' was one description of Fraenkel. It works for MacKinnon, too. Iris worshipped both.

His philosophy tutorials, given from his battered armchair, or to some male students from his bath, or while lying on his back under his table, sucking a razor-blade which, when not cutting the table, he sometimes turned over and over in his lips or hands, were notably dramatic (Iris when later an Oxford don herself would sometimes imitate the prone tutorial, not the razor-blade). Or he would sharpen up to a dozen pencils. If he had been fire-watching the night before, he stayed proudly in the boilersuit worn for that purpose. He was skilful at making you feel something very important was happening.[63] When he got to something impossible to explain, he would protrude his tongue with his upper denture balanced on the end. Nervous tutees had been known to edge backwards, so as not to have to catch the denture if it fell. Sometimes he talked out of one of his room's two windows. To hear him, you put your head out of the other, like another gargoyle. Once he rolled himself up in the carpet, like Beatrix Potter's Tom Kitten caught in the pastry. Such gimmicks developed the logic of an argument. However bizarre they are to read about, they did not feel false. Certainly not, in any case, to Iris. Like many Oxford characters of the day MacKinnon was profoundly eccentric. When David Pears suggested that he consciously overdid it, Iris, who reverenced him, was exasperated by the imputation. Tom Stoppard drew heavily on MacKinnon stories when creating 'George', the Professor of Moral Philosophy in his play *Jumpers* (1972).[64]

MacKinnon had been a legend even while a schoolboy at Winchester,[65] and to a cold eye he could appear comical. One such saw him as absolutely devoted to philosophy and dedicated to his students, deeply religious, yet rather absurd, a joke Wykehamist-scholar in the way he talked – a mixture of pedantry and madness – and not in the first rank of philosophers. But his writings do less than justice to his true impact, which was face-to-face. Iris wrote of his resonant voice-type as 'the slightly alcoholic crafty coyness of a well-marked Wykehamist'.[66] Some felt an undercurrent of menace.[67] His native Argyllshire featured, and he liked to speak of leaving the tea he brewed to 'infuse'. Huge, shambling, broad-shouldered, very powerful, dark-suited, ham-fisted and maladroit – he once crushed a glass at a Balliol dinner – he told one wartime student that he had so terrible a conscience about not being in the forces that he lived in his college rooms, and left his newly-married wife living twenty or thirty yards away, working far too hard in order to justify himself.[68] During public lectures, as the outward expression of inward mental travail, he would famously stab himself with his pen with remarkable vigour, and grasp his shaggy, beetling brow. Detractors saw him as a cut-price English version of Simone Weil: tortured, but on terms with a large intelligentsia-following, which included unbelievers.

One day he said to Dennis Nineham, future Regius Professor of Divinity at Cambridge, 'The only time I can fit you in is Sunday morning at 11 o'clock. Will you guarantee that you go to church first?' Nineham rightly replied that whether or not he went to church first was his own business.* This sense, however importunate, that everyone's soul hung in the balance points to some legacies in Iris's thinking. MacKinnon was at the tail end of the Oxford Idealist tradition, refusing to believe in the demise of metaphysics, a Kantian and post-Kantian idealist.[69] His dominant interest was the philosophy of religion, and in 1960 he was to be

---

* Nineham nonetheless turned up at Keble: there was no answer when he knocked, until a voice from behind another door said, 'Come in.' Nineham went in, and found MacKinnon in his bath. He motioned to Nineham to sit on the lavatory seat and read his essay. When MacKinnon had finished his bath, he rose and complained, 'I haven't got a towel.' He opened the door and shouted, 'Mabel, Mabel!' (the scout). She didn't come, and he complained, 'This is always happening: I think that girl thinks I'm *queer* or something.' So Nineham volunteered to get a towel. MacKinnon dressed in the most astonishing and terrible clothes, and they adjourned to the Lamb and Flag, where he bought Nineham a whisky, himself a double, then paced up and down the crowded bar, completing the tutorial, unaware of the effect his rhetoric was having on the other drinkers: 'You see WHEN Kant says this, he MEANS to say that, and THIS is CRUCIAL,' in his unique Scots-Wykehamist brogue. This continued for thirty minutes, and the drinkers – all servicemen – went completely silent. When he'd finished, the entire bar broke into entranced applause at this exotic manifestation. MacKinnon was genuinely nonplussed, and blushed deeply. He was 'not a self-conscious eccentric but a genuine one'. Nineham, like Vera Crane, identified MacKinnon as Rozanov in *The Philosopher's Pupil*, an alarming figure to his students: Rozanov, unlike MacKinnon, maltreats them.

appointed to the Norris-Hulse Chair of Divinity at Cambridge. The title of his inaugural lecture – 'Borderlands of Theology' – is evocative. Philosophy and theology are somehow to be brought back together.

Already in the 1940s, when he had published only two books of basic theology, MacKinnon's thinking points towards attitudes Iris would later adopt wholesale. That those thinkers especially are to be commended who 'live out ... the consequences of [their own] attitude of mind', moral philosophy being the study of 'what in the last resort can only be lived', a central tenet of her *The Sovereignty of Good*. If life must bear witness to philosophy, then enquiry into the 'good life' still matters; those who call ethics a 'bogus subject' are usually posturing, and 'the kind of mystery which tends to gather round ... notions of good and evil' cannot easily be dispelled. That it is a pious superstition to believe that pain necessarily ennobles: like Iris, MacKinnon was fascinated by pain. That those whose experience is deepest may be inarticulate. That intellectual integrity is something at least partly moral in character. That the fundamental sin is pride. That it is dangerous to seek the good of one's fellows 'in blind oblivion of the poor stuff of which one is oneself made'. That the field of personal experience must be taken into account; that the individual should be approached with a sense of his or her 'unconditional worth'.[70] That 'only a suffering Christ could help', who might teach how to 'displace the self from the centre'.[71]

George Steiner has written of MacKinnon as 'that most searching of modern British moral philosophers'.[72] His absolute dedication to and impact on his students is remarkable. Many speak of feeling uniquely and accurately *apprehended* by him; Iris among them. Mary Midgley remembered: 'He was capable of giving one a full two hours tutorial and saying "We need more time, you'd better come back on Thursday."' Seeing how busy he was – he was rumoured to teach eighty hours a week, the number of students swollen by army and naval cadets on short courses, as well as his Oxford undergraduates now coming up termly, not annually – that kind of attention, and his meticulous courtesy also, were staggering.[73] David Pears, disenchanted with his course, owed his becoming a professional philosopher mainly to MacKinnon's patient encouragement and inspiration. Philippa Bosanquet, not given to hyperbole, described him as 'holy' – 'No one has influenced me more . . . He *created* me' – while tellingly defining holiness as 'an absolute lack of sense of proportion'. He taught both Philippa and Iris how to care for the afflicted: lovingly, imaginatively, with limitless patience. He showed them how to look after people. When Vera Hoar was ill with depression, MacKinnon alone dealt with her with skill as well as sympathy. Nor were such recollections restricted to his wartime students. A much later pupil has described how the profundity and moral passion of MacKinnon's thinking, and his obsessive preoccupation with the difficulty and the danger of truthful speech, created in most of those who knew him 'a sense of deep affection, puzzlement, a kind of awe'.[74] His legacy in Iris and Philippa's thought was that philosophy is central to how you live your life.

Philippa Bosanquet came up to Somerville to read Philosophy, Politics and Economics (PPE) in 1939. Her chief memory of Iris before 1942 was of herself nominating an alternative candidate to Iris as President of Somerville Junior Common Room Committee. She feared both that Communists were generally a nuisance, and also that Iris might convene too many meetings. Since Philippa's nominee won – unlike Iris, she was someone not at all prominent – others must have shared her fears. There were limits to Iris's popularity, constituencies immune to her charm. Enid Stoye, reading history, felt Iris despised her group of friends for their political conservatism and Christianity, and that Iris within herself stood apart from all groups. She and Iris disliked each other. Stoye felt Iris had a covering of ice.

In the summer of 1942, MacKinnon mentioned to Iris that Philippa was ill – she had suffered, partly under the stress of studying with her august tutors, a suspected recrudescence of childhood abdominal tuberculosis and was corseted in plaster-of-Paris, stuck at home, struggling with Finals. The mother of Philippa's flatmate Anne Cobbe saw to it that MacKinnon and Thomas Balogh – a brilliant but abrasive teacher – gave Philippa tutorials in her lodgings. It is typical of MacKinnon's skill at involving others in practical solicitude that he told Iris, 'Philippa might appreciate a friendly visit.' Iris, hitherto a somewhat distant and glamorous figure, one year senior, arrived at Philippa's lodgings at 2 Bradmore Road with a bunch of wildflowers. 'I recall the joy with which I found her,' wrote Iris later, her 'life-long best friend'.[75] Iris chronicled the ups and downs of this friendship, over nearly sixty years, more than any other.[76] Philippa's mother had been born in the White House, her grandfather Grover Cleveland twice President of the United States, and she had been mainly brought up with her sister Marion by governesses in the North of England. Like Iris she was self-possessed, strong-willed, intelligent. Also attractive, and in those days unconfident, she was for Iris the 'good sister' Iris had never had. MacKinnon greatly influenced both. He 'cared about goodness', was the keeper of Iris and Philippa's goodness, saw himself as a steadying influence against (in his view) their wartime bohemianism. They were in awe of him. Around 1990 Iris and Philippa were staggered to discover MacKinnon's true age. He was born in 1912. They had thought him much older, an ancient prophet-figure, a holy man whom they revered.

6

When Iris met the French writer and critic Raymond Queneau in 1946, he noted in his journal that she had formerly been a CP member for four years. So, if card-carrying, she did not tear up her card until 1942, probably on the advice of the Party itself when she entered the Treasury.[77] Iris's disdainful comments, after going down in 1942, on the political commitments of the average student show that her world-view had not yet changed.[78] She wrote to Philippa in late 1942, 'I feel that when anyone really thinks about [politics] there is only one conclusion! But maybe I'm prejudiced.'[79] Later, she wished she had been a bit less high-minded at Oxford, and a bit more frivolous. She thought £5 for a ticket for a Commem Ball a 'terrible waste of money'[80] – £5 was exactly the then large sum Anne Cloake once begged off Mary

Midgley for an undisclosed political cause. 'They [CP members and sympathisers] lived a very exciting life,' Mary commented, with irony. By 1938 the Moscow treason trials were documented. By 1940 Arthur Koestler's *Darkness at Noon* was published. Mary – uneasily – admired the courage and whole-heartedness of those who like Iris, Anne and Leonie Marsh could 'jump' into the Party, but she could not follow them. Yet like most of their set, Mary was politically active, and the CP was scarcely the only outlet for political passion. 'Buy the Tuppeny Strachey,' 'Char' and Susie Williams-Ellis would cry, selling their uncle John Strachey's pamphlet *Why You Should be a Socialist*.

Opinions vary as to whether – Frank apart – Iris proselytised. Vera Hoar, who came up only in 1940, remembered: 'she never thrust Marxism down one's throat; she just waited patiently for you to see the light. Though she once told me she had her doubts about whether dialectical materialism was philosophically sound.' 'Char' Williams-Ellis noted that Iris 'was a diligent and persuasive missionary for the CP and I did even go along to one or two meetings at her urging'. Iris's copy of *A Handbook of Marxism* (Left Book Club Edition, edited by Emile Burns, with 'Not For Sale to the General Public' clearly printed on it), though little annotated, was much-thumbed. She admired Lenin's *State and Revolution*.* Iris later spoke of her CP years as having taught her from the inside how a small, ruthless group of individuals can wield destructive power, and compared a dictatorial CP branch with an IRA cell. But it is hard to see what 'destruction' the wartime CPGB effected. The nearest and most sensitive example is the 'recruitment' by Leonie and Iris of Frank in 1939. Philip Toynbee's memoir *Friends Apart* makes uncomfortable reading: 'The Oxford CP practised dishonesty almost as a principle . . . the Party was, of course, indelicate, authoritarian and possessive . . . [displaying] a crudity of judgement which . . . extended to a bluff insensitivity about love affairs . . . There was a "line" for love; there was almost a line for friendship.'[81]

---

* Iris wrote to Raymond Queneau on 27 February 1949 *à propos* this book: 'how rationalistic I must have been at 19'.

But Frank had his own political journey. He had been a rebel even at Winchester. He was more than ready for conversion, and his own man. 'Almost any undergraduate who wanted to stop Hitler was then easy game for the Communists,'[82] wrote Denis Healey, and Toynbee recalls the 'marvellous atmosphere of conspiracy and purpose'[83] which they generated. The Labour Party in 1935 had permitted fusion of Communist and Socialist societies at the universities,[84] and there were close Labour links with CP headquarters on Hythe Bridge Street. Since then the University Labour Federation had been under CP domination. The Labour Club at Oxford, dominated by Communists, had over a thousand members; nearly all its committee were in the CP.[85] But then all of the committees of the League of Nations Union, the Liberal Club, the Student Christian Movement, two of the five Conservative Club committee, and two even of the ten British Union of Fascists were also in the CP.[86] It helps give the atmosphere of the times to point out that Robert Conquest, later to pioneer the objective history of Stalinism, while an open Communist, was a member of the university's conservative Carlton Club, with the approval of both bodies, and that the CP included John Biggs-Davidson, later Chairman of the right-wing Monday Club.[87] Probably there were dons also in the CP. Donald MacKinnon, who was not, certainly had instinctively radical social and political principles* – the oft-repeated tale of his climbing under the table to bite the calf of a visiting Anglican bishop has only symbolic truth: he was at odds with what would later be termed the Establishment.

Of the over two hundred CP student-members at Oxford, thirty were 'open', among them Robert Conquest, Denis Healey and Iris. She could scarcely have been more open. Her CP membership was referred to in June 1939 in *Cherwell*. Moreover, in the first newsletter of the *Old Froebelian*, 1940–41, while Iris's peers modestly vouchsafe merely that they are serving in the Air Ministry, are humbly 'one of the people on the Home Front', or 'work

---

* See MacKinnon's *Times* obituary, 4 March 1994. In 1953 he edited *Christian Faith and Communist Faith*, a series of studies by members of the Anglican Communion.

in a canteen at Marylebone',[88] Iris on the same page, having reported that she got a second in Mods and is now doing Greats, then heroically boasts, 'I am a member of the Communist Party.' Indeed a dramatic announcement. Meeting fellow-Froebelian Garth Underwood for the first time for eight years in Foyle's bookshop in March 1940,[89] she declared her CP membership. She was until June 1941 consistently unsympathetic to the war effort.

The first Executive Committee of the Oxford University Labour Club (OULC) Iris attended was on 19 April 1940, just after 'schools' for Mods;[90] she soon made her mark. In summer 1940 she represents 'culture' on the committee and proposes a meeting on Ireland.[91] (When the following year Kingsley Amis, also in the 'student' branch of the CP in his first year at Oxford, was co-appointed to take over 'this sector of the front' – culture – he interpreted the job less strenuously, as 'gramophone recitals' rather than, for example, working-class Oxford history. His CP membership, he later claimed, involved little more than meeting girls, 'trying to read Marx, Lenin and Plekhanov (aargh), going to meetings, speaking at meetings . . .'.[92] Some – like Lilian Eldridge – became members mainly in order to go to Saturday-night 'hops' at Ruskin.)

April 1940 was an interesting month in Oxford Labour politics. Roy Jenkins and Tony Crosland, both nauseated by the CP rubric that the Red Army was fighting to liberate the tiny, brave Finnish people from the reactionary rule of President Mannerheim[93] (just as it had, in collusion with the Nazis, 'liberated' the Poles), broke with the OULC and set up a much bigger Democratic Socialist Club, with Crosland as Chairman and Jenkins as Treasurer. Meanwhile the tiny official rump-OULC continued to support the USSR despite its invasion of Finland, Iris remaining 'apparently rigid on the Stalinist line'.[94] While the German armies were chasing the British Expeditionary Force across the fields of Picardy, towards Dunkirk, Jenkins spent fruitless weeks attempting to sort out the assets and liabilities of the rival groups, writing to 'Dear Miss Murdoch' as OULC Co-Treasurer and receiving humourless answers from her addressed to 'Dear Comrade Jenkins'. 'Student politics,' Jenkins later reflected, 'have rarely been notable for their sense of proportion.'[95] The Labour Party took no great interest: the OULC, as Crosland's widow Susan would write, resembled 'the sex life of the amoeba – dividing itself constantly'.[96]

Mary Midgley joined Crosland on the Dem-Soc committee – where, to great acclaim, Roy Jenkins was famous for singing 'Frankie and Johnnie'. On 1 May 1940 the Communists, trying to hold a May Day meeting, were pelted with tomatoes, oranges, rotten eggs and stink-bombs as they marched over Magdalen Bridge and up the 'High'.[97] Mary extemporised a comic verse about the 'Fascist' tomato Iris was cross at having to wash out of her hair.* But that summer after the fall of France, when Britain was fighting Hitler entirely alone, the two factions were still squabbling, both sides using Marxist arguments.[98] In winter 1941 Iris is OULC Secretary, in summer Chairman. She appears a competent minute-taker – one predecessor contributed almost as many doodles as notes – and a conscientious and effective chairwoman. Life had become, in one of her expressively breathless lists, 'one long committee meeting, with intervals in which interminable letters, articles, resolutions, protests, exhortations and minimum programmes have to be drafted'.[99]

On 22 June 1941 the Germans invaded the USSR, which now made it into an anti-Fascist war of which 'we' *did* approve. Iris told Mary that the CP had again to spend a week sorting out the Party line. During this turmoil Leo Pliatzky cut his ties with the Party: Hitler's invasion of Russia for him gave the lie to the former Party *diktat.* Similarly Iris told Margaret Stanier that disillusionment – not yet with Marxism, but with the Party for abandoning its opposition to the war effort – had made her consider quitting it. Even after she gave up office, the OULC nominated her to oppose a Democratic Socialist Club speaker.[100] By October 1941 a motion pinned into the minute book pressed for the opening of a second front for 'the safety of the USSR, of this country, of the whole world'. Negotiations to heal the split between OULC and DSC proceeded fruitlessly until 1943.[101]

---

* It showed her 'in her true colours as a Red'.

7

On 17 October 1940 Iris's signature in the Bodleian Library register sits immediately before Philip Larkin's,[102] a reminder that hard scholarly work continued too, throughout her last two years. Results came out after vivas in the Ashmolean in June 1942. Mary had a *viva voce*, or face-to-face examination.[103] Iris didn't, and quite wrongly feared the worst. In the event both got firsts, Iris's 'unquestioned'. Isobel Henderson arranged a dinner party in a smart restaurant for Iris and Mary, her only Greats finalists at Somerville that year, and invited two distinguished sages to enter-tain the girls: J.B. Trend, Mozart-scholar, translator, musicologist, and the polymath A.L. Rowse. Iris and Mary were very tired, though quite willing to be interested, but Rowse showed off, ate up the available space, was conceited and self-centred, and this exhausted and confused them. 'Did we learn something new this evening?' Mary asked Iris, as they stumbled home through bright moonlight on St Giles.

> 'O yes, I think so,' declared Iris, gazing up at the enor-mous moon. 'I do think so. Trend is a good man and Rowse is a bad man.' At which exact but grotesquely unfashionable judgement we both fell about laughing so helplessly that the rare passers-by looked round in alarm and all the cats ran away.[104]

Mary thought Iris's diagnosis was 'dead right' and that it put the evening in perspective. Rowse's showing-off battered at them. Imperfect behaviour can make the young feel inadequate, irrationally guilty. It was a great relief to Mary to have Iris's (Mani-chaean) perspective.[105] (Iris and Rowse later got on. Despite hav-ing little or no sexual interest in women, he once took bizarre pleasure in pulling her hair in a taxi.[106] Monsters great and small interested her.)

In one of a series of letters expressing her impatience for Finals to be over and for war work and 'real life' to begin, Iris wrote to Frank, serving overseas, 'I suppose I hanker for the dramatic &

heroic – ridiculous. I can almost see myself joining the WRNS just to demonstrate my vicarious suffering for Leningrad – & my contempt of [*sic*] Oxford'; and, later, 'ATS seems more and more probable. Teaching or Civil Service also conceivable';[107] she also thought she might nurse or fill shells.[108] A central register had been set up for bright women undergraduates, and dons spared from teaching, willing to carry out war work in the short-staffed civil service. Mary got the Ministry of Production, Philippa the Nuffield Social Survey under G.D.H. Cole in Oxford. Iris was interviewed,[109] and for some days was anxious in case her CP membership prejudiced her chances of a job. Finally the buff-coloured HM Stationery envelope arrived, inviting her to the governmental department with the greatest self-conceit, the Treasury, which favoured those who had undergone the *formation professionelle* of cold baths and irregular Greek verbs that shaped the English ruling class for centuries. 'Iris Murdoch has of late been no more a roving, and her old haunts know her not,' she wrote to the *Badminton School Magazine.*[110]

Recalling Oxford in wartime, she later wrote of how often one heard the announcement: 'Extra coaches will be added to the end of this train.'[111] On one such train, in early July 1942, only ten days after having sat her Finals, Iris left Oxford for London. She sent the news that she was a temporary Assistant Principal to Frank.[112] 'But do not please on this account say Irushka is dead, long live Miss Murdoch, an official in the Treasury.' 'Bureaucrat' was a dirty word to them both.*

---

* Frank always used the word pejoratively. See the 'poisonous-looking' bureaucrat Iris was dancing with when he first saw her, and Iris's condescension when mentioning to Frank that of the first-year intake of Somerville 'lasses' in 1941, 'half of them are bureaucrats'. Among these new students were two non-bureaucrats – Chitra Rudingerova – one of the Czech partly Jewish girls from Badminton (first name from Tagore) who came up in 1941, whom BMB asked Iris to take under her wing. Chitra thought Iris marvellous, quiet and somehow fey, not quite in the real world – her quietness hiding or exemplifying great power. Marjorie Boulton came up in 1941 too, an unconfident Staffordshire girl reading English, who would be a lifelong friend. See also M.R.D. Foot to Frank Thompson, 28 November 1942: 'I promise you the "charms of bureaucracy" shall not enslave me.' This was not, averred Frank's future sister-in-law Dorothy Thompson, who joined the Communist Party aged fifteen in 1939, an uncommon attitude: the short stories of Mikhail Zoschenko, *The Woman who Couldn't Read Stories* (translated around 1945), are both pro-Party and satirical of bureaucracy.

6

This Love Business
1942–1943

Two weeks after her arrival in London in July 1942,[1] Iris wrote to Philippa Bosanquet that she now lived

> in a fantastic world, ringing with telephonic voices, & peopled by strange fictional personalities such as Lords Commissioners of His Majesty's Treasury . . . (Oxford has nothing on the Treasury as far as tradition goes.) I can't believe that it's me writing these peremptory letters & telling people over the phone where they get off . . . all I do at present feels like play-acting.[2]

She sat at a 'desk 8 feet square amid heaps of blue files tied up with tape' devising new regulations 'with names like 1437/ 63538 90m.(14) &tc',[3] sharing a 'lofty airy office on the 3rd floor' working in 'Establishments', in what was then called the New Public Offices on the corner of Great George Street and White-hall, looking straight onto the north front of Westminster Abbey.[4] Her room-mate at one point was 'a charming but excessively talkative staff-officer in whose company work is virtually imposs-ible'.[5] Iris sometimes fled to the Treasury library. Haughty pre-war Treasury tradition meant Lords Commissioners issuing Letters of Permission. Wartime procedure was more informal, and letters coming into the department went first, to their surprise, to the new, young 'Assistant Principals' (AP's) such as Pat Shaw (later Lady Trend), Peggy Stebbing (later Pyke-Lees) and Iris. They had considerable power, looking up precedents and drafting official letters, which they passed on up to one of the two Principals 'to' whom they worked.[6]

In Iris's second novel, *The Flight from the Enchanter* (1956), a small army of energetic, ambitious and effective young women alone understand the workings of the fictional 'SELIB',* to the terror of at least one male colleague. This may reflect Iris's war work. In September 1939 there was one notable woman in the Treasury – Evelyn (later Baroness) Sharp, an Assistant Secretary,[7] and by 1941 the then thirteen women were still regarded as odd creatures. By 1943, following Iris's arrival, their number had gone up to twenty-three. They acted on their own initiative, did not always consult their seniors or let things go via committee. Because they were *Treasury* APs, they dealt directly with heads of other Civil Service divisions.[8]

Was Iris 'Treasury material'? Senior Treasury 'top brass' are famously statesmen in disguise, carrying with them a mass of interrelated exact knowledge, extreme day-to-day precision, intellectual detachment and *realpolitik*. While generally the Treasury was loosening up, and in measurable ways, Iris had landed in its stuffiest and narrowest division. Other departments looked outwards towards the wider world. 'Establishments'[9] looked inward, dealing with the internal workings of the civil service itself – discipline, pay, emoluments, rooms, complaints, requests to move.[10] Iris spent much time on what she called 'certain pay questions'[11] – calculating what increments those civil servants who had been seconded for war work should be entitled to receive at the end of hostilities; otherwise known – a standing Bayley joke, this – as *Notional Promotion in Absentia*. She was also secretary to three committees, one designated to 'investigate causes of delay'. She wrote to Frank:

> I still lose more files & overlook more important letters than anyone else in the Treasury . . . I'm learning a hell of a lot of new things about how our curious country is

* Special European Labour Immigration Board. Probably based on the European Voluntary Worker scheme (EVW), through which Iris's friends the Jančars (see Chapter 9) came to Britain.

governed – & I'm even beginning to think that Administration is a serious & interesting activity.[12]

Her colleagues were 'decent and endowed with senses of
humour',[13] and Michael Foot reassured Frank that August that
Iris was 'in good heart, but grown very quiet'.[14] She was none the
less frustrated. Frank had written from Cairo in June 1942 inviting
her to 'Join the WAAF, get a job as a cipher operator, and come
out here. I'd love to see you again. I'd love to see anyone who
makes sense.'[15] Iris's was not a 'bad' war, though, being Iris, she
chafed at her 'cushy job' when the rest of Europe was 'taking it on
the chin'. She voiced her disaffection to Frank on 24 November:

> Lord, lord. I get so damnably restless . . . I would volun-
> teer for *anything* that would be certain to take me abroad.
> Unfortunately there is no guarantee given one when one
> joins the women's forces & anyway the Treasury would
> never let me go; for, inefficient as I am, I am filling a very
> necessary post in a semi-skilled sort of way. Sometimes I
> think it's quite bloody being a woman. So much of one's
> life has to consist in having an attitude (I hope you follow
> this, which is a little condensed.) . . .
>
> I should of course like you to be a hero – but I doubt
> if I could accept the risk – & I am quite certain you have
> all the qualities of a stout fella, without the necessity of
> a vulgar display . . . I miss that unanxious society in which
> we trusted each other & were gentle as well as gay . . .
> The Treasury yields a number of pleasant men and
> women who, besides being very intelligent (& some of
> them very beautiful) are good company over a beer or
> whiskey. But they lack a certain redness of the blood –
> a certain human gentleness and sensitiveness. On the
> other hand, my Soho, Bloomsbury & Chelsea acquaint-
> anceship is widening also. 'The Swiss' in Old Compton
> Street, 'The Wellington' in Wardour Street* & 'The Lord
> Nelson' in King's Road are the clubs [*sic*] which I fre-

---

* The Swiss and the Wellington, like the Wheatsheaf, Black Horse and Fitzroy, were
well-known for their literary-bohemian ambience, and formed part of a familiar
pub-crawl. See e.g. Tambimuttu, ed. Jane Williams, *Bridge Between Two Worlds* (Peter
Owen, 1989), pp.75ff.

quent in search of the Ultimate Human Beings – and knowledge & experience & freedom. A strange society – composed of restless incomplete ambitious people who live in a chaotic and random way, never caring about the next five minutes, drunk every night without exception from 6 o'clock onwards, homeless & unfamilied, living in pubs & copulating upon the floors of other people's flats. Poetry is perhaps the only thing taken seriously by them all – & the only name they all respect is T.S. Eliot. *Politics they do not understand or care about* [my emphasis]. Their thought & their poetry is concerned with subtleties of personal relations – with the creation of the unexpected in words – 'dredging the horrible from unseen places behind cloaks and mirrors'.

Perhaps it is a betrayal to make friends with these people while our armies are fighting in North Africa. But I cannot help finding these off-scourings of *Horizon* a goodly company in some ways – they seem, indefinably, to be better human beings than these smiling Treasury people who drink, but never too much, & who never in any sense give themselves away. They are queer & unreliable, many of them – but they meet you in a level human sort of way, without the miles & miles of frigid protective atmosphere between. They have a sort of freedom, too, which I envy. I think it arises from a complete lack of any sense of responsibility – (so of course my envy is not whole-hearted. I may be flying blind at present, but I would not cast *all* the instruments overboard . . .) . . . I write a bit. I read a lot – am having an orgy of Edmund Wilson at the moment – (good on literature, superficial on history) . . .

. . . I feel in a peculiar sort of way that I mustn't let you down – yet don't quite know how to set about it. I don't think I believe any more in clean hands & a pure heart . . . I am on First Aid Duty tonight at the Treasury – an oasis of peace in a far too full life. I must go down to bed pretty soon (We had one casualty tonight. Great excitement. A man with a cut finger. Christ.)

I think of you often. May the gods guard you. Goodnight, my gentle Frank –

Much love to you. Iris.

2

One of the first things Iris did when she got to London was to start learning Russian, with Malvina Steen, a White Russian émigrée living behind Peter Jones department store in Sloane Square. While she found Steen 'learned without being intelligent', the Treasury intellectuals were 'intelligent without being learned'.[16] Yet there were compensations. She was pleased to discover, on greeting Peggy Stebbing's arrival – Iris had a strong handshake – that Peggy was the niece of Susan Stebbing, philosopher-author of the recent Pelican *Thinking to Some Purpose.** Peggy later married the poet Walter Pyke-Lees, also in the Treasury, and his war diaries show that, alone among women PAs, the Pyke-Lees called Iris by her first name, without any stuffy 'Miss Murdoch'. Three or four Treasury personnel had died in the air raids of May 1941, but Iris's time was quieter, as her ironical comment about the cut finger makes clear. On one of the regular fire-watch duty nights she donned her tin helmet, went up to the roof of the Treasury, and found herself in the company of A.W. Gomme, annotator of Thucydides.

Few of Iris's Treasury colleagues seem to have been invited to her flat.[17] The 'frigid protective atmosphere' she ascribed to Treasury mores was possibly also created by her shyness, giving an unconscious personal edge to her complaint. Peggy Stebbing, by contrast, was delighted by the relative informality of the wartime Treasury: although the department had a name as a 'heavy hand', Peggy thought the Treasury essentially enablers, and found the atmosphere so informal and unstuffy that when the bombing was bad she went into the country with her Principal Assistant Secretary, Edward Hayle.

Iris's hair was still shoulder-length, fairish, pinned up in something that was never quite a bun. She hoped that this created an effect 'less arty and juvenile'.[18] At tea-time each day she would stretch out her arms and yawn, then her hands would come

* Susan Stebbing had died the week before.

down and pluck out two hairpins, sending her hair cascading down onto her shoulders. Some of the Treasury's young men, stimulated by this very mild bohemianism, would come by to witness the spectacle – one which recurs at the end of *The Flight from the Enchanter*. Iris was in more than one sense learning to let her hair down, as well as noting that some colleagues found this harder to do.

Above all there was London. One autumn morning after another night of fire-watching[19] with Pat Shaw, the pair went out to breakfast together. Most Treasury staff crossed the road to the ABC, but Iris instead proposed they walk up to Leicester Square, where she threw back her shoulders, breathed in 'a deep gallon of air' and declared, 'The heart of London! The smell of London!' She staggered Shaw on another occasion by saying that she was going to be a don after the war. That made her seem both more grown-up than any of her colleagues, and more seri- ous. Untidy hair apart, Iris had an inner beauty, was one of a kind, very alive and somehow fey. She was thought politically aware, very private, intently watchful, empathetic, never casual, always friendly. She dressed neatly rather than smartly, and some- times her stockings had holes which, by the codes of the day 'could be the result of an accident. A darn was a sign of poverty.'[20] She gave herself no airs, was 'who she was'. Her voice was Oxford, with a slight but distinct brogue. It is possible that she provided a shoulder for secretaries to weep on.[21]

Iris and her colleagues worked a six-day week, until at least 6 p.m. on weekdays, 4 p.m. Saturdays, fixing, for example, 'new pay scales for Civil Service nurses'. They got very hungry: it was necessary to queue even for a penny bun. Some Treasury staff ate at the National Gallery where, for those with civil service passes, a meal cost one shilling and tuppence. There were only twelve days off per year, and no Bank Holidays. If you lingered over lunch, you had to stay until perhaps 7 p.m.[22] Many were exhausted when they got home and could think of nothing except supper and sleep. Iris later wrote, 'I was the slave of circumstance at 23.'[23] Yet she had two advantages over her peers. One was the super-abundance of energy noted at Somerville, an energy that enabled her to write one letter to Frank at 3 a.m.,* and sometimes to write poetry and fiction through the night, until the Tube trains started again in the small hours.† She had wanted, after Finals, to 'learn jujitso, German, translate Sophocles, learn to draw decently, buy expensive & crazy presents for my friends – really go into the subject of comparative mythology – read many very basic books about politics – learn about America, psychology, animals, my God I could go on for ever'.

Her other advantage was that she had found for herself a most unusual, magical and much discussed flat, only half a mile from work. Many of her peers had long journeys to the Treasury, or shared tiny rooms with a landlady on the premises, on their very small salaries (Iris earned £5 per week in 1942, which went up to £5.10s in 1944, plus a £40 a year war bonus 'kindly withheld for her until after hostilities'[24]). Home in Chiswick had been bombed, probably in the winter of 1941; her parents had by then in any case already moved to Blackpool with the Ministry of Health, where she visited them.[25] By mid-August Iris had discovered a studio flat to let for £60 a year unfurnished, on a three-year protected tenancy.[26] It would give her a base: 'London swarms with acquaintances whom individually I like but who collectively are making hay of my life!' she told Frank. The new flat, Iris's first, was owned by a Mrs Royalton-Kisch, aged about ninety-four and probably in a nursing-home. Iris was independent. She was also in a place and a time where she would live out, if not (like a character in *The Red and the Green*) 'the true and entire history of her heart', at least some critical chapters of that curious history.

---

* A letter to Paddy O'Regan is also dated 3.30 a.m., and one of her poems was completed at 4.30 a.m.
† Barbara Mitchell met Iris by prior arrangement at the Pillars of Hercules pub in Soho in 1943, and learnt that Iris was writing from the time the last Underground train left St James's Park at night to the time the first one started in the morning. In 1944, by contrast, when Philippa Foot anxiously walked the City streets, Iris slept soundly.

3

In July 1942 Iris wrote to Philippa: 'Best prospect for a flat is probably a single room in Gerrard Place – with a wonderful view of the blitz & practically no plumbing.' But she did considerably better, and by mid-August[27] found the flat which, a year later, would accommodate Philippa too, and which fifty-eight years later was still 'in the family', tenanted by Philippa's sister Marion. Iris called it a 'studio-flat ... of quite indescribable charm ... of utterly irresistible personality ... with some 6 square miles of window to guard, in blitz & blackout'.[28]

A few hundred yards from Buckingham Palace is a sliver of land called Brewer's Green, in what was once an area of breweries – Stagg's, Green's, Elliott's and the Artillery – all now long gone. Number 5 Seaforth Place nearby was always known to Iris and Philippa simply as 'Seaforth'. The tiny alley off Buckingham Gate was marked by a narrow cleft with a white post in the middle of it, and has no other front door. The flat belonged to the stables servicing a curious chain of pubs serving only non-alcoholic drinks, which provided rest-places for the poor.[29] Even today 'Seaforth' is a tiny, ancient white cube curiously beached in an era strange to it, an ensemble so closed off and secret that it seems, like the mysterious enclosures of Iris's Gothic fictions, a little lost world on its own.[30]

At street level was an empty garage or warehouse where the brewers once stabled their horses; their loose-boxes survived the war. The places on the wall where the halters were attached are visible today. Inside, a little bit of brown linoleum in the hall and a steep, uncovered stairway (with a very narrow, windowless bathroom fuelled by a geyser tucked under the stairs to the left – you could not stand up in the bath) led to the spacious first floor above the stalls. When you reached the top you were in the roughly converted old brewer's granary, twenty-five feet square and interrupted only by the staircase slicing up the middle, which Iris grandly termed 'the atrium'.[31] To the left of this was a corridor where she soon placed an ancient gas-stove, to make a kitchen[32] twenty-five feet long by eight feet wide, with a small dark window looking out onto a mews containing first-floor drawing offices over garages, and interrupted by an approach just wide enough for a coach and horses to enter the coach-houses on Spencer Street. This kitchen had an ill-fitting greenhouse roof of overlapping glass panes, and so was boiling hot in summer, freezing in winter and dripping when it rained. It contained a primitive improvised stand, pitcher and ewer, and water could be scooped up with a jug from the zinc-lined water-tank nesting under a ringed, wooden-hinged hatch-door at the top of the stairs. There was no water, hot or cold, in the kitchen, so washing-up was done downstairs in the bathroom.

To the right of the atrium, beyond what resembled a proscenium arch from which hung simple blue curtains, was the living-room, once the brewer's hayloft, similar in size to the granary/atrium. A large skylight on the left looked towards the St James's Court Hotel; two windows on the other side fronted – only a few feet away, like an alley in Palermo – the Territorial Army drill-halls, one for Artillery, one for Scottish conscripts.[33] Iris put in bookshelves on either side of an old-fashioned Edwardian gas-fire in the living-room, with an elegantly curved chimney-breast. This gas-fire, its perforated porcelain columns giving a 'few pale inches of war-time gas',[34] was the only heating – useful for making toast, too – though the ancient gas-oven could also be turned on, on a bitter winter night. Earlier groom-tenants had had some sort of *pied-à-terre* in the flat. Into what had probably been their bread-oven set into the wall, Iris put extra bookshelves, still there today. In January 1943 she wrote to Frank: 'I have a pleasant flat near St James's Park . . . which . . . is rapidly becoming so full of volumes of poetry of all eras & languages that I shall have to go & camp on the railway line (or feed 'em to the mice, after they've finished their present strict diet of airgraphs*).'[35] The mice had been eating Frank's letters.

---

* An airgraph was written on a single quarto sheet, then microfilmed and taken by flying-boat to its destination (Poole harbour in Dorset to Karachi took only three days), where it was developed, magnified, put into a manila envelope and delivered.

Lacking any inner doors, the flat effectively constituted one huge 'modern' open-plan space, seventy feet long. Being in so old a building, it also lacks straight lines or true right-angles. There is a gentle swept-back angle between atrium and kitchen, probably to ease the passage of hay. A delightful old coachman survived and was a source of lore about the place, until the coach-houses were demolished, and the character of the whole area changed, by the building of the new Westminster City Hall in 1960.[36]

Not that the wider world, especially in wartime, left Seaforth Place untouched. It was near enough to Whitehall to hear Big Ben, and to Westminster Cathedral to hear the angelus. For some friends living out of London, this very central flat was 'a convenient hotel'. Close friends believe that, on CP advice, Iris nominally left the Party just before joining the Treasury in order to disarm suspicion, while remaining for much of the war what the Party called an 'underground' (i.e. clandestine) member, one of those who paid no dues but could be expected to attend some branch meetings.[37] Leonie Marsh indeed reported Iris in July 1943 'unchanged in the slightest particular of manner, voice, dress or *Weltanschauung* [world-view]'.[38] Three scrupulous letters from Seaforth – undated but probably early in 1943 – to Marjorie Boulton, still up at Somerville until 1944, and seeking Iris's advice about joining the CP, support this view. Iris is anxious to proffer only 'objective' advice to the then impressionable Boulton. 'Oxford is not typical of the Party,' she wrote in one, implying that she knew the London CP also. In another:

> Whatever happens you mustn't dramatise this business & join us on the crest of a wave of emotion. Our organisation is in many ways intensely prosaic & often even sordid. There are bitter domestic quarrels – & sometimes the framework seems unbearably rigid & the people stupidly dogmatic. It is very easy to lose the beautiful clear vision & the joy of comradeship . . . there are two main things. Do you agree with our general policy? And then – more disquieting to me – your religious views . . .

> . . . Soon (I hope) you'll feel the deep quiet certainty
> that nothing can shake.*

CP members were required to feed information about their war work to the Party, which Iris, out of an idealism she would later see as misplaced, duly did: presumably, given her junior status, information of little moment about colleagues and Treasury doings. The CP explicitly trained its members to a habit of systematic dissimulation, which caused some to quit. The moral pressure to accept the resulting isolation from most of those around one was undoubtedly extreme: one's reaction to that pressure might largely depend on one's personal relations with the people who were calling on one to accept it. It would be thrilling to imagine Iris-as-Communist-mole imperilling the security of the realm, but at the level that she was employed, this is not likely. On the other hand, if she had had information of greater moment to pass on, she would probably have done so.

The capacity to operate clandestinely resembles the capacity to run love relationships concurrently: both evidence that warm-yet-cool ability to enter into, and operate within, many other people's worlds that Keats, in a famous letter, admired in Shakespeare (now read by certain critics as a spy in the Catholic cause). Training in dissimulation also throws some light on, even if it cannot altogether explain, the co-existence within Iris of a striking outward stillness or serenity with an equally turbulent inner world. But it is extraordinary that she attempted to be a loyal 'cadre' for so long: she had too much sense and heart to be loyal to that kind of political clique, and detested, once she properly understood it, Stalinist tyranny.[39]

Her Treasury colleague Walter Pyke-Lees mentioned Iris's Communism casually and tolerantly to his future wife and co-

---

* All three letters are undated, but c1942–43. Iris also wrote: 'I am more sorry than I can say that your dawning interest in the Party should have coincided with an era of bloodiness really unparalleled in my experience of our extremely imperfect organisation . . . Oxford is not typical of the Party, & this recent fracas not typical of Oxford'; 'Serious political work (as opposed to the Labour Party) does tend to shorten tempers, fray nerves, & . . . produce the text brandishing dogmatist.' Marjorie was finally deterred from joining the Party by the ten-shilling subscription.

colleague Peggy Stebbing, who recalled it as being, with some exceptions, 'understood, in a civilised spirit', Russia being at that time Britain's newest ally. There is little direct evidence about when or why she severed her links with the Party. CPGB archives up to 1942 are now in Moscow, and the absence of the name 'Iris Murdoch' from the 1943 CP list of members[40] proves nothing: 'underground' members, by definition, were not listed. In the spring of 1943 Iris proselytised (unsuccessfully) the ex-Magpie Ruth Kingsbury (later Mills), who, though unconvinced, nonetheless bought at Iris's suggestion a Russian grammar and a Tolstoy short story in Russian. Iris's poet friend Paul Potts, recalled as sympathetic to the CP,[41] was a close friend of George Orwell, who had bravely unmasked the USSR, notably in 'Inside the Whale'. If it is true that the CP held meetings in Iris's flat with her agreement, but in her absence,[42] they were probably of some dull, perhaps 'bureaucratic' committee in whose doings she took no interest.[43] No such events are recalled after Philippa moved in in October 1943, and a reasonable guess is that Iris had started a withdrawal, probably painfully, by 1944, under the influence of the politically clearer-sighted Thomas Balogh, sufficiently anti-Communist as a thirteen-year-old schoolboy in Budapest after its 'Socialist revolution' of 1919 to take potshots with a rifle at Bela Kun's troops.[44] Frank Thompson's future sister-in-law Dorothy[45] was from September 1944 attending what would have been Iris's local Victoria/Pimlico branch of the CP, but never met Iris at the Dolphin Square meetings.

There was much in wartime London to worry a tender social conscience: one and a half million homeless alone by May 1941. There were many air raids, and people from the devastated East End were sleeping in bunks on the platforms of Tube stations such as St James's Park, more or less underneath the Seaforth flat. They 'trekked into central London each night and out to work in the mornings. Strangers sheltering in doorways would sometimes accompany each other home,' Philippa recalled. The constant rumble and vibration of the District and Circle Line trains beneath the flat Iris was later to use in *The Time of the Angels*. She relished 'both the noise and the shaking'.[46] On nights when the bombs fell heavily, Iris or Philippa if alone in the flat would on occasion shelter in the bathtub under the stairs, Iris having carefully reasoned that a tin hat protected against shrapnel, and the closest item they had to a tin hat (albeit upside-down) was a bath.[47] When a V2 took out three largish houses on the other side of the St James's Court Hotel – which must have protected them – they lost windows and frames; these were soon repaired.

Visitors were surprised by how big the flat looked. It had very little furniture, some of it at orange-box level. In those days of rationing and coupons, everything was rather bare – food, clothing, furnishing alike. Iris's bohemianism also tended to make her avoid any hint of luxury, even if she could have afforded it. The aesthetic minimalism was impressive. There were two armchairs by the gas-fire, one of them Mary Midgley's,[48] a table and chairs. Having found the flat in August 1942, she moved in by September.[49] In October she wrote to Frank that she was settled more or less into both her flat and her job.

4

In March 1941 Frank, having transferred the previous August from the Royal Artillery to 'Phantom', a small communications and intelligence unit, was posted to the Middle East. He and Iris met before this at least once in London, and visited Westminster Cathedral together, Frank lighting a candle to the Madonna. He left behind with Iris a ring-bound folder of his typed poems predating this departure, including a handwritten 'To Irushka' in heroic mode, later damned by him as 'Hooey'. He sailed, from Clydeside via Cape Town, to Cairo, disgusted by the disparity between the slum-like conditions and diet of the men and the six-course meals and menu-cards taken for granted by the officers. In November 1941, after two months with septicaemia in the Australian Hospital in Damascus, but now back in Cairo, he wrote to his parents that he had just heard from Iris, 'gloomy and as always when she hasn't seen me for a long time, full of affection'. For over three years they continued their correspondence, and many of their letters survive.[50] Iris was in 1991 to judge her war-time letters 'very affectionate but a bit stilted, young person's letters'.[51] Of this 'stilted' tone, one early instance was sent to Frank around December 1939: 'I am particularly distressed that you are worried about the world. I was, but am much less so now – remember, your environment is probably less likely to induce clear thought than mine is.' Here is Iris-as-perpetual-Head-Girl, a role she did not easily outgrow.[52]

But generally these gifted, energetic letters, which Iris refers to as a 'flow of talk',[53] are alive even now. Frank repeatedly makes clear how good they were to receive: 'It seems strange to compare your gentle letters with flint but the simile has this much aptness. They strike fire immediately. And when one arrives, as has yours ... I am impelled forthwith to answer it.'[54] Iris made clear how intensely lonely she felt in busy London, and how 'much in need of intellectual intimacy'. Frank's was, uniquely, 'the patient mind which is prepared to comprehend my own & toss me back the ball of my thought'.[55]

Iris's habitually intense reserve inspired awe throughout her life. To the absent Frank she now started to reveal the 'inward' unconfident soul who suffered ambition and insecurity, was lost and confused in the ordinary way of young mortals. Instead of Iris always consoling Frank, Frank now increasingly 'plays the man' and cheers Iris up when she is despondent. With few other friends does she ever reveal herself thus.

Of Frank's growing importance to Iris there is plenty of evidence, from letters, from friends and from Iris herself, who in 1996 was distressed to recall the terrible waiting which went on and on, week by week, more than half a century before, through much of 1944, to find out where Frank was and what had happened to him. By demonstrating his independence in joining up, he had significantly shifted the balance of power between them. Moreover, as he wrote to his parents, 'an Englishman of our class seems to change more between 20 and 23 than at any other time'.[56] He, one year younger, was in some ways growing up faster than she. He had less choice. He was known in North Africa by his men as 'the gaffer', and to play the officer at twenty-one and twenty-two required him to act ten years older than he was. He now wrote to his brother: 'The OULC looked needlessly bohemian to outside observers. The men (I was a very bad offender) were often unwashed and wore the most ridiculous clothes. Many of the women did the same and both conducted the most tangled and nauseating love affairs in public, while the rest of the university kept its sex life fairly decorous behind closed doors.'[57] He could measure the distance between the callow youth he once had been and the young man he was becoming. When Iris wrote to Frank that 'the more letters I get from you, the more I admire you', she was expressing no more and no less than the truth.

What of Frank? He wrote to Iris that there were only four people in England to whom he could speak almost as clearly on paper as with his lips: 'Three of them are my closest kin and the other one is you.'[58] He got close to other women, corresponded with a number, but did not cherish their letters as he did hers.[59] Even his family was told that, if they wished, they should make copies of their letters before sending them to him. He had acquired so many sackfuls that he could not keep them all. Iris's letters alone, he kept.[60]

A relationship maintained only by letter must be precarious. How much belonged to the realm of fantasy? Iris after all had not been a body to him 'for nearly 4 years', he wrote in April 1944. The sinister vagaries of wartime postal delivery alone might delight a Thomas Hardy. Just as Frank may never have learnt that he had in 1944 been gazetted Major, so Iris does not understand that he had, in September 1942, been promoted Captain, until half a year later. These were frustrations to which both refer. Letters matter intensely to Frank. He gets 'down' when they are delayed, feeling it impossible to believe he has 'kin' anywhere; then, when a letter arrives, 'feels as though home were only a five minute walk away'. In October 1942 he wrote to Iris:

> Three years and a bit since I joined the Army. More than that since you & I first exchanged Weltanschauungs in a room in Ruskin. Now I am 22 instead of 18, and you are 23, almost a matron. Looks like being another three years straight before we meet again. We shall probably

find we have both changed out of all knowing and have nothing any longer in common. Write whenever you can. An airgraph is a pleasant way of saying 'I havent forgotten you'. But a letter is a golden gift, a winged gift – worth more than a half the world to a mortal in depression.[61]

Iris wrote that she had found that reciting Homeric hexameters went very well with the rhythm of the Tube train. Frank replied:

I'm greatly cheered by the picture of staid Iris Murdoch reading Homer in the Underground. Does the train ever stop suddenly, leaving your words to ring out in all their natural clarity? If so, many must be the tired stock-broker whose heart is melted and his vision beautified. Doubt if I could construe a line of Homer now.

Iris and Frank's four-year correspondence betokens the tenacity of their feeling, as does the quality of their letters. In January 1942 he translated Pushkin's short early poem 'I loved you once' (*'Ya vas Lyubil'*), managing to convey the explosive compression, and also the calm, peace, and sheer stylishness, of the twenty-year-old Pushkin's Russian:

I loved you once in silent desperation.
Shyness and envy wracked me numb with pain.
I loved you once. God grant such adoration
So true, so gentle, comes your way again.

He also wrote a story about a certain Gunner Perkins who wishes to express his passion by letter to his girlfriend Helen, rather than thoughts about books and politics. 'If only he had had the courage before he left. Now it was too late, you could never break down barriers by letter.' 'Helen' is an interesting *nom-de-guerre* for Iris: the Greeks died at Troy for another Helen. Interesting too, in the light of Frank's wartime career, is this passage from Iris in a letter, of 24 November 1942, in which she celebrates Allied progress, but worries that it is terrible to 'rejoice in something which totals up to such a sum of human anguish' – especially when one is 'snug in Whitehall' oneself:

[L]ately I reread *The Seven Pillars* [*of Wisdom*]. I feel a
sort of reverence for that book – for that man [T.E.
Lawrence] – which it is hard to describe. To live such a
swift life of action & yet not simplify everything to the
point of inhumanity – to let the agonizing complexities
of situations twist your heart instead of tying your hands
– that is real human greatness – *it is that sort of person I
would leave everything to follow.* [My emphasis.]

Iris is unusual among liberal novelists in admiring soldiers. She
later recalled lying on the floor and watching the V1s 'tottering
past the window' – a brilliantly chosen phrase for the movement
of the mass-produced buzz-bomb, propelled by its unsteady 'pulse-
jet'.[62] While destroying many wartime writings, she saved a brief
account of her reactions when bombs fell near the Hungarian
economist Nickie Kaldor's flat in Chelsea Cloisters[63] in March
1944: the thirty-second crash, the rocking of the house, the pat-
tering fall of debris which taps the window, and the fact that 'I
cannot stop watching my own reaction even when there is no-one
about before whom I want to keep up appearances.'

Iris's obsession with T.E. Lawrence – an acquaintance of the
Thompsons, whom Frank met as a child – shared by Simone de
Beauvoir and Simone Weil, was lifelong, and the ascetic warriors
in her novels – Felix in *An Unofficial Rose*; General James Arrowby
in *The Sea, The Sea*; Pat Dumay in *The Red and the Green*; even
James in *The Bell*, whose simple piety relates to his coming from
'an old military family' – owe something to this 'world-changer
who never lost his capacity to doubt',[64] as well as something to the
figure of Frank. Iris's encouragement helped persuade another
admirer, Paddy O'Regan, to join the Special Operations Executive
(SOE),[65] set up by Churchill in 1940 to 'set Europe ablaze' by
supplying arms and other support to guerrilla and sabotage
groups. This was a dangerous move, to say the least; Hitler had
ordered in the autumn of 1942 that any Allied soldier found
involved in clandestine activities could be shot on sight, and part
of the routine training involved an explanation of the extreme
risks involved.[66] O'Regan would win an MC and bar. Frank had
his own motives for volunteering for SOE, on 5 September 1943.

The unfolding logic of his and Iris's love-at-long-distance may also have played a role in his deciding to make this move, as his choice of the name 'Helen' suggests. Iris began as the 'unmoved mover'. By 1943 she was, in some sense, increasingly in love with the absent Frank.

5

They felt affinity. During 1942 Iris's forms of opening address to Frank move from 'Greetings, my brave and beautiful buccaneer' (January), to 'Dearly beloved' (April), to 'Frank, my wild & gentle chevalier' (October), to 'Frank, my brave & beloved' (November), to, on 22 January 1943, a simple 'Darling'. Her valedictions are mostly pleas to him not to get hurt: 'Frank, old friend, I love hearing your voice crying in the wilderness – cry often, & at great length – & oh, for Christ's sake don't get hurt in this business' (April/May 1942); 'And oh, Keep Safe. The gods protect you' (29 July 1943). He is for his part no less inventive: 'Irushka, flaxen-haired light of wisdom!' (June 1942); 'My green-haired Sybil' (July 1942), though shyer of open displays of affection.

Both are highly intelligent, politically aware – 'Old Campaigner' is another of Iris's soubriquets for Frank – both by 1942 believing the war is not only to protect a bad old world from Fascism, but to help forge a new one. Both are writers in the making. His father had some of Frank's letters published in the *New Statesman*, and a story in the *Manchester Guardian*, and Frank thought he might be a journalist after the war. Iris reviewed for the *Adelphi* and began to write novels.* Both are romantics, and remind each other of this[67] – romantic idealists in their political hopes, their liking for high diction, but also in what they expect from others. On 20 March 1943 Iris writes: 'Oh Frank, I wonder what the future holds for us all – shall we ever make out of the dreamy idealistic stuff of our lives any hard & real thing? You will perhaps. Your inconsequent romanticism has the requisite streak

* See Chapter 7.

of realism in it – I think I am just a dreamer. Shout in my ear, please. Much love, old pirate – I.'

Frank is the more brilliant linguist – indeed at one point, in Bulgaria, he is saved by a bullet being fired into his dictionary. Both learn new languages for pleasure, and Frank their literatures too. He attributed importance to this because, in the new post-war Europe-of-the-heart in which he so passionately believed, the acquisition of languages is to help overcome misunderstanding and mutual ignorance. In learning Russian Iris was probably partly imitating Frank, who had started aged fifteen at Winchester, and now translated not only Pushkin, but also Gogol, Gusyev and Lermontov. Both were of course also intensely pro-Russian for political reasons. After he picks up Italian, she tries to do the same: 'incredibly easy as you say'.[68] Frank also picked up Serbo-Croat, Bulgarian, Polish and modern Greek, faltering only with Arabic. She goes beyond him once, arriving at the Turkish Embassy and demanding to be taught Turkish – in order, mysteriously, to improve her post-war job prospects, about which she feels 'cynical'. Frank, who refers to this new interest of hers on 2 June 1943, is studying a Turkish grammar by that August.

They tried to share their reading, too. While still at Somerville in 1941 she was reading Proust: 'He too teaches one to forgive[69] – a point I'm learning from all quarters just now. Characteristic of all great writers? Shakespeare – Tolstoy – James Joyce – for the last of whom I'm feeling an enormous enthusiasm . . . and everything that survives of Tacitus – except the *Germania*. I tremble and adore.'[70] On 24 December 1941 she mentions Mallarmé and Gorky's *Mother*, which both loved, and 'I have been reading Virginia Woolf, the darling dangerous woman, & am in a state of extreme nervous self-consciousness. The most selfish of all states to be in.' She pledges herself on his recommendation ready to read 'Bachtin' (i.e. Bakhtin), 'even if this means borrowing it from Bodley'.[71] In November 1942 she read Pushkin (in Russian), Edmund Wilson and Pindar. The following October Proust, Joyce, de Montherlant, Woolf ('quite incapable of writing anything straight again'), Balzac's *Eugenie Grandet* ('left me cold') and Celine ('What a gorgeous language – how much one is exiled from. How much more they are exiled from'). He read *Penguin New Writing* before her,[72] sending her his translations from the Russian. Both read Louis Aragon's *Crève-Coeur*,[73] an iconic text enjoying cult success, banned in Britain probably because it addressed Dunkirk, but smuggled in from France, acclaimed by Cyril Connolly and Charles Morgan for its poetry and patriotism alike.* In 1943 Frank sends her Mayakovsky and she sends him poems by the 'New Apocalyptics', the 'Poetry (London) gang, the sensibility boys who think with their stomach'.[74] They argue about Henry James, whom Iris likes considerably more than does Frank. Both accuse themselves of being 'intellectual snob'. In March 1943 they discuss *Antony and Cleopatra*.

In October 1943, while undergoing a sabotage and parachute training course in the Lebanon, with a view to helping – as he then thought – the partisans in occupied Greece, Frank requested a photograph. Iris obliged with a visit to Polyfoto, then recipro-cated the request. There is an odd sympathetic magic about the fact that both succumbed to jaundice, although this ailment (or, rather, symptom) was commoner then than it is now. Frank suf-fered it at the Indian hospital near Hamadan in Persia in October 1942 – whence he wrote home about Iris's first in Greats, joking that the war had saved him from the indignity of getting a lower degree than her – Iris a year later, with her parents in Blackpool: 'You have had this curious complaint.'[75]

Frank once wrote: 'Without going all James Barry, . . . the real enduring people have kept something of the child within them.' Here lies one key to their growing affinity. His friend Gabriel Carritt always spoke of Frank's '*sancta simplicitas*'. Iris saw this. She had her own too.

---

* Frank to Iris, 14 August 1943: 'Michael [Foot] has sent me *Crève-Coeur* . . . Aragon has scored several bulls.' Iris later sent a copy to David Hicks which had to be cleared by the censor.

6

On 22 January 1943, settled alike into her flat and her job, Iris wrote Frank a ten-page letter that is by turns playful – 'Darling, the mice have been eating your letters again,' it starts – then serious, lyrical, informative and, in a familiar wartime mode, resolutely undramatic. She does not 'mind how many dangers you face, so long as I don't know at the time, & you emerge in good condition – & don't suffer miseries en route of course'. She shares with him her writerly ambitions, pondering hopefully Aldous Huxley's doctrine that, for a writer, 'it is not what one has experienced but what one *does* with what one has experienced that matters'. She imparts news of mutual friends, reports on her reading – Wilfred Owen, Ann Ridler, the Beveridge plan ('a fine piece of work, thorough and equitable', though she is anxious about the chances of this blueprint for the post-war Welfare State being fully realised), 'numerous moderns'. She describes her life, the emptiness she feels in his absence, and the intellectual intimacy which she strongly implies that only he now offers her (Philippa had not yet joined her in Seaforth Place). After reporting that she is 'hellishly lonely', despite being in 'great and beautiful and exciting London', she continues:

> I should tell you that I have parted company with my virginity. This I regard as in every way a good thing. I feel calmer & freer – relieved from something which was obsessing me, & made free of a new field of experience. There have been two men. I don't think I love either of them – but I like them & I know that no damage has been done. I wonder how you react to this – if at all? Don't be angry with me – deep down in your heart. (I know you are far too Emancipated to be angry on the surface.) I am not just going wild. In spite of a certain amount of wild talk I still live my life with deliberation.

If she had cared for him less, Iris would not have thought Frank worth this proximate candour. Her painful belated honesty is a token of love, the more so in that friends thought her loss

of virginity had happened before she left Oxford.[76] The exact
sequence is obscure. Noel Eldridge, whom she had met through
Oxford student journalism – *Oxford Forward, Cherwell* and the
short-lived *Kingdom Come* – had asked her to marry him, arguing
light-heartedly that, as he was almost certain to be killed, she
could at least enjoy a modest war widow's pension. Iris later told
John Bayley, 'laughing and weeping', that she had told Noel she
would not marry him, but was willing to sleep with him instead.
He was indeed shot and killed by a sniper somewhere along
the Bologna–Rimini road, having rejoined the Queen's Royal
Regiment fighting the Germans in Italy, in September 1944.

Noel's twin sister Lilian Eldridge in 1998 recognised the playfulness of Noel's bid,[77] a playfulness Iris could express too. Noel
wrote to his mother around November 1939:

> The sanest attitude I think is The Murdoch's: she is
> announcing that she wants the literary remains of all her
> friends and is going to make lots of money with a slim
> anthology when the war ends. I've refused to give her
> anything yet as I'm holding out for a cash payment.

Iris kept all her life many slim volumes of verse that had
belonged to Eldridge: Auden's 1930 poems, Herbert Read, David
Gascoyne, Paul Eluard, Caudwell, Francis Thompson, and an
Imagist anthology.

Leo Pliatzky believed, by contrast, that he was Iris's first lover,
very broadly construed, just as she was, after Leonie Marsh, his
second. He spoke of the unusual parental complaisance of Rene
and Hughes, who allowed him and Iris to be unchaperoned in
her room in Chiswick. Iris later recalled a time when Leo tried
to undress her in his rooms at Corpus, and she wept. Noel Eldridge and Leo are not the only contenders,[78] and the different
stories which different friends were told reflect Iris's intention
not to cause hurt, as much as a positive desire to mystify, though
she was certainly capable of mystification.[79] It is hard to know
how much weight to give to her jest, delighting in her own 'modernity', to Margaret Stanier[80] that there was perhaps only one
man in Oxford she had *not* had an affair with:[81] bohemianism was

for her generation often part of the same revolt against bourgeois conventionality as Communism.[82] Walking across Westminster Bridge one midnight in 1943, Iris told Clare Campbell that she had recently lost her virginity and was sad about it (though the man 'was very kind', she added when they recapped this decades later). Clare had no idea how to respond. She recalls that Iris could not at this time hear without crying the theme song from a film, 'Oh the Pity of it All'.

Frank knew and disliked Noel Eldridge, whom he once, probably from jealousy, called to Iris 'that snake', but Leo was his good friend. Indeed Leo and Frank ran into each other in a Field Army Workshop in North Africa in September 1943, and drank a can each of warm beer together. One perplexity of Frank and Iris's friendship is that almost all the male friends to whom she refers in her letters to him – Leo, Noel Martin, David Hicks, Noel Eldridge, Michael Foot – were at some time in love with her. A number were at some point her lovers. When, in a letter dated 29 January 1942, she asks Frank for news of Leo, Hal Lidderdale and David Hicks, she is in sober fact asking him for news of three of his many potential rivals. Frank and Hal also met during the war, in Libya in July 1943; Iris heard of this meeting through Hal. The imaginative importance she accorded each man is another matter. She lost touch with Eldridge, for example, well before his death – he married after a brief courtship in 1943.* Hal and David became her lifelong friends. Frank, on the other hand, never her lover, preoccupied her all her life. And she played her cards close to her chest, one admirer rarely being told of rival-claimants.

The war, like the decade following it, was a period of sexual and emotional experimentation – something long claimed as a natural right by men, with whom Iris in some ways easily identified. The 'wild talk' she tells Frank about shows in an early letter to Philippa, two months after they had first properly met:

---

* Noel married Jane Brown McNab, and then introduced his wife and mother casually on the street. Two weeks later he was sent abroad. He and his wife never saw one another again.

I have a great many friends in London – I have lunch
or dinner with a different person every day – but I get
no satisfaction or consolation from them, & our relations
seem superficial & even chilly. I feel like going out &
picking up the first man I meet that's willing, simply for
the sake of a more intense relationship of any description
with another human being.[83]

This has an air of Lawrentian bravura, indicative of the itch
for emancipation. Fifty years after the war Iris recalled 'Hammersmith Palais de Danse with Susie Williams-Ellis, and we danced
with soldiers, and they were so sweet and gentle. Waltz.'[84] This
was dancing for the love of it: her own range of acquaintance
was large enough to provide her with a lover if she needed one.
It is a paradox about Iris that she managed to run an increasingly
complicated love-life, while continuing to appear to many
observers chaste if not chilly. Anne Cloake and Leonie Marsh
were two Somerville friends from the OULC. Anne, who thought
she had taught Iris the facts of life, always referred to her as a
prim blue-stocking.[85] Leonie found Iris in 1942 virginal, and as
late as 1944–45 the novelist Mulk Raj Anand, later a Minister in
the Indian government, remarked to Vera Hoar in a pub that
'Iris was always virginal.' Frank, too, in his complex reply to Iris's
confession, reports his fear that she had been wedded to 'a cold
virginity'.

The myth of a cold virginity was one Iris had difficulties in
dispelling. She had written to Frank one year before: 'Gentle
gloom bloody hell. I get so sick of that myth. I'm not a Blessed
Damozel you know, at least not any more. There isn't even a trace
of Burne-Jones – & the faint aroma of incense has perished in
the high wind . . .' The 'Blessed Damozel' reference amounts to
a standing joke in their circle, possibly an uncomfortable one.*

---

* The letter was dated 29 January 1942. Compare Iris to Clare Campbell, April
1941: 'I am inebriating myself with French poetry and Malory, and becoming more
romantic and unphilosophical every day. Soon I shall turn into a pre-Raphaelite
bubble (Holman Hunt variety) and float away before the breeze . . .'. Compare also
Frank to Iris, 27 July 1942, *à propos* the conceit that Iris has green hair: 'a good
green, mind you, none of yr ghoulish pre-Raphaelite stuff'; and on 17 October 1942
Frank thinks he has 'written to you before about the Noble Passion of Dante Gabriel

Iris had also written to Frank from Oxford: 'I haven't a face any more. I am prepared to give up the clear contours & the cutting edge which were formerly my ideal. I feel generally iconoclastic, and the eikon I most want to smash is the pretty golden image inside myself I've preserved so carefully. Completeness terrifies me – I have no more pat answers – I want to hurl myself down into the melee & the mud & I dont care how filthy it is . . .' It was the Blessed Damozel image of herself she wished to smash, one in which, with its pressure of intense sexual idealisation, Frank had some investment. Iris's *nostalgie de la boue* is one reply.

7

Iris's letter took twelve weeks to reach Frank in the Levant. He replied at comparable length on 22 April: 'I could have no cause for anger. Nor can I, since I am not conventional after the modern fashion, be unreservedly glad without due reflection.'

He lists two 'stumbling-blocks' or possible problems. He understands that his is not the only tendency towards idealisation: 'I know of course, that your men are not ordinary men but parfit gentle knights. But it will take years of sorrow to realise how violently misogynistic most men are *au fond*.' His second 'stumbling-block' points to the impact of her news on him. He writes of 'a theory which I'm still engaged in formulating . . . I, you see, have messed up my sex-life . . . [with] a most terrible dichotomy by which women fall into two categories – Women it would be rather nice to sleep with provided one didn't have to talk with them for more than five minutes/women one really likes *avec lesquelles il ne vaut pas s'embeter dans un lit.'* This classic dualism, he perfectly realises, insults both kinds of women. He had expressed it three years earlier to his brother:

Rossetti' for the wombat, and wishes Rossetti had painted wombats instead of 'Blessed Damozels & all that poppycock'.
* Roughly: 'with whom it's not worthwhile bothering oneself in bed'.

My chief concern is looking for a woman ... There are
plenty to pick up on the streets but few one wants ...
The trouble is, I expect rather a lot of a woman. She's
got to be one I can talk to, and if she is, she's probably
not sexual enough or else she's clever enough to see
through me. I've had friendships with several girls, like
my beloved Iris, but it never gets farther than that. That's
the trouble with idealistic women, and if a woman's not
an idealist, I don't want her. Enough of this muck. A few
months in the army is bound to lower my standards.[86]

Three years had not lowered his standards, and his biographer
believes that they were never so lowered.[87] Frank goes on to refer
Iris to the oft-hymned joys of a honeymoon in which both parties
are virgin: 'To medicine me from this would probably take years
of psychotherapy combined with the best type of free love ...
But having suffered all this, I am coming to the conclusion that
it is better to abstain altogether until one falls head over heels
in love ... I remember thinking ... often ... that a good love-
affair would do you the devil of a lot of good.' He feared that
she was wedded to 'a cold virginity from which it would be yearly
more difficult to free yourself. So, on balance, it is obviously a
subject for joy. If I've said anything here that is clumsy or stupid,
forgive me. I'm afraid there is no finesse about me, Irushka.' He
ends, tellingly: 'Do write me more long letters like your last. I
talk a lot of baloney when I answer, but maybe I understand more
than I let on.'

Frank's reply contains an interesting polemic against introspection. He improbably claims that, unlike Iris, he has no books of
poetry with him, and says that, on the one hand 'unless you are
an introvert, you have not the vision to look into other people's
minds', on the other 'Tolstoi & Chehov went as far into the minds
of our fellow-men as it is profitable *or seemly* to go.' This seems
in context like a *caveat* against pursuing dangerous lines of
enquiry. Iris, who would write to Frank when depressed that she
was 'feeling rather Chehov tonight', saw in him someone who,
like T.E. Lawrence, could rise above the mere introspection to
which her desk- and pub-bound life constrained her.

He must have known that, had Iris cared for him less, she would not have thought him worth her confession. The coldness of his analysis is his only mild punishment, and means of self-protection. Before writing it, he went and sat in a Greek Orthodox church. She had earlier enquired whether his apparently inviolable good spirits were 'stiff upper lip on your part? Give me a line on that.' His mother Theo also complained to him that 'You never say when you are down.' He replied to Iris that he was 'far too malleable' to keep a 'stiff upper lip'.

This is bravado. Three weeks before, on 18 May 1943, Frank had written to his parents asking them to tear up his will,[88] together with the letter he had left to accompany it – almost certainly a letter to Iris, or making mention of her. Within a month, also, M.R.D. Foot, to whom alone of his correspondents he was willing to sound vulnerable,[89] received from him a 'wildly melancholiac letter' which so disturbed him that it prompted two letters in reply urging him not to despair, until Frank angrily persuaded Michael that his fears were 'baseless'. 'Faced with stark horror I prefer to grapple with it silently and alone,' he said, *à propos* watching a companion parachute to his death. Had he just 'roman-candled' in love? 'Half-man, half-boy', he had described himself to Iris in 1939, and his growing older did not prevent him from finding tears in his eyes on leaving his unit – his father touchingly wrote that his description of this parting was worthy of Tolstoy. Nor did it prevent him from weeping the following year – in SOE, and with the end of the menace of Fascism finally in view – to think of the new Europe they were to build after the war.

Iris's announcement of the loss of her virginity did not change the direction of Frank's attachment. On 22 July 1943 in Libya he met their mutual friend Hal Lidderdale, 'a small dark-eyed humanist' and Captain in No. 2 Anti-Aircraft battery, and they agreed about the complacent and stupid ethos of their respective officers' messes.

> Hal and I are really rivals for Iris, but the fair object of
> our rivalry is so remote in time and space that it only

serves to cement our friendship. At the moment I think
Hal's leading quite comfortably, [as] Iris goes to stay
with his mother.[90]

Iris wrote to Frank in spring 1943: 'As a matter of interest,
how have you fared with women in the East? I don't mean from
the grand passion point of view, but just from the sex experience
point of view.' Very 'Ursula and Gudrun', this rehearsed casualness, and that cunningly placed word 'just', would-be worldly,
downplaying the 'merely' physical aspects of sexuality. It seems
to betoken the hope that an equivalent confession to her own
from Frank would lessen any sense of guilt on her part, although
she would certainly have been jealous, too. 'Do you spend your
days lying with lovely Iranians? How do you feel about that racket
now? It's terrible, Frank, how little we know really in spite of fairly
frequent letters of how the other party is developing in these fast
and fatal years. Perhaps we shouldn't pry into each other's minds
... God what a difference half an hour's conversation would
make.'

8

Frank had other ways of learning about Iris. Leo Pliatzky wrote
to him: 'I have continued to hear from Iris at intervals, though
nothing in the last week or two and nothing at all unusual. She
finds the world tragic and moving, but that is not unusual. I shall
not be writing to her for some time ... But when I do I shall
convey your undying affection – perhaps a little more articulately
than you have so far managed to do.'[91]

On one of Iris's visits to Oxford before June 1943,[92] when Vera
Hoar took her Finals, she thought that Iris looked particularly
radiant. 'Go and sleep with some man ... it's a technique that
has to be learnt,' Iris sagely advised, a briskly matter-of-fact
memory that might be set against another. There was also the
emotional Iris who, as Leo noted, found the world in general
'tragic and moving'. Iris sometimes found love so, too. A Senior

Staff Officer at the Treasury, W.C. Roberts, MBE, saw her travelling home on a bus one winter evening in the 1943 blackout, the bus windows covered in scrim against bomb blast. (The war years found him writing the long – anonymous, of course – *His Majesty's Stationery Office Blue Book: A Digest of Pension Law*, with whose rulings on Civil Service pensions and conditions of service Iris would have been familiar.) Iris was peering out into the gloom through the little rectangle which was left clear and he realised with distress that she was silently sobbing, the tears running down her face. Treasury reserve was overcome and he moved to put a comforting arm about her.

'Miss Murdoch, what is the matter? Can I help in any way?'

'No thank you. I'm quite all right. It's just this love business,' she cried.

'Never mind,' he said, thinking it indiscreet to enquire further and having faith in both her common sense and her intelligence.[93] 'I'm sure it will work out all right in the end.'[94]

7

'A la Guerre, comme à la Guerre'
1943–1944

I ris's wartime letters, though kind, abound in anti-sentimental
pragmatism. While consoling Michael Foot on his hurt on
the occasion of Leonie Marsh's marriage, she remarks to
Frank, 'This sort of damn silly fidelity is rare enough in this bloody
matter-of-fact *chacun-pour-soi* existence.' This grim note of '*à la
guerre, comme à la guerre*' recurs. In November 1942 she wrote that
she missed Frank's 'burly self', and 'like all sensible people, I am
searching out substitutes'. Two months later, after recounting to
Frank her loss of virginity, she comments:

> Ersatz? Well, yes, a bit – but then all life is rather ersatz
> now, since the genuine articles have been separated from
> us – & he is a fool who does not go ahead on the basis
> of what he has.

This is bitter-sweet consolation, especially for one whose standards for marriage were, in Frank's own words, '1860 Baptist
Chapel'. He wanted both an idealistic wife who would believe
'crazily' that 'the whole of life can be cast anew',[1] and children.
Meanwhile Iris's lovers, she implies, are *inferior imitations* or substitutes for Frank himself, tokens of how much he is missed. Finally,
in March 1943 she writes:

> It isn't as if we all had endless lives & could say 'OK we'll
> put all that off till a better time'. Christ, this is the only
> time we've got, poor wretches, & we must make the best
> of it – our only lives and short enough of youth to enjoy
> them to the full.

Such briskness could sound cruel. When Iris reported to a friend that she had decided she was stronger than 'David' from the OULC, with whom she had spent a night, it is hard not to wonder how the chap in question felt about the verdict, albeit presumably unspoken. In one of her best novels, *A Fairly Honourable Defeat*, the devilish Julius taunts his listener, and the reader, by proclaiming that 'Human beings are essentially finders of substitutes. They never really see each other at all.' For the wise the first proposition might be true, but not the second.

Iris at this time was not wise, despite Frank's idealisation of her, and nor did the exigencies of war, with its endless sense of a nightmare present full of longing and dread, cut off from its future, necessarily encourage wisdom. 'How the war changed my life I only now begin to see and feel,' she noted in 1977;[2] and later: 'There is a kind of intensity, even rage, about that time when I had no notion what the future held.'[3] Though she never wrote directly about the war in her novels, her experiences during it inform all her fiction. She put photos of the narrow alley outside Seaforth into her album. The flat and the famous hothouse emotional atmosphere of the war alike incubated within her imagination.[4]

2

In the autumn of 1943 Philippa Bosanquet moved from Oxford to London. She worked as an economics research assistant at Chatham House in St James's Square on the prospects for post-war European economic reconstruction with American capital, together with representatives of governments-in-exile.[5] At first she lived sometimes in her close friend Anne Cobbe's rather grand flat in Weymouth Street, Marylebone, where she and Anne had a couple to look after them, but found this constricting (if meals are being prepared, you have to say when you will be in for them). So she gravitated more and more to the simplicity and freedom of Seaforth Place. But she was also looking for a place of her own, and found a rather flea-ridden but attractive flat in Fitzroy

Street, into which she put a bit of furniture. It was only when Iris said she supposed they would in future spend half the week together in Seaforth and the other half in Fitzroy Street that they started to laugh and realised it would be much easier for them both to stay where they were. So Philippa never moved in to the Fitzroy Street place, and by mid-October was living full-time with Iris, where she stayed until spring 1945. Chatham House was within walking distance. In 1944 the time of V1 and V2 rockets began: going to work in the mornings they would find various buildings had disappeared in the night;[6] they stepped through the resultant debris.[7]

On Philippa's first night Iris explained that she had insufficient blankets, and showed Philippa how to pull down the blackout material from the skylight to cover her bed. They were often cold. The ancient gas-cooker supplemented the single feeble gas-fire on bitter winter nights, when the girls went to bed fully dressed, even wearing their overcoats, taking hot-water bottles with them – by the end of the war, when rubber gave out, unyielding stone bottles. (Philippa, noting later how often hot-water bottles appeared in Iris's fiction, was unsurprised.) The Lyons tea-shop across Victoria Street gave them breakfast warmth, tea or coffee and sticky buns. Sometimes, though not often, older, richer friends like Thomas Balogh or Nickie Kaldor – those 'cloistered aliens, with un-British [i.e. left-wing] views', as Churchill remarked in the House of Commons, originally Philippa's friends, later very much Iris's also – would take them out to l'Etoile in Charlotte Street or the Gay Hussar. The men paid for the meal, as was then customary. The five-shilling limit on restaurant meals did something for social justice during that time of strict rationing. While clothes rationing did not worry them over-much, the fact that they had only three pairs of shoes between the two of them was troublesome, given the amount of walking that had to be done. The extremely broken-down and frayed state of Iris's shoes much impressed Philippa's sister Marion when they first met in a Chinese restaurant (one favoured dish: a plate, only, of plain boiled rice), more even than Iris's fairly elderly raincoat, which was to become a trademark, and her lack of make-up.

When Iris's single pair had eventually to be mended, Philippa lent her a pair of hers, and complained bitterly that she got them back as 'flat bottom boats', which was how they were from then on referred to.

Iris later recalled

> the good times at Seaforth, and how much we laughed together – 'the scene changes to Illyria' (as we leave the supper table uncleared): I had forgotten that. The cheese and cabbage. How P pulled down the blackout. The bomb that arrived just before the alarm clock went off (not quite so gay). P ironing my blouse with desperate slowness as I chafe to go out to a party . . . [8]

They were still young and 'ready for silliness', laughing a good deal, and with a closeness based on shared jokes and gossip about boyfriends. Once they decided to tell each other of the men who had asked to marry them. Philippa's 'list' was soon done. As Iris's went on and on Philippa asked crossly whether it might not save time if Iris listed the men who had *not* yet asked her to marry them.[9] Philippa had in 1942 become one of the unsatisfactory Thomas Balogh's girls. He had, he told a wartime colleague, a 'penchant for blue-stockings'. Charming and interesting to talk to when he wished but also sometimes violently irascible, rude and arrogant, selfish and unscrupulous, Balogh worked partly at Balliol, partly at the Institute of Statistics, which he had helped to found, in the New Bodleian, and partly on 'hush-hush' work in London,[10] whose importance he possibly exaggerated, staying each Wednesday in Nickie Kaldor's flat in Chelsea Cloisters. Philippa and Iris took care of each other – Philippa's health was for years precarious – not just in the light of Donald MacKinnon's ethic, but because of the natural protective anxiety of each and their easy affection for each other. MacKinnon stayed in touch with his protégées, worrying about Iris's wildness and bohemianism, perhaps unnecessarily.

On one occasion Iris helped an impoverished, distressed civil service friend to have an unwanted pregnancy safely terminated, a common enough wartime scenario. The girl concerned expressed lifelong gratitude towards Iris, who had 'taken upon herself the whole misery of the situation'. The event was celebrated by a party in Redcliffe Road, with the sailor who had impregnated her present. Iris was anything but light-hearted about this; indeed the sailor hoped she might be absent from the party, in case her presence turned it into a 'wake' (Iris did appear, bottle in hand and lugubrious). In a similar spirit she helped disseminate information, then hard to get, about contraception: both acts symptomatic of her regard for the freedom of women.

If politics generally played any part in their existence, it was probably no more than joining in the Trafalgar Square demonstrations for a 'Second Front *NOW!*' Iris struck Philippa by coming in from work and getting instantly into a book. Serious and orderly, she tidied things away if Philippa left them out.[11] Having been brought up mainly by governesses, Philippa still felt very ignorant and under-educated. Iris introduced her to the joys of Beckett's *Murphy*,* which they located with difficulty through a borough library, of Queneau's *Pierrot mon ami*,[12] of Dickens and of Proust, whole passages of whose *Le Côté de Guermantes* Book II Iris transcribed in a wartime journal, together with passages from *Murphy*. They had few, if any, quarrels. Having no fridge or larder, Iris kept food in her cupboard, where Philippa once commented on the strange odours it produced. And Iris was dilatory about 'Taking Measures' against the many mice which had eaten more than one of Frank's letters, and which left her 'sentimental with a fringe of annoyance'. Though she did at one stage start chemical warfare[13] she would, she wrote to Frank, encounter them on the stairs, and liked their 'nice long tails'. Philippa would jest, on their going to sleep, about whether Iris had remembered to leave out enough of their scant rations for them. Even Iris did not, on the other hand, collaborate with the rats, the sound of whose scrabblings was magnified behind the bathroom walls.

Iris loved ballet,[14] and Leonid Massine of all male dancers – 'one appreciates ballet with one's whole body';[15] both liked films –

* Denis Healey had introduced Iris to *Murphy*: see his *Time of my Life*.

especially René Clair's *Sous les toits de Paris*. They visited Philippa's grand home in Kirkleatham, North Yorkshire, where Iris's informality irritated Philippa's American mother. Kitchen staff were now absent because of the war, and Iris, strong-willed and without a by-your-leave, went to make sandwiches; on another occasion she pushed her plate away and put her head on the table. They also went to occasional parties in London, often on foot, and gave two, the first in autumn 1943, the second in May 1944.[16] Both the Hungarian expatriate economists Balogh and Nickie Kaldor (known to some as 'Buda' and 'Pest'), Dorothy Thom and Vera Hoar from Somerville, Mervyn James and Vernon Saunders[17] from Oriel, Jane Degras and her ex-burglar and author boyfriend Mark Benny, Stevie Smith and Tambimuttu came. Guests brought a bottle. James Meary Tambimuttu – 'a darling & has beautiful hair', wrote Iris[18] – editor of the leading poetry magazine of the 1940s, the bi-monthly *Poetry London*, and protégé of T.S. Eliot, had arrived in 1938 from Ceylon almost penniless.[19] The predicament of such uprooted people always awoke in Iris interest and compassion.

One escape from the cold of the flat was into the bohemian pub-life of 'Fitzrovia' – less an area of North Soho than a state of mind.[20] Iris danced with Dylan Thomas at the Gargoyle. She visited the Pillars of Hercules pub in Greek Street, met Dan Davin the Irish-New Zealand novelist and, in the Wheatsheaf, wild Mulk Raj Anand.[21] Arthur Koestler, whom she loathed, propositioned her insultingly at a party, and was rejected. She lent Ruth Kingsbury's Corona 4 typewriter to the Canadian prolet-kult prairie-poet and close friend of Orwell Paul Potts, who declined to return it, his need, as he put it, 'being greater than yours'.*[22] Keidrych Rhys – editor of *Poetry Wales* – gave her books and offered to marry her. She drank with Tambi, and tried to get a poem published in *Poetry London*, without success.[23]

---

* Iris, very put out, sent Ruth a cheque for £5 or £10 after the war, which Ruth declined to encash.

3

Iris, who had been writing stories and poems since she was a small child, was now starting to conceive of herself as an apprentice writer, as well as a 'bemused intellectual misfit'.[24] She did not dissent when Philippa said she had an entry in an imaginary diary reading 'Mem.: to make my mark.' Philippa was never in doubt that Iris would one day do something extraordinary. Iris wrote several fictions before publishing *Under the Net* in 1954 – sometimes she gave the figure as four, on one occasion six. A number were destroyed by her around 1986.[25] In the late autumn of 1944 she submitted her second novel, completed that July, to Tambimuttu's mentor T.S. Eliot at Faber & Faber, receiving a letter of rejection from the great man himself. He was right to reject it, she later thought, though the lack of any encouragement from him meant that she did not venture to apply to Faber again. For his part, Eliot had done her a favour. These early novels were 'too personal'. By the time she published successfully, she had learnt to burn the confessional and subjective out of her writing. Iris had entrusted part of one novel to a Somerville friend, Margaret Stanier, living in the country during the worst of the bombing, and told her she might if she wished read what Iris had written. Stanier, to whom about six manuscript notebooks were entrusted, recalls now only a heroine called Mary, who partly lived in Paris, and a group of young English characters. Iris later reported the novel 'lost in a taxi'. Friends were surprised that she had done nothing to retrieve it.[26] It is probable that this loss was a convenient fiction (as well as a homage to T.E. Lawrence, who had similarly lost a draft of *Seven Pillars of Wisdom*) to cover the pain and embarrassment of Eliot's rejection, which elsewhere she ascribed to wartime paper shortage. 'I so hate the sight of it, I haven't the heart to try any other publisher,' she wrote in February 1945.[27]

Iris's 1943 letters to Frank abound in references to her desire to write. In January:

I have no time to live my own life – at a time when my own life feels of intense value & interest to me. Jesus God how I want to write. I want to write a long, long & exceedingly obscure novel objectifying the queer conflicts I find within myself & observe in the characters of others. Like Proust I want to escape from the eternal push and rattle of time into the coolness & poise of a work of art.

In July: 'My chief thought will probably be "Whether or not I am a writer" – a thought which has obsessed me all the year, & grows in proportion daily, like an angel I am wrestling with.' And in August: 'Writing is the only activity which makes me feel, "Only I could produce *this*."' Philippa, who read one of Iris's wartime novels, recalls a character called Stuart who sprang up some steps out of the underground 'erect with longing', a *double entendre* Iris presumably did not intend, and if so a symptom of the mysterious innocence accompanying her love-life. John Bayley recalled a paragraph about the 'little red bee' of desire which the heroine, detached if not disassociated, is surprised and possibly irritated to register within her brain, while a boor puts a hairy leg over hers in bed, murmuring in her ear: 'You know you want it.'

Fragments of three 'lost' novels survive. The earliest, on a few loose leaves, features characters called (indeed) Stuart and also Peter, Damien, Benedicta, Hilary and Morgen. The second, volume IV of which was started in January 1945, is some pages of an otherwise lost manuscript with the characters John, Valery, Pete, an Oxford classicist called only 'The Professor',[28] and Christie, 'a *mystic*' (Iris's emphasis) who loves Mark. Set in Oxford and London, it has a pleasing reference – considering the direction Iris's Platonism would take her twenty years later – to the statue of Eros in Piccadilly Circus, 'high above the gyrating traffic', 'poised and still, most gross & simple, a most refined & strange little god'. The Professor struggles with being incarnate, being attracted to girls, and appears a cross between Fraenkel and MacKinnon.

Mark, who wishes to write a book on Pindar, Frank's favourite Greek poet, is a heroic portrait of Frank. He is acutely focused as having the rare combination of 'great intelligence with great warmth'. Mozart's '*Voi che Sapete*', which Iris had heard in Frank's rooms in New College in spring 1939, makes an appearance. Mark 'wants to act, he wants to commit himself', and feels consumed by a flame of love enabling him to rise above 'the mud of ambiguity' and indecision in which the others are embroiled. He is to be offered an Oxford Fellowship but may reject it. A lengthy analysis of the last free Spanish elections, in February 1936, must be there to deck out Mark/Frank's political passion. Frank was profoundly affected by the death of his friend Anthony Carritt with the International Brigade in 1937, and saw the Second World War as a continuation of that struggle by other means. Mark identifies more with Lenin than with Christ, since Lenin is 'less concerned with the value of his individual righteousness', and is thus the more completely self-effacing of the two.

A.N. Wilson once wittily remarked that Iris joined the Communist Party for 'religious' reasons.[29] She left it for religious reasons too. The choice between Lenin and Christ might be said to underpin her only wartime publications, three reviews in the *Adelphi* in 1943 and 1944. The magazine's founder John Middleton Murry, who in 1931 had published *The Necessity of Communism*, now veered towards the semi-mystical, seeing life as a spiritual search. The *Adelphi* explored spirituality without orthodoxy. Possibly MacKinnon suggested that Iris write for it.[30] In her first review, in January–March 1943, of 'Nicodemus's' *Midnight Hour*, she three times disclaims being, herself, a Christian. This is indeed to 'protest too much'. In 1941 she had, in a *New Statesman* letter written on behalf of the OULC, attacked the philosopher C.E.M. Joad's 'liberal ethics of the nineteenth century' and his facile invocation to 'truth, beauty, goodness and love' alike. At that time she held Plato in contempt. Her 1943 review marks a turn towards a later position, which would purge and reconstruct those ethics, and invoked Plato to do so. She now attempts to imagine and understand the wartime Christian 'spiritual pilgrimage' in the book under review. 'Nicodemus' (a name taken from St John, 3: 1–4) was the *nom-de plume* of one Melville Salter Chaning-Pearce, and the book, an intimate spiritual journal, charted his dark night of the soul as a failed ordin-

and. How, asks Iris, do his spiritual struggle and quest connect with 'Malta and Stalingrad and Coventry'?

> One may sympathise with this horror that turns its face utterly from this world as from a place of unrelieved filth and corruption – but the problem of the 'return to the Cave' remains a very real one for Christianity.

She identifies herself, too, with the figure of the 'artist', as the following passage, with its echo of Auden's December 1938 poem 'The Novelist', who 'suffers dully all the wrongs of man', makes clear:

> [Nicodemus] compares the apartness of the artist with that of the saint. But the artist is not 'apart' in this sense. He sees the earth freshly and strangely; but he is inside the things he sees and speaks of, as well as outside them. He is of their substance, he suffers with them. Of saints I know nothing.

In the succeeding reviews she notes, again, the necessity that Christianity grapple with the real world before it can win the respect of her disaffected generation. Christianity needs to condemn 'a disintegrating capitalist society which can offer only an endless prospect of exploitation and war', and must take sides in the choice between 'some form of' Socialism and Fascism, and champion that common life which is, for the majority, 'such an all-absorbing, degrading and hopeless affair'.[31]

The advocacy merely of 'some form of' Socialism, like her 1942 championing of the Fitzrovia bohemians despite their 'utter lack of any political sense', suggests a weakening of Iris's doctrinaire Communism. A passionate religious sense can perfectly well coexist with an impassioned political radicalism, as the careers of Walter Benjamin and Simone Weil alike make clear, both mystics, both Marxists. Yet Iris, like Orwell, often opposes religion and politics. In many letters to Frank she talks about her growing interest in Christianity. In spring 1942, and awaiting life after Finals:

> After June I must a) read the Bible and b) go into the history of the Roman Catholic Church which *fascinates*

me . . . Christianity, you know, when you get away from it a bit and really see it, is a most amazing and almost incredible phenomenon. How does it look from Galilee? What a beautiful, queer, unexpected world it is. Christ, what a miserable, humiliated, broken, & altogether bloody world it is. I do believe in the future though – I believe tremendously. My God, we'll make something of this hole-&-corner planet of ours . . .

In autumn 1942 she is 'reading a great deal, mainly theology at the moment which you mightn't approve of, but don't worry, Jesus won't get me'. By 6 July 1943, strikingly: 'Better than being an Epicurean, to be a Kantian, *and better still to believe in the True Gospel*' (my emphasis). Early July 1943 was a crucial time in both Iris and Frank's stories. She adds how unbearable she finds the 'suppression of the individual most Eastern philosophies have at their heart'. The following month, 'I am re-reading large sections of the Bible.' MacKinnon, despite crises and breaks in their friendship, feared for Iris's soul and worked towards her Christian conversion. Although he asked Philippa, a little sententiously and inappropriately, to look after Iris, MacKinnon could appreciate Philippa's own idea of her role – to make Iris laugh, to help keep her happy. When Philippa asked him whether she needed to be a Christian too, he replied after some thought, 'No; it's not necessary.'

Frank, who, apart from the image of the Madonna, then hated Roman Catholicism, nonetheless wrote to another friend, a Christian pacifist,[32] that of Christ's sayings he 'liked best the one about losing one's life and gaining it'; and, thinking Christ's death an even more splendid gesture than Socrates', wrote his best-known poem, 'Polliciti Meliora: an epitaph for my Friends', informed by the sentiment of self-sacrifice. Other English soldier-poets either fought in wars we remember little of (Sir Philip Sidney) or which generated poetry out of futile human sacrifice (Brooke, Owen). Frank's, though the rhetoric was low-key, was a just war:

> As one who, gazing at a vista
> Of beauty, sees the clouds close in
> And turns his back in sorrow, hearing
> The thunderclaps begin

So we, whose life was all before us,
Our hearts with sunlight filled,
Left in the hills our books and flowers,
Descended, and were killed

Write on the stone no words of sadness,
– Only the gladness due
That we, who asked the most of living,
Knew how to give it too.

4

By the time Iris was writing about Christie and Mark, her and Philippa's lives had undergone an interlude as strange and painful as anything in her fiction, and the little red bee had not been inactive. With the capricious and improbable symmetry that marks her fictional imagination, she and Philippa exchanged lovers. Two years later Iris wrote to Philippa: 'One doesn't – as I know you realize – get over an *histoire* like that of 1944 very quickly. When one has behaved as I then behaved to two people one loves, the hurt and the sense of guilt go very deep.' At the time it seemed to happen with an unconscious logic of its own.

The original love-quartet of Michael in love with Leonie, who loved Frank, who loved Iris, had been decisively broken by Leonie marrying Tony Platt in January 1941. Leonie would not see Michael at that point, and Iris, as she wrote to Frank, consoled him. 'Dear old Michael. A lost soul too.' He was grateful, buying her a box of expensive Turkish cigarettes for Christmas that year, and making her sole beneficiary of an early will; indeed, soon he was head over heels in love with her, pursuing her, by his own account, for months. They went away together for a weekend at Betty Pinney's (who did not care for Iris) in Dorset early in 1943. Iris, torn and undecided, finally refused him. Michael wrote to Frank on 2 April about working with the sense of feeling knocked down.

On 9 July 1943 she finally told him that she would spend the night with him, in his pleasantly austere rooms above a printer's shop[33] at 48 Rochester Row,[34] not far from Seaforth. Michael, an Army Captain on the Intelligence Staff, was working at Combined Operations HQ at Richmond Terrace, opposite Downing Street, with a view over the Thames. He handled a good deal of secret information. Above all, he knew that that night the invasion of Sicily was to start, although he could not tell Iris. He did not then know – though he shortly guessed from a letter-code – that Frank was taking part in the landings, near Catania.

'Who says that one swallow doesn't make a summer?' asked Michael rhetorically, shortly after. In fact this was an inauspicious start to an unhappy affair, which dragged on until early the following year. Michael had been at Winchester with Frank, and in becoming his lover Iris was arguably getting as close to Frank himself as she could manage. She was not able to conceal this from Michael, who perceived himself a 'stand-in'. In September she wrote but did not send Frank a love poem, 'For WFT', whose conceit is that when they were physically close in Oxford, she measured their distance: now they are separated he is close to her heart.* Michael noted uneasily Iris's growing preoccupation with Frank, feeling that she and Frank were kindred 'free spirits'. They were, for example, more serious about their writing, and about literature in general, than was Michael. They all wrote and circulated their poems to each other, and Iris had told Frank that Michael's poems revealed 'a very sensitive appreciation of the beautiful & an intense desire for it. Like most of our juvenilia . . .', but lacked 'clarity & originality'. By contrast she wrote to Frank in October 1943 that he must be changing a great deal, though 'it's hard for me to measure the stuff of the change from your

---

* 'For WFT': Not far from the green garden, folded in/Your room, your story & your arms, I guaged [*sic*]/With a heart quietly beating the long/Long gulf between us. Summer hung/Its colours on the window, & a song/Swept over us from the gramophone./Now, in a sad September, gilt with leaves, I am without you, & as many miles/Of sea and mountain part us, as my thoughts/Could then imagine of our separateness./[Yet you speak simply & your human voice/Gentle as ever: deleted] Yet, listening at last, I have caught/That human echo in your tone that might/Call me to love. Nearer, far nearer to my heart/You lie now, distantly in your grief's desert than/When all your candid years did homage then' (16 September 1943). Frank had begun a flirtation with his Greek teacher Maroula Thalis in August, and was possibly writing less frequently to Iris that summer.

letters – which are in the old vein, though so much more adult
& so infinitely enriched'. In the same letter she requests his photograph, and promises one of her own. That she was bedding his
friend cannot have been comfortable for her. The sense of being
a stand-in for a Frank whom, he noted, Iris now in some sense
loved, was also acutely uncomfortable for Michael. They had been
friendly rivals at school,[35] and had exchanged many letters during
the war. That July Michael apologised for baselessly accusing
Frank of melancholy, and added that Iris was reported as 'missing
life in the pursuit of art'.

Iris was Michael's first lover, and though he knew he was not
hers, she did not appear to him experienced either. He had
won where Frank had failed, without much joy, though their
lovemaking was eventually unbroken even by air raids. He tried
to cook meals for Iris; she never. He was scrupulous about wartime
decorum and secrecy, never telling her about Combined Operations, or enquiring what work she was doing, assuming – quite
wrongly – that it was of national importance. Yet when a coded
address on a letter from Frank revealed to Michael that he was
in Sicily, his gentlemanly willingness to put Iris's peace of mind,
and indeed Iris and Frank's 'cause', before his own, made him
tell Iris. So, on the 'baking breathless hot evening' of Thursday,
29 July, a day she had penned a short lyric 'For Michael: Bettis-
combe in July', Iris also wrote to Frank wondering 'greatly
whether . . . you are in Sicily' and requesting a postcard 'enumer-
ating the Sicilian antiquities which you have preserved from the
British hordes'.

In September 1943 Philippa borrowed 'Tommy' Balogh's
empty cottage in Dorchester (outside Oxford) for a week,[36] and
Iris accompanied her. Iris bought Hölderlin's poems,[37] got asthma
when a pan of fat caught fire, sent an ecstatic postcard home
about the beauty of the countryside. Philippa moved into Seaforth
that October, and they gave a party to which Tommy came. Soon
Iris informed Philippa that she and Balogh were now also lovers.
Philippa, who like many of Tommy's girls had had an 'off-on'
relationship with him for two years and then thought herself
disengaged, was nonetheless aggrieved and jealous at the sheer

speed with which he had moved from one flatmate to the other, not to speak of the rapidity of Iris's move, or the deception of both, and spent a sleepless night. The lines from 'The Agamemnon Class 1939', about how *then* – before the war – they had known nothing of 'betrayal of lover or friend' take on new force. Philippa read, much later, *The Black Prince* with its meditation on the perils of introducing friends: 'Of course one fears treachery. What human fear is deeper?' For an interlude she felt herself excluded. Iris was like a force of nature.

Michael suffered very directly from Iris's divided affections, while she, in thrall to Balogh,[38] averted her gaze. Early in 1944, moreover, egged on by Balogh, who while willing to run more than one affair at a time himself would not tolerate a rival,[39] she with some cruelty gave Michael his marching orders. *A la guerre, comme à la guerre.* 'It has not been a good winter,' Michael wrote to Frank on Easter Sunday 1944, without naming any of the participants, 'and it all ends in dumb failure and tighter twists than before. It's one of many stories you shall hear from one of us after the war.' Michael had a recurrent vivid dream of a friendly and reassuring Frank appearing in his rooms to grasp his hand. But each time, before they could talk, the dream ended, the dream-Frank vanishing away.

In Iris's absence, Michael, disconsolate, paid a visit to Seaforth in April 1944. Iris had some time before pointed Philippa out distantly to him in the tea-shop in Victoria Street.[40] Now he left a note at the empty flat, mentioning a time that he might call again. Philippa, who had not before set eyes on him but who hated the careless cruelty with which he had been dispatched by Iris and Tommy, fell in love at first sight. Michael was both heartbreakingly beautiful and also unhappy. They were soon lovers, most happily and successfully. The comic properties of the situation were then clear to none of them. The times lent themselves to intensity.

'There *were* roses round the door,' Iris tried to reassure Philippa of her ill-fated affair with Tommy, with whom there were 'idyllic' weekends at his Dorchester cottage. She had a pet name for him;[41] marriage was spoken of.[42] Philippa thought she had the better bargain, and time proved her right. It was Balogh who caused Iris those tears on the bus; happiness absorbed Philippa and Michael. On one early occasion Philippa banished Iris from the flat, to avoid Michael being hurt by seeing her, and because they wanted to be by themselves. 'All right, I'm going, I'm going,' Iris cried, collecting her things. It was time for her to feel excluded and rejected.

A period of trial awaited them all. Michael had joined the SAS* in February, was stationed in Scotland for much of that spring, training as a parachutist and coming down intermittently to London. By May 1944 he was in a tent at Moor Park, just outside London, HQ of 'Boy' Browning, who was in command of all airborne troops. He and Philippa were engaged that June. Michael had been absent one night helping bring home an agent from France, as Philippa much later discovered, and he forewarned her that he might suddenly disappear again, and was not to be questioned. At his request she sewed into his uniform a compass, a silk road-map of France, and a file. On 15 July her birthday present to Iris was Alex Comfort's book of poems *Elegies*, inscribed merely, 'Iris from Pip'. In late August, a month in which Iris was anxiously awaiting news of Frank, Michael disappeared. Philippa wore his watch and looked after his bicycle and waited. MacKinnon wrote daily letters which brought some comfort. Philippa, when sleepless with worry, would walk the streets of bombed-out London at night, as far as the City and back.

5

Frank, taking part in the 10 July invasion of Sicily, led his unit with distinction,† although there is no record of his ever having fired in anger. Leonie Marsh wrote to him that 'one day the "good" will triumph', and that his gun tended to jam because

---

* The Special Air Service was formed in October 1941 as a parachutist-commando unit, initially for use in the Middle East.
† He began training with Phantom for the Sicilian landings some time after February 1943.

he had 'real brotherly love in him' and so did not wish to kill.[43] Like his father, Frank was 'more & more inclined to Buddhism'.* Iris too wrote to him, 'There is no bitterness in your letters.'[44] Approaching the Sicilian coast, most of the landing force feared a 'barren, waterless, disease and sirocco-scourged island peopled with imbeciles and murderers'. For Frank, by contrast, Sicily was the island Theocritus, the Emperor Frederick and Matthew Arnold had all hymned, 'an eclogue' itself, where Pindar had eulogised the tyrants of Syracuse, and where Aeschylus lay buried at Gela.

On the long night-time approach Frank encouraged his unit, dished out the rum ration, lit up his pipe. Two mortar shells killed the crew of the landing craft as they landed, setting the stern ablaze. Another took most of the arm and leg off a fellow a few paces in front, who fell, groaning. To calm his badly shaken men, Frank led the way to a safe wadi reeking of thyme and mint and nearby lemon groves, encouraging them to start blackberrying. Looking at him a little oddly, they joined in. 'The English, whom Europe understands so little and needs so much' – a reciprocal state of affairs, he noted – 'had returned to her after two years of absence.' He spent some hours tramping out of his way to return a tuppeny-ha'penny watch stolen from a child of sixteen by a British soldier, meditating mordantly that when the Germans conquered an East European town they, by contrast, shot 50,000 inhabitants and sent the best-looking girls to military brothels.

He read *War and Peace* in Italian: 'However villainous the character', the great Russian novelists 'never for one moment let you forget his humanity'. In Malta on 15 July there were so many courting couples he felt 'sick with envy', and the incurious philistinism of most of his brother-officers made him feel estranged. They stayed in the mess playing cards; he roamed and looked, trying to understand what he was watching and recording in his journals and letters.

---

* In January 1944 he wrote to his 'folks' that this year he would have the chance of following one of the Buddha's eight-fold paths: Right Living.

He had written to Iris on 23 May from Alexandria:

> Today I want to talk to you about the Greeks because
> they are staunch anti-Fascists, because they are simply
> among the best people I have met, because they are very
> much the same Greeks who fought at Scamander and
> Marathon, drove their chariot by the weeping firs on the
> Hill of Kronos or packed the slopes of the Acropolos to
> hear the Agamemnon . . .

Peter Wright, who met Frank in Cairo, was also working in
SOE Greek section. They found attending briefings agonising.
Frank had chosen Greece partly because he was a Greek scholar,
mainly because he was so impressed by the bravery of the CP-led
resistance groups ELAS and EAM. British policy was nominally
to support all genuine resistance movements, but in fact, it
became clear, the British gave the Communist-led groups credit
only grudgingly, if at all, for brave and effective action, and sometimes distorted intelligence reports to give the royalist Zervas
equal – and undeserved – credit. Frank, furious, negotiated a
posting in Serbia. He struck Wright as a 'fine dreamer, a versatile
scholar and a true internationalist'. Wright saw Frank just before
his departure for Macedonia, cheerful, confident, keenly aware
that he was going not merely on an adventure, but to help liberate
Europe from Fascism.

6

Letter-writing, of course, is a performance art, as Frank implicitly
acknowledged in addressing Iris's enthusiasm for *Antony and Cleopatra* a year before:

> I too am very fond of [it]. There is something uncanny
> about the way in which these slightly sordid middle-aged
> lovers, who have talked very little but drivel for the first
> three acts, suddenly rise in the last two to the very pin-
> nacle of poetry, and blaze their trail across the mind of
> humanity for all time. It is in a way a promise to all of

us lesser folks ... that we might, in our time and on our own level, provided we still have the grace to be dissatisfied, know a moment like Antony's.

He had expressed one kind of self-dramatisation earlier in the war when he wrote facetiously, 'I am, if anything, too brilliant. I am afraid that this, my precocity, will prove a flash in the pan. I shall be burned out at 23. I must seek an early death to keep my fame untarnished and immortal.' By December 1943 he now 'harbour[s] a good deal of malice' towards that pseudo-heroic mode which had accompanied his volunteering three months before for parachute duties. Demoralised in base camp, he wrote to Iris about the detail of life in Cairo; and:

> I still press for active work because it suits my tempera-
> ment better than sitting in an office ... [But] it won't
> be a tragedy if I survive the war. I can see so many evil
> and petty men surviving well entrenched. For all my vices,
> I don't think I am either of these. Every man of good
> will is going to be badly needed in the years that lie
> ahead ... [I] don't say it to reassure you, nor even myself.

To his family he wrote: 'I find that more and more of my delight in living comes from isolated moments of perception. The Nile at sunrise, a tortoise-shell cat ... a small girl in a grey frock, with long black cavalier curls ... picking white chrysan-thema, and the last white roses before the frost.' And with a greater rhetorical up-beat:

> My Christmas message to you is one of greater hope than
> I have ever had in my life before. There is a spirit abroad
> in Europe finer and braver than anything that tired conti-
> nent has known for centuries and which cannot be withs-
> tood. You can, if you like, think of it in terms of politics,
> but it is broader and more generous than any dogma. It
> is the confident will of whole peoples who have known
> the utmost humiliation and suffering and have tri-
> umphed over it to build their own life once and for all
> ... all that is required from Britain, America and the
> USSR is imagination, help and sympathy.

'No sicker epitaph for the Second World War', as Frank's brother E.P. Thompson observed, was ever written.[45] Frank goes on: '1944 is going to be a good year though a terrible one,' and on 26 December 1943 he wrote to Iris of arriving at a watershed in his life, and of 'profoundly moving experiences':

> I have had the honour to meet and talk to some of the best people in the world. People whom, when the truth is known, Europe will recognise as among the finest and toughest she has ever borne. Meeting them has made me utterly disgusted with some aspects of my present life, reminding me that all my waking hours should be dedicated to one purpose only. This sounds like all new year's resolutions, but in this case I think I shall soon have a change in my way of living which will give me a real chance. Nothing else matters. We must crush the Nazis and build our whole life anew.
>
> 'If we should meet again, why then, we'll smile.' If not, why then those that follow us will be able to smile far more happily and honestly in the world we all helped to make. No men are more disarming in their gaiety than these men our allies, who have known more suffering than we can easily imagine.

7

Frank wrote to Leo Pliatzky saying he was to go on a special mission, quoting the *Aeneid*. He was very fit. He had learnt Serbo-Croat – 'plum-easy' – and Bulgarian too – 'simply Russian as a Turk would talk it' – and early noted that 'even the old peasant Bulgars will turn in the end – just you see'. On the night of 25 January 1944 he was dropped, with supplies, onto the high Serbian plateau at Dobro Polje. Code-named 'Claridges', his mission was to remain on the Serb-Bulgarian frontier and act as a base for the four men in 'Mulligatawny', led by Major Mostyn Davies, which was alone to move into Bulgaria. The plan was ill-conceived and ill-executed.

It began badly. For two months on snowy, mountainous terrain, hunted from camp to camp, the missions evaded capture. Bad weather was blamed for the unpredictability of drops of supplies. On 18 March more than ten thousand troops, mainly Bulgarian, encircled the whole South Serbian plateau. Partisans and refugees repeatedly escaped from ambush, at terrible cost in terms of casualties. An old mill by a stream, with Frank, Davies and a wireless-telegraphy operator within it, was attacked by hand-grenade on the twenty-second or twenty-third. Only Frank got out alive, through a back window, hiding for a day or two in the snow, then in a haystack, until rescued by a peasant, who showed a small partisan unit how to reach him. Together with two Mulliga-tawny survivors they moved towards Macedonia where, in Tergovi-ste on 21 April, Frank at last found time to write three letters.

To his parents he laconically writes that he 'now hold[s] the record for the twenty yards sprint for three major battle areas'. He misses England, 'where they really know how to organise Spring. But I want to see dog's tooth violets and red winged blackbirds before I go over the hill.' To his brother E.P., then engaged in the long assault on Monte Cassino, he promises a post-war walking tour, with frequent stops at pubs. And to Iris he writes a letter, citing *Agamemnon* 418–19, and making clear that he has, from her letters, put together a picture of events at home.

> Irushka!
> Sorry I haven't written for so long. Old Brotoloig seems to have been monopolising my attention. I know forgiveness is one of your chief virtues. Three air-mail letter-cards from you, bringing me up to the end of JAN.

'Brotoloigos' is the Homeric epithet for Ares, god of war, mean-ing plague-like or baneful. Iris had clearly been unhappy. The stoicism, sweetness, warmth and intelligence of Frank's letter is remarkable, written as it self-effacingly is in the midst of so many perils.

> . . . You know quite well there's no danger of your suc-cumbing to [weariness of soul]. You have springs within you that will never fail . . . I can't say precisely what your

role in life will be, but I should say it will certainly be a literary-humanistic one.

A whimsical prologue envisages the different kinds of *literatteur* Iris, Hal, Leo and Michael Foot might be after the war. 'Does this restore your faith in yourself & your mission? It certainly should ... I can't think why you are so interested in MORALS. Chiefly a question of the liver and digestive organs I assure you.' The important task of the moment, he argues, is by contrast 'the question of building a new communal ethic'. He continues:

My own list of priorities is as follows:

1. People and everything to do with people, their habits, their loves and hates, their arts, their languages. Everything of importance revolves around people.

2. Animals and flowers. These bring me a constant undercurrent of joy. Just now I'm revelling in plum blossom and young lambs and the first leaves on the briar roses. One doesn't need any more than these. I couldn't wish for better company.

These are enough for a hundred lifetimes. And yet I must confess to being very fond of food and drink also.

I envy you and Michael in one way. All this time you are doing important things like falling in and out of love – things which broaden and deepen and strengthen the character more surely than anything else. I can honestly say I've never been in love. When I pined for you I was too young to know what I was doing – no offence meant. Since then I haven't lost an hour's sleep over any of Eve's daughters. This means I'm growing up lop-sided, an overgrown boy. Ah well, – I shall find time, Cassius, I shall find time.

All the same, I don't think you should fall for 'emotional fascists' – Try to avoid that.

This 'emotional fascist' – a recurrent psychological type in Iris's life – is Balogh, over whom her Treasury work was now suffering, and who cost her many tears. It is impossible to judge how hard-won is Frank's tone of dispassionate objectivity. He had had romantic friendships, Iris knew, with two girls, one Polish, one

Greek,* and had written some time before to Iris as 'soul-sister', relishing the phrase's Shelleyan and incestuous ambiguities. And certainly he had other matters to worry about. The lack of irony in his account of the character-forming 'importance' of falling in and out of love is breathtaking, a simplicity capable of stinging.

Julius Caesar, that great play about friendship and betrayal, had provided the *leitmotiv* of his December letter, with Brutus's 'If we should meet again' from Act V. He now quotes Brutus from the following scene about finding time, later, to grieve for the death of Cassius, after the battle of Philippi: 'Friends, I owe more tears/ To this dead man than you shall see me pay.' The ironies of 'I shall find time, Cassius, I shall find time' are almost unbearable. Time was exactly what was now in short supply, and he knew it.

On 17 May he marched with the 2nd Sofia Partisan Brigade from the Serbian frontier into the heart of Bulgaria, where conditions were worse. It was a fateful move, a 'military folly of the first order'.[46] The brave but inexperienced Bulgarian partisans were, as he reported 'too badly armed and scattered to be made into serious nation-wide force before big day'; a less charitable observer called them a horror-comic army.[47] Bulgaria, moreover, unlike Yugoslavia, though not at war with the USSR, was an Axis ally. The Bulgarian occupation of Thrace and Macedonia was noted for its brutality – 'most murders were accompanied by torture, most rapes ... ended with murder',[48] and the partisans knew that their end, if caught, would be messy. Frank had wired SOE Cairo on 29 April, requesting 'general direction soonest'. He received no answer.

As in good tragedy, many malign forces were at work. There was the 'characteristic military balls-up' that dropped Frank's new wireless operator – Sergeant Kenneth Scott – and his code-book in two very different places. Then SOE headquarters was moving from Cairo to under-staffed Bari in Italy, where Frank's desperate pleas for food and arms had to be decoded and recoded, in both directions, with a resultant delay of two to three days even in messages being received. 'Pinpoints' for drops were persistently

---

* Corporal Emilia Krzyprowna and Maroula Thalis.

lost under pressure of enemy advance. Cairo received no message from Frank after 11 May. By the time the matter of the code-book was sorted out he was in Bulgaria, involved in running battles and wild marches across mountains. Scott's wireless equipment, always dicey as well as heavy, requiring a mule to carry it, fell into a river during one ambush. They covered fifty kilometres a day across pathless ground for nine days without a break under conditions of terrible hardship. Once during a march Frank, exhausted, fell asleep and dropped over a small cliff into a river. They were by now lice-ridden – 'Enemy number 2', they would joke. They had had no food for fifteen days, and were so hungry they ate live wood-snails and unripe cherries. It may have been the need for food that drove them, despite a government bribe for the head of each partisan of up to 50,000 lev, to a village, where they bought bread – Frank putting his cap beneath his chin to catch each crumb. On 31 May 1944 they were betrayed.

Near Litakovo, north of Sofia, Major Frank Thompson – wearing the British uniform that should have protected him – was captured together with his unit. They were tied up, kicked, spat at by villagers angered by the Allied bombing of Sofia, beaten with fists, pistols, rifles and once, during the interrogations that continued by day and by night, a truncheon. A Gestapo officer was present.[49] They were sometimes deprived of sleep, and there were terrible cries from the cells where the women were held. His gentle colleague Yordanka was raped, then killed.

Raina Sharova, who claimed to have been an eye-witness, gave a theatrical, oft-repeated and unreliable account of the last days.[50] It ran as follows. Frank may have been tortured.[51] His claims for protection as a prisoner of war under the Geneva Convention were ignored. He revealed nothing. During his imprisonment he was calm and observant despite a fever. After an old peasant woman spoke up bravely in his defence, Frank and his companions were given bread and onions to eat.[52] On 18 January he had written that even the death of a democrat is in a sense creative: 'One or ten or a hundred new democrats are created by his example.' 'I don't despair,' he answered a query in Bulgarian, 'but time flies very fast.'[53] The decapitated heads of colleagues appeared, piked, in the square.

The villagers could not be persuaded to enact the lynching the authorities required, and during a staged trial Frank much impressed his hearers by calmly smoking his pipe while leaning against a pillar, dismissing the interpreter and answering questions in idiomatic Bulgarian.[54] He avowed Communism at this trial. Found guilty around 7 June,[55] when the second front that he so longed for was finally opening in Normandy, he was taken with his men and four other officers for execution.

> Major Thompson took charge of the condemned men and led them to the castle. As they marched off before the assembled people, he raised a clenched fist, the salute of the Fatherland Front which the Allies were helping. A gendarme struck his arm down, but Thompson called out to the people, 'I give you the Salute of Freedom!' All the men died raising this salute. The spectators were sobbing, many present declared the scene was one of the most moving in all Bulgarian history, that the men's amazing courage was the work of the English Officer who carried their spirits, as well as his own.[56]

They were hurriedly buried in an unmarked grave. A volume of Catullus was found in Frank's pocket, and a Byzantine coin, sewn into his tunic, was kept by a collaborator. These, in time, were returned to Iris.[57]

8

The last letters of Bulgarian partisans, generally apologising for the troubles they had brought upon their parents, were often doctored as Party declarations.[58] Thus too the authorised, pious version of Frank's death – dying with Botev's 'Song of Freedom' on his lips – gave a heroic ancestry and legitimacy to the new Bulgarian Communist regime. Iris had no reason to disbelieve it. Some of it – the bread and onions, and also Frank's courage – is true.[59] But now, after the fall of Communism, Litakovo villagers say emphatically that there was no 'trial' of any kind, merely brutal interrogation.* Litakovo was a killing-ground for partisans, where none survived. Those who had offered them food or shelter were treated with 'exceptional cruelty' – the atmosphere was terrifying, uncontrolled and wild. The villagers had witnessed bodies, some decomposing, dragged into the village behind carts for weeks, and had also been forced to witness executions and then walk, or even dance to a band playing, around the bodies to show disrespect. Some victims were beaten to death in the public square. Sashka Razgradlian, a nineteen-year-old Jewish partisan from Sofia, was in late May raped, forced to dig her own grave, and buried alive.

Naku Staminov, then twelve years old, whose parents' house fronted the square, followed a group of about twelve partisans including Frank, the tallest and handsomest and strongest, who was chewing something. Frank wore a green jacket with a zip-fastener, and Naku later recognised his picture in a newspaper as that of the foreigner whose murder he had unexpectedly watched. The partisans were surrounded by gendarmerie but seemed calm. Later Naku learned they had been told a lie: they believed they were being marched to another village. There was complete silence; then they were shot in a ditch. Frank half-turned, shouting something furiously in English before being raked with fire across the shoulders. The bodies were then injected – presumably with poison – to ensure that there had

---

* They include Todorka Kotseva, pro-gymnasium headmistress, official guide to the monument and the events of 1944, familiar with evidence collected from villagers for a 1986 exhibition; the Litakovo Mayor Svetlana Toderova; and the partisan Slavcho Trunski, Frank's acting General, speaking two weeks before his death, in November 1999. Trunski is a key witness, for as Bulgaria's Deputy Minister of Defence the two books he had written on Frank gave currency to the story of the staged trial. Robert Conquest, press attaché to the Allied Control Commission in Bulgaria from 1944 to 1947, suggested to Topencharov, then Director of Press, that something be done to honour Frank, which would redound to the credit of the Bulgarian Communist Party's image, as well as to that of the British. The naming of a railway station near Sofia after Frank, and his reburial with his mother Theo and his brother E.P. present, followed. Though he did not know, or know of, Sharova, Conquest is 'sure the trial story was a later invention' (letter to the author, 17 December 1999), and believes that at most a 'drumhead' trial without speeches might have occurred. There is nothing in Znepolski's *Memoirs* (1998) about a trial.

been no mistake. Frank was the last to stop convulsing. A ring was cut off his finger with a knife. Naku was sick with terror for months afterwards. He thought normal life could never begin again.*

9

E.P. Thompson's *Beyond the Frontier* movingly analyses the forces that led up to this moment. The very small, weak Bulgarian partisan forces were attacking a regime which both Britain and a by now rapidly advancing Russia were alike – and competitively – wooing. The Cold War, which saw a global extension of such rivalries, was in view. On 6 April 1944 Churchill minuted: 'We are purging all our secret establishments of Communists because we know they owe no allegiance to us or our cause and will always betray secrets to the Soviet.'[60]

It is a sick irony that Frank Thompson, that gentle and gifted apostle of internationalism, may have been among the Cold War's first victims. 'How wonderful it would be to call Europe one's fatherland, and think of Krakow, Munich, Rome, Arles, Madrid as one's own cities.' Was he still a Communist? He had praised Communism to the partisans, without avowing the creed himself, perhaps doubting that he would be believed. He was not in contact with the headquarters of the CPGB in King Street, near Covent Garden market, or with the Comintern, and E.P. thought his Communism, which went with a deep sense of democracy,

---

* The report of the Allied Control Commission's official inquiry, recently uncovered in Bulgaria, corroborates Naku Staminov. Frank Thompson was shot on the orders of Captain Stoianov, who was tried and condemned for exceeding his authority, illegally ordering subordinates to shoot Thompson without due sentence. Stoianov was summarily executed on 11 September 1944 in Litakovo, one month before Iris learnt of Frank's death. Six subordinates were tried by the Novoselski and Botevgradski People's Courts, sentenced to death and executed: Georgi Manov, Dicho Dichev and Boris Tomov for their role in the interrogation; Stoian Lazarov, Angel Stanchev and Ilia Tupankov for their role in the execution. Only Tupankov admitted his guilt. He and Manov both claimed that Stoianov had confessed that he himself shot Thompson. Source: state archives in Vielki Tarnovo, letter N-4454/19–20 December 1945.

would have died at the Kostov trials of 1949, although a friend disputes this.[61] Frank was, in late 1942, shocked by the number of people Stalin had *personally* ordered to be poisoned.[62] He wrote from Cairo, shortly before embarking for Serbia, 'When the Communists come to power after the war, as they surely will, I will be the first to be hung as a heretic':[63] he knew he was exactly the kind of independent-minded sympathiser who would soonest be purged in post-war Eastern Europe.

His politics, instinctively humanitarian, are quickly summarised. He hoped that the war was to forge a new and better world order, not defend a bad, old one. He wanted full employment, a welfare state, and believed there would be no world peace without world government. He told the partisans he 'respected' Communists, and certainly he had a strong attachment to the war aims of the Soviet Union.[64] There was also within him a patriotic Englishman with a sentimental attachment to the English countryside, who thought Communism a 'cold and rational creed' and who in 1942 told E.P. 'how very rarely I've found myself marching down the stream-lined autobahn of my socialist theory'. Though so massively well-read, and in so many languages, he once boasted that he had never read *Das Kapital*.*[65]

Frank believed many things more interesting than politics, and that 'art and literature' were 'paramount'. He saw himself as a 'left intellectual, unkempt, talkative, lazy', missing his own set, with their 'homewoven ties and untidy hair whose ideas and emotions are in such a mess but who know better than anyone how to make a friend and keep one'. He described his mind as 'more inclined to love than analyse', and rebuked his brother, 'It's a mistake to hate people because of their class.' He knew, though he came from an opposing, bohemian-intellectual England, that 'the best fighting regiments were blue-blooded', even if they were fighting merely 'to save the lunch tent at Ascot'. He felt compassion for the homesickness of the soldiers whose letters he had, as an officer, to censor; for his comrades ('my major has been captured, poor old boy'); for those Sicilians prisoners who, having

---

* This was in 1941. His biographer believes that he later remedied this omission.

just shot at the British, now begged for mercy. He grieved for how much men and women had suffered 'for millennia',[66] growing up and dying 'in filth and flies and stench'. He wrote:

> In a world as filthy as it is today, one should remember
> how helpless and lonely the individual human being is;
> and that kindliness, especially when it costs so little, is a
> policy that justifies itself.

Whitehall and Moscow alike had each by 1944 some interest in the failure of such missions as Frank's. Moscow, together with the exiled Bulgarian Communist leader Dimitrov, mistrusted the Bulgarian brand of Communism.[67] Dimitrov encouraged the missions to enter the country, where their lives would be in even greater danger than in Serbia. The royalist Bulgarian authorities for their part wanted an end to Western stimulation of partisan activity as one price for their change of allegiance. E.P. Thompson argues that there was 'very heavy and specific weeding' of the British archives that demonstrated 'expending' of Communists at the time of Frank's death, and that the authorities would not have ordered the execution of a uniformed British officer unless some gesture or signal had passed offering licence: 'Somebody winked.'[68] As Peregrine Worsthorne, like Frank a member of Phantom, put it: 'In executing Major Thompson, the Bulgarian authorities were doing the British government's dirty work.'[69] Michael Foot, later the leading historian of SOE, disputes this: 'Everyone in SOE or SAS . . . knew that his chances of trouble if captured were high . . . It was part of one's routine training.'[70]

Whatever the truth of the matter, Frank died bravely, yet has never been posthumously decorated. In Communist Bulgaria he was a national hero, and is remembered today.* The railway station near Sofia named after him shows him, in bas-relief, still smoking his pipe.

---

* The British Liaison Officers were represented first as heroes against Fascism, then as imperialist agents, and finally, after 1991, as Soviet agents intent on establishing Soviet hegemony. See E.P. Thompson, *Beyond the Frontier*, p.41.

10

For months the Thompsons at Bledlow in Buckinghamshire were tormented by the usual bogus messages sent on Scott's captured wireless transmitter, implying that Frank was still alive. On 27 September a 'Missing, Believed Killed' notice appeared in *The Times*. More than a week later Philippa, at work in Chatham House, was alerted to this by Donald MacKinnon. On her return to Seaforth she found Iris in the kitchen, and broke the news.[71] Iris wept. Confirmation of Frank's death came in the new year, and over the following years the details gradually came together.

In 1988 Iris was reported as saying that, though not engaged, she and Frank would have married.[72] In fact she had told Michael Foot (of whom Philippa then learnt that he was missing, probably a prisoner, and feared terribly that autumn and winter that the Germans might take him with them as they retreated through the Mannheim Gap) that she would not marry until she was thirty-five, and then to a civil servant. In the event she was only two years out. 'Frank was the person I thought about'[73] is a more scrupulous recollection.

The idea of marrying Frank represents a later wish, and indeed in July 1980 she vividly dreamt that she had somehow married both John Bayley and Frank, and was nervous of how this *ménage-à-trois* would work out. But both her husbands were evidently so sweet-tempered and so civilised that, within the dream, they all got along splendidly, and were happy together.

> A dream about Frank. I was with Frank and he told me he loved me. (As he did on that day in autumn 1938[74] in New College.) I was very moved but not sure what I felt (as then). He went away and I then realised I loved him. (As I really did come to love him later.) In the dream, realising I loved him I felt great joy at the thought that I could tell him now, and I sent for him. He appeared at the top of a steep slope, dressed as a soldier, with a black cap on. As I climbed up the slope towards him I felt sudden dismay, thinking I cannot marry him,

I am married already. Then I thought, it is all right, I can be married to both him and John. We met and were somehow very happy and yet awkward too.

11

'When the war ends', Frank had written in his last letter to his brother, 'whether I'm there or not', E.P. should meet Iris, a good philosopher and 'Compleat Humanist' – they could work out E.P.'s scheme of 'dialectical idealism' together. Around the end of 1945 Iris wrote at length to E.P., or Palmer as she always called him,[75] from Innsbruck, to help with the family's plans to publish *There is a Spirit in Europe* with Gollancz, commemorating Frank:

> He is so much more than the odd collection of things one remembers. One gets mixed up too with all the feelings of sickness about not having loved him enough – which was true at the start, though not later. And the sheer sickness of loss. You have a difficult job. Then his opinions, his splendid positive uncompromising faith in the world's people. Oneself, one goes on changing, & can't argue out with him one's shifts of opinion on the USSR, one's compromises with life. It's not easy to write about him, even a few paragraphs of a letter, he was pure gold.

'I felt very unhappy and very proud when I read his letters through,' Iris wrote to Frank's mother Theo on 21 November 1945; Theo had visited Iris at Seaforth.[76] Fifty years later, in 1996, Iris wrote, 'It is all so moving and so near,'[77] and indeed she thought about Frank all her life. In 1995 his 'Polliciti Meliora' was read on television on the fiftieth anniversary of VJ-Day by Edward Fox, and transmitted worldwide. There were to be two books dealing with his life and death before *Beyond the Frontier*.[78] Slavcho Trunski's *Grateful Bulgaria* and Stowers Johnson's *Agents Extraordinary*, which Iris hated for its portrayal of Frank as a grim and fanatical megalomaniac trying to be Lawrence of Bulgaria,[79] rashly and romantically leading his men towards the false dawn of a liberated Bulgaria. She was particularly incensed that a film based on Frank's life, tailored for an American audience, would omit all mention of his Communism. It was never made. Her Frank 'had a horror of violence'[80] and never dreamt of himself as a hero but was 'delicate, scrupulous and tender . . . never the victim of dreams of violence or illusions of grandeur'.[81] She wrote to Trunski:

> He was a very various person . . . gentle, quiet, very reticent and modest and also eccentric in a very English way. He didn't seem in the least framed to be a soldier. In fact he was very like . . . a sort of English hero who is very, very quiet and is interested in flowers and birds . . . One wouldn't have imagined him as a soldier, but he was, when it came to it, a very good and brave soldier . . . he was a very absolute man . . . This absoluteness, courage, this feeling of being willing to make sacrifices was part of his character. One wasn't surprised when he became the kind of hero he was. We who loved Frank waited most anxiously to see him again, but when it was not to be, one felt that it was as he would have wished it. He died for a cause that he believed in . . . I think he was someone who was very happy . . . and died in a way he would have understood or approved, if one can say that about somebody's death when they die so young.

She wrote to Palmer around 1980 that 'In a sense of course it wasn't worth it, nothing in the subsequent state of the world seems worth it in relation to such destruction, because of the complex nature of causality and because of the shabbiness of the outcome. And yet of course –'. The sentence is left deliberately unfinished. When Iris's *alter ego* says in *The Black Prince* that she reveres no one except great artists and 'those who say No to tyrants'; or when at the end of *The Red and the Green* Frances thinks of the 'inconceivably brave' Irish dead of Easter 1916, 'made young and perfect for ever', Iris is surely thinking of Frank.* *The Book and the Brotherhood*, too, envisages a confrontation

---

* E.P. Thompson also compares Frank's death with the 'symbolic confrontation' of Easter 1916. *Beyond the Frontier*, p.42.

with a figure who, like the dead Frank, has never moved ideologically while the world around him has compromised its ideals.

Perhaps Iris captured the sense of grief and of mysterious causality best in the long poem she dedicated, in 1977, to Frank's memory, 'The Agamemnon Class, 1939', ingeniously conflating the deaths of Frank in Thrace, and Achilles on the 'windy plains of Troy'. It ends:

> What was it for? Guides tell a garbled tale.
> The hero's tomb is a disputed mound.
> What really happened on the windy plain?
> The young are bored by stories of war.
> And you, the other young, who stayed there
> In the land of the past, are courteous and pale,
> Aloof, holding your fates.
> We have to tell you that it was not in vain.
> Even grief dates, and even Niobe
> At last was fed, and you
> Are all pain, and yet without pain,
> As is the way of the dead.
>
> No one can rebuild that town
> And the soldier who came home
> Has entered the machine of a continued doom.
> Only the sky and the sea
> Are unpolluted and old
> And godless with innocence.
> And twilight comes to the chasm,
> And to the sea's expanse
> And the terrible bright Greek air fades away.

II

Storm and Stress
1944–1956

'*Question de chercher un maitre, problème important et dangereux.*'
Letter to Raymond Queneau, 28 February 1946

8

A Madcap Tale
1944–1946

'We are all interested in sexual relations,' Frank's brother later wrote.

> We are all willing to moralise about them at the drop of a hat . . . We have scarcely begun to establish the facts before we begin to mix them up with our own moralising additives: scandalised, or apologetic, or admiring or condescending. What we make of her is already mixed up with what we have made of ourselves; it is something different from her own taut, unrelenting self-making . . .
>
> . . . [She] needs no one's condescension. She was poor in nothing. She was never beaten. And the final evidence lies in that part of her which remained 'a child to the end of the chapter'. For that part of her – the refusal to become careful and 'knowing', the resilient assent to new experience – is exactly that part which most of us are careful to cauterise, and then to protect with the callouses of our worldly-wise complicities.

This is E.P. Thompson on Mary Wollstonecraft;[1] but the fact that his remarks seem as true of Iris Murdoch points to something radical, pioneering and uncompromising in both, in their different ages. 'Like Socrates, perhaps, love is the only subject on which I am really expert?' Iris later wondered;[2] love and power the matters in which she was well-versed.

2

Iris's love for the Frank who remained, with others of pre-war Oxford, a figure on a Grecian urn, forever young and forever loved, makes for a noble, simplified tale. The truth is more complex. An angry letter of Michael Foot's to Frank on 25 May 1943 warned him against taking suicidal risks in his longing to finish either Fascism or himself: 'Neither a true choice nor a true opposition.' Leo Pliatzky, too, feared that Frank took foolhardy risks at the end. Iris objected: 'He would have found the tensions unbearable later, it's true, but he . . . so much knew how to enjoy living. I cannot regard him as a suicide, however noble-minded.'[3] If Frank's avowal a few weeks before his death that 'I can honestly say I've never been in love' was partly self-protection, then any carelessness of his own survival – especially in the fateful decision to enter Bulgaria[4] – could also be read as peevish, reckless, even vengeful. Michael Kullman, an intensely self-destructive *âme damnée* and prize student of Isaiah Berlin, reminded Iris of Frank in May 1953, with his torrent of restless talk;[5] six weeks later, at an Oxford party, a friend of Frank's since Winchester[6] spoke of him. Iris noted that 'a strong far off thing' touched her in the middle of the froth of cleverness and flirtation. Had Frank survived, his impact might have been shorter-lived. By dying so young he marked Iris indelibly, lived always within her imagination, an emblem of gentle strength, courage, truth. She wrote in 1967: 'I miss him . . . more and more. It almost seems as if wanting to see him & talk to him were something real and possible.'[7]

During 1944–45 Iris read much Henry James and identified strongly with his heroines – 'the rather splendid but definitely unsound character whom the author slowly & ruthlessly crushes in the second volume'.[8] Like the story of Isabel Archer in *The Portrait of a Lady*, Iris's younger life abounds – to borrow James's idiom – in a degree of headstrong foolishness that must gratify the severest of judges, and constitute an appeal to the understanding of others. It may cheer the hostile or puzzle admirers that she claimed what some men assume as a birthright, the right to run close friendships and even love-affairs concurrently. 'What she felt about each . . . was totally genuine and without guile,' John Bayley later commented.[9] If this was (in her) a symptom of largeness of soul, it did not always make for happiness. '*Amour-euse/ heureuse* are contradictions in my universe of discourse,'[10] she wrote. The period of 1938–56, containing especially the 'lucid abnormality'* of the war years and their aftermath, resembles James Joyce's years in Dublin. The adventures of their youth, meditated upon and inwardly digested for the next forty years, provided both with the experience that their fiction shares with us.

There are, as in much modern narrative, problems of perspective. Many a Murdoch novel ends with a sudden and vertiginous shift in point-of-view, where we unexpectedly discover that one character has obsessively for years loved a highly improbable other.[11] Frank, Franz Steiner, Elias Canetti and John Bayley possess the imaginative foreground. But a 1946 interlude conveys the arbitrariness of the time. What happens, Iris's novels show, owes much to chance – because the heart is giddy, its desires 'crooked as corkscrews'. Backtracking is necessary.

3

Iris was all her life a prolific correspondent. To Philippa Foot she wrote in 1968, 'I can live in letters'; a recurrent idea, too, in her journals. Face-to-face communication, except with remarkably few close friends, could be shy and inhibited. On paper, being a writer, she experienced freedom. The epistolary habit had started while she was still at school in the 1930s, as her romance, sight unseen, with James Henderson Scott makes clear.[12] In October 1945 she wrote, 'When I was younger, I remember, I loved writing long letters to all sorts of people – a kind of exhibitionism I

---

* The phrase is Elizabeth Bowen's. See Roy Foster's introduction to *The Heat of the Day* (Vintage, 1998), p.6. Compare Iris to David Hicks, September 1944: 'These distances & irrevocable partings & keepings apart & all this business of not being one's own master . . . One's life is being lived unnaturally.'

daresay'; and that December, 'I'm very talkative on paper.'[13] The war was the last great age of letter-writing.[14] Like visits to the mothers of soldier-friends posted overseas,[15] letter-writing was morale-building. Iris describes her wartime letters as 'talk', or direct address. It was conversation by other means, 'living on paper'.[16] That letter-writing is also a matter of the invention of *personae* or masks she is half-aware: 'one persists in considering the other person as something quite separate from his letters'.[17]

On 28 February 1946 Iris wrote to Hal Lidderdale from Austria, listening to the warm Italian wind roaring about the house and causing melted snow to fall from the roof in a series of shattering crashes. She wrote to convey *une histoire de fous* (a 'madcap tale'). Ten days before, their mutual friend David Hicks had written to jilt her, after a rapid engagement two months earlier. She wanted to render some account of herself.

4

One Oxford contemporary believed Iris's reserve in 1938 a function 'not of shyness but of self-confidence'.[18] It was both. Despite the appearance of assurance, she had often felt as a student 'tongue-tied & unsure of myself & frightened of everyone',[19] admiring the confidence that took so many older Somervillians both into the Party and into same-sex love-affairs. She found particularly glamorous the quiet but 'wild' and 'adorable'[20] Lucy Klatschko (later Sister Marian) and the 'very dashing' Carol Stewart (later Graham-Harrison) for 'having much more of the jungle animal than my own contemporaries & successors'. Unlike that fully pre-war Oxford generation, hers, because of the war, had 'not had enough decent men around to develop the fighting instincts'.[21]

These stalwarts came up to Oxford in 1936, two years before Iris. David Hicks pursued both – Lucy 'relentlessly'.[22] She thought him a conventional enough chap whose wild and carefree *persona* was assumed.[23] Hal Lidderdale described David as a 'lissom gallant' with a shock of dark hair and formidable physical strength.[24]

Good-looking, saturnine, talented, penniless, very attractive and, like Iris, a frustrated writer and poet, he also had the reputation of a Don Juan. He had a dry wit and did not suffer fools gladly. He had been spoiled by his teacher-mother, and his sisters were in awe of him.

The imaginative appeal of Frank, a year younger than Iris, lay in his heroic idealism. David's was earthbound. He was the first man to kiss her, one evening in her first term in autumn 1938 at 124 Walton Street, probably in his flat, the first to awaken in her physical passion, 'in addition to a great tenderness . . . [and] the absolute romantic devotion of . . . extreme youth'. She was fresh from school; he, three years her senior, must have seemed mature and sophisticated. She spent the snowy Boxing Day evening of 1938 with David's family in Palmer's Green, North London.[25] Early in January 1939, nettled by the directness with which she tried to sympathise with a momentary sense of inadequacy, and vexed, she believed, by her 'quaint virginity cult', he rejected her, making 'a few unpleasant remarks'. She was proud. This stung. David had graduated from Worcester College in 1938 and was taking a Diploma of Education before departing England in the summer of 1939. He spent the war teaching English for the British Council in Egypt and Persia. Iris and he did not meet again until November 1945, nearly seven years later. 'Time. Funny substance. I feel differently about it these days,' she wrote to Leo. 'So much of one's life is in a state of suspension.'[26]

The laws of love – of '*Oh, qu'ils sont pittoresques, les trains manqués*'* – determined that she brooded about him: 'You must have met me at an impressionable age.'[27] A much-loved only child whose parents, by her own admission, had brought her up too leniently, head girl and a 'star' at both her schools, Iris resembled – as David wrote to her in 1939 – a 'fairy-tale princess'.[28] 'It must be the way I do my hair – I shall have to change it.' Fairy-tale princesses, following some statutory ordeal, are generally granted their secret wish. A 'golden girl for whom the waters parted',[29]

---

* Jules Laforgue, from an untitled late poem: 'How picturesque do those trains later seem to us that we failed to catch.'

she had grown used to conquest. Gaining an outstanding first in 1942 further helped: 'You dreary Firsts, with your built-in-for-life sense of superiority!' as one of her novel characters puts it.[30] David, the 'twisted satyr of Palmer's Green', had dared to turn her down, with a youthful, casual brutality that rankled. His witticisms bruised her, and she rallied pugnaciously, a Beatrice to his Benedick, though she records that she tended towards sounding 'earnest' and silly, he to being smart and sounding slick. He had accurately predicted that she would get only a second in Mods. She minded the prediction.

She wrote him (but did not send) many poems, one subtitled 'DH (may he rot)';[31] and a single yearly letter from 1940 to 1943, waiting a year to answer his first reply. In 1941 she enquires with rehearsed casualness whether he happens now to be married to Alastine Bell, with whom he had been obsessively in love, 'or not'. By 1943, in answer to his second reply, she brings him news of Alastine's marriage to Graham Lehmann. She comments in her fifth, in January 1944, 'your memory is accurate. We met remarkably little. I suppose I have a myth-making mind – I certainly invented a character for you . . . I should be happy to start again from scratch.' After Frank's death she wrote to David frequently. She closely tied her two writing-habits together – letters, novels – when she wrote from Brussels in 1945. They had then not met for nearly seven years:

> Write to me now, David. I feel lonely. Let me hear your 'authentic accents' or I shall begin to think after all that you're just someone that I invented – a character out of my unsuccessful novels.

Indeed she requests 'an up-to-date photograph . . . I find I've entirely forgotten what you look like. And I hate not to know what my friends look like.' From Brussels in the autumn of 1945, Boxing Day 1938 now seemed 'the essence of a dream'.[32]

5

'When this war is over,' wrote Frank in August 1942, 'there will have to be an enormous deal of kindness to atone for all the senseless hate & suffering of these years.' He wrote of the need for a 'new communal ethic'. The United Nations Relief and Rehabilitation Administration (UNRRA),* the first agency to operate in the name of the United Nations, was designed to address the predicament of the entire populations of liberated countries,[33] including the enormous and unprecedented problems of housing, clothing, feeding and finally – with luck – rehabilitating the more than eight million refugees who even in 1944 found themselves homeless, stateless and adrift (in post-war Europe a year later, the figure was very much larger). Torn from their homes, battered into despair, many had been treated as 'animals or slaves'.[34]

Iris wrote to Hicks in January 1944, 'I am not at all built to be a civil servant. I am inefficient & administration depresses me.' She wished to escape out of 'this half-baked intellectualism into UNRRA's Europe & do some thoroughly menial & absorbing job ... then come back to England at the age of 29 and play the experienced woman round what's left of Bloomsbury'. In addition to writing novels, she wished to teach philosophy at a university, but sought wider experience first. In May 1944 the thought of spending the post-war years in England appalled her 'to the point of suicidal mania', partly because she wanted to escape an emotional tangle. She separated painfully in the early summer of 1944 from 'utterly adorable but wicked' Balogh, and claimed by September no longer to be 'bleeding at every artery'[35] – but was having a 'rather decorous affaire [*sic*] with a French diplomat, which is at any rate good for my French'.[36] (Since this diplomat, Olivier Wormser, was, like another wartime lover, an

---

* The precursor of the Office of the UN High Commissioner for Refugees, which leads today's humanitarian efforts for refugees worldwide.

acquaintance of Balogh's, these affaires may have been partly revenge for Balogh's infidelities).[37]

The day after D-Day, Wednesday, 7 June, when Frank was waiting to be shot,[38] Iris listened, much moved, to the live radio reporting of the Normandy landings, feeling 'a sensation of wanting to cry & cheer at the same time that I can't remember having before except at certain moments in the Spanish War . . . it's good to see the bloody English people getting really thrilled about something'. She applied to join UNRRA the same month, giving Nickie Kaldor, Eduard Frankel (*sic*), Isobel Henderson, Donald MacKinnon and BMB as referees. She wanted to work on the 'relief' side – it might mean going abroad and attaining first-hand experience. Throughout the war she had complained: 'I feel very bitterly about the second-handness of most of my knowledge of life,'[39] and felt 'savage jealousy' of those – mainly men – who had escaped England for the duration.[40] Her application form records that she wanted 'to serve the liberated peoples . . . whether in a refugee camp or at a desk, being as near as possible to the actual scene', and expresses particular interest in France.

Alas, she got 'rehabilitation' instead: 'Who is going to listen to UNRRA on rehabilitation?' It meant staying in London, and she started work at the European Regional Office of UNRRA at 11 Portland Place by Monday, 12 June 1944.[41] Her plans to use 'disgraceful string-pulling' to get abroad – 'the number of people I know in influential positions who are devoted to my cause has increased in the last year' – came to nothing. That September she was refused a job on a flying-squad through inability to ride a motorbike.[42] She was stuck with UNRRA in London for a further vexing fifteen months.

Though in later life she was to speak of her two years with UNRRA as 'one of the most wonderful things I ever did',[43] the London period was full of frustrations. The outfit was run,

> not by quiet bowler-hats from Ealing & Dagenham who at least behave approximately like gentlemen, but by the citizens of Milwaukee & Cincinnati & New Haven, Conn., let loose in their myriads to deal a death-blow to tottering Europe. They do not sit on office stools but lounge, with

cellulose belts & nylon braces, behind enormous desks,
& chew gum & call their fellow citizens by their christian
names . . .*

Iris became fond of some of them, notwithstanding their tendency to mistake her for a clerk or girl messenger, but judged it
a pretty unstable show. At her level a jungle life prevailed. As well
as go-getting Americans and Canadians UNRRA in London was
'rather too full of inept British civil servants (. . . me, for
instance), uncoordinated foreigners with Special Ideas & an
imperfect command of English. Pretty fair chaos. V. many noble-
hearted good-intentioned people – [who] drown in the general
flood of mediocrity & muddle.' So it amounted to 'a very mad
show, full of extremely nice people with no *esprit de corps* & no
glimmering of an idea how to make an Administration go'.[44] To
Leo she wrote: 'All is chaos as usual at UNRRA . . . At the moment
I am working a ten hour day, getting supplies out to Displaced
Persons, and that is good. But next week?'[45] She especially liked
the Czechs her work brought her into contact with, and – though
feeling lost, disaffected and depressed – quipped dispassionately
that a little social success 'relieves & rehabilitates' her vanity. In
November 1944 she visited the Rehabilitation Centre in Egham,
Surrey.[46] It was sometimes hard to see how any of her work was
helping Europe's eight million displaced people.

In December 1944 she wrote to David Hicks recounting the
death of 'my old friend Frank Thompson'. She had over the years
commended Frank to Hicks – 'a pleasant chap in case you ever
run into him in Cairo' – fearing simultaneously that he might be
too young and also too simple and warm-hearted for David's
tastes. Now, in successive letters, she candidly mourns him. 'He
was a brilliant & full-blooded creature', and 'one of the best men
I ever knew'. She also reports Noel Eldridge's death – 'one of
those "hopeless" characters that contrive to be terribly lovable'.[47]
She questions the urge to praise people when there's no longer

---

* 21 July 1945. Jo Grimond, then UNRRA's Director of Personnel for Europe,
agreed: 'I . . . watched the smothering of the British system by the American . . . But
the American methods did not suit the British.' *Memoirs* (London, 1979), p.139.

any point in it – 'A sort of conscience-money perhaps.' The war no longer seems a peculiar interval after which one would simply pick up where pre-war existence left off. The 'golden lads & lasses period . . . all very golden & beautiful & pure-hearted' had gone, and for good. Paris was liberated on 25 August 1944. By that December, though the war in Europe still had half a year to run and there were pockets of German resistance to the north, it had become 'a city one's friends go off to for a week and come back from. Even books are coming across the Channel . . . very refreshing & exciting.'[48] Iris could now 'sniff the post-war political atmosphere'.

Winter 1945 was real, with snow and cold, and that 'absolute failure of the imagination to conceive of ever being warm & human again'.[49] She read the German philosopher and social scientist Wilhelm Dilthey.[50] UNRRA frustrated her intensely: 'Nothing practical is ever decided', they were 'stooges to the military', and she felt 'sick & degraded and incompetent'. In March she was back after a long bout of 'flu in the familiar atmosphere of 'inactivity & gossip & intrigue for better jobs'. Her 'incompetence & dreamy unpracticalness . . . prevent[ed her] landing a real job'. She had been rereading Dostoevsky's *The Possessed* and found it the 'greatest novel in the world'. She liked the way it

> battered its way through one's spirit & effects a Coperni-
> can revolution in one's thought . . . One has to go down
> into the pit with the man – it's no use standing on the
> brink & peering . . . If ever I taught ethics to students
> I'd make them read that sort of thing.

The complex Austrian poet Rilke, too, with his lyrical ability to make abstract ideas tangible, for whom poetry was a religious vocation, makes her excited, bewildered and 'melted', causing 'that liquefaction of the inner organs which fine poetry produces'. She drew solace from him over the following year, especially from his *Letters to a Young Poet*.

In late February Michael Foot cast up as a result of a prisoner-of-war exchange the previous November: the Germans demanded and got four of their men with Iron Crosses in exchange for a prisoner who had 'given them so much trouble'. It turned out that in the late summer of 1944 his party had run into a German patrol in the tiny occupied enclave of Saint-Nazaire. Of about a hundred SAS men taken prisoner that year, Michael was one of only six who returned alive, repatriated on a stretcher after months in a hospital in Rennes, shaven-headed, with a broken skull, standing and walking with difficulty. His top vertebra had been cracked by a collaborator's pitchfork and his left side – face included – paralysed during his fourth brave attempt to escape. Philippa soon moved out of Seaforth, first to Michael's flat in Rochester Row, where a fieldmouse with tufted ears sometimes lodged in the gas-oven. (Always hospitable, they named the fieldmouse 'Nova' after the film-star Nova Pilbeam; her residence sometimes necessitated a cold supper.) They were married that June. Philippa soon returned to Somerville to study philosophy on the grant she had been promised when she went down.[51] Iris, though a little envious, still wished to wander before settling down, and noted: 'Philippa is much the better philosopher than me.'[52] Michael resumed his studies at New College.

Iris, left to her own devices, spent the March days in a 'slightly irritated dream'. She lost her temper with an anti-Yalta Pole for whom she none the less felt sorry.[53] She walked up and down her long and spacious attic and brewed tea at hourly intervals and wrote and read poetry and stood at the window watching the trains go by.* She visited the tufted ducks in St James's Park and felt lonely. The 'affaire' with Balogh was over: he had married an 'extroverted . . . hunting and shooting woman with lots of money'.[54] Her French diplomat had returned to liberated Paris. Frank was no more. Sometimes, especially after a French film, she felt 'desperate again for human intimacy & a man & the insanities of being in love'.[55] VE-Day, 8 May, found her at a party at Treasury Principal Hilary Sinclair's flat just off the Strand, with something villainous to drink (he was teetotal), then joining the crowds milling in St James's Park and finally doing 'all the right

---

* To and from St James's Park station; now wholly underground, at that time it had trains travelling above-ground.

things ... such as dancing in Piccadilly at 2am'.[56] The return to the National Gallery in early June of about fifty pictures from a disused slate mine in north Wales – 'Sir Kenneth Clark's favourites, I suppose' – filled her with 'heavenly bliss': 'The Van Eyck man and pregnant wife. Bellini & Mantegna agonies. Titian Noli me Tangere. Rubens's Bacchus & Ariadne ... Rembrandt's portraits of self & of an old lady. His small Woman Bathing (Lovely!). A delicious Claude fading into blue blue blue . . .' She was delirious with the first shock. During the war there had commonly been one single picture on display each month. The new abundance by contrast felt 'really', she wrote emphatically, like peace.[57]

By now the UNRRA wheels were fully turning at last and she had far too much to do. Although a year in UNRRA had shown her that universal brotherhood is not a condition that comes naturally to people,[58] she could sometimes see that what one did in one's office had some remote connexion with someone or other over there being fed, clothed, calmed, who wouldn't otherwise be.

She wished from late 1944 that she felt more confidence in the Labour Party, with whose politics she actively engaged, by the following May sitting on the interviewing board to look at the chaps who had 'the effrontery' to offer themselves as possible Labour candidates for Westminster – she found them 'uniformly frightful (ignorant, opinionated, careerist, insensitive)'.* Iris also underwent a change in her view of the USSR at some undisclosed point,[59] and became disillusioned with the CP. In late May 1945 she was also reading Koestler's brilliant, complex, prophetic *The Yogi and the Commissar* – demythologising sequel to his savagely anti-Communist *Darkness at Noon* – with its bleak survey of the Soviet experiment ('The End of an Illusion'), and called it 'nasty, clever'.[60] Possibly what was 'nasty' was Koestler's unmasking of the wilful self-duping of the European left, of the irrational surrender of their critical faculties when confronted by the naked horror of USSR state terrorism, of deportations and atrocities,

---

* Jeremy Hutchinson (at that point married to Peggy Ashcroft), who applied from Caserta in Italy and is therefore excluded from Iris's scorn, won; he stood against Frank's childhood friend Bill Carritt for the CP.

labour camps and systematic lying. He called, without turning his back on the political, for a recovery of the spiritual and contemplative, analysing the difficulties of that recovery. Neither the saint nor the revolutionary could save us, argued Koestler, only some synthesis of the two. Since his schooldays he had never 'ceased to marvel each year at the fool [he] had been the year before'.[61] It may be inferred that Iris felt similarly: only Koestler saw, she wrote, 'what are the *real* moral problems of now'.[62]

Tommy Balogh strongly felt that the Labour Party approach was the right one.[63] His Hungarian origins and wartime contacts might also have helped sensitise Iris to Soviet intentions *vis-à-vis* smaller neighbouring countries, having watched how they had eaten up the Baltic states. If this chronology is accurate, Iris had been in the Party for between five and six years. Her recorded nostalgia for it lasted until 1953, when she wrote of Sartre's novels that 'all who felt the Spanish War as a personal wound, and all disappointed and vainly passionate lovers of Communism will hear these novels speak to them'.[64] She had greeted the liberation of Paris on 25 August 1944 with the hope that something in post-war Europe would be neither Americanised nor Russianised.[65] Late in 1945 she recorded 'shifts of opinion about the USSR';[66] and by February 1946 Raymond Queneau observed that she had left the CP for the Labour Party. On 27 July 1945, after Attlee's landslide election victory, she wrote ecstatically: 'Oh wonderful people of Britain! After all the ballyhoo and eyewash, they've had the guts to vote against Winston! . . . I can't help feeling that to be young is very heaven!'[67]

That month she expects shortly to leave to work either on a 'welfare' supply programme for DPs or to be sent to Frankfurt. In early August she visits Westminster Cathedral, watches a boy fall impetuously to his knees with bowed head and listens to the faint chink and rattle of his rosary. She finds it 'inexpressibly moving' and is reminded of a young Guards officer she once met on a railway station in Scotland, with a kestrel on his wrist which had been with him all through the war. 'The sudden rush of feeling, blinding, darkening.' The candles flickering before the saints also bring to mind 'how Frank once lit a candle to the

Virgin Mary. I am glad he was here with me . . . Coming out, I see a high bank of pure white cloud with the sun upon it. It seems to be the light which fills the world. Blinded with joy I sing in my heart.'[68] On 11 August – VJ-Day – Londoners were showering torn paper, in imitation of New York.

Finally, after another month of waiting, UNRRA sent Iris abroad for ten months; not to Frankfurt as she expected, but to Austria, via a spell in Brussels.[69] On Tuesday, 4 September she witnessed Brussels's *Fête de la Libération*. It was her first real time abroad since Geneva and the League of Nations ten years before. Ostend reminded her less of Belfast than she expected, more of a Cornish fishing village. Bruges's beauty was 'unbearable' and its Memlings exquisite. In Antwerp, after seeing the cathedral by moonlight and following a brass band about at eleven at night, she ended up in a café drinking cognac by herself, 'still stunned with admiration of this wonderful continental habit of having no licensing hours'. Brussels was glorious. The cobbled streets, the soft twitter of French and harsher music of Flemish, the indefinitely open thousand and one cafés for talking the new ideas in for hours on end were sources of intoxication. The ridiculous little dogs, the way everyone rode on the running boards of the little clanging trams and never paid their fare, were others.[70] She wrote to Marjorie Boulton:

> Did you ever yearn in your more romantic & decadent youth, for a glittering Huxleyan Europe of wit & poetry & talk? There are moments now when I feel that, suddenly, I am in the midst of it, & it's good. Other times I feel it is in the midst of me – & I get a frisson of joy to think that I am of *this* age, *this* Europe – saved or damned with it.[71]

In her office in Brussels she hung an expensive reproduction of Brueghel's *Fall of Icarus* – 'one of the most poetic of great pictures'.

As for Seaforth, Philippa's sister Marion Bosanquet had moved in, Iris helping to sustain the fiction that they shared the protected tenancy of sixty guineas per year. There Marion stayed for the following fifty and more years. Iris still spoke nostalgically of the flat as late as 1994.[72]

6

Iris was glad to be away from London and from the remains of old entanglements and bitternesses, though she was 'desolated & furious' not to have been there when David Hicks finally returned. After nearly seven years apart, and with home leave for David withdrawn at the last moment, they missed each other by a week, and counted themselves 'star-crossed'. The war, and now its aftermath, meant that 'everyone's lives are being mucked up', as she had earlier noted: it 'disturbed all one's feelings of the future very profoundly'.[73]

If to Marjorie Boulton she emphasised café-talk, to David she dilated on loneliness. Twenty minutes with a highbrow Brussels bookseller – almost certainly Ernest Collet, who, when feeling low, would announce from time to time, '*Demain je vais partir pour le Congo Belge*' – was, she now claimed, her only real conversation in Brussels. (In fact she ran into Noel Martin who was driving a jeep in the Place du Nord and they had dinner, during which she talked of Balogh; she also met Hal Lidderdale.[74] In *The Sea, The Sea* she called this 'that rather moving time of the reunion of survivors'.[75]) The bookseller and she discussed the '*roman existentialist*', and he used the term with a casualness that showed it – to her excitement – to be 'an accepted usage!' That she is in a partly French-speaking city is a matter for joy and consolation. She reads Julien Gracq's *Un Beau tenebreux*. The desire of the 'modern French school' philosophically to denude life in their novels fascinates her.

Iris's love-affair – she spells it 'affaire' – with France and all things French was of its epoch, an intoxication of the British intelligentsia which Koestler had lampooned as 'French 'flu'.*

---

* *Tribune*, 6 November 1943: the essay is included in Koestler's *The Yogi and the Commissar*. Koestler attacked Aragon, Gide and the intoxication of the British

Doris Lessing would write fifty years later: 'there is no way now of telling how powerful a dream France was then ... now that our cooking and our coffee and our clothes are good, it is hard to remember how people yearned for France, as for civilization itself'.[76] In 1944 Iris longed to travel and meet 'above all French people! How far, I wonder, will one be able to – with no money, & with a nagging useless irresolute sort of conscience?' She noted after the liberation of Paris that 'London has shown considerable restrained enthusiasm ... & one sees tricolours about'; and 'if France lives, Europe will live'. Her letters are full of cries of enthusiasm about French people, French films, French songs, Baudelaire and Mauriac '& the dangerous intellects of the Church & Giraudoux & Aragon & Jeanne d'Arc and what have you'. She quipped that 'the French are the real Master-race',[77] while French Existentialists induce an 'intellectual exaltation' that recalls for her an ecstatic phrase she loved from Valery – '*pluie/Ou on se jette à genoux*'.[78] While cooling her heels in London throughout 1945 she was getting 'fascinating stuff' over from France:

> As a result of late repercussions from Kierkegaard & Kafka the French novelist seems to be in a dilemma, wondering whether to write a philosophical essay or a novel. Some, like Albert Camus, write first one & then the other ... a lot of exciting & maybe good literature seems to be getting written. I'm quite intoxicated by all this. The intellectual fumes are strangely mixed, very strong, overpowering.[79]

In Brussels she discovers 'a *wonderful* novelist ... and ... Sartre's mistress' – Simone de Beauvoir[80] – 'her first play now running magnificently in Paris', and dreams that she meets her.[81] 'I propose to hang around a lot in Paris in the next ten years or so,' she warns David. Two features of the new Existentialist climate compel her; both connect with novel-writing. Firstly, 'what excites me more than the philosophy itself is the extraordinary bunch of good novelists it is inspiring'.[82] Secondly, 'the fact that the

---

intelligentsia with all things French. See D. Johnson on J. Bennett's *Aragon, Londres et la France libre* in *Times Literary Supplement*, 10 December 1999, p.28.

Church is very much with them still' makes them, for Iris 'far more exciting than the English novelists . . . it is still the eternal Good & Evil which is in question'.[83] (Not all her pleasures were highbrow: she bought a paperback of Gabriel Chevallier's satirical 1934 novel *Clochemerle* that September too.) She typifies Existentialism, acclaimed as the 'new philosophy of France & the philosophy of this age' thus:

> . . . a group of theories descended from Hegel & Kierkegaard, via Jaspers & Heidigger [*sic*] & now incarnated in Jean Paul Sartre (non Catholic variety) & Gabriel Marcel (Catholic variety) and others. It's anti-metaphysical & phenomenalist in flavour – concerned with the concrete puzzle of personal existence, rather than with general theories about the universe . . . it's a theory of the self, & the self's attitude to death.[84]

In early November, moreover, she met Sartre in person. He was in Brussels to lecture on Existentialism, being mobbed by larger crowds than Chico Marx (whom, probably because David was a Marx Brothers fan, Iris telephoned[85]). Iris was introduced to Sartre at a select gathering after the lecture, and met him again at an interminable café-séance the following day. These were their only meetings.[86] To Hal Lidderdale she described Sartre as

> small. Simple in manner, squints alarmingly. I am busily reading everything of his I can lay my hands on. The excitement – I remember nothing like it since the days of discovering Keats & Shelley & Coleridge when I was very young.[87]

To David:

> His talk is ruthlessly gorgeously lucid – & I begin to like his ideas more & more. He's accused by many of being a corruptor of the youth (*philosophe pernicieux, mauvais maître* as an article that I read this morning started) – he's certainly excessively obsessed, in his novels, with the more horrid aspects of sex. But his writing and talking on morals – will, liberty, choice – is hard & lucid &

invigorating. It's the real thing – so exciting, & so sobering, to meet at last – after turning away in despair from
the shallow stupid milk & water 'ethics' of English 'moralists' like Ross & Prichard ... Nietzsche's and Schopen-
hauer's great big mistakes are worth infinitely more than
the colourless finicky liberalism of our Rosses & Cook
Wilsons.*

Yesterday, another joy, I heard Charles Trenet sing
... There's something magical about almost any toler-
able song ... It was wonderful.[88]

Sartre wrote 'philosophy, novels, plays, cinema, journalism!'[89]
No wonder the stuffy English were suspicious of such versatility.
Iris thought his moral philosophy was exactly what Oxford
philosophy needed to have injected in its veins to rejuvenate it.
By December 1945 she is reading *Being and Nothingness*. Sartre
had signed her copy. It gave her the feeling that it was possible,
after nearly four years of war work, to get back to philosophy
again.

7

By December 1945 something else momentous had happened.
She and David met again. Iris arranged to leave Brussels on Thursday, 16 November, after both phoning and writing to him to
finalise their arrangements. She returned to Brussels two weeks
later. During the visit to London she re-read Frank's letters and
felt 'very unhappy and very proud'.[90] The intervening days were,
she told Hal, 'a tornado ... ten days that positively shook the
world'. On the second day she and David decided to marry, and
would have completed the business at once, 'only there wasn't
enough time'. Iris was alarmed that his parents evidently doubted

---

* Sir W.D. Ross (1877–1971) and H.A. Prichard (1871–1947) were among the
major figures in Oxford moral philosophy in the first half of the twentieth century.
John Cook Wilson (1849–1915), a respected philosopher who published little and
whose work has not stood the test of time. Iris and Mary Midgley had had to read
his *Statement and Inference* (1926) as Greats students.

whether she had a strong sense of humour. She also felt tongue-tied and overwhelmed by shyness in front of his friends. Nonetheless they were now officially engaged. Immediately on her return to Brussels she wrote to him: 'It would have been so dreadful if we had not fallen in love, after that build-up.'

The build-up had indeed been extraordinary. As a student Iris had written apologetically to Paddy O'Regan: 'my physical affections come & go like the wind, and enjoy, like a butterfly, the blossom nearest to them'.[91] There were exceptions, and she was later able to write about obsessional love in, for example, *The Sea, The Sea*, because she inhabited it from inside. Over nearly seven years of separation, but especially during 1945, she had written to David, tried to picture his life, to interest him in her separate existence and history, pursued him long and with ingenuity. She was, at least until their November meeting, making most of the running. He was more casual about his movements, about giving her his address, indeed about replying.

While Frank loved Iris's 'lofty' vein, and mirrored it, David, four years older than Frank, scorns and questions it. While her letters to Frank show her idealism and fastidiousness, those to David on occasion affect a tone of cool and disenchanted worldliness, sometimes of sexual frankness, as if vying with him to sound emancipated. His letters to her before 1946 have not survived, but hers show that he is puzzled by her attempt to demonstrate how grown-up she has become, how remote from the adolescent 'fairy-tale princess' of 1938. In 1941, in comparing him to Alcibiades, she implies that he too has 'all the qualities of greatness except character', and recalls how at Oxford 'I loved you, & hated you'. 'There are remarkably few men who have ever stirred me to any passion,' she wrote in 1943. 'You, for reasons which I can't conceive of, were one of the few.' He would be a nice bloke, she adds, if he could get over his tendency to 'sneer at people & hurt them unnecessarily'. In 1944: 'You were always a casual, cynical chap.' In March 1945 she testifies: 'You've always had a fairly electrical effect.' And, a few weeks before their re-meeting, she writes to him that he has two faces, 'a dark one & a bright one':

You used to be rather a cruel & insolent young brute, David. Sometimes the only adequate reply would have been a slap in the face . . . you are a wild, bad character & . . . I am a more sober goody-goody character . . . [Yet] you know without my telling you, how much everything that is wild in you is bound up with the things I love most in you . . .

8

Iris tried to interest David in the strange story of Seaforth, and in her novel-writing. She suffers 'many extremities for love'. A letter started on 20 May 1944 ran:

I am afraid I am not yet really eligible for inclusion among the harlots of history. I still take my love very seriously & let it tear my guts out every time – & although at the moment I am actually running two affaires concurrently that doesn't signify as only one is *pour plaisir*, the other being completed from a sense of duty only. Also I am very inept and keep involving myself in excruciatingly embarrassing situations . . . & feel that there is no depth of pain & humiliation to which I cannot descend where such matters are concerned.

Complaints about loneliness led to what she termed an 'eagle-eyed searching for a different sort of relationship'. During 1945 she wrote him thirty letters. His interest was actively ignited. She told him about Fitzrovia; he was frequenting its pubs. It was a world she just

ran away from in the end [since for a woman] it's more difficult to cope with that sort of society & appear neither a whore nor a blue-stocking . . . Soho abounds in people with some talent & ability, but not much solid ferro-concrete intelligence . . . And oh, the vanity of so many of those Bohemians! I liked a lot of them very well . . . But relationships were always stormy – People turned out so often to be childish & malicious.

So volatile were Tambimuttu and his 'set' that one had to 'develop a sort of shockproof relationship to cope'. The month before their meeting was a time for candour. David had evidently blazed a trail through some of the girls frequenting Fitzrovia, and found them disappointing; Iris declared herself (in a letter she later disavowed as trying falsely to mirror his cynicism) simultaneously jealous and available. In September she feels 'despair & loneliness & self-hatred' yet writes in her 'old lofty vein'. The tone of her letters leading up to their meeting that November is penitent, not about taking lovers, but about the hurt which can be entailed. Her discovery that she can cold-bloodedly hurt others as well as brood on her own hurt leads to a discussion of the religious sense. She promises soon to tell him 'the Story of my Life . . . Not so eventful, but dismal & bitter the way lives tend to become. One wants to be pitied? One wants, more, to be judged . . . I have done things I could weep with shame about . . . You should be wary too . . . I have far more of the bitch about me than you've probably ever realised.' It is perfectly feasible, she notes, to be both a 'bitch' and a prude.

In November, within days of departing for London, she writes, crucially:

> there are certain subtle treasons that are hard to describe. In general, I notice a tendency to want to be loved, & not engage myself in return – that, plus a really dangerous lack of decision & will power where other people's feelings are concerned. A sort of paralysis, maybe, before the picture of myself which I see in someone who loves me. Mortal sin; hell, not purgatory . . . The real crash as far as my self-esteem & general psychological security was concerned was this Hungarian story . . . The whole process took about 18 months & left me in a state of utter despair & self-hatred.

It had been a quadrilateral tale that would make 'rather a good psychological novel', and began, she recounts, when she took Michael Foot – 'terribly tense & tangled emotionally, very intelligent, honest & good' – as a lover from misguided generosity. He was in love with her; she was sorry for him; like so many

Wykehamists, Frank for a while included, he left school unsure of his sexuality; and he was likely to be sent abroad at any moment. In the midst of this, the 'brilliant & darling Pip Bosanquet, very tender & adorable, yet morally tough & subtle, & with lots of will & self-control' came to lodge at Seaforth. Philippa was then breaking off her relations with Balogh, 'a horribly clever Hungarian Jew . . . age 38, very brilliant & attractive & (without really realizing it himself) quite unscrupulous. Self-deception to infinity.' Iris and Balogh fell terribly in love, were at first 'insanely happy'. Having hitherto 'shunned the unrestrained in human relations', she discovered in herself 'extravagant cravings for affection'.[92] Balogh, though promiscuous, did not tolerate rivals. Somehow Iris 'managed to avert my eyes' to the 'rather hideous' sufferings they visited on Michael.

Iris depicts herself to David, in her infatuation, as 'utterly devoid of will-power', and Balogh, as one might when transferring responsibility to another, as the 'devil incarnate'. It was, she argues, love for Balogh that prompted her casual cruelty.

> It was my first introduction to complete passionate love. It was also my first introduction to hate . . . Pip & I continued to live together at Seaforth almost till the end – it was fantastic – we wept almost continually. I saw my relation with her gradually being destroyed, by my own fault, yet I did nothing to save it. She behaved wonderfully throughout. My God, I did love her . . . more than I ever thought I could love any woman.

Finally, she recounts that Philippa fell in love with Michael, 'most successfully salvaged what was left after my behaviour, & married him & they are now living happily in Oxford'.

There are two other men she wants David to know about, 'not because they come into the story directly, but because I rather loved them, & lost them, about the same time, when I was looking round for support'. One is Frank, whose bravery and death she again evokes; the other Donald MacKinnon.

> Donald is rather like Bernanos's country priest[93] – he carries his love for people & his mistrust of himself almost

to the edge of insanity. Yet he is lucid and unsentimental
& tough & really *good* in the strong brave way which is
real goodness, & not self-love with a twist. He's also,
incidentally, a philosopher of the first quality. I think I'll
always be a bit in love with Donald, in a Mary Magdalen-
Christ sort of way. After meeting him one really understands how the impact of one personality could change
one's view of the universe, & how these people at Galilee
got up & followed without any hesitation. I learnt all
sorts of things from Donald. Then a moment came when
his wife began to imagine (wrongly I am sure) that he
was falling in love with me.

As a result Donald broke off their friendship,[94] which, she says,
'must have needed a great strength and courage for which I
admire & love him. Not I mean because he's in love with me –
he isn't – but because he must have known his intervention could
have been decisive.' The reference to herself as Mary Magdalene,
to Donald as Christ, the demonising of Balogh, relate also to the
dramatic underside of Iris's religious nature. In two contemporary
letters she refers to Arthur Koestler, *à propos* his *Yogi and Commissar*, as 'Satan', noting that 'the best moralists are satanic'. Heidegger later was 'possibly Lucifer in person'.[95] The cases are
distinct but the tendency similar. Her imagination lent itself to
allegory. And Balogh was not her only demonic male lover. David
came (for her) from the same stable. Nor were these her last.

9

'*These people & these events are part of me,*' she ended her account
to David. 'There are lots of other people, of course, & lots of
other men, before & since, & some of them important, but not
so much . . .' Twenty-three years later, she remarked to Laura
Cecil that 'there were friendships which influenced me deeply
when I was younger, and something to do with them is in my
books because it is within me'.[96] The 'dragon-eating-its-own-tail'
aspect of her plotting, as she put it, her love of symmetrical

pairings, her sense of a group of people living through some unconscious myth, of dark irrational forces: all of these have one origin in Seaforth. Another aspect is a recurring constellation of a hesitant lover, a bold warrior and an absent sage.[97]

The 1943–44 reversals marked an epoch, a charged memory always. For Iris, Seaforth and sexual love meant loss of Eden. For Michael and Philippa Foot, Seaforth meant only the place they first met. Thomas Balogh, who often had other women around when she was seeing him – 'Peggy Joseph and Margaret Stewart. Probably others as well'[98] – meant little to Philippa. Michael (who declined years later, on being formally introduced, to shake Balogh by the hand) noted in passing that Iris 'made a formidable enemy', but recovered well and was otherwise untouched. Iris and he met, though not often, in later years. For Iris the *scale* of events was different. She had hurt her own better self, lost a 'family'. Some lines from 'Agamemnon Class, 1939' gain in significance: the assertions that members of Fraenkel's class 'ruled a chaste soul' and knew nothing yet either of pain, sin, guilt or death, or of 'betrayal of lover and friend'. It is no accident that her 'saint' Stuart in *The Good Apprentice* wants to retain innocence by never entering the 'machine' of sexual love;* nor that Ducane in *The Nice and the Good* finds the origins of war, slavery and 'all man's inhumanity to man' in the 'cool, self-justifying selfishness of quite ordinary people'.

War produced tales stranger than Seaforth; while many peacetime marriages involved less allowable, and daily, cruelties. Nonetheless if Seaforth was Iris's first home-made family, the predatory face of love – Racine's '*Vénus toute entière à sa proie attachée*' – destroyed it. By 1945 her adoptive father MacKinnon was incommunicado, one 'brother' dead, another married and estranged, and Philippa was thoroughly attached to Michael. This stood between them, as Iris wrote to David: 'There are some

---

* The theme recurs. Otto in *The Italian Girl*: 'To be good is just never to lose [innocence]'; Theo in *The Nice and the Good*, longs to 'regain at least the untempered innocence of a well-guarded child'; Lucius in *Henry and Cato* writes a haiku elegising lost innocence; Daisy in *Nuns and Soldiers* ends up seeking innocence, 'a quest suited to human powers'.

things no friendship can survive. I still feel sick when I think of her & Michael – & they must feel the same when they think of me.'[99] 'Losing you, & losing you *in that way*,' she later wrote to Philippa, 'was one of the worst things that ever happened to me.'

Twenty years later Iris recalled this as a time when she felt 'rejected by D[onald] & P[hilippa]' but saved by someone Donald had introduced her to: 'J[esus] C[hrist]'. It is not surprising that from 1945 on she refused entirely to separate religion and philosophy, or that their willingness to engage with religion is precisely what commends certain Existentialist writers to her. In her letters after the madcap London days, she declares hers precipitately to be an 'essentially religious nature ... These germs in the blood must be confessed to.' How is such a nature to be defined? 'A certain sense of sin combined with a certain sense of beauty? Something like that ...' David, by contrast, thinks religion is only faith in dogma. This, for Iris, is not a necessary part of it, 'though I daresay a sort of humility & submission is'. She accepts that she has it, he hasn't, and she will have to go to mass in the cathedral all by herself.[100]

10

'Disasters I've met with lately make me mistrust relationships which go on from writing to meeting ... though there may be bombs I give up expecting angels through the roof.'[101] Iris's expectations of 'angels through the roof', and her propensity for disasters alike, were not in fact so easily exhausted. Her letters to David after their London idyll show that extreme mixture of hope and fear that accompanies falling in love.

Immediately on her return to Brussels following their engagement she has the 'general idea of what a curious sort of bastard you are, but ... I do want to marry you (fully realizing how often we should annoy each other)'. She also wished to bear his children.[102] Away from him she feels 'such a dipsomaniac for affection & tendresse', and is conscious of him constantly, even in dreams. He wrote gloomily about the prospect of marriage, feeling 'doubts & terrors'.[103] Iris rallies on 7 December: 'You may have sown what you consider to be a decent crop of wild oats, but I certainly haven't finished sowing mine.' Their partnership represents not bourgeois respectability, she further reassures him – though she does plan to send their sons to Winchester – but 'the great wide sea & peril & a high wind'. A 'modern', open marriage is assumed by Iris, partly, one senses, because such are the only terms on which David is willing to commit himself. So on 3 December: 'I've no desire just yet to be unfaithful to you! I'll let you know when that happens. You too please . . . I wonder will you often want other women when we're married?'

She had that day caught herself referring to him in conversation as 'my fiancé'. This gave her a shock: she had her own doubts and terrors. She is worried that David in London had shown no interest in the typescript of her latest novel. She feels she knows him much better than he knows her: 'You were so incurious! That frightened me.' His letters are few and 'highly unsatisfactory', his descriptions of Prague 'meagre', and she showers him with questions. By 31 December 'our days in London seem like a wonderful dream'. She looks forward to 'struggling' with his dark, 'demonic' side, and with him, and hopes he will talk to her: 'Talk with someone I love is so essential – in fact it is *the* thing, & all physical things somehow merge with it.' On his lack of curiosity about her she writes: 'I suspect that you are more concerned about my effect on you than about me myself. You self-centred blighter.' In January: 'I wonder, can you manage me, with my needs & demands – my great arrogance & my great yearning to submit?' She warns him: 'You are going to have a wife with expensive tastes. (Kierkegaard at two guineas a volume, & so on) . . .'

She ponders whether she will drag him out to restaurants to eat, on the salary of a bright snappy job, or selfishly bury herself in books, dreamily emerging to make him some ghastly undercooked meal. Children are to be postponed until prosperity returns; she has seen what it is like for DPs – 'a full-time job for these people to get enough food & clothes to go on living at all properly'. She records a deep irrational desire to be dominated, to be held – 'together with a savage joyous disinclination to submit easily'. In early February: 'Sometimes I'm afraid & feel that I will be a very difficult person to be married to – nervy & selfish & ambitious . . . I'm so frightened because I feel I don't know you.'

11

On 21 January 1946 David wrote to Iris, who had arrived in Austria in mid-December, to confess that he had fallen in love with a girl both refer to as the 'Dornford Yates heroine', Molly Purchase. This letter did not arrive until 18 February. 'Pig dog, another courier has come, bringing no letter from you!' Iris wrote at the end of January. Her letters during this month-long interim have a pathos born of her ignorance of the blow that is on its way.

In mid-December she is drunk with the beauty of Salzburg, its 'endless sunslashed mountains' surrounding a city 'bedraggled & poor & dirty with the war & the melting snow'. She loves its swift river, the dozens of fine arrogant ecclesiastical squares with ironwork doorways. Even Tyrolean hats are complimented. 'My German is dreadful', she twice reports. The opera house is an American cinema.[104] She learns to ski, six thousand feet up over Zell-am-See: 'Oh David, what a sensation! . . . The blazing sun on the snow, the air, the sunburnt faces, the sounds that carry for miles, the sea of mountain peaks all round . . . Yes.' She visits Hitler's house at Berchtesgaden, and the enormous SS barracks that had housed two thousand troops before being 'wrecked & blasted' in the raids the previous February, now entirely desolate and deserted. Only the bell of a woodsleigh passing along the road interrupts the total silence.[105]

On Wednesday, 20 December she moved to Innsbruck, head-quarters of the French zone in Austria, and had an Austrian Christmas, up in the snow.[106] Eagerly anticipating the 'trials & high winds' of her and David's life together, she is now Communications Officer, liaising with the French Army. UNRRA have requisitioned a hotel – Mariabrunn – at an altitude of a thousand feet. There are views over to Italy, and she goes to work by mountain railway. A *téléphérique*, leaving from the door, takes her straight up the mountain for skiing and sunbathing: 'At weekends one walks or skis or just looks in dumb joy at the view.'

She wrote to David at once on arrival. A recent thaw meant the lower slopes of the mountains were 'green, summits in the clouds, much nearer & higher than at Salzburg, town beautiful, medieval & twisted & condensed & full of arches & courtyards & baroque buildings & an adorable river'. Her chief is 'a French colonel of *devastating* sex appeal, age 60 or so'. A car crosses the Brenner each week, bringing their wine ration over from Italy. There is wine *ad lib* at lunch and dinner, also cognac, and when the liquor ration arrives 'we have orgies & drink ourselves nearly insensible'. '*La France, les montagnes* ... What more could the heart desire?' A Persian princess called Djemboulate, who knows David, and sings beautifully in Russian, appeals to Iris's romantic heart, while her sad story 'makes one shut up about the food & cigarette shortage'. The move soon after to US Army rations, 'from penury to paradise', presumably relieves both. Iris runs round the refugee camps in a jeep – 'interesting, though sobering'.

She and David have been discussing the religious philosopher Martin Buber, whose development of what he termed 'I-Thou' spirituality profoundly influenced theology and ethics. She also commends Gabriel Marcel, whose Catholic Existentialism was often opposed to Sartre's atheistical variety. Not all pleasures are cerebral. On 13 January: 'sometimes I feel vaguely restless, point of view sex, & rather like kissing *n'importe qui*'. A week later she confesses that at an all-night blind, a birthday party, she fell gladly into the arms of a handsome young French driver, but 'it wasn't in the nature of a conscious act. Don't worry.' She also records 'pure ecstatic tenderness and joy' at watching a pair of beautiful twenty-four-year-old Parisian ex-Maquisards, escapees from PoW camps, one with the Croix-de-Guerre. They remind her of the two Arab boys from *Seven Pillars of Wisdom*. It was like watching squirrels or birds at play. She describes herself as dependent on tenderness to the point of making herself a victim, a noteworthy description. Within a short time she feels she had better confess that she has been to bed once with André, the more beautiful, Italianate and younger of the two Parisians: 'A fully conscious act, which I do not regret at all, unless it upsets you, & please don't let it.' Not that such acts are without consequence. Shifts in the emotional balance of power, she notes, upset the office for days. It is curious that the dalliance with the handsome driver is explained on the grounds that this 'wasn't in the nature of a conscious act' at all, while that with André is excused on the opposite grounds that it was 'a fully conscious act'. Iris was later to say that the problem with Existentialism was that it 'either made your responsibility absolute or it abolishes it'.[107] Probably both uncharacteristic confessions are half-conscious bribes to the nervous Hicks, whom she fears might flee at anything but an 'open' relationship.

She found in Innsbruck 'no one there who has any sort of intellectual finish or even general knowledge'. When she is reading Max Brod's book on Kafka they all ask, 'Who is Kafka?' The absence of soul-mates made her dependence on faraway and intelligent David all the greater. It may have added to the shock of what, to Hal, she described as his 'long, lyrical letter' of rejection,

> saying he has met in Prague a WONDERFUL (English) girl, that he is very much in love with her, & suggesting in a final line or two that maybe we'd better call our arrangements off. I wrote back at once, saying, yes, call them off, but don't be in too much of a hurry marrying the D[ornford] Y[ates] heroine.

It is typical both of her generosity of spirit and of her pride – in her almost identical – that when she finally receives David's letter, Iris, who felt smashed-up for some time, sympathises with the painful suspense *he* must have undergone awaiting her reply: 'Don't fret at all about me.' And: 'Remember that you've just nearly made one mistake – don't go & make another.' To Leo Pliatzky she wrote that she was now cured of her infatuation – otherwise she 'would have gone on pining for D for years'. To Hal she claimed, after the initial shock, 'extreme relief, &

amazement at this period of temporary insanity . . . a very narrow
escape'. It left her with 'an increased horror of all ties, especially
marital' and a fear of her propensity for 'choosing the second-
rate'.

Thus she kept her courage up and options open, Hal still
counting himself an admirer, and unmarried. Many then thought
Iris beautiful or even glamorous,[108] some pretty, one '*furieusement
belle*'[109] and almost all attractive. But the Jančars, Slovene refugees
she met that spring, recall her as 'a plain Jane'. Rejection hit her
hard, and her looks suffered. Philippa, who saw her later that
summer, intuited that she had suffered a blow. Indeed Iris was
still smarting. In late May David answers her 'querulous' letter of
16 April:

> I like you enormously, better than anyone I can think
> of. But was worried at the thought of being married to
> you. Probably the same with anyone else, but it seemed
> more terrifying in your case. Brain, will and womb, you
> are formidable . . .

Together she and David achieved the feat of turning their
erstwhile passion into friendship. She probably helped financially
when he had no money. She was right about his precipitate move:
his first marriage lasted only a few years. But Iris took him and
his second wife Katherine Messenger out to dinner at the Ran-
dolph Hotel when they were too poor for a honeymoon on 1
June 1953, came up to Shropshire for his seventieth birthday in
March 1986, and they met and wrote to each other often over
the years in between. 'Something of me is stored up with you in
a way that I can never regret,' and 'everything to do with you still
has so many echoes & resonances in all parts of me', she wrote
early in the 1950s.[110] She copied into her journal a generous and
moving letter he wrote in praise of her fiction in the 1970s, and
wrote twice to condole with him when his son Barney, after a
long depressive illness, committed suicide in 1978, aged twenty-
two; David feared his sons suffered from his undisguised contempt
for traditional religion.[111] Katherine considered that David and
Iris would have made a disastrous marriage – both living, perhaps

too much, through the imagination. David kept her letters, back
to 1938, and had a recurrent dream of her about once a month
in which he was always struggling to

> do something absurd like helping recalcitrant people to
> climb a vertical mudbank, or dashing to give a lecture
> on an unknown subject without notes, and being quietly
> surveyed by a Beatrice-like figure, at the top, or in the
> audience.[112]

12

David tried to reassure Iris, after their 'madcap tale' was done,
that 'you do remain a whole person, with your ability to spring
intact'. This oddly echoes Frank's final letter to her. He too had
said that she had 'springs within you that will never fail'. Indeed,
in one letter to David, written in the very bad months of early
1944, Iris had written, 'I feel, even at the lowest moment, such
endless vitality inside me'; this was a time when she evidently
contrived to work hard on her Russian vocabulary, draw pleasure
from reading about Persian art[113] and support Marjorie Boulton
with love and strength of purpose when her father died suddenly.

Natural resilience and life-force apart, Iris also had a special
means to hand by which she was able to process and sublimate
her experiences. She was, after all, an apprentice writer. Five days
after her return from the madcap days in London with David she
wrote to him, seated on the bed with her feet on the radiator,
from a cold Dutch monastery near Haaren where she was completing the latest UNRRA Field Training Course. The London visit,
she wrote, had given her 'copy' for her current novel, which is
partly concerned with a young man 'who makes a dream picture
of a woman he has known, writes her into a novel, & then meets
her again after a long interval ... I can use [this] even if you
can't.'

This is coolly pragmatic, distantly anticipating the plot of *The
Sea, The Sea*. She already believed that a good novelist should be
somehow absent from her work, yet knew this to be a challenge.

She had told him that her second novel, completed in July 1944, was less bad than her first, which 'was extremely bad & ought to be torn up', but the second was 'much harder to write since none of the characters is altogether me whereas in the other they all were'.[114] Now she complains that 'I'm in the middle of another novel ... but it's bad ... I spend so much time cutting a figure to myself & so little time being myself.' Her characters 'are like children – either they're dull & lifeless or else they give you no peace',[115] and presciently, 'Trouble is, I get to love my characters too much – with the bad ones, I see so clearly just why they're like that, & that it isn't really their fault – & they become positively loveable & ruin all my plans'.[116]

Her January letters continue this meditation. On the thirteenth: 'In my own work I do seek formal perfection & economy. I am not at all a raconteur.' By the nineteenth she is 'fed up with my novel ... My efforts to "expel myself" from the characters & give them an independent life has resulted in their becoming thoroughly tiresome & unreal. For the central character ... a rather charming dreamy though ineffectual youth, I am developing a passionate hatred.' This youth was presumably Mark, based on Frank. She now wants to change the ending so he will 'jolly well not triumph over his difficulties in the end ... Yet it means a lot to have these people about me as I walk along a road & wonder what exactly they will do when the next crisis comes.' On the twenty-seventh: 'My characters seem to me a lot of silly spoilt nervy pseudo intellectuals without any real joy or real Angst in them.' She quotes in German Rilke's famous lines from *Letters to a Young Poet* about the overriding importance of aesthetic *urgency*. On 4 February, her current novel is 'very bad'. She is accordingly depressed. Rilke still consoles her. Her skiing is improving.

9

Displaced Persons
1946–1947

I ris received David Hicks's letter breaking their engagement
on Monday, 18 February 1946. Two days before, on Saturday
the sixteenth, she met Raymond Queneau. She recorded,
years later, the first moment of seeing him in the snow outside
the UNRRA office, turning away in the wind. He had arrived in
Innsbruck, capital of the French Zone – 'a sad city' hard hit by
the war – from Vienna the previous day, and was staying with the
French Surrealist writer Maxime Alexandre. He met Iris, '*une fille
épatante*', at four in the afternoon. Iris in turn told Hal Lidderdale
she had met 'a charming ex-Surrealist' whom she wrongly thought
'in the French Army'.[1]

Queneau had been demobbed in 1940, but the conference
about 'The Crisis in French Literature' he was addressing was
organised by the French army of occupation. He had quarrelled
with the Surrealist André Breton, briefly married to his wife's
sister, more than a decade before, probably objecting to Breton's
aesthetic indiscipline as much as his defection from the family.
Surrealism had nonetheless touched him deeply, and was to
influence Iris too.

It was a meeting with the 'very avant-garde man' that Iris had
long hoped for: 'Part of me wants to be Raymond Queneau,
another wants to be Thomas Mann.'[2] She had introduced Philippa
to Queneau's novel *Pierrot mon ami* (1943) – presumably one of
the books brought back for her from liberated Paris in 1944[3] –
which both read with enthusiasm. The previous December Ernest
Collet, back in Brussels from a trip to Paris, had been helping

secure her translation rights for Queneau's novels, and she noted with excitement that Queneau 'wants to see me'. She was planning to translate him first and secure permission later, though 'I'm not sure my obscene vocabulary is large enough in English.' Iris's 'not wholly successful' translation of *Pierrot mon ami* would be rejected by the publisher John Lehmann in November that year.[4] The playful iconoclasm and audacious linguistic fireworks of Queneau's brilliant comic writing must have posed problems. Nonetheless he influenced her first published novel *Under the Net* (1954), whose narrator-hero treasures *Pierrot mon ami*, and is translating a French novelist called Breteuil just as Iris was translating Queneau.

One of Iris's roles at Innsbruck was liaising with the French, which included interpreting, and she and Queneau always spoke French together,[5] her only approximately fluent second spoken language, though she had some reading knowledge in German, Italian and Russian. Iris understood French very well, writing it in fluent idiom, and spoke it badly, with a strong accent.[6] She and Queneau had a long conversation, and 'understood each another perfectly'. He felt wholly won over and charmed. He was deeply read in English, knew his Sterne, Lewis Carroll and Shakespeare well, and translated from English too.[7] He introduced Iris to Erskine Caldwell and William Faulkner; she later held that it was he who had invented the term 'franglais'.[8] He had a magpie passion for learning, puzzles and lists. They drove together, watching the snow moving on the windscreen, '*comme un petit bateau*', Iris recorded. The friendship had importance for both for a decade.

The afternoon of their meeting they climbed up to Igls at 2,900 feet, and drank '*fine*' until late at night. Queneau noted Iris's sadness. The following day they climbed a higher peak, the Patscher Kofel (7,264 feet), watched a snow-storm from a hut full of French Alpine troops, and Queneau felt their understanding growing in strength. He spoke to her of his psychoanalysis. Iris left Queneau at six in the evening and he sought her out the following Thursday, the day following his forty-third birthday, in the Club Franco-Allié, but the unspecified public talks both were engaged in left them little chance to speak, and they made 'tender' adieux. Queneau describes her thus: 'Irishwoman. Big. Blonde. Common-sensical. A little bun. A peaked cap. A decided walk, somewhat heavy, military. Beautiful eyes, charming smile . . .'; and summarises her career: '4 years in the CP, nowadays Labour'. He mentions Oxford, the Treasury, her acquaintances with Belgian Surrealists,[9] her knowledge of recent French literature, the fact that she was reading *L'Etre et le néant*, her completion of two novels, and Faber's rejection of the second. The novel she was writing in 1946 – not yet *Under the Net* – has already taken thrust from her reading of *Pierrot mon ami*. His dossier continues: 'She loves Kierkegaard. Is interested in the problems of blacks. Likes [Henry Miller's] *Colossus of Maroussi*.' He plans to send her Miller's *Tropic of Cancer*.

Iris, suppliant, asks him whether it vexed him to talk about his work, at which he succinctly comments: 'Yes, in other circumstances. Now, why not? And above all with her . . .' She wished to know whether he had precise political opinions. Indeed he, too, had twice been close to the CP and had left it. The entry concludes: 'She is weary. Her work interests her sufficiently. She skis.' For her part Iris would later say of this complex writer born in Le Havre, of Norman *petit bourgeois* origins, that he had a tremendous presence, was both bear-like and sphinx-like, and that when questioned would ponder carefully before replying. She found something monumental about him, yet something absolutely 'funny and humorous' too. He had a 'very beautiful head'.[10]

Queneau had other girlfriends: one Marianne Hillblom; Janine, whom he later married; and a mysterious 'X', with whom he makes love in a taxi in a scene reminiscent of Henry Miller, involving his reaching a sexual climax while willing himself (successfully) not to ejaculate, an effort of hygiene that 'exhausted [him] all morning'. Given such outspokenness, his chaste descriptions of meetings with Iris are to be taken at face value.[11] They met again in Paris when Iris visited in 1948, after which she wrote to him that, though loving him a lot, 'I am after all a sensible person! For I am indeed *en fin de compte* so sensible and calm and full of the English virtues.' She gave his address as a *poste restante* to her parents during a 1950 visit. To the scholar Walter Redfern, working on Queneau soon after his death in 1976, she wrote, 'I knew RQ well, he was a friend ... I think he (especially *Pierrot*) influenced U[*nder the*] N[*et*].[12] He was a natural, absolute, philosopher ... a very reflective man, & in many ways, I think, a melancholy, unhappy man. What *joie de vivre* in his work, though!'[13] Among the first of the 114 surviving letters she wrote him, many in English, is one in which she refers to the 'important and dangerous' question of finding a literary 'master'.[14] He was her first. When she came to dedicate *Under the Net* to Queneau, she wrote to him that 'it has certain affinities with *Pierrot*'.[15]

2

At the end of January 1946 Iris wrote a furious and upset letter under the influence of Sliwowitz: 'How *irrevocably* broken so many lives have been in this war ... Nothing, nothing nothing ahead for these people.'[16] A twenty-four-year-old DP Yugoslav driver, having smashed up an UNRRA truck and therefore afraid to return to HQ, had made a dash to the Italian frontier with a loaded pistol. Iris helped bring him back, he crying all the way, in a jeep. 'Put him in the cooler,' said the 'hard cynical swine' at HQ with a laugh, eager for the maximum penalty in revenge for the loss of one wretched truck. Iris railed at the stupidity of the man being committed to trial on a charge of carrying firearms, but noted realistically, 'DPs are either apathetic or inclined to be thugs or crooks – they've had to be, to survive.' In the event, the French repatriated him: 'All a bloody business.' She predicted that he (as a King Peter partisan*) would probably end up being shot willy-nilly by Tito's men. The prediction was almost certainly accurate. Before the war the Communist Party in Yugoslavia had two thousand members: its domination of the post-war country, helped by Allied wartime support, was not achieved without

---

* Yugoslav resistance to Hitler was chiefly divided between Communists, following Tito, and royalists, led by Mihailovic. Churchill was persuaded by 1943 to back the former, who were enemies of the latter.

terror. Between 700,000 and 800,000 Yugoslav lives had been lost between 1941 and 1945, many in brutal civil war.

UNRRA was due to take over fully from the military in Austria by 1 March 1946, and Iris's arrival in December 1945 made her part of the advance-guard. Once there her opinion of UNRRA personnel generally went up. Liberation from the German Reich had meant for many Austrians only a decrease in rations to subsistence level, and a doubtful future under military occupation. The UNRRA Chief of Mission noted that the Austrian nation owed its survival to UNRRA aid.[17] The daily ration in Austria was the lowest of any UNRRA-assisted country, the diet in Vienna mostly bread and potatoes, and there had been an increase in deaths from tuberculosis. There were temptations – a few UNRRA recruits got involved in the black market, which was mainly run by Yugoslavs. Iris observed Red Cross parcels changing hands fast in exchange for anything from motor cars to women.[18] But most UNRRA personnel were prepared to do difficult or dull jobs. The Americans showed up well, particularly their efficient women, often trained in welfare and willing, like nurses, to turn their hand to anything.

Iris noted later of her UNRRA years how instructive it was to witness a 'complete breakdown of society',[19] and recalled four separate postings. Innsbruck, at a distance from the DP camps, involved office-work in setting up and financing them, and making pacts with the local authorities to be of mutual use. Since there were hardly any shops, very little to eat, and transport had broken down, semi-official bartering was necessary to obtain food, medicine, blankets, fuel and transport. Cigarettes counted as international currency. Iris wrote to Frank's brother Palmer[20] that she was leading a curious desert-island life with a few people and a few books and very many mountains,

> dealing with the touchy French and the sullen but courteous Austrians, and the thousands of tragic displaced persons who are collected in this pocket between Italy and Switzerland – bad hats many of them by now, after so much survival of the fittest discipline, and hard to do anything for.[21]

She later called Innsbruck a desolate hole.

On arrival at Puch[22] in the American zone,* she was brusquely asked why, if she could not type, she had been sent? Soon she was involved in setting up a telephone exchange instead. Here was a disorderly camp, with frequent fights. She met Serbs who were 'wild & handsome & dramatic & frightfully nice', and as late as 1990 there are roll-calls of Serbian names in her journals – 'A note I made, in memory of the UNRRA camps. Branislav Djekic, Radovan . . . , Dragomir Pardanjac. Handsome Serbs. Also: Boris Leontic . . . (Draga and Djekic, with help from me and Mrs Lewis, came to England, I saw something of Draga. Then lost touch.) March 14. Thinking of Branislav Djekic and Dragomir Pardanjac – should they have gone home? Draga cd have had hopes for his boy. What happened to Draga?'

The Serbs had nowhere to go because they had been in the army, pro-Mihailovic (and thus – though this is unmentioned by Iris – belonging to one of the factions complicit in Frank's death). Everyone wanted to go to America, the dream country far from the bitter racial and political conflicts of Europe,[23] or, failing that, England or possibly France. Iris helped one or two to get to England. One – probably Draga – got a job as a butler in some grand house, but was not happy there. He had a wife and child, little English, and no skills. Iris later wrote to David Hicks to solicit his help over Draga, and, after losing touch, advertised unsuccessfully in *The Times* in an attempt to find him.

Food was so scarce that the Burgomaster of Vienna faced riots.[24] There was an astronomically priced black market, 'corrupt as hell', with one pound of butter quoted at £2.10s, and fifty kilos exchanged against a good fur coat. Mismanagements in high places between UNRRA and the French military authorities resulted in particularly bad food shortages for the DPs that March, and UNRRA was reduced, Iris wrote, to scrounging in Italy and even 'buying up old French cavalry horses'.[25] As the official his-

---

* According to the 'UNRRA Austrian Mission Directory of Personnel' (dated 20 May 1946, Vienna), Puch was in Area I HQ Land Salzburg in the American Zone, one of twelve camps, a large camp with eleven on its team (the average-size UNRRA team was seven and a half).

torian put it, methods combined 'the devious, the bold and the opportunistic',[26] but the end was the same: to look after the welfare of DPs. Iris helped send a wagon round to the British Army camp to beg for left-over food. Her work also involved identifying newcomers, finding out what they were up to and where they wanted to go, finding them somewhere to sleep and procuring blankets. The camps became overcrowded, and there was ill-feeling between the nationalities, but also 'just general misery & crossness & so forth'. The worst tragedies often involved the elderly: 'Nobody wanted them.' Youngsters with skills could live on the hope that they would one day find a new home, and a new country.

3

Iris arrived at UNRRA HQ in Klagenfurt by late March.[27] She travelled via divided Vienna, memorably depicted in Graham Greene's *The Third Man*, in which 'one still climbs over mountains of debris in the streets'.[28] Amongst the rubble blocking the once fashionable Kaernter Strasse was the carcase of a burnt-out tank, while the opera company bravely went on playing in the Teater an der Wien to an audience wrapped in blankets.[29] She visited the Kunsthistorisches Museum and communed long, identifying with 'the long middle-period [self-portrait] of the gazing romantic Rembrandt'. She was still 'young and did not know my life'.[30] The mystery of the portrait appealed, and she later put its 'enormous Socratic head' into *The Sandcastle*, where the painter is described as seeking the truth.[31] She wrote in low spirits to Philippa:

> Dearest, your christmas letter did eventually reach me, two months late ... I was in Vienna and dancing one evening in the gorgeous Kinsky palace – the British officers club, for once we British have done ourselves well in Wien. And the GHQ is at Schönbrunn! which is intact down to the last shimmering pinnacle on the chandeliers ... Vienna was extraordinary. Mountains of masonry and bricks in every street, ruins all golden in

an *intense* sun – the Opera is a magnificent shell, and the cathedral has lost its roof & is horribly blasted but looks beautiful. The general effect, under this blue sky and mad sun, was of a very touching beauty and dignity. *Life* too – music, plays, exhibitions – & they are already rebuilding the main buildings. But oh the streets – 7 maids with 7 mops . . . Yet as one walks the Ringstrasse, between trees, one feels in a great city. Lots of Russians, picturesque and well-armed. UNRRA rife with anti-Soviet stories I fear – but one progressive typist did say to me 'I'd be bored to tears in Vienna if it wasn't for the Red Army.'

Since the Vienna interlude I have come to work at Klagenfurt HQ British Zone Austria . . . Here we are living . . . on the shores of an *exquisite* lake, the Worthersee, 10 km out of Klagenfurt. Intensely blue, still, mountain and forest surround, castle reflecting, altogether precious. I gaze at it in perpetual amazement. The work here is as futile as ever and I am more cut off from the camps and the DPs than I was at Innsbruck, which is a pity.

(Thirty years later, on a return visit to Klagenfurt, she saw 'the Marietta, where I lived in 1946, just the same only enlarged. I recall the golden-eyed goat who danced on his hind legs in the courtyard, and the martins' nests along the open gallery.'[32])

Klagenfurt was a short interlude before her final posting at Graz, probably from late April until late June, in a front-line camp, Hochsteingasse, once a Hitler Youth camp, now a dormitory – set up by British Allied Military Government authority – for students who had contrived to be accepted at the University of Graz.[33] Hochsteingasse was run by a Scots director, Miss Margaret Jaboor, 'the most wonderful woman . . . tremendously practical . . . & an absolutely perfect colleague', with help from a Mrs Lewis. Here there was a kind of hope. On 7 March 1946 there were 208 students from twelve national groupings, of which the seventy-six Slovenes were by far the largest, followed by forty Ukrainians, twenty-five White Russians and Croats, nine Albanians – who nonetheless got together a football team before departing for

Vienna – and eight bleakly described as 'stateless'. German was the *lingua franca* of the camps, and the more fluently it was spoken, the less grammatically. The leader of the Slovene group, a moving spirit behind the whole enterprise, was a strikingly red-haired medical student, Jože Jančar. Iris stayed in touch over the following fifty years with Jože and his wife Marija (*née* Hribar), daughter of a successful farmer, and also then a medical student. 'I got the head boy into medical school,' Iris later misremembered: a large and unexpected cheque from her in 1950, when despair at his poverty nearly forced Jože to abandon his studies, enabled him to complete them instead.

Refugees play a significant role in Iris's imaginative universe and fiction alike, displacement hereafter a spiritual as well as a political condition. At Cambridge in 1947 her four closest friends were to be an Indian, a Palestinian, an Italian-speaking Jewish Egyptian and an Austrian half-Jew; the philosophy scene at Cambridge was dominated by another expatriate, Ludwig Wittgenstein. On being criticised in 1957 for portraying characters in her first two published novels who are misfits, oddities, exiles or displaced, all with something of the refugee about them, Iris replied that 'we are not so comfortable in society as our grandfathers were. Society itself has become problematic and unreliable. So it is that the person who is literally an exile, the refugee, seems an appropriate symbol for the man of the present time.' Modern man is not at home, in his society, in his world. But, she added, she also 'likes and approves of eccentric and unsettled people'.[34] In 1982 Iris remarked to Susan Hill, about refugees in her novels: 'These are images of human suffering, kinds of people that one has met. Such persons are windows through which one looks into terrible worlds.'[35]

The Jančars' story bears recounting, and can stand for others Iris encountered.

4

Jože, son of a village organist, spent a year in the notorious Gonars concentration camp in Italy in 1942, where the partisans tried to kill him, followed by a week in the death cell at Ljubljana. After 1943 he was working with the Yugoslav underground, helping in hospitals and treating those who were fighting Nazis and Communists alike.

The Jančars were typical victims of post-war chaos. By early 1945 the Yugoslav Communists were murdering, as if in a frenzy, such large numbers of their opponents near the Austrian–Slovene border that for years afterward peasants there would find corpses thrown to the surface by underground rivers.[36] As leader of an organisation for young Catholic workers Jože was an obvious target. He and Marija fled their homes in the greatest possible haste, without passports, for what they hoped would be at most a two-week absence, after which they believed the British 8th Army would sort out Slovenia. They were to stay in Austria for three years, and never went back.

Nigel Nicolson, then with the British 5th Corps in Carinthia – and just about to be summoned back to London to work on regimental history with his fellow-Grenadier Second Lieutenant John Bayley – spent the first weeks of peace in southern Austria, which he described as 'the sump of Europe', into which soldiers of many nationalities, and thousands of refugee civilians, had flooded to escape captivity or oppression by the Russians or Tito's partisans, seeking British protection.[37] On 12 May 1945 Nicolson observed a ten-mile column of 30,000 Germans, Slovenes, Serbs, Croats and White Russians marching out of Yugoslavia towards a very makeshift camp at Viktring,*[38] south of Klagenfurt, where there was nothing to eat and no amenities.

Most had opposed and feared Tito, whom Churchill had been persuaded to back against the Royalist Chetniks. The Croats had accepted German command and committed atrocities, but the

---

* 'Vetrinje' in Slovene.

majority, like the Jančars, never accepted German leadership. They simply did not wish to live under Communism, and their only crime was a terror of being returned, against their will, to a regime ready and willing, after civil war, to butcher them. After emerging at the border from a long, wet, frightening tunnel, full of refugees shouting in all languages, the Jančars sighted English Tommies – who promptly stripped Marija of her watch. An instinctive anglophile, the shock of this theft was one of the great disappointments of her life. Jančar became Sanitary Inspector at the camp, digging ditches and latrines. Sulphonamide and DDT helped keep epidemics at bay.

The simultaneous and brutal British repatriation of 40,000 Cossacks to certain death in Stalin's Russia has since been much publicised – there were dozens of suicides; the soldiers used rifle butts, pick handles, bayonets and finally flame-throwers to force people onto the trucks and trains[39] – but that of the dissident Yugoslavs is less well-known.[40] Ordered in writing on 17 May 1945, probably as part of a secret deal with Tito, it lasted from 19 May until the end of that month, at the rate of two trains per day, consisting of old padlocked cattle-trucks, each carrying 1,500 people. Soldiers of the Welsh Guards battalion, in charge at the station and on the verge of mutiny, were instructed to assure the Yugoslavs that the trains were headed for Italy. This lie was at once exposed by the last-minute boarding of Tito's partisans, who had been hiding in nearby bushes and in the station buildings. After some hours the prisoners were unloaded at Kočevje, ninety miles to the south-east, stripped, wired in pairs, shot in the neck and their bodies flung into a pit. Nigel Nicolson later wrote: 'It was the most horrible experience of my life'; and Anthony Crosland, on the Intelligence staff of the 6th Armoured Division, said: 'It was the most nauseating and cold-blooded act of war I have ever taken part in.'[41] Marija's twenty-two-year-old brother Anton was among those the British repatriated to certain death. Following a protest to General Alexander on 4 June, six thousand refugees, some from the Viktring monastery, were at the very last moment spared repatriation. They included the Jančars. There is an echo of all this in *Flight from the Enchanter*, where an arbitrary line determines which refugees in England are sent home.

The survivors were very afraid of the British. Those who trusted them had, after all, been sent back and killed, while some who mistrusted them had survived; and fear made them good observers. As John Corsellis has described in *Slovenian Phoenix*, the Slovenes picked themselves up after the double tragedy and, with astonishing courage, resisting many pressures to accept 'voluntary repatriation', gradually made new lives for themselves. Their Catholicism, nationalism, and the fact that there were children in nearly all the camps,[42] meant that they had to keep going.

Jože played a key role in the opening of the camp for university students at Graz. He hiked across the Italian border in August 1945 to try to get Slovene students accepted at Padua University, and soon after, with the intervention and active help of John Corsellis in the Friends Ambulance Unit, and the backing of the UNRRA Area Director Mr Cornwell, contrived after many exertions, and despite the chauvinism of the authorities, to have them accepted at Graz University. They studied in German. Hochsteingasse was the dormitory camp for those DPs enrolled at Graz, a student camp to be run by UNRRA. They moved in at the beginning of February 1946,* and Iris joined them in April.

The students 'created a community life of outstanding quality, educationally, culturally, and socially'.[43] Morale was high. There was a camp newspaper, a volunteer fire service which adopted fancy-dress on occasion, and, above all, a sense of the future. Jože was student spokesman and leader. They wore for a while white overalls purloined from some army store which made them resemble – in Jože's eyes – Sunday painters like Churchill. Iris noted the sense of comradeship.[44] The closeness to the Yugoslav border was dangerous – the Yugoslavs fomented trouble, particularly persecuting the 'intelligentsia'. UNRRA may rarely and involuntarily have been involved in forcible repatriation, through CP infiltration or through concern to see DPs return to their country of origin,[45] but after the Cold War began in earnest,

---

* After two and a half months in the Keplerschule, Keplerstrasse, Graz.

resettlement as much as repatriation became official alternative policies. Iris watched while a Tito man in full rig, with his big boots and his Rolls-Royce, appeared at the camp to attempt to persuade his fellow countrymen to come home. They nearly lynched him. In mid-April, her view of Tito appears cool, distanced, inquisitive and politically naive:

> Another shadow that falls here (or ray of light, whichever you prefer) is that of Tito, who is the local ogre for half the population, & Joan of Arc for the other. Up in the hills the other day . . . I heard the peasants talking a Slav tongue. This is the territory which Tito claims . . . Violent contradictory stories about Yugoslavia circulate all the time & now & then the factions shoot off a few rounds of ammunition. I would love to get into Yugoslavia to find out what is happening, but I gather entry is impossible at present.[46]

5

The main problem in Graz, after repatriation, was lack of food, a *leitmotiv* of Iris's stay. The DPs were on six hundred calories per day (under the military they had had 850), compared to a normal 2,500 or more, a diet so close to starvation that girls were missing their periods: 'in the morning unsweetened black slush, presumably coffee, even for children. At midday watery soup made from Army Supply surplus with a few morsels of macaroni, beans or potato or meat fibres in it . . . having 380 calories . . . For supper unsweetened blackish coffee again.' Bread was poor, and one day a loaf would be shared between five people, the next between ten or even more. The diarist Franc Pernišek feared that starvation of the 'serf' refugees – who fared worse than native Austrians – was an UNRRA ruse to get as many possible to go home.

When Indian rice arrived at Hochsteingasse, a play about Indians was improvised. When potatoes arrived, Iris held the key to the warehouse and Jože persuaded her to allow the refugees to take them out while she turned a blind eye. He found a packet of sweets in his pocket immediately afterwards. Iris later told him they were for Marija.

Iris wore a British officer's uniform – khaki jacket with pink shoulder-tabs carrying red-and-white flashes reading UNRRA, over a khaki skirt – but was generally 'improperly dressed', never donning the peaked cap which Margaret Jaboor wore for official visits. Her hair, too, invited comment: fringed, dishevelled, over-hanging her eyes. The students in the philosophy barracks, the most bohemian and cheeky, would wolf-whistle at her approach, and nicknamed her 'Čopka' (from *chopka*, a kind of little hen whose wattles hang over its eyes): 'Here comes Čopka!'

The Jančars thought Iris 'a shy young girl, introverted, non-communicative', thoughtful and kind in dealing with the students' problems, but too naive and convoluted. Although nearly twenty-seven, she reminded them of a student. Miss Jaboor was more effective. In her forties, aggressive, she fought for them and, in private, would condemn the repatriations as both a tragedy and a 'nonsense'. The students honoured her – and it was a singular honour – by calling her 'Mutti' ('Mummy'). Her continuing work for refugees was to be rewarded by an OBE. She was remembered for her love of her fellow human beings, and for forgiving their failings – 'And at times there [was] a lot to forgive.'[47] Iris, by contrast with Miss Jaboor, offered no direct criticism of Communism. The Jančars wrongly recalled Iris as Deputy Director of the camp, although UNRRA personnel had no military rank but a civilian grade determining their salary. Iris called herself the 'lowest Commissioned Officer . . . at the scene', and Miss Jaboor later confirmed that her position was in fact very junior.[48] Her scope for independent manoeuvre was accordingly circum-scribed.

Late in 1947, a year after Iris's departure, Jože, now seriously ill with TB, was again arrested, under the Steele–Tito agreement, according to which refugees alleged by Tito to be guilty of a war crime might be returned to Yugoslavia. John Corsellis and Margaret Jaboor, among others, did all they could to get him released. Marija thought this arrest was caused by Jože's work as the first Chairman of the Slovene Students' Group. He could at that time have qualified as a doctor within a few months but, fearing kidnap by the Yugoslavs after their failure to have him extradited, he did not dare remain in Graz and set about trying to emigrate instead, thus delaying his qualification by many years. As for Marija, she gave up her prospective career as a doctor for good.

By early 1948 Jože and Marija were on their way to Britain as European Voluntary Workers, nominally to work either in the mines or in agriculture. To their distress, since only single volunteers were eligible they were split up, he to a camp near Cambridge, where Iris was then studying, she to Preston.

6

Iris resigned from UNRRA with effect from 1 July 1946[49] and went home via Paris, where she bought a second hardback copy of Sartre's *l'Etre et la néant* three days later, and met up with Queneau. The pain of David Hicks's rejection was soon absorbed, it may be conjectured, within the larger one of Balogh's, of which a later friend wrote in 1952, 'This affair, more than anything else, tore her life apart. She never got completely over it.'[50] Iris spoke of Balogh to Noel Martin in Brussels in September 1945, to Leo Pliatzky in the late summer of 1946, to Franz Steiner in 1952, and to Nickie Kaldor in November 1954.

Frank, too, was evidently on her mind. In his last letter he had gently reproached her, addressing her various painful love-complications, that he, by contrast, felt able to win a continence contest with Hippolytus. The previous June Iris had translated Euripides' *Hippolytus* 'into rather harsh verse – long lines & syllable [sic] sticking out in all directions. Soothing, but hardly successful.'[51] She was now also in contact with Frank's brother Edward (Palmer), whom she helped collect material for the commemorative *There is a Spirit in Europe*.

By March 1946 she had applied to Newnham College, Cambridge, to do a D.Phil., and she also put in for a lectureship in philosophy at Sheffield University. Although UNRRA was due to fold anyway by June 1947 (succeeded by the Office of the United Nations High Commissioner for Refugees), Leo recalled this as one of the few times Hughes was cross with her, as she was giving up a not inconsiderable salary of £550: junior academics earned considerably less. She also contrived to get a reference from Donald MacKinnon for an application to study, with the help of a Commonwealth Scholarship, at Vassar College in New York State. This was 'a last gesture which I do want to make toward the academic life! After this I shall chuck my academic ambitions!'[52] Vassar was the college Frank's mother Theo had attended.

Iris won the place at Vassar and a Commonwealth Scholarship, but in the space on the US visa application form where the prospective visitor is asked whether they have ever been a member of the CP – where more worldly contemporaries would wisely write 'no' – puritanical and literal-minded Iris wrote 'yes'. She was thus prevented by the McCarren Act from entering the United States. Iris had been longing to go to America, and wrote succinctly to Leo that September: 'US visa refused; reason: ex-member of CP! My view of the US now hits an altogether new low!'[53] Bertrand Russell, the government Minister Hugh Gaitskell, the Thompson family's neighbour and friend Gilbert Murray[54] and Justice Felix Frankfurter became involved on her behalf, 'but the act is made of iron'.* For the rest of her life, any visit she planned to America would necessitate a separate waiver.[55] To Hal Lidderdale that September, who had railed against the Cold War in an 'anti-weather tirade', she wrote: 'Can one *rely* on 100 aspirins, or is a tube train safer?'[56] Eight gloomy months later she hoped that reading André Maurois, Martin Buber and T.H. White's *Mistress Masham's Repose* would drive away 'gloomy forebodings & suicide plans'.[57]

Here – despite public disavowal[58] – was one source of Iris's disaffection with the United States. Although America in real

---

* Jeffrey Meyers, 'The Art of Fiction', *Paris Review* 115, 1990, p.210. Denis Healey also wrote 'Yes', but Gaitskell pleaded successfully on his behalf, mentioning the work Healey had done separating Labour from the CP. Congress decided separately, Healey recalls, on each and every case.

life contained much that fascinated both Bayleys (including such friends as Al and Nay Lebowitz, she an academic, he a lawyer, in St Louis), it is in her fiction the land to which, like Henry James in *The Golden Bowl*, she exiles characters at the end of two novels;[59] or the place where neurotically stiff English intellectuals go to liberate themselves, arriving back home in a state of unacceptable exuberance.[60] The good Vietnam draft-resister Ludwig in *An Accidental Man* and Maisie Tether in *The Message to the Planet* are American exceptions to the rule that her major characters be British. 'I never feel at home there,' she later confessed; it was 'so raw & unworked, I hate not walking, & absence of urban life'.[61] Unlike most visitors, she was permitted, after each 'waiver', only one visit every twelve months. In 1963 she was for this reason vexingly obliged to remain in Canada while John visited New York State. The help of Katharine Graham, owner and editor of the *Washington Post*, was called upon – unsuccessfully – to try to get Iris in.

Iris, who came from a family of 'wanderers' cut off from their Irish roots, and, having worked with displaced persons, identified with the condition of exile, later recording a dramatic '1946 fear that I would get nowhere, would hang around and ultimately become a DP myself'.[62] The failure of her attempt to get to Vassar left her depressed, lost, lacking the sense of a future. She was unemployed from July 1946 until she went up to Cambridge in October 1947, and her financial situation was dire.[63] Under a photograph of herself taken that bitter winter of 1946–47, in a cold and snowy London, she wrote in her photograph album a single, expressive word: 'Nadir'.

7

Despite 'nostalgia for the extreme Left',[64] Iris felt positively drawn towards Anglo-Catholicism.[65] Between 3 and 9 October 1946 she made her first visit to Malling Abbey in Kent, and to Dame Magdalene Mary Euan-Smith, its notable Abbess. Malling is an Anglican Benedictine community and abbey together, originally founded in 1090, refounded after 1916. Iris had written to Queneau a fortnight earlier that this was a time of 'particular desolation and difficulty'.[66] The visit was the first of three.* Donald MacKinnon suggested that Iris visit Malling after asking for advice from a Pusey House† priest.[67] The Abbess had a reputation of 'being good with difficult cases'.[68] In 1940 MacKinnon had been one of a group of young theologians who, under Dom Gregory Dix's lead, wrote shilling booklets for the Dacre Press, associated with Malling, and he sent the Abbess his BBC radio scripts. MacKinnon was that year (as all her life‡) much on Iris's mind.

Iris's upbringing was not exclusively free-thinking. Many years later she wrote to Philippa: 'I got [religion] in childhood which I think you didn't.'[69] Both her mother's and her father's relatives had the habit of giving her the Gospels as a gift, with bright pointers towards helpful quotations, and she kept many of these.§ During the pre-war summer holidays when Iris stayed with her paternal Chapman cousins in Portrush,[70] one friend remembers family prayers after dinner, Uncle Willy, treasurer to the Apsley Gospel Hall Brethren in Donegall Pass, reading from the Bible and praying.[71] With her maternal 'cousin' Eva Lee, moreover, the family attended revivalist meetings, Eva's family being involved with the evangelical 'Crusaders'. In 1985 Iris would record that

---

* Her second visit was 6–7 August 1948; her third 2–4 August 1949, during a retreat taken by 'dogmatic' Canon Dart.
† A small Anglo-Catholic house in St Giles, Oxford, for work among students.
‡ Evidenced e.g. by journals. Comparison of the structure of her Gifford lectures, published as *Metaphysics as a Guide to Morals* (London, 1992), shows a resemblance to MacKinnon's some years earlier – see Donald MacKinnon, *The Problem of Metaphysics* (Cambridge, 1974), *passim.* Both Iris Murdoch and MacKinnon, for example, explore the relationship between morality, metaphysics and the tragic.
§ For Christmas 1929 her grandmother Louisa Murdoch gave her a Bible with the inscription '. . . with love from Grannie: Psalms 119 and 105'. One of the many copies of the New Testament she carefully kept by her in her London flat has '. . . with love from Eva. Revelation 3.20' written in it. This was given to her by her maternal quasi-cousin Eva Lee on the occasion of her thirteenth birthday. Iris kept *Daily Light on the Daily Path: A Devotional Text Book for Every Day in the Year; in the Very Words of the Bible* (many editions from 1861 to 1983) from November 1934. Another New Testament arrived for Easter 1939, with the handwritten inscription, 'I am the Way the Truth the Life, John. 14 vi'. Another (New English Bible translation) came in March 1961 from Cousin Muriel, 'with Love and memory of another happy visit'.

the verse 'Wide, wide as the ocean, high as the heavens above, deep, deep as the deepest sea is my saviour's love' brought back 'memories of evangelical meetings in Ireland'.[72] Of Ireland's evangelical Christianity she wrote, 'singing was the best part of the thing where some light shone'.[73] Cousin Sybil recalled Iris taking her grandmother to a Chiswick church that was 'high'. Louisa, affronted, refused to put any money into the collecting-dish; Iris went off and wept.[74] Sybil believes Iris may simply have been trying to oblige in taking Louisa to church, and was affronted when she failed, Louisa smelling Papism. Cousin Muriel gritted her teeth through another such service with Iris in the late 1940s.

Even at the height of her CP involvement in 1940–41 Iris had written to Paddy O'Regan, after an account of watching Liverpudlians picking furniture out of the ruins of their bombed houses:

> You are worried that I may, in a rush of external activities, forget about my soul . . . My trouble is that I am obsessed with my soul . . . I was not made for action, I hate action, I loathe political activity of any sort beyond reading Engels & enjoying the intellectual refinements of Marxism. I have to force myself to be active – my spirit is forever returning to the still centre, & I have to drive it out again into the world of movement & change . . . my journey is just beginning. One cannot have a harmony that does not contain the universe . . . and that . . . means changing the social system.[75]

Conversion was not then uncommon among philosophers – Elizabeth Anscombe, Peter Geach and Michael Dummett all converted to Catholicism. Novelists too – Muriel Spark, William Golding, perhaps later Doris Lessing – had conversion experiences. The rationalist culture of the 1920s and 1930s was thought to have led to Dachau, Hiroshima and the Second World War. A sense of 'there must be something more' was prevalent, and there were mass conversions under Bishop Stephen Neill's mission to Oxford University in February 1947, the Sheldonian packed to overflowing for five nights in succession. Circumstantial evidence suggests that Iris may have attended. Father Martin Jarrett-Kerr, normally posted in South Africa, claimed to have received her first

confession:[76] she catechised him sternly about the South African
political scene, alarming him with her moral passion and vehemence. He was assistant missionary to Bishop Neill on that
occasion. At the point after the war where Iris engages with Existentialism, with its doctrine of self-liberation, she also engages
with Christianity, with its investment in self-purgation.

Guests to Malling Abbey live in a separate building within the
grounds, have their own rooms, keep silence after Compline at
9 p.m. until 10.30 the following morning, attend the Mass and
office, with whose Latin Iris had no problems. They have their own
fourteenth-century pilgrim chapel in the gatehouse for prayers,
readings or talk, and they help in the spacious gardens. The guest
chapel abutted the transept where the nuns prayed, at a right
angle, so that the nuns could be heard but not seen. Much of
this was borrowed wholesale for *The Bell.*

Iris was greeted by the guest sister, Sister Elizabeth, who gave
readings during the otherwise silent meal-times. With one or two
other younger sisters, Sister Perpetua saw Iris in the parlour which
still in those days had wooden grilles through which nuns and
guests conversed. She recalled talking about Iris's work in the DP
camps in Austria, and was struck by the frank, open expression
of her face, her short fair hair, general simplicity, warmth and
ability to enter sympathetically into the problems of others.[77] Iris
also spoke to the Abbess through the widely separated wooden
bars. She wrote to Philippa: 'When I see you I will tell you about
the Abbess, tho' I daresay you know about her already.' Dame
Mary, daughter of a doctor, was the fifth child of a typical Victorian upper-middle-class family. She was warm, outgoing and
had the gift of concentrating entirely on the concerns of the
person she was addressing. Her spiritual influence ranged far
beyond the community at Malling. Though an atheist herself,
Philippa was sufficiently touched by how helped Iris had been to
send the Abbess a small donation: 'So peaceful & moving that
place,' wrote Iris. 'What a sick world.'

One New Year's Eve in Oxford, perhaps 1946–47, Iris and
Philippa's sister Marion were alone with a friend of Marion's.
'Oh, do talk to us,' Marion pleaded with Iris, who demurred. She

was concentrating instead on making New Year's resolutions: 'It's very important, to make them, and to keep them, it could alter the whole direction of life.' Such talk of changing one's life distantly echoes a conversation she had with her first cousin Cleaver Chapman about Christianity. Iris asked Cleaver how you became a Christian. Cleaver, who stayed for life with the Brethren, replied that you simply 'Let Christ into your life and He will take away your sins.' Iris scornfully, vehemently replied, 'It can't *possibly* be as easy as that.' She evidently felt that in order to be 'saved' you had to do something strenuous and continuing, engage yourself in an arduous quest.

During the night of 20 January 1947 she had a dream of Christ and the Virgin Mary inaugurated by angels resembling birds of prey so vivid and brilliant it felt like 'not a dream, but a vision'. Both Donald MacKinnon and her father figured in the dream, which she was thirty years later to give to Anne Cavidge in *Nuns and Soldiers*. On 2 March 1947 she heard Gervase Mathew preach a sermon at Westminster Cathedral on 'the life of charity, the compassion of God, & the temptation to despair after sin'. He cited a medieval English churchman: 'If all the sin in London is like a little spark of flame – the compassion of God is like the Thames.' She was to criticise Existentialists for their 'dramatic, solipsistic, romantic and anti-social exaltation of the individual'.[78] Her journals suggest her own complicity in the dramatic.

On 5 April 1947:

> Urge towards drama is fundamental. I am 'full of representations of myself' (see Ruysbroek*). Need for self-expression, to speak, may seem to conflict . . . I am using novels to slough off my lesser selves – instead of a means to self-knowledge and greater inwardness. Hence my 'moral vulgarity'.
>
> The escape from drama? (Need of not drifting away from politics.) In love. In simple relations with people,

---

* Jan van Ruysbroeck (1293–1381; sometimes spelled 'Ruusbroec'), influential Flemish Christian mystic, whose gentleness gained him the epithet 'the good prior'. He wrote four extensive treatises and seven lesser works; the Church declared him 'blessed' in 1908.

animals, things. Face to face with great art – which gives feeling of humility & admiration – or great intellectual world. (S.K[ierkegaard]. [Gabriel] Marcel). Drama besets me – when alone often, walking along road &tc. This corrupts my inner life – I must attend to that fact. In relations with people I'm not intimate with, & want to impress . . . What goes on in my head is 4/5 unnecessary or bad. Fantasies, self-pity, self-torture. Need for wholeness, simplicity. To hope, to see new vision of myself . . . 'Nothing better' than a good person.[79]

8

To David Hicks in September 1946 she was upbeat, painting her recovery as complete: 'I have rarely felt more insouciante & generally more serene.'[80] Writing to Philippa three weeks later, just after her return from Malling, she is by contrast remorseful for past sins, full of hopeful gratitude about the renewal of their friendship despite all: 'You are infinitely precious to me.' Only since coming back from Austria, she says, has she realised the Seaforth 'events' fully as things that she did, as apart from things she suffered (in fact she had brooded on them continuously[81]). She now lived them again, seeing her own responsibility. This had been not pleasant, but it was necessary. She apologises to both Philippa and Michael 'most humbly'. She has been 'very deep in the pit over this affair', her love remaining 'as deep & as tender as ever'. Philippa evidently replied with characteristic generosity, and Iris spoke of their friendship as 'this precious central thing in my life', giving courage and calm of mind – something it was, through many changes, to remain. She knew she had been hateful to Michael, but what had caused that is 'dead & cut away. Now that I am out of the despair & frenzy I feel the strength to change myself. I have learnt a lot from these horrors . . . most of [what is bad] has now died. My darling, please be patient . . . it is long way back [*sic*] & I have still far to go & many knots to untie. Don't let go your hold – all shall be well. We now have a phone: Chiswick 1913.'[82]

In October Philippa had acquired Existentialist essays from Paris that Iris wished to read. Iris also re-read Max Brod on Kafka, and felt Brod was 'never able to measure the great man – the talented bloke's comments on the genius'. Baffled by Kant and Hegel, she compares herself to the German Romantic Idealist Herder, a 'poetically-fervid, largely enthusiastic & essentially historical soul'. She had always had a 'wicked penchant for those who make their errors in a big way'.[83] On 11 November 1946 she saw Michael and Philippa and wrote with relief that 'peace & joy [are] possible for me again'. Seeing Pip was 'freedom & life after being entombed for so long'. She finds 'joy in our constant love & in our whole world of thought & feeling together. There is no one who can be to me what you are. Hope Michael didn't find it too much a strain . . .'

Something forced in these cries of joy meets something deeply felt. Constraint governed the friendship for some years. But living as Iris was outside the social context provided by a career, contact with Philippa, whose talent for philosophy she always rated above her own, mattered greatly:

> I haven't had a real conversation with anyone since I was last in Oxford . . . I just flounder about with the same old problems. I just don't see how any intellectual institution could ever dream of employing me. Not having anyone to talk to about the stuff, or indeed about anything else that matters, is sometimes sheer agony. I lose all sense of my reality as a thinker.[84]

When the bad news about Vassar came, she was reading Unamuno, Heidegger, Sartre, Berdyaev. Oxford was 'more "logical positivist" than ever, & anyone interested in psychology, history or religion is regarded as "romantic" & ergo unsound. Sartre is mentioned only with derision & no one reads Kierkegaard.' She saw Sartre's *Huis Clos* in London and judged it 'formidable'. The critics hated it: 'Alas my country.'[85] She contemplated studying philosophy at Reading,[86] wrote later, at MacKinnon's suggestion, to Bangor for details of a post there, thought of Cardiff too.[87] She was also 'struggling with Kant & Hegel & trying to get a hard intellectual grip on certain problems which I only grasp imaginatively & emotionally. I'm still not sure whether I can really think philosophically at all. However. I shall probably push off to Paris for a while . . . or maybe I'll wait till next spring. Winter in Paris would be no fun.'[88]

A friend (probably Philippa) sent her notice of a Sarah Smithson studentship in philosophy at Newnham College, Cambridge, and in spring 1947 she was accepted. She thought of studying the philosophy of Husserl,[89] but claimed no one had heard of him. Money was short, and at the end of July she applied for a Ministry of Education grant for an additional £50 or £100 to eke out Newnham's cash, giving MacKinnon as referee.

9

The year 1947 was not all gloom. In February, while reading philosophy to prepare to go up to Newnham, and rekindling her friendship with Philippa, Iris also made a foray to St Ives in Cornwall with its community of painters.[90] Anne Willett – with whom Michael Foot had spent his last free evening before his capture in occupied Brittany – saw her in a Soho jazz club, dancing away from her partner, gazing into a world which was not there. In the summer Iris, Mary Scrutton and Tom Greeves took their bicycles and food to Paris on a shoestring budget, and probably at Montmartre visited an early example of the Rotor, a hollow drum inside which people stood and then discovered, as it rotated faster and faster and the floor sank away beneath them, that they were hanging vertically, stuck to the walls by sheer centrifugal force. Tom and Mary were content to watch this spectacle from above. Iris (typically, in Mary's view) at once volunteered to go inside and have the Experience. It seemed to do her no harm. She also saw Queneau on her own.[91]

This was the first of a series of annual visits.[92] Iris later recalled 'various *boites*, including homosexual ones'[93] and getting mixed up with a criminal whom she thought to help, who stole a lot of her belongings before vanishing. The man, later arrested, sent her begging letters from prison; what she sent included soap and was returned to her. (Later she wrote that she had 'probably experienced everything', which was 'not the same as knowing everything'.[94]) She met Marcel Mouloudji,[95] whose novel *Enrico* won the Prix Pléiade in 1945, and saw Edith Piaf and the Compagnons de la Chanson on stage. She and Queneau listened to Juliette Greco in a *boîte*; Greco was at that time singing the classic bitter-sweet golden song about the passing of youth and love that Queneau had written for her, '*Si tu t'imagines*'. Iris watched her with a blonde woman-lover,[96] and was interested when Queneau explained that Greco 'did not like only men'.[97] Anne Willett also saw her in 1947 at the Café Flore in Saint-Germain, where black marketeers were accepting money from Jews wishing to be shipped illegally into Israel. Iris would stand and listen to the café-talk amongst, for example, the actor Roger Blin, Henry Miller and the writer Jacques Prévert, whose *Paroles* (1946) she acquired. Simone de Beauvoir was always accompanied by a different young man, never by Sartre. Iris made it plain, despite an invitation to join in and sit down, that standing and listening were what she preferred.

When Jake in *Under the Net* is entranced by being cabled at the Brasserie Lipp opposite Café Flore, one can feel Iris's excitement at her own new-found cosmopolitanism inhabiting Jake's. Indeed she noted wistfully the message, probably from Queneau, '*Chère Iris, je serai certainement au Flore entre 7.30 et 8*';[98] and received the 'first poem to be written to me on a metro ticket', probably also by Queneau. Paris was to be a 'necessary' city all her life, a Mecca. Angus Wilson sighted her there in the 1970s, happily whistling with her head in the air and her hands in her pockets, like a schoolboy.

10

Iris's association with Donald MacKinnon had undergone a break in the autumn of 1943, when the friendship aroused his wife Lois's strong resentment. MacKinnon, wise in so many ways, lacked the common sense to introduce favoured undergraduates to his wife, 'normalising' such friendships. Both Lois and Iris were passionate philo-Semites,[99] both painted and they doubtless had other interests in common. Perhaps fearing being outnumbered, MacKinnon did not encourage meetings even between his wife and mother. On 28 February 1947 Iris recorded:

> The thought came to me yesterday that my love for D[onald] will always be a source of profound joy to me, beyond all the conflicts & paradoxes, even when I can't see him. This brought me great peace.[100]

During Holy Week 1947 they met again from three to seven, probably in London one Tuesday afternoon when he was on his way back to Oxford from Wells. 'I shall never forget that week, never. There was a kind of agony,' he wrote. The oft-repeated, unascribed quotation from Iris's journals, 'I would go into the dark, if it meant light for you,' may belong to this period: she and MacKinnon shared the heady cocktail of dramatic intensity, religious and erotic passion and guilt which she satirised in *The Red and the Green*[101] and gently mocked in her sequence of tormented gay male seekers, starting with Michael Meade in *The Bell.* MacKinnon spoke later of 'foolish, fantasy-ridden efforts' to help her, and Lois recalled that he advised Iris not to repeat her perception of herself as a mixture of the revolutionary Rosa Luxemburg, the philosopher Susan Stebbing and the feminist writer Simone de Beauvoir.[102]

MacKinnon's feelings were now engaged. Iris had confided to him difficulties about her love-life when a student. It could not have escaped his attention that Thomas Balogh was seven years older than him, while for her part Iris always thought Donald older than he actually was. Her ethic of 'sexual generosity', Lois believed, could be a source of disturbance. He later told Lois, who identified Iris at this period as his 'sacred' love, herself as his 'profane', that duplicity then ruled his life: the theologian Karl Barth had just such an intense liaison with Fraülein von Kirchbaum which, though also chaste, hurt his marriage, excluding his wife and condemning her to loneliness. Lois saw Iris as formidable, promiscuous, vain; and, in collecting admirers, merciless. No doubt Iris appeared a twentieth-century Lou-Andreas Salomé. Iris noted that she saw Donald as 'Christ' and herself as Mary Magdalene, that model penitent out of whom, we are told, Christ had cast 'seven devils'.[103] She 'would always be a little in love with Donald'.[104] Lois was in a position dryly to note that between Christ and her husband Donald there were a few minor differences, that the role of the Magdalene entailed half-conscious flirtation – 'He did once hold my hand,' Iris remarked[105] – and that the drama left her, a young and insecure wife, role-less.

MacKinnon confided in each about the other. Iris pilloried her own early habit of selfish idealisation in *A Fairly Honourable Defeat* in the character of Morgan, who invented pictures of friends before persecuting them with those pictures. That said, the episode shows Iris at her least attractive. Never short of admirers, she was willing to continue clandestine communication that she knew to be hurtful to Donald's wife: on leaving Keble in September 1947 Lois had to suffer the indignity of receiving the 'very tactful' sympathy of the head porter, who could not escape witnessing such communication, whether in the form of visits, telephone calls or letters. Though neither guileless nor free from duplicity or concealment, Iris nonetheless protested her 'innocence'. Perhaps she saw this emotional intimacy with another woman's husband as no more than her natural right.

Lois later noted the resemblance, in *The Sandcastle*, between the difficult marriage of Nan and Mor troubled by the advent of Rain Carter, and Iris's threat to her marriage. Theological differences between the MacKinnons[106] become in that novel differences about Mor's political career, and while Rain was partly modelled on one of Iris's students, she is also given Iris's Riley car, her interest in the problems of human portraiture – painterly rather than novelistic – her love of swimming, and her ability to cry. If Iris intended to echo the MacKinnons in *The Sandcastle* this was cruel, recalling Michael Foot's observation that she made a 'formidable enemy': indeed Iris later lamented that she had been 'unfair to Nan'.[107] MacKinnon's humane wisdom is displaced onto Bledyard ('Who can look reverently enough upon another human face?'[108]) The gambit by which Nan wins Mor back at the end is echoed in the fortunate move the MacKinnons made that year for him to take up the Regius Chair of Moral Philosophy in Aberdeen.*

In April Iris noted: 'desperate mood today. Bitter thoughts seem to tear down ... what I am trying to build.'[109] In May 'depression after letter from D[onald]',[110] whose birthday she notes on 27 August, and who, drinking heavily, was now breaking his ties with the South. He once more broke matters off, putting it thus: 'It's all a matter in the end of keeping to a true care for I[ris]. And that I shall achieve. One's so overlaid by corruption.'[111] In June Iris wrote in her journal, 'Gloomy interval. Angst, nausée, & all the bag of tricks.'[112] On the Feast of the Assumption in mid-August[113] she thought much and peacefully of Donald, and cited his quotation from Graham Greene's *The Power and the Glory* 'that loving God, like loving other people, is wanting to protect Him from oneself'. She transcribed his writings, for example that modern doubt was not speculative but a state of mind, almost a state of being, while 'integrity is to be achieved in Christ alone',[114] and bought him Kathleen Raine's recent verse collection *Living in Time.*

Later she lamented that human frailty – 'mine, theirs' – lay behind the whole tangle. Meanwhile the MacKinnons were settling into a handsome eighteenth-century house and walled garden opposite St Machar's Cathedral in Aberdeen. About this move Iris expressed 'tormented ... misery ... God knows I'm in some ways an interested party.'[115] She and MacKinnon met once thereafter, by chance, in the 1960s, when he, now Norris-Hulse Professor of Divinity in Cambridge, declined her invitation to visit her in London. He returned home pale and, unusually for him, early for lunch.

---

* Mor and Nan are almost certainly composite portraits, for which another Oxford couple, unrelated to the MacKinnons, also 'sat'.

11

Iris continued to demonstrate a writer's consoling capacity to
create explanatory myths. Listening to Sartre's *The Flies* on the
Third Programme on Tuesday, 29 July, she wondered: 'Myths.
What is it to invent a new myth?'[116] Sartre had taken the *Oresteia*
– Fraenkel's *Oresteia* and indeed Frank's *Oresteia* – replaying it in
Paris under the very noses of the Germans to make propaganda
for violent resistance. What could she do with it? During the night
she lay awake and rewrote the Orestes story in her mind's eye to
make something very different and 'highly autobiographical'. Her
version resembles Peter Brook's production of *A Midsummer
Night's Dream*: all the characters are doubled. Orestes is twinned
with Agamemnon and Aegisthus, Electra with Clytemnestra. Iris
– as in her six novels narrated in the first person by a man –
identifies with the male hero, Orestes, who has been sent into
exile – Austria, but also the state of being unable to meet MacKinnon – during which time (s)he is 'tormented by the Erinyes of
selfish uncreative remorse'. Electra – The Abbess/possibly also
Philippa – persuades the guilt-ridden Orestes to make the creative
act of true repentance: for example, visiting Malling. Orestes
kills Aegisthus and Clytemnestra and is able to see Agamemnon/
MacKinnon again, no longer blinded by self-hatred and remorse.
As well as her exile from Donald, there are oblique references
to Seaforth.

12

In August 1947 Iris was still sick at heart, unable to work: 'Life's
been disintegrated in a nightmarish way for so long now, one
almost forgets what it would be like to feel normal & secure &
loved. Wrong of course to have this nostalgia & to feel in exile.
One's life just is this endless attempt to integrate & where that
attempt is is home.'[117] She stayed at Bledlow for two nights with
Frank's recently widowed mother Theo, just returned from a trip

to Bulgaria with Palmer.[118] Theo did not entirely approve of Iris.[119] Born in 1892 of New England missionary stock, she probably found her bohemianism disconcerting. She would have told Iris about attending the deeply moving official ceremony in Litakovo to honour Frank and his fallen comrades,[120] and she probably then gave Iris the volume of Catullus that had been found on Frank's body after he was shot.[121]

Iris arrived at Cambridge in early October.[122] Her rooms were in The Pightle, a small house on Newnham Walk, next to the Principal's Lodge. She bought a kettle and admired the Renaissance buildings reflected in the Cam. Philippa sent her a gown. Iris read *The Plague*, which she felt was a great novel, ambiguous, mysterious, absurd; Queneau was jealous of her admiration for it. If she felt displaced, she before long found in Simone Weil's *Need for Roots* and *Gravity and Grace* a way of thinking that put decentring and displacement at the centre.[123] One of the worst evils committed by totalitarian dictators entailed the uprooting of entire peoples; yet the moral life *itself* was a task of unselfing, *ascesis*, or voluntary deracination. Weil resolves the paradox by speaking of 'moral levels' above which the agent cannot proceed without danger. Only for the saintly, Weil appeared to argue, can virtue have no fixed address. It was through Weil too, the only woman among Iris's great teachers, that she encountered Plato anew.[124] 'I call Sartre "romantic" and would not call her so,' Iris wrote in her journal,[125] and noted 'Virtue is knowledge/is attention' in the margin of Weil's *Intuitions Pré-Chrétiennes*.[126]

10

Cambridge
1947–1948

Cambridge in 1947 was full of women, 'unsettled, impatient, restless', not yet permitted to graduate,[1] whom the writer Elizabeth Sewell tried to enfranchise by starting a 'Union of Women Graduates'. Iris, 'really a stranger', did not join, and never seemed to fit in.[2] Sewell was impressed that Iris had written several unpublished novels, including one about a Greek statue that comes to life.

Through Sewell, Iris met the Italian-speaking Jewish Alexandrian Pierre Riches. They travelled to Italy together in 1948. His later conversion to Catholicism, his further becoming a Catholic priest, and his exotic background and patrician friends all fascinated her. He was the first of a long series of gay or bisexual men friends, all of whom remained important to her, and one of his yellow sapphires, she assured him, made an appearance in *The Flight from the Enchanter*. Six years after his becoming a priest, Iris remarked, 'But you don't seem to have changed at all!' He was as world-loving as ever, not an Alexandrian for nothing. For his part he watched her 'going overboard' for new people with enormous warmth, her enthusiasm properly Irish, while her intelligence kept things somewhat in proportion. He saw in her a remarkable combination of great warm-heartedness together with shyness and reserve.

Although her official Cambridge lodgings were on Newnham Walk, Iris spent most of her time at Trinity – 'almost living there', she would say – in the spacious set of rooms occupied by Wasfi Hijab, a Palestinian postgraduate from Nablus, anxious about the coming war over the partition of Palestine, after which he was uprooted,[3] and with Kanti Shah, from south India, whose grace and beauty she admired.[4] Both had studied with Wittgenstein, and Shah's notes on Wittgenstein's lectures on Philosophical Psychology in 1946–47 later formed part of the book of that name.[5] Iris found 'the beauty of the place and the cool slow tempo of [their] endless discussions ... healing'.[6] She at once changed her supervisor 'very politely' from C.D. Broad to John Wisdom,[7] whom she described to Queneau as a 'disciple of Wittgenstein (the great master of logical positivism, who alas is retiring)'. She wondered whether Wisdom would 'come to meet' her or would 'amuse himself cutting me up'.[8]

Shah and Hijab wished to save money by getting Iris to cook for them. Moslem Hijab ate meat, while the Hindu Shah was vegetarian. Should Iris mix the meat fat and the vegetable fat, or keep them scrupulously separate? 'Such things are much more important than philosophy.'[9] Fifty years later Hijab recalled a particularly good apple stew.[10] The eminent mathematical-logician-to-be Georg Kreisel, always known by his surname alone, whom Wittgenstein greatly respected and admired,[11] was a research student at Trinity. Hijab's recollection that Kreisel was an occasional visitor to Hijab's rooms in Trinity[12] seems more accurate than Iris's, that the four of them always 'went around together, we ate together, we argued together, and we talked all night together, and so on, and this was a very important year of my life';[13] Kreisel thought Iris's friendship with Shah and Hijab owed something to her weird propensity 'for finding stray dogs *noble*'.(She found *all* her friends noble.) Kreisel, sponsored as a refugee by Stanley Baldwin, half-Jewish and very Austrian, schooled at Rugby, described himself wittily as 'the kind of alien England could afford'.

Certainly Iris found all three 'touching' – a key word. The words 'moved', and 'deeply moved', 'touched' and 'profoundly touched' recur often in her journals, constituting their background music. With Shah and Hijab she discussed philosophy, talking and asking 'incessantly' about Wittgenstein.* She had

---

* John Vinelott, reading Moral Sciences at Queen's 1946–50, witnessed these discussions. Other participants were Stephen Toulmin, Norman Malcolm, John Wisdom and Peter Minkus.

arrived too late, to her bitter regret, to listen to him lecture: in the summer just prior to her going up, Wittgenstein had resigned his chair as from 31 December, keeping his rooms for one last Sabbatical term. That Christmas he would decamp to Ireland. Since Iris could not sit at the feet of the Master, she listened carefully to those who had been close to him:[14] Hijab even dreamed of Wittgenstein at night.[15] They had a single topic: 'Wittgenstein, Wittgenstein, and Wittgenstein'.[16] On New Year's Day 1978 Iris pondered, 'How far has the fact that I have known *very well* certain people (Eliz [Anscombe], Yorick [Smythies], Kreisel, Hijab) who were *imprinted* by Wittgenstein affected my work as a writer?'

Her first two novels are structured round a court or cabal with a charismatic Master at its centre, who, unwittingly (*Under the Net*) or deliberately (*The Flight from the Enchanter*), 'imprints' all his disciples deeply. Hugo in *Under the Net* is a portrait of Wittgenstein's star pupil Yorick Smythies, after 1937 often the only person permitted to take notes in Wittgenstein's lectures.[17] But many of her novels interrogate the 'anxiety of influence' itself. Iris saw Wittgenstein as both numinous and later as demonic. She dreamt of him all her life (never of Sartre), gave *Tractatus* aphorisms to the mystical Nigel in *Bruno's Dream*, and started *Nuns and Soldiers* teasingly: '"Wittgenstein – ". "Yes?" said the Count.' Part of what doubtless fascinated her was the way he commandeered his students' lives, humiliated and sometimes excommunicated them. She wrote to Queneau that the atmosphere around Wittgenstein was 'emotional and esoteric';[18] and later spoke of him as evil: he had abandoned old friends, 'harshly criticized Jewish refugee-philosophers' – probably his combative ex-disciple Friedrich Waissman – ruined careers by telling promising students to give up philosophy – including Smythies.[19] Wittgenstein, she later noted, could, like Kreisel, 'destroy the very inward part of someone's self-respect'.[20] He was ferocious and destructive. Yet, if she continued to admire him, it was probably his obstinate and at times difficult lucidity which influenced Oxford analytical philosophy generally, and is observable in her own best work.

Iris, Shah and Hijab went on the river Cam[21] – they were

impressed that she could punt – visited Suffolk, and in July 1948 she cycled with Shah in the Cotswolds and in Dorset[22] before a visit to Paris. With Kreisel, discussion of moral philosophy floundered. On 31 May 1948 Hijab explained to Kreisel 'what are moral problems' – a powerful induction, Iris noted, 'like when one begins to distinguish virgins from non-virgins . . . Kreisel now classifies people according to whether they have moral problems – (Stage 1!). A feat.' Over dinner with Kreisel a year later Iris wished to determine the moral meaning and ownership of acts, as if – as she put her own sense of the urgency of this issue – 'on the Day of Judgement'. Kreisel, by contrast, diminished the notion of moral responsibility by reducing it to a symptom of neurotic 'guilt' or anxiety. He cited how the typists at the Admiralty, where he had worked during the war, felt ashamed of their sex lives 'until they found that everyone else's was the same! . . . He said he often didn't feel acts, moral or mathematical, as his. They just occurred, and to regard them as his was self importance!' The exclamation marks measure Iris's amused interest in their difference of outlook.

Iris transcribed Kreisel's letters – he referred to them as 'soliloquies' – into her journals over the succeeding fifty years, more by far than those of any other correspondent. Wittgenstein was 'our eternal topic'.[23] Kreisel's views on how unoriginal Wittgenstein was, and how scrappy his knowledge of other philosophers, are given to Guy in *Nuns and Soldiers*. It was for her a defining characteristic of friendship that one does not catalogue one's friends' qualities: 'When I get to know someone well . . . I don't index them – they *are* for me.'[24] For half a century she nonetheless records variously Kreisel's brilliance, wit and sheer 'dotty' solipsistic strangeness, his amoralism, cruelty, ambiguous vanity and obscenity; though not his taste for a fashionable world, nor the boastfulness noted in the unusual Festschrift dedicated to him.[25] Kreisel and Elizabeth Anscombe are the unnamed pair who, as John Bayley later and furiously learnt, went into Iris's room in Park Town in her absence in 1951 and made fish soup there, ruining a blue silk-chiffon scarf given her by Rene by straining the soup through it.[26] The mess and stink left behind resulted in

Iris being thrown out of her lodgings. 'Forgiveness' was not in question: Iris's friendship came unconditionally. A.J. Ayer delighted Kreisel by saying that he was a juvenile delinquent, 'but only on the surface'.

Iris told Kreisel she sometimes found his casualness disturbing. His apartness and moral solipsism fascinated her. She understood why she should wish to write to him, but not why he should like to write to her. In 1971 she dedicated *An Accidental Man* to him. In January 1994 she noted him 'as beautiful & charming & *unique* as ever'. When a third party suggested to Kreisel that he was one model for the Satanic Julius King in *A Fairly Honourable Defeat*,[27] Iris characteristically protested that he was 'too noble'. Possibly he was insufficiently interested in others to have been the main prototype for the unsettlingly perceptive and coolly detached Julius, for whom there was in any case a more disturbing model; while Hijab recalled Kreisel vividly,[28] to Kreisel both Hijab and Shah were 'wholly without interest'.[29] Kreisel, however, was one model for Marcus Vallar in *The Message to the Planet*,[30] who is brilliant and solitary to the point of near-autism, and given to bouts of random cruelty that devastate its victims.

2

Within three weeks of arriving in Cambridge Iris met Wittgenstein. Trinity, where she so frequently was, had been Wittgenstein's college, more off than on, since 1912. Elizabeth Anscombe, Wittgenstein's premier pupil, would translate and give Iris a copy of his *Investigations*, the revolutionary handbook of the second phase of his thinking, only in May 1953. Meanwhile his *Brown* and *Blue Books* were circulating in typewritten form, like *samizdat* literature behind the Iron Curtain, and generating a comparable excitement. Iris had mentioned Wittgenstein to Frank in a letter of 5 July 1943, and had talked about him with Anscombe in 1944. After some preliminary 'devastating' skirmishing with Anscombe, who, like John Wisdom, might effect an entree to Wittgenstein, Iris met him on Thursday, 23 October

1947. He had two narrow, empty, barracks-like rooms, K.10 in Whewell's Court, at the top of a Gothic tower, with no books or bathroom,[31] only two deckchairs and a camp bed. She thought him very good-looking, rather small, with a sharpish, intent, alert face and 'those very piercing eyes. He had a trampish sort of appearance.' He said to her, 'It's as if I have an apple tree in my garden & everyone is carting away the apples & sending them all over the world. And you ask: may I have an apple from your tree.' She remarked, 'Yes, but I'm never sure when I'm given an apple whether it really is from your tree.' 'True. I should say though they are not good apples . . .'. He also said, 'What's the good of having one philosophical discussion? It's like having one piano lesson.' Wittgenstein famously did not think women, in any case, could do philosophy: 'men are foul, but women are viler' he would remark.[32] Elizabeth Anscombe was an honorary male.

Wittgenstein's extraordinary directness of approach, the absence of any paraphernalia or conventional framework, his denuded setting, all unnerved Iris. There was a naked confrontation of personalities. She met him once more, never got to know him well, always thought of him with awe and alarm. He and the differently alarming and influential John Austin, she later said, were 'the most extraordinary men among us'.[33] Since she was too late to hear Wittgenstein lecture, his influence reached her mainly through disciples such as Elizabeth Anscombe and Yorick Smythies, whose personal style ('authenticity') and philosophic style were seen to coincide:

> The ruthless authenticity of Elizabeth makes me feel more & more ashamed of the vague self-indulgent way in which I have been philosophizing. I must make a tremendous effort if I am to get any sort of philosophical clarity or truth out of the sea of fascinating dramatic, psychological, moral & other ideas in which I've been immersed.[34]

One week after meeting him, while reading the *Brown Book*, Iris asked: 'What are the main points of the Wittgenstein revolution? . . . What's happening? The solidity seems to go. "We act like automatons much of the time'' True in a way.' Her focus was not on the discontinuities between early and later Wittgenstein but on the effect of his philosophy generally on our conception of ourselves. He had an excessive suspicion of the inner life.[35] Two days later, she asked herself, 'Will I admit I acted like automaton? I might.'[36] This message she found also in Freud: that we, and our motives, are dark to ourselves. 'I am obscure to myself. I don't coincide with my life. (This is basis of metaphysics)', she wrote on 4 November,[37] noting on the same day that 'Julian of Norwich* is just as self-certifying as Wittgenstein'. And she criticised Wittgenstein's as 'a world without magic', objecting from the first to the divorce he pressed between fact and value: 'Our imagination is immediately & continuously at work on our experience. There are no "brute data".'[38]

The idea that important aspects of human behaviour are mechanical she had also noted that 21 June, after listening to a talk on Kafka's importance at the Anglo-French Art Centre. 'Four themes . . . : guilt, the loneliness of man, a certain mechanism in action (one irrevocable act sets off a whole train of apparently necessary actions . . . An automatism of the individual versus an automatism of the Order – & no real contact) and the instability of the universe (its disintegration).' The speaker had part of a concentration camp journal read out to show its Kafkaesque quality. Kafka, Iris notes, was one who sees the forces at work in the world more clearly than we, and so can 'prophesy'. He always mattered greatly: she hoped to be influenced by him.[39] Roquentin's plight in Sartre's *Nausea*, she noted, was that of a philosopher, while K's in *The Castle* was 'that of everyman'. Kafka's model, not Sartre's, she strongly implies, is the one she wishes to follow.[40]

---

* Dame Julian of Norwich, the fourteenth-century mystic and anchoress, was important to Iris. The Norwich chapel in which she conducted her long retreat, destroyed by enemy action in 1942, was restored and rededicated on 8 May 1953. The phrase 'All shall be well, and all manner of thing shall be well,' from Dame Julian's still vivid and energetic and much-loved *Revelations of Divine Love*, is repeated – often ironically – in many of Iris's novels.

3

There is an amiable counterpoint of philosophic discussion and everyday observation in Iris's journals of this period, as if philosophy and quotidian life might be connected, not kept apart. In the middle of recording a discussion, in Trinity College Gardens, of – as it might be – 'logical space', or why it should happen to be that we do not remember backwards (i.e. like the backtracking of a film), she will note the luminous blueness of Shah's shirt glowing immensely in the evening light. 12 June 1948: 'Back from Oxford. A world of women. I reflected, talking with Mary [Midgley], Pip [Philippa Foot] & Elizabeth [Anscombe], how much I love them.' Or on phenomenology in action: 'Walking this afternoon toward Kings – I wanted the crocuses (mauve & white) to enter into me – they would not – until the chapel bell began to toll – then I was penetrated by the colour.'[41]

Iris never adopted the tone of detailed casuistry that long marked official British philosophy. Kreisel recalled that, by contrast, when she gave papers at the Moral Sciences Club she was noted for 'saying it with roses'. 'There simply isn't very much to be said about your ideas,' he wrote in 1968, and Iris commented, 'This is fairly devastating, but is the kind of thing I can take from Kreisel!' It brought to her mind the awful occasion on 3 June 1948 when Hijab walked out of the Moral Sciences Club after her paper on 'Objectivity and Description' in Richard Braithwaite's rooms because he felt there was nothing to be said about it.[42] It was not that Iris was casual or lacked discipline. What put her at odds with 'dried-up' orthodox philosophy was that she was simply interested, as philosophers once in the golden age all were, in everything on earth. She refused, ever, to honour contemporary proscriptions which might limit her intellectual curiosity or reduce her to a blue-stocking.

Being half-artist and half-intellectual, Iris felt entirely at home nowhere. Talking with Dylan Thomas at a party given by the writer and editor Kay Dick in December 1948, she decided that she best liked the company of 'artists, or rather Bohemians, not intellectuals'. Among intellectuals, by contrast, she felt herself 'all warmth & solidity'. Yet, once having come to this conclusion, meeting the 'brutishness and emotional opaqueness' of bohemian Tambimuttu's world, or even of Ernest Collet's world, made her feel that she must be an intellectual again, after all.

4

Six days before meeting Wittgenstein, Iris wrote in her journal:

> For me philosophical problems are the problems of my
> own life . . . Reading Sartre or [Gabriel] Marcel, we say:
> yes, that rings a bell. I recognise that & *that*'s how I work,
> is it? . . . Is this psychology?[43]

It was precisely their trespass over the frontier between philosophy and psychology that enabled rarely noticed aspects of our being – such as 'Angst, nausée, & all the bag of tricks'[44] – to be at last categorised by Existentialist philosophers. This excited her. 'Do please explain Existentialism to me,' John Willett's mother would say to Iris during the war. On 31 July 1947 Iris returned to Badminton, and felt 'BOGUS'[45] explaining Existentialism there. Broadcasting twice about Existentialism in March 1950, and writing the first monograph on Sartre,[46] she was now explaining matters to a wider audience. Excitingly, 'The war was over, Europe was in ruins, we had emerged from a long captivity', and Sartre's philosophy was an inspiration to many who felt 'they must, and *could*, make out of all that misery and chaos a better world for it had now been revealed that anything was possible'.[47] 'Anything was possible' is ironic.

Iris's quarrel with Sartre goes back to her first encounter with him, and extends into her first novel. It was, she wrote to Queneau, as if Sartre were 'repeating a spell: Be like me, be like me. Almost ready to say: yes dammit, I am.' But she was not quite spellbound.[48] In October 1947: 'There is something demonic about Sartre which is part of his fascination.' Like Wittgenstein, Sartre, by diminishing the inner life, over-privileged the first person. Neither thinker sufficiently respected – or allowed themselves to be touched by – the Other.[49] Although Sartre explored consciousness and value, topics then outlawed from British philosophy, and of equal interest to Iris as would-be novelist and philosopher, *Being and Nothingness* recognised no value 'except a Luciferian private will which in effect exalted unprincipled "sincerity", bizarre originality, and irresponsible courage'.[50] This will was attached to a heroic consciousness, inalienably and ineluctably free, belonging nowhere, confronting the 'given' in the form of existing society, history, tradition, other people. The enemy was dead bourgeois conventionality.

Iris felt equivocal about this isolated 'outsider'-hero for whom 'rational awareness was in inverse proportion to social integration'. Existentialism's promise of freedom was bogus. When one 'leapt' in the moment, repetitive patterns emerged:[51] one's behaviour in fact looked mechanical. Later she thought she had begun as 'a kind of' Existentialist believing in freedom, before coming to understand that love – and goodness – were paramount; and in 1970 she opposed the Existentialist hero (in the novels of Sartre, Camus, Lawrence, Hemingway, Kingsley Amis) to what she termed the 'mystical' hero (in those of Muriel Spark, Patrick White, Saul Bellow, Greene, Golding and – in one draft for this essay – herself).[52] Here she argued that humility is a more apt response to our world than egoism. But the urge to find an accurate description of our condition drove both her philosophy and her fiction from the start. Jake in *Under the Net* is a solipsist, and the novel comically charts his awakening out of solipsism towards a better understanding of the nature and needs of others. Hugo, the novel's saint or mystic, is Jake's awakener. Iris's notes for *Under the Net* pose the question: 'How to bring religion in?'

She gave two evening talks on Sartre and Existentialism that October – probably at partly bombed-out St Anne's church in Old Compton Street, Soho.[53] Her notes on Sartre at this point owe something to Gabriel Marcel's objections to Sartre – she introduced Marcel at the same venue. Echoing Marcel, she noted that Sartre's heroes are heroic not in terms of self-mastery, but merely as bandits. Existentialism, 'an anguished, tortured liberalism', was excessively individualistic. Sartre 'does not give value to the other as such. Hence he does not conceive of [the] fact of love,' a subject on which she judged him '*affreusement détraqué*[54] and simplistic. Sartre reduced love to a 'battle between two hypnotists in a closed room'.[55] Though she attacked her own formulation ('pretty tepid effort'), she charged Sartre with 'a drunken, luciferian, refusal of those calls of which love would make man conscious – love, & not that phantom of it which arises when it reflects itself, instead of accomplishing itself'.

Indeed, Sartre's admission of the importance of the Other was relative, not absolute, 'authorised by us'. 'Sartre is dangerous . . . [and] Sartrian man merely a sex maniac with an incomprehensible liberty, alone in the world.' Most damagingly, his philosophy, with its emphasis on morality as action, and its deep distrust of Freud, did not allow for any real core to personality. In this, as in other ways, her mature philosophy would argue, Existentialism increasingly resembled the British tradition; and she levels similar criticisms at Wittgenstein, ascribing the current crisis in philosophy to precisely such defaults.

In her monograph *Sartre, Romantic Rationalist* Iris famously criticised British empiricism, and the Oxford philosopher Gilbert Ryle's *Concept of Mind*, elegantly unmasking Ryle's pretensions to a value-free neutrality. Ryle's world, so far from being value-free, was one where people do no more than 'play cricket, cook cakes, make simple decisions, remember their childhood and go to the circus'. Ryle ignored, by contrast, the worlds in which we 'commit sins, fall in love, say prayers or join the Communist Party'.[56] Sin, love, prayer and politics: for Iris, no idle list of omissions. 'We know,' she memorably ends this brilliant study, 'that the real lesson to be taught is that the human person is precious and unique; but we seem unable to set it forth except in terms of ideology and abstraction.' Sartre's impatience, fatal to the novelist proper, 'with the stuff of human life' was to blame. Although Simone Weil is absent from her monograph, Iris also rejected Sartre's questioning of the 'authenticity' of suffering. She favoured Weil's Aeschylean account of 'affliction' (*malheur*), which seemed better matched to the horrors of the time.

If her own characters' predicament is Existentialist, their solution is not. It was not that Existentialism was wrong to remind its adherents to live in the present moment. More that it underestimated, unlike religious disciplines, the difficulties of doing so. Existentialism left out of account the daunting power of the personality and of its secret, obsessive, fantasy-ridden inner life. It praised being in the present but ignored the training necessary to the attempt. The messy incompleteness of things provoked in Sartre 'nausea', but might also more appropriately induce a healing reverence before the sheer alien, pointless multiplicity of the world.

Mary Warnock rightly observes that the Existentialist theory of life is intrinsically theatrical,[57] and for that reason objectionable. Iris's picturing of Sartre became increasingly deadly;* but even in 1947 she opposes his 'authentic' hero to Dostoesvky's good men – Myshkin in *The Idiot*, Alyosha in *The Brothers Karamazov*. 28 September 1947: '"Learning what goodness is" is changing oneself.' Bertrand Russell, in a famous essay, opposed Mysticism and Logic, as if a mystic or saint were by definition an irrationalist or a dreamer. Iris's saints, so far from inhabiting an alternative reality, are attuned to the here-and-now. Attention – that crucial concept in Simone Weil – and looking, valued above 'will', 'movement' and the 'leap' of choice, are the indispensable preliminaries to moral action. And attention and looking were what Sartre ignored.

5

'Man is a creature who makes pictures of himself, and then comes to resemble the picture,' wrote Iris in 1957.[58] Simone de Beauvoir's English translator Roger Senhouse wrote to Iris that the

---

* Her comments on Sartre in the introduction to the second edition of her monograph (1987) are studiously polite about the sententiousness of his later work. Sartre is versatile, courageous, learned, talented, clever. He 'lived his own time to the full'. But by 1992 and *Metaphysics as a Guide to Morals* (pp.377, 463) Sartre is a demonic figure, envisaging the Other as the enemy, his *nausée* 'the horror of those who can

moeurs treated in de Beauvoir's *She Came to Stay* were widely followed by the younger generation of Parisian café-goers.[59] The 'Existentialist' phase in Iris's own self-invention illustrates this – a phase of caprices, of seeing through illusions and of Gidean *gestes arbitraires* and *actes gratuites*. Some love pursuits were, arguably, risky adventures of the will and manifested a happy bohemian disregard for convention.* The husband of one ex-Somervillian friend was startled in the 1940s when Iris, during what he had until that moment taken to be a quite different kind of conversation, concluded sagely, 'So we're *not* going to go to bed, then . . .'. A slightly later triangular involvement in which a different woman-friend unnerved Iris by showing her her journal record of Iris's affair with her husband, with which she had for reasons of sex and power colluded, recalled (very broadly) *She Came to Stay*.[60] Later an entry in Iris's journal: 'Then I began to kiss her passionately and was desiring her very much. Understanding of what it would be to be a man, feeling very violent & positive, wanting to strike her body like an instrument' immediately precedes a love-passage with the husband in question.[61] And she is given to examining herself for signs of insincerity, and to praising others – e.g. Elizabeth Anscombe – for their 'ruthless authenticity'.[62] She, too, tried not to mind what others thought. Seated alone on the evening of 22 April 1953 in the bar of the Eastgate Hotel in Oxford, she reflects: 'How little I care about that sort of "eccentricity". Insight into how perhaps odd old ladies in white stockings, or madmen, don't care either. (Being "conspicuous", I mean.),' a comment echoed the following month: 'How I hate & despise embarrassment.'[63]

Iris kept a journal all her life, albeit she did not write in it every day. Most journals after her marriage in 1956 read as a mixture of informal personal memoranda, observations, aphorisms, reminiscences, dreams (both hers and John Bayley's), diaries of foreign

---

no longer love or attend to or even really see the contingent, and fear it as a threat to their imaginary freedom and self-regarding authenticity'.

* No accident that in 1959 in her essay 'The Sublime and the Good' she would condemn convention and neurosis equally as 'the two great enemies of love' (see *Existentialists and Mystics*, p.217)

trips, ideas for novels (marked 'N') and for philosophy (marked 'P'), all jostling together, often in compressed form, unselfconsciously. Here was a writer's quarry. Pre-marriage journals have on occasion an uncanny emotional intensity. Friends, sometimes appearing under their initials, are often identifiable.

13 December 1948. I need a strongbox to keep this damn diary in. Probably I ought to destroy all the entries of the last 3 weeks. Why am I unwilling to? . . . Must root out the weak desire for an audience (the lurking feeling eg that I write this diary *for* someone – E[lizabeth], P[hilippa], D[onald], or X, *l'inconnu*, I still believe in l'inconnu –?). Way to sincerity, a long way.

30 January 1949. BS [unidentified] lectured me on politics & the old nostalgia stirred, part conscience, part guilt, part sheer romanticism and part sheer bloody hatred of the present set-up. To no end, but it stirred. It occurs to me that I entertain the idea: 'One day I shall return to the party', and the idea 'One day I shall join the Roman church' like two escape valves. It is not that I am utterly unserious about them – but they not held close, but part of some far project . . . Thought later: what marks one out as a confined person, with no dimension of greatness? Some lack of sweep, some surreptitious idolatry. In my case, I feel there must be some will to please which is on my face like a birthmark. Who lacks this smallness? D[onald], and Pippa [Philippa], unconfined people, and E[lizabeth] too.

18 May 1952. Looking back in this diary. What an unstable person I seem to be . . . I shall be to blame if I don't build now where I know it is strong, in the centre, through loneliness. (Aloneness) . . . I wrote today on the top of my lecture paper: marriage, an idea of reason!

14 June 1952. There is a lot which I don't put into this diary, because it would be too discreditable – & maybe even more painful. (At least – no major item omitted but certain angles altered – and painful incidents omitted.)

27 October 1958. The instinct to keep a diary: to preserve certain moments *for ever.*

Journal-keeping, acting, letter-writing and the writing of fiction are – *inter alia* – all ways of inventing and expressing, and hence also of outliving and shedding, *personae*. Each entails communicating with, and performing in front of, an audience, real or imagined (*'l'inconnu'*). While the stories Iris tells in her novels are not her own, in the early journals (and letters[64]) she accuses herself of exhibitionism.

After a lecture by Elizabeth Anscombe on 'the past' in October 1947, Iris reflects about what she might feel if presented with documentary evidence – for example, journals – about her forgotten past:[65] 'Suppose I were given evidence about what I thought at the time. My diaries etc. I think I wd not accept that evidence. I'd still feel I didn't know what my past really was.' Over many pages of reflection, she reaches towards a distinction between a 'frozen' and an 'unfrozen' past. So long as one lives, one's relationship with one's past *should* keep shifting, since *'re-thinking one's past is a constant responsibility'*, an operation of conscience in evidence, for example, when it comes to thinking about one's enemies. Since one 'shdnt hate "so-&-so" stuck in yr past, you can, in a way, un-hate them in your past too'. The first essay in *The Sovereignty of Good* (1970) would famously describe a mother-in-law learning to 'un-despise' her daughter-in-law.

6

A few weeks after Iris's arrival in Cambridge she contacted Father Denis Marsh, a friar all his life, at the time chaplain to Cambridge's Anglican Franciscan house, heading their successful attempt to influence those involved in higher education, a simple believer who left theological sophistication to others. She felt, and would continue to feel, divided between two authoritarian forms of belief, before rejecting both: 'Joining the CP was at least a gesture of solidarity with sufferers. This is in a way joining their enemies . . . I am crying. Crocodile tears.'[66] When in April 1950 she gave a talk on Communism to a conference of clergy and youth leaders in Carmarthen she appeared still a fellow-traveller.[67]

Although an unidentified CP friend criticised her paper, and quoted Browning's 'Lost Leader' – 'Never glad confident morning again' – accusing her of desertion, she nonetheless told her audience that Marxism's 'terrific ethical power ... and force' could still command the allegiance of morally scrupulous and idealistic people: 'While there is injustice or oppression anywhere, they cannot rest.' Marxism was a moral code, a metaphysic, a religion, 'answering the spiritual as well as the material needs of tens of millions', and Christians must learn from Communists. She argued for a dogmatic pacifism, even against Stalinism, which was 'not imperialistic' – and even if it were, Christians should be willing to be 'martyred' (sic) for the sake of the ideal. Better Red than see the world undergo 'an atom war'.

'Have I ever really modified my profound choice of my style of life?' she soon charged herself. 'Today I was imagining a conversation (my thoughts are damnably dramatic at present – indeed usually are) in which someone taxed me with *d'être devenue chrétienne*, and I replied *J'ai changé de technique, c'est tout.*'* A humorous habit of addressing friends as 'Comrades and Citizens', as of singing the satirical CP song about the Independent Labour Party – 'Just now there are but two of us, but soon there will be three' – stayed with her; so did her search for believable authority. There was no moment in Iris's career when she was not 'touched' – to use the recurrent word – by the plight of the Insulted and the Injured. Her untitled 1945 'Stuart' novel contains a woman character who, when it's 'more than half the world's population that's so hurt and bedraggled, ... doesn't worry'; but none the less 'when she pities ... half dies with pity ... If there was only one human creature in the world that was being starved & ill-treated ... she'd probably weep for hours & not be happy till something had been done.' This is one persona of that Iris who, as her novels show in some strange, surreal and even sinister ways, experienced an extreme protective anxiety about her world and

---

* 'Someone taxed me with having become Christian and I replied, "I've merely altered my technique."' Journal entry, December 1948.

all it contained; yet for whom the ability to experience pathos, to be touched, was the sign of a whole heart.

> *21 February 1949.* Had a curious hesitation today about burning a sheet of paper. There is a sort of animism which I recognize in myself & in my parents. We are surrounded by live & rather pathetic objects. I connect this with my sentimentality & general softness.*

Such protective anxiety never goes away, but attaches itself, as in later Dickens and Dostoevsky, to the individual case, without hope of complete cure. Iris never took the orthodox line that no alleviation of suffering should occur lest this delay the revolution ('tinkering with the mechanism rather than replacing it'), but does what she can to help others now. On Thursday, 22 April 1948, the Jančars arrived in England, after TB and imprisonment, as 'European Voluntary Workers'. The following day Jože appeared in Iris's room at Newnham, having walked the fourteen miles from RAF camp West Wratting with only one pound in the world. Since EVW accepted single persons only, he was wretchedly separated from Marija in Preston, yet 'completely intoxicated with happiness & freedom & hope! Thank God for such people ... He hopes to get some humble job in a hospital, & finish his studies later.'[68] In his excitement at seeing her Jančar's little English disappeared, and he told her happily: 'Iris – I have become a letter from my wife.'

A week later she took him to London for the day to see the public-spirited Duchess of Atholl – in the 1930s pilloried as the 'Red Duchess' – in her Knightsbridge flat. Iris hoped she might help Jančar. He had never before met a Duchess. This one wore dark clothes and a splendid brooch. Things went well after, in good Hapsburg style, he elected to greet her by kissing her hand. Speaking to him in excellent French and German, she proposed that he first spend a year trying to learn English so that 'we can

---

* For the legendary superstitiousness of Irish Protestants see Roy Foster, *Paddy and Mr Punch*, p.221 et seq. See also Iris's journal, 1945 (no date): 'an animism – embracing cats, buses, stones ... a tenderness for all things. Such as my mother has.'

get you into Oxbridge'. Duchesses apart, this was also Jančar's first trip to London, so Iris took him, via Nelson's Column and the Houses of Parliament, to Westminster Cathedral. 'Do you believe in God?' she asked him, more than once. Jančar: 'Yes I do.' Both knelt and prayed, Iris taking out a rosary and telling her beads. She was charmed when he referred to them both as philosophers – '*Wir Philosophen* . . . ' (We philosophers . . .) – while she struck him as a confused seeker (spiritually, politically): 'If Iris had a god, she could never discover its name.'

In the end the only college Jože could get into to complete his medical studies was Galway, where, on St Patrick's Day 1950, desperate as he had no money to pay his rent, and hoping at best to be deported back to his wife in England, a cheque from Iris for £100 – no mean sum in those days, representing some months' salary – arrived out of the blue. Iris also helped get Marija a job as nurse at Badminton, where she taught a little German too, and was intimidated by BMB. The next year Iris was godmother to their first child, Sonja,* BMB and Iris both attending the baptism. Later still, after a distinguished career, Jančar rose to be Vice-President of the Royal College of Psychiatrists.

7

The episode shows Iris as what Kipling (and later John Bayley) called 'little-friend-to-all-the-world', or Madonna della Misericordia. As in the famous Piero della Francesca picture of that name, she took dozens, perhaps hundreds of souls, both renowned and wholly unknown, inside the protection of her capacious cloak, often for life, writing concerned and nurturing letters to them over the decades, fretful and yet calm and wise. But this is one part only of her story. She was also seen as a vamp or flirt, albeit

---

* The first of many: as well as Sonja she was to be godmother to Angus and Joanna Macintyre's son Ben; Vera and Donald Crane's daughter Frances; Hal and Mary Lidderdale's daughter Norah; Christopher Gillberg's son Theo; Paul and Penny Levi's daughter Tatiana. To her ex-student Nicolas Veto she declined the honour around 1967, but said she would act as 'honorary' godmother.

inordinately high-minded, which is not necessarily either the least confusing kind to deal with, or the least self-deceived sort to be. John Bayley later observed that the most successful vamps are those who appear subdued, un-showy and even uninterested in what they are up to, simply waiting for someone else to make the running, and concealing any desire for success in the field of battle. Dominic de Grunne, already cited as seeing Iris as a puritan idealist (see Chapter 1), in fact saw her half in that light, and half as a seductress, the two halves at war with each other. It was partly how she then saw herself: 'Flirting is fine, but to be a flirt is not ... Despite the impossibility of flirting by yourself, flirts are traditionally considered to be women.' The very concept of flirtation privileges the male.[69]

'She stared at men & whistled after them,' Iris imagined, in June 1953, of a possible novel-character never incorporated into a published work. Yet the idea of role-reversal fascinated her all her life, and to some degree she lived it. She records with no selfconsciousness both 'homosexual' (she does not use the word 'lesbian') dreams, and the possibility of exchange of tendernesses, from time to time, with a loved woman-friend. One later lesbian affair was intensely important to her. In so many ways 'emancipated' herself, Iris's feminism shifts in successive decades, and she was suspicious of the notion of women being separated off for 'progressive' reasons into new ghettos. In 1970 she recorded a fear that 'Women's Lib [might] mix up what makes one miserable because one is a woman with what makes one miserable because one is a human being,' and later felt that 'lots of present day literary criticism, feminism etc.' were simply not worth pursuing in detail. There is no period, however, in which the cause of women's rights is not close to her heart.

The writer Adam Phillips connects flirtation with that once fashionable philosophic concept 'contingency' – a word much used by Iris, meaning all that we cannot easily tame or make sense of, all that resists the desire for our story to take a particular shape, rather than stay open, undecided, unresolved. The ability to learn openness to contingency is a virtue her fiction and philosophy alike are famous for commending. Hers was in some sense a personality without frontiers. She had the gift Keats praised in Shakespeare, that of 'negative capability': that wise passivity and receptivity which allows those so gifted to be touched by, and to enter into, the lives, thoughts and emotions – the private worlds – of many others. Rosemary Cramp was typical of many friends in finding Iris's capacity to enter so fully into the worlds of others enthralling. Yet emotional promiscuity could be one aspect of negative capability, so that, as some observed, Iris's life sometimes appeared to be a series of *engouements*, leading even Iris herself to wonder about what she, much later, termed her 'silliness'.

To put the same point another way: loving others was her way both of knowing them, and of losing herself. And loving her world was her way of realising or imagining it. As for the willingness to allow oneself to feel touched, it led naturally to the desire, in turn, to touch. 21 February 1949: 'Moved by a sense of his [x's] integrity. (Has this sort of "being moved" any value? There is a sort of sexual thrill in it sometimes. But it raises a Q about what one *does*.)' The question about 'what one does' runs through these pre-marriage journals. That she did not trouble to edit them suggests both how remote, by 1990, this earlier persona seemed to her and how innocent.

> *29 June 1952.* Coming back, a further folly. I told F[erruccio] R[ossi-Landi]* I wd see him, & came by taxi from the station. It was very hot. We spoke of his Milan love – sitting on F's bed, with our knees almost touching. As I was about to leave, I couldn't resist making a gesture, & in a moment F had his arms about me. It was a kiss that I had wanted long, & he too, & we could not have resisted further at that moment. Is this wrong? . . . I must be in control.
>
> *11 October 1952.* M[aurice] C[harlton]† was here just now; he suddenly appeared, offering to do Mods teaching . . . I asked him to stay. We drank coca-cola. He talked

---

* Semiotician, linguist and translator of Gilbert Ryle's *Concept of Mind* into Italian.
† Maurice Charlton (1926–94), with a double first in Mods and Greats, in 1952 a medical student at Hertford College, later a leading medical authority on epilepsy. See John Bayley's *Iris: A Memoir of Iris Murdoch*.

of his work. He looks much better, less small and drawn, a new beauty in his face. We were both very tense . . . I wanted to embrace him. I am sure he wanted the same. We avoided each other's eyes. MC is dynamite. I ought to avoid him.

6 May 1953. Just back from a principal election meeting. G[eoffrey de Ste] C[roix]* offered me a lift in his car. I accepted it, remembering the last time. When we got to K[ing] E[dward] S[treet], we sat in the car talking – then as I was about to get out he seized my hand & kissed it, & then kissed me on the lips . . . How strangely moving these momentary meetings are. Earlier in the day [xx] was here, with his tender cynicism. It is foolish to invite such tendernesses, however slender. But I find them irresistible. There has never been a moment when I have trembled on the brink of such an exchange & drawn back.

6 October 1953. Found myself thinking of Hans Motz† last night . . . I can see his strong hard face, more purely man than most of the men I know. Last night I was desiring him, or wanting, at any rate, a first kiss. The metaphysics of the first kiss . . . The impossibility of marriage, of having only one man.

She was young, very attractive, built for happiness. 'The impossibility of marriage, of having only one man' is not the dictum of one lacking in confidence, and though she sometimes felt 'that these casual friendly liaisons are wrong',[70] in her they seem blameless. Nickie Kaldor, for a while much taken with her, said, 'It's like something she gives out.' Olivier Todd, who knew her from Cambridge in 1947,[71] found her, despite her quietness and ethereal quality – neither here nor there but *elsewhere* during conversations – '*une personalité frappante*', and noted the asymmetrical quality to her affairs, Iris being less involved than the

---

* 1910–99, author of the standard work on accounting in the ancient world; he had just moved from Birkbeck College and the LSE to New College, Oxford. He met Iris through Hal Lidderdale, with whom he had worked in a filter-room in the Middle East during the war.

† 1909–87, first Professor of Engineering at Oxford, at St Catherine's.

other. To what extent should the attractive feel responsible for the sufferings of their admirers? Her journals hint at her care in avoiding Feydeau-like collisions (and render the night in *The Red and the Green* when four suitors independently visit Lady Millie exaggerated realism rather than, as some have criticised, fantasy). She enjoyed admiration and was also susceptible, rarely, at any point in her life, out of love, indeed frequently in love with more than one person at a time. She had the courage required to be vulnerable together with the prudence to keep options open. E.M. Forster once wrote that love drives novel characters more than it does people in real life: if so, Iris may be an exception. She noted humorously, 'I am a hand and wrist fetishist. Only some men wear gloves so one never knows,' but it was the intellectual and moral qualities of her male lovers, rather than their beauty (the latter sometimes apparent only to Iris), that usually appealed, and the drama of an affair was as important as its passion. Power and vanity apart, she wanted to learn and was, despite all, shy. To all she was remorselessly kind.

On 16 November 1968, on discovering and rereading her diaries from 1945 onwards she wrote: 'That business of falling in love with A, then with B, then with C (all madly) seems a bit sickening,' and noted what an 'ass' she then appeared. 'I mustn't live in this torment of emotion (Empty words – I shall always live so.),' she by contrast wrote on 15 August 1952. It is no accident that in her May 1952 diary she associated two apparently opposed desirables: loneliness and marriage. John Bayley would, in the very best sense, provide both. Meanwhile there were adventures. She did not identify with Queneau's picaresque Pierrot for nothing.

The combination of susceptibility and unwillingness to make final commitments – of a soft heart and a strong will – was powerful; many were enchanted, some confused. The novelist and critic Rachel Trickett, who returned to Oxford in 1950, aptly observed that, so intensely magnetic was Iris, it was small wonder if she should also be 'all over the place', emotionally speaking. There was a distinction between the idle dalliances of youth and 'the real thing' – yet the distinction was not always clear. The advent of John Bayley helped bring proportion.

8

Admirers may be disturbed by the notion of Iris, like King Lear, not being ague-proof. But part of her intellectual legacy is a revival of the idea of the soul, an entity divided and at war between low, half-conscious motives, and higher ideals. Without having pondered her own frailties, she could not have argued this with clarity or force; and her writings would lack their charge of truth. She had noted to David Hicks in 1945 'a tendency to want to be loved, and not engage myself in return', echoing this in her journal ten years later: 'I always want to have it both ways – to give moderately and yet have full attention.'[72] Yeats's father once pointed out that *all* creativity can be seen in some sense as a frustrated bid for love;[73] indeed Iris noted on 4 April 1948: 'All speech is seduction.' Within 'speech' may be included the writing of fiction. In 1964 she noted to a friend '25 years of being told in the most extravagant terms' that she was beautiful.[74] 'One of my fundamental assumptions,' she asserted more baldly, during an *imbroglio* in December 1948, 'is that I have the power to seduce anyone.'[75]

9

The most brilliant of her generation of British philosophers, Elizabeth Anscombe was from 1946 a Research Fellow at Somerville, becoming a Fellow in 1964. If other colleges were less appreciative of her remarkable qualities than was Somerville, her mix of bohemianism and fiercely expressed scorn for the frivolity of the Oxford philosophical faculty may help account for this.

'Do you stay awake worrying about the existence of the external world?' Anscombe asked Mary Warnock, who did not. Fair without being blonde, of fine profile, broad noble brow and extraordinary stamina, Anscombe was both poor and unselfconscious enough to collect cigarette stubs from the gutter, and appears in Iris's journals being pilloried for wearing trousers at early Mass, living at 27 St John's Street in a squalor that Iris, tolerant in such matters, finds noteworthy, and getting arrested for wandering about with her hair down at 5 a.m., then refusing to give her name to the police. She was married from 1941 to Peter Geach, with whom, since he worked at Cambridge and then Birmingham, she practised what they termed 'telegamy' – marriage at a distance. Iris repeatedly pays homage to Anscombe and to Yorick Smythies, Wittgenstein's leading students. Reading Norman Malcolm's life of Wittgenstein in 1958 brings back suddenly to Iris 'all that E[lizabeth] A[nscombe] and Yorick once "taught" me, were for me . . . ten years ago. A real sense of a great demand, & a hatred of the frivolous & insincere.'[76] One of her students thought Anscombe detectable within the serenely Buddha-like chain-smoking corner-shop newspaper-seller Mrs Tinckham, much given to silences, in *Under the Net*.[77] (The phrase 'pathologically discreet,' used of Mrs Tinckham, was, however, originally invented by Heinz Cassirer for Philippa Foot.)

What Iris termed a three-day 'courtship' between herself and Anscombe started on Friday, 10 December 1948. Iris noted in herself a feeling of curious detachment, 'almost frivolous. A vague sexual excitement.' When her delightful colleague at St Anne's, the quarter-Burmese Economics tutor Peter Ady – despite her first name a woman, and one who hunted and dressed well – came in to drink gin and talk of candidates, Iris found herself contemplating her 'with a sort of desire. Inclination to kiss her neck. (Something affected in all this.) I feel as light as a feather, can't even see myself as bloody or in danger or a menace to others.' Twenty-two pages of self-examination follow, full of hope and fear, seven excised, in which Iris appears to have wished to purchase love at the price of passion, but, with considerable ado and regret, renounces this yearning for the sake of peace of mind. She contemplates what she at first fears to be Anscombe's lack of 'generosity, gentleness, douceur, tendresse, of all that for me lights up & gives grace to my attachments to people', but is then startled to realise how dangerous these qualities are, 'especially in their corrupted form in me'. Yorick Smythies helps her to see that, on the contrary, it is essential for all concerned that no further idle emotions be aroused or aired. Iris went to Mass and prayed that she might genuinely desire the well-being of all concerned, and to confession with Father Dalby of the non-denominational, though vaguely Benedictine, High Anglo-Catholic Cowley Fathers on the Iffley Road, who suggested that she get the nuns at Malling to pray for her also.

On learning that Anscombe was going to visit Wittgenstein in Ireland, Iris was doubtful whether Wittgenstein would positively discourage this courtship. If told that one had seduced number-less women, Iris reflected, Wittgenstein might not be at all moved; yet some frivolous remark about it would send him into a rage – an idea that gets into *The Nice and the Good*.[78]

> What he hated were styles and attitudes rather than sins
> ... (Do anything so long as you take it seriously!) ...
> He wouldn't necessarily mind what foul thing you did,
> so long as you didn't *talk* about it in a certain way ... I
> feel that they [Anscombe and Wittgenstein] tend the
> same way thro' an excessive attention to intellectual style
> – and *moral* style. Yet what looks like attention to style at
> one level is real seriousness at another. The style *is* a
> symptom. (I see this in myself – relation of my 'bad style'
> to my real badness.)

In February 1958 Iris wrote:

> It strikes me now for the first time as remarkable that in
> all that time E and I never touched each other, except
> for my touching her arm on the first evening. That lent
> to the thing much of its special intensity. I suffered very
> much, especially from the quality of E's contempt for
> me. But I wd not have wanted any of it not to happen.[79]

Friendship survived; fifty years later Anscombe remembered Iris as 'someone who was obviously extremely attractive in a way which didn't quite work with me. I mean we didn't become close friends ... and I don't think we ever quite managed to work out what we meant to each other.'[80] In 1993 Iris dedicated *Metaphysics as a Guide to Morals* to her 'old friend-foe', as she had described Anscombe to Queneau.[81]

10

A woman character who conducts numerous emotional intimacies simultaneously recurs in Iris's fiction:[82] Anna Quentin in *Under the Net*, charged with 'emotional promiscuity' and with having a character which was 'not all it should be', who significantly 'yearns for love as a poet yearns for an audience' – or indeed a novelist yearns; Antonia in *A Severed Head*; Lady Millie in *The Red and the Green*; Morgan in *A Fairly Honourable Defeat*. They are dealt with with comic severity. The sequence comes to an end by 1980 in *Nuns and Soldiers*, where Anne Cavidge enters a convent having lived a wild youth and then wholly gone beyond it. Her youth had been

> a carnival, a maelstrom, a festival of popularity and per-
> sonality and sex. She obtained a First . . . [while simul-
> taneously devoting] energy, thought and feeling to love
> affairs. There were so many jostling men . . . dazzling
> choices . . . flattering vistas. She became skilful at con-
> ducting two, even three, affairs at the same time, keeping
> the victims happy by lying.

Yet Anne is attracted, too, by 'the idea of holiness, of becoming good in some more positive sense', and quits the world without regret. She does not later judge her sins therein too harshly, indulging no morbid sense of guilt: 'Everything was provisional and moved so fast; others behaved quite as wildly as she'; more-over her early life had been in itself 'a teaching, something laid down from the very start'.[83] Anne owes something both to Iris's imaginings of a fellow-Somervillian (Lucy Klatschko) who entered a convent in 1954, and to Iris herself, apprenticed to learning how to love everybody dispassionately.

There are moments throughout Iris's fiction when physical touch takes on an importance not necessarily ceded to it in ordi-nary life. 'Only take someone's hand in a certain way . . . and the world is changed for ever,' says the narrator of *The Black Prince*. In *The Bell* the first scandal breaks merely because Toby and Nick are disturbed holding hands. In *The Unicorn* our view of Hannah shifts dramatically when, while Dennis Nolan is busy cutting her hair, her hand 'nuzzles' into his jacket pocket. In *The Good Apprentice* we are told of the good character Stuart that he may yet break out, and are led to understand that this breaking out might possibly involve his touching young Meredith; we are somehow reassured that he 'already knew intuitively about the terrible *untouchable* sufferings of others'.[84] Respecting the distance that separates us all, he can none the less build bridges. Iris's 1982 Gifford lectures were dedicated to the proposition that 'chaste love teaches'. No doubt the debacles of the early 1940s gave to the problematics of 'touch' a special potency.

11

Iris's fiction, like her life, is a story of 'touchment', a nonce-word she coins and uses exclusively for thinking about and watching her husband John Bayley: 'Puss [i.e. Bayley] at St Ant's holding broken wine glass by stem. Touchment.' Women and gay men in her fiction are often willing to allow the world to touch them. There are also 'touchy' and vain persons, some (not all) of them men. Is not 'touchiness' a defensive symptom of our refusal to permit the world, precisely, to touch us? What other novelist would give to her character a thought about 'how moving a dog's nostrils were, moist and dark', identifying herself with all of that dog's intense, involuntary sensitivity and responsiveness?[85] Iris – oddly – defines the good man in the 1980s, both in *The Good Apprentice* and also in interview, as 'cold and dead',[86] by which she partly means chaste. She herself learnt not to be 'touchy' or easily upsettable.[87]

Of the deeply sympathetic gay character Simon Foster in *A Fairly Honourable Defeat,* we are told that his philosophy had been: 'One offers oneself in various quarters and one hopes for love. The love he had hoped for was real love. But the search had had its lighter side.' This is not a bad summing-up of Iris's search either, where 'lighter' could of course mean less morally serious, but also happier.

11

St Anne's
1948–1952

In April 1948 Philippa Foot sent Iris details of a philosophy tutorship at St Anne's College, Oxford. Iris felt odd about applying. She had once acted as secretary to an UNRRA committee of which Miss 'Plummer' (*sic*) – St Anne's Principal, Miss Plumer – was chairman; this tried both their tempers. She also felt sick at the idea of competing with her old friend Mary Midgley. But by 11 July she had won the job – Mary cheering herself up afterwards in the Foots' garden in Park Town, North Oxford, by decapitating some gladioli (shades of Frank Thompson digging up the irises at Boar's Hill in 1939).

During the summer Iris read, *inter alia*, Rousseau's *Social Contract*, set text for the following year, and also Tacitus' *Germania*, noting of the Romans that 'if they had to be imperialists they might at least have done the job properly & civilised the Germans!' As well as philosophy, she at first taught 'some accursed Latin'[1], looking after the few Classics students St Anne's attracted each year. Women's colleges were still struggling, and tutors were asked to 'fill in'. Iris lengthened her skirts for the 'New Look' – a mode she would stay loyal to after it had ceased to be fashionable and laugh when this was pointed out – said farewell to Hijab when he left for Palestine and then, after the cycling holiday with Shah, to him also: 'It breaks the heart.' As for Iris's love for Philippa, '*ça continue, ça reste, ça me donne de la paix*'.*

Philippa and Michael, expert and kindly rescuers, partly under

---

* 'This continues, stays, and is a source of inner peace.'

Donald MacKinnon's tuition, took in Iris as a weekend guest in 1947 at their house at 16 Park Town, and as a formal lodger for more than a year from late July 1948.[2] Jokes about having to go to the rent tribunal as the Foots are 'grossly undercharging' her do not disguise Iris's alarm about her presence offending Michael: living with the Foots seemed 'daring'.[3] The arrangement worked, but all thought it odd, and when Philippa had to be absent, Iris's journal suggests that she found meeting Michael on the staircase as peculiar as he did meeting her.[4] She hated what she termed 'mislaying' anyone (1965: 'How did I mislay Queneau?'), as if her own carelessness were always in question. Conversation with Philippa was unbroken but relations were sometimes constrained: intimacy had lapsed.

Iris's plots – and opening chapters – sometimes present a Shakespearian 'court' so interconnected as to dizzy the reader, and demand concentration. In the interests of clarity, this biography follows a few strands only. The presentation of such inter-relationships in the fiction accurately reflects the extraordinary degree to which, mid-century, educated middle- and upper-class British persons knew one another; and also the complexities of family life after divorce became commoner in the 1960s and 1970s.

Park Town, where Iris had been in digs as a student, is a distinguished 1850s neo-Regency quasi-circular close. The Foot household and its neighbours in 1948 reflect the interrelatedness of a Murdoch novel. Honor Smith, a distinguished neurologist lodging at the top flat in number 16, was daughter of that Irish Lady Bicester who had admired Iris's Magpie acting on 29 August 1939. She was now Senior Research Fellow at St Hugh's. Soon afterwards living at number 25, she and Iris's old Greats tutor Isobel Henderson, who lived at number 30, later planned to end their days together. Honor Smith's erstwhile fellow neurological researcher Peter Daniel later married Philippa's sister Marion; they lived happily together at Seaforth.

Iris's predecessor on the middle floor at number 16, Prue Smith, working for the new BBC Third Programme, commissioned two broadcasts from Iris in 1949. Smith knew Iris as a philosopher who always carried a novel written during the war in her suitcase, which she was so foolish as still to hope to get published: 'She has a lovely voice. I can strongly recommend her.' 'Dear Prue,' Iris wrote on 8 November, 'What I had in mind was to discuss the conception certain French novelists have of their vocation: that they are to picture the "situation of man", the human consciousness caught in the act of making its own world &tc ... I could discuss all this in relation to Sartre and Queneau, who represent two entirely different types of "metaphysical novelist".' With unnecessary but not untypical secretiveness, she added that this wholly anodyne letter was 'for your private eye' only.[5] 'The Novelist as Metaphysician' and a second talk, 'The Existentialist Hero',[6] were broadcast on the Third Programme on 26 February and 6 March 1950, Iris receiving forty guineas plus expenses. Sartre's and de Beauvoir's characters, she argued, are appealing

> but they are never enchanting – and the worlds in which they live are without magic and without terror. There is here none of the enticing mystery of the unknown ... and none of the demonic powers we feel in Dostoevsky. There is not even the nightmarishness of the absurd Kafka expresses. Sartre's nightmares are thoroughly intelligible. This is ... an unpoetical and unromantic literary tradition ... This fact alone, that there is no mystery, would falsify their claim to be true pictures of the situation of man.

Here is a programme for her own fiction: to restore poetry, mystery, nightmare, terror, opacity to modern fiction and also to criticise Sartre's 'dramatic, solipsistic, romantic and anti-social exaltation of the individual':[7] 'We are not yet resigned to absurdity, and our only hope lies in not becoming resigned.'[8]

2

St Anne's was different from other women's colleges. Originally confusingly called the 'Oxford Society for Home Students', suggesting a correspondence or domestic science college, or a body of extramural students, its name changed to St Anne's Society in 1942. At this point most tutors still taught in their own homes, and earned less than those of other women's colleges. In 1948 it was still designated a 'Society', and poorly endowed, its dream to become a college, and thus have Fellows rather than tutors, realised only in 1952.

There was no college accommodation before then, and no formal dining-room until 1960. No student lived in until 1953, when ten houses on Bevington Road were bought: large numbers, living mainly in hostels, were needed to cover the overheads.* Fellows were very good about dining at the hostels in turn, and students were happy when Iris came: 'She was very beautiful, with a calm, steady regard. She . . . listened kindly and was a most courteous guest,' remembered one.[9] St Anne's was sometimes willing to take a risk on a girl who had failed to get into the more prestigious colleges which had a joint entrance exam, and there were some odd and interesting students (called 'Principal's funnies' later, under Lady Ogilvie). It had other advantages, too, beyond being easier to get into. Anne Moses, later married to Wallace Robson, who read English 1950–53, found at St Anne's the 'most exciting' of women's college senior common rooms, full of young, brilliant and often beautiful dons. Chic Peter Ady was not exactly conventional: among other attachments to both sexes, she was later involved with Rose Dugdale, whose identification with the IRA led Dugdale to terrorism and to prison. Neither exacting Dorothy Bednarowska, one of three splendid English tutors, beautiful, cool Jennifer Hart who taught history, nor Iris

* In 1950, out of 257 students, 213 lived in hostels, four with parents, five with guardians, seventeen with 'hostesses', and eighteen were mature students in 'approved houses'.

were hide-bound. Hart, arriving in 1952, found it a friendly place, with only nine tutors, 'unstuffy, liberal and generally go-ahead'. St Anne's alone was willing to defy the convention that frowned on a candidate who was married or pregnant, or who wished to marry her tutor.[10] Moreover by the early 1960s, under Lady Ogilvie's tutelage, and with notably brilliant teaching in English, excellent exam results were achieved.

Miss Plumer, despising the dons as unworldly, was an efficient and strict disciplinarian, always getting up earlier than anyone else,[11] a field-marshal's daughter and a tactician. When she gathered that one student was having an affair, she asked the junior common room, aghast, 'How am I to know that she isn't one of many?' Another student sensibly replied, 'You have no way of knowing, Miss Plumer.' She rusticated the student in question on hearsay evidence, over the Christmas break, to the later consternation of the dons. Iris gave her student Jennifer Dawson the impression that she found Miss Plumer (whose deformed shoulder scared Dawson) imperious and autocratic. 'If you *must* have children,' Plumer advised one lecturer, 'kindly ensure that you have them in the University Vacation.' If she could appear a narrow-minded martinet, she could also show practical kindness, and it was much to her credit that St Anne's moved so smoothly towards college status. On her retirement in 1953 Iris was involved in canvassing for Plumer's successor, writing to Hal's sister Jane Lidderdale, a civil servant;[12] Iris also went, with her kindly Scots colleague Kirsty Morrison, to see T.S. Eliot about the possible candidacy of the then editor of the *New Statesman* Janet Adam Smith;[13] the latter recalled Iris at the time of the interview wearing a man's peaked cap, very 'present', very attentive, and (probably) voting for her.[14] In the end Lady Ogilvie was elected; though watchful, she could be liberal,[15] and she transformed St Anne's for the good.[16]

Iris was widely thought to be adored by her St Anne's colleagues, a number of whom typified (in Lord David Cecil's good-humoured phrase) 'old-fashioned lesbians of the highest type'.[17] Yet at governing board meetings Jennifer Hart cannot have been the only one to be mildly irritated by Iris on occasion reading more interesting matter under the table: Iris is unrepresented in college governing records. Hart was annoyed, too, by Iris's being referred to as *the* expert on moral problems. Iris would never send anyone down, no matter how ill they behaved, preferring to tear her hair while saying she didn't know *what* to do. Her interest lay very much in teaching, and she was dedicated, generally liked and admired by her students.

Nonetheless a disparate range of opinion survives about Iris as tutor. Gabriele Taylor, later Tutor in Philosophy at St Anne's herself, found Iris, despite a reputation for disliking lecturing, a brilliant lecturer, good at indicating new directions for enquiry, but was surprised that she siphoned off first-year tutorials in Logic to her as an inexperienced postgraduate without coming back to confer about how they were doing. A number speak of her as a superb teacher, enabling and respectful,[18] and the effect of her teaching as life-changing.[19] Others found her unfocused. Deirdre Levinson felt disenchanted when Iris dedicated her Sartre book '*To my parents*': to some students she was fighting their own generational battles.[20] Ann Louise Wilkinson (later Luthi), the rusticated student, recalls that for her year ridding themselves of their virginities was seen as important, and their love-lives took up much of their time. Iris seemed (to her) to be leading the same life as her students – she was once discovered by one of her pupils[21] lying in the long grass of the Parks with a lover, she even on occasion went to the same bohemian parties, and once she and a student climbed the Parks gates together.[22] By 1953, Iris had twice been thrown out of lodgings by indignant landladies.[23]

Many recall Iris sitting or lying on the floor, even during an admissions interview, or lying on a sofa, sometimes bare of stockings, splattered with mud after riding through puddles on her bike, a mop of fair hair over her eyes, or giving a tutorial with wet hair, having just washed it. When Katrin Fitzherbert was interviewed in 1955 Iris asked why she wanted to study philosophy. Fitzherbert replied, 'I want to be wise'; Iris collapsed into peals of laughter. Some days later, when the letter offering her a place arrived, she finally forgave Iris.[24] It was, after all, what Iris herself sought, too.

3

Oxford brought, at last, outward stability. Iris found the city, though not in general pretentious or snobbish, stiffer and more formal than London. One antidote lay with that aspect of post-war Oxford summed up by Maurice Bowra as 'the era of the dancing economists'. A group of the beautiful people – 'posh Labour', in Mary Warnock's phrase* – decided that they could combine being influential intellectuals with spare-time dancing.

Around 1950 Ian and 'Dobs' Little gave the first of two dances at Burcot Grange, an eighteenth-century brick house with modern additions on the Thames.[25] Dancing was to a radiogram: there was no band. High-spirited parties, with much cheerful rudeness, they were frequently copied on a smaller scale.[26] An entire pig was staked and roasted. Trinity College's butler made a cup; no one knew how strong it was: there was gin disguised by orange with white wine, an orange liqueur and soda. This may help account for the number of people who proposed to Iris, whose inner radiance Ian Little recalled: 'she would shine'.[27] There may have been sixty or seventy guests. Tony Crosland, then Labour MP for South Gloucestershire, came. Hugh Gaitskell, the Chancellor of the Exchequer, complained that the music wasn't loud enough, but it was at full volume: the sheer crush of people absorbed the sound. Gavin Faringdon, the Socialist peer from Buscott where the Magpies had played, was there. A huge ring was formed, a dance extemporised. More and more people joined until the ring got too big, and many fell – or, as Mary Warnock recalls, *jumped* – into the Thames. Iris went to the second party which was in fancy-dress, in June 1952, with Peter Ady. Tony Quinton, fellow of All Souls, and his fiancée Marcelle Wegier went as Arabs, the austere Magdalen economist David Worswick, robed in a sheet, as Nero. Thomas Balogh, unrecorded by Iris, was

---

* Mary Warnock, *A Memoir: People and Places* (London, 2000), pp.157 *et seq.* Among those whose presence Warnock records are Hugh Dalton, Douglas Jay and Richard Crossman.

a Chinese grandee, in Mary Warnock's memory an exceptionally predatory one.[28] Iris drank a great deal. Worswick kissed her; the budding historian Asa Briggs, at once 'completely and totally'[29] in love with Iris, and soon important to her, was 'very charming'; he danced better than she. In the car going back Peter Ady made a declaration of love and they kissed 'with equal passion'. Iris, who 'would have needed little prompting to spend the night with her', was ashamed afterwards at having been so drunk.

There were other antidotes to stiffness. John and Jean Jones, she a painter who had met Iris in Cambridge, he a Law Fellow and later an English don, living at Holywell Cottage, and their circle of friends, were one, and thought by some to be one model (there were others) for the kindly, hospitable, ambiguous host-and-hostess figures who dominate Iris's novels of the 1960s and 1970s. Another was that 'happy band of free spirits' and hard-drinking companions (the Horse and Jockey on the Woodstock Road was one favourite), many of them Irish or Antipodean or both, who represented to her 'a piece of London broken loose': the novelist Joyce Cary;[30] the painter Gerald Wilde, whose bohemianism caused him wrongly to be cited as model for Gully Jimson in Cary's *The Horse's Mouth*,[31] lodging free from February 1949 on the Woodstock Road with Wendy Campbell-Purdie, who acted as 'land-lady, spiritual director and friend to a miscellany of talented persons';[32] Dan Davin, the Irish-New Zealand novelist and executive at the Clarendon Press, and his wife Win; trousered Enid Starkie, whose biography of Rimbaud Iris read in 1947.[33] Iris often wore trousers too, that mutinous signal of independence, displaying that one was an emancipated post-war woman.[34] She never wore gloves and was amazed when others did.[35] She gained a reputation for going about, sometimes be-sandalled,[36] 'without a thought for her dress or a penny in her pocket'.[37]

Also living in Park Town was another companionate spirit, Audrey Beecham, profoundly eccentric niece to the conductor Sir Thomas, sharing both his arbitrary quality and boundless self-confidence, very butch – liking all-in wrestling – genuinely bohemian and unexpected. She had lived in Paris and fallen in love with Anaïs Nin, done gun-running for the Anarchists in Spain, been improbably pursued by Maurice Bowra who was carried away by her transsexual charm. Convinced that there were terrorists in the next house, she turned out to be perfectly right: they were deported. Beecham lent Iris Henry Miller books.

The novel Iris was then writing, with the (to put it mildly) unpromising title 'Our Lady of the Bosky Gates' – the excuse being that it was a modern imitation of Ancient Greek[38] – involved a semi-bogus spiritual seeker known as the Guardian who, having travelled in Tibet and met the Dalai Lama, finds he can communicate with the statue of a Greek goddess, possibly Aphrodite.[39] The statue comes to life. 1949, ten years before the Chinese embarked on their brutal crushing of the country, is an early year to take an interest in Tibet. Iris's interest flowered in *The Sea, The Sea* in 1978. In June 1949 Audrey Beecham talked to her of Tibetan Buddhism, 'where religious concepts were not "contaminated" by morality – i.e. the rules were technical – *how* to reach certain states of mind, which were accounted better than others'.

4

Iris was teaching moral and political philosophy, principally to students of PPE and of Greats: 'Plato, Aristotle, Kant, Descartes, Berkeley, Hume, moral philosophy . . .' she wrote to Queneau.[40] Her quarrel with the constrictions of the exam-led curriculum – connected to her dispute with Oxford philosophy itself – made her want to range more freely: she asked some 1949 students to read Lenin's *State and Revolution.*[41] Students from other colleges and disciplines, especially mature postgraduates, profited most, while those most needful of coaching for 'Schools' sometimes expressed frustration, finding her diffuse. She would write blaming herself if a student did badly in the exams.[42] Stronger students enjoyed precisely the fact that Iris could be 'blithe and insouciante' about the curriculum.[43] Many ex-St Anne's students, like the novelist Penelope Lively, even fifty years later referred to her as 'Miss Murdoch':[44] she could help others 'open up' without dropping her own guard. And judging by the number of students whose weddings she attended, she was very popular.

It is somehow typical of Iris that her first student in 1948 should have been Mother Grant, a nun in the Sacred Heart order, later seriously to investigate Hinduism, then in her last year reading Greats. Tall, blue-eyed, black-veiled, habited and with goffered cap around her face, she was supposed to go out only when essential. Tutorials took place at 16 Park Town, Iris seated on the hearth-rug. She gave as one tutorial essay-topic 'Space, time and individuation', and relentlessly challenged each statement Mother Grant (a thoroughgoing Thomist) made: 'Could you say a little more about that, Mother Grant?'[45] They also met often, outside tutorials, at the St Anne's hostel at 11 Norham Gardens, where Iris's journals suggest that they discussed religion, Mother Grant evidently continuing by letter a conversation they had had about the 'rottenness of our desires'.

> *1 March 1949.* To tea with Mother Grant. Felt very great affection for her, & was immediately afraid & spoke of 'snakes' & 'loss of nerve'. She said that she held me in her heart. A great feeling of gladness & humility where she is concerned. MG told me: when she was a child she was worried about the interminable list of people to pray for; later she understood a 'lived solidarity in Christ'.

Mother Grant was later co-Acharya of an ashram in Pune (then Poona), the ecumenical 'Christ Prem Seva Ashram', together with Anglicans and Hindus. Iris firmly and romantically believed that the Vatican, in a fit of absent-mindedness, had given her permission. In fact the Vatican knew nothing of these ashrams' existence: the local Bishops encouraged them.[46] She wore *salwar kameez* (tunic and trousers), became expert on the texts of Sankaracarya, and was sometimes known, to her pleasure, as Mataji (Little Mother). Iris's own ecumenicalism – her feeling that Christianity needed to be revitalised by exactly the kind of reflection in which Mother Grant was involved – meant that such developments were of great interest to her. In 1948 she would sometimes make reference to 'your Church', which made Mother Grant feel personally responsible for its vagaries. She knew that Iris, carrying a Latin missal, sometimes went to Mass at Blackfriars, and felt that they met at some profound and wordless level transcending faiths, Iris's absolute honesty and integrity making it necessary to dwell on essentials: 'The thing that has struck me most about Iris is her sheer goodness.'[47] Iris, characteristically, blamed herself when Mother Grant just missed a first. They stayed in touch and met, if rarely, once in India and also in Oxford.

Also of continuing importance was Julian Chrysostomides, who went up in 1951, after a rejection from St Hugh's. She had cried for two days. 'Tell me your story!' said Iris. Her English had been so poor, they told her, once she had the courage to ask, that they had been unable to decide whether she was stupid or intelligent. Iris accepted her to read Classics, and taught her 'probingly, imaginatively' in her third and fourth years, in 1954 and 1955. In December 1954, because she looked sad and a foreigner, Iris said, 'I want to look after you!' and took her home for Christmas. When Julian's father died, Iris arranged for her to stay at a hotel in Paris, near her; Iris met her at the Gare du Nord, where she (Iris) rushed to help an old lady with her bags. She and Julian went to the Rodin museum, the Bois de Boulogne, the Jeu de Paume. Iris introduced her to English poetry, they went for frequent walks and picnics, and Iris was, for solitary Julian, her England,[48] manifesting only its better aspects: humanity, humour, tolerance. Iris introduced her to three of her 'gurus': Canetti, Momigliano, Fraenkel.

Julian saw Iris as vulnerable despite great inner strength. Iris helped her write letters, helped her with her mortgage when she needed such help, helped accelerate her British naturalisation in 1962. Iris would claim that all the best poets – Yeats, Sheridan, Wilde, Swift – were Anglo-Irish; in due course Julian visited the Dublin 'cousins'. Iris was enchanted when she learned of Julian's twin brother Nikos, and of how, when one twin cried, the other cried too: the depth of this love fascinated her. Julian was not offended when Iris put her picture of her to imaginative use in the character of Rain Carter, who is simultaneously proud and humble, in *The Sandcastle*; something they did not discuss. They met at least twice a year over the next half-century.

Jennifer Dawson read history from 1949 to 1952, and in 1961 published the novel *The Ha-Ha*, about the experience of mental breakdown. She had Iris as tutor in political theory in 1951 for what was supposed to be one term, but turned – so spendthrift was Iris of her time – into a year, tutorials often running on an extra half-hour. Iris, uninterested in clothes or make-up, wearing flat-heeled Brevitt Bouncer shoes, lisle stockings (nylons were expensive) and Sloppy Joe sweaters, cycled to St Anne's, smiling as if she had a secret joy. Her room at that time in Musgrave House, 1 South Parks Road, was big, bare, with one picture on the wall. A coffee-bar on the other side of the front door enabled Iris to go out and bring her students coffee.

The syllabus should have been Hobbes, Locke and Rousseau's *Social Contract*, which both she and Dawson hated. So instead they studied Plato, then utopias (More, Swift, Rousseau, Oakeshott's theory of the state, which Iris attacked: it was not enough for the ship of state merely to 'stay afloat' as he argued – more should be possible) and Simone Weil's *Waiting on God*, which fascinated Iris, who read it in French. 'Miss Murdoch', as Dawson, like Penelope Lively, still thought of her fifty years later, was so brilliant: why was she so nice to her? Iris often carried a string bag with bottles of beer in it, which they sometimes drank. Hating waffle, obscurity, pretension, she would ask, 'What is the *cash-value* of this?' That forced Dawson to learn clarity, and to write lucidly too. Encouraging precision, Iris would ask: 'Wouldn't one think this argument rather bizarre?'; she was fond of that impersonal locution, 'one'. (Dawson finally looked up 'bizarre' in a diction-ary.) They wistfully discussed the meaning of life, as if they hoped to find it. A perfectly rational society would have no poetry or history, Dawson once said, to which Iris riposted, 'Come off it: there'd still be the history of the railways, the water-supply and the Trade Unions. And there would always be love and death.' Once, in a discussion of *déjà vu*, Iris suggested Dawson read the myth of the Cave in Plato's *Republic*, *à propos* the cave-like half-life we seem to inhabit. Iris had a genius for connecting the prose and the passion of life,[49] and Dawson would leave each tutorial excited by the world she had been shown.

5

Iris seemed to appreciate, too, the mature Greats students Gerry Hughes and John Ashton, both Jesuits from Campion Hall, studying ethics. Hughes recalls that her room had very low furniture and an unused, unmade-up divan bed on which she would sit, curled up, *spiralled* up, playing with her hair, listening with the most intense interest. Once, flustered because she had unwittingly made a girl cry by saying, 'Don't you think that it's immoral to say you LOVE somebody whom you don't LIKE?', she poured them each a gin. She was demanding, challenging and stretching, had so many backgrounds, analytic, Marxist, Existentialist – you never knew which angle she would approach from: she could set Sartre's *Existentialisme est-il un Humanisme?*, or the proceedings of the First or Second Internationale for tutorial essays. She encouraged Hughes to trust himself, to go to the heart of the matter. Ashton so enjoyed his tutorials he asked for and got extra ones on political philosophy, where she set him off reading Kierkegaard, Weil, Marx, Lenin – no one else would offer so varied a reading-list. One essay topic goes to the heart of her concerns, both as novelist and philosopher: 'Liberalism cannot succeed as a creed until it purges itself of its romantic elements.' (It was Ashton whom she startled when he quoted St Augustine by asking, 'Have you any evidence that he was *a good man?*') She wore flouncy, billowing clothes, deflected questions about herself, and her quality for him is generosity: of mind and spirit and with her time, of which she gave freely, especially when she helped see him through the crisis of leaving the Order.

Iris was supervisor to A.D. Nuttall and Stephen Medcalf, who went on to distinguished careers as literary critics, and who came to her in 1959 as graduate students writing on literature and philosophy. For Nuttall, who produced out of his work with Iris the unclassifiable *Two Concepts of Allegory*, Iris had to read Prudentia's long, boring *Psychomachia*. Her tremendously, disquietingly messy room in no way detracted from her painstaking efficiency as a supervisor, writing detailed and helpful notes. She supported Nuttall when he (an atheist) married a Catholic, and gave the couple a very generous cheque. Medcalf too was helped and influenced. At his first tutorial with Iris in Hilary term 1960, she had for him the look of some being one might expect to find living quietly underground at the end of a deserted garden, at once faintly 'unearthly and of the earth, earthy, like a kobold'. Hugo Dyson, their Merton tutor, said simply of the strong impression Iris made during that first meeting: 'She's suffered.'

6

Oxford then saw itself, to some degree rightly, as the philosophical centre of the world.[50] A word sometimes used by that richly talented generation of philosophers of Iris on her return is 'exotic'. Mary Warnock, who conceived herself a stay-at-home, saw Iris as an 'exotic' who had actually had a 'proper war' and been abroad, to the Austrian camps, to Paris. She admired Iris's insight into other people's ideas and her ability to put these to use, which she found reminiscent of Coleridge.[51] Warnock was not alone in thinking Iris's Sartre book brilliant, and Iris herself 'unearthly, legendary, sophisticated, extraordinary'. David Pears, a good friend, recalls her as very beautiful and, since she had arrived from Cambridge, regarded as the person who knew about Wittgenstein, there being a great mystery in Oxford about what Wittgenstein was thinking: it was wrongly supposed that she had grown close to him. Richard Wollheim, who taught in London, remembers her first at a summer weekend joint session of the Aristotelian Society and Mind, tossing her hair back in debate like someone out of a social novel by Aldous Huxley, very striking, determined and emancipated. Tony Quinton felt her reputation was helped by the fact that she was working on Sartre; Anthony Kenny, based in Oxford after 1963, was struck by the way she concentrated totally on whoever she was talking to, never looking over anyone's shoulder to see who else was around, and by her gift for taking everyone seriously. Peter Strawson was enormously impressed by her beauty and intensity alike, her lack of either vanity or conceit, and had no difficulty with the 'strenuousness' of her moral philosophy; Stuart Hampshire, both a friend from around 1950 and later a polemical opponent,[52] felt that her presence was of positive assistance to analytical philosophers, redeeming them from the constant accusation that they were

> philistines, a dried-up lot, that all the literary splendours of the idealist movement had been done away with and everything was thin and precise and dry. The fact that someone like Iris minded about it, took it seriously, was part of it, had all these friends, made an enormous difference.[53]

A now forgotten storm accompanied the publication in 1959 of Ernest Gellner's *Words and Things*, famously attacking Oxford philosophy, which Iris defended vigorously, reviewing the book unfavourably.[54] She appears, indeed, even to have considered writing a higher degree on 'meaning and thought'[55] which would have taken issue with Gilbert Ryle and A.J. Ayer, to whose viewpoints she had both ethical and logical objections, and accordingly to have consulted Henry Price, Wykeham Professor of Logic. Yet Oxford philosophy, however much Iris enlivened it, never entirely constituted home territory. While it is true that Bernard Williams saw her in the 1950s, together with Michael Dummett, Elizabeth Anscombe, Philippa Foot and David Pears, as a valuable mainstream Wittgensteinian,[56] and Dummett himself felt that she was always held in great respect, others, watching her courageously developing her own original views, thought her 'exotic' in the sense of unassimilated. Philippa Foot: 'We were interested in moral language, she was interested in the moral life . . . She left us, in the end.' Isaiah Berlin declared her in a private *boutade* a 'lady not known for the clarity of her views'. To her developing Platonism* he and a few others would later declare themselves 'allergic'.

When recognition of her philosophic originality finally came,

---

* The novel-form, as D.H. Lawrence saw, is 'incapable of the Absolute', and given over to the clash and claims of competing voices. See Peter J. Conradi, *The Saint and the Artist*, which argues that Iris's fiction challenges her own Platonism.

it would be from a less provincial tradition, one more open to Continental Europe and mostly working in North America: John McDowell, Stanley Cavell, Charles Taylor, Cora Diamond,[57] Martha Nussbaum, Mark Platts[58]. After Schools in 1955 Taylor went on to do an Oxford D.Phil., and found Iris tremendously helpful in two ways. Firstly, she herself was daring to explore those interesting philosophical issues declared out of bounds; secondly, the sheer quality of her listening when he visited her to try to sort out his confused ideas 'was extraordinary; that and her questions. It helped enormously.' He found much of what she wrote helpful and suggestive. She was a leading 'role model' to him and others trying 'to break out of the post-positivist analytic box', a teacher to whom he owed much; while John McDowell would in the 1970s read and re-read *The Sovereignty of Good* and declare himself pervasively influenced.[59]

Iris was never invited to John Austin's central Saturday-morning 'kindergartens' where minute and combative investigation among younger tutorial Fellows took place. Example: 'Why can you say "*highly entertaining* but not *highly good*"?' Here Austin, shortish with thin curving nose and thin lips, was as terrifying as possible, with a taste for self-congratulatory complicity. Eventually Philippa was invited and felt obliged to attend both Austin's Saturdays and, after 1959, and despite the fact that both events were overwhelmingly male, Ayer's rival Tuesday *soirées* also. Iris came to neither. Michael Dummett felt that Oxford's narrowness was Gilbert Ryle's fault as much as Austin's. Ryle, author of *The Concept of Mind*, resembled a Prussian general, tall, well-set-up, operating from Magdalen.[60] Iris, typically, though she made Ryle a polemical opponent in *Sartre*, liked the man himself. He lent her Heidegger's *Sein und Zeit*[61] – pointing to considerable openness to non-Oxonian thought – 'with a nice note' early in 1949, and she later poured her heart out while he sucked on his pipe.

Philosophy, as Iris noted, was then at its driest, morality being treated as a special subject dealt with by various technical devices '(emotive utterances, imperatives &tc). Fact [was] firmly separated from value, and value was insubstantial,'[62] the moral agent reduced to an isolated will and intellect choosing afresh and *ex nihilo*, moment by moment. This picture, she felt, was not merely excessively individualistic, but inaccurate and wrong. She noted that Ryle 'describes the mind without its unconsc[ious] or even involuntary side – and so fails to describe it . . . This simply will not do. The mind R describes is controlled by me – when I imagine *I* fancy, pretend, *know how* to etc. This may do for deliberate imagining, but what of the picture that surges up?'

'The picture that surges up' correctly suggests that she declined to give up her belief in the inner life, or in 'introspectabilia', about which (in her view) Wittgenstein, Ryle and Ayer all had excessive suspicion. Iris was never impressed by fashion; her entire *oeuvre*, philosophic and novelistic alike, is given to exploring the 'soul-picture' under attack. Her first paper to the Philosophical Society – the faculty's in-house colloquium – was thus aptly on 'The Stream of Consciousness'.[63] Ryle was in the chair. Geoffrey Warnock, a disciple of Austin, made a rough or tart respondent, and was, as Isaiah Berlin reported, deeply unsympathetic: 'Have you ever seen a machine for making spaghetti? That was what it was like. Iris put in large lumps of dough, and Warnock extracted very *very* thin strings.'[64] Stuart Hampshire none the less told her she had been 'gallant', which Iris noted ruefully 'was the best that cd be said'. In that forum she later introduced a discussion with Gabriel Marcel – skilfully translating between the Oxford and the French philosophical dialects, without strain – 'probably no one else could have done it,' thought one observer.[65]

Her first Aristotelian Society Paper, given in Bedford Square, London, on 9 June 1952 and entitled 'Nostalgia for the Particular', was equally disputatious. David Pears and Mary Warnock alike recalled the abrasiveness of Ayer, whose viewpoint it challenged and who patronised Iris 'in a philistine way'.[66] Both also thought it a good counterblast to Ryle's quasi-behaviourism, a head-on attack on his advocacy of an image-less world, and a defence, once more,[67] of the 'inner life'. Here Iris memorably observed that it is 'difficult to describe the smell of the Paris metro or what it is *like* to hold a mouse in one's hand'. As Pears noted, Iris was at war with the desiccation, the detailed casuistry, of contemporary philosophy, seeking herself what the American philosopher William James famously called a 'tender-minded' approach; one in which, as in the Renaissance, the sense of wonder at nature is not at odds with the desire to understand it.[68] Her journal entry for 14 December 1951 – 'Good = saintly?' – suggests her distance from the surrounding philosophical scene.

7

Iris wanted a more inclusive philosophy, and struggled to find it elsewhere, in meetings of the High Anglican group called the 'Metaphysicals'. There were at first eight 'members', and Iris was present, a 'wistful seeker', at the inaugural meeting late in 1948.[69] Their aims were to explore how far the anti-metaphysical bias of analytic (linguistic) philosophy could be resisted; how far you could make a good philosophical basis for a religious metaphysics; and to show that theological discourse had real philosophical meaning. They met three or four times a term in one or other of the members' rooms. It was very informal, with one person elected to start un-minuted discussion with a few remarks.

The leading voices among the Metaphysicals were Eric Mascall, Austin Farrer and Basil Mitchell. Dennis Nineham, Chaplain-Fellow at Queen's College when he and Iris first met, was the most sceptical male participant; Iris, the only woman, would say very little. Dressed informally, 'like a fisher-girl',[70] she would sit on the floor, rather like a kitten, her knees bent up in front of her, usually in front of another participant, to the occasional embarrassment of Mascall, a strange, kindly, old-fashioned celibate Anglo-Catholic clergyman. The Metaphysicals were his brainchild, the intention being to get like-minded people together, and the first meeting happened in his rooms in Christ Church. Elfin, occasionally waspish Farrer, leading Oxford theologian, Warden of Keble and mystic who in his exceeding shyness and brilliance recalled 'a sort of male Iris',[71] attended. So did Richard Hare, then Fellow of Balliol, still visibly suffering from having had a bad war, and somewhat withdrawn. Iris (like Philippa) felt that Hare, a dominant voice in moral philosophy, a topic undervalued at Oxford, urged too restrictive a conception of moral discourse, and she took exception to his prioritising of the will. Experience of the war years – separations, losses – had taught Mitchell that 'love was the one thing necessary'.[72] Ian Crombie, Fellow of Wadham and friend of Donald MacKinnon, who said what he thought succinctly and then stopped, and kind, bleak, solitary Michael Foster, teaching philosophy at Christ Church, a tortured soul, his lips permanently aquiver, were also at that inaugural meeting.* Iris gave a 'paper' (unrecorded) on 25 October 1950.

In the book born of these discussions, *Faith and Logic: Oxford Essays in Philosophical Theology* (ed. B. Mitchell, London, 1957), Iris's contribution, though unspecified, is acknowledged. The influence went in both directions. In the only record she kept of a meeting,[73] on 6 May 1953, with Hare, Foster, Mitchell and Keble's chaplain Christopher Stead also present, Michael Foster's comment: '[This] account of moral judgement is too existentialist – it is all a matter of "decision". I would like to speak of a contemplative element,' strongly anticipates Iris's line, in its conflation of British and French voluntarisms, and its invoking of contemplation as antidote. Foster, again like Iris, argued that the 'ordinary language' philosophers purported to analyse and interpret was in fact deeply theory-laden, and that it proposed an unavowed metaphysics which they should acknowledge and defend. Dennis Nineham's interest in Rudolf Bultmann (1884–1976), who, influenced by Heidegger, urged a demythologisation of the New Testament, on which he gave a paper, once again prefigures Iris's. When Iris left the group – probably late in 1953[74] – she explained that, as far as the Church was concerned, she was 'more of a fellow-traveller than a Party member'.[75] Mitchell protested that the group would be the stronger for such a member, but she would have none of it.

---

* Foster killed himself c1955, and was the first suicide to be given a full Christian burial, D.A. Demant preaching an impressive sermon about how it was time the Church woke up to the fact that for some people life was simply unbearable.

Iris engaged in a Socratic Club dialogue (on the 'Existentialist Political Myth') during Hilary term 1952,[76] and hymned that institution forty years later. The Socratic Club was started by Stella Aldwinckle in 1941, with C.S. Lewis as President, originally to propagate Christianity among undergraduates. Meetings were large, with sixty to a hundred students; either one speaker, or two who held dialogue with each other, generally in college junior common rooms. Speakers included Anscombe with her monocle and cheroot,[77] devastating C.S. Lewis on the subject of miracles,[78] C.E.M. Joad (of *The Brains Trust*), the polymath writer Jacob Bronowski and Austin Farrer. Iris liked the club's bold attempts to reintroduce philosophy and theology, which had not in the twentieth century been on speaking terms,[79] to each other, and its courage in raising true-to-life issues that might elsewhere be deemed non-admissible. Buddhism, Communism, Existentialism and Wittgensteinian philosophy were all permissible topics.

Iris had met the striking Stella Aldwinckle in 1941 at Somerville when she was a Marxist student and Aldwinckle, attached to the college as representative of the Oxford Pastorate, proselytised with the Student Christian Movement. Now she was Women's Officer for the evangelical St Aldate's Church, much involved in the post-war Christian resurgence, and a potent if not always popular force in Oxford, starting the Horsemanship Club as well as the Socratic. Many found her a trying, simple-minded, self-righteous woman who, after some conversion experience, overestimated her own capacities. She had bought an old farmhouse in South Hinksey where she lived in a semi-rustic state with her horses, often appearing in riding gear like a land-girl. Iris was very impressed that she had driven a cart drawn by six pairs of mules when a farmer in South Africa. She wrote Iris sentimental letters, arousing in her a curious mixture of 'coquetry & brutality', and was unclear how Iris could be interested in 'someone so unsophisticated'. But Iris appreciated her innocence and freshness – 'she is still as if fifteen' – and thought her wise, with 'her strange narrow-eyed weather-beaten & wrinkled, yet so young, face'.

I told her she was like a sybil. And I told her that the strange mingling of masculine & feminine in her was a mystery that moved me deeply. She said it was odd that something which had caused her such grief should move me, and so bring joy to her. I hope, I would pray if I could, that I may do her no harm. Her pure heartedness may do me some good.

This recalls Iris's wartime letter to Frank about not believing any more in 'clean hands and a pure heart'.[80] Perhaps only someone irremediably innocent makes such observations and expresses such wishes. 'May I not harm [so-and-so]' is a refrain in Iris's journals, repeated in relation to admirers of both sexes.[81] A later friend of Iris's, Frances Partridge, who shrewdly recorded late Bloomsbury in her many journals, observed more harshly of herself: 'What appalling selfishness, what smug desire to be always in the right, what craving always to be liked, what hypocrisy can be concealed by aversion to causing pain . . .'.[82]

On a drive from London to Oxford up the old A40, Aldwinckle told Iris to stop the car in a layby; they walked half a mile to a wood where nightingales were magically singing. Iris shared Aldwinckle's Platonism, her exaggerated sense that metaphysics was undervalued by the Oxford 'school' (the subtitle of Peter Strawson's 1959 *Individuals*, after all, was 'An Essay in Descriptive Metaphysics'). In 1990 Iris wrote an introduction to Aldwinckle's poem 'Christ's Shadow in Plato's Cave: A Meditation on the Substance of Love'.

8

Rosemary Cramp, an undergraduate at St Anne's from 1947, and fellow-lecturer, in Anglo-Saxon, from 1950, later dedicatee of *The Sea, The Sea*, was close to Iris, and noticed how Iris's friends belonged to different courts or worlds, and also that she had the gift of keeping friends, all of whom loved her. Iris once asked her meditatively whether she didn't agree 'that any worthwhile person ought to have at least *some* Jewish blood?' Cramp, from

deep in wildest gentile Leicestershire, was nonplussed. Iris sometimes forgot to eat. She would enjoy Cramp's trout and almonds,
then say, 'Darling I'd have eaten *anything*. I hadn't eaten for a
day and half.' Iris later called her a 'lovely and wonderful girl',
remembering the time they lay drunk on the floor of her room
at Norham Gardens and Cramp read her the whole of *Beowulf*,
'and I understood every word. *Eheu fugaces.*' Very much under
Iris's spell, and finding Iris's capacity to enter into others' worlds
enthralling, she read all that Iris read, including de Beauvoir's
Second Sex, a book whose 'fierce war-like manner'[83] Iris believed
fifty years ahead of its time. Iris, like de Beauvoir, insisted that
women laboured under atavistic constraints.

Cramp observed Iris moving unhappily from person to person,
perhaps in revolt against such constraints, unbesmirched and
uncorrupted by the relative wildness of her private life. (Iris's
judgement was sometimes harsher: she charged herself with lying
to all and sundry; and her novels demonstrate that she thought
the temptations of vanity and power in matters of love both difficult – and important – to avoid.) The whirligig continued. There
were minor players such as diffident, anglophile political scientist
'Tino' de Marchi, who sponsored *Occidente*, a non-Communist
Resistance paper in Italy during the war, who loved his Lancia
and the Muffin Coffee Bar on Oxford's North Parade, and started
a dining-club, the Cavour, where everyone had to sport a green
waistcoat – he became much more important as a friend than a
lover. Iris (later, Iris and John) visited his chocolate-manufacturer-
father outside Como, with his black boxer dogs, one called 'Eliot';
and she dedicated *The Black Prince* to Tino. She was also attached
to the Viennese Professor of Engineering Hans Motz,[84] and to
Marxologist and anglicised Berliner George Lichtheim, who saw
himself as a 'burnt-out case' and, after two earlier attempts, killed
himself in 1973.[85]

There were also major players, who expected, if not marriage,
at least proximate fidelity, and were hurt when neither were to
be. In January 1949, on an odd, lonely, saddening walk, the
talkative Fred Broadie, an 'old man of the sea' with a passionate
love of philosophical discussion, told Iris how he had seen her,

every week, waiting for Elizabeth Anscombe outside Schools before he knew her, and how Anscombe 'was the Queen', Iris flushing for pleasure when Anscombe came out: 'He's hellish observant.' Before the war Broadie had been a café violinist with Mabel Steedman ('a terrible sweet scent of the thirties from those old programmes,' Iris commented) when the eminent Manchester philosopher Samuel Alexander 'discovered' him. After the war, during which he was wounded while serving in the RAF, he became one of many protégés of MacKinnon, who helped him into Balliol. At first thinking him a blunt instrument, Iris soon changed her mind and was 'profoundly touched . . . that I may not harm him'. By June she 'absolutely cannot get B out of my head'; in July there are rows, he accusing her of insincerity, she fearing being 'swallowed', losing her integrity.

> *23 July 1949.* B. continues to amaze me. Today when I was really angry, shouting at him, he quietly insisted that we should do philosophy, & in the end I had to laugh.
>
> *31 July 1949.* He talked of Judaism, said he had been often to the synagogue since his mother's death, that he had been there that morning and held the tables of the law in his hand. I saw him then as wise and strange and rooted in the past, in old things and deep things. I had never thought I would see him as a religious person, but now he seems to me very religious.

She found his 'naive frank joy' in the countryside, and buildings, 'poetic', and he brought that out in her too. Broadie, wanting more from Iris than she was prepared to offer, ended the relationship in November 1949. Iris wrote back telling him to 'resist the fatalistic daimon'.[86]

In February 1950 she met and liked Wallace Robson, recovering from a breakdown, who told her he wanted a shoulder to weep on. He had been a star pupil of David Cecil's and was now English Fellow at Lincoln, a wonderful talker, Johnsonian in appearance and manner, resembling to some a very warmhearted, modest, subtle and learned lorry-driver, albeit a brilliant and complicated one. Both liked pubs, and Iris appreciated his deep knowledge and understanding of English Literature and his willingness to share it with her. He later married, very happily, Anne Moses, who had loved him for a decade, then a student at St Anne's and a perceptive observer of his and Iris's affair.

Iris and Robson's two-year relationship culminated in a semi-formal engagement, Iris meeting his Irish Catholic mother and sister, while he met Rene and Hughes, to whom Iris sent Robson's greetings in January 1952, when they were seeing the New Year in together at Dover. She wrote, too, to Hal about 'a rather intense situation – & the thought of marriage comes into my head'. She constantly quarrelled with Robson, whom she unfairly describes – perhaps placating Hal, who also wished to marry her[87] – as a 'very neurotic creature. Perhaps something too much of violence here on both sides. I don't know what will come of it . . . (Don't speak of this to anyone – all is so unclear).' The description seems one-sided. On 9 January 1952 she noted: 'Some good days at Dover. Felt very certain. There is a directness of contact which is good. I'm moody tho'. Yesterday he was in London and had one of his "unreasonable" fits. Today fearful depression. I wish I could understand my feelings.' On 12 January: 'WR is the shadow of the great man I wanted to marry. I am the shadow of the great woman I wanted to be. We are a pair of shadows. But perhaps we can move toward reality together.' In mid-February they sat in the Mitre and Iris attacked him for not reverencing people – 'meaning me'. She ended the relationship late in April 1952, and described her departure in a felicitous phrase that neatly undoes itself: she had left him 'definitively (I think)'. (The wartime habit of postponing decisions until 'after the duration' died hard with her.) The relationship was not an easy one. Iris's heart resembled an old-fashioned wardrobe, both capacious and full (as she noted[88]) of unexpected compartments; Robson's description of her as 'monumentally unfaithful' does not sound exaggerated.

In October 1950 she had met and fallen for the political philosopher Michael Oakeshott, who offered the possibility of the unhappy love she noted, without understanding it, that she needed: 'I hope Michael doesn't break my heart before Easter.' As for the 'terrible pain and frenzy' this inflicted on Robson, she felt 'bad about it but not bad enough. All a very unhappy business.' Iris's St Anne's colleague Jennifer Hart had an affair with Oakeshott soon afterwards, recalling him as highly attractive, easy-going, lazy, addicted to 'love at first sight', going 'overboard' for a new lover. She remembered his twinkling eyes, boyish bohemianism (he still resembled an undergraduate when he reached eighty) and disregard for convention and ostentation.[89] Both Iris and Oakeshott will have been opposed to a scientistic rationalism in philosophy. Both were incurable romantics. Iris at this point disliked his right-wing political pessimism and his distrust of utopias alike,[90] his 'lazy philosophy based on refusal to think or do anything'.[91] None of this prevented her *engouement*:

> There is *no doubt* about this. I was sure, even before we met at Marble Arch. Agonizingly sure now. A deep pain of joy and fear in my heart. Can't work or eat, just want to wander around thinking about M. What is he thinking today? I must try to work. I am making myself sick with emotion.
>
> *Later.* Feeling perfectly demented about M. I don't know how I can get through today without seeing him. Yet I can't decently call upon him again before tomorrow.

Two months after the affair had begun, both cried when he announced his attachment to a third party. 'Accept the end & grimly draw a line,' wrote Iris, who did literally this across the page.

By October 1951 she and Robson had a *rapprochement*. In November he is 'increasingly precious to me – his gentleness, violence, wit, all a language I understand. We communicate perfectly'; she has no doubt she is falling in love with him, feeling 'blinding clarity'. Though they parted in April 1952, the affair again re-ignited after Iris was bereaved later that year, then once more, and finally, lapsed, to his pain and fury: 'I loved the way she thought and talked. I loved her mind.'[92] Some 1953 meetings were painful, Iris at one point comparing him to a great fish she had seen dying by the river, and wondering why she did not feel more distress. (Of another lover who stayed 'stricken', she commented coolly that it was like knocking someone down and then coming back, years later, and finding them still suffering by the roadside: a tender heart, it seems, can also be a callous one, though some grace about her meant that she rarely forfeited regard.) In November Robson wrote, 'Dear little one, I'm so afraid of losing your friendship through being such a bore. And through constantly saying cross things.' Such words made Iris 'sad & humble'; in 1955 he took sabbatical leave in Australia. A reconciliation was first refused by Iris, and took place only after both parties married, Iris writing 'beautifully' when Robson's sister died young, in 1964, that she would always love him. He and Anne moved to Edinburgh once he got the Masson Chair in English there. Shortly before his death in 1993, he out of the blue reflected that 'Iris was always so mysterious,' wondering whether it had been this that he had loved in her.

9

Iris and the distinguished Jewish Italian Arnoldo Momigliano probably met while she was still an undergraduate. They were close friends by May 1952. A short, neat and bespectacled man, of very wide and deep culture and sometimes comical English, brilliant and touchy to a fault, he, his wife and daughter arrived in England in April 1939. During the war he was close to Iris's tutor Isobel Henderson, and later to the sociologist Jean Floud, but he always referred to Iris differently. His wife Gemma accepted these attachments, and Iris met her and liked both her and their daughter Anna-Laura. Momigliano's parents had been deported and killed by the Germans late in 1943. In 1951 he became Professor of Ancient History at University College, London. Every Saturday he came up to Oxford to work at the Ashmolean or Bodleian libraries. He spent Saturdays, after 4 p.m., with Iris in her flat, talking about the ancient world; they read the *Divine Comedy* together in Italian, and Iris referred to him always as one of her great teachers. Iris's enthusiasm for Dante, whose work is well represented in her library, dates from this time; it would cause her to make Martin in *A Severed Head*, quoting from Dante's *Rime*, which had been Momigliano's 1953 birthday present to her, speak of the 'terrible figure of Love' which has struck him to the ground, standing over him with the same sword with which he killed Dido.[93] Momigliano wrote to her that Dante now always sounded to him with the soft undertone of her Irish Oxford Italian.[94] Iris would make him a salad supper; he would hold her hand and kiss her, leaving punctually at 11.30 to walk to his room in the Old Parsonage hotel on Banbury Road. In August of 1952 and of 1953, and again in 1955, they travelled together in Italy. On the first journey they were lovers.[95]

In January 1953 Iris noted a dialogue so intensely dramatised and 'literary' as to be halfway to partaking in a novel:

> I saw A. this evening. His love was moving and enormously saddening. I found myself saying to him 'poor darling'. He said – you are grieving for the pain you will cause me one day. I said: whatever pain I may cause you I shall be with you to suffer it. He said, 'I believe you can do miracles.' Oh, may I be able to manage this one!

In a novel of hers such high-mindedness would quickly merit a comic come-uppance. Soon, wishing to find the point where she could release her tenderness for him, she noted that his demands bred a bitter resistance in her.[96] In April 1953 the death of Maud Gonne at eighty-eight – Yeats's muse, just as Iris was Momigliano's – prompted him to write to her of her many mental and sentimental commitments; but Iris was his life, he lived in fullness only when with her. This relationship, too, could be tricky. There was both rancour, and a break of many years, after Iris's marriage in 1956. He asked her to return all the books he had given her, noting angrily a certain lack of integrity in her – a capacity for misleading and covering herself from open accusation of telling lies by using a lawyer's devices; for her part Iris at one vexed point retorted, 'You are the kind of person who forces others to lie to you.'

When she saw him four feet away at a reception at the Italian Institute in September 1968, she swiftly fled: 'He was talking & might not have seen me . . . I was shaken, but not too much. Felt sad, sad.' In 1977, on 19 February ('a day when things happen'[97]), after twenty years, they met again, and he wrote, 'Our reconciliation is a fact'; after this she had dreams of pursuing him in crowds. On 18 July 1979, in the quad just outside the Bodleian Library, he handed her the copy of Dante's *Rime* he had first given her in 1953, and which she had returned to him in 1956. Inside she found a birthday card inscribed 'To Iris with my heart: A. July 15 1954'. Beneath this he had added, 'July 1979 A'. He said, 'You were a beast!' and laughed. In 1983 she dedicated *The Philosopher's Pupil* to him. Six weeks after his death on 1 September 1987, his widow Gemma wrote to Iris: 'I often think to hear his voice calling me from another room; or opening the door of the room where I am working, and asking: "*Che cosa fai adesso?*"'

10

There were breaks in the intensity, moments when comedy looked in. In early 1952 there was a 'very comical demarche' *à propos* Kreisel and the smuggling of gold sovereigns into France.

On Tuesday, 4 March Iris was unsettled by a telephone call from Anscombe saying that she was going to Paris with Kreisel and Gabriel Andrew Dirac, son of the physicist at King's College London, and that it would make all the difference if Iris came too. She cancelled all her tutorials and took the 9.50 train to London to get her passport, it now seeming most desirable 'to be in Paris with K and E'. Anscombe, by this stage, had received a letter from Kreisel with the phrase: 'Of course you know the purpose of this trip?', following which she had contracted 'flu. Iris interpreted Kreisel's question as Anscombe did, and felt undecided as to whether to proceed without her. At ten on the Wednesday Kreisel rang and Iris deprecated what she imagined were the conditions – '(going to bed)'.

K. scornful – nothing like *that.* 'But you would be
expected to carry something'. I decline – return to Ox.
& busy myself fixing all tutorials on again. Chez E I find
out that the dark phrases refer to what Dirac calls the
cunt carriage of sovereigns. Helpless with laughter. K's
coolness and naiveté beyond belief.

You could then buy gold sovereigns cheaply in London and
sell them at twice the rate in Paris, thus earning yourself a large
illegal profit. Dirac, after taking his own cut, wished as a Communist in this manner to subvert the capitalist system. The incident
shows Iris as something other than a humourless blue-stocking:
she was sometimes a prig but, despite hating sexual innuendo,
not a prude.* She also had more luck, or more good sense – or
both – than another of Dirac's victims. The journalist Jeffrey
Bernard's first wife Anna, similarly recruited by Dirac, went to
Holloway Prison for a month and was then given two years' probation in January 1954 for carrying £1,653-worth of gold and
platinum in a pouch strapped to her back, rather than in the
Rabelaisian fashion Kreisel had, not untypically, contrived to
suggest.[98]

* John Bayley believes Brian Aldiss's account of their visit to China in October 1979
in *The Twinkling of an Eye* (London, 1998), pp. 348–9, to be apocryphal. In one
town Chinese women enquired as to whether it was true that the genital arrangement
of Western women differed from that of Chinese, being east-west, rather than north-
south. While Aldiss recorded that Iris took the women into a separate room to show
them that all women were sisters under the skirt, Bayley is sure that the demonstration
was purely diagrammatic, and on paper. See also Iris's journal, 28 May 1990: 'Offering from Brian Medlin: "There was a young man from Cape Cod/Who didn't believe
in a God./His name was Ken Tucker,/The bleeder, the fucker,/The bugger, the
bastard, the sod." (Very cheering.)'

12

Franz Baermann Steiner
1951–1952

On 4 May 1952 Iris, returning from a holiday at the Court Hotel, Charmouth in Dorset where she had missed her journal – 'things I would have told it are lost now' – wrote, 'Much, much since last I wrote in here.' One week before she had made Wallace Robson understand that their relationship was 'impossible'. She thought of him all week, but he seemed far off, receding into the past with terrible speed: 'I don't *feel* it now, as in the past – all my crying was done before. I just . . . am deeply sad.'

She was living in two unfurnished rooms at 13 King Edward Street costing £7 a month[1] – if only this were Russia, she reported cheerfully, the landlady, who fully returned her dislike, and who the following year after eighteen months 'chucked her out', would be 'destined to be killed with a hatchet'.[2] (In June 1953 Iris moved to a couple of basement rooms at 48 Southmoor Road, owned by Dr Alice Stewart of Lady Margaret Hall. Here she called herself 'slave to the Aga', which it was her duty to tend, and bought an old canoe to take out on the dark canal which ran at the bottom of the garden. 'Bathing in summer, rheumatism in winter,' she wrote to David Hicks. She liked listening to the sedge-warblers, and watching the swans.) Among the letters awaiting her from admirers was a 'lovely' one from 'F': 'I belong to you quietly without dialectic, tho' you will never belong to me.' 'F' was Franz Baermann Steiner, who had written into his diary on Friday, 11 May 1951, 'Enter Iris Murdoch'. He had seen her once before, in 1941, and remembered it well.[3] During 1951, a lonely year,[4] Iris and Franz met six times, mostly for a drink in the Lamb and Flag pub.

Iris first mentions this new acquaintanceship nine months later, in February 1952. On 3 March they discussed their differing understandings of the past in the Golden Cross pub. He remarked: 'A cut-off past is in a way easier to convey to another than a continuous one. You have a shorter unit. When the past is continuous it mixes with present consciousness and is harder to comprehend.' Iris, trying to understand his mood as he spoke of his home city, Prague, a city he liked to compare for its provincialism and artistic vitality with Dublin, for the first time took his hand. Franz, surprised, asked, 'Am I talking too much with my hands?' Understanding that Iris simply wanted to express a wish to be closer, he told her he felt almost frightened. He wrote her a letter starting: '*Was doch die Sprache für ein seltsames Ding ist*' – how strange language is.[5]

Franz Steiner was slight, short-sighted, balding, moustachioed, disorganised, absent-minded, sometimes unshaven.[6] Born an Austrian citizen on 12 October 1909 in Karlin, a middle-class Prague suburb, he spoke that lost Prague German of Rilke and Kafka's youth which now survived only among educated Czech Jews. His father in the 1920s bought a shop selling waxed cloth, leather goods and linoleum, and from the autumn of 1934 they lived in a flat on the top floor of the Susicky Palace. Educated at the German State Gymnasium on Stepanska Street – earlier attended by Kafka's friend and biographer Max Brod and the writer Franz Werfel, both of whom he knew – and at home in the coffee-house culture of middle Europe, he gave poetry readings in the bookshop of Fritz Baum, co-founder of *Freie Gruppe Prag*. After a brief flirtation with Marxism, he went in 1930 to the Hebrew University in Jerusalem to study Arabic, and grew close to another intimate of Kafka's, S.H. Bergman. Franz identified with Kafka as writer and Jewish mystic. In 1935 he was awarded his first D.Phil., on the history of Arabic language roots, from the Charles University in Prague. He became an eccentric Zionist who spoke Arabic and wanted a *rapprochement* between these two, as he saw it, colonised peoples, Jews and Arabs. The child of non-practising Jews, he began to emphasise his Jewishness.

On the boat to England in late autumn 1936 to attend the

London School of Economics seminars of Bronislaw Malinowski, who had established modern British anthropology after the First World War, fellow Jewish refugees, to seem English, started puffing on pipes they had bought on board. Franz, put off by this, stuck to cigarettes. In July 1937 he returned to Prague for his only field trip – studying the gypsies of sub-Carpathian Ruthenia. Early the following year he again left for England. The break in his past he spoke of to Iris in the Golden Cross happened then. He had a last picture of his parents, seated in sunshine on a park bench,[7] but the Munich Agreement of 1938 and the betrayal of Czechoslovakia to the Nazis meant he could not return. In May 1939 his father wrote to him: 'The horror of the time is the way in which people fail. All their worst characteristics multiply, so that the neighbour on whom you were counting suddenly disappears or just walks over you. Everyone thinks only of themselves.'[8] One month after the war began Franz registered for his second doctorate, entitled 'A Comparative Study of the Forms of Slavery'. This choice of subject was determined by his need to bear witness to what was happening to his homeland, family and fellow Jews. Internalising the persecutions, and assuming responsibility for the pain of those afflicted, he described his research as a sacrifice, or penance.

One friend, the marine archaeologist Honor Frost, recalled him as bird-like, bent, frail, with his small black moustache, terribly vulnerable, his emotions all close to the surface, often upset. She remembered his extreme modesty, sensibility, goodness – 'always adorable, ironic, self-deprecatory'. He would keep bills and railway tickets and – like Stendhal on the tram ticket in Livorno – write *vers données* on them which he would later work up into poems. The anthropologist Professor Srinivas recalled a small, foreign-looking man, wearing a shabby mackintosh over his suit. Franz was incapable of dealing with authorities. Often very poor, he spent what money he had on the books strewn chaotically about his room with his papers, nothing on clothes. His poetry is essentially religious.[9] An idealist and mystic – influenced by Boehme, Lao Tse and the Bhagavad Gita – Buddhist, Taoist, Jewish and Muslim ideas converge in his poetry. Pre-war

Franz had been a carefree, fun-loving, life-affirming satyr,[10] a self-confident cheerful youth whose often overpowering sensuality got in the way of long-term relationships; being a poet, he was naturally said to be 'highly sensitive to beauty'. A pre-war engagement to a New Zealand girl came to nothing. In April 1940 his mother wrote to him, dreaming of 'when you come home, how I will clean everything for your arrival!'; she knew this was a dream.

His friend the deaf poet David Wright recorded the post-war Steiner as 'learned, caustic', 'broken and not defeated', 'comic in courage':

> Franz, barely forty, an old man already:
> His face had a scorched look. It is my fancy
> Those burnings – books, then bodies, the nightmare
> Of middle Europe, unimagined here –
> Withered the skin of this lean survivor,
> Always unlucky Franz, man without family
> In exile from his language, living on.[11]

2

'Always unlucky Franz' nonetheless had strokes of good fortune, of which his reciprocated love for Iris was not the least. Around Christmas 1938 the retired Classicist and Magdalen Fellow Christopher Cookson invited Franz to visit for a few days: he stayed happily for ten years, until Cookson's death. In 1944 Tambimuttu, thanks to David Wright, published some of Franz's poems in the fat issue 10 of *Poetry London*. Stephen Spender wrote admiringly, Paul Celan later expressed appreciation too, and Adorno admired his prose. In early 1939 his charismatic acquaintance Elias Canetti contacted Steiner two weeks after his arrival in England. Their friendship prospered, albeit with an interruption, and was fruitful for both; Honor Frost recalled Franz as – her word – one of Canetti's 'creatures'.

There were also setbacks. On 22 November 1932 his beloved younger sister Suse – of whom Iris always reminded him – had died, aged nineteen, in just a few days, from a streptococcal infection. When he left Prague he also left behind his early fiction, plays, and some eight hundred poems. All disappeared on the arrest of his parents. Then, in the spring of 1942, on the train between London and Oxford, the heavy suitcase containing his collection of materials for his D.Phil. – records, drafts, research – three years' work, was lost. (This was almost a tradition among anthropologists in the early 1940s: Edmund Leach lost his notes in Burma, Max Gluckmann his in a canoe on the Zambesi, and Ruth Pardee hers under a palm tree where she hid them on the invasion of Sumatra.[12]) One version has Franz's bag stolen from the guard's van; another – recalling T. E. Lawrence's loss at the same station (Reading) around Christmas 1919 of a draft of *Seven Pillars* – has Franz depositing his case at the lavatory entrance while changing trains and on his return being handed a case belonging to a luckless nurse. Great Western Railways sent him £50 in compensation. He telephoned Honor Frost, 'All my work! All my work! But this is just like me!' Frost, like most of us, would have howled. Franz, resigned, set about patiently reconstructing his thesis from scratch.

For much of the war he had no news of his parents. Then on 24 July 1945 his childhood friend and fellow writer Hans Gunther Adler wrote to tell him that he had survived internment in the camps. Adler had watched his first wife Gertrud – they had married to get deported together on the same Gestapo 'list' – choose, when her mother was selected to be gassed at the Auschwitz ramp on 14 October 1944, to die with her; and on the same transport he had seen the mother of Bettina Gross – his second-wife-to-be – similarly refuse to abandon her sister. Franz's steadfast parents were with Adler in Theresienstadt from July until mid-October 1942. He had tried to be a son to them, to help them as much as he could, to reduce the bitterness of their suffering. He was unable to prevent their being sent to their deaths in Treblinka. In one of his novels Adler writes, of the incommunicability of such loss: 'How does one address a human being who has not died?'

Franz's work was his way of living through tragedy, even a source of joy. That summer he enquired of the anthropologist

A.R. Radcliffe-Brown about the distinction between 'work' & 'labour'. Radcliffe-Brown asked, 'Got any letter from home?' Franz replied, 'Both my parents are dead, that's what I hear.' Radcliffe-Brown: 'Oh dear! Have you looked up Firth?'[13]

Franz would say that the news of his parents' deaths finally 'broke his heart', and this seems no idle metaphor. To his close friend the poet Michael Hamburger, his heart disease seemed less like a physical condition than an after-effect of that blow;[14] Iris too considered him 'one of Hitler's victims'. From Franz's greatest poem, 'Prayer in the Garden', begun on the anniversary of his father's birthday in 1947: 'A great, a mighty frost has entered my heart', and his father is 'The noblest presence ever shown to me'. In 1946 he was diagnosed after a fainting fit as suffering a nervous breakdown; in 1948 his chest pains were put down to 'hypertension'. The next year, when attempts to publish a collection of his poems – *In Babylon's Niches* – floundered, he was hospitalised for weeks in the Radcliffe Infirmary after his first heart attack; a nurse recalled him as a frail-bodied, eagle-spirited gentleman.

Despite attending synagogue irregularly, Franz perceived himself (and was seen by others) from 1939 as a profoundly religious traditional Jew, placing faith in none but Yahweh. He believed the Jews should have headed for India, where, as he wrote to Gandhi – who published ill-considered advice to the Jews in *Harijan** – they would have been simply one more caste, and not stigmatised as in Europe. In 1943 he wrote that 'A life without suffering is useless. A world without suffering is useless.' Religion was the ground we have to communicate about the possibility of ending suffering. He recited the daily prayers, usually silently. Judaism alone offered the riches to 'transvalue his suffering'.

---

* On 20 July 1946. Gandhi was concerned that Muslim sovereignty of the Holy Land should not be ceded as a result of the war; some felt that a desire to demonstrate solidarity with fellow-Indian Muslims underlay his pronouncement, which was by no means his first on this topic. In 1938, ten days after Kristallnacht, he advised German Jews to practise non-violence.

3

Franz was set apart by ill health, by tragedy, by learning. For his first D.Phil. he took courses in Siberian ethnology and Turkish studies. He had a working knowledge of Classical and Modern Arabic, differing degrees of competence in six Slavonic languages, could read Dutch, the Scandinavian tongues, and others.* When he let slip to Edward Evans-Pritchard, greatest of English anthropologists, that he knew Hebrew, he had the unpleasant feeling of having shown too much of himself: 'In England you mustn't be a Jack-of-all-Trades.' (Frank too had met Evans-Pritchard, in Syria on 7 June 1942: drinking arak, they watched a French general dance with his mistress, and discussed the coming decline of Europe and ascendancy of Asia.) Evans-Pritchard later helped publish Franz's *Taboo*.[15] In 1952 Franz was starting Chinese, and attempting a book on economics. He had wide-ranging interests: shamanism, arrow studies, boat-building and the sociology of the elephant were among his studies, and his posthumously published work on taboo profoundly influenced Mary Douglas, especially in writing *Purity and Danger*. She thought him far better-qualified than any other anthropologist in Oxford, despite his single field trip, and more modest too.

A polymath observer of English culture with a strong sense of whimsy, a quaint, acerbic humour, and a love of puns, his talk could be quizzical and light-hearted, his erudite wit and wisdom admired and sometimes feared.[16] He was direct, simple, touchy, took vast delight in small things, was lonely and valorous.[17] He could also be illogical, intolerant, difficult, imperious, and sharp when it came to exposing dishonesty, smugness and cant. His favourite writers had been E.T.A. Hoffmann, Dostoevsky, Rilke, Kafka, Adalbert Stifter; in many of these a guilt-ridden inner world confronts a wicked political scene. He now also studied Donne, Milton, Blake, Wordsworth, Keats, Hopkins, Eliot. He adored

---

* Hebrew, Turkish, Armenian, Persian, Malay, English, French, Russian, Greek and Latin, Spanish, Italian, Czech, Yiddish.

dancing. Naturalised as British in 1950, he, like his new compatriots, favoured freedom and distance in personal relationships. By nature reticent, he did not open up easily. He would say: 'If you are sick and penniless, have no relatives left alive and no friends, and no hopes for the future, pray that you may find yourself in England.'

But there was much in Britain that was inhospitable to émigrés. Franz made more friends in Spain in ten weeks than in eighteen years in England. Despite having a Czech D.Phil., he had to complete a second, *British* doctorate, in July 1950. He was nonplussed by assimilated Anglo-Jews, disliked British weather and imperialism, and saw before others how the will to *power over*, and the will to *knowledge of*, other societies were inseparable in old-fashioned anthropology. To Adler he wrote that the English were so backward in the human sciences that 'it makes one shudder. Many subjects couldn't be taught without émigrés. At the BM they don't even have an expert on Armenian, they can't even catalogue the relevant publications properly.'[18] A late journal entry makes clear how insufferable he, like Canetti, often thought the English intelligentsia, deploring their

> mixture of moral insanity and secularised puritanism, killing any ideas, but 'better', 'more moral' than anyone else. This is the suicidal renunciation of ideas by the English. This is the root of sterility. Even when this renunciation is seen as a noble sacrifice, and proposes no alternatives, it remains a kind of lethargy. A lethargy broken by the aesthetic rebellion of small, nervous bird voices . . .

In 1950 Franz was appointed Lecturer in Social Anthropology at the Anthropological Institute in Oxford, a large Victorian family house on South Parks Road. He went to the regular Friday-afternoon seminar and to drinks afterwards in the King's Arms; his presence helped make Oxford anthropology distinct. He gave his groundbreaking lectures on 'Taboo' – and on the organisation of labour, kinship, slavery, language and society – which inaugurated a revolution in anthropological thought. He denounced the separation of society and culture – 'Meanings are generated in social life; society has to be studied as part of a system of beliefs.' He would talk to students as he rested on a chair on the half-landing to catch his breath on his way to the first-floor lecture-room. He looked frail, older than his years. He was giving the first series of lectures in a British university on the German sociologist Georg Simmel, remembered, among other matters, for pro-pounding a theory of the cultural *Kreis* or circle in his study of small groups, which Franz, Canetti and Iris each lived out. Each was secretive, kept their friends apart, living in more than one circle at a time. Franz commuted between 10 Norham Road in Oxford and, in London, a Notting Hill Gate room containing his library. He vacillated between loneliness and sociability; between acceptance of an early death and hope for a new life, including marriage and children. It was probably in April 1952 that he asked a friend which of two women she thought he ought to marry: one Viennese, the other Iris.[19]

4

Iris's sense that she had always something new to learn constitutes her special aliveness and humility. In the 1960s she recorded of her Royal College of Art colleague Frederic Samson that he 'is the latest of my Jewish teachers, of whom the first was Fraenkel and the most beloved Franz'. Franz continued Wallace Robson's role of deepening her understanding of literature. She wrote in her journal on Sunday, 4 May 1952: 'talking yesterday with F. in the Crown: poetry and philosophy are close after all – I see it now.' Rilke's sensibility overwhelmed his poetic thought, she learnt, while in Eliot, often, there is mere versified thought. 'So much about this I learnt from W[allace] – and now from F[ranz]. I am trying to feel more than I do – as if sheer will could do something for him. Sadness.'

A dozen entries precede Franz's departure for a summer holi-day with his fellow anthropologist Julian Pitt-Rivers in Spain, and show Iris's feelings shifting from the 'willed' towards something deeper. They spent the vivid blue evening of Saturday, 17 May together at the Victoria Arms. She had been reading Franz's poems. The river was very still. They queued for drinks and listened to a saxophone. 'God help me to become better,' she prayed the next day, remembering Franz's gentle face and anxious, loving eyes, and also Wallace, over whose hurt she brooded. 'Let me see the way. Let me try to see – God be with W.' Four days later (Thursday, 22 May) she and Franz studied German together and Iris noticed in him 'a curious grace. (Like Shah it occurs to me.)' Franz was brown and remarkably muscular, considering he could take no exercise. 'He said: a time will come when I will see you every day. I said: not now. He said: I know not now, but it will come. He said too he was a little bit like W[allace], meaning possessive. Felt a deep quiet strength of tenderness for him. Peace.'

They met on Sunday, 1 June, a weekend crowded with other points of interest, including Arnoldo Momigliano, who was jealous of Franz,[20] and with whom she walked along the river at Abingdon while he read her Italian poetry and they laughed a lot: 'Tired now – and wanting to create silence about me.' Eight days later she travelled to London to give her paper 'Nostalgia for the Particular',[21] taking the midnight train back and 'surprised & very moved' that Franz met her at Oxford. On her thirty-third birthday that July Franz gave her a wine-glass together with a little German poem:

> *Dieses Weinglas schenk ich Dir,*
> *Trink aus ihm, trink aus mir*
> *Wahr das schöne gleich Gewicht*
> *Und zerbrich uns beide nicht.*

> (I give you this wine-glass.
> Drink from it, drink from me,
> Preserve the beautiful balance
> And don't break either of us.)

The crushing of a wine-glass beneath the groom's heel is a crucial symbolic moment at a Jewish wedding. Two weeks later

Iris visited BMB at Little Grange and prayed 'that I should not have done harm, after all – that I may not do harm'. She saw Franz off on his way to Spain, in heavy rain, from London on Friday, 15 August: 'he was cheerful. I was very sad to leave him.' A photograph shows them together, she duffle-coated in the uncertain weather, and clearly in love. (In Paris nine days later she nonetheless sent Queneau a fourteen-sided declaration of love from the Gare d'Austerlitz; his reply soon made clear that he, at least, was *hors de combat*.) She spent time in Italy with Momigliano, later regretting that she had not gone with Franz to Andalusia. The growing strength of her feeling is evident. A week before he left she had walked with Franz again by the river.[22] She had lent him the manuscript of *Under the Net*, and was delighted by his reaction: 'It is a Slav type of humour.' More detailed response came from him immediately on his return from Spain: it is possible that she entrusted him with the second half of the first draft for the summer.[23] She mentioned having written the novel to few; Franz alone was permitted to read it. She greeted him at Oxford station on his return on Saturday, 18 October,[24] bringing a bunch of gentians as a welcome-home gift, then transcribing the poem he wrote about this – '*Enzian brachte sie mir*' – into her journal. On Monday, 17 November, she wrote:

> In the evening, chez Franz. He was in pain. I stayed with him till late. He said: now you are getting fonder of me, not because I am decent or industrious or good, but just because I am in pain. Today I saw him again. He was better. He said, touching my hair, I don't want this to fade. I said, why choose this, it will all fade. He said, I know this, it is very close to me. It occurred to me that I didn't really know it. It was abstract. On Saturday I talked of religion with F. He said, in answer to my asking if he believed in God, that he *loved* God. In him, it seemed no affectation.

Later, she accused herself of having recorded 'stupidities' rather than so many more important things, and set out, in pages of lamentation, some omissions.

5

Franz too kept a journal.[25] On Saturday, 18 October, back from Spain, he saw the lights of Oxford with delight. There stood Iris on the railway platform, in trousers and grey duffle-coat, serious yet laughing, 'lovely to see', holding her small posy of gentians. Being fit and well, she dragged his massive suitcases into the house at Norham Road while he, almost dying of fear and shame, arranged the gentians in a wine-glass. They talked of a thousand things at the same time, crouched on the floor like children, pressing against each other, and he spoke further about *Under the Net*. The 'child-like' description looks forward almost two years to 14 May 1954, when she and John Bayley would prattle together about anything and everything – a sure sign her heart was opened. Franz commented only on passages in her novel that he had very much liked, they agreed on those needing reworking, and he reproached himself later that he hadn't been sufficiently encouraging. What made him happiest is how difficult it was for her to leave. He 'wallowed' in reminiscences, prayed and went to bed very happy.

The next day, a Sunday, Iris came for two hours after lunch, 'soaking wet from rain, the dear creature'. They discussed Fraenkel. 'Does the old man love her?' wondered Franz, answering himself ruefully, 'Can't imagine anyone knowing her without falling in love.' Their reading together of Goethe's 'Bride of Corinth', influenced by the Classical distych, inspired him to write his 'small poem' about the flowers.* She helped him unpack, he showing her the folder in which he stored all early versions of his poems, beautifully ordered, apologising for his vanity in the

---

* Iris later copied out the poem: 'Wed Oct. 22nd. A poem from Franz for some gentians which I brought him: "*Enzian brachte sie mir und stellte die Blüten ins Weinglas,/ O das bereite Gefass, immer erwartet es uns./ Kelche im Kelch und satt von der blaue verbotener Berge,/ Da das Krankliche Herz kaum zu ertraumen mehr wagt./ Zwölf an der Zahl sind die edlen sanft geoffneten Sterne,/ Keusch im farblosen Rund, leben mein sinnliches Jahr./ Wie, seid ihr Kinder des Weins? ihr monate siegricher Blaue?/ Nein, die Ältern seid ihr: Kindschaft beseligt den Rausch.*"'

English fashion. 'But you *are* vain!' she replied simply yet with emphasis, as if registering something to which she had long ago been reconciled. Franz, greatly affected, a trifle hurt, was haunted by the exchange all evening. They met on nineteen days of those four weeks, and during those times when they are not together she is constantly on his mind. When he opened the *Observer* on 26 October his eye at once caught a picture of and a short article about Thomas Balogh. Franz had heard Balogh lecture on economics years before, and his arrogance and 'utter vanity' repelled him. The photograph showed a handsome, clever and successful man. He knew that Iris had been his mistress and that this affair, more than anything else, 'tore her life apart. She never got completely over it.'[26]

From Franz's journal:

Monday, 20 October. What wouldn't I give to sing & accompany myself on a guitar! How happy it would make Iris! I'd give all my versifying. (And how she would tell me off for wanting to make such a swap).

Tuesday, 21 October. After 8.30 Iris came & stayed for almost 3 hours, the angel. We talked about everything & nothing . . . She arrived in funny checkered trousers & an almost masculine jacket. For quite a while we spoke in German . . . Tomorrow I shall go and see her. At least she can lock her room.

Wednesday, 22 October. Then to her. She has a bad cold, raised temperature, and her face all swollen. Wishing to spare my feelings, she told me that today it was not possible, gently, as one would tell a child that today it can't have its toy but would have to wait for another day. Whenever she looks least beautiful I love her most . . . Pain in the arm and the wrist. 12.30 to bed.

Thursday, 23 October. Again & again I thought about last night. How I keep puzzling her endlessly as if I were the sole specimen of an unknown species, a little dog with feathers or a bird with six legs instead of wings. It may well be I really am like that but I chose to interpret her remarks as words of love . . . I'll have to give up smoking before it's too late. But, how, how? . . . Now I

know what makes me wonder at her surprise over my
strange eccentricity. Her sense of wonder & surprise is
motherly ... How I prayed to God to take care of her
and thanked him for her.

Franz's heart condition gave their love-affair both its urgency
and also a tormented check to that urgency, as if, as in the Tristan
myth – Franz being a myth-connoisseur – there were a sword in
the bed. Saturday, 25 October: 'Were there ever two people who
loved each other so much and were experienced, that at the same
time were so afraid of each other?' Sometimes he feared that
things were as they were because 'she had decided to give herself
in order to comfort me, and her feelings were not obeying her',
recalling Iris's May entry about 'trying to feel more than I do'.
He goes on, 'Then she talked me out of this desperate suppo-
sition, and in the end it happened. But she was afraid because
of my heart. Neither of us made a single spontaneous movement,
each disappointed the other.' They lay in a draught from the
window, he thinking about Iris's cold, she worrying about his
heart. His journey home was sad. He listened to the owls hooting,
the leaves rustling, and the following day, brooding and fearing
a strong reaction on her part, did not dare leave the house. She
had no telephone. Again and again he imagined the door opening, her entering, saying: 'Darling this is perhaps the last time we
can see each other,' or maybe just horrific silence. If there were
no letter in the morning ending it all, he fixed his hopes upon
a meeting they had agreed on next day to visit Elizabeth
Anscombe at 27 St John Street. 'To bed at 1.15 ... to the left of
my heart sits a little mouse gnawing away. Dear God, what can I
do to deserve that woman?'

He had indeed put himself in a cage with imaginary bars. Like
a good wife fetching her man from work – as he optimistically
expressed it – Iris, 'beautiful, loving, tender', collected him at
6 p.m. from the Institute. 'What a fool I am, so fickle. Not at all
like this steadfast creature.' After Anscombe they drank a bottle
of Beaujolais over dinner. Both drank and smoked plentifully, he
aware of the dangers, unable to stop: 'The most beautiful hours

since my arrival in Oxford.' Iris, though tired, was filled with enthusiasm. For the first time she found fault with one of his poems. Franz told her a lot, about a previous girlfriend, Mary, and about the Carpathians. 'To bed at 12.15. A glorious day, completely free from pain.'

Not seeing her for even two days at the end of the month he found unbearable: 'Living separately is only for young people.' Other women who attracted him recalled Iris. Addressing a Spanish girl gave him such joy he went down on his knees and prayed. He did not speak to a 'ravishing' nineteen-year-old Swedish girl at the British Council because of Iris, since he 'liked her too much'. Smiling his most engaging smile at a French barmaid called Nadette – she had a walk whose vibration he 'felt in his sex organ, even when she is at the far end of the room' – he is suddenly reminded 'how much Iris loves my smile, so I wiped it off my face, and this absurd grimace was mirrored on her face as she listened with great attention'. He invited Nadette to a dance; she came accompanied by a friend for protection. The combination of cold night air and dancing brought on hellish chest pains; his eyes were riveted on the gramophone needle that was working its way towards his release: 'I shall never forget that dance. It was like dancing with the devil.' His liaison with Iris was semi-public, in that they decided to have lunch together on 30 October at the Abingdon Arms, where Nadette worked, to put an end to stupid talk about 'his' French girl.

6

Franz recorded each meeting, each absence, each telephone call. They felt to him like a couple, and he wanted the arrangement solemnised. As they listened to Mozart's string quartet K.593, Iris described her room in St Anne's so vividly he felt he was walking around in it. The blue jar he had brought from Spain, looking proud and content with its rough bright colour. The picture she had painted as a slip of a girl, a still life of sensuous yet stern primroses (or coltsfoot), by the side of a copy of Joyce's *Ulysses*, against a curiously empty yet intense blue background. On Friday, 31 October in the Child and Eagle pub they drank beer and he watched her order for herself, not for the first time, a ham sandwich. So interested in general in Jewishness, she was unaware that in certain moods he objected to being offered ham: 'I shouldn't be so bothered about that,' he reproached himself, fearing that she was slipping away from him.[27] But 'intimate understanding' survived. He was overjoyed that his blood pressure had improved, felt hopeful for the future. She looked in through the window, saw him bent over his prayer book, resting on his elbows, his hands against his ears. 'What were you puzzling over?' she said as she entered, bringing a posy of violets. The doctor was satisfied with him. She was pale and radiant, all the little hairs on her face displaying 'the purest goodness'. They agreed to meet on Sunday evening, and went to the pub for a while. He admired the violets, whose long stems he put into a tall glass, describing them at length and admiringly to himself: 'How she unconsciously expresses herself in all her presents.' Throughout a lecture at the University Jewish Society he saw in his mind's eye her face, interested, amused, now and then rejecting and so making him aware that this or that humorous remark was cheap. He was always able to visualise her face exactly, her hands not as clearly. Browsing in Simmel to prepare the following Monday's lecture, he felt stupid, too much in love to work: 'Silly old tom-cat,' he reproached himself. As they grew closer he repeatedly felt – as on the following evening, when she stayed until midnight – that 'we've never been as close as this' before. After she left he worked on his lecture till three in the morning.

The Monday was glorious: one of those spring-like English days you get in late autumn. They met and walked about Portmeadow, enjoying the fields, willows, the white sails, 'all those small ordinary, sparkling things'. A gaggle of geese thrilled Iris. On Tuesday, 4 November he had not seen her all day, yet felt her presence so strongly that he didn't miss her. He noticed during his lecture that the movements of his hands had started to imitate hers:

She's changing my life. But how can we belong to each
other without getting married? I'm not going to talk
about that to her. She is afraid of it. The wish must come
from her.

He called on her that Thursday, 6 November, after dinner.
She was exhausted, having eaten nothing since the morning, just
taught through the day, 'poor angel'. In the disorderly kitchen
he talked her into eating something. They 'just kept looking at
each other, like young lovers', scarcely talking sensibly.

We undressed, but on the draughty sofa my pains became
once again severe. She was the more sensible of the two
of us, told me to have a rest, and then helped me into
my clothes. All that with so much concern, goodness,
love and tact that this evening brought us closer to each
other than a successful union.

Next day he lectured miserably. Evans-Pritchard had recommended him for the Chair in Sociology at the University of Jerusalem, and the possibility of a choice between Jerusalem and Iris
horrified him. His heart condition prevented his going to her
now the weather had become colder. Many evenings Iris arrived
at his lodgings late, flicking a stone against his window to attract
his attention – once, when she was tipsy, a big one. She was often
tired after a full day's work and on one occasion also after a debate
at the Socratic Club where she opened discussion. It seemed like
a miracle to him: she arrived so tired and absent-minded and
then slowly became peaceful and happy. They read German
poetry:[28] 'How happy we were,' Franz wrote, and he quoted '*Ver-
weile doch!*' from Goethe's *Faust*, inviting the happy hour to linger.

7

Franz's entries that November are dominated by Kafka, whom
both admired.[29] His poem 'Kafka in England' concerns the gap
between those who had lived through or felt the guilt of witnessing the Holocaust, and those English who had done neither.

Iris, however, was always accounted one who 'understood'.* A translation of Kafka's *Letters to Milena* was coming out; Franz was a little afraid of this Milena, who reminded him that, like Kafka, that other, older 'Franz', he was in love with a gentile girl whom he did not know how to make his own. Like Kafka, too, he was mortally ill. And like Kafka, he suffered from excess of scruple: 'How disgusting even unintentional lies are. One can't correct them without making a big issue out of nothing.' He bought *Letters to Milena* the day they appeared, the day he also heard of the death of a Spanish baby for whom he and Iris had, in August, bought a present in London.[30] Kafka's letters made him sad. Much in them seemed to him unworthy of such a noble human being: 'The longing to find shelter in the beloved, to find, at long last, a home in another human being – and at the same time such fear of the bed.' These letters, he feared, would bring joy to few people and would only strengthen the tendency to interpret Kafka 'psychologically'. What was noble in them reminded him of Canetti, while Kafka's

> shameful way of burdening the beloved, as fiancé, with one's own problems instead of unburdening her from marital problems, and over and above that, entangle her in a correspondence . . . , to exploit the energy of a more vital human being – that is me, unfortunately, unfortunately.[31]

As he read the letters he told himself: 'That's just what I don't want, I don't want a mistress, even if it's necessary to pass through *that* phase; I want a firmer tie, something which she and I wd feel to be a marriage, a container for love in which she can forever radiate.' Meanwhile his need for a nurse as well as a beloved was pressing. After a dinner-party with her in Headington he came home alone and, entering the unheated room, was 'knocked down' by pain. When the electric fire went out he could neither

* On 7 August she had noted: 'F. said: The Jews identified themselves more with the illegal immigrants than with the concentration camp victims. It was the people in motion, the archetype. This was a propos of "Gebet im Garten" – I said, why pick on us. Charming story of young Jew who started to eat pig after the farmer had killed a calf for him!'

insert a coin nor undress himself. Afraid he would have to go back into hospital, he fought for breath, writhing in a pain not spasmodic enough to be a thrombosis or angina, but (he hoped) stress on the heart as a result of continuous smoking, extreme cold and the big meal. Medicaments did not help. The 'hell' lasted two hours. When he could breathe again he read the *Kaddish* (prayers for the dead), scribbled a farewell note to Iris, and undressed. The pain went on for another hour, during which he endlessly reproached himself and tried to read 'poor Kafka'. He was so exhausted that he fell asleep without offering a prayer of thanks for his recovery. Iris, when he recounted all this two days later, gripped and would not let go of his hand.

Their last discussions concern religion.[32] Iris asked him whether he believed in God. He replied that he could not use the word 'believe' because, among other things, it misinterpreted his relationship with God: he could only say that he loved Him. He skirted lamely around the most important thing for him, wondering how he could talk about such heartfelt matters, 'least of all to this seriously questioning angel'. He tried to speak of his understanding of Judaism, in painfully brittle words: the dual relationship of God – to the individual as creator, and to the people as spouse ('*Gefreier*'*). Then she spoke: about her ignorant 'groping' for truth; her feelings of guilt because of her past life; her ties to the Anglican Church. Only within the framework of *that* Church could she imagine a realisation of the religious life. Had sentence been pronounced on Franz? He listened, half turning away, silently praying for mercy, that all might not be lost, his heart thumping a grand march of breathlessness: 'Thank God she didn't see how things were with me.' They read Kafka's story 'Josephine, the Singer' together. The pains began, and 'once again made everything impossible': 'That the dear, modest girl should have to go through this farce of undressing to no purpose seemed to me like a physical punishment. Yet she was so loving, so touchingly kind to me. Quite suddenly the beloved was a nurse. Despite all the pain, I felt happy in her care.' Finally she sat,

* Franz's handwriting is very hard to decode: '*Befreier*' would be 'deliverer'.

dressed, by his side holding his hand, comforting him as much as possible. When he felt better he read her his poem, 'Spaziergang'. She found it somewhat dependent on Eliot and not unlike Rilke, with reference to the line, '*Die ganze Gestalt ist der Toten*': 'She's becoming a good critic. Nonetheless she likes the poem very much. She left at 12.30. I stayed awake for a long time, prayed, thanked God for her, and asked Him to bless her.'

They continued their discussion of religion and the conduct of life on the morning of Sunday, the sixteenth, after which he noted: 'How dark life is, when I'm not hearing her voice, her steps. How meaningless it would be without her. I mustn't lose her.' Night pains caused him to cancel the next day's lecture. He stayed at home, read Kafka, slept a great deal. Tea, toasted cheese, dry figs and apples made his lunch. That afternoon his doctor[33] prescribed teobromine-phenobarbitone for his pain, took his blood pressure ('170. – Not bad'), warned him against sexual excess. Franz commented: 'Poor Franz. I should marry a Jewish girl and then all would be well.' Iris came at 4.15 with half a bottle of sherry, which they almost emptied. 'I was once again touched by the same things. She is so full of concern – if only she knew, that with one short sentence she could give me lasting joy.' After she left, the pain started again, cramp-like in the wrist and the middle of the chest.

His final diary entry, on Tuesday, 18 November, ran as follows:

A warmer day . . . What have I achieved? My poems are unpublished, all was in vain. My illness comes and goes as it likes. I have the love of the best woman I can imagine and she won't marry me. I still don't know whether I'm any good as a scientist. Recently she said, 'You certainly are a religious person (religious in English usage means pious) but you're not really a good person'. If she says so it must be true. When I looked at her in horror she smiled her dearest smile and said, 'But it doesn't matter. Not to me.' The night was unbearable. Paul Eluard, that noble poet has passed away as well.

Around this time Honor Frost took Franz to see a friend's paintings.[34] There was a Tarot pack which he cut. 'Yes, I know,' he said, in the resigned tone she remembered from when he had lost his suitcase: like a character in grand opera, he had contrived to draw the card for 'Death'. On the evening of Wednesday the twenty-sixth Franz showed Iris his poem '*Über dem Tod*'. He said, 'Notice it is "*dem*" not "*der*" – not "*About* death", but "*Above* death".' Iris, tired after meetings, puzzled away at it and couldn't understand. 'Never mind it,' said Franz, tossing it aside. 'You relax now and be quiet.'

8

Franz died the following evening. He had recently turned forty-three. Iris formally registered the death: 'I was with him on so many days. I did not expect this.'[35] One of Franz's aphorisms had been that, in matters of love, the more faithless is the stronger. Until that last week, Iris's strength had, in every sense, exceeded his, and her time, energy and love, though increasingly devoted to Franz, were also shared with others. Now it was he who (like Frank before him) had unequivocally deserted her, an act worthy of respect, the relative balance of strengths changed for good. Other suitors thus vanquished, she was flooded, as can happen in bereavement, with pain and remorse, with tormented longing, with a love deferred for good, hence unappeasable. 'How does one write sincerely about great pain?' she interrogated herself.

> *7 December 1952*. My love for F. which was becoming such a broad serene river, now is a raging torrent.
> *21 December 1952*. F. saying, as I knelt by him: Darling, I do want to get better for you ... Even then I didn't see or understand anything. Sick and rent with misery. The way F's eyes gleamed through his glasses – & I wept over him only a few days before, & he said: You do love me. *Was für Steinereien hast du heute gemacht?**
> *26 December 1952*. When I told F. he was foolish, he

---

* 'What have you done for old Steiner today?'

said: Oh Darling, you don't know how foolish ... F.
needed me. [We] could have built a universe together
... F ... created me by his love. Misery today, tying up
F's letters ... Every day there are things I would like to
ask F. I can't stop yet the gesture of turning towards him.
Franz.

28 December 1952. The reality of death. How all trivial
references to it now sound different. One wonders: but
don't all these people *know?*

18 January 1953. It suddenly strikes me as funny (&
as I think this I am crying) that the only *legal* right I have
where Franz is concerned is the ownership of his body!
(I received yesterday the deed giving me the rights over
the grave space.) Everything else has passed, legally
speaking, into the hands of others.

9

That Friday, 28 November, Iris interrupted Barbara Mitchell's
Latin class at St Anne's in tears and took her outside to cancel
their lunch-date; a note on her door in Hartland House cancelled
all further tutorials that term. The funeral was at 1 p.m. at
Oxford's Jewish Cemetery, a day of brilliant, bleak, cold sunshine
after early snow. Seven of Franz's London friends, including Adler
and Canetti, were there, and some sixty people from Oxford,
many from the institute. There were neither flowers nor speeches,
but the customary prayers, including the *Kaddish*, greatest of Jewish prayers, for the dead. Iris stood apart from the others and
near the grave, chief mourner.[36] Dressed unconventionally for a
funeral in her usual day-clothes, she looked 'utterly desolate'.[37]
It had been Philippa, who baby-sat for Michael and Anne
Dummett that weekend with Iris, at Iris's urgent request, who
had bought Iris news of Frank Thompson's death eight years
before: her desolation over Franz was quite different.

She wrote to David Hicks that she was not in good shape at
present, having

lately lost, by death, the person who was closest to me, whom I loved very dearly, whom I would very probably have married, if things had gone on as they were going. I can't at the moment see how one recovers from such a loss. It was sudden & unexpected . . . I wasn't ready for it. We were both so full of the future. And now I simply don't know what to do.[38]

On the Sunday she fell in the snow, breaking a little vase of Franz's and wrenching her ankle, a sprain bad enough to have to have her leg set for a week in plaster. Friends and admirers tried to console her. Her St Anne's colleague Elaine Griffeths took her to talk for an hour with John Jones[39] who, with his wife Jean, was 'so kind. But they are so young and so happy'. Asa Briggs, first to sign his name on Iris's plaster cast, said: 'It is not an empty world.' It seemed empty, though Iris noticed people's kindness, even their love. Wallace Robson told her over sherry that he loved her deeply, and asked if this was any consolation. Handsome Ferruccio Rossi-Landi,[40] with whom she had had a happy, brief liaison, said conventionally that 'the dead are out of trouble & our relation with them is made perfect'. Arnoldo Momigliano was in fear for himself, his desperate love kindling no warmth in her; he noted Iris's terrible rhythmic weeping, like that of a distraught child. Iris said to Adler, in Oxford for two days dividing up Franz's things, 'You have known F. so long & so well.' He replied: 'Yes, but you loved him & one day of love tells you more than years of friendship.' And he added: 'Franz was loved for the first time.' Franz had kept all Iris's letters, had indeed kept everything, even each silly note arranging a *rendez-vous*. In London with the Adlers on 10 December, Bettina Adler wanted to speak to Iris alone, of a 'great light', and how Franz was happy and protected at the last. Iris felt moved by her sincerity and simplicity. But it was no use. 'No love is any use,' she reflected. Two days later she wrote to Queneau, apologising for her 'foolish' August letter: 'My whole existence seems to me now a tissue of foolishness.' Franz, she told him, whom she loved very deeply, had been, by contrast, 'daily bread'.

Even in deep grief, her imagination was active. She collected her memories, fearing they would fade, tried to catch his voice and intonation. The way he said, 'A warm night – or ees eet feelthy?' The way he asked, 'What ees eet?' The way he would wave down his hand 'Indyed.' She recalled a day that summer when they lunched in the Parks, and she delighted him by cutting the cheese with a blade of grass.

22 November. 20th anniversary of F's sister's death.

30 November. What can I do with such a degree of misery? . . . How I overtook him on my bicycle in Parks Rd in the summer, and how his eyes shone so glad thro' his glasses & he ran a little toward me – & I took his briefcase from him. And how we lay in the grass in the parks and he took photos of me. And how he would say 'indyed!', and whistle like a bird, & move his ears. And how I wd feel him moving them when he lay against my breast & we would both laugh. Mein Franz – dein Franz indeed – & more than you know. Ganz Steinerisch. Steiner and Steinerism. These things are as nearly unbearable as anything I have known. I love him. I don't know what I can do with such pain. How to face it.

In agony. No overcoming death.

I only met F. a year ago in the summer. Except for that encounter in 1941 which he remembered so well . . .

Demented with grief. I don't know what to do.

Though 'in such pain as never before', the urge to record little things, to notate the psychopathology of grief, remained. When at last she ate some food, the taste surprised her. She noted, too, the *distance* of ordinary things, their lack of any contact with her; how all love, which might have consoled for anything else, was as nothing here. And 'how boring bereaved people are. They have only one subject.' Yet she knew her own strength, too, and what would, as she believed, serve it. 'The horror of feeling indestructible. I can bear all this grief and more without breaking.'

10

Franz joined Frank in Iris's private pantheon of martyrs.[41] She sanctified both.[42] Others vouchsafe that Franz could be difficult and moody, could speak ill of third parties, had an envious anxiety that he might lose one friend to another, a love of control,[43] was thought solipsistic. Iris herself had told him he was 'not really a good person'. Here she is silent, all is sanitised. Since 'Good = Saintly' and there were no saints, there were also no entirely good people either. His character improved retrospectively. About such a tendency to idealise absence she wrote sharply at the end of *The Unicorn*: 'She [Hannah] was like the rest of us. She loved what wasn't there, what was absent. This can be dangerous ... She could not really love the people she saw, she could not afford to, it would have made the limitations of her life too painful.'

When Iris telephoned Adler in London to bring him news of Franz's death, he at once asked, 'By his own hand?' 'Hitler's victims', a later journal-entry, annotates this exchange. It was Franz who that August brought Iris the news of the suicide of Tommy, son of the refugee and ex-disciple of Wittgenstein, Friedrich Waissman – his wife had killed herself earlier. 'All violent & hurtful & senseless,' Iris noted.[44]

In 1988 Iris elegised Franz, a 'cheerful, happy person, very tender, very full of feeling', and

> certainly one of Hitler's victims. But, though so terribly sad and wounded, he was one of the best people I ever met, with a remarkable capacity for enjoyment. He was gentle and good and full of spirit and imagination. He was ... a very good poet. I loved him greatly ... I still miss him.

The best muses are unattainable – 'Think you, if Laura had been Petrarch's wife, he would have written sonnets all his life?'[45] Or if Minnie Temple had not died, Henry James would still have created Millie Theale? In her last, unpublished book of philosophy, on Heidegger, Iris wrote of those who resisted Nazism and

Stalinism as 'reflections of pure goodness, a proof of [Good's] connexion with us as a reality, as a real possibility'.[46] Frank and Franz – probably also a later friend, the Soviet dissident Vladimir Bukovsky – were on her mind. She again associated Frank and Franz when she wrote that 'They were both of them full of truth and pure in heart.'[47] If Frank helped inspire her characterisation of virtuous soldiers, Franz helped inspire her scholar-saints Peter Saward, Willy Kost and Tallis Browne,[48] all of them isolated figures. The good slave in *Acastos* echoes Franz too when, on being asked whether he believed in God, can reply only that he loved Him. Of course Frank and Franz's goodness shone the brighter because of the darkness of that to which they were opposed: like Muriel Spark and William Golding in particular, Iris came of that generation of writers whose ability to create a world is defined by the need to oppose Hitler, which led to Golding's quest, in *Lord of the Flies*, to understand the blackness within Jack and Roger, the goodness of Ralph and Simon. The courage of both Frank and Franz was to stand *against*. Thus they expressed their different styles of practical idealism, which constitute their legacy for her.

She records that Franz influenced her, especially her views on religion, but does not vouchsafe *how*. Adler's son Jeremy suggested three aspects: the religious sense itself, guilt, and an impassioned sense of good and evil. Bettina Adler agreed that, coming from a harmonious home, Iris felt the evil of the world more keenly than most; and that she saw in Franz both an absolutely truthful attempt to see the evil of the world, and how, though 'none of us could cope with it', an understanding of the powers of Good, in the Bible, in poetry, and in good things in the world, perhaps good people, were the only means we have of opposing it.[49] 'Prayer in the Garden' remains to Michael Hamburger 'one of the few valid and adequate responses in poetry to events literally unspeakable and beyond the range of good sense, decorum or realistic presentation', a long poem that 'exposed the raw nerve of his anguish and of his faith'. Here Franz utters the unspeakable by negating the will and identity of the speaker; the dead can be 'uttered' only from a posture of complete self-abasement. The poet, 'wounded' into his own inwardness, must bear witness to the transcending of all taboos, to the defilement of all that is held sacred, accepting his own spiritual death as a condition of witness – a martyr taking on himself the world's pain.

For Mary Douglas, Franz single-handedly invented the 'sociology of danger'[50] and that reading of 'taboo' that relates it not to aberration, but to the sacred. He himself became, because of what he had endured, both sacred and taboo, coming from the place where Nazism undid all taboos, so questioning the idea of the sacred itself. The Dachau survivor Willy Kost in *The Nice and the Good*, inspired by Franz, is also both sacred and taboo. His Trescombe neighbours leave anxious gifts outside his cottage door, unconsciously appeasing a source of danger, propitiating one whose ill luck makes him an object of holy dread. If Iris argued later for a recovery of our sense of the sacred, Franz fed this, and taught her to view the world in terms of the relations between what is taboo or forbidden and what is holy. They held in common an essentially religious vision that reverenced difference or otherness and privileged the sense of wonder, a mistrust of systems and of modernity, a fascination with exile, a belief that the ancient gods or powers now reappear as impersonal forces.[51] For both, the truth must be grounded in pain. Iris could look steadily at the terrible aspects of human existence. Friendship with Franz strengthened this.

11

Iris had lunch that foggy December of 1952 with her old Somerville friend Lucy Klatschko. In general Lucy found communication with Iris easy and delightful, Iris entering so much into other people's lives in a self-effacing way. But Iris was so upset that a great friend of hers had just died – 'a Jewish refugee who was a brilliant poet' – that this meeting was memorably different. Iris only stated the fact and said nothing more: not even his name. The meal was silent and strained.

343

Lucy was working for Thomas Thorpe, a bookseller near the publisher John Murray on Albemarle Street, a 'horrible man' who secretly ate buns and pinched the behinds of the girl assistants. She consoled herself by reading as many books against the Catholic Church as she could find, only to discover, to her horrified and dismayed interest, that she was gradually becoming persuaded by the power of that which was being attacked. By Christmas 1952 she was received into the Church. On 23 March 1953 she wrote to Iris, 'I don't think I will become a nun on account of the Rev. Mother Superior!' but on 1 May 1954 she was accepted at Stanbrook Abbey near Worcester as a postulant, living out the next half-century there. These developments were later of great interest to Iris. She wrote in her journal on 12 January 1994: 'Lucy's life – to imagine it . . .'

Meanwhile, she recorded on 10 December 1952 that there was only one person she now really wanted to see: Elias Canetti. 'I telephoned Canetti when the pain was unbearable, but he was not there.'

13

Conversations with a Prince
1952–1956

Franz had introduced Iris and Elias Canetti.[1] On the evening of Christmas Day 1952 Canetti phoned her at her parents' house in Chiswick at a quarter to eight and asked her to come and see him in Hampstead. They drank in the North Star pub on the Finchley Road and adjourned to his flat in nearby Compayne Gardens, Canetti speaking that night on transformation (*Verwandlung*), or how one divides oneself into many *personae*. Iris saw dangers in this, but soon noted in him many aspects and faces – a veritable 'Hindu pantheon'. Canetti spoke with a curious, almost naive, confident directness, finding her 'interesting', seeming capable of great affection, and not wanting her to go, but to stay talking, which she did, until 1.30 on Boxing Day morning when he reluctantly found her a taxi.[2] She was moved by him for the first time, feared to be too direct, but reflected, 'I think there can be no harm here, even if I were to love him' – a thought which brought her back to Franz with pain: *they* could have 'built a universe together'. By January 1953 Iris and Canetti had started a three-year love-affair,[3] of central and continuing and passionate importance to both, Iris feeling 'stunned misery, astonishment', and despite herself 'a sort of joy in Canetti mingling with an acute consciousness of Franz and the cruelty of his absence'. She wrote on 10 January from Chiswick:

> It is midnight. [Canetti][4] was here for five hours. He fills me with wonder and delight and fear. I told him: you are a great city of which I am learning now the main thoroughfares, which roads lead to the river. Later I shall

explore each quarter carefully. He said: will you ask for any changes? Do you approve of the cathedral? And what will you do with this city? Live in it. We spoke of the out-of-time character of what C. means by 'myth' – contrasted with the step-by-step future planning movement of Kafka. The viewpoint is that to be achieved. The concentration into the small creatures, the small scale – which shews the powerfulness of the individual so much more tensely. I am amazed at the scale of C's thought. How *much* he intends. He said: I want to approach freshly, as the early Greeks or those who broke with scholasticism. He makes me believe in the possibility of understanding. (How much Ox. philos. glories in the impossibility!) We laughed very much, C. keeping up a stream of pompous-sounding discussion in an audible voice for my parents' benefit in intervals of kissing me violently. He is a bull, a lion, an angel. I told him – most like a beast & most like an angel. He said – what I would wish. He lay there, beautiful as a landsknecht. When he left I gave him one of my fossil stones shaped like a heart. I spoke of how he was bound in my mind to Franz . . .

The loss of Franz precipitated an affair of which he would have been jealous; Iris tried, in her mind's eye, to give Franz reassurance. Soon obsessively in love, she noted that Canetti is 'the only reality these days'. It says much about their secretiveness that, in 1999, no surviving friend knew that they had been lovers, rather than friends.

2

Canetti was known always only by his surname like 'Socrates' or 'Confucius'[5] – never, even to his wife Veza, by his Christian name ('Canetti is a genius,' she would say, 'but he is not a Goethe'[6]). Canetti would say he had yet to become worthy of his Christian name Elias – since it betokened a little Elijah or prophet of God. Such modesty was not habitual. 'Don't you think Canetti is exactly like God?' Madame Meyer, the wife of the then French Cultural

Attaché, was asked, to which she riposted, 'Yes. But is God like Canetti?'[7] The story shocked him.

He was born in Ruschuk in Bulgaria in 1905, with Ladino, the medieval Spanish spoken by Sephardi Jews, his first language; he would tell of proud Sephardim enshrining in their Balkan houses the great house-keys they took with them after their expulsion from Spain in 1492.[8] His intense pride in this patrician inheritance marked a life rich in further displacements. His polyglot merchant father moved the family to Didsbury, Manchester, from 1911, where Canetti learned English, which he spoke without accent, and French; at the age of eight, in Vienna, his gifted, possessive mother obliged him, with a fiercely cruel singleness of will, to learn German in weeks. Knowing many languages is one way of not being tied to any single identity; as an adult he similarly travelled on a Nansen passport, invented for citizens displaced by the treaties of 1919.[9] Though schooled in Lausanne and Zurich, and having sojourned in Berlin, Vienna remained the capital of his interior universe, German its chosen tongue. He had a talent for sniffing out great artists, and his memoirs contain memorable cameo-portraits of Karl Kraus, Thomas Mann, Robert Musil, Alban Berg, Bertolt Brecht, Georg Grosz, Isaac Babel, Hermann Broch and others. 'The dog of his age', he joked of himself.

Canetti arrived in England from Vienna, via Paris, early in 1939 with his wife Venetiana Taubner-Calderon – a proto-feminist whose articles in Viennese papers were humbly signed 'Veza Magd' (Veza the Maid) – also Sephardi, known always as Veza, and a gifted writer;[10] through her he had escaped from his mother, probably the only human being who ever dominated him. They were closely pursued by Friedl Benedikt, second daughter[11] of Ernst Martin Benedikt, owner of the *Neue Freie Presse* and painter,[12] both well-evoked in the third volume of Canetti's memoirs, *The Play of the Eyes*. The other Benedikts escaped to Sweden: Friedl alone, who had fallen in love with Canetti through his novel *Die Blendung* (1935) and had taken trouble to meet him, followed him to London.* She

---

* Friedl used her sister Susie as a lookout to alert her when Canetti was approaching, so she could prepare herself. Susie Ovadia (*née* Benedikt), letter to author.

came for Canetti, and her letters suggest that they were happy together – 'My life and his are bound together for ever, he taught me to write and to live and has been good to me . . .'.[13]

Canetti and Veza soon moved to Amersham, on the outskirts of London, where his affair with Anna Mahler, an earlier 'official' mistress,[14] was followed by a lifelong liaison with the painter Marie-Louise von Motesiczky, leading student of Max Beckmann. He addressed Marie-Louise always as '*Sie*' rather than the familiar '*Du*', affecting the old-world decorum of Laclos's *Liaisons Dangereuses*, a world with whose elaborate erotic plotting he had affinity. Probably Friedl and Marie-Louise knew little of one another:[15] Friedl lived in Hampstead, at 35 Downshire Hill, of which her first cousin Margaret Gardiner left her in charge:[16] 'Margaret, don't you think life is absolute hell, every single *minute* of it?' Friedl would ask. Neither Canetti, Veza nor Friedl had any money; all were in bohemian style ready to share their last penny. Finding a Christmas present for Canetti that satisfied a practical need without demeaning him could be hard. Yet he gravitated easily towards wealth.

At the time Iris met Canetti, his habit of working late at night, then moving nomadically – 'as if hunted'[17] – between a variety of neatly book-lined safe-houses – a seedy flat at 14 Crawford Street, Marylebone, another in Compayne Gardens, Hampstead, belonging to Marie-Louise but used by Veza – was well-established. He visited friends separately, living a double, sometimes a triple life, holding court in the coffee-shops of Hampstead, which recreated a lost '*Mitteleuropa*'. When Iris was asked how he fitted his wife into his busy round of visits, she replied airily, 'Oh, he sees her at four in the afternoon.'[18] Both Canetti and Veza insisted that Veza be treated with all the respect due to a Wife Number One in a classical Chinese household: 'Canetti can have as many mistresses as he likes, I don't care, for I am Veza Canetti, and no one else can call themselves that.' She revered him – '*Ich verehre ihn*' – expressing amazement to other women that they did not fall in love with Canetti.[19] Iris at first took Canetti, as she did everyone, at his own valuation, reverencing Veza too, loving his 'genius' and 'Viennese' sophistication alike, charmed when he sagely remarked of Rene: 'How young she is – and more than pretty. She could have a young lover any day yet she loves your father!' He was what Germans call a *Sitzriese*, a short man who, sitting, manifests great power. His face resembled Strindberg's, his hair standing on end as if made of bronze, his extraordinary eyes 'some colour or other', sometimes very ferocious, at others 'suddenly full of glittering lights like a flirtatious milkmaid'.

Die Blendung was translated by Veronica Wedgwood and published to acclaim in Britain in 1946 as *Auto da Fé*.[20] The novel is a Georg Grosz-like black comedy of justified paranoia. Susan Sontag, whose brilliant championing of his work helped win Canetti the Nobel Prize for Literature in 1981,[21] noted that it was impossible not to regard the derangement of its monomaniac hero, the book-man Peter Kien, as other than a variation on his author's most cherished exaggerations; that it is animated by an exceptionally inventive, delirious, hatred of women (Canetti's mother accurately predicted that women would worship him for its misogyny[22]). Kien resembles Aschenbach (in Thomas Mann's *Death in Venice*) or Unrath (in *The Blue Angel*), full of intellectual vanity. The animal stupidity of his housekeeper Therese, and the fanatical greed of the grotesque dwarf *Ost-Jude* Fischerle, a portrait Canetti later regretted and uneasily defended, in the light of the 'catastrophe' that overcame all Europe,[23] help destroy Kien and his library.

Canetti soon spoke to Iris of a good man called Abraham Sonne, who had shown him that the 'evil' that his book is replete with was 'not the evil I have in me now':[24] 'He gave me the right to be what I am.' Iris recalled Sonne in her own notebooks forty years later. Those wishing to honour Iris's reputation must fight the temptation to blacken Canetti's. Since he aroused strong emotions of admiration, subservience, fear and dislike, this is not always easy. Their friendship survived until his death in 1994, and he claimed to be proud to have lived to see twenty-five of her novels published, while she considered him always a genius to whom she introduced only close friends.[25] The task of evoking him justly is made the harder by his investment in *Verwandlung*, or transformation – the great theme of his work and life – the poet being, in his view, Master of Transformations, or shape-shifter.[26] His embargo on any biography being written until thirty years after his death is read by friends as a plea for the feelings of survivors; by others, since few will then be alive who remember the first-hand truth, as mythomania.

An experience of self-transformation, a 'blooding', a return journey to the underworld: these were what the writer in Iris was looking for. If there is something 'willed' about the untried Iris's rapid subjection to the 'monster' whom she wished to tame, thus establishing her place in the cult, there is also something involuntary. Canetti, in one of his 'transformations', touches all her male enchanter-figures, from *A Severed Head* and *The Unicorn* to *The Sea, The Sea*. He would sometimes proudly claim to have been her discoverer. If he helped 'make' her a writer, it was not quite in the manner that he assumed: an *argument* with him is latent throughout. Oxford philosophy, in the very century of Stalin and Hitler, had tended to evacuate the ideas of Good and Evil and render them idle functions of the choosing will. Canetti claimed to the poet Kathleen Raine, who he felt was too starry-eyed to understand, to have introduced Iris to an understanding of evil: Iris 'respected' evil, Raine not. Through Canetti Iris discovered something about the workings of power, and her own complicity in this. If so, it made her a better writer.

3

Franz Steiner was said to have been on the phone when he collapsed and died, leaving the receiver dangling.[27] Canetti, however, would say that Iris proposed marriage to Franz, whose heart, like that of the Duke of Gloucester in *King Lear*, unable to bear the strain of joy, 'burst smilingly'.[28] This proposal-tale is an expurgated, prettified version of the story that obsessed Canetti all his life, with which he shocked many, from the 1950s until shortly before his death.[29] He claimed that lovemaking was too much for Franz's heart, and, implausibly, that Iris laid out his body. He sometimes added, falsely, that she beat on his London door in distress, begging his help.[30] True, Franz had not known love with-out pain since he was thirty-nine, and his doctor warned him against sexual excess. Much also casts doubt on Iris's 1988 state-ment that she last saw him on the evening before his death, and that they parted happily in the expectation of meeting again soon.[31] A January 1953 journal entry reads, 'I haven't seen death before,' and a later recollection about awakening Franz, 'coming into his room suddenly before he died, and how for a moment there was a look of fear on his face. How can I bear to remember this?' not to speak of the sheer intensity of her grief and sense of responsibility alike, could support the view that he died in her arms. 'Iris Murdoch' appears on his death certificate as the person formally registering his passing. It was surely she who left open his manuscript poems at the 'beautiful' text which Louis Dumont, paying his last respects the following morning, recognised as related to the event: probably '*Über dem Tod*'.[32]

The exact circumstances of Franz's death do not finally matter. Canetti's need to retell the tale is more significant, disclosing as it does his own fear of women. It was *for Canetti* that love was fraught with mortal dangers. 'How did I know so certainly that C. could never bear to spend a whole night with anybody?' asked Iris in Janu-ary 1953: a habitual pattern she would give to the misogynistic and power-obsessed Charles Arrowby in *The Sea, The Sea*.

Franz's death was followed by a great fog, one she recalled vividly forty years later. Fogs feature in Iris's novels as a concrete metaphor for obfuscation, or a bewitchment of the intelligence, of which Canetti's variant tales of Franz's death are a first symp-tom. Both *A Severed Head* and *The Time of the Angels* contain enchanters and power-figures as well as memorable fogs. It is fitting that her relationship with the original enchanter should have begun during England's worst winter-fog ever. Visibility was down to less than twenty yards.[33] There were accidents on the roads, trains delayed, air traffic diverted, bus services suspended. Twelve thousand people died in central London alone of respirat-ory and heart failure.[34] The fog penetrated indoors: at Sadler's Wells *La Traviata* was halted when the audience could no longer see the stage.

4

Franz told Iris, 'Everyone tells everything to Canetti!': 'He could make a stone speak.'[35] She found herself, on Monday, 12 January 1953, after he had boasted of how the St Ives painters had all rushed to tell him their secrets, seated on his knee, telling him much about herself (a thing she had vowed she never would), about events at Seaforth in 1943, her loss of MacKinnon,[36] and 'other even more secret things'. When she asked if he believed that she loved him, he replied, 'Yes, but I don't yet see which of various ways this will develop.' 'You are like God the Father,' she replied angrily. 'Whatever I shall do you will have foreseen it and understood it even before I have myself' – a sentence repeated in *The Flight from the Enchanter* where the leaves fleeing Shelley's west wind, 'like ghosts from an enchanter fleeing', are in fact driven by that wind. He replied, 'You are speaking exactly like Friedl, even to the very words!' On her leaving he gave her an American edition of *Die Blendung*, writing in it: 'To Iris in great hopes, Elias Canetti. 12 January 1953.' By day she tormented herself; at night there were nightmares about death. Canetti built up for her a picture of her relations with Franz, who had 'captured her spiritually',[37] giving her as few self-reproaches as possible. After thus confiding in him, she felt better. He was a 'liberating figure'.[38]

Many recall Canetti's ability, like the shamans who fascinated him, to call to the surface memories, thoughts and secret wishes of which his acquaintances had been unaware, as if tapping or unlocking the unconscious itself. They felt elevated in the attention they received, and carried away.[39] He had complete patience. He did not interrupt. He listened as if you had something vital to tell him, and he, everything to learn. His answers were never prepackaged or formulaic. He responded on the spot, here and now, in an answer tailor-made for you and for no one else, devoting himself with uncanny intensity to whomsoever he was speaking, with enormous intellectual-spiritual energy and imagination.[40] He could prepare for a meeting by reading *all* of a writer's works in advance. Thus he could, partly by flattery, enter into others and, through an intense power of curiosity, transform himself. Those who met him once only still recalled the experience fifty years later.[41] Canetti wrote: 'I love to tell people who they really are. I am proud of my ability to instil in them a belief in themselves.'[42]

Such Svengali-like power can be misused. Gunther Adler, when angered by Canetti, would describe him as a conceited hunter of human beings who, deliberately amusing and inspiring at the beginning, charmed people into his maw, playing unpredictably with them, keeping them at arm's length, answering letters with a capricious unpredictability from which Franz and, later, Iris suffered.[43]

5

Canetti's qualities, positive and negative, are so contradictory that it is hard to see how they belong within the same person. It is no accident that when Iris first portrayed him, in *The Flight from the Enchanter*, she gave him eyes of different colours and then divided him into two: cunning Mischa Fox, effortlessly superior and god-like, and Calvin Blick, his Smerdyakov-like double, manipulative and wicked.* The habit of the age is to assume that what is deepest must be what is darkest; Canetti had virtues too. He had a massive polymath intelligence and an original mind – neither qualities widely appreciated by the English. He could be self-sacrificingly generous, magnanimous in print about others, and funny, an excellent mimic. Though then very poor, he at once wrote a cheque for £100 when the writer Kay Dick, after a suicide attempt in 1963, was in financial difficulties. He was thoughtful in his gifts – often of valuable books. According to Kathleen Raine the most widely learned and intelligent man she knew, he prodigally expended his time, intelligence and (perhaps) compassion on

---

* In *The Brothers Karamazov* the illegitimate Smerdyakov carries out the murder of his father that he intuits his half-brother Ivan desires.

others.[44] Like Socrates, it was hard to imagine him away from the city. He didn't think the universe a good place, and said the Day of Judgement would happen when the human race arose with one voice to condemn God – the Jewish God (Iris followed him in considering the Christian 'lie' about the conquest of death by Jesus deeply vulgar). He was both concerned that someone would speak a word for poor humanity, yet despised 'us' too. He was interested in 'his creatures'; and would have liked to remake the world and do it better. He said to Iris in January 1954: 'It's not so much that I disbelieve in God – but I hate him.'

Canetti had abundant self-conceit. The novelist Dan Jacobson recalls him at a party held by Sonia Orwell for Saul Bellow, the two egotistical writers manoeuvring carefully around each other, Canetti playing prince-in-exile among the tepid English, and immovable. Neither was in any rush to reconcile his views with yours. Though distinctly a man of the left politically, Canetti had a great respect for power and a liking for the affluent and patrician: there were hostess-patrons – the author Gladys Hunt-ingdon,[45] with whose family in Hyde Park Gardens (and in Amberley) he lived when he first arrived in England in 1939; Diana Spearman in Lord North Street, Westminster, associated with the magazine *Time and Tide*; Flora Solomon in Mayfair, daughter of the Tsar's banker and once mistress to Kerensky. He arrived knowing no one; ten years later he consorted with 'painters, cabinet ministers, sculptors, intellectuals, film actresses'.[46]

Canetti, an acclaimed writer, attracted what Iris called 'apostles' or 'creatures'. Oxford 1938 reappears in Hampstead trans-formed: David Hicks's friend the 'dashing' Carol Stewart trans-lated Canetti's *Crowds and Power* (published in English in 1962); John Willett, who stage-lit Frank Thompson's *It Can Happen Here*; the artist Milein Cosman, who drew Iris in 1941, and her husband Hans Keller: all were neighbours and friends of Canetti's. So were the writers Bernice Rubens and Rudi Nassauer. Gwenda David, literary 'scout' for the American publisher Viking, lived at 44 Well Walk, Hampstead. At number 21 were Clement Glock, who painted scenery at Covent Garden, and her husband William, future head of music at the BBC. The poet Kathleen Raine and

ABOVE IM's mother, Irene ('Rene') Alice Cooper Murdoch, *née* Richardson.

RIGHT 'Few knew him': IM's father, Wills John Hughes Murdoch, Second Lieutenant, First King Edward's Horse, 1918.

LEFT Rene and Hughes in Ireland, c.1930.

BELOW Rene, Hughes and baby Iris.

BELOW Rene and Iris, aged two, Dalkey, August 1921.

RIGHT Seaside picnic on Portstewart strand, mid-1930s. Clockwise from bottom left: Cousin Sybil, Uncle Willy, Aunt Sarah Chapman, Hughes, IM, Rene, Grandmother Louisa Murdoch.

BELOW Cousin Victor Bell, Rene, IM, c.1933.

LEFT 4 Eastbourne Road, Chiswick, where IM and her family moved in about 1926.

BELOW In the back garden at Eastbourne Road, *c*.1927.

RIGHT 'The Powers',
Badminton School, summer
1937. Centre row, left to right:
'Ski' Webb-Johnson, music
mistress; housemistress Lucy
Rendall ('LJR'), who taught
PT; headmistress Beatrice May
Baker ('BMB').

BELOW Badminton, summer
1937. Back row, left to right:
Anne Leech, Marion Finch,
IM. In front of Marion Finch
is Eleanor Leach, daughter of
the potter Bernard Leach.

BELOW BMB in later years.

Group portrait, Somerville College, Oxford, 1938: 1. IM, 2. Anne Cloake,
3. Margaret Stanier, 4. 'Char' Williams-Ellis, 5. Mary Scrutton, 6. Princess
Natalya Galitzine, 7. Leonie Marsh, 8. Enid Stoye.

ABOVE The Magpie Players
'wolfing' food: Bucklebury,
22 August 1939. Left to right:
Tom Fletcher, IM, Hugh Vaughan
James.

RIGHT 'This ['Play of the
Weather'] should amuse the
sixpennies anyhow.' IM (far left, as
little boy) petitions Jupiter (Tom
Fletcher, with umbrella) for snow
to make snowballs with. Fellow
petitioners, left to right: Moira
Dunbar, Joanne Yexley, Hugh
Vaughan James, Denys Becher.

'Mother of God preserve me from the simple sewing machine': IM and Joanne Yexley on the Magpies tour.

A postcard home on the brink of war, 30 August 1939.

Magpie Players
The Cotswolds,   Keep the card!

POSTCARD PICTURE
BY JUDGES' LTD., HASTINGS
ENGLAND

Had a superb audience at
Bicester yesterday, & Lady
Bicester gave us lunch (off
silver plate!) & was par-
ticularly taken with my
acting. Have had a quiet
afternoon here — a beautiful
little place. Bibury has
unexpectedly cancelled our
performance — Crisis, I suppose.
We are most wonderfully
oblivious of the international situation. love I

Mr & Mrs Murdoch
4 Eastbourne Rd.
Chiswick
London
W. 4.

ABOVE IM in the grounds of Somerville.

RIGHT 'Gentle lioness' look, 1939.

'Nonsense! Unspeakable!': Eduard Fraenkel at work.

'This man is a jewel': Donald MacKinnon.

ABOVE 'Brilliant and darling Pip': Philippa Bosanquet, 1942.

RIGHT 'Tangled, intelligent, honest and good': Michael (M.R.D.) Foot, summer 1943.

OPPOSITE Seaforth Place, where IM lived from 1942 to 1945.

ABOVE Noel Eldridge as editor of *Cherwell*.

LEFT 'Tommy' Balogh, his 'perfect beauty marred only by a receding hairline'.

ABOVE Frank Thompson (front left) with his parents and younger brother Edward (Palmer), 1939.

RIGHT Second Lieutenant Thompson, 'Phantom', in the Libyan desert, spring 1942. The pipe made him look conveniently older than his twenty-one years.

'Send me a photo': Captain Thompson, SOE, Cairo, late 1943.

Sir Aymer Maxwell, Canetti's travelling companion in Morocco, were other 'apostles'. Probably Aymer[47] and Flora Solomon helped support Canetti. Raine obsessively, unhappily loved the homosexual Aymer's younger brother Gavin Maxwell, author of *Ring of Bright Water*, another 'apostle', and also predominantly homosexual. Both he *and* Raine employed Canetti as confidant,[48] although Gavin Maxwell said: 'None of us needs Canetti as much as Canetti needs us.'[49] Aymer called him 'The Master'. Carol Stewart remembered: 'He ruled over both men and women.' As at court, not everyone stayed in favour. Close friends were given a code – ring three times, put the phone down, dial again – to distinguish them from bores and enemies.

Canetti could be intensely secretive. His memoirs typically report only that Veza 'did not clap' when he first saw her at the critic and satirist Karl Kraus's lectures in Vienna. Many believed that one of her arms was deformed or paralysed; in fact she had lost it in a car crash at two years of age, and wore a prosthesis concealed by a brown leather glove. When she with stubborn persistence typed Canetti's writings, or laid a tray, or made *Apfel-strudel*,[50] it was with one hand only. (Asked on one occasion about Veza's missing arm, Anne Hamburger – so terrifying did she consider Canetti – suggested that he had probably bitten it off.)

After Veza's death in 1962 Canetti lived part-time for eleven years with his second wife Hera Buschor and their baby daughter Johanna in Zurich before his long-term London mistress Marie-Louise von Motesiczky discovered the extent of the change in his situation. He was jealous, paranoiac and a mythomaniac who, in the words of Friedl's sister Susie, 'loved creating and undoing human relations and toying with people, watching their reactions as a scientist might watch his white mice'.[51] Susie once saw Canetti drill Friedl in preparation for a grand party, probably at the Glocks'. She had never witnessed such a detailed set of instructions, of warlike strategies and tactics. It was like Clausewitz, Friedl acting as delighted lieutenant to Canetti's dictator.

He liked to appear a man of the highest moral scruple,[52] yet spoke offensively of friends,[53] and, being intensely suspicious, was not a fount of truthfulness, adroit at making mischief. Michael and Anne Hamburger were shocked, on April Fool's Day 1952, when his cruelty uncharacteristically lacked finesse. They were with Franz in his Notting Hill flat when Canetti rang up to announce, 'Congratulations! Your book of poems has appeared!' Canetti knew that Franz's health was broken, and that publication of his poems meant everything to him. When the trick was explained, Franz changed colour but carried it off with courage, and his last journal suggests he bore no grudge. Iris regretted, decades later, what she termed this 'hurtful joke'.[54] To explain why he preferred to be invited out alone, Canetti sometimes claimed his wife was schizophrenic. As to other tricks – claiming that the painter Milein Cosman had a glass eye, or trying to talk into existence an affair between two St Ives painters[55] – the malignity, as Coleridge observed of Iago, seems motiveless.

In November Iris's first book, *Sartre, Romantic Rationalist*, was published in tiny print on what resembled wartime austerity paper by Bowes & Bowes, in their series 'Studies in Modern European Literature and Thought', which ran from Samuel Beckett to Zamyatin. It was praised, and deservedly so. If Iris had, as a thinker, two modes, one lapidary and compressed, the other discursive or rambling, this study belonged in the first category. It is a brilliant work, authoritative and, despite its brevity, wide-ranging. It revealed a novelist's capacity to sink and merge her personality within the mind of another, and criticised Sartre's ideas and novels accessibly. It is still among the very best studies of Sartre in English.

Canetti scorned Iris's implicit use of the Tolstoyan novel as an appropriate modern paradigm, and they discussed the need for the modern novel to invent its own myth. What most disturbs in Canetti rests on a confusion of life and literature. He seems to belong inside a novel, as when claiming that the English bored him because they were 'not wicked enough'. Kathleen Raine observed that he had 'studied evil more closely' than she, had 'specialised in it'. She saw him as a puppet-master lacking any sense of the sacred, thinking himself invisible. Not for nothing are the characters in *Auto da Fé* tormented worms. Iris spoke often of the type of the artist – to which she opposed the saint – as the man consciously, aesthetically, creating his own myth; making, in other words, of his life a work of art, and in so doing risking becoming an arch-individualist or 'demonic egotist'. Canetti told her that myths came out of the region where religions come from, and took hold of him with a sort of authority so that he could not see things otherwise: 'Either a situation has this quality or not.'

6

Those who liberate, Iris noted in *A Severed Head,* can also enslave. She knew whereof she spoke. She had recorded to David Hicks 'a deep irrational desire to be dominated, to be held – together with a savage joyous disinclination to submit easily'. Canetti satisfied such fantasies. On 8 February 1953 she noted how he 'held me savagely between his knees & grasps my hair and forces my head back. His power. He subjugates me completely. Only such a complete intellectual & moral ascendancy could hold me.' Her descriptions of lovemaking with Canetti (often, as he preferred, in an armchair) are noteworthy, first of all, because – as she acknowledges with amazement – out of character. 'Why do I now write down such things? I never have in the past. A measure of my love for C. & my certainty.' Secondly because of the sheer oddness, even by bohemian standards, that Veza should let Iris into the flat, and later make a meal for the three of them. While Veza and Friedl became enemies, Veza and Iris stayed friends. Veza appears here a mixture of wise white witch and kindlier Madame Merle from Henry James's *The Portrait of a Lady,* colluding in middle life with the affairs of the man she loves, inviting Iris after her own death to take care of Canetti (which, through friendship, Iris attempted). Lastly the sado-masochism of the relationship carries for Iris an electrifying charge. In his forceful lovemaking Canetti was a Zeus, a 'great superb beast'. 24 March 1953:

> C. has all possible mythological meaning for me. And he reaches far far beyond my view. Physically, he is violent, never quiet, with me. He takes me quickly, suddenly,

in one movement as it were – and he kisses me restlessly,
& savagely draws back my head. There is no tender quiet
resting, as there was with Franz. When we are satisfied
we do not lie together, but contemplate each other with
a sort of amused hostility. He is an angel-demon, terrible
in his detachment and the mystery of his suffering.

When she wrote on 30 March that 'I sometimes feel that C.
doesn't believe a word that I say. But people oughtn't to believe
me so readily. A lot that I say isn't true,' or that she was not
interested in his estimate of her *own* real wishes, all she was interested in was the state of *his* inclinations, we seem to find ourselves
– apart from the reversal of sexes – inside the world of Count
Leopold von Sacher-Masoch's *Venus in Furs*. She did not judge a
proclivity for masochism harshly; it was one part only of her highly
complex nature. Indeed, when in *The Black Prince* Bradley Pearson
announces, 'Of course Shakespeare was a masochist,' masochism
is idealised as one aspect of the mystery of negative capability
itself, of that healing surrender to the otherness of the world
which is for Iris an aspect of virtue.[56] But Canetti, as John Bayley
observed, was one who 'had an air of keeping, at every moment,
every advantage'.[57] Small wonder that Iris, who with other men
felt her acts to have a sort of grace and ease, with Canetti felt
clumsy, a dolt.

7

Franz noted to Gunther Adler that, despite his childish atheism,
Canetti was 'really important, a very rare human being, passionately engaging as a friend, selfless, and quite unreliable'.[58] Canetti
liked to talk with Franz about life-myths, Franz holding in his
head 'all the myths of humankind' and Canetti playing father to
him. Both wrote aphorisms. Canetti liked the way Franz spoke
slowly, with reticence, always thinking carefully about what he was
saying. All three – Adler, Canetti, Steiner – to some degree
resented England.

Franz had quarrelled bitterly with Canetti during the war about who owed more in his writings to the other – which of them was the greater poet – but in his final weeks he compared Canetti favourably with Kafka.[59] Canetti blamed their quarrel on the 'very desirable' Friedl, on her life-loving mischievousness and sensuality; she had been full of her triumph over the quarrelling friends, both of whom wanted her, and when Canetti told her the story, Iris felt 'oddly responsible' for Friedl, angry with her too. After the quarrel Franz sent Canetti a quotation from the Talmud: 'No man can consent that another have dominion over his soul.' Canetti 'cut' Franz for two years. Mastery was at stake; power, too.

The twentieth century, our world, it has often been observed, is the work of Hitler.[60] Just as Franz intended his doctorate on slavery as an atonement for and an attempt accurately to apprehend the Holocaust, and as Gunther Adler wrote his monumental, pioneering *Theresienstadt 1941–45*[61] scrutinising the Nazi machinery of genocide – transports, administrative structures, accommodation, diet, health – with a systematic eye, so Canetti at the outbreak of war devoted himself exclusively to writing his parallel study of the phenomenon of mass behaviour, *Crowds and Power*.[62] It was triggered by his experience in Vienna in July 1927 of witnessing a bloody demonstration against the acquittal of two murderers of Social Democrats, which ended with ninety wounded or shot dead and the Palace of Justice set alight, and took him twenty years. Franz, Canetti and Adler – friends of each other and of Iris – were thus all moved by the temper of the times to look into the workings of power at its most extreme.

Adler's increasingly desperate, detailed pleas to Canetti from April to August 1939 to help him escape from Prague and the Nazi threat there went unanswered. There might have been many such claims, and underwriting an incoming refugee's solvency cost £500; Canetti would not have had the means to help with one. His silence was a source of bitterness: after the war Adler during a heated moment felt reproached by Veza for having survived without Canetti ordaining that survival. In an interview Adler said Veza was disturbed by the events of the war, and never recovered. How could Canetti and Veza not be disturbed by the cataclysm? In the copy of *Crowds and Power* that Canetti gave Adler, survivor of Auschwitz and Theresienstadt, he wrote, 'To Günther, who experienced what I wrote about'. But in Canetti the emphasis on power and victimhood fell differently. He wrote in German, the language he stayed fiercely loyal to – 'the Germans had had so much taken away from them, it was not right that they should lose their language too'.[63] He might have enjoyed the savage quip that the Germans would never be able to forgive the Jews for Auschwitz. Many saw in *Crowds and Power* 'a message of forgiveness from a Jewish writer to the German people'.[64] But had Canetti earned by suffering, as Franz and Adler unquestionably had, the 'right' to offer such forgiveness? (Of Adler it was once said that he forgave the Germans everything, and Canetti nothing.) Canetti had not,[65] unlike them, lost his country, his family, nor – since he knew English before German – his language. But his authority to speak for a whole culture was that of the *Dichter* or authoritative 'seer' who owns all available truth. That this is a convention actively mistrusted in these islands was one reason he hated the English and their accursed 'modesty', and forbade publication of his autobiographies in Britain. The story Canetti told of travelling to Auschwitz in 1945 with the Red Cross, and speaking to surviving children in German, was probably apocryphal: '*Meine Name! Meine Name!*' they begged, having forgotten their names – he purportedly telling them what those names once were.[66] It sounds in magisterial character, but was typical myth-making. The travel he preferred was in his mind. With disarming apparent candour he wrote: 'I would have a purer relationship to Machiavelli if I were not also interested in power; here my path crosses his in a complicated and intimate way. For me, power still is evil absolute.'[67] That he, more than most writers, was a *Macht-Mensch* – one who seeks, consolidates, and hangs onto power – renders such high-minded protestation rhetorical, or fatuous.

Readers of *Crowds and Power*, which is partly an anti-religious tract, will recognise Saul Bellow's satire in *Herzog* of Banowitch's 'gruesome and crazy book' on power-systems as psychosis, reflecting Hitler's and Stalin's achievements in corpse-making, and relating them to the way we all masticate and chew each other:

Fairly inhuman, and full of vile paranoid hypotheses such
as that crowds are fundamentally cannibalistic, that
people standing secretly terrify the sitting, that smiling
teeth are the weapons of hunger, that the tyrant is mad
for the sight of (possible edible?) corpses about him.[68]

One leaves *Crowds and Power* overwhelmed by the reduction of
the entire panorama of human history to what Lenin termed
'Who: Whom': the triumph of survivors who delight in cruelty.
Canetti's crowd is as much a sub-human monster as a community
offering fellowship and resistance to tyranny,[69] and his brief final
piety about being 'against power' reads feebly. Why should we
believe it? He has offered no analysis of how the power-instinct –
whose tenacity over millennia he spent twenty years remorselessly
demonstrating – can be attenuated. Here is history reduced to
slaughterhouse, blood-lust, will to power. The secret mythologies
upon which all human affairs permanently rest are delight in
power, and joy in killing.

8

One source of obfuscation in Iris and Canetti's love-affair was
that each was trying to survive the death or dying of a former
lover, and experiencing survivor-guilt, that great – not merely
Jewish – theme of the day. Canetti never paid attention to his
own Nietzschean decree that survivors feel lasting triumphal joy
at outliving others. When Veza died in 1962 he contemplated
suicide, and made of her flat in Thurloe Road, Hampstead[70] (to
the disgust of some[71]) a shrine to her memory. And Iris was
touched and obsessed by the fact that Canetti's mistress Friedl
Benedikt was dying, aged thirty-six, in the American Hospital in
Paris, of Hodgkin's Disease. Perhaps identifying with Canetti's
dying ex-lover, whom Iris physically resembled,[72] was one way
of attenuating the guilt involved in 'betraying' her own dead
lover, Franz. Canetti methodically assisted this identification. On
10 January 1953, when Iris spoke of how he was bound in her
mind to Franz, he replied by speaking of Friedl, and said – which

pleased her profoundly – 'I feel that you are helping to keep Friedl alive.'

> He has clearly been meditating a lot about Friedl & me. He said he had written 'hundreds of pages' about me, about the myth, the story. I don't feel any fear at this. After all, I am working at this also. I told him he knew all the things that I wanted to know. He said and very much more! Let us have none of this English modesty!

Friedl was the *leitmotiv* of their love throughout 1953 and 1954. Othello wooed Desdemona with tales of derring-do; Canetti wooed Iris with tales of Friedl. In March 1951 he had written to Friedl's sister Susie: '*Ich liebe Friedl nicht mehr. Ich werde nie mehr mit ihr leben*' ('I don't love Friedl any more. I will never live with her [again]'). This can have made him feel no less guilty when, that year, Friedl became seriously ill. This guilt Iris, willingly, if unwittingly, took upon herself. She was an ideal scapegoat: credulous, soft-hearted, masochistic, intensely imaginative. When she wrote to console him about Friedl's illness, Canetti replied that her letters had helped, adding, 'You did what she would have done.' Soon she was writing constantly, sometimes twice a day, to Canetti: 'What a sad air a letter can have when it records momentary things which are past when the other person gets it . . . But writing down such things is a kind of charm to bring you into the present . . .'.[73] Friedl was a leading topic: 'How strangely little I resent C's identifying me with Friedl,' Iris early noted: 'I continue her for him, through me he enjoys her again.' He told her her arms 'were just like Friedl's'. When she half-playfully struck him in the face he said Friedl had never dared do the same, while implying that Friedl needed and liked a degree of physical duress. He told Iris, on one of his madder lifelong hobby-horses[74] (which she would address in *The Good Apprentice*): 'There were times when I thought I had come into this world to abolish death.' And: 'I loathe & despise myself for not being able to stop death.' Where Jesus Christ failed, Canetti was to succeed. Iris wrote to say she wanted to give Friedl her blood.

In March 1953 Iris dreamed that Friedl telephoned her and

they chatted at length. This dream-Friedl was very friendly, called Iris by her first name, wanted to meet. 'I didn't ask her surname,' Iris noted, after discussing Friedl with Veza the same month. Soon Canetti, in Paris, wrote to Iris that he had sat beside Friedl and had lied to her that Aymer Maxwell was making a ballet of her first book, had even taken a theatre. At the end of the month Friedl seemed a little better, and Iris recorded her sense of devastation: 'I am a rotten thing. The "aesthetic" conclusion was that she should die & C. should console himself with me.' There are two ways of overcoming jealousy, she noted: one, by becoming absorbed in one's own activity, the other by trying to love the person concerned. She prayed for Friedl and 'went in spirit to her aid'; and wrote, 'About Friedl. What evil there is in me . . .'

On the last day of March Canetti told Iris the tale of Friedl's love-affair with a 'dwarf in Sweden' – the Hungarian painter Endre Nemes – who tore her clothes to ribbons (a scene Iris would write into *A Fairly Honourable Defeat*) before raping her and slashing his own pictures. When the affair turned to knives and murderous hatred, Canetti wrote Friedl a letter ordering her to leave Nemes at once. She soon found a kind and generous lover in the American Allan Forbes. Now writing about Friedl all the time, Canetti advised Allan to do the same (he did not). Iris wept, her tears partly sympathetic, partly jealous, when Canetti romanced that Allan had won Friedl by promising her a Caribbean island, just as Friedl had once offered Canetti 'one of her islands' off Sweden. (Allan belonged to the old 'brahmin' Boston Forbeses, who owned a small island, Naushon, off Martha's Vineyard; Friedl's mother's family owned one island only: Ångholm. Neither island was within either's gift.[75]) Three days later, at 5 p.m. on 3 April, Good Friday, in the middle of a tremendous thunderstorm, and with Susie by her side, Friedl died. Her sufferings had been terrible.[76] Susie's last conversation with her, on Maundy Thursday, was about how the intention of an act may be good and its result evil, and vice versa (perhaps even Canetti had genuinely *intended* good by Friedl . . .). Allan and Susie, though wishing to have her cremated on the spot, drove Friedl's body in awful procession back for burial to the tilted graveyard of Grinzing, outside Vienna. Canetti had decreed this by phone.

Friedl's death did not end Iris's identification. She noted, 'The thing that one forgets. That one doesn't face death in the fullness of one's strength.' The two continued to meet in Iris's dreams, and she and Canetti went on pilgrimage around the places in Hampstead associated with her. Friedl and Canetti had made love on a bench in the gardens of St John's College. Had anyone else ever made love in broad daylight in an Oxford college garden, he wondered? Iris carved Friedl's name into that bench. In June Canetti 'lashed out' and terrified her over something she had written to him about Friedl. Weeping, Iris wrote a reply at once, angry with him too, telling him again that he was like God, 'passing by my good deeds & striking me for a bad one'. When Allan Forbes came to England after Friedl's death, Canetti wondered if he would see the resemblance between Iris and Friedl. (What he in the event said was, 'How marvellously beautiful she looked'; and 'You won't change about Iris, will you?' She recalled to him the actress Falconetti in Carl Dreyer's 1928 film *The Passion of Joan of Arc*: a Gothic/Renaissance look, naïve, simple, strong.) On New Year's Eve 1953, Iris recorded that she wanted 'to *be* Friedl', while Canetti reassured her early in 1954 that he did not love her merely 'because of that', fearing she might identify herself too much. As late as November 1954, after a holiday in Italy when Iris angered Veza, Canetti patiently explained: 'your appearing suddenly like that in Milan, just as we arrived, made her identify you with Friedl. F. used always to do that, having waited perhaps for hours at a corner.'

Friedl's last, unpublished novel concerns an adolescent whose persona is being stolen by an older man. Iris admired Friedl's books. All three of her published novels – written under the *nom de plume* 'Anna Sebastian', and admired by Angus Wilson[77] – are dedicated to Canetti. Iris's dedication of *The Flight from the Enchanter* 'To Elias Canetti' imitates Friedl's '*dem Dichter Elias Canetti, meinem grossen Meister*' – 'to the poet Elias Canetti, my great master' (in her 1950 novel *The Dreams*). So does her attempt to evoke Canetti through the central character Mischa Fox, just as Friedl had done with the hero of her surreal novel *The Monster* (1944). Jonathan Crisp is an insolent, contemptuous, demonic Lord of the Universe and of misrule, a vacuum-cleaner salesman, rent-racketeer, voyeur, ingenious solicitor of confidences, rapist, freeloader, liar, Casanova, Svengali. He has elegant mistresses and a nostalgia for the working class. Sex is part of his will to power. Though intensely promiscuous, his attractiveness is a 'given', never explained. He slowly amasses a crowd of bourgeois and workers as his slaves, who finally kneel, one after another, to kiss his shoes. He communes with God as with an envied sibling, God having more worshippers than he. Friedl confessed to Canetti, weeping, that Crisp was him. When Canetti told Iris of this, in May 1953, he quoted to her from *The Monster.* 'Down on your knees, Kate!' laughing at her as he did so. He then told her how much he'd liked *Under the Net,* 'its pattern of overlapping pairs . . . & the pupil-teacher couple'. Friedl wrote in 1944 to her parents in Sweden that *The Monster* was an attempt to show how Hitlers are made.

9

Friedl's sister Susie had alerted Canetti when Endre Nemes went mad. Iris wrote: 'The thought I might one day meet, not Friedl, that would be too much, but even Susi [*sic*] or Allen [*sic*] is like thinking of meeting a character out of a Greek play. "Oh, let me introduce you. Have you met Antigone?"' Nothing shows so clearly Canetti's ability to turn his life into myth, into literature, as well as how intensely Iris was under his spell.

Nearly fifty years after Friedl's death, both Susie, who knew Canetti from 1936 until his death in 1994, and Allan Forbes thought her illness grew from guilt. Forbes ascribed it to survivor-guilt, Susie to guilt over her treatment of Canetti, who could neither be fully with her, nor let her grow up and be happy elsewhere. Friedl wrote in her diary: 'I have lived in your light, but could not find my own.'[78] Unlike Iris, who angered Canetti by recovering, Friedl never got over her childish awe and quasi-religious love of Canetti. He invented rules and punishments for her that governed most aspects of her day, especially writing. Doubtless Friedl, who was bohemian and chaotic but strong of will, gave as good as she got. Their relationship, in current jargon, was 'co-dependent'. The rules included love-affairs. He did not believe she should be allowed full sexual happiness (it might impede her creativity), yet personally choreographed a number of her affairs. Forbes found a way of co-existing with Friedl's fixation on Canetti. Nemes was maddened by it. A Sephardi Swede (Ivar Iverus) with whom Canetti decreed Friedl should have an affair for her own protection while fleeing Austria was also badly hurt. Susie turned against Canetti when he spoke of 'giving up' Friedl to Allan: he never really let go of her, wanting both her and Allan within his power – thus Iris recorded – treating them 'like little dogs', another aspect of Canetti that Iris would exploit in *The Sea, The Sea.*

Friedl's tales that Canetti imprisoned, beat[79] and spied on her may be partly fantastical. What is certain is that when she became happily pregnant by the writer Willy Goldman, Canetti told her he would never see her again if she had the child.[80] The threat worked. He thought a child sapped creativity; and he was certainly jealous of Goldman too: 'Another had replaced him in a most sensitive role,' thought Forbes, and the abortion was Friedl's 'punishment'.[81] The story gives substance to Veza's claim that Canetti put her through abortions too.[82] He offended the Benedikts in *The Play of the Eyes* by insinuating that the girl who had *really* attracted him in Vienna in 1936 was Susie, not Friedl at all. In the American Hospital in February 1952, the dying Friedl was so ashamed of her appearance that she refused to let Canetti see her. So his story (of lying to Friedl that Aymer Maxwell was turning Friedl's novel into a ballet) was for Iris's benefit. Meanwhile, waiting in the hospital corridor, he distressed Susie by praising her walk, which he said excited him.

Mischa Fox's only public act of power in *The Flight from the Enchanter* consists in his buying up the Suffragette paper *The Artemis*.[83] The novel itself never explains why, though Fox is described as 'not, to put it mildly, a supporter of female emancipation'.[84] Canetti, though somewhat of a prude,[85] was attracted to many women, and Gwenda David was anxious for her teenage daughter when he was around; making love to a woman, Canetti believed, was one way of mastering her. When Allan Forbes arrived in London, Canetti took him under his wing, showed him about, and, to help console him, installed him in a room opposite Bernice Rubens, choreographing an affair between them. Since he simultaneously aided and abetted the affair Rubens's husband Rudi Nassauer was engaged in, this arrangement had the advantage of symmetry, one Nassauer explored in a *roman-à-clef, The Cuckoo* (1962), in which Canetti appeared, to his disgust, as the fanatically tidy, over-defended character Klein, or 'Small' (Iris used the name for two power-figures, Honor Klein in *A Severed Head* and the tyrannical General Klein in her play *The Servants and the Snow*). Rubens came to detest Canetti's puppet-mastering, and found in his fascination with the maimed and suicidal a repellent mixture of sentimentality and cruelty; Susie believed that Canetti was genuinely torn between wishing to be a good man and the proclivities of novelist, inventor and fabulist. Things took off and went their own way.

10

Friedl and Iris were two of many Galateas whom Canetti fostered. But, Pygmalion-like, he would often claim to have made Iris a writer as he had done for Friedl. He advised her sagely to write for an hour a day, 'perhaps half-formulated thoughts, anything'. She had been keeping such a journal for a decade. As often with Canetti, truth has to be detected within a fog of myth. He told John and Anne Willett that he had rummaged through Iris's belongings and, finding unpublished writings, decided something should be done with them. In his final book, *Aufzeichnungen*, Canetti credited Franz with having 'discovered' Iris, claiming that Franz's last letter commended Iris's first novel to him.[86]

Iris's journal is matter-of-fact about lending Canetti the first notebook of her novel, 'small & dry as a walnut'. On 28 March 1953 she finished the entire second draft and noted, 'I can see very clearly how bad it is. It is very romantic & sentimental, even what is intellectual in it is intellectual in a romantic way. If anything saves it from complete wreck it is a sort of vitality & joy that lifts it a little – perhaps,' adding, 'I shall let C. have it.'[87] Gwenda David, talent scout for Viking, never learnt who had posted what became *Under the Net* through her large letterbox designed for manuscripts at 44 Well Walk. This has all the marks of mystification associated with Canetti, but Iris would surely have been published sooner or later, without such intervention. Gwenda David danced with Ian Parsons from Chatto & Windus at a dinner Victor Gollancz was giving – infuriatingly, she had to buy full evening dress for £11 – and told Parsons she had a novel that might interest him, sending it to Norah Smallwood at Chatto on 5 August. By 3 October Iris noted, 'Chatto's taking my novel – and Viking Press. But sadness over all.' This is the sole reference to either publishing house,[88] and her only reference to the literary life, in sixty years of journals: her success was instantaneous. She was unsure what to call this novel, playing with such awful titles as 'Up the Ladder and Down the Wall: A Reflective Pursuit', or (from Addison's version of Psalm 19) 'In Solemn Silence All'. Gwenda David came to stay in Iris's smart new top-floor flat in Beaumont Street, Oxford, where the dust was so thick Gwenda wrote her name in it, and a writer-protégée called Winnie Scott proposed the title *Under the Net* instead.

Some months into her affair with Canetti Iris started to understand him, and herself, better. In the first month she wrote: 'I have considered the possibility of your turning out to be completely diabolical!' She reflected on her need for an unhappy love, which Canetti, with his 'separateness and brutality', satisfied. Canetti confessed he came into the Porcupine pub on Charing Cross Road and watched Iris and Momigliano unobserved on 21 March 1953.[89] That he is partly a figure of light, partly of darkness preoccupied Iris: 'Is his flattery of me a cunning way of keeping me close, while not committing himself to me at all? I must have been very impressed by his demonishness today to be able to suspect this.' On 1 April she noted: 'Canetti claimed "Good has to become demonic, in our age, in real life. Unless it can live idyllically . . ." What is it for C. to be a manichee? He believes in real forces of evil – & is ready to use evil to serve good, if he can.'[90] 'Is his positive idea of good subject to anything transcendent?' Iris's and Kathleen Raine's views tally closely. On 29 May Iris, distressed by recognising him in Friedl's Jonathan Crisp, wrote Canetti a 'foolish' letter about good and evil, noting that he took a positive pleasure in lying and deceiving, 'tho' always for the best of motives . . . great power inspires fear, even when it's not misused, and one considers it evil or a sort of defence'. However he misused her, she could not stop belonging to him completely. Yet she quoted Franz's remark, 'One man cannot be God to another.' On 28 June she notes that she believes in a kind of unseen reality, he does not, and connects this with his willingness to deceive people for their own good.

Clement Glock identified a Holy Family in the coterie, with Canetti – of course – as God the Father, and Veza the Madonna. The atmosphere of power-play and paranoia awoke Iris further. On 13 May she records Canetti as having asked: 'What would you say if I told you I had been to Oxford to watch you? And if I found you had deceived me, what a scene! A tornado would be nothing. And how you would enjoy it! When C. speaks so I feel sad. He is almost capable of such a thing. And this is something in him I find hard to understand.' On 10 July Aymer Maxwell feared Canetti might destroy him with a thunderbolt, and pushed Iris into admitting Canetti was a 'great writer'. Soon Canetti warned her against Aymer, who would 'do anything he could to drive a wedge between us, even to trying to seduce me'. He added, 'If you do do anything you regret, remember that I am merciful! I should be furiously angry – but I am merciful.' Iris 'was exasperated extremely by this – but touched too, in an absurd way'.

More of the atmosphere surrounding Canetti is evoked by a scene in the Cosmo café-restaurant in Swiss Cottage in December 1953, where Aymer Maxwell seemed to Iris gentle and faunlike. She was touched by Aymer's devotion: missing Canetti for a moment in the restaurant he said, 'Where is the master? (*Canetti,*

c'est le maître.)' Canetti later protested, 'Aymer is a werewolf – I
am taming a werewolf.' Spirited, coltish-looking Clement Glock
was cruel both to Aymer – 'you are weak!' – and to Canetti,
savagely: 'When you are dead I will draw you, when you are lying
dead. And I'll publish a book about you, and how I helped you!'
Canetti, unperturbed connoisseur of the instincts, said to Iris
later: 'Her desire to survive; she really saw me lying dead and
exulted.' For many years Iris remembered a conversation at Carol
Stewart's at 8 Kent Terrace, Regent's Park, when Canetti had said
how deep was the desire to survive, outlive.

In January 1954 she had been moved, turning the dial on the
radio, suddenly to hear Canetti from Stuttgart recite his play *The
Comedy of Vanities*: she was then translating it into English. The
same month she recorded a comic, happy dialogue at Compayne
Gardens. Canetti was playing Mozart on the gramophone, and
when she told him he looked like a pirate in repose, he riposted
that he would sell her for two hundred doubloons.

> I. But think – the nearest white woman is 500 miles away!
> C. Not at all! I captured three yesterday. They're in the
> next cave. All virgins.
> I. Well I don't care – I'll take a look at the buyer, &
> then decide whether I'll argue!
> C. Now you'll go! And I was just beginning to think I'd
> disguise one of the others as you. The buyer is a horrible
> old Turk.
> I. Yes, please do that! Think how useful I could be – I
> could darn your socks & do the accounts of your raids.
> C. Well, you'd have to teach this woman English. I've
> described you to the Turk – & he's a man I do a lot of
> business with.
> I. He won't have minded your descriptions – he probably
> knows what a dreadful liar you are. But you turn the
> women over to me. I'll train them for you. I'll do any-
> thing for you. I'll be your slave.
> C. You are my slave! Ho Ho Ho! But now I'm in two
> minds. What else can you do?
> I. I can write you a poem – now if you like.
> C. A woman, write poetry!

Sitting up, she then wrote, very rapidly, a sonnet, her 'first poem for C', of which she later recalled only scattered lines. 'C. after holding it upside down, & saying "is this writing?" and "It's a message to my enemies," made me read it. Then he said – all right, you stay? I said how long? He said, forever.'

Earlier she had told him of how Gunther Adler saved his life in the concentration camp by writing love poems for the Nazis. The connexion between her love poems and Adler's is not obvious. But she came to see that the Jewish expatriates whom she loved, who fought as expatriates will, who had undergone the worst their century had to offer, carried within themselves, as it were, an understanding that she and other British people lacked. What Canetti showed in *Crowds and Power*, and what he was, were, in Iris's view, challenges to English liberal humanism. Even the best of expatriate lives showed that 'those to whom evil is done, do evil in return'.[91] The intensity of what they had undergone carried 'truth'; their experience of 'enslavement' suggesting something about us all, especially to one already fascinated by Plato's allegory of the Cave and the Sun, which proposed enslavement as the human norm, a myth which (for Iris) illuminated the disturbances of the age. Jews in her novels are sometimes idealised; and the notable Jew who is not – Julius King in *A Fairly Honourable Defeat* – is demonised instead. Canetti was what she termed an 'alien god', whose entry into situations altered them.

It is the main point of *The Flight from the Enchanter* that those enslaved to Mischa Fox/Canetti are enslaved voluntarily. The 'alien god' can rule only because his creatures surrender their will. Virginia Woolf once noted: 'Hitlers are bred by slaves.'[92] The karmic 'blame' of power is thus shared between bully and victim, resting on an act of collusion, and the victims of power, as Iris expressed this in *The Unicorn*, 'infected too', passing on the virus to others. Some of what is monstrous in Canetti may be symptomatic of what is monstrous in all of us, and in the last century. Henry James opposed European corruption and American innocence. Iris's novels often oppose English ignorance and European understanding.

11

Iris thought she was weaker than Friedl. Certainly she struggled
with Canetti's influence, too, throughout her life. His radical
atheism probably played its part in her leaving the Anglo-Catholic
Metaphysicals in 1953.

Even in January 1953 she wrote:

> I notice already his influence upon me – about 'power'
> for instance. (Should the virtuous have power? I dis-
> cussed with two political theory pupils!) I shall have to
> remake my attitude to religion. (Am I excessively 'open
> to influence'? Franz influenced me very much. Now C's
> influence operates in a rather different way.)

She told him about Momigliano, and about Asa Briggs, who
would comfort her about the various complications of her life
and teach her modern history in front of a blazing log fire at
Worcester College. She told Canetti, too, about her tendency to
collect around her what she termed a 'family', her divided 'loyalty'
to the members of which had caused her to be unfaithful to
Franz. It was surely from her anguished remorse about this that
he helped liberate her.

Doubtless she came to fear him as her own darker 'double'.
His genius for collecting 'creatures' funds *The Flight from the
Enchanter* and, more darkly, *A Fairly Honourable Defeat*; hers lies
behind Morgan's feckless emotional greed in the same novel and
behind the figure of Hannah Crean-Smith, Anglo-Irish half-
ascetic, half-vamp, centre of a court of admirers in *The Unicorn*.
Both Iris and Canetti were secretive, leading complicated private
lives, keeping friends and lovers in compartments. 'Holding them
& yet hurling them away. A sort of solar system. Until they are
suspended at a certain distance by a force of gravity. Until they
find an orbit,'[93] could describe either Canetti or herself. Both had
within them, as well as warmth and vulnerability, that ice-splinter
without which art is not made. Both were highly attractive to
others, and neither always told the truth. On 23 May 1953 Iris

reflected: 'How for years one might keep up a facade of casualness & deceive others about one's relations with a certain person. I do this – or hope I do!' Precisely one week later she complained that Canetti 'has no right to deceive me for my own peace of mind. It is a deep offence.' The juxtaposition is ironic; months later she lamented 'that I have told lies to all those I loved most deeply, not once but continually'.

Both loved animals. Both were spellbinding enchanters who elicited intimacy by holding themselves intact, aloof. To the hostile they were 'wreckers', who 'ate people up'. Iris's Cambridge contemporary Olivier Todd, who then confided only in her about his illegitimacy, later wondered whether her reserve betokened the odour of '*sulfur ou des roses*'.[94] Of Anna Quentin in *Under the Net*, Iris wrote: 'to anyone who will take the trouble to become attached to her she will give a devoted, generous, imaginative and completely uncapricious attention, that is still a calculated avoidance of self-surrender'. Anna was one aspect of Iris. Of Momigliano's putting himself in her power, she noted, 'terrifying ... To wield such power is wicked.' The love-victims of Anna Quentin become resigned to the liberal scope of her affections while remaining 'just as much her *slave* as ever'.[95] How was love-energy to be purified so that one did good, rather than enslaving? What distinguished Iris's love-affairs from Canetti's?

Her friend and co-philosopher Patrick Gardiner intuited that something in Iris's past had introduced her to the idea of evil.[96] The events of 1943–44 – her abandonment of Michael Foot and taking up with Thomas Balogh – started that process; those of 1952–56 continued it. Canetti represented the artist-as-manipulative-and-sadistic-mythomaniac who had struck a Faustian bargain, the mystifier-enchanter Iris feared turning into, whom indeed she might have become. Her assertion that the structure of good literary works is to do with 'erotic mysteries and deep, dark struggles between good and evil'[97] owes much to these years. As Kathleen Raine accurately observed, Canetti's quarrel with God is an ancient Jewish tradition going back as far as the Book of Job. Iris's quarrel with Canetti reflects that tradition; the Hebrew 'deuteragonist' was Satan. Canetti acts deuteragonist in many of Iris's novels. Her unpublished poem-cycle of the 1950s, 'Conversations with a Prince', at one stage had the working title 'Conversations with a Tyrant'. Her novels oppose 'Good' and 'Power', asking questions of 'authority' which Canetti rendered urgent. In *The Bell* the Abbess defines Good as, not powerless, but 'nonpowerful'; in *The Unicorn* only the good man stands outside and magically heals power-conceived-of-as-sickness. And power, though most critics failed to see this, was as deep an obsession in Iris's work as in Canetti's.

In 1964 Marie-Louise von Motesiczky and Iris were sitting quietly in Marie-Louise's Hampstead studio, she painting Iris's portrait for St Anne's,[98] when Canetti suddenly appeared through the side door. He startled them both – 'on purpose of course', Iris objectively reported. Then he made Marie-Louise show her the portrait. Iris thought it 'wonderful, terrible, so sad and frightening, me with the demons. How did she know?' Canetti had done her lasting service. He had shown her to herself; and something of the corruptible relationship between pity and power.

12

During a talk Iris gave at Wedgwood Memorial College in 1955, John Wain and Richard Lyne,[99] who had been carelessly tilting back in their chairs, were so electrified by the measured elegance of her response to one question, its truth and incisiveness – 'I am not persuaded that being in love is necessarily a mode of knowledge of the beloved' – that their chairs overbalanced and both crashed to the floor. Iris glared at them.[100]

If enslaved herself, an improbable rescuer was to hand. On 5 February 1954 she noted the laughter of a new admirer who lived at St Antony's College. His name was John Bayley, and he came to fear Canetti as 'Pluto, god of the Underworld, with a crocodile smile, wanting to whisk Iris off to Hades'.[101] A poem Iris wrote that March depicts Canetti 'always elsewhere: maybe in an aeroplane or in someone's Bentley/Or standing like Socrates in a London street'. Bayley, by contrast, was accessible and here.

Meanwhile Iris had underestimated her own strength, which came from different sources. When Ferruccio Rossi-Landi described 'women', she recognised herself.

> They have no hierarchy of interests. Each thing is an absolute then they pass on. That is why a woman is stronger than a man. She puts her whole being into getting some momentary thing.

Iris felt that she too underwent the impression of the moment, then passed on. Her own native good sense, that of a cheerful, prudent Ulsterwoman, played its part, too, in the coming struggle.

14

An Ideal Co-Child
1953–1956

John Bayley has recorded sighting Iris on her bike before knowing her name or anything about her, thinking her to be superior, mysterious, with no 'past', and hoping that she was waiting for him to arrive.[1] A cocktail party given by Elaine Griffeths, who taught English at St Anne's, brought them face to face. Iris's manner on those early occasions was kindly but repressive, avoiding intimacy. He did not admire her looks. He believed her to be old, wise and plain, and hoped therefore that he had minimal competition. Each of these assumptions, he later decided, bore further thought.

John and his colleague Patrick Gardiner threw a party for the publication of Iris's book on Sartre in November 1953, serving 'Black Velvet', which they had read about in Evelyn Waugh, a mixture of Guinness and champagne slightly more disgusting than it sounds. Iris was discouraging too. She does not mention John in her journal until February 1954: 'a dear man' whom she had visited at his college. In March they met three times, at her Southmoor Road basement flat, or his first-floor room in St Antony's, a new college which as yet had only postgraduate teaching. John taught a little at Wadham and New Colleges at one pound an hour, and, with a small grant from the army, got by on £200 a year. St Antony's had been an Anglican convent, his room once a nun's cell.

Soon they gave each other feedback, over *vin rosé*, on drafts they had exchanged of each other's first novels. They sang German and English songs together; John played his descant recorder. When he accompanied her back to Southmoor Road – both on bikes – on turning to hand over some books of hers he had carried back, he stood in her way and kissed her firmly on the lips. It had no prelude and, she wrote, 'delighted me very much'. It is no accident that her earliest references to John associate him with 'gay & sweet *laughter*', 'suppressed *laughter*'. Her entry, 'O the calming externality of an Englishman after the upsetting inwardness of these continentals!'[2] was not *à propos* John, but it could have been. He had a happy, solitary temperament, and carried around with him always a sense of joyous carnival, of holiday. Four days after that first kiss they stayed up till 4 a.m., he confiding in her about his earlier love for a woman who wanted to be separate and alone. Iris spoke to him vehemently 'about love & about his work, feeling a deep concern for him'. She grieved at leaving him and was tempted to run into St Antony's the following morning. Iris was playing the woman of the world; John the *ingénu* or child.

When John, who did not think matters were going well, that night disparaged Charles Morgan's novel *The Fountain*, Iris defended its depiction of physical desire. Noel Martin had sent her in 1942 a Morgan quotation which travelled with her:[3] 'The freedoms of the spirit are not attained by violence of the will, but by an infinite patience of the imagination.' Today *The Fountain* seems a slack and portentous spiritual adventure-story, full of grimly high-minded *Schöngeisterei*,* with no spark of comedy. Its influence on Iris is nonetheless discernible, with its Platonic quest-motif, its discovery that inner freedom can be found within enclosures (castles, monasteries), its patrician brooding on the contemplative life, and its crisis merely a *conversation* between two men locked in a love-hate relation, in which the wiser (Narwitz) teaches the more callow (Lewis). The crisis of *Under the Net* also consists in nothing more than a hospital conversation – marvellously comical and touching – in which Hugo teaches Jake, 'God is a task. God is a detail. It all lies close to your hand.'

---

* The cult of noble souls. See Ian Buruma, *Voltaire's Coconuts* (London, 1999), p.68, for a history of the term.

At a dance at St Antony's on Friday, 14 May, Dee Wells watched Iris and John whooping and galloping around the two rooms, Iris dressed strangely; Wells was asking her future husband A.J. Ayer, whom she had just met for the first time, about white rabbits and coloured handkerchiefs. He retorted, 'I did not say I was a *magician* – I am a *logician*.' Iris had twice fallen down the stairs to the old crypt where the dance was held. She noted 'extraordinary events' and that she had fallen truly in love with John, who

> was, is, certainly very deeply in love with me. Since then, all sense of time & place has been dissolved. Does this endless capacity for new loves shew – what? that I am very shallow, unstable? I can't think this. God knows what I can do for, or with, JB – but I shall try not to harm or hurt him. What can I do? His wide undeceiving eyes, his laugh, his strange Byzantine figure, his hands (which I examined the other day – 'I'd have washed them if I'd known this was going to happen!') He delights me in a thousand ways & fills me with laughter & joy . . .

They kissed and, like children, talked and talked. Two weeks later she recorded:

> Terrible intensity of life. I must not leave tasks undone. Extraordinary need for JB. His laughter, his poems, his letters. His helplessness & emotion in the face of my attachment to him is very touching. He said 'I feel like a dog overwhelmed by being given an enormous bone. I can't pick it up, can only lick the corners!'

To some they made an improbable couple, Iris so fine-looking, John, as one friend quipped, the runt of the litter of three brothers – slight, balding, myopic, uncoordinated – and yet also, with his brilliance and his confident modesty, 'the best argument against eugenics we have'. Iris admired John's slim grace, and gave his 'white flank' when they bathed naked in the Thames that July to Toby in *The Bell*. She had explained to him at the dance that her situation was not simple, naming Momigliano, Asa Briggs and Canetti as important to her too. 'I can give but a sort of constancy,' she extemporised in one of many poems to him, this one on 23 May; and 'So many others in my life have place/ How can I dare to look you in the face?' On 15 June they were at another dance, at St Anne's, from which she dragged him away to walk back through pouring rain, having indeed experienced sudden jealousy about Asa Briggs who was there with a different partner. The incident is doubtless one of those which made Iris in 1968 disclaim 'identification with the ass that I then was'. The 1954 Iris noted that

> the who am I to be jealous? aspect doesn't stop me being in great pain. At the very same time I am in delight & grief over JB. I have never seen such an undefended mortal. (Except perhaps Shah, of whom he reminds me oddly . . . in . . . his extreme slimness & grace.) The other night I . . . kissed him & his cheeks tasted salt – he had been weeping very much. I am overwhelmed by his gentleness and self-effacing sensitive love.

John *particularly* enjoyed this part of the evening – Iris weeping and talking of suicide. He explained that he couldn't but enjoy being alone with her, whatever was going on. His willingness to accommodate Iris *as she was* comes over clearly, together with a (to her) healing lack of curiosity about the detail of her trouble. She later recorded his comment 'emotions for their own sake'. She and John were soon lovers, she being his first, at twenty-nine.

John went home to Kent one week after the momentous St Antony's dance and cabled Iris: 'The *Sunday Times* has made it clear/Perilla's in her proper sphere'. In that journal J.W. Lambert had praised *Under the Net*, whose publication the same week as the dance anyone vainer than Iris would have recorded. Asa Briggs saw signs of pre-publication nerves. The same month during a tutorial her student Gabriele Taylor registered that Iris was not concentrating as she should. 'There is something I want to show you,' she said. She went to a cupboard and produced a copy of *Under the Net*, published on 20 May. She was clearly thrilled and philosophy, for once, forgotten.

2

Iris had decided to 'chuck' her earlier attempt at a novel, 'Our Lady of the Bosky Gates' on 27 October 1949, asking herself, 'What sort of novel shall I write?':

> Vague reduplications of my own situation must be rejected ... A tale of someone making a choice! ... Some simple frame. In form of a diary? (cf. *La Nausée*) Half in Paris, half in London – some ex-lover confidant in Paris. The task – to break a liaison, achieve something intellectual? Introduce a 'rub' – of the Xavière variety.[4] ... Some cool other female in London. Light on relation with women. How shall religion come in?

She later wrote the aphorism: 'Everything that is deep loves a mask'. Although *Under the Net* is not strictly a 'diary', male first-person narrative liberated her. She had hit upon an idiom in which she felt instinctively at home, and to which she would return, which enabled her to speak confidently through a masculine *persona*. (It was also a way of championing that inner life philosophers neglected. Philosophy undervalued the inner life, but a first-person narrative could still display its potency, strangeness and consequentiality, its shape as a 'pilgrimage'.) If her first-person novels are often among her best work, it is also because the form granted her the freedom of involuntariness. It is no accident that each of her first-person male narrators is the same age as Iris at the time of the novel's composition, from Jake in *Under the Net*, in his early thirties, to Charles Arrowby in *The Sea, The Sea*, who, like Iris in 1978, is sixty-ish. Both Jake and Charles are, for all the evident differences between them, like Iris, short persons who blush and like swimming.

Like Iris, Jake Donaghue is an Irish Londoner who has 'shattered nerves', who was once in the Young Communist League and is now disaffected, who is translating a French novelist just as Iris had translated Queneau's *Pierrot mon ami* – and who like Iris is about to turn into a novelist in his own right. London is a real presence, almost another character in the novel. Jake jests that Dave Gellner, being Jewish, could afford to live at a 'contingent address' – off the Goldhawk Road – whereas he is not sure that he could. The address in the notebooks for *Under the Net* – Iris's parental home, 4 Eastbourne Road – is in Chiswick, 'contingent', as the novel jokes, 'to the point of nausea'; her schoolgirl poems expressed routine contempt for suburbia.

The instrument of Jake's education is Hugo Belfounder. Those who see Wittgenstein in Hugo are not wholly misled: both have Central European origins, a tormented love-life, a care for their boots, give up their fortune, are associated with hospital work, employ the word 'decent' as high commendation. So keenly did Wittgenstein's pupils emulate him, even to his Austrian accent,[5] that when he gave a lecture at Cornell University in New York, one student asked, 'Who is that old man imitating Norman Malcolm?'[6] Malcolm was another of the holy fool-disciples Wittgenstein sometimes preferred in philosophy, the main conveyer of his ideas to the United States.

But Hugo was based on a different holy fool. 'What a poor image of Yorick Hugo Belfounder is! But this is unkind to Hugo. The fault is mine,' Iris noted. Wittgenstein's star pupil Yorick Smythies resembled a cross between Hamlet and the first gravedigger, thin, stooped, myopic, tall, pure of heart, given to the slow catechising that Wittgenstein favoured as a method of investigation, and to strange abstinences. He read Plotinus at the age of five. Friends use of him precisely the same parlance as Iris of Hugo: he was 'totally truthful',[7] to the point of wild eccentricity. Like Hugo torn between Anna and Sadie, Yorick in real life was divided between two loves (neither of whom, however, resembled the Quentin sisters). Like Hugo, finally apprenticed to a Nottingham watchmaker, Yorick aspired to become a bus conductor but, Iris noted, was the only person in the history of the bus company to fail the theory test. They muddled him with complex situations so that he could not give the correct change;[8] when he accidentally pressed part of the ticket-punching gadget which conductors wore around their necks, 'great sausages' of rolled-up tickets came spewing out.

During his single driving-lesson the instructor left the car as Yorick drove on and off the pavement.

Though Iris in 1977 wrote to Chatto pleading for a philosophical work by Yorick to be taken seriously by them,[9] his only known publication is a review of Bertrand Russell's *History of Western Philosophy*, a book he feared would encourage slipshod thinking.[10] He lived mainly as a librarian; Wittgenstein wrote a warm testimonial. Yorick for Iris was a wise counsellor, quick, sensitive, humorous, an excellent listener. When he died in 1980, she wrote his death into the novel she was then composing, *The Philosopher's Pupil*, where Hugo leaves his clocks to 'that writer-chap, I forget his name' – in other words to Jake Donaghue. Before this a schizophrenic breakdown caused him to hide behind trees, making strange utterances ('soft soap'; 'Heil Hitler'). Like Elizabeth Anscombe, Smythies was a Catholic convert and a pacifist. A record of conversations with Yorick kept by his friend Peter Daniel from 1952 makes clear his wide culture, his wholly original views, his religious passion, his belief that ordinary consciousness is unfree since enslaved to sin, his attraction to Buddhism (when a film of *Under the Net* was discussed in 1956, Iris proposed to simplify the philosophy by making it Buddhist[11]), his preoccupation with saintliness. He believed in human 'transformation'. He wished we had recorded conversations between a saint and an ordinary worldly person. He wondered why no saint has left us rules for living – they themselves must have them, but not such as we could follow, like: 'Think of nothing for one hour.' It would be good if, at the end, one were praying all the time. The kindest and most charitable Christians he met were his fellow-inmates in the mental hospital following his breakdown. Saints, though suffering, were still happy. He found the anonymous mystical *Cloud of Unknowing* helpful. He was not so unworldly as to be unable to see that many Oxford dons were bored and jealous. He took snuff.

Iris shared Yorick's concern with sin and saintliness, and his love of the great mystics; also of Kafka and of Murasaki's *The Tale of Genji*. Yorick helped Iris through a number of emotional crises. The wise fool Hugo, in the novel, cuts through Jake's illusions about who loves whom, but also, by his very mode of being, reawakens in Jake a humility and a related sense of wonder. 'It's just one of the wonders of the world,' are the final words. The novel concerns a re-enchantment of the ordinary, the redemption of particulars, a re-christening of the eyes. Hugo stands in this process for the puritan ideal of silence, to which art must of necessity be opposed, but by which it may also be refreshed; Jake for the necessary compromises of art.

In July 1953, after completing the novel, Iris rowed Yorick Smythies in her canoe as far as the Plough pub at Wolvercote.

> . . . a long conversation in which Y. was more like Hugo than it's possible to imagine. A diary couldn't but be 'a lie'. All art was a lie. Only the Bible was not a fabrication. Chaucer, Dante? Perhaps Chaucer was all right . . . I said, some people's trade is writing, & if it's possible to sin in it, this doesn't differentiate it from any other trade. Y. said – it's different because it involves judging. He agreed later perhaps this only differentiated it from simple manual jobs. All others were 'tainted' in some similar way! I said too – there must be people who try to purify ideas & speech. You advocate some terrible dichotomy – tainted speech or silence.

Jake writes up such conversations with Hugo as a pretentious dialogue called 'The Silencer'; while Anna Quentin, who loves Hugo, creates out of his influence an equally silent mime theatre in Hammersmith. Being nobly unselfconscious and living without self-image, Hugo is unable to recognise these reflections. The quarrel between Hugo and Jake is the first of many treatments in Iris's work of the fruitful war between 'the saint and the artist' – for 'artist' read 'arch-individualist'.[12] She came to think of *Under the Net* as immature.[13] Jake and Hugo are together for only half an hour during the entire book, and Hugo's saintliness is not immediately clear to the reader, remaining itself in the realm of theory.

3

Iris wrote to Queneau to tell him he was the book's dedicatee. Jake's hearing Anna sing on the wireless at the end refers to Sartre's *La Nausée*, where Roquentin hears Josephine Baker;[14] a private reference is to Iris and Queneau listening to Juliette Greco, perhaps singing Queneau's '*Si tu t'imagines*'. The casualness of Queneau's reply to her letter hurt her – 'When I think of the letter I would have got from Franz . . . !' He was bemused by the way Jake breaks into other people's flats in their absence, and enquired whether this were a peculiar old English tradition. Iris reassured him: 'No!' – only Jake and she had this 'nomadic insecurity'.[15] *Under the Net* tries to copy Queneau's *Pierrot mon ami* and Beckett's *Murphy*, both of which are among its charming, feckless, bohemian hack-hero Jake Donaghue's few and treasured possessions, but it resembles neither closely. Its humour is very different from the owlish pedantry of *Murphy*. Iris admired 'that vertiginous heart-breaking absurdity which Queneau achieves by his ambiguous serio-comic play'.[16] Like Queneau's *Pierrot mon ami*, *Under the Net* concerns *petites gens* and is picaresque and unexpected. But its marvellously lyrical evocations of London and of Paris, its wit and endless comic invention, its philosophic theme yet lightness of touch, make it unlike either book. In her journals Iris calls it 'a philosophical adventure story': the title alludes to Wittgenstein's *Tractatus*, 6, 341, the net of discourse behind which the world's particulars hide, which can separate us from our world, yet simultaneously connect us. Sartre is here too; but where *La Nausée* presented the contingency of the world as the enemy, *Under the Net* presents some healing surrender to its otherness as a precondition for happiness and creativity alike.

Anna Quentin is a *persona* Iris wished to shed. Anna – like Iris in her grief over Frank and Franz – has a 'taste for tragedy', taking life 'intensely and very hard'. Her character moreover 'was not all that it should be', her existence 'one long act of disloyalty'. She is constantly involved in 'secrecy and lying in order to conceal from each of her friends the fact that she was so closely bound up with the others'. Sometimes she tries deadening by small, steady shocks the sharpness of jealousy, so that her enslaved victim becomes resigned to 'the liberal scope of her affections'.[17] When Jake memorably pursues the woman he takes to be Anna through Paris on the glorious fourteenth of July – '*Alors, chérie*' – Anna's double finally addresses him. He has mistaken Anna for a lady of easy virtue. Another judgement comes when the authoritative Hugo, his voice 'edged with fury', portrays Anna both as a 'frenzied maenad' and also as less intelligent than her sister Sadie.

By Iris's standards the novel grew slowly. One year into writing she notes that only 'a dash to the summit [is] worth attempting'. May 1952 journal entries make clear her identification with Jake, the narrator who then believed his sidekick Finn to be a relative, and a character called Rosina, later dropped, also features. In March 1953 she compares the novel to 'a crop of clover – not much in itself, but it cleans the soil'. In June she asks, 'Is it "symbolic"? No more & no less than anything else that happens to human beings.'

On *Under the Net*'s publication the *Times Literary Supplement* hailed a 'brilliant talent' that, despite a lack of 'fit' between characters and plot, promised great things. Kingsley Amis in the *Spectator* admired her 'complete control of her material'; she was 'a distinguished novelist of a rare kind'. John Betjeman in the *Telegraph* disdained the novel's 'intellectuals, washouts, and seedy characters in general', its excesses of farce and fantasy. Canetti enjoyed Angus Wilson's grudging quip in the *Observer* that here all was 'Wein, Weib and Wittgenstein'.* The *Guardian* dismissed the novel as 'sentimental . . . strictly for those who can take their fantasy neat'. Philippa Foot was amazed by the wit Iris had hidden from the world and could express only in writing; Asa Briggs was struck by her ability to turn common experience into poetry. Iris's father Hughes was proud, and spoke of the novel to his bank manager.[18] Julian Chrysostomides saw how happy and not at all vain Iris was when an Oxford bookseller congratulated her:

---

* 'Wine, women, and Wittgenstein'. (Information from Allan Forbes, letter to author.)

'You must have worked very hard to produce this!' She grew, John observed, in self-confidence. A possible translation into French was a 'dazzling vision to me of course'.[19] Chatto had what sounds like a record-breaking number of copies (215,000)[20] printed for the Reprint Society book club.

4

On 30 June John wrote to a depressed, tired Iris at Chiswick: 'Darling, don't ever give me up: I could live in any contradiction indefinitely with you, and never mind the mornings when one wakes early & alone.' Iris had been seen with John at a party for the marriage of J.B. Priestley and Jacquetta Hawkes, and reported by a 'snake-in-the-grass' to Canetti, whose letter filled her with foreboding. Having tried not to think about the approaching crisis, she now felt 'terror & wretchedness mixed with relief . . . What sort of living in contradiction can I offer [John] now?' Canetti interrogated Iris, who was consumed by guilt towards both lovers. He was 'very gentle and very firm, continually turning my head towards him & making me look into his eyes while he questioned relentlessly'. He told her it was as well she had not seen him when he was really angry.

> Not that he would have beaten me, though he might, but he would have said things which couldn't be unsaid . . . I am very glad & relieved to have told him. There remains the problem of how to get the required bounds to my relations with John without doing some irreparable damage to that gentle beast. I feel full of grief – and will feel even more so when I face the details of this. I have a considerable capacity for dividing my mind (rather my heart) into compartments and giving apparently a full attention to a number of people at once. Then, as now, I am suddenly trapped – & this causes pain to others.

Canetti was 'the king', yet Iris saw little of him, having to 'live on a myth in intervals of seeing the flesh & blood man'. Meanwhile it was hard for her not to love those who surrounded her. Fear prevented her feeling a full joy in Canetti – whereas she could 'bring measureless joy to [Momigliano] or to JB. I am terribly to blame for all this duplicity. (I feel this when it is being unsuccessful.)' She also feared hurting John, 'a totally innocent person'. Canetti's conditions – that she and John break off sexual relations – made her feel 'as if a Ford lorry had driven straight through me . . . miserable and half crazy'. She explained these conditions to John who arrived at Victoria station, 'slouching out with his rucksack' on 3 July, his delighted smile visible from far away. They stopped at a pub.

> I began to tell him. Interrupted. Then we went to Trafalgar Square & we stood beside the lions. I told him about C. and how I felt we had no choice but to 'set bounds', to be friends not lovers. It sounded crazy. We walked up & down a bit & then leaned against the monument. (J. said in his letter of this morning: 'it must have been like clubbing a kitten.') My knees were giving way. J. said – 'it wasn't important before. Now it is.' We had a drink in St Martin's Lane & tried to eat but couldn't. J. talked wildly of going to see C. I told him not to. I wanted terribly to embrace & kiss him, & told him so. He said – 'we'll go to the London Library'. We went there, & I followed J. upstairs. It was fantastic. We walked up & down the long dark alleys of books. Always there was here & there a reader, hidden. We kept climbing up more & more iron stairways. At last we found a floor where there was no one. We leaned against the shelves in the half darkness & clung to each other. J. wept. After a long time we went out, & I came with him in the taxi to Paddington. What will come of all this?

On Iris's thirty-fourth birthday on 15 July Canetti gave her a copy of the *Ching P'ing Mei*, a book (perhaps unsurprisingly) about a man with six wives, inscribing it 'To Iris – for her second novel with great expectations'. On his birthday, ten days later, he twice told her he loved her, and then regretted this; she joked that he need not say it again for two years. There is no record of Canetti proposing any self-denying ordinance for himself, but

John and she obeyed his edict. When she proposed John's coming
to meet BMB in August his deliberate misquoting of Dante's '*la
tua volontade è mia pace*' – in your will is my peace – delighted
her. Photographs of Iris and John in his room at St Antony's
before Canetti's decree show him happy, concentrating on the
cotton cord he has rigged up to operate the camera at long-
distance. Those Iris took in Paris that summer show him miserable: he hated Paris, and Iris insisted they stay in separate little
hotels. By September they once again were lovers, meeting at a
friend's flat in West Halkin Street in London.

Iris was depressed about her new novel-in-progress, *The Flight
from the Enchanter*, which seemed to her emotional, shapeless,
repetitive. 'Another failure. If I imagined I now knew "how to
do it" I was wrong. Not a great writer in training, but a mediocre
writer who had a single stroke of luck? (I *will not* believe this.)
. . . A terrible haste has infected my work. Not exactly that I grudge
time to the writing of each piece – but a sort of metaphysical
sense of rush. Be quieter in the soul.' She rarely discussed her
creative depressions with anybody. John's sureness of instinct
helped.

> *4 August.* JB rang up this morning. His voice was consol-
> ing. How can I describe how remarkable he is? . . . A
> grace of soul – humility, simplicity, and a way of being
> very acute & subtle without ever protecting oneself by
> placing & despising other people. (J. in a letter today:
> 'You don't know how earthy & inconsiderable I am –
> how completely without enlightenment of any kind.')

In Oxford that October she noted that:

> . . . courage, courage, courage is the secret of all . . . I
> know I can overcome the hurts from my work and from
> other people . . . At such moments a yearning for union
> with this infinite joins with the sheer sense of creative
> energy. My task after all to write – thank God for this
> much of a solution.

5

Within days of finishing *Under the Net* Iris registered the approach of *The Flight from the Enchanter*. In March 1953: 'The next thing. Which is already present, only I have not yet turned to look at it. Like a king whose bride has been brought from a far country. But he continues to look out of the window, though he can hear the rustle of her dress.' That spring she made a first draft, in which the main characters are Jewish, and Peter Saward, based on Franz and named Kostalanetz, is writing a history of the Jews. On 10 July: 'Astonishing progress since my last entry. The novel now stands up, as a completed plan, all characters present, all scenes planned, many small details in! If only my wise Jew were not such a bore.'

She decided to 'unmake' this and start again. Her second draft generalised the conditions of rootlessness and of enslavement. Here she invented not only the mysterious Fox, the demonic Polish brothers to whom Rosa is enslaved and the dressmaker Nina (a half-rhyme for Veza; Marie-Louise von Motesiczky's well-known picture *At the Dress-makers* may have suggested her profession) but gentile English characters too. Annette Cockeyne is deracinated by being a diplomat's daughter, speaking four languages, none perfectly. Rosa Keepe tries to uproot herself from a Campden Hill Square background by working in a factory, recalling Simone Weil's working for Renault, while Agnes Casement is upwardly mobile instead, acquiring a typist as her own 'slave'. Even the foolish Rainborough suffers a small deracination when the wistaria in his Belgravia garden is cut down to make room for a neighbouring hospital.

This final draft was finished in February 1955, when Iris was increasingly drawn to John, and her relations with Canetti unresolved. 'When will you tell Canetti?' John would ask. 'I don't want to lose him at the moment,' she would reply. 'He's very jealous.' The fugitive autumn leaves in Shelley's 'Ode to the West Wind' are secretly driven by that greater power. So Rosa's defection from Fox, like Iris's from Canetti, obeys the enchanter's secret wish. Fox's power – like Shelley's 'unseen presence' – is literally inexplicable. If there is a literary parallel, it is Thomas Mann's short story 'Mario and the Magician' (1930), a prophetic anti-Hitlerite fable where a conjuror-hypnotist bewitches his audience, and the voluntary enslavement of that audience is as blameworthy as are the manipulations of the Magician himself.

No one knows Fox's age, what country he comes from, or can fathom his apparent omniscience. Rainborough stands in for all Fox's 'creatures' in asking anxiously, 'Did he say anything about me?' Annette, like the younger Iris, positively wills her enslavement to him, suffering the illusion that she can thereby 'liberate [his] soul from captivity';[21] while Rosa, like an older and wiser Iris, dislikes his assertions of power and finds the 'strength to flee ... the demon'.[22] Isolated Nina (Franz had noted that slaves were 'kinless'[23]), captive to her fear of Fox, finally escapes, not to Australia as she plans, but by throwing herself out of the window to her death. Fox's power is ceded to him by his creatures, who *will* their own enslavement. Both parties are complicit; an analysis of power running throughout Iris's *oeuvre*.

Although Iris denied putting Franz or Canetti into her work,[24] both shadow *The Flight from the Enchanter*, whose opening meditation concerns the vulnerability of monsters. Annette thinks of Dante's condemned minotaur in the twelfth canto of the *Inferno*: 'Why should the poor minotaur be suffering in hell?' He hadn't *asked* to be born a monster. This softens our judgement on Mischa Fox, named for his cunning, inspired by Canetti: what is monstrous deserves our pity. Yet monstrosity, the novel also suggests, is bred out of an ambiguity within the experience of pity itself, which may be corrupted into cruelty and power. The inward nature of that protective anxiety Iris had vicariously felt about Friedl, and which Canetti (like Fox) recorded especially about the fate of animals – 'Why do animals suffer death? What is their original sin?'[25] – is closely examined in the novel.

Iris made her mystery-man Fox wealthy, because it disguised Canetti who was then poor, and because wealth can fascinate as a power-source. We forget that he is a newsaper magnate: the point is never developed. He is given Canetti's moustache, also one blue and one brown eye, pointing to a divided nature, and is 'famous for being famous'. Much is merely stated of him: that he is 'capable of enormous cruelty'; that the 'sight of little independent things annoys him' – he wants them in his power; that he is capable of taking a careful revenge after ten years; that he has collected around London 'dozens of enslaved beings' waiting to do his will whom, as Saward observes, he drives mad; that his parties are carefully constructed plots for the forcing of various dramas; that, dragon-like, he eats up young girls and, for Rosa, is sometimes the 'very figure of evil'.

Little of his power-broking, his 'oriental magic', is actually shown. One of the best scenes has him arriving unannounced at Rainborough's when the latter in panic has shut away young Annette, bare-breasted, in a cupboard. Fox talks, with a poetry both sinister and interminable, about the protean and malleable nature of women and their need to be broken; his *Schadenfreude* or malicious joy, both towards Rainborough, whose predicament he intuits, and towards women, is simultaneously comical and disturbing. Fox enjoys disquieting others. The crisis of the novel, also funny and sinister, is a Dostoevskian *skandal*, a party in Fox's palazzo where a goldfish bowl gets smashed and a fish, by mistake, 'saved' in a decanter of gin. His inviting Agnes Casement is typical of Canetti, who would make a point both of discovering his friends' secrets, and also of paying attention in social gatherings to the least probable guest.

Iris solves the aesthetic problem that Canetti/Fox is morally mixed, at a time when she was in thrall to Canetti, by giving him a wicked double, Calvin Blick, who is 'the dark half of Mischa Fox's mind. That's how Mischa can be so innocent.' Blick argues that reality 'is a cipher with many solutions, all of them right ones', a view Carol Stewart recalls as close to Canetti's,[26] and is opposed in this foggy relativism by the good Peter Saward, who argues on the final page by contrast for a humble striving towards truths which may be unreachable. Peter, like Franz, is a scholar-saint in his forties whose beloved sister has died, and who, also like Franz after the loss of his thesis in 1942, at the end patiently has to restart his work. He is dying of TB as was Franz of heart failure, and Rosa's proposal of marriage to him on the last page, just after she has dreamt that he is dead, reflects Franz's last days. 'He did not defend himself by placing others. He did not defend himself' – a description recalling Iris's view of John as well as of Franz. Saward plays saint to Mischa's artist, as necessary to the others as an object of contemplation and speculation as is the cunning Fox himself. Evil (in Fox) and Good (in Saward) embody forces half-independent of society, the drama of whose opposition is the secret dynamo of the novelistic world.

The novel memorably distances its tone – surreal (Annette swinging from a chandelier), lightly comic, Lewis Carroll-like, fantastic – from its grim subject-matter. The worst we know of Mischa Fox, reputed to cry when reading the newspapers, is that as a boy he killed a kitten. 'If the gods kill us, it is not for their sport, but because we fill them with such intolerable compassion, a sort of nausea,' he comments. Hitler, mentioned once only, who killed those he had rendered piteous by uprooting, is a real presence. When Fox asks Peter whether he does not feel that everything in the universe requires his protection, 'even this matchbox', Peter demurs, observing how close in Mischa lie the springs of pity and of cruelty. The protective anxiety that preoccupied Iris during 1943 and again in 1953 is displayed here in a new light. It holds her as much as snobbery and memory obsess Proust.

Canetti's own writings, also tender towards animals, are memorable when encountering what is maimed or not whole – the anonymous human sack at the end of *The Voices of Marrakesh* that produces a single note;[27] the paralysed young cripple Thomas Marek whose mother pushes him around on a wagon, whom he befriends near Vienna in his memoirs.[28] He liked to rescue those '*in extremis*'. In *The Flight from the Enchanter* a bird with only one foot (in real life sighted by Iris with Momigliano at Kew) fascinates Mischa. How will it manage in a storm? The novel examines the connexions between pity and power, sentimentality and cruelty, like Ezra Pound in Canto XXX. Rainborough is predator to Annette, victim to Agnes Casement; but most play both victim and predator. Only Peter Saward and Annette's mother stand outside the web of enslavement, which reaches one comic apogee in the persecutions the old Suffragette Mrs Wingfield visits on her companion Miss Foy: 'Would you say old Foy was a virgin? . . . She isn't!' Agnes Casement too, who nearly swallows Rainborough whole, shows Iris's consistent refusal to depict women only as victims.

6

When Rosa flees from Mischa in Italy towards the end of the novel, Iris was enacting her own symbolic liberation from Canetti, one which in real life she had not yet achieved. Liberation took one further year. Finally at Gwenda David's party for the publication of the novel in March 1956 the enchanter announced to John: 'I like you.' Iris had begged his blessing the previous month, and, though he remained ambivalent and jealous, she had apparently won it, he surrounding her 'with a sort of positive radiant concern, very deliberate, as everything that he does'. She felt 'deep deep relief at being free; and joy at all the freedom & simplicity of my love for JB. Back again in a world of simplicity & truth. Truth bought at *that* price.' Canetti was nonetheless angry when she left the party with John, without having greeted him; his refusal afterwards to come to the phone to speak to her – she tried several times – she now felt 'objective enough . . . to see . . . as vanity on his part and just dislike it'. She did not ask John his impressions of Canetti, and he gave none. In April 1956 she put her hands in Canetti's hair, saying he was Moses and that she was searching for his horns. He said: 'Yes, the horns which you put there!' He was gentle, that day.

Iris could display in fiction an objectivity she had not achieved in life. Hence the value to her of her art; and hence also the related 'spiritual' dimension of marriage, about which she was having frequent dreams. In December 1955 she noted:

> The possibility of becoming a better writer, (??A great writer??) after certain *renunciations*. Thinking of marriage makes me realize the extent to which my writing up to

now [*sic*] has an aspect of sheer personal *adornment*. I
have wanted, with its help, to make myself more desirable
& interesting, a centre of attention. By dropping all that,
the possibility of a power & a freedom I now do not
dream of.

The possibility of marriage was on her mind from late 1955.
She wanted yet feared it. John wrote to her early in 1956:

> If John Cranko's Josephine could get at me perhaps she
> would turn me into a bat. Then I could be (life's
> ambition) small, and no trouble, and furry and gently
> fruit-eating. I could hang inconspicuously upside down
> in the corner of your ceiling while you did your work or
> entertained your lovers, and since I should be pretty
> witless and nearly blind my presence would not upset
> you. But, as you said, this being always near is only a
> dream. If I was a bat, it would be pointless. If I was me,
> it would be both unseemly and impossible. Forgive this
> drunken letter. The only bat I am is *bâteau ivre*. My head
> is frail *comme un papillon de maie*. But my heart, so obstin-
> ately wanting to be given, is firm as a rock. At least, it's
> givable all right, but not acceptable.

Mischa Fox had announced that women have a Protean, shape-
shifting nature, and that the way to deal with Proteus was to hang
onto him while he changed form. So, when he despaired, Iris
would comfort John: 'Simply hang onto me as if I were Proteus,
and I'll assume my real nature.' On 15 February 1956: 'I cannot
help being swept now toward JB . . . with a great force of joy &
love. What will come I don't know, probably marriage.' Formally,
they were 'engaged'.[29] Yet the event remained unsure: 'I hesitated
and hesitated and hesitated'.[30]

7

One day in 1955 Iris took Julian Chrysostomides to St Antony's,
where a cat had littered in John's rooms. Julian felt the affinity
between Iris and John at once. It was as if they were so much a

part of one another that there were no barriers between them. Each was part of the other; a deep intuitive understanding linked them: 'She chose well!' Susan Gardiner witnessed the tension and passion John felt for two years. He was seen gazing up at Iris's window and following her, while Iris appeared 'radiant, luminous, like a Fra Angelico'; John was also sighted climbing out of her flat window the odd morning.[31] He constantly read the runes. That she took him to Badminton to meet BMB in August 1954 was a sign of hope. That BMB remarked to Iris, 'My dear, he doesn't look very strong,' was ominous (he cheered himself up by buying a jumper). Being permitted to teach Iris to drive that year was a positive sign. Even crashing her Hillman Minx *en route* from London into a stationary lorry was happily forgiven. Helping her replace the Hillman with a dark-green 1946 Riley with black wings, which she loved and put into *The Sandcastle*, brought hope. So did driving her to London in the Riley in February 1956, to take Rene and Hughes out, first to eat at La Coquille, then to the musical *Salad Days*: 'a lovely evening', Iris noted. When in October 1955 Iris left out in her Beaumont Street flat, to which John had a key, her journal account of her affair with Canetti, he was deeply upset. Nor, in 1955–56, were his rivals only men: Audrey Beecham was reported as remarking, perhaps optimistically, that Iris was 'one of us' – i.e. lesbian – until 'that horrid little man' took her away. In the autumn of 1955 Iris and Brigid Brophy were close; the following spring Iris and Peter Ady holidayed in Burgundy, their second French jaunt. Ady later commented that no other intimate friend was so 'unintelligible' to her as Iris.

Soon Iris had also met John's formidable, strong-willed and beautiful mother Olivia* and his engaging father (Frederick – except to Olivia, to whom uniquely he was 'Jack') at 'Nettlepole', the Bayley house at Pluckley, near Charing, in Kent, with its

---

* John Bayley, in *Iris: A Memoir*, states (p.66) that his mother had a moment of hesitation when introduced to Mrs Murdoch and her daughter: 'Which of them had her son just married?' This is one of a number of moments of poetic licence: the uncertainty about whether Rene or her daughter had married John was in reality expressed by his aunt 'Flummie' (Florisse) from Chicago. Iris and her future mother-in-law were acquainted by then.

occasional butler. They were more anxious than Iris's parents about what was going to come of this relationship in which Iris was six years senior and had – distinctly – an 'odd past'. John's mother uttered a strangely expressive phrase by which Iris was much amused, 'She's like a little bull!' This referred to Iris's resolute stride – '*une démarche decidée*', Queneau had written – holding her head slightly down, a determined expression on her face. She looked as if she was really going somewhere, knew what she was about.

In Michaelmas term 1954 John had written his first critical book, *Romantic Survival,* which discriminated between surviving 'Romanticisms' and showed Auden and Yeats recolonising the modern urban world and in so doing giving it back to us afresh – a thesis relevant to Iris's fiction. 'In our moments of most acute observation', she wrote praising Surrealism, we see a world that is 'strange and startling'.[32] Her best writing startles us with exactly such strangeness. In 1955 John won a Fellowship at New College and a splendid set of rooms. His prospects were improving.

The writer Brigid Brophy, a new friend, spoke in April 1956 to Iris of her own 'loss of identity' during her engagement. Iris was having continual dreams about marriage. In that month *The Sandcastle,* which had taken a year to write, was finished and at the typist. Hughes was operated on – lung cancer was found, one lung removed and the cavity, as was then customary, filled with ping-pong balls. In the evenings at her parents' home there was an atmosphere of sadness and doom.

> Sense of deep psychological upset. I dreamt last night that I was getting on famously with Wittgenstein . . . In the dream I was very pleased, & afraid because JB was due to arrive & I feared some clash. Hesitation always between the son and the father. Now that I seem to be choosing the son, I am anxious about the father's atti-tude. This comes in with deep anxieties about my own father . . .

She was choosing the child: 'How utterly without fear are my relations with JB.' John's favourite brother Michael had tied up

John's shoes until he was seven and a half. At nine John and his mother had sailed to the Caribbean to help pre-empt incipient TB. A much loved and indulged delicate youngest son, John early learnt that his wit could charm and flatter; at his wedding his mother would remark, 'John is such a chatterbox.' He inherited from his maternal Heanan grandfather a very Irish desire, and ability, to please. At eighteen, in the autumn of 1943, down from Eton and at the end of his first leave from the Grenadier Guards, where fellow-soldiers helped him on with his puttees, he (wearing uniform) took a red-sailed yacht onto the Round Pond at Kensington Gardens, and was mortified when his mother reported that a fellow Grenadier officer, passing by with his girlfriend, had looked much amused. 'Child-soldiers,' Iris commented in May 1978; John received his call-up papers before his eighteenth birthday.

In 1945, after active service in Belgium on the 'second front' and in Norway, he escaped from London without permission to Target Force* in Germany, to get away from having to work with his senior officer Nigel Nicolson, whom he charged in a farewell letter with '*Grenadierismus*' – officious pomposity. Nicolson generously pursued neither offence. John's stammer, worsened by criticism, prevented his giving parade-ground orders as Second Lieutenant, and when stationed at Windsor, where he was in training as a three-inch-mortar officer, his Sergeant-Major gave orders in his stead; it also necessitated a friend (he claimed few as a student) reading out his Newdigate Prize-winning poem 'Eldorado' for him in the Sheldonian in 1950. It was no accident that in his accomplished first novel *In Another Country* (1955), admired by Elizabeth Bowen, whose influence in it is clear, John chose the name 'Childers' for his own character.

He signed himself to Iris 'child' or 'your child'. The six-year age-difference excited him. His admiration for Hannibal, he would jest, was partly because the Carthaginians practised

---

* Known also as 'T-force', it was an Intelligence unit engaged both in headhunting German scientists and in requisitioning items from German factories for use in Britain.

child-sacrifice: he did not appreciate competition.* Iris early noted that he was free from guilt. He detested responsibility and still found it most soothing being driven around by his forceful, elegant mother at home in Kent on her charitable visits, sometimes taking patients to mental hospital. His mother 'paralysed' him into a benign passivity. The prospect of adult life having to start filled him with gloom, and he felt no urge to accelerate the process. In Iris he had found his 'ideal co-child'.[33] Together they could be babes in the wood, and she liked, always, watching him play. On 7 April 1969: 'Puss has been trying to dye some daffodils blue – not so far as I can see with any success whatsoever.'

Iris's July 1956 visit to stay with Elizabeth Bowen at Bowen's Court, County Cork was critical. She had met Bowen for dinner at the Cecils' Oxford house at 7 Linton Road, and they had liked each other. Lord David Cecil, at the time a Fellow of New College, who acted as mentor or father-figure to John, though later very fond of Iris, at first wondered if she had a sense of humour. He and his wife Rachel kept a protective eye on John, and on the progress of the affair in general. Bowen was very enthusiastic about Iris and liked watching her develop, liked the *idea*, Stuart Hampshire recalled, of a woman novelist operating out of Oxford. Indeed Iris influenced the aesthetic daring and escape from realism in Bowen's final novel *Eva Trout* in 1969.[34] They also had Protestant Irishness in common. Photographs of Iris's 1956 visit to Bowen in Ireland show the ambience of Bowen's Court in its final days (the house was sold three years later), Iris watching intently a company that included Lady Ursula Vernon, daughter of 'Bend Or', second Duke of Westminster – thought by neighbours to be a model for Hannah in *The Unicorn* – and Eddie Sackville-West, dilettante writer, Catholic neighbour and heir to Knole. She was much struck when Bowen hymned her late husband Alan Cameron, older than her and less distinguished, a

---

* Possibly because she had a child in John, the desire for children which Iris had expressed in 1945–46 to David Hicks now lapsed. In 1989 (on BBC TV's *Bookmark*) she added that by 1956 she was no longer young enough to raise a family. John Bayley in *Iris: A Memoir of Iris Murdoch* says the topic of their having children was never discussed.

schools inspector for Oxfordshire and gloomy First World War veteran: 'I couldn't buy a pair of shoes without him,' Bowen confided. Here was a successful writer who had found marriage essential to her stability. Iris thought hard about this.

None of this stopped Iris's last-minute anxious fear in late July that she could not marry John because of her commitments to two philosophers who were variously attached to her and whom she did not wish to estrange: John Simopoulos, half-Jewish gay son of the Greek Ambassador to London, whose 'strong black eyes, down-drawn wry-smiling mouth, quick glances' she records liking more and more; and David Pears, who in 1998 spoke of Iris's quality of 'luminous goodness ... when she came into a room, you felt better', and whose article in *Mind* on the incongruity of counterparts she put into *Under the Net*.[35] John somehow intuited that quietness was his strongest card. For his part Simopoulos also recalled the importance to Iris of Hans Motz. Had John spoken of the 'rights' their understanding gave him, Iris might have fled. Something of this touch-and-go quality is captured by the apparent casualness with which Iris noted, in the margin of her journal, and after having torn out the two and a half previous pages, the words: 'August 14. Married John.'

8

The wedding, in an Oxford register office, followed by a party at New College, was an extemporised affair. John wore his demob suit and bought an engagement ring at a pawnbrokers; Iris a bright-blue silk dress a friend of Rene's had made,[36] obscured by a mackintosh ('I've just been to a wedding where the bride wore a mac,' reported John's school-friend John Grigg, then Lord Altrincham before he, on principle, renounced his peerage). Iris hailed that morning in Beaumont Street an ex-St Anne's student – Antonia Gianetti[37] – and conjured, then opened, a bottle of champagne, from which each happily took a swig on the street, Iris explaining that she was about to be married. A confusion about 'Mrs Bayleys' dispirited her. Since John's mother Olivia, his sister-in-law Agnes, and Iris – now Mrs J.O. Bayley – were all there, John's colleague John Buxton remarked, 'Everyone here is called Mrs Bayley.' '*That* brought the full horror of the situation home to me!' Iris commented gloomily to John. While they were waiting for Rene's train to arrive – nursing Hughes delayed her – Iris cheered John up by saying, 'Oh what a relief to have got it all over.' He fervently agreed: the sense of *détente*, of 'no more bloody emotions' was welcome.

They took his Austin 10 van, nicknamed 'Alligator', to Henley, then to the Jersey Arms at Middleton Stoney, finally to France and Italy for three weeks, a time well described in John's *Iris: A Memoir*. Over-excitement and the strain of the previous days gave John a spastic colon which doubled him up with pain. He took belladonna to relax the muscles. Iris was sympathetic; John grateful. They stopped at a pub and had another of John's experimental drinks – gin and peppermint – which helped too. When, weeks later, they got to Borgo San Sepolcro they disputed the meaning of Piero's great *Resurrection*. John, following Aldous Huxley,* saw the Christ-figure as a pagan nature-god; Iris was intent on a Christian meaning.

9

6 *October 1956.* It is somehow typical of the way things are now that the only time I find to write this diary is 5 minutes when JB has gone to get the car so that we can go out & visit the Cecils at Cranborne. I am happy. It is very strange now to read the entries above. *et haec meminisse iuvabit.* Life has such a quality of simplicity, warmth and joy . . . Hope that this diary may improve in quality. Now that there will be fewer entries of the type: 'so & so kissed me and asked me out to dinner', perhaps I shall be able to record something of importance! . . . And for such deep consideration of the consequences

---

* 'More like a Plutarchian hero,' thought Huxley in 'The Best Picture', in *On Art and Artists* (London, 1923), pp.197–202.

of my past actions I have plenty of other motives and occasions. I have these, but I don't do it, or hardly.

Some of Iris's Oxford friends were gloomy about her marriage, fearing lest she might be throwing herself away. Boon companions wanted her to belong uniquely to them, a figure of infinite charm, potential and mystery, and there were knowing comments that such a marriage could not last. Gentle Noel Martin made one unscheduled visit. One woman admirer would arrive unannounced and invite Iris out on her own. Hal Lidderdale on his motorbike would include Iris in a series of visits to old flames. One tactic if presumptuous admirers attempted to exclude John – most did not – was to 'poke' them verbally. He enjoyed the comedy of human vanity and liked watching conceited persons jump. But he worked to accommodate everyone, and no friends were 'mislaid' by the transition. Doubtless the move out of Oxford to the country, which Iris urgently desired, helped.

'Why,' Iris would later say, 'should I be cheated of happiness?' She told Rosemary Cramp that each year she loved John more and more, indeed that all time spent away from him was time wasted. In *The Black Prince* she would write, 'Writing should be like getting married. One should not make a move until one cannot believe one's luck.' Both Iris and John had been lucky. Philippa Foot saw that she had chosen one of the few men who, though outwardly easy-going and timid, was 'up to her', who had extraordinary hidden strengths. John Simopoulos would call it a marriage made in heaven, and saw how John both anchored and liberated her.

John adored Iris's mysterious way of being present yet distant; her face that expressed so much yet gave away so little. Of course there were alarums and excursions; the 'contradictions' he had declared himself willing to live in would make themselves apparent. Iris's sentence in her journal about 'simplicity, warmth and joy' is in a later hand and ink, a truth grasped retrospectively. But they were married. He felt about her 'silliness', rather as a country yokel might feel about an urban intellectual, reverencing that intellectual's formidable superiority, while seeing that it was clearly not achieved without other costs. It was what he most loved in her, what most moved him. The Latin tag – *et haec meminisse iuvabit* – from *Aeneid*, I, 203 – implied that painful matters might in future be seen in a new light.* Marriage and novel-writing alike would assist that transmutation.

10

Marriage provided what generals called a 'base for operations'. Iris did not want a bourgeois or conventional marriage. This arrangement procured her a child-wife in John, who cooked, or assembled, picnic meals – '*Wind-in-the-Willows* food', she called it in *The Sea, The Sea* – and who would modestly prefer to say that he acted more as 'comic relief' to Iris than as a sheet-anchor. His absence of intensity and his common sense alike were tonic, preventing her other deep friendships from becoming too serious, giving her a pretext for keeping them light. Her protean gift for changing with different friends he saw as Shakespearian, while A.N. Wilson, later John's student, then friend, saw John ascribe to Iris what was essentially his own negative capability, and believed he acted as Prospero, 'a sort of controller of the demons and spirits who flew in and out of her consciousness'.[38]

But he, as much as she, had a personality without frontiers, with his own relaxed and humorous availability to everyone, the gift of intuitive sympathy developed 'to an astonishingly high degree'[39] and an 'Ariel'-like impulsiveness, a brilliant whimsical ability to fly with each and every idea. When in 1956 Isaiah Berlin and David Cecil circulated a petition urging Britain to move into Suez against Egypt's President Nasser, John signed. When, shortly after, a letter opposing this view appeared in the *Guardian*, John signed that too. He explained to Cecil, 'I agreed with both.' He had a saving irresponsibility about him, of which Iris's intensity

---

* '*Forsan et haec olim meminisse iuvabit*'. Translated in *The Oxford Dictionary of Quotations*, ed. Jackson, as 'the day may dawn when this plight will be sweet to remember'; in W.F. Jackson Knight's translation of *The Aeneid* (Penguin), as 'perhaps one day you will enjoy looking back even on what you now endure.'

stood in need. He could put things back in proportion, by releasing the *independent* child in her – Canetti invested in dependent children. New College wits started a game which involved inventing the least probable statements by friends. The phrase for Isaiah Berlin, easily bruised, was 'I don't mind what people say.' For the elegant Stuart Hampshire, 'My feet are killing me.' For John, 'I'm afraid with me it's a matter of principle.' Not that he lacked decorum or tact – quite the contrary – but he did not take to those who 'preen and peacock themselves' on their own rectitude.[40]

John was, Iris believed, 'the greatest literary critic in England since Coleridge',[41] and was soon reviewing novels weekly for the *Spectator*, working on an influential study of James's *Golden Bowl*, Chaucer's *Troilus and Criseyde* and Shakespeare's *Othello*. *The Characters of Love: A Study in the Literature of Personality* (1960) called for a revival of the idea of 'character' as central to literature. John had the gift of total recall for poetry and prose alike, with a good reading knowledge of French and German, and later Russian. He was a living encyclopedia and walking concordance of European history and literature. He knew about cars, engines, hand-guns, battles, birds, fishes, flowers, popular songs and ballads. A gifted listener and an acutely perceptive observer with a retentive memory, he was not as unworldly as he sometimes appeared.

Iris was acquiring a family, something she had felt deprived of. John's paternal grandfather had written *Times* third leaders and helped start the magazine *Tit-bits* in the 1870s; perhaps his own journalistic flair came from that side of the family. His maternal grandfather was a wealthy Irish builder whose family converted to Anglicanism. His mother sometimes played as a result 'more English than the English'. His eldest brother David, taken POW in Italy, and returning evangelical and Low Church, was an engineer. John's beloved middle brother Michael, seriously wounded in 1944, was a career soldier. Iris and Michael's first meeting shortly before the wedding was unpropitious. John got Michael, serving at Windsor Castle, to drive them to the Catherine Wheel pub in Henley. Michael, cross to be using up his petrol ration, was crosser still when John announced that he was disappearing (he had a meeting to discuss Schools), leaving him to buy supper for, then drive back to Oxford, a woman he did not yet know, nor at that first meeting much care for or find attractive. Iris quizzed him through the frosty meal about his army career and his life, getting his 'résumé'. It was a poor start. If the Bayleys at first were cool to Iris or Bayley *père* hostile, she never showed she minded. They warmed to her later.

John also provided new social worlds, in which Iris felt more at home than he. On the basis of his parents' living during the war in Gerrards Cross, just outside London, uniquely happy years,[42] he would boast of being 'suburban'. He and Michael were the first Bayleys to have gone into the Grenadier Guards, which might not have happened in peacetime. Michael's commanding officer Miles Fitzalan-Howard (from 1975 Duke of Norfolk) and his wife Anne, friends of Michael's from the 1940s, became friends also of Iris and John. His mother Olivia was proud of having been presented at court; his godmother Eulalia Salisbury-Jones, known as 'Aunt John', sister to an equerry, was connected by marriage to Lord Saye and Seele. Iris was much more at ease in a fashionable setting, indeed in all settings, than John. With her he relaxed and flowered. For her, A.N. Wilson later wrote, the 'weasels and the stoats had been seen off and Toad Hall repossessed; Ithaca . . . regained and the suitors gone . . . Iris's wild earlier selves would find a happy resting-place and turn themselves into fiction.'[43]

11

Soon she wrote, 'Love for J. deepening in all sorts of tender and absurd mythologies.' Their house was 'Dogers'. Both were cats named 'Puss', both were mice, and 'mouse' could suffix any other word. She had a Valentine card painted by John in 1980 mounted and framed. Entitled 'Flags of Old Catland' – one was 'The Fighting Mouse', based on the old Fighting Man of Wessex – it showed the two of them as adjacent countries, separated by a river, joined by a railway, representing two separate selves who shared what Swift called the 'little languages' of love. Small wonder that Morgan in *A Fairly Honourable Defeat* defines happy marriage as 'like animals together in a hutch'.

Canetti remarked that Iris's conversation with John about books was ceaseless. Her novels show much indirect influence.[44] When he enthused about Henry James's *The Golden Bowl* her novels – *A Severed Head, An Unofficial Rose* – became Jamesian. When he wrote a brilliant study of Tolstoy, his ideas about Tolstoy found their way into *The Nice and the Good*. When he praised Dostoevsky's *Notes from Underground,*[45] her novels – *A Word Child, The Black Prince* – took on the form of that fable. John Goode would argue in the *New Left Review* that they together constituted a neo-liberal criticism,[46] both believing against fashion that a high pleasure in literature came from the creation of character; Shakespeare and Tolstoy accomplishing that creation best. The same importance is given to the author's love of his characters in Iris's essays as in John's criticism.

Iris liked to quote an early Auden poem, later excluded from the canon by Auden, which starts, 'It's no use raising a shout . . .'. She would quote the lines, 'I've come a very long way to prove:/ No land, no water and *no love*';[47] their cynicism upset John. Yet it was a legendarily happy marriage. John had army ice-skates from Norway in 1945, which they shared during the bitter winter of 1963, one holding onto the other's coat-tails, on the frozen Cherwell, on canals, even on Blenheim Lake. Iris tried wearing the left skate, John the right, which never seemed to work particularly well. When in 1981 John for the third time broke his leg – something he had managed in 1958 and again in 1972 – they drove to Banbury hospital through snow, he with his good leg working the accelerator, she with a foot on the clutch. When in 1997 Iris had to be tested for diabetes and supplied some urine, in order both to keep the hospital on their toes and also to get two results for the price of one, John mixed in a little of his own.

It was at times hard to distinguish between them. Which view came from whom? The novelist Angus Wilson and his partner Tony Garrett were in 1972 shown the identical room 'in an unbelievable state of chaos' by John, later by Iris, and told by each that it belonged to the other. I was assured by both, on different occasions, that they disliked cats, but that the other was fond of them. Iris was cross when *Encounter* omitted the footnote to her landmark 1961 essay 'Against Dryness', 'My argument owes much to the ideas of my husband John Bayley.' Conversely John's notion that the art-work, 'like a human being, [has] a life of its own which is ultimately mysterious and irreducible',[48] occurs first in Iris's 1947 journal.

III

Wise Child
1956–1999

'I suppose I have a myth-making mind.'
Letter to David Hicks, January 1944

'Uncle Tim shared this lack of identity. They sometimes discussed it. Does everyone feel like this, Benet had wondered. Tim had said no, not everyone did, admitting that it was a gift, an intimation of a deep truth: "I am nothing." This was, it seemed, one of those states, achieved usually by many years of intense meditation, which may be offered by the gods "free of charge" to certain individuals.'
Jackson's Dilemma, p.11

15

Cedar Lodge
1956–1961

Living with 'mad land-ladies' in 'gloomy rooms in Oxford ... with terrible gas-meters' was over.[1] 'We have,' wrote Iris, 'bought a country house.'[2] Fourteen miles out of Oxford, off a winding lane in the straggling village of Steeple Aston, and immediately opposite the old school, is a stout old farmhouse built around 1725, substantially added to a century later. The church bells are audible inside. Cedar Lodge cost £3,500, and John got a college mortgage for a sum equal to that which Iris soon inherited from a wealthy great-uncle.[3] The house is fairly long but thin, and, having no damp-proof course on the north side, chilly and damp except in summer. There are two Georgian bays on each floor of the main house, with side windows, and a lunette above at the back. From a lobby you enter a south-facing drawing-room giving on to the big, rambling garden, with its many springs sloping steeply down to a muddy, shallow, stream-fed fish-pond, where in the early days Iris liked to swim, John trailing down in his dressing-gown. There were golden carp that a heron ate. The pond kept drying up – John struggling to keep it open. April 1961: 'Puss very sweet playing with his pond.' Iris loved watching John play.

Iris, a city-girl, loved the idea of living in the country; indeed John believed this was one reason she agreed to marry. Unlike other suitors, he was prepared for the rigours of a country existence. While he was waiting anxiously for her to make up her mind, he asked her, 'Well is there *anything* that appeals to you about the idea of being married?' Iris considered for a moment, and said, 'Well, yes. I rather like to think of you coming home in the evening, and me rushing out to say, "Darling: *the badgers have broken into the garden.*" July 1992: 'This little picture of our life together touched him very much. He said (today) that he did not think that he would have been much good at evicting badgers!' Iris's natural start as a novelist had been urban. *Under the Net* and *The Flight from the Enchanter* were London novels; *The Sandcastle*, completed in March 1956, before her marriage, suburban. The first novel written in Steeple Aston, and showing something of the imagination and spirit of the place, was *The Bell*, which many think her best. Before she went to live in the country, Iris might not have done it so convincingly. Though only fourteen miles from Oxford, Steeple Aston was then a real country village inhabited by country people.

It was still a 'deference culture', with squire and vicar held in respect. Iris and John, living in the ex-squire's house, were considered odd birds. The hunt would visit, once killing a fox in a field the Bayleys had bought, much to Iris's displeasure, which she forcibly expressed. The huntsmen were apologetic. During the thirty years they lived there the village changed greatly, only the Rector Michael Hayter remaining. He did not believe in the Christian story but was persuaded by the faith of Patsie, his tall wife, thinking, 'I love the woman, and she believes the story implicitly, therefore it is no trouble for me to do so.' The Tankerville-Chamberlaynes, previous owners of Cedar Lodge as run-down as the house itself, kept horses, and were reputed to sit in full evening-dress on antiquated car-seats to a dinner of tinned pilchards and raw tomatoes. Bayley bohemianism succeeded such broken-down gentility. They inherited a Mr and Mrs Grantham who cleaned and gardened for a while, but the Bayleys did not really want others in the house, and in due course they left.

The house was in a bad way, and comparatively cheap because only a mile or so from the big airfield at Upper Heyford, leased to the USAF and very noisy: about one night a week an immense tanker would zoom in, three hundred feet above the house. Iris and John would turn over and go back to sleep. Iris put such flights into a draft for Mitzi and Charlotte's funny and sad 'idyllic' Surrey cottage in *An Accidental Man*. There were aerial displays sometimes – one gets into *The Bell*, though probably that episode derives from a display at Giddington, Oxford's airfield, which had fascinated Iris.

To the left of the lobby, beyond a box-room, was an unused 'library', painted dark red, the shelves gilt-edged, with an old tapestry in need of re-stitching; log fires burned here during parties. To get to the kitchen quarters you turned sharp right onto a long corridor with a warren of smallish rooms off it on the road-fronting side, past pantries and an old scullery (which had a well that supplied the water-tank by an electric pump that often broke down until, after twenty years, the local health authorities insisted the Bayleys go onto mains water). Here Iris washed up, and John put in a sauna in 1970 for her arthritis; they enjoyed it like children, then forgot about it. Turning left you reached three very dark rooms *en suite*: an unused dining-room; a small kitchen with a range, in which John had his chair, wrote, and lived half the time, the other half being in bed, where he also read and wrote; beyond that a room with the electric stove. The house was never warm, and only half-lived-in. They knew theoretically where all the rooms were, but never had a sense of quite dominating the house, and had a fantasy that there might be somebody else living in some part of it they had never found.

It was indeed shared by mice, whom they early on watched planning to confiscate Iris's Mars bar. Some gentlemanly rats, there for generations, commuted, coming home late at night after a busy day, one, in an excited state because the drains had gone wrong, in 1964 startling John on the stairs. Disconcerted, he slept that night with a walking stick by the bed. A rather tempting veal and ham pie which they had been much looking forward to mysteriously disappeared – leading to the conceit that whenever something got unaccountably lost (not infrequent) it had 'gone to Pieland' to join the missing pie. Eventually something was done about the rats.

Other rooms could be entered only from outside; one of them, the so-called 'groom's bed-chamber', just opposite the back door, they never really came to grips with. The beautiful loose-boxes stayed full of rubbish of all kinds. A gardener's earth-closet had an uncanny atmosphere. All this may have contributed to their slightly haunted sense of sharing the house with persons unknown. Initially they lived simply in the kitchen. Around 1965 their builder Mr Palmer – and his 'dogs' (i.e. workers), as Iris called them – put in a reinforced steel joist and joined a small dining-room to the hall space, to make one fine big open room. This was the first room you entered, giving directly onto the garden. It made the house even colder. When a boiler was finally put in, it never worked well. John painted the new drawing-room Georgian green, and the upstairs corridor Chinese red, to cheer them up.

They did a minimum of upkeep, both being too busy, and not caring much either. In those days people lived more primitively. The house was fearfully cold in winter. Frequently the roof leaked very badly. A valley-gutter filled up with snow, leaking furiously onto the exact spot where they lay in bed, John once waking up to a steady stream of water pouring onto his face. This was considered a good joke. There was no real heating except for an electric fire which had the habit of blowing the fuse and making the trip-switch jump out, which it did at the slightest opportunity, plunging them into darkness.

2

In a tumbledown greenhouse, lying sideways on the floor and very green, they found a good Victorian marble bust of Venus, 'thrown in' with the house. Here they created 'Iris's wallow', a pond in which she could swim, six feet deep, ten feet long by eight feet wide, lined with plastic inside concrete. John laid immersion heater elements on the bottom, which when switched on sent up a cloud of bubbles through water of uncertain quality. The system was perfectly safe, and the baby green tench and perch Mr Palmer, a keen fisherman, gave them never minded either being heated or swum with. A note with skull and crossbones none the less warned against swimming with the system switched on. When Angus Wilson in 1972 noticed a single-bar electric fire hanging above the wallow from an overhead crossbar by a piece of string, John replied with a look of concerned technical seriousness, 'The mornings in Oxfordshire can be very cold.'[4] John painted the surround with an Etruscan motif from Volterra, and fixed a picturesque ceramic Poseidon above. Iris clambered through smilax (ground-herb) to get into the pool.

Iris planted a liquidambar, John a silver birch, and her letters show an informed knowledge of plants and of gardening.[5] After two years, she planted old-fashioned roses – Mme Alfred Carrière, York and Lancaster, *Rosa mundi*, Zéphirine de Drouhin – near one of a number of springs, close to a concrete path with box growing alongside. They were very proud of them, but they were perhaps planted too closely together, and some succumbed to black spot. 'Captain John Ingram' went almost entirely black. This right-hand part of the garden became facetiously known as 'Iris's concentration camp for roses'. She also, idiosyncratically, planted giant hogweed seeds, admiring the architectural qualities of the mature plant more than others do. There was no terrace at first, but more than two acres of rough uncut grass. The mowing problem was solved eventually by 'letting all the grass grow naturally', while John created 'rides' through it, for walking about. John collected three slate mortuary slabs, with neat plug-holes for bodily fluids, which lived outside, one incorporated as a working surface by an unsuspecting later owner into the newly smartened kitchen. Lady Violet Powell, wife of the novelist Anthony, was struck by the number of ageing Volkswagen Beetle cars secreted about the garden, which John reassured her were, 'of course, a hedge against inflation'.

3

Upstairs they disposed of their space 'extravagantly'. They shared a big bedroom with a fine large bed obtained at auction for one pound. Iris moved her study twice, starting at the east end upstairs, and ending at the west, where she faced out onto the south-facing gardens, and enjoyed watching generations of foxes and fox-cubs at play; they made their way into *The Philosopher's Pupil.* John had a work-room, and there was also a spare bedroom at the end of the corridor. Soon both got glandular fever, Iris not too badly, but both were laid up. Being ill together was a new and interesting experience.

Iris liked to entertain, and found the house magical. John's brother Michael, despite the Sellotape on window-cracks, agreed. Her old school-friend Margaret Orpen, now Lintott, recalled ancient newspapers all over the floor, everywhere, including upstairs, and an air of total chaos, Iris paying for taxis for students who had struggled out by bus. Katherine Duncan-Jones found the house elegant, and was charmed by John's habit of chopping up ground elder instead of watercress during ramshackle lunches resembling high teas. Not everyone agreed with Tony Quinton that, while Cedar Lodge was smelly, all the different smells happily cancelled each other out. Fastidious Stuart Hampshire laughed uneasily at the recollection of his fears of the possible consequences of going there to eat: it was 'beyond bohemianism', outdoing Miss Havisham in *Great Expectations.* There were hats everywhere, and all manner of stones (philosopher's stones, perhaps? They get into novel after novel, demanding to be loved and made sense of). There were liberal collections of dust. Genial John Grigg and his wife Patsy were close friends of the Bayleys, the two Johns having been friends at Eton while Patsy, a fellow-Ulsterwoman, had been taught maths at school by Iris's first cousin Muriel Chapman. The Bayleys were frequent guests at the Griggs' houses in Blackheath, at Tamariu in Spain and at Guisachon in Inverness-shire, and all four travelled successfully together, in the USSR (1963), India (1967), the Greek islands and Menton (1973). The Griggs only ever stayed one night at Cedar Lodge.

John did the cooking at dinner parties, reheating college food. Once he attempted an ambitious '*sauce verte*' for the Powells, A.N. Wilson and Katherine Duncan-Jones, which Wilson recalled fondly as tongue-in-green-slime. A much-heralded '*surprise-*

pudding of Iris's', to general astonishment and after quite a long build-up, consisted in each guest being awarded, from off a huge tray, a single Mr Kipling cake. Stuart Hampshire felt charmed by the unselfconsciousness of it all. Eric Christiansen, history don and younger colleague at New College, thought Iris and John were all the better hosts for seeming to be guests at their own parties, Iris's intense interest in others untainted by any malice or gossip of the Bowra school. She had a way of staring down at her glass, listening very carefully to the speaker, possibly indicating also that the glass was empty. She loved the crowded room, the voices, the possibility of multiplying pleasure through many conversations.

4

1 September 1954. Some sad domestic picture The woman whose life work is being gay & tender in some slightly artificial way. The *job* of being a woman.

The Sandcastle, finished in January 1956, was published in May of the following year, and dedicated to John, whose stammer may be echoed in the speech defect of the novel's 'saint', the art-master Bledyard. He, like John, is an Old Etonian and, like Hugo in *Under the Net* also, what Iris termed an 'anti-art artist', one who renounces, for puritanical reasons, his own talent. Following the success in 1955 of *In Another Country*, John ceased for thirty-five years writing novels: Iris's career was 'simply too meteoric'. Iris lost her copy of John's novel, inscribed in his hand 'Horror-Comic for IM from John Bayley, March 26th 1955' in (it may be surmised) Bowen's Court, where she had perhaps brought it for Elizabeth Bowen to read: by a coincidence that belongs within her fictional world, her second cousin Max Wright found and bought it in a Belfast second-hand bookshop forty years later.

The Sandcastle differs from its predecessors, and takes a love-triangle as its theme. The schoolmaster Mor, unhappily married to the bullying Nan, falls in love with the proud and humble Rain Carter, who has come to paint the portrait of the retired

headmaster Demoyte. Rain was inspired by Iris's student Julian
Chrysostomides, whose proud humility and excellent French are
noted in her journals, and who had told Iris about the sadness,
during her Greek childhood, of watching sandcastles crumble in
the tideless Mediterranean. Iris was much struck, both by the
story, which provides a central unifying image in the novel, and
by Julian herself:

> She is a magical girl. Her detached integrity & pride . . .
> As if she had risen out of the animal world – & yet as a
> divine being – she is warmth, simplicity, & [has] a kind
> of small fierce strength like a beast. (All this is exact.)

The novel, though not her strongest, has memorable scenes.
The way Nan and Mor can no longer communicate except
through appeals to the memory of their deceased dog Liffey is
well observed. The school, the garden, Demoyte's worldly desire
to see Mor win his love; Rain's Riley (in real life Iris's) falling
into the river and having to be rescued; Nan's lonely final victory.
Rain is idealised – she is magical, fey, her 'gaiety and tenderness'
not quite in the real world of the book – while Nan is seen only
from outside, or – in Iris's word – 'coerced': *The Sacred and Profane
Love Machine* is a much more disturbing and subversive later novel
about a love-triangle. Raymond Mortimer, finding almost all *The
Sandcastle*'s characters more interesting than its hero, noted
further that he had no idea why any of Murdoch's characters
behave as they do, but felt her novels retained a dreamlike conviction.[6] The novels are indeed surrealistic in the sense of dreamlike;
and Nan's carefully staged victory over Rain at the end shows Iris
as concerned, for all her rhetoric about the novel as a 'house fit
for free characters to live in', with matters deeper than freedom.
Her characters are enslaved to one another and also to what she
would eloquently term unconscious 'life-myths'.

5

The month after the novel appeared Iris wrote to her redoubtable and parsimonious publisher at Chatto & Windus, the alarming, legendary Norah Smallwood, who increasingly ran the firm herself and on old-fashioned lines, 'No, don't bother to send cuttings thanks. I'd rather not bother with seeing them. Except for the ones one sees anyway.' A bad review, she would famously later say, matters less than whether it is raining in Patagonia,[7] arguing also that any novelist who is any good knows what is wrong with her work without being told. She was lucky in Smallwood, a thin, domineering, elegant woman with apple-red cheeks and dazzling ice-blue eyes,[8] who was clearly both fond and very proud of her, and, perhaps, indulged her. Smallwood loved Iris's 'infinite capacity for listening'.[9]

Iris was fortunate in her American editor, Marshall Best at Viking, in a quite different way. Best always sent her a careful reader's report on each novel, with praise for what had succeeded and also suggestions for changes, a practice Smallwood would later resent being criticised for defaulting on. 'We seem,' Best wrote to Iris in 1961, 'to do more of this telling you how well your intentions come across than English publishers do.' While irritated that Viking had changed Rain's Riley into a Jaguar without telling her (American readers 'could not be expected to have heard of' the former car[10]), she was at this stage grateful to be published, and still biddable, thinking carefully about Best's suggestions, sometimes giving ground, allowing cuts, for example, in the Lefty/Jake scene in *Under the Net*, but willing to stand her ground also. She was, wrote Gwenda David to Best, 'a firm but delightful woman. A rare soul who knows her own mind.'[11] Best thought the figure of the gipsy in *The Sandcastle* weak. Iris agreed that he was weak, and incongruous, yet, while ceding other cuts and changes, feared that the novel would be further weakened if the gipsy were taken out, since he is Rain's 'shadow', relating Rain to Mor's daughter Felicity, with whom Rain was also to be identified. She made changes that tried to clarify these points.[12]

These two letter-runs, from Smallwood and Best, also bring out Iris's kindness, and conscientious impracticality. She apologises for constantly badgering Smallwood about manuscripts from hopeful author-friends – she read and criticised these first with utmost care – including her mother's window-cleaner Christopher Hood, whom Chatto indeed successfully published (and whom Iris always encouraged), and also about jobs for friends ('Have you by any chance, now or in prospect, a possible job for an intelligent young woman?'[13]). 'The business side is rather beyond me, I'm afraid . . . I fear I may cause you more and more trouble,' she apologised, and indeed often lost contracts and records of royalty statements. Her depression at the thought of photographs of herself in a bookshop display suggests her shy absence of ordinary vanity. For one 1959 foreign contract requiring witnessing by a notary, she loses the form ('Please don't be cross with me. Is it possible to send fresh copies?'), then sends it witnessed only by John, after four months finally getting it witnessed properly. She was only once notably angry, typically on John's and not her own behalf, when the opening pages of his Tolstoy book were ill-set in 1966.

6

Iris's fourth novel, *The Bell,* was finished in January 1958 and appeared that November. Despite tragic events, and a moving ending, it is also a comedy in which most characters survive and renew themselves. The central character Michael Meade, failed priest, failed schoolmaster and chaste homosexual, has left schoolmastering fourteen years earlier because of a love-affair, unconsummated, with his adolescent pupil Nick Fawley. Nick, probably influenced by an evangelical preacher, exposed Michael to the headmaster. Michael has given up his Palladian house, Imber Court, to become the centre for a lay religious community. Nick's sister Catherine, with whom he is rumoured to have had a Byronic affair, is to enter the neighbouring Abbey as a postulant when Nick turns up, a tormented drunkard in bad need of Michael's help. Michael's clumsy inability to supply this is a factor contributing to Nick's vengeful suicide.

Catherine and Nick, demonic siblings, contrast with two innocents: Toby Gashe, marking time while waiting to go up to Oxford, and immature, attractive Dora Greenfield – her first name referring to David Copperfield's child-wife – bullied by her pompous, unhappy historian husband Paul, who is studying medieval documents at the abbey. Dora and Toby recover the legendary bell of the title from the lake (its having been cast by one 'Belfounder' links it with Hugo in *Under the Net*: both stand in for the numinous) and substitute it for a new bell which is, like Catherine, about to enter the abbey. Nick now stages a second scandal by compelling Toby to expose Michael's tenderness for him: like many Murdoch characters, Michael makes the same mistake twice. Catherine, who turns out to be schizophrenic and in love with Michael too, attempts to drown herself. Nick shoots his head off. The unstable world of Imber Court dissolves, swallowed by the abbey. Toby seems unscathed, Dora learns the confidence to leave her husband, to value herself, and to swim – almost in itself a sign of moral competence. Michael, romantic unfortunate that he is, faces up to the indignities of survival.

7

The philosopher Dorothy Emmet, with whose thinking about the need for a *rapprochement* between religion and philosophy Iris was in sympathy, discounted George Steiner's view that *The Bell* owed something to the 'Epiphany Philosophers'[14] who, led by Richard Braithwaite and Margaret Masterman, explored the possibilities of the religious life in a residential group at 11 Millington Road in Cambridge, but not until the 1960s. Such misattributions are compliments to the novel's truth to its times – the Bishop of Ely finally permitted Braithwaite to be baptised without believing in God, and regarding the Church only as a useful vehicle for propagating 'agapeistic morality'. *The Bell* concerns, in part, such hunger for the spiritual in a post-theistic age.

Some sources are clear. Michael, first of many muddled gay male 'seekers', is animated wonderfully from within: Iris's own search for peace of mind at Malling from 1946 to 1949 lay behind the troubled quests of her leading characters. Imber Abbey's guest chapel, at right angles to and separated by an iron grille from the nave, was inspired by Malling, which, precisely like Imber, combines Anglican Benedictine community and abbey. Malling's notable Abbess Dame Magdalene Mary Euan-Smith has a 'marked affinity' with Imber's abbess, who describes Nick as a '*mauvais sujet*'. Three weeks after *The Bell*'s publication Iris thought of visiting Malling but hesitated, perhaps concerned about Malling susceptibilities.

On 1 May 1954 Iris's old Somervillian friend the 'wild' Lucy Klatschko had been accepted as postulant at Stanbrook Abbey, and later assumed that *The Bell* drew on Stanbrook. Iris had written to her: 'May it be all that you hope ... Take me with you as much as you can.'[15] Two months later she had gone to stay.[16]

> *18 July 1954*. Dressed in her own clothes, black & white, & a veil & black cloak she looked like someone acting in a play as a nun. In the chapel in the morning I identified her, among several black clad figures with their backs to me, by her black gym shoes. Then she extinguished the candles on the altar. It was like being at a play.
>
> Later we went for a walk, & we lay down in a hayfield. L. said she wanted to roll on the grass, & did so. (It was a secluded field.)
>
> She asked if I had cigarettes. Fortunately I had – & she smoked one in a lonely lane, leaning against a gate & looking warily up & down to see if anyone was coming. It was all gloriously improper & very strange. She said that for the first month she wept continuously, her tears falling onto the altar rails & into the soup. Now, she said, she could not leave. She asked me how she looked, whether she looked like a nun – as there were no mirrors in the Abbey. (No mirrors.) I was moved to see her, sad to leave her.

Lucy, now Sister Marian, would, unlike Catherine, be happy in convent life, but may have suggested the figure of the reluctant or divided postulant. Iris told Honor Tracy, who reported it to Sister Marian, 'that she was always against your leaving the world, "though not against *idea* as *such*" – so like Iris! . . . What a curious mixture she is of arrogance – for who is she, or anyone, to approve or not? – and warm understanding and sympathy. But she loves you very much and is always asking about you.'

One of the joys of the novel is the way its author, who later admitted to identifying, 'a little, with the Abbess', in fact animates all her characters, not least Dora, who discovers the joys of classical music at the end of the book. This new pleasure prefigures Iris's own move from the emotional response to music she reported to the critic Harold Hobson, to a more comprehensive appreciation. The Bayleys acquired a cherished gramophone, and the growth of the titles in their record collection Iris transcribed on journal-page after page.

Iris claimed as *donnée* for the novel an involuntary vision of Toby approaching in the headlights of Michael's Land Rover. In August 1954 she was touring in France with John Simopoulos, future dedicatee of *The Bell*, a sixteen-year-old Marlborough protégé of Simopoulos and the boy's elder sister, who was about to go up to St Anne's. She noted between Laon and Rheims a 'picture in the headlights' of the car: Simopoulos running to rescue a drunken, reeling cyclist who promptly gave him a crucifix. Iris denied that Nick and Toby owed anything to 'real life', and indeed her happy account of the journey is wholly remote from the Imber melodrama. The echo between the two 'pictures in the headlights', the real one with the crucifix, the other imaginary, is still of note. So is the echo between the innocent tenderness, in Iris's mind, between her and Donald MacKinnon which threatened his marriage, and the intensity of a taboo being broken when Michael merely kisses Nick.

8

'Those who hope, by retiring from the world, to earn a holiday from human frailty, in themselves and others, are usually disappointed,' comments *The Bell*'s wise (abbess-like) narrative voice. Indeed the bossy and wrong-headed Mrs Mark – wonderfully 'caught' – continues the quarrels with her husband she entered the community to escape. The Abbess calls the Imber Court inmates a 'kind of sick people, disturbed and hunted by God',* who can live neither in the world nor out of it. Iris treats them with gentle irony. Her contemporary essay 'A House of Theory' champions a Morris-ite Guild Socialism sympathetic to 'the vision of an ideal community in which work would once again be creative and meaningful and human brotherhood be restored'.[17]

While the abbess and her nuns are idealised pictures of the beauty of holiness, the bishop, like most of Iris's churchmen, is worldly. *The Bell* is her first novel to be fuelled by Platonism, in which Good substitutes for God, and any authentic spiritual tradition, including appreciation of the visual arts – Dora in the National Gallery confronting Gainsborough's portrait of his two daughters – provides a means of ascent. For Iris all spiritual pilgrimage entails the purification of desire. So the medallions of Imber Court bear the motto '*Amor Vita Mea*' (Love is my Life), and the ancient bell is inscribed '*Ego Vox Amoris Sum*' (I am the Voice of Love). Michael knows that his religion and his sexual passion 'arose deeply from the same source';[18] we are not being invited simply to collapse the former into the latter.

When Harold Hobson objected to Iris's obscurity, she pointed him towards the clarity of the argument underlying *The Bell*. The second leader of the Imber community, James Tayper-Pace, preaches that the chief requirement of the good life is to 'live without any image of oneself'. This is only half-true, and James indeed lacks self-awareness. Michael's sermon the following week

* Recalling Karl Barth's description of the Jews as '*Krank an Gott*'.

argues, by contrast, for knowing one's own moral level, and not attempting too much too fast. The quarrel between James and Michael is echoed in *The Sovereignty of Good* when Iris asks, 'What of the command, "Be ye therefore perfect"?' This is James's line. To it she opposes Michael's 'Would it not be more sensible to say "Be ye therefore slightly improved"?' She argues that the 'idea of perfection' can help mediate between these two positions. The Abbess in *The Bell* earlier proposed exactly such a mediation: 'Our duty ... is not necessarily to seek the highest regardless of the realities of our spiritual life as it in fact is, but to seek that place, that task, those people, which will make our spiritual life ... grow and flourish.'

9

The Bell, Iris would say, was a 'lucky' novel. Here everything had come together and worked. Sister Marian worried to Iris that the 'sex imbroglios' of her novels reduced the characters, made them unreal and would be bad for people – meaning the nuns whom she felt needed protection. Iris, annoyed, said that her 'more discerning readers would understand', and created a character called Marian in *The Unicorn* who suffers from too much innocence. *The Bell* was welcomed and applauded. To the *New Statesman* it marked Iris as 'the foremost novelist of her generation'; to *The Times*, it was a 'joy ... running over with purpose and intelligence'; to Frank Kermode in the *Spectator* it showed a 'steady gain in power' in a writer possessing 'altogether exceptional intelligence and vitality'; while the *TLS* praised in it the rare conjunction of a 'brilliant imagination and a passionate concern for conveying ... moral concepts'.[19] It brought her commercial success: Chatto printed 30,000 hardback copies within ten weeks.

It also brought fame. Iris judged the prestigious Prix Formentor (for two years running, first in Majorca, then Corfu), with its strongly leftist, anti-fascist and pro-third-world undercurrent, with the jury having the tough task of subjecting the literary output of each country to multi-national scrutiny. Yale University invited her for one month in the autumn of 1959, where she gave a talk on 'The Sublime and the Beautiful Revisited', later published as an article. Lord Snowdon photographed her in college looking as if John had just given her a pudding-basin haircut. John himself was so disturbed and astonished by the imaginative intensity his outwardly placid wife had revealed in *The Bell* that he could not at first read its immediate successors, but pretended to have done so.

The Bayleys often did not bother to answer the telephone (which, from the kitchen with the door closed, was inaudible), and gave their mothers and close friends Canetti's telephone-code to filter out calls from them – 'We live *entre deux mères*,' they would joke. Iris was soon painstakingly answering a dozen fan letters, by hand, every day; in less than a week in 1964 there were seventy.[20] Given how sympathetically and adventurously she had treated homosexuality, she surely now had a gay following, as well as one interested in religious matters; the trials of Peter Wildeblood, Lord Montagu of Beaulieu and Michael Pitt-Rivers rendered homosexuality newsworthy, as did Wildeblood's brave book *Against the Law* (1955). Every novel she wrote after *The Bell* has at least one homosexual character. She had an unusual tendency to imagine that even some of her happily married men-friends must be secretly bisexual.

Journalists got at her, as she wrote to Vera Crane in 1957:

> Press: Well, Miss M, do you intend to do so-and-so, such-and-such, and so-and-so?
> Oneself: I don't really know – maybe, but I haven't made any plans at all . . .
> Press report: Miss M told us that she intends to do so-and-so, such-and-such, and so-and-so.[21]

A journalistic scandal, as in Dostoevsky's *The Devils*, had helped to finish off the lay community in *The Bell*; and there was no end, as she later put it, to the spite of journalists. Fame did not alter her; she hated always the idea of being taken for 'a touchy grandee'.[22] Most writers are rightly made happy by success. A few go insane with vanity. Iris differed. So far from her head being turned, she was 'nauseated by the stream of imbecile praise for *The Bell*'. Three aspects of this response invite comment. Firstly, the great success of *The Bell* dispirited her. Secondly, she badly wanted to improve as a writer. Lastly, she wanted to be *attacked* 'in the right way'. And she cast about for the right person to attack her.

10

Iris's father Hughes had retired from his 'personal grade'[23] of Assistant Registrar General working at Somerset House on census returns six years before. He appeared to be carrying out private research for 'devious' Sir George North, as some colleagues thought him, but no one quite understood what he did.[24] Both Hughes and Irene smoked very heavily – not unusual in those days. Irene probably smoked ordinary Players, the standard cigarette for the time, while Hughes was fond of the delightfully named Sweet Afton (in fact also made by Players), with a name out of a Robert Burns poem ('Flow gently, sweet Afton, among thy green braes . . .'). Just before Christmas 1956 they learnt that he had cancer in his remaining lung.

> Rene told me, in my bedroom, late one night. I did not see how she cd manage. She wanted Doodle not to know. After some terrible days she has adjusted herself and now is bravely cheerful with him . . . a terrible sense of nightmare hangs over the time.

At first cheerful and not in great discomfort, Hughes soon weakened. Visits home became 'very sad', and Rene bravely settled into a routine of cheerful care. Hughes sold John and Iris his first editions as an 'investment', suddenly wanting them away, but unable to bear parting with them on the Charing Cross Road at low prices. 'Sadness hangs over this time,' wrote Iris. By January 1958 he was much iller, and despondent. One bore it, Iris noted, by a 'curious averting of attention, almost withdrawal of sympathy

... One lives deliberately at a trivial moment to moment level. Anything else would be too terrible.' Rene expected every morning when she came in to find him dead – and then would see the bed clothes moving and know he was still alive.

Except for a curious delusion about a cablegram to come from New York about a horse running in a race, Hughes was lucid and even joking till the last. He died on the afternoon of Saturday, 1 March 1958, aged sixty-seven. Rene was talking to him, when suddenly he threw himself back across the bed, gasping, became unconscious, and died very quickly. After receiving a police message at Steeple Aston, Iris and John drove down at once through the fog, arriving around eleven. It was 'a terrible arrival. Rene ... frantic with grief.' Iris went up at once and saw him, seeming 'so small & wasted on the bed'. Among the six mourners at the funeral, near Syon House, the following Wednesday, were no ex-colleagues.[25]

> He was so gentle, so quiet, so kind – so without pretensions & ambitions – few knew him or knew how good he was. He taught me so much.

Three weeks later John broke his leg – like Austen Gibson Gray in *An Accidental Man* he was subject to mishap – the first of three times. Trying to start the car with the starting handle when it was in gear, it jumped forward, pinning him against the garage wall. He called to Iris, upstairs, 'Darling, come quickly, come quickly.' When she got there he told her to put the car into neutral, and it moved back. She drove him to the Radcliffe hospital. It took months for his leg to recover, during which Iris had a happy unexpected meeting with her erstwhile lover Michael Oakeshott, to whom she gave, at his request, advice about the progress of an unhappy affair.

That summer John and Iris took Rene to Dublin to house-hunt, staying at the Shelbourne Hotel:

> As we drove round Dun Laoghaire & Sandy Cove in a hired car, so many memories. Saw a lovely house at Killiney, with a view of the bay between palms & eucalyp-

tus trees. But R. thought it might be too lonely, & the
hill too steep. Everyone so kindly in Ireland, & Dublin
so slow & eighteenth century.

Back at Steeple Aston, Iris was writing throughout 1958 a novel
entitled 'Jerusalem', about an old man, which ends with a Dublin
episode; four of her next five novels have an Irish connexion.
The garden absorbed and delighted her and she measured how
happy and lucky she was. By November, and publication of *The
Bell*, her mood swung. On John's advice she completed 'Jerusalem', but thought it – rightly – a work 'without a heart'. This was
the 'Trades Union' novel she would refer to in interviews. The
Utopian Jerusalem Socialists of the title believe in Guild Socialism
of the kind she had advocated in 'A House of Theory', which was
republished in *Partisan Review*. But their theories about taxation,
community and equality do not engage with the fog-bound reverie
of the narrator, perhaps the most solipsistic of all her first-person
narrators. He is a world-famous and sexually potent eighty-year-
old architect who designed the Utopian 'Shakespeare House',
which memorably burns down and is, at the end, to be rebuilt
by a Jerusalemite Labour government. The other characters
remain, like the narrator's complex love-life, too remote to
engage the reader. Iris tied the manuscript up with string early
in February 1959, writing on it: '*Abandoned. Not on any account for
publication ever.*' 'Few regrets now, because I feel quite clear about
it,' she wrote in her journal. She recycled a number of the names
– Lynch-Gibbon, Georgie Hands, and so on – giving them to
quite different characters in *A Severed Head*.

As well as feeling nauseated by praise of *The Bell*, Iris was generally fed up with her work, and 'sunk in a sort of mush of insincerity
and imprecise thinking & facile success ... If I could only see
how to get, in my writing, out of the second class and into the
first.'

Her hopes of Yorick Smythies, who had been helpful during
earlier difficulties, were disappointed. He displayed his absolute
and exhilarating seriousness, producing a typescript concerning
'headings', the 'forms' of speech which *divide* us from what is

supposed to be being described: 'How very like Hugo Yorick remains. I am deeply impressed by the way he stays with the *same* problems.' John tried drawing a picture of her 'spiritual crisis', making it look 'just like a friendly old crocodile'. This cheered her up, but she also wanted 'the reality of being profoundly attacked'. Brigid Brophy had written 'rejecting' her work, Iris noted, but Iris felt that Brophy's motives were 'not pure enough . . . also she distinguishes between me and my work, and the person who is to help me must not do that'. Harshness only helped, she reflected, when accompanied by love, or at least affectionate respect of some sort. Or when it came from something impersonal, such as a religious institution: 'Very few people can give one in a way that invigorates a sense of one's second-rateness.' She needed 'a foothold to get into a completely different region. A new discipline.' She could not stand 'this smell of success'.

She considered making a religious retreat. 'Religion gives one a machinery here,' even though she disbelieved in God. 'At Stanbrook? Not Malling.' She went to neither. It was infernally cold. They had the east end of the house redecorated. John was in bed with a bad ear. Snowdrops and aconites were in flower, and she noted the beauty of the snowdrops she placed in John's room 'with the pale clear green mark at the edge of the bell'. Having abandoned the Jerusalem novel she was attempting a poem-series which she had typed up, writing 'To those for whom these poems were written, they are now dedicated' on the front page. One, above which she wrote the initials of both Frank Thompson and Franz Steiner, ends: 'Precious dead,/I cannot follow there where you go on/Nor love you quite so finely as I did once. My love lacks in detail now. Forgive/To grieve for little matters is to live.' Although she had mysteriously appeared in a *Spectator* leader in 1954 linked to two 'Movement' poets where, presumably, a token woman was required,* she accurately noted that hers was 'not really bad poetry but mediocre. I wish I could

---

* *Spectator*, 1 October 1954. The poets were Donald Davie and Thom Gunn; three novelists were K. Amis, IM and John Wain. See Blake Morrison, *The Movement* (Oxford, 1980) pp.1–2.

write poetry.' Her odd frame of mind persisted; she felt an 'unutterable longing for what is not'. Though there were ready tears she diagnosed her mood as not altogether depression. Sometimes it felt

> more like being utterly *possessed* by some sort of blind love, love of everything, the birds, the trees, the logs in the fire, the pieces of coke. And such a feeling can't help being somehow sad. Yet at the same time quite stuck in work. Extraordinary inward agitation with no apparent cause. At a time like this I see and know that all art is ultimately love but this knowledge lies dark in me and I have not the courage and the goodness required to do anything with it . . .

In fact her diagnosis that 'being stuck in fiction-writing' underlay her depression sounds exact. She would later say that she would 'hate to be alive and not writing a novel',[26] and when asked how long she paused between completing one fiction and starting to think about the next, reply, 'About half an hour.'[27] She now, most unusually, found herself between novels, and resembled an addict suffering withdrawal symptoms. She wrote to Canetti, asking him to help her find fresh possibilities of self-knowledge. Although they seldom met now, she felt the need to go back and 'try again to understand and feel the impact of things which I find only in him'. She sought the 'lively grasp of a standard . . . the *bite* of truth'.

> Last Thursday I saw EC in London, day of dreadful fog (memories of our original fog). We talked of my work and this was very helpful. C. said the stuff I have written so far is weak and sentimental. I avoid unpleasant things, do not 'let rip' enough. I should let things come out from much deeper within me. Let the *cutting edge* of my mind come out in my fiction. At present, I am afraid of offending and hurting people. (True: this is the basis of much that is wrong in my life too.) Nothing I write draws any blood. C's talk was invigorating. I feel unutterably tired and limp at present, but things *will* live again.

Soon she had the idea for a new novel, which would deal with a topic that fascinated and alarmed her in equal measure: incest. 'Too upsetting & dangerous? The theme of loving one's sibling, always near to my heart – but to attack it directly –?' She started reading up on it. By Easter she was working well. On 29 March, Rene's birthday, the house at 4 Eastbourne Road in which Iris had spent her childhood was sold. John and Iris, since Rene could not bear it, saw the furniture out for her. Iris rescued an old teak garden-bench Rene had nearly sold to the neighbours. She installed it at Cedar Lodge instead.

11

A 1955 poem about the pain of Iris's frozen friendship with Philippa and Michael Foot – 'Musical Evening for Three' – lamented that 'the structure of the past remains intact'. On 28 April 1959 came 'almost incredible news': Pip and Michael were parting. The past was frozen no longer.

> I had thought of them as so indissolubly connected & somehow of that part of my history concerning them as so completely ended. (How immediately one falls into egoism.) I feel extremely disturbed. M. has apparently fallen in love with his secretary in London . . . & is going to marry her . . . An extraordinary sense of time rolling backward. And honestly a certain sense of relief at the removal of the barrier between P. and me which M. constituted. I wrote at once to P. saying I sent my old love – & she replied quickly saying this meant a lot. How hard it is to *take in* . . . Such a strange sensation . . . of seeing P. as it were *alone.*

Over the next three weeks Iris thought a lot about Philippa, and at once a flurry of letters began. Somehow she '*trusted* P's mind, & knew myself safe in it, even when I thought I wd not ever speak to her frankly again'. Iris sent 'all [my] old love . . . a long time in store but . . . scarcely diminished . . . Losing you, & losing you in that way, was one of the worst things that ever happened to me ... I have thought of you so much in these years & dreamed painfully of you too.' In two remarkable letters Philippa

> could not think of seeing me without being frank, that to 'find' me again meant very much to her ... She spoke here very directly to my heart. I replied that I had not hoped to speak frankly to her again, and I was filled with joy at the prospect. 14 years since I talked openly with P. A strange sense here of reconquering my past. That old desire for 'justification'. Yet not just that, for the main thing is *joy* at the prospect of discovering and loving P again ... My heart founders with concern.

Before they met Iris had anxious dreams. They drank Chianti and, unable to eat lunch, discussed recent events. 'If you want to *leave* someone, the need to do it *ruthlessly*, leaving no place for discussion etc.', Iris reflected. They reminisced about Seaforth, and wept. Philippa too had grieved over losing Iris and had dreamt persistently of seeking her in vain. Iris was torn with love for her '& a terrible inability to speak & manage'. It was, for Iris, 'strange & overwhelming to recover a whole area of one's being one thought was lost'.

> How strong the old structure is of my love for her. In some way, the parting of those two *reopens my own past*. It is as if they, together, closed a door for me, ended a certain piece of my history, & closed the book. Now that they are parting that force is no longer exerted.

In October she wrote to Philippa: 'I'm very glad the future contains you. It makes a lot of difference to that tract.'

12

A quasi-mythical view of Iris's working methods has the new novel gestating for between nine months and a year, a time she would describe as tormented, with a terrifying, dizzy-making sense of myriad possibilities and of floating unrelated fragments, after whose resolution she would announce triumphantly to John, 'I've finished it!' At this point she had blocked out an elaborate scene-by-scene plan detailing each successive conversation and piece of action. All that then remained was the pleasurable part, the mere writing of the novel itself, always longhand with her Mont Blanc fountain pen. John read the novels only once they reached galley form.

Iris's manuscripts show how carefully she planned each fiction.[28] Loose-leaf pages may include elaborate background research, such as notes for young Penn's Australian background in *An Unofficial Rose*, which built her confidence, though little of this 'local colour' appears in the published book. In the dozen or so holograph notebooks that comprised the first draft she would write only on the right-hand page, leaving the left free for later head-girl-like observations, such as '*Curtail this rot!*' when a conversation had gone on too long; '*Make more Kafka-esque*' of Book 2, Chapter 10 of *A Fairly Honourable Defeat*; or, with engagingly painstaking dottiness, considering that that novel is more a romance than a piece of realism, '*Check visibility of Milky Way in Hammersmith*' for *Bruno's Dream* (results of careful research: '*Stars visible in Hammersmith, not Milky Way*'). 'Shax' (Shakespeare) is often invoked. She discovered the anonymous choric part-voices in *An Accidental Man* experimentally, halfway through the second draft. Sometimes she instinctively chose incidents or sense-details, only later worrying about how to motivate and render them plausible. When she is dissatisfied with a passage, she scores it through diagonally and rewrites it on the following pages. Finally she would write out, in a hand clear enough for her typist, a loose-leaf second draft, which might differ in substance as well as in detail from the first.[29] A remark of John's scribbled in the margin of 'Jerusalem' makes clear that she did (if rarely) solicit his help; he also contributed a paragraph on Dora to *The Bell*.[30]

Iris lent currency to the idea that she devised her novels on a deterministic plan, ruthlessly executed. She would accordingly lament lacking the courage at a late stage to take out the central characters and leave only peripheral ones, as if this could open up the book and liberate its characters from her puppet-mastering. In fact she left herself considerable freedom of manoeuvre throughout. She decided halfway through a late draft of *A Word Child* to 'kill off' the Impiatts' twin children, who until then had playfully challenged Hilary Burde to guess the humorous or sinister contents of a box they presented to him on each of his visits. The Impiatts metamorphosed into a 'childless couple full of good works'. There were other false starts. The Lynch-Gibbon family first appear in 'Jerusalem', abandoned in February 1959. From June she put new Lynch-Gibbons into what became *A Severed Head*, with most relationships as we now know them, but set in the west of Ireland in what was later to become the landscape of *The Unicorn*, with peat fires, a bog that periodically floods, and three country houses containing Anglo-Irish neighbours who 'uphold, in a hostile country, their religion and their class'. Palmer is Martin's partner in the wine trade, which has a Dublin office. Georgie is Martin's secretary, a Catholic peasant girl from County Mayo whom he pleasurably beats. Her disreputable land-agent brother Theo blackmails Martin. Alexander 'Fielding', in love with Antonia, is not yet Martin's elder brother. There are Catholic and Protestant priests, a debutante called the Hon. Sybil Aston-Greene, and Honor Klein is an anthropological expert on 'taboo'; Franz's book of that name was posthumously published in 1956. Franz's theme, later picked up by Mary Douglas in *Purity and Danger*, is the relation between what is forbidden and what is sacred. Many characters spend their weekends in the west of Ireland, natural home of the primitive forces Honor studies.

13

On her return from Yale at Christmas 1959, Iris abandoned this as a false start, writing on it 'Never for Publication'. Discarded characters were recycled: Theo recurs as Fivey in *The Nice and the Good*; the biddable maid Kathleen as Adelaide in *Bruno's Dream* and as Patsie in *The Time of the Angels*. During 1960 she compressed the action within a narrow segment of London – Knightsbridge, Chelsea –

with excursions only to Oxfordshire and Cambridge, and told the story dramatically, so that the reader and fall-guy narrator Martin Lynch-Gibbon alike suffer the same appalling narrative surprises together. *A Severed Head* is the best of her intensely stylised Restoration comedies of manners. It took a familiar contemporary theme – the mandarin educated by passion – and made of it something different from Thomas Mann's high aesthetic drama in *Death in Venice* or the nihilistic farce of Nabokov's *Lolita*. Martin Lynch-Gibbon is an intelligent, priggish, forty-one-year-old wine merchant with a frustrated interest in military history which he reads and, a little, writes. John furnished relevant details, and his old school-friend the historian Michael Jaffé was cited by some as one model for Martin, who describes his state of mind at the beginning as one of 'degenerate innocence'. He has stayed in business to support his fashionable, extravagant wife Antonia. Acquaintances sometimes mistake her for his mother. They occupy separate bedrooms.

Martin's younger mistress Georgie Hands now lectures in economics at the LSE, and loves him with so intelligent a restraint that with her he can put himself greatly at ease. Antonia and Georgie are opposites, Antonia a bossy, ageing, predatory society beauty, self-dramatising, frivolous, fascinated by powerful men – which Martin, to her, is not – using her sexual *will* to extend her territory. Just as Antonia takes Martin for granted, so Martin does the same with Georgie, who has had an abortion at his request and whose desire to see New York he has out of cowardice frustrated. Antonia is inside 'society', Georgie 'outside'. Martin plays father (or master) to Georgie, son (or slave) to Antonia.

This analysis of human relations in power-terms reflects what Iris owed to Canetti and Simone Weil alike, those oddly similar thinkers.* Martin fears meeting his sister Rosemary who, divorced herself, has a sharp appetite for news of other failed marriages and may feign a distress that secretly hides a '*glow of excitement and pleasure*' analogous to that '*felt at the death of acquaintance*':

---

* As Susan Sontag pointed out in 'Mind as Passion', *New York Review of Books*, 25 September 1980.

this is pure Canetti (as is Martin's avowal of atheism as he 'cannot imagine an omnipotent sentient being sufficiently cruel to create the world we inhabit',[31] a view Iris on occasion echoed). The novel abounds in emotional *realpolitik*, which also exemplifies Iris's view of Weil: 'Until we become good we are at the mercy of mechanical forces . . . All beings tend to use all the power at their disposal.' Honor, the book's interpreter of totem and taboo, who is indeed only half-human, connects spirit not with love, but with power. The book opposes the polite and the primitive. Power drives the plot as much as love.

14

Iris feared the novel might be 'just a quite private thing which others will regard with surprise or dislike'.[32] Yorick Smythies thought it 'foul'; at some point, too, she quarrelled with Fraenkel about her fiction. It is hard now to recall that her erotic imbroglios and willingness to confront 'incest' were then found pioneering, hence provocative. Reviews were mixed. The *Spectator* thought it her most masterful so far, consigning the earlier novels to juvenilia. Dan Jacobson in the *New Statesman* wrote most perceptively, finding its virtuosity less satisfying than that of *The Bell*, but recognising that Honor is to this novel what the Abbey was to the former, and what Hugo and Fox were to *Under the Net* and *The Flight from the Enchanter* respectively: central images of spiritual power. He admired Iris's simple moral intensity, pointed out that 'simplicity is what only the greatest writers achieve', and singled out for attention the sculptor Alexander's exchange with Martin, who speaks first:

> 'I envy you,' I said. 'You have a technique for discovering more about what is real.'
> 'So have you,' said Alexander. 'It is called morality.'

In the *Observer* Philip Toynbee, deeply uneasy about Iris's talent – he had priggishly found the pub-crawl in *Under the Net* 'deplorable' – found *A Severed Head* both immensely readable and

435

preposterous. He wholly missed that the book is, as others saw, 'almost unbearably funny'.[33] Iris's worst novels are indeed sentimental melodramas written in high diction. But to miss the comedy in the best is to miss not a detail, but their heart. Small wonder that Toynbee was reminded of the worst of Charles Morgan's self-indulgent affectation, and chivalrously hoped her later novels might improve. The *TLS* found all the characters except Georgie dislikeable, noting, as did Rebecca West later, that this 'brilliantly enjoyable' book resembled Congreve's comedy *The Way of the World,* but ended with the 'familiar feeling' after reading Murdoch that there is some 'central, large, and simple meaning which one has, somehow, just missed'. And Barbara Everett in the *Critical Quarterly,* sympathetic to Iris's contention that reality could be precisely apprehended by giving up selfish illusion, thought the novels so far progressively illuminated this, while wondering whether this highly stylised novel had not so fully achieved her purposes that it was hard to see 'how she could effect any further, new crystallisation'. A prophecy other critics would soon endorse.[34]

16

Island of Spells
1961–1965

Over a family Christmas in 1962 at Nettlepole in Kent, after John's mother had cheerfully asked, 'What's all this about Felix Meecham [in *An Unofficial Rose*] and Michael?' Iris, at once white and silent with anger, was later discovered upstairs in her room, upset. Drawing from life was taboo. Although she argued that people were generally far odder than they admitted to their psychotherapists, and that the novelist's task was to 'reveal the secret' of this oddness, these were 'imaginary secrets', not real ones. Iris had written to Michael Bayley, then stationed in Singapore, while composing *An Unofficial Rose*, seeking advice over the question of how and when Felix might, as an Intelligence Officer in the Far East, have learnt French; Michael replied that he would have had prior knowledge of French to be so employed in the first place. She had similarly enlisted help from her St Anne's colleague the historian Marjorie Reeves over medieval bells for *The Bell*, researched wine merchants with Rudi Nassauer's help for *A Severed Head*, and would request help about woodcuts and engraving from Reynolds Stone for *The Italian Girl*[1] and about the Treasury (where he was Under-Secretary from 1967) and (later) Jewishness from Leo Pliatzky for *A Fairly Honourable Defeat*: 'Don't forget yr homewk. I want a) brief description of desk & in-tray covering coloured folders &tc b) one or two topics, names of committees – these cd be fictitious as long as plausible.'[2] 'I am practically a Jew myself,' she wrote to him enthusiastically in 1977.

Both Michael Bayley and Felix Meecham, however, were

solitary bachelor career soldiers – Michael rising to be Brigadier. The physical description of Felix reminded one family friend of Michael, who disliked Felix as a 'stuffed shirt'. Others later thought the very different Polish 'Count' in *Nuns and Soldiers* recalled Michael. Felix and the Count differ widely, by nationality and temperament, which might suggest that, where Iris borrowed, it was 'situational logic' that she took, not 'character' as such. Asa Briggs believed that while Iris never copied people, reshaping life into art instead, she nevertheless never dreamt people up entirely either. The novelist, she wrote, is one who stores up and treasures particulars. Like many novelists, she might put 'bits' of friends' lives or stories to work. Humphrey's career in *An Unofficial Rose* is based on that of Sir Owen O'Malley,[3] a slight acquaintance of the Bayleys who lived in Oxford from December 1958 with his wife the popular novelist Ann Bridge;[4] like Humphrey, he had been 'drummed out of the diplomatic' for an indiscretion. Nor was Iris's own life immune to plunder. Behind both Honor Klein's unexpected return to marry Martin at the end of *A Severed Head*, and also Lisa's equally surprising return – through a window – to marry Danby towards the end of *Bruno's Dream*, lay that precipitate 1956 journal comment: 'August 14. Married John.' Julius and Tallis's struggle for Morgan's soul in *A Fairly Honourable Defeat*, moreover, mirrors Canetti and John's two-year struggle for hers.

Dogs were fair game.* So were 'details', which she collected, as Eric Christiansen, John's colleague at New College, recalled:

> When told that A had thrown her drink at B and had then bitten C in the leg, she asked
> – Now . . . at what point exactly did she say those words 'I have been wanting to do this for a very long time?' After the wine was thrown? Or it wouldn't have been a surprise, and she might have missed. Would she not have said 'do *that*', rather than '*this*', if the action were completed?

---

* Tadg in *The Unicorn* was the Griggs' golden labrador Crumpet; the papillon Zed in *The Philosopher's Pupil* was based on Diana Avebury's three-legged, shrill-barking Zelda; Anax in *The Green Knight* on my and my partner Jim O'Neill's blue merle collie Cloudy.

– Possibly. But it was after. I know it wasn't during.
– Look here, this is not by any chance fiction is it?

But Iris stoutly maintained that she never drew her characters from life, a practice she held morally abhorrent – 'bad form' – which would inhibit her. When friends saw themselves in her books, she said, this was generally 'vanity' on their part.[5]

Since Iris did acknowledge Hugo in *Under the Net* as a portrait of Yorick Smythies, this is not the whole story. The architectural critic Stephen Gardiner, a friend from 1965, believed she made another exception to her rule when he inspired Danby in *Bruno's Dream*, whom she told him was her 'one happy character'. When Philippa Foot, dedicatee of *The Red and the Green*, identified the opposition therein between hidebound Andrew and the wilder Pat as reflecting a contrast between her ex-husband Michael and Frank Thompson, Iris replied (though the real Frank was unlike Pat Dumay) that no one else understood either her, *or* her books, better than Philippa. She also put an unmistakable portrait of her and Philippa's friendship into *The Nice and the Good*. Perhaps the sin against the Holy Ghost was to use fiction – like Dostoevsky brutally parodying Turgenev as Karmazinov in *The Devils* – for purposes of hatred or revenge. 'To touch another person's past,' a journal entry proposes, of a novelist-friend who had written a *roman-à-clef*, 'is sacrilege ... The attempt to circumscribe another person in this way inspires *hatred*.' Hers, by contrast, were 'characters of love'.

She did have cause for concern. No fewer than four people – Lord David Cecil, BMB, J.B. Priestley and Elizabeth Bowen – were separately offended by the old man in *Bruno's Dream*, the differences of sex and condition between them suggesting that Iris had 'universalised' the condition of old age quite successfully. Of the four, BMB was 'the most sporting'. Resemblances between the plot of *The Sacred and Profane Love Machine* and her own life offended Rebecca West, whom Iris scarcely knew. West, after a coldness at one or two parties for which Iris could not account, wrote saying that, from what she had recently learnt of Iris, she now doubted whether Iris had copied West's life. Iris's reply,

hoping to be acquitted from 'any such rotten act'[6] – one she
called unkind and disgraceful – secured a friendly conclusion to
the *contretemps*. (Among the novelists in whose work West 'recognised' her life were, unbeknownst to Iris, Wyndham Lewis, Hugh
Walpole, Storm Jameson, Muriel Spark, H.G. Wells, and one
Phyllis Paul.[7]) More seriously, her already fragile friendship with
Donald MacKinnon was dealt a death-blow when he believed he
had been treated satirically as Barnabas Drumm in *The Red and
the Green*, a characterisation in which she 'nails' the mixture of
sexuality, religion and neurotic guilt which was arguably his least
helpful legacy. Iris, reporting herself 'sickened' and 'stunned',
denied the imputation with fury and distress:

> I had not even thought of Donald in connection with
> Barney, except for there being one *Tenebrae* quotation
> which B used which D used too . . . if anything Barney
> is a picture of myself. How long these threads of responsi-
> bility stretch. Oh God . . . But I am so sorry for D & sorry
> he has been hurt, & of course human frailty . . . lies
> behind the whole *extraordinary* tangle.

Others 'recognised' and were offended by this characterisation.
Barney is one of Iris's gentle Dostoevskian holy fools as well as a
whiskey-drenched self-deceiving seeker and failed priest;
unhappily married, he acts as servile dog to the vamp-like Millie,
whom he adores but will never gain. That Barney's wife Kathleen
is one of her 'saintly' characters, while in real life Lois MacKinnon
and Iris were not friends, does not rule out the uncomfortable
possibility that she had drawn an unconscious portrait – leading to
an 'open season' for identifications. (Iris was not forgiven; she
never learned that in 1992, two years before his death, MacKinnon
denounced her to the effect that 'there was real evil there' at a semi-
formal dinner to celebrate London University's award to him of an
honorary doctorate. Nor did the row of 1965 prevent her in 1983
creating Rozanov in *The Philosopher's Pupil*, who reminded others[8]
of the magisterial and menacing aspects of MacKinnon.)

When Victoria Glendinning asked Iris whether Hannah in *The
Unicorn* was based on Lady Ursula Vernon, Iris fiercely replied

that of course she was *not*. People refused to believe, she added, in the independent powers of imagination. To attest that power, she cited the way the Drumm marriage was said (by others) to be based on Elizabeth Bowen's to Alan Cameron. But the fictional marriage was celibate. How, Iris asked, could she, who never witnessed Bowen's marriage, possibly have made any assumption about it? (Quite recently a letter came to light showing that Bowen's marriage was indeed celibate. Iris retained a child's prescient ability to access her own unconscious intuition, together with an adult's willingness to deny it.[9])

To warn the American biographer Jeffrey Meyers off trying to trace them back to life, Iris wrote disingenuously that *all* her characters were aspects of herself, 'which I suppose is rather boring'. In fact she hoped to absent herself from her novels too. To Harold Hobson she said in 1962 that of her novels she liked *The Flight from the Enchanter* and *A Severed Head* best because they were 'myths more organically connected with myself. They are full of me. They are for that reason less good.'[10] Her essays warn against the lesser value of fictions presenting 'puppets in the exteriorisation of some closely locked psychological conflict' in the author's mind.[11] Art is not the expression of personality, it is a question rather of 'the continual expelling of oneself from the matter in hand', and Romantic writers externalising 'a personal conflict in a tightly conceived self-contained myth' are producing inferior art.[12] Yet her identifying her characters as 'imaginary siblings' does suggest a relationship with the author, a quasi-genetic one. Her characters were company to her, like family; the novel finished, it was as if they had gone to Australia.[13] Her novels' capacity to wound friends, to be written 'close to the knuckle', however involuntarily, might be taken as a sign, for all their famous stylisation and contrivance, of their *general* truthfulness to life, regardless of whether Iris acknowledged (or recalled) where their inspiration came from; just as her general readers 'recognised' themselves and so came back for more. That her later characters are sometimes harder to trace back to real-life models might also connect with the fact that her last books are not always her strongest.

Even when a character or situation can be traced back to one in 'real life', this does not necessarily illuminate the book. The knowledge that Anna Quentin is based on a persona of herself that Iris wished to outgrow does not radically shift our original view of Anna; that Hugo is a portrait of Yorick Smythies may influence how we read *Under the Net*'s idea-play, but not how we read its fantastic invention, humour, witty observation, or love-plot. 'No libel difficulties cd possibly arise,' Iris assured Viking.[14] The understanding that Mischa Fox is based on Canetti, by con-trast, does redirect our attention to a darker Fox exercising power not always benignly.[15] And Canetti's influence both on and within the novels merits discussion. That he arguably helped inspire characters as different from one another as Fox, Julius King and Charles Arrowby,* as Franz Steiner helped inspire the equally different Peter Saward, Willy Kost and Tallis Browne,† underlines the truism that there can be no exact congruence between real life and fiction.

Iris, during her 1982 Gifford lectures, echoed Canetti in main-taining that 'true writers encounter their characters *after* they've created them'.[16] Exactly this happened after she had created Anne Cavidge in *Nuns and Soldiers*, then met Marjorie Locke (Sister Ann Teresa), who had left the Anglican-Augustinian convent of St Mary's, Wantage, after fifteen years there, rather as Cavidge left *her* convent.[17] Locke, unlike Cavidge, never lost her faith, but like Cavidge, found her Abbess difficult, and recognised the accuracy of Iris's description of arriving bravely back in the world without friends or knowhow, like an ex-prisoner. She and Iris exchanged many hundreds of letters.[18]

John Bayley believed Iris's characters could not be traced back to life for two different reasons: because the raising of the imagin-ative temperature is so intense and transformative; and because of the way that after 1960 she elevates her characters involuntarily – and comically – to so high a social pitch.

---

* In *The Flight from the Enchanter, A Fairly Honourable Defeat* and *The Sea, The Sea.*
† In, respectively, *The Flight from the Enchanter, The Nice and the Good* and *A Fairly Honourable Defeat.*

2

The social range of the first four novels had been unremarkable: bohemians and refugees in the first two, schoolmasters in *The Sandcastle*, motley seekers in *The Bell*. With *A Severed Head* there is a marked shift upwards, into what Angus Wilson irritably termed 'expenses-sheet pseudo-elegance', while the 'civilised sensitiveness' of its successor, *An Unofficial Rose*, struck him as false. Unlike Virginia Woolf's, none of Murdoch's characters regards their 'way of living in its social, economic sense with any questioning whatever ... [they] approach such things as the Boulestin Restaurant or a chateau-bottled wine with an awe ... which suggests that their creator is not entirely at ease in her chosen environment'.[19]

Wilson missed the point that Iris's naming of *A Severed Head*'s wines after roses suggested ironic distance; since he had published in 1958 a novel centring, like *An Unofficial Rose*, on a nursery,* rivalry may underlie his criticisms, which miss the point of that book's title. This refers not to the 'snobbish distinction between shrub and hybrid tea roses', but to Rupert Brooke contrasting in 'Grantchester' the officious gardens of Wilhelmine Berlin with the wild 'unofficial' dog-rose that blows about 'an English hedge'. The opposition is echoed between the forceful and mediocre artist Randall Peronett and his good, 'formless' wife Anne, with whom he stage-manages a public row to gain a pretext to leave her. What is most alive here is the believable weakness of the men and the different power of women-characters, the witch-like half lesbian Emma Sands, her lover Lindsay, the pert and obsessed Miranda, the 'deadness' of the good Anne, and the battle of wills between these. The snobbery Wilson detects in Murdoch can be a thoroughly useful vice for a novelist to investigate: we no longer blame James, Proust, Compton-Burnett, Waugh or Muriel Spark for evoking social worlds which delight or appal them because

* *The Middle Age of Mrs Eliot.*

they were stylishly strange to their own authors. And Iris, like Elizabeth Bowen, saw England itself with foreign eyes.*

In August 1963 the dying Louis MacNeice, offered anything he wanted, asked for a novel of Iris's.[20] Although her sales in the 1960s did not suffer – British hardback sales were in excess of 20,000 for all her novels of that decade[21] – and even her slightest fiction from that time has something of interest, the sixties did not, as critics noted, produce her best work. The decade bridges the brio of her early novels, in which she spreads her wings and tries out disparate novel-forms, and her maturity in the 1970s.

Angus Wilson accurately saw that Iris was now neo-Jamesian. James, she said, was 'a pattern man too'. One point of the 'high' social world in *A Severed Head* was precisely to contrast the 'primal' appetites and impulses (violence/incest) that are unmasked within it. But Wilson was also right to think Iris had private investment in claiming such worlds. It is noteworthy that, following the death of her father, an identification with the old ruling order in Ireland gets into her fiction. She, John and Rene travelled to Ireland in summer 1958 and 1959, making their pilgrimage to Drum Manor. Martin Lynch-Gibbon in *A Severed Head* is Anglo-Irish on his father's side; Grayhallock in *An Unofficial Rose*, whence the Peronetts acquired their eighteenth-century linen wealth, recalls the name of one house from which the Richardsons stemmed. *The Unicorn* is set in a fictionalised County Clare; while the plot may borrow from Lady Ursula Vernon, the names of characters, like many from *The Red and the Green*, stem from Rene's family. Given the modesty of Iris's background, this was seen by some as solipsistic fantasising.[22] A running joke about upwardly mobile women links a number of the novels, from Madge Casement in *Under the Net* to Pinn in *The Sacred and Profane Love Machine*, 'socially speaking, in fairly rapid motion'. If Iris mythologised her background, Shakespeare too had fantasies about gentility. When in the 1970s, at a party of Anne Wignall's (a friend they had met through David Cecil), Iris mischievously initiated a

---

* Even her anglophilia, it could be argued, has an outsider's passion, as in the references in *Jackson's Dilemma* to 'the beauty and nobility of [England's] history'.

conversation about what social class the guests, who included Olivia Manning and J.G. Farrell, thought they belonged to – they boasted of being lower-middle class – she alone vouchsafed no reply.[23] Most of her first-person narrators, from Jake in *Under the Net* to Charles in *The Sea, The Sea*, are from poor backgrounds. A number of her 'saints' are from rich ones – Old Etonian Bledyard in *The Sandcastle*, Wykehamist James in *The Sea, The Sea*.

3

Despite finding the teetotal existence of her Belfast relatives hard going, Iris was fond of these cousins, and gave introductions to them to friends such as Asa Briggs, who met the Chapman cousins in Belfast. Julian Chrysostomides met both Eva and Billy Lee, manager from 1955 of the Dargle and Bray laundry, and the Harold Murdochs with their two prosperous hardware shops in Dun Laoghaire. Iris took care in Ireland to visit family. Attending with Philip Larkin in 1965 a celebration for Maurice Bowra at Queen's University, the Bayleys visited her Chapman cousins. When John gave a talk on Pushkin at Clandeboye House in 1980, Cleaver, Muriel and Sybil came, John borrowing his hostess Lady Dufferin's car so that Iris could visit her Aunt Ella. When Iris was awarded honorary doctorates at Queen's University Belfast in 1977, at Trinity College, Dublin in 1985 and at Coleraine University in 1993, cousins and connexions were invited, as they were to Steeple Aston and to the London flat. As late as 1964 she maintained crossly and implausibly that she had an Irish accent 'you could cut with a knife ... I may have misleading Oxford overtones – but the vowels are Irish.'[24]

She was capable of portraying a Dublin closer to that of her own childhood, especially that of her Bell first cousins, with whom she was rarely in touch.* Probably after her return from Glengariff

---

* Although during lean times in the 1960s Iris would, if alerted, send a generous and welcome gift, Victor's widow Connie recalls meeting her only once; while Rose, widow of Iris's youngest Bell cousin, and Iris never met.

in 1954, when she recorded childhood memories of 'the post-cards in Aunt Noonie's shop with sentimental "I wish cap-tions"',[25] she wrote the short story 'Something Special',[26] about young Yvonne Geary who lives in her working-class Protestant mother's Dun Laoghaire stationer's shop on Upper George's Street; Iris's closest Dublin connexion Eva Robinson (later, Lee) lived with her foster-mother Mrs Walton in the latter's newspaper shop on Upper George's Street. 'Yvonne' resembles 'Eva', and the paternity of both is mysterious. The Anglican Mariner's Church where Mrs Walton and Eva attended Revivalist meetings run by the 'Crusaders' makes an appearance, as do the rocks on Dun Laoghaire beach where young Iris and Eva sat during sum-mer holidays.[27] Iris distinctly downgraded Eva socially;[28] young Yvonne Geary shares a bed with her shop-owner mother. She is courted by a tender-hearted Jewish tailor's assistant, Sam Gold-man, whose religion is no impediment. Sam would 'bring the children up Church of Ireland', says Yvonne's mother. 'It's better than the other lot with the little priest after them the whole time and bobbing their hats at the chapel doors so you can't even have a peaceful ride on the tram.'

The title, 'Something Special', refers to Yvonne's fantasy of escape from poverty, and is repeated in the Christmas card she finds glamorous but her mother declines to order; in the diamond ring her mother feels confident Sam will tempt her with; in the surreal treat Sam procures for her after they visit a louche downstairs bar, Kimballs, where they witness a near-brawl. Sam takes Yvonne to see a huge fallen tree on St Stephen's Green, which he finds poetic and she confusing. After running away she announces that they will marry. 'And why, may I ask, did your Majesty decide it just tonight?' asks her mother. 'For nothing,' she replies before a night of tears, 'for nothing, for nothing.' 'The long night was ahead,' the story ends. 'Something Special' recalls Joyce in its detailed, detached naturalism, but its lyrical unexpectedness is pure Murdoch. Yvonne has her author's capricious longing to surrender yet remain independent. 'How absurdly his small feet turned out as he stood there' may recall Iris's view of her future husband's feet. Iris's ambivalence about marriage in 1955 helps fuel Yvonne's conflicting emotions.

Eva Robinson, born in 1912, would have reached Yvonne's age in 1936, when her foster-mother Mrs Walton had moved from stationer to owner and manager of the nursing home at 16 Mellifont Avenue. The newsagent's recurs in Iris's work: Bradley Pearson in *The Black Prince*, born in a paper-shop, fantasises that he slept under the counter. Eva's fate differed from Yvonne's. She worked in 1936 as secretary to Jacob's Biscuits advertising manager – the factory was an insurrectionary redoubt during the 1916 Rising – and married a fellow-Anglican, Billy Lee, in 1941. Together they took in the elderly Mrs Walton, and Iris's grandmother Elizabeth Jane ('Bessie') Richardson, until their deaths.[29] Planning a visit to Dublin in summer 1945, where she would soon be godmother to the second of Eva's four sons, Arnold, Iris noted, in a reprise of Yeats,[30] that she now felt not of any particular country: 'There's Ireland, there's England – but if I have a fatherland, it would be something like the literature of England perhaps.' She described Ireland as 'island of spells, provincial pigsty. ("Little brittle magic nation dim of mind"; Joyce, of course).'[31]

Iris was proud, in October 1964, to be the first woman ever to address the 'illustrious' Philosophical Society at Trinity College, Dublin, her topic 'Job: Prophet of Modern Nihilism'. She was interested to find how strongly she felt against Job and pro God, though finding God's reply to Job questioning his sufferings magnificently irrelevant. The straight answer was: 'You suffer, you are good. So what?'[32] 'It was odd and very moving to be thus feted in my native city.'[33] Dublin looked beautiful in a slight mist. She finished her Irish novel *The Red and the Green* the week she returned to Steeple Aston.

4

Iris saw Ireland in the 1950s as 'something of a dream country where everything happens with a difference'.[34] The first draft of *A Severed Head* was set in the west of Ireland, the region Joyce's Gabriel Conroy in 'The Dead' was bitterly rebuked for not visiting;

where the young Yeats projected magic; and whose myth-like primitiveness Synge mapped in *The Aran Islands.* County Clare inspires *The Unicorn*: the Scarren with its carnivorous plants stands in for the Burren, the great cliffs are based on those of Moher. Its gentry may owe their whiskey to the worlds of Honor Tracy in Mayo or of Bowen in Cork, but their names are from Iris's family. Effingham Cooper takes his first name from Iris's grandfather, and 'Cooper' from *his* father. Denis Nolan's surname is that of Iris's grandmother Bessie and her sister, Eva's grandmother Anna Nolan.[35] But this is not a real, but a fantastical fairytale Gothic world, with a Platonic topography, a bog that floods at seven-year intervals, an ocean that kills, a megalith 'seemingly pointless yet dreadfully significant' and an imprisoned heroine out of a fairy-tale.

It has living sources too. Neighbours of Lady Ursula Vernon at 'Fairyfield', Kinsale, County Cork, saw striking parallels with the rotting house running on whiskey; her increasingly paralysed husband Stephen had a handsome valet, Gerard, who behaved like an adopted son and was widely supposed to be Stephen's lover. Kinsale opinion accepted quite easily that the Vernons had 'separate arrangements'. Stephen became more and more dependent on Gerard, upon whom he 'doted', and though Gerard married and had a family and lived in the gate lodge, when Stephen died Gerard inherited the house.[36] Another *donnée*, well-known in the west, and a stock Irish-Gothic reference, was the thirty-year imprisonment in the eighteenth century of the wife of Robert Bellfield, later first Earl of Belvedere, allowed to see only servants as her great beauty decayed. She had either committed adultery with her husband's brother or was bullied into a false confession by her husband in 1742. She had at first a good wardrobe and plenty of servants, but though a carriage was kept for her use, she was never allowed to pass the boundaries of the Park. After, like Hannah, an attempt to escape, she was confined to her room. She emerged only on her husband's death in 1772, broken, white-haired, unearthly. Contemporary commentators like Mrs Delany took the view that all this was a reasonable enough punishment, considering the provocation.[37]

448

'People can't just be shut up. We're not living in the Middle Ages.' 'We are here,' runs one exchange in the novel.[38] Iris advised Chatto against mentioning Ireland in any pre-publicity or jacket-blurb (as it is never named in Henry Green's *Loving*). We are being invited outside society, the better to understand the forces – love and power – that govern it.[39] 'Such a swift passage; such an appalling mystery,' Pip Lejour observes when he catches and kills a trout, while readers are invited to apprehend human existence as analogously fragile and mysterious. To say that Ireland seems here Iris's chosen 'spiritual home' – and not, as Tracy liked to observe, her physical or material home – is not an idle metaphor.

A moment of earned shock, classically Murdochian, comes when we learn that Hannah's gaoler Gerald Scottow regularly visits *inter alia* Marrakesh – a private resonance. Iris wrote on 27 January 1953: 'What a joke if C[anetti] is in Marrakesh all this time, while I am writing letters to him every other day.' All her power-figures somewhere echo Canetti. The frisson comes also from the contrast between the brooding, inward-looking, 'timeless' intensity the novel has created, and an aspect of modernity whose co-existence with this we are forced to acknowledge. Flying between County Clare and Marrakesh, or even New York, where Hannah's husband courts his beautiful male painter-lover, in 1962 was feasible: Shannon international airport had opened. On watching an aeroplane descend, Effingham thinks, 'There was life, indifferent life, beautiful life going forward.'[40]

The Bayleys famously had no television. The last musical they saw was *Salad Days* in 1956; the last film *The French Connection* in 1972. Yet William Golding praised Iris, especially in 1973 with *The Black Prince*, for achieving what he found hard: locating her work believably in the twentieth century. His testimony that her novels possess actuality is valuable. She colonised the century and gave it back to us as myth. She does this best in the 1970s, but the formula of psychological-myth versus modernity recurs throughout. Sometimes an aspect of the twentieth-century world is inserted, as it were within inverted commas, into the mythology. In *Under the Net* the cold-cure centre, Sadie's smart hairdressing shop, the Hammersmith theatre. In *An Unofficial Rose* and *A Fairly Honourable Defeat* alike, sinister telephones, and in *The Sacred and Profane Love Machine* a tape-recorder playing the voice of dead Sophie, have disturbing roles. In *The Nice and the Good* the waste-disposal unit in which Kate Gray's glove gets caught has its own '*mana*'; so does a disused railway line in *A Fairly Honourable Defeat*.[41] In *The Good Apprentice* a hot-air balloon is sighted from claustrophobic Seegard. In *The Green Knight* the 'solution' to Joan Blacket's intercontinental marriage problem is a fax machine. Such emblematically selected features of modernity seem as poetically mysterious as the 'mythical' intensity they enliven and contradict.

5

'My novels are too full of thought,' Iris had bitterly lamented to David Hicks in 1945; thought, as is well known, being something the British are not at ease with. David Pears had a long conversation with Iris about her developing Platonism at a St Anne's dinner. They spoke of Plato's myth of the Cave and the Sun (see Chapter 17), which she was coming to see as the central image of man's pilgrimage away from egoistic blindness towards the Good; and discussed the old medieval ontological argument about God's existence, which Iris maintained should now be re-invented for Good, not God. She announced that she would write a novel about these matters, accordingly dedicating *The Unicorn* to Pears. Teaching at Berkeley in 1964, he asked friends to explain the book. He was not alone in finding it obscure.*

Iris wanted a secular religion: *The Unicorn* concerns her theme that life is – or should be – a spiritual quest or pilgrimage. She projects herself into the heroine Hannah Crean-Smith, imprisoned for seven years in Gaze Castle by her husband for

---

* Ivy Compton-Burnett remarked (undated) of Iris to Francis King, 'I do wish that she had not got involved in philosophy. If she had studied domestic science or trained to be a Norland nurse, I'm sure her books would have been much better' (Francis King, *Yesterday Came Suddenly*, p.227).

450

her infidelity and violence, and now attempting to 'purify' her suffering, a woman 'much given to looking at herself in mirrors'.[42] Iris ridiculed the famous critic who noticed that Crean-Smith is an anagram of 'Christ-Name' or 'Christ-Mean'.[43] Critical books about Iris have not lacked in high-mindedness, as titles such as *Fables of Unselfing, Work for the Spirit* and *Figures of Good* make clear. They perhaps take too literally that Iris who, of the cast of characters making up *The Bell*, identified 'a little' with the Abbess, the voice of wise counsel itself. In her journals, by contrast, she often charges herself with the twin vices of vanity and 'silliness', recalling, for all her formidable powers of intellect and imagination, *The Bell*'s attractive, emotionally muddled, silly Dora, bad-mouthed by James as a 'bitch'. It is almost certainly because readers sense this Dora-Iris that they accept the Abbess-Iris too, without feeling that the author is, as George Eliot now sometimes reads, a conceited, governessy, talking head.

The ambiguities of Hannah, part-wise, part-silly, part-seeker, part-vamp, fuel the novel, which is again structured round a court. Where Hugo was the unconscious good centre of the court in *Under the Net*, Mischa the bad centre in *Flight*, Hannah is centre of another cult. Her gaolers are her worshippers, and she has the same mysterious ability to compel love from both sexes that Iris herself evinced, and which made, in June 1940, Paddy O'Regan's present of C.S. Lewis's *The Allegory of Love* an appropriately emblematic gift. It is not Iris's gentility that matters within Hannah so much as what she in 1952 termed 'my slightly sinister ambiguous religious vein', recalled both by the tarot card known as 'La Papessa'[44] and by her realisation, around 1949, that 'all that for me lights up & gives grace to my attachments to people' – she lists 'generosity, gentleness, douceur, tendresse' – are 'dangerous' (her word) 'especially in their *corrupted form* in me' (my emphasis). The temptation to see Hannah as a saint is given pause when she early 'nuzzles' her hand into Denis's pocket while he cuts her hair. Hannah is given Iris's habit of bursting into tears on hearing music;[45] given, also, a wounded bat whose strange little doggy face disturbs Marian Taylor. Iris and John (who cut her hair, making it look chewed) discovered the bat while she was writing the first draft in August 1961: 'A sick bat we nursed today I found dead. While it was crawling around it looked up at me and our eyes met – an odd sense of communion. If stroked, it opened its mouth and squeaked, shewing sharp little teeth.' Hannah feels a strange affinity with the bat held in a box, like her, a prisoner. The word 'vamp' derives from 'vampire'; the bat is Hannah's kin.

'How mysterious day and night are, this endless procession of dark and light . . . I think such sad thoughts – of people in trouble and afraid, all lonely people, all prisoners,'[46] Hannah announces. Such urges towards sympathy and rescue figured with an analogous sinister poetry in *The Flight from the Enchanter,* where Mischa felt such intolerable compassion – 'a sort of nausea' – for creature-kind that he had as a child killed small animals, including a kitten. The Iris who was unable to have a home-help or secretary though well able to afford them, because 'you end up running their private lives and doing everything for them',[47] lies behind such creepy moments as much as Canetti. She was always susceptible to the twin sentiments of protective anxiety and desire to rescue. 'May I not harm so-and-so' is no accidental journal-refrain. Fox drowning a pitiable kitten is echoed by Monty in *The Sacred and Profane Love Machine* strangling his hostile wife Sophie, dying of cancer, because of a tormented 'wild awful pity' for her suffering.[48] Among the most memorable moments in Iris's novels are attempts to free birds, animals, fish: Jake and Finn releasing the dog Mr Mars; Dora rescuing a butterfly and forgetting Paul's valise; Morgan's frantic surreal attempts to liberate a pigeon from Piccadilly Circus Underground station's escalator; Gabriel's purchase of a live fish[49] (based on a real fish Iris bribed children to release while staying with the Griggs in Spain in 1974). Such animals recall her trapped women: Annette in the cupboard; Hannah in her demesne; Hartley in Charles's inner room.

Iris's journals have their own rescue-sagas, some quixotic. Carolyn Ste Croix, daughter of Iris's friend the ancient historian Geoffrey Ste Croix, had been a St Anne's student and was a friend.[50] Her suicide, a carefully planned operation on 31 January 1964, was not discovered until 9 February, and Iris spoke memorably, unscripted at her graveside. Iris saw Carolyn as 'slim, pretty, beautifully dressed'[51] – others as small, mousy, bespectacled, with an unsatisfactory relationship with an amiable Turk whom she called 'my wog'. Iris had taken her to Paris to try to cheer her up in April 1957, and got her a job as temporary research assistant to J. B. Priestley. In August 1963 Carolyn stayed the weekend at Cedar Lodge, 'very gloomy and suicidal, worse than ever. She has dyed her hair gold and now has a sort of pale doomed look ... my love for her is too feeble, it struggles to reach her but is soon tired.'

One false alarm occurred when Iris in a panic rang up 'about a dozen people in Cambridge' and had the police break into Carolyn's house using a ladder. Carolyn was out at a cinema. Following this she had promised Iris that '"Suicide is out" ... in that curiously cheerful way she had. I ought not to have believed her, ought to have organized people to watch her, ought to have gone to see her *often*, loved her better. But I did love her and am so appalled and wretched now, and so terribly sad and full of regrets.' Carolyn kept fifty of Iris's and John's many letters and cards to her, in a gold gift-box, during her long depression. Suicides in Iris's fiction are usually caused by the sheer inattention of those surrounding the stricken one. When John defended Carolyn's right to take her life, suggesting that it was the right course for her, Iris was coldly angry. She reproached herself bitterly for not having 'taken charge' more, wished she had introduced Carolyn and Donald MacKinnon, who sent a priest to the funeral to say, 'Professor MacKinnon knew about Carolyn. He said he thought you'd be here today.' Iris noted: 'She cd have been saved by love, a great deal of love, whatever the psychiatrists could or couldn't manage – I feel sick and stifled with misery about this.' 'One could,' she wrote to a friend, 'be damned for such failures.'[52] Later, she thought her sense of guilty responsibility a form of vanity: 'Some people just *cannot* cope with life "manfully". This is hard for the healthy ones to understand.'[53]

6

The Unicorn, like so much of Iris's fiction, concerns itself with the nature of 'goodness' in a post-Christian age. Its apparatus borrows from Simone Weil's view of Plato. Chapter 12 is the heart of the idea-play. Max Lejour, observer of Hannah's drama from Riders – named after the good and bad horses who compete for government of the soul in the *Phaedrus* – is based on Fraenkel, who lamented to Iris his lack of wisdom in 1952. Max too says he has 'never done a hand's turn' in practical morality. Like Fraenkel he sings to a plainsong chant of his own the Chorus from Aeschylus' *Agamemnon*: 'Zeus, who leads men into the ways of understanding, has established the rule that we must learn by suffering. As sad care, with memories of pain, comes dropping upon the heart in sleep, so even against our will does wisdom come upon us.' He says to Effingham:

> Recall the idea of Até which was so real to the Greeks. Até is the name of the almost automatic transfer of suffering. Power is a form of Até. The victims of power, and any power has its victims, are themselves infected. They have then to pass it on, to use power on others. This is evil, and the crude image of the all-powerful God is a sacrilege. Good is not completely powerless. For to be powerless, to be a complete victim, may be another source of power. But Good is non-powerful. And it is in the good that Até is finally quenched, when it encounters a pure being who only suffers and does not attempt to pass the suffering on.

Most critics rightly decode this poetically dense passage through Weil's Aeschylean ideas on 'affliction', which degrades all but the good person – and 'good' to Weil does not mean what we normally mean by it, but approximates to saintliness. Whether Hannah is such a being or not is one topic of *The Unicorn*. Canetti is here too. In 1953 he spoke to Iris about giving orders: 'How every order leaves a *stachel* [thorn, barb or sting] in the spirit, of the exact form of that order; how the primitive form of the

order is the roar of the hunting beast that makes others flee. . . .
He said of religions – the great religions represent this hier-
archical need for orders. Of Christianity: its centre – apart from
the question of resurrection – is the transformation of the
hunting pack into the wailing pack – the pack that laments the
loss of one of its number. We are all of us both hunters and
tormenters.'

Such ideas had in 1962 been published in Canetti's *Crowds
and Power*, to which Iris gave one of only two favourable
reviews.[54] The provocative idea of victim-guilt was topical in 1963,
the year of Hannah Arendt's *Eichmann in Jerusalem*, with its
scandalous implication of Arendt's fellow-Jews in their own
sufferings.

7

Iris completed the final draft of *The Unicorn* in 1962, convinced
it was 'no good, a nightmarish claustrophobic little book'.[55]
Indeed, there is too much plot, too little comedy: it remains
more interesting than it is good. The progressive revelation that
what rules the stylish world, once more, is sexual slavery, is
formulaic. No one but Denis is free of the chain of sexual power-
and-victimhood. Such freedom, for Iris, would resemble being
free from the chain of Buddhist karma, the good man alone
being neither bully nor victim.* The book's real power and
fascination lie in its poetry, its evocations of place and person
and time of day. The Hymn to Zeus from Aeschylus' *Agamemnon*
which Max sings, in Iris's own translation, contributes to the
elegiac mood, as does '*Le vent se lève. Il faut tenter de vivre*'† from
Valéry's '*Cimetière Marin*' (a favourite poem, alluded to in three
novels[56]), and Landor's *Imaginary Conversations* yields an un-

---

* Mischa Fox killed the little animals he pitied; Iris, who often spoke of how she
'loved' all her characters, sometimes 'coerced' those characters, like Mischa's little
animals, in patterns that she, not they, have willed. Thus, too, her plots chastise the
characters she cherishes.
† 'The wind is rising; we must attempt the task of living.'

ascribed, edited quotation on the last page: 'There are no voices that are not soon mute, there is no name, with whatever emphasis of passionate love repeated, of which the echoes are not faint at last.'

The Times was mystified by *The Unicorn*. The *Tablet* thought it her best novel, liking its improbability; so did the *Month*. It should not be surprising that the American critic Robert Scholes read it as Christian allegory. But *The Unicorn* is neo-Platonic. To Iris's Hungarian postgraduate student Nicolas Veto, writing his thesis on Simone Weil under her supervision, she acknowledged that 'Unicorn is full of Simone Weil, tho' few (apparently) are those who spot that greater source of my "wisdom".' Her philosophy, she said, always turns into theology, which is 'awkward for me as I don't believe in God'.[57] The co-existence in the novel of the willed and the quaint, combined with the deliberate absence of social or historical elements, made it hard going for some. Although it was later a set text for the *Agrégation* (teachers' exam) in France, Continental European publishers were reluctant to bring it out in translation.

8

The romance of marriage, the narrator of 'Jerusalem' observed, is based on a sentimental fallacy – 'One can love, be in love with, more than one person at a time.' Iris had married John for laughter as much as passion, he declaring himself willing to live in any contradiction 'indefinitely'. It was never uncommon for her to become fascinated by someone new, but he trusted her scrupulousness, in turn providing unfailing background support, 'earthing' her. (Perhaps, he wondered, Shakespeare often fell in love while being, like Iris, inwardly self-contained.) Their partnership was seriously threatened once, leading to her resigning her Fellowship at St Anne's. In 1962–63 the college magazine announced that 'Iris Murdoch has resigned in order to devote more time to writing,' and had been duly elected Honorary Fellow.[58] She had indeed felt divided between teaching and writing for years;* one reason her early novels were set in summer was that she had only that season free to write. The reason she resigned,[59] however, was to free herself from a mutually obsessional attachment to a woman colleague that threatened scandal, and that alarmed the Principal of St Anne's, Lady Ogilvie, enough for her gently to warn Iris, to which she did not take kindly. Far from writing full time, she soon took up teaching in London at the Royal College of Art, albeit of a less time-consuming kind.

Since the Irish for 'Club of Women' is '*Cumann na mBan*', Iris and John would lightly refer to this Oxford colleague as the Chumman. She was exceptional, original, able, a brilliant cook, passionate and dogmatic, with great magnetism, bossiness, possessiveness, and capacity for being wrapped up in her students. Extremely left-wing, she would threaten periodically to resign. She was thought by some to have inspired Honor Klein in *A Severed Head*. Aggressive and difficult people, John observed, liked Iris, because she relaxed them, taking their 'stuff' on board.

Their acquaintanceship went back to 1952. In February 1959 Iris wrote:

> In the same line of thought: I am becoming very attached to –. She said to me the other day in her brisk manner 'There are no hidden depths. Everything I have is on view!' How untrue this is. I have no idea whether [she] has any physical apprehension of me comparable to mine of her, and whether when our hands touch when she lights my cigarette she too trembles.

Three months later Iris feels 'precariously emotional' about her, and by the summer of 1961 a note about 'anxiety and arranging' suggests matters had gone far. That August Iris had a dream John found significant. The Bayleys, playing on a railway platform, saw their toy train fall underneath a real train: the world of drama

---

* Marshall Best of Viking wrote to Iris on 16 October 1956: 'We were all glad to hear from Gwenda David that you are serious enough about your writing to want to give up the University work. I hope you succeed in breaking loose and that other books will burgeon as a result.' Iris wrote to Vera Crane on 23 November 1957: 'I will stop lecturing from next summer, & teach a smaller number of hours – which will leave more time to write.'

and passion outside was menacing the innocent Cedar Lodge
play-world. By now the woman reviled Iris for not leaving John
and setting up home with her instead; if Iris would not do that,
she should at least have a 'proper relationship' with her. It was
probably at this time that at least one St Anne's student was moved
at her own request to another tutor, finding Iris's habit of 'looking
out of the window and talking about love', or lying mutely on
the floor for the statutory hour with her eyes closed, less than
fully helpful.

> *4 November 1961.* I meet [her] in the Lamb and Flag
> after the class on Fridays . . . She is calmer in some ways,
> but there is despair.
>
> *26 June 1962.* It looks as if [she] and I are through. I
> can hardly write for misery and tears. How true it was,
> what she said on Day one, 'We have let a destroyer loose.'
> Yet I can't believe it. I left hysterically last night after the
> New Hall dinner. She wanted to drive me back, I was so
> drunk, & I wouldn't let her. Her face as the door . . .
> slowly closed. I just don't know what to do or how to
> manage without her.
>
> *5 July 1962.* Of course we aren't through – but can
> we go on like this? I wish I were not so decisively and
> hopelessly divided from my chance of ordinary happiness
> . . . . exiling myself from it.
>
> *6 August 1962.* A moment of curious peace, or not
> peace exactly . . . but silence . . . she came to Steeple
> Aston for the first time and we read . . . in the garden.
> We were both very much on edge and – obviously hated
> it. She was very hostile and bullying when we next met,
> spoke contemptuously about 'English homes and gar-
> dens', and generally treated me with harshness and con-
> tempt. Not unusual of course . . . I have told [her] I must
> resign . . . Yet I have not 'decided' for her anger [6 pages
> excised]. Puss is very dear.

Soon, the decision to leave St Anne's achieved, Iris records her
joy in being able to 'see' the world again, 'being able to look at
things. A sense of freedom & looking, and the whole world, given
again, one's consolation. Also everyday life with puss.' 'There is

no substitute,' she wrote in *A Severed Head*, 'for the comfort supplied by the utterly taken-for granted relationship.' On 9
December 1966: 'How lonely I was all those years with [her].'
When she met the Slovene Jože Jančar again on 15 May 1967:
'If I ask what I have been doing for 16 years I suppose the answer
is getting married, getting used to being married, & getting away
from –.' On 17 November 1968: 'How awful the business with –
was. Reading of my sufferings I think it quite scandalous that I
survived them!'

Liberation, however, obscured in her memory wonderful things
they had shared: this saddened her. She dreamt, in May 1976,
of a joyous reconciliation in a Dublin cellar-bar. In waking life
she religiously avoided, always, those parts of Oxford where a
chance meeting might occur. Her depictions of same-sex love
between women were, in the 1960s, unpredictable. Violet Ever-
creech in *The Unicorn* is lonely and predatory; Emma Sands in
An Unofficial Rose sinister yet winning; in *A Severed Head* Martin's
secretaries, Miss Seelhaft and Miss Hernshaw, have the only happy
relationship in the novel.

9

'*The Italian Girl* is *A S[evered]* H[*ead*] in reverse, the spell repeated
backwards.'[60] In the 1960s Iris was sometimes repeating a formula,
as well as trying to transmute her Platonism into intelligible public
rhetoric. In 1963 Marshall Best was dissatisfied with *The Italian Girl*
and warned Iris that she might this time annoy her readership: 'I
think you come near to justifying the charge sometimes made
against you ... that you are playing games with your reader,
deliberately holding back your meanings until he wonders if they
are really there.' The character of Maggie baffled him at the end.
Norah Smallwood agreed, and was very interested to see how
Iris would react, writing to Best: 'between you and me, in our
experience we have in the past made suggestions, and while she
has received them very charmingly, she has seldom ... taken
them into account.' Iris agreed that the book was flawed, and

Maggie was weak, but did not now want to go back to it. 'Much as I love and admire her,' Best wrote to Smallwood, 'I hate this lack of professionalism and this unwillingness to take herself seriously as a novelist. She does say, and apparently means it, that she wouldn't mind a bit if we skipped this book and waited for another.' Smallwood agreed that it was odd that someone as good as Iris 'is not interested in making good better. Can it be that she is so bursting with ideas that there is little time to do all that she wants?'[61]

Smallwood accordingly wrote to Iris lamenting that, while she liked and admired the book, 'I'd like it even better if you gave that final re-touching'. Anthony Burgess, who would later name *The Bell* as one of the best novels of its epoch,[62] thought *The Italian Girl* showed that Iris's reputation was grossly inflated. P.N. Furbank blamed Oxford for the book's disappointments.[63] Iris's friend Honor Tracy's hostile review in the *New Republic* caused a temporary rift;[64] Tracy's question therein as to why 'Miss Murdoch chose to set *The Unicorn* in Ireland when she so plainly is not at home there' may also have stung.

Perhaps she wrote too fast. When Viking queried the kitchen scene at the end of *The Red and the Green*, Iris conceded to Smallwood, 'They're right of course and it worried me a lot.' She 'might try to rethink the end of the book', and perhaps tried, but it was 'pretty old hat by now and I'm involved in something else'. Late in 1965 Best noted that this criticism – that her taking insufficient pains with her books prevented her full realisation as a novelist – recurred more frequently. Smallwood shrewdly hypothesised that Iris, always 'seeking and thinking', clarified something *to herself* in writing, and was therefore unfussed by critical reception. Nor were her sales affected. Smallwood noted that Gwenda David knew of one unnamed 'considerable influence' on Iris who, if run into, might be very helpful. But Canetti – it was certainly he – did not then materialise. As for Iris, she well knew that she was as much the victim of her creative *daemon* as its mistress. She wondered gloomily when her 'obsessional phase as a novelist would end?'[65]

Meanwhile a triumphant, uproariously successful adaptation

for the stage, with J.B. Priestley, of *A Severed Head* opened at the Criterion Theatre in June 1963. It was strongly cast, with Robert Hardy as Martin and Paul Eddington as Palmer. This was by far the best of the three stage adaptations of Iris's novels, running for 1,111 performances, and brought her nearly £18,000 in its first two years. 'You don't really *like* the theatre, do you Duckie?' Priestley, however, sagely noted. Before long Iris was in a position to meditate making what she tactfully called 'some loans' to various impecunious friends and relations. 'Don't forget, before you give it all away,' Smallwood had cautioned as early as 1962, 'you have still got to pay tax on it.'

In February 1964 Iris and John began big alterations to Cedar Lodge, putting in a new staircase and enlarging the hall. This produced a large space for entertaining in, which was even colder than before. Soon they bought an adjoining cottage and old barn, and could boast more than six acres. It was going very cheap, they had large ideas at that time, hoping that friends might stay in it, and here was a way of ensuring good neighbours. They never did much with this acquisition, feeling uneasy about the added responsibility. People used to graze their horses uninvited on the land; the barn remained unconverted; an amiably unscrupulous student dumped spoil, John and Iris, complaisant as ever, agreeing. An eyesore resulted.

10

Iris researched *The Red and the Green* hard, even learning some Gaelic.[66] She described the novel as a good textbook to learn Irish history from, and was pleased when the Irish historian and politician Conor Cruise O'Brien wrote to her praising it. The action takes place during one week of April 1916, leading up to the Easter Rising. Chapter 2, a seminar on the history of Ireland, gives the January 1801 Act of Union as its major disaster, since it demoralised the country's ruling class. 'Ireland's real past is the ascendancy,' ventures one character, who reminds us that, the early-nineteenth-century leader Daniel O'Connell excepted, the great Irish patriots have all been Protestants. Doubtless Iris is mythologising her own family here, as at Oxford in 1939 when she first referred in print to the Anglo-Irish as 'a special breed'. Following Yeats and Bowen, she appears to have adopted the historian W.E.H. Lecky's idealisation of the eighteenth-century Ascendancy.[67] This chapter, too, idealises the Protestant land-lords, 'those aristocrats who think themselves superior both to the English and to the Irish', while Anglo-Irish writers have 'always written the best English'. The family name of Barney Drumm recalls that of the original Richardson demesne, Drum Manor, and Barney's mother was indeed a Richardson. But those who reduce the novel to that particular mythologisation[68] miss others as potent – the book in effect explores many aspects of Iris's inheritance – and ignore the fact that the only character with social pretensions – the betrousered, cigar-smoking Lady Millie Kinnard, who conducts target practice in her boudoir – is also bankrupt, highly promiscuous, and bad. Millie is (presumably) partly based on Countess Constance Markievicz, grandee and rebel. She is the earthiest of all Iris's projections of the 'vamp'-figure. Her lively exoticism is opposed to the dullness, provincialism and occasional stupidity of the English cousins.

At Oxford in 1940 Iris had given a paper to the Irish Club on James Connolly, a Marxist praised by Lenin for fusing, during bitter social struggle, class militancy and revolutionary national-ism. Connolly is a background figure in *The Red and the Green*, but righteous pity for the plight of the Dublin poor is shared even by 'English' Frances as much as by her Catholic Dumay cousins. The Easter Rising had in Connolly a Socialist presence, as well as, in Padraic Pearse, a mystical and martyrological wing, which of course won out in the end. There are glimpses of real poverty throughout the book – one in Chapter 7 borrowed directly from Mrs Marmeladov's death in *Crime and Punishment*. The action, despite forays to Millie's two smart houses, in Upper Mount Street and 'Rathblane' in the Wicklow mountains, is set mainly in middle-class Dublin; genteel and 'English' Dun Laog-haire (then Kingstown) once more, with the Mariner's Church and salt-water baths familiar to Iris from visits to Eva Robinson;

and Blessington Street. W.L. Webb in the *Guardian* noted the author's love showing in the 'vivid and exact descriptions of Dalkey and environs and the clear wet evening light in Dublin streets'.[69]

Iris invents an Anglo-Irish cousinry of some complexity, with branches on both sides of the Irish Sea, and cousins both Anglican and Catholic, a family dramatising within itself Ireland's historical tensions, making them immediate and personal. She said that the book concerned 'the awful tensions involved in being Irish',[70] and claimed Catholic relatives herself.[71] The most interesting autobiographical reference is that she places the novel's 'representative' Catholic 'rebel' family, Kathleen and Barney Drumm, and Barney's stepsons Pat and Cathal Dumay, within the seedy gentility of the house on Blessington Street where she was born, a street Eva Lee recalled being raided in 1921 by the Black and Tans. This suggests one quixotic main thrust, pro-Nationalist, pro-'rebel'.* Doubtless gentle Willie Pearse's fate – shot in 1916 because he loved his famous, fanatical brother Padraic enough to be at his side wherever he went, whatever he did[72] – lies behind Cathal's fatal love for his fanatical elder brother, named 'Pat'.

Chapter 4 opens with Andrew Chase-White – like Hughes a Second Lieutenant in King Edward's Horse, born in Canada rather as Hughes was in New Zealand – observing an evangelical meeting with a hundred youthful voices and their boisterous mentors singing, 'Over and over, like a mighty sea/Comes the love of JESUS rolling over me!' in a marquee with a large red banner above it reading 'Children's Special Service Mission' and 'Saved by the Blood of the Lamb'. Iris and her parents probably attended the Crusaders' Revivalist meetings at the Mariner's Church in Dun Laoghaire; her journals recall evangelical hymns. Andrew laments that religion in Ireland is a matter of choosing between one appalling vulgarity and another, meaning the Catholic Church and the Church of Ireland, more 'Low Church', as it was,

---

* Although Iris's two younger Bell cousins both married Catholics, it might be objected that for an Irish Protestant to identify with a Catholic is itself a patriarchal Ascendancy posture.

than Anglicanism in England. He does not mention the famous third term in Lyons's Irish historiography – the dissenting tradition of (mainly) the North – to which Hughes's family belonged. Since the novel is set in Dublin, the Non-Conformist tradition is less relevant.

The epilogue to *The Red and the Green*, set in 1938 during the Spanish Civil War, creates another echo, between the martyrs of Easter 1916 and those of the Spanish war, in which Iris and Frank had taken such interest.[73] Frances and Millie might be seen as respectable and louche sides of the same 'plump' girl,* both of whom are nearly attached (sexually; or maritally) to Andrew, while secretly loving Pat. Millie wickedly destroys Andrew, and her character is just as interesting an element of the novel as the Easter Rising itself, although some found the crisis, in which four of the book's menfolk visit her during a single night, 'just like comic opera',[74] improbable.

The contrast between Millie's promiscuity and Pat's fierce chastity – resembling that of the revolutionary Rakhmetov in Chernyshevsky's *What is to be Done?* (1863) – was overlooked. Irish reviews were generally good. Sean Lucy in the *Irish Independent* noted how painstakingly Iris had researched, though he quarrelled with the novel's 'sometimes intense blend of fantasy and realism'. (The weekly *Hibernia*, of a later novel, found precisely this blend, which Iris had defended to Harold Hobson,† 'highly *Irish*'.) Sean O'Faolain in the *Irish Times* admired her courage and venturousness, while caring less for her taste for baroque melodrama. He praised the way the 'twisted poetry in all her work flowers from the reek of common life'.[75] Her sometimes uncertain grasp of Irish speech-patterns passed without remark.[76]

---

* Iris acknowledged her identification with Frances: see *Iris Murdoch Newsletter*, no. 14, autumn 2000, p.12.
† 'If fantasy and realism are visible as separate aspects in a novel, the novel is likely to be a failure. If you ask how they are divided in Shakespeare you recognise how meaningless the question is [that Murdoch alternates fantasy and reality]. In real life the fantastic and the ordinary, the plain and symbolic are often indissolubly joined, and I think the best novels explore and exhibit life without disjoining them.' Harold Hobson, 'Lunch with Iris Murdoch', *Sunday Times*, 11 March 1962.

11

The Easter Rising mistook its enemy. The British government had been ready to cede Home Rule to Ireland. Ulster Presbyterians – often strongly radical in 1798, when Murdochs and Richardsons were probably on the same United Ireland side – objected to Home Rule in 1912, and should logically have been the target of Nationalist anger in 1916.[77] Indeed, while the Murdochs would have been anti-Nationalist in 1916, some Protestant Richardsons, especially after the British executed sixteen 'rebels', were pro-independence.[78] Within four years of *The Red and the Green*'s publication, the Troubles recommenced in Northern Ireland, and Iris's loyalties swung violently. It became the one novel she felt equivocal about.[79] It had romanticised violence, idealising the Catholic Nationalist cause, investing in that self-perpetuating mythology of blood-sacrifice on which the IRA fed.

The Troubles were the one topic that could move Iris to tears of anger and distress: 'One's heart is broken over Ireland.'[80] On that subject she was able henceforth wildly to lose her temper, even with old friends. 12 June 1983: 'Mary Scrutton [Midgley] here, after being in court in Banbury for breaking the peace at the demo [against Cruise missiles] at Heyford Base! Very good indeed to see her. Argument about Ireland, however.' She wrote to Midgley defending the hardline Protestant leader Ian Paisley: 'That he is emotional and angry is not surprising, after 12–15 years of murderous IRA activity . . . All this business is deep in my soul I'm afraid.' She now evinced the laager-mentality of the Ulster Protestant who, she felt, unlike Northern Irish Catholics, had no hinterland. No occasion is recorded on which she allowed that Northern Catholics had, in 1968, distinct and legitimate grievances. Honor Tracy, though Catholic, agreed: 'It is the Stone Age ferocity of the native Irish Catholics in the north which brings these atrocious deeds about.'[81] Iris's brother-in-law Michael Bayley was stationed in Ulster from 1969 for two years; there was a disturbing level of alleged support within the Irish Republic for the IRA. Her cousin Sybil's husband Reggie Livingston, specialist

in vascular surgery at Belfast's Royal Victoria Hospital, often operated on and helped save victims of terrorism. One terribly injured
visiting notable required fifty-eight pints of blood. His car had
had bricks thrown at it; and paramilitaries fired into the operating
theatre.

In 1982 Iris remarked, 'It's a terrible thing to be Irish.'[82] In
July 1985, after receiving an honorary D.Litt at Trinity College,
Dublin, 'I am always disturbed by visiting Ireland – demonic
island, so charming & so mad.'[83] The pro-IRA attitude of the
American Irish she found 'particularly sickening'.[84] Labour Party
policy on Northern Ireland was a leading cause in her voting
Tory in the 1980s. For her Ireland became 'unthinkable'. After
The Red and the Green it was certainly unwriteable. She tried while
gestating *The Book and the Brotherhood* to oppose within it an Irish
Catholic and an Irish Protestant,[85] but failed. Her later attitude
is prefigured by *The Red and the Green*'s epilogue, where Ireland
in 1938 is bitterly called a 'provincial dump living on German
capital which cannot even make its own cheese'; this is echoed by
the Irish Peregrine Arbelow in *The Sea, The Sea* when he mordantly
compares how the Jews suffer – 'wittily' – how the Poles suffer –
'tragically' – and how the Irish suffer: 'like a bawling cow in a
bog'. Being Irish is so 'awful' that even being Scottish is better.
Anti-Irish wit is itself an old Irish tradition.

17

What a Decade!
1965–1969

On 17 January 1965, having finished with *The Red and the Green*, Iris recorded feeling rather lost and lonely without her characters. Shadows of another novel were about, but 'such grim melancholy stuff'. 'There seems so little choice,' she mourned. There was as yet no unifying fire to the new novel, and she sought to stave it off, slow it down. Nonetheless she completed a first draft of *The Time of the Angels* between April and August, and the second by 17 October. Two weeks later she had decided to re-read the whole of Shakespeare, and studied the plays over four years. 'I wish I could see what to do to write a masterpiece. I've written ten novels and that's enough. If not a masterpiece now, no point in writing anything. Shakespeare, Shakespeare.' The contrast between the choicelessness with which her own artistic *daemon* dictated what she wrote, and Shakespeare's glorious scope and freedom, preoccupied her.

She sat in the newly enlarged Georgian-green-painted drawing room at Cedar Lodge reading the comedies, starting with *The Tempest, Twelfth Night, Much Ado* and *Midsummer Night's Dream*. 'An odd experience, not quite like anything else. The plays seem so exceedingly *short*. One has so filled them out with thoughts & imaginings there is a great aura round each.' *As You Like It* had 'a sort of lucidity I could fawn upon. If only, if only.' She could sense a new novel waiting, but did not want to 'whistle' for it too soon. *Henry IV Part I* provoked an 'oh marvellous!', *Troilus* the child-like question, 'With what purpose does Shakespeare have Achilles kill Hector in that sinister way?'

467

She had started to transfer *The Nice and the Good* from notebooks to loose-leaf, commenting dispassionately, 'It looks as if it will be very long.' The Shakespeare reading-programme continued into 1967 and 1968 when she studied the tragedies, and was, by contrast, 'absolutely fed up . . . to the teeth' by her own *Bruno's Dream*. In February 1969 she read *Lear* and, again, *The Tempest*, noting, 'Reading *The Tempest* immediately tears stream down. Why?' She thought about that play throughout the spring of 1969. It concerned 'power undoing itself in favour of love';[1] 'the triumph of spiritual (free) power over magical (obsessional) power'. It was about the 'role of forgiveness'.[2]

In the same spirit of self-improvement that led her to study Shakespeare, she dedicated the whole of 1969 to the writing of plays – there would be four – forswearing fiction. She was trying to take seriously those critics who thought she wrote her novels too fast. It occurred to her out of the blue in May that all her novels concerned a conflict between two men. 'Sometimes this is obvious, sometimes in the background. Jake and Hugo. Randall and Felix. Ducane and Biranne. Miles and Danby. etc etc.' On 4 June 1969 she wrote in her journal: 'Still infernally cold. Came out late evening into blue pink dark scene, the evening star shewing very chaste, blackbirds. Star at once vanished behind cloud, got message simply: WAIT. Yes, wait.' The spirit who said 'wait' didn't tell her whether or not she should work like a demon at something else while she was waiting. She waited, writing plays for a year. Though craving success, she feared herself untalented as a playwright;[3] perhaps she hoped play-writing might also improve her fiction. The first play, *The Three Arrows*, materialised 'straight on the line from the unconscious', a place 'absolutely hidden' from her view. She abandoned one play – termed only 'FN' – in depression. Another, *Joanna, Joanna*, was (rightly) never performed, but the plot was stolen and improved upon in the novel *A Word Child*. On the last day of the 1960s ('What a decade!') she felt the shadow of a new novel, *An Accidental Man*. 'What comes,' she noted, 'is always so very surprising.' On 13 January 1970: 'Odd how different the atmosphere of one novel is from another. This new one is a completely different world, an unexpected & somehow unrecognizable one. Where has all this come from?' She decided simultaneously to write verses for one year before attempting a poem. 'Now I think rather six months, and *then* try. That will be till March 9.' In February she got 'stuck' with *An Accidental Man*: 'A ghastly feeling of one's mind deployed as a dreary broken down sort of suburb in some corner of which one is trapped and whining.' If only, she entreated, 'my obsessional period as a novelist could be over'. She invoked Shakespeare, praying for some spark from his genius to descend upon her.

2

Within months of resigning from St Anne's[4] in 1963, Iris was on the staff of the General Studies department of the Royal College of Art on Kensington Gore, with a starting salary of £515 per year, as a one-day-a-week tutor (Wednesdays), drawing a quarter of a tutor's salary until August 1967.[5] Early in their married life the Bayleys had met Lucy and Christopher Cornford while visiting Dominic de Grunne at his French château; Christopher Cornford, Dean of General Studies, invited Iris to teach in June 1963.[6] Younger brother of the poet (John) killed in Spain, son of another poet (Frances) and of the great classicist and scholar of Plato (F.M.), at whose house outside Cambridge (Conduit Head) the Bayleys often stayed, he was tall, beautifully mannered, Peter Pan-ish, a wonderful talker without being a gossip, fey, libertarian, aristocratic, a good dancer and squash-player (he liked to win), a strong idealist, a painter.[7] In 1958 Christopher and Lucy Cornford and John Grigg weekended at Steeple Aston. They played 'adverbs'. Christopher, impersonating a Cambridge 'skit', told the story of Bertrand Russell coming to the staircase where G.E. Moore was residing and knocking meticulously on Moore's door. 'Come in,' said Moore. '*Very well,*' 'Russell' replied – at this point Cornford produced a masterly imitation of Russell's excessively slow, precise and deliberate tones – '*If that – is what – you wish.*' Cornford designed the covers for four of Iris's novels, starting

with *The Unicorn.*[8] He was not a 'solid administrator' but an artist
by temperament, which caused rows with his first-cousin-once-
removed, Robin Darwin, then Principal of the RCA.* Not all
agreed that Darwin was the rudest man they had ever met. Some
who had known his father claimed he had been ruder. Many
thought he did not treat Cornford well. 'A curious personality.
Minotaur, or Ass's Head? A bit of both. Indeed they are perhaps
the same thing,' Iris commented, finding Darwin attractive.

The RCA in the 1960s was both maverick and small, with only
thirty students in the largest department (Painting) and perhaps
three hundred in all. It was a splendid anomaly. Funded directly
by a Treasury official, it was independent both of local authorities
(unlike normal art schools) and (unlike universities) the University Grants Committee. Other art schools were inspected by the
Ministry of Education, and taught a centrally examined agreed
syllabus: not the RCA. A non-residential postgraduate college, it
was also a patrician club with sinecures for friends and relations.
Darwin (great-grandson of Charles), who had taught art at Eton
from 1933 to 1938, wanted artists and designers to have 'amused
and well-tempered minds', a wording suggestive of the eighteenth-century clubman he partly was. The Senior Common
Room, dear to his heart, moved from Cromwell Road to Kensington Gore around 1961. Fine wines and food were available, wearing a tie was obligatory for men. 'Extraordinary Members'
included E.M. Forster, John Minton and Francis Bacon, whom
Iris wished to meet: 'I am probably too romantic about painters
– I want to project my own dream life as a painter,' she accurately
noted.[9] Now she would see the 'sensual, physical, sexual world of
painters and sculptors'[10] at first hand. Darwin valued the input
of visiting intellectuals. Isaiah Berlin lectured on Marx, Julian
Huxley on Darwin and T.H. Huxley, George Steiner excited students with de Sade, Raymond Chandler spoke of writing for *Black
Mask* magazine. Such luminaries as Kenneth Clark, John Betjeman, Elisabeth Frink, John Summerson and ex-student David

---

* Darwin was Principal from 1948. In 1967, when the Royal College of Art acquired
university status, he became Rector.

Hockney visited, or were listed as doing so. As Hockney resentfully, accurately observed, Darwin wanted the RCA to be a university. Specifically, he wanted it to be Cambridge.

Iris rented a small dusty, tidy flat[11] at 59 Harcourt Terrace,
SW10, off Redcliffe Square, and spent Tuesday and Wednesday
nights[12] there in term time. The flat was convenient for visiting
her mother, now living two Tube stops away at 97 Comeragh
Road in Barons Court, and groups of students could be invited
for drinks.[13] Iris associated London with a 'holiday feeling'[14] – a
feeling John in no way shared; Iris alone was the 'terrific London
gadabout',[15] and joy in the city gets into many of her novels. She
now had the first London base of her own since 1945. As in 1942,
she picked up her Russian lessons, and appears to have thought
of sitting Russian O-level.[16] Leo Pliatzky, in the Treasury and
soon to be Under-Secretary, had at work her identical wartime
telephone number: Whitehall 1234. She found Leo at various
times difficult, stiff, shy, amorous despite being married, and a
useful source of current civil service lore. Such old valued friendships could now be picked up again.

London had greatly changed. Barriers of class and custom and
discipline were coming down. The mixture of patrician staff
and rebel-bohemian students at the RCA was novel. Ossie Clark
and Zandra Rhodes were both students of fashion design; the
former's diaries (published in 1999) show the experimental and
iconoclastic drug-taking, sex-obsessed lifestyle that was common
to many. Though the students had not necessarily read Witkova's
Born Under Saturn, their lives could be appropriately Caravaggio-
esque. The rock bands Pink Floyd (studying at the Central School
of Architecture) and The Animals (from Newcastle) frequented
the student bar; some Film Department students startled Cornford by shooting The Who smashing their musical instruments;
Charlie Watts (of The Rolling Stones) married a painting
student;[17] Ian Dury was another painting student. Reg Gadney,
a later RCA tutor (in 1982 he would write a notable four-part
adaptation of *The Bell* for BBC2) who had had a religious upbringing was as shocked, fascinated, delighted and appalled as was
Iris by the amorality and anarchism of the students, and by the

crackpot rivalries,[18] unending scandals and fights, both emotional and sometimes physical, of the staff: the latter may have played some role in her decision, in 1967, to move on.

Cornford and General Studies were disliked equally – his department was seen as a closet of wayward left-wing intellectuals, when other lecturers were anti-intellectual and sometimes right-wing. The Schools of Painting and of Graphic Design were then adjacent to the Victoria and Albert Museum. Although their students – part *idiots savants*, part half-educated 'sharp city boys on the make'[19] – had to pass General Studies, they still needed an incentive to spend fifteen minutes walking up Exhibition Road to what they persisted in pejoratively calling the Department of Words;[20] they had a genuine but *mute* inspired rapport with their given medium.[21]

Tutors had latitude as to how they taught. Each of Iris's students came to a fortnightly tutorial. In 1964–65 she had four tutorial groups,[22] working on Sartre, Gabriel Marcel, Kierkegaard's *Fear and Trembling* and J.S. Mill's *Utilitarianism*. Some students wrote dissertations under her supervision. The 'blurb' for her course promised exploration of the moral and political 'mythologies' which have often found expression in literary form. In 1967 she was looking for a postgraduate student whom she would pay to mark 'about 40 or 50 I think' essays on Sartre, as she 'had to go away'. The person concerned, she wrote to Richard Wollheim,[23] need not be a Sartre expert, suggesting no exorbitant expectations on either side.

The Coldstream and Summerson Reports from 1960 to 1962 had urged that all tertiary students have an examinable level of literacy. Gaining a diploma thus became contingent on demonstrating intellectual attainment in a 12,000-word dissertation in General Studies, which was of necessity partly 'instant culture', and partly remedial work, as students were of startlingly mixed ability. David Hockney, an RCA student from 1959 to 1962, wished to devote himself to painting without being sidetracked.[24] R.B. Kitaj and Hockney had left the year before, Hockney almost failing because his illustrated, hastily written General Studies essay on Fauvism was chaotically argued. An Academic Board subcommittee conveniently found that *all* the dissertation marks were 'un-sound', and Hockney, who had won a Gold Medal for draughtsmanship, gained his diploma.[25] The function of the General Studies Department's courses was, as Iris put it on the RCA interview board to appoint Cornford's successor in 1979,[26] 'to get artists to read books – to raise their gaze'. Some students, even when literate, had never read a book.

Michael Jaffé called General Studies a 'home for failed geniuses'. Lance Beales, co-founder with Allen Lane of Penguin Non-Fiction,[27] lectured on Contemporary Britain. Jan Hevesy taught two courses on the History of Science, and helped many students suffering with anorexia, for which he was later perhaps unjustly sacked. There were options on the Arts 1789–1918, and 1918 to the present day, and on European Cinema. Dominic de Grunne, teaching African, Polynesian and Chinese Art, and Poetry and Philosophy from 1968, found the students easily bored with the past, which he could bring alive for them only by showing its contemporary 'relevance'.

Iris gave in 1965–66 twenty-four lectures on 'Moral and Political Pictures of Man'. Some felt that attending these was like eavesdropping on a soliloquy. She communed aloud with herself, frowning a trifle nervously in a corner about a philosophic problem, while her listeners overheard. Her dissertation topics for 1964–65 are, reasonably enough, lists of her philosophical obsessions: 'Compare and contrast Mill's picture of "the good man" with that of Kierkegaard'; and, *à propos* the latter's distinction between the ethical and the religious, 'What are the merits and the dangers of the idea of going "beyond the ethical"?' She supervised dissertations, gave lectures, group seminars and individual tutorials for extra-curricular discussion. The fashion designer Janice Wainwright found Iris very shy, but noted her interest in collecting details – for example of dress – for her fiction. Wainwright's friend Sandra Keenan, whom Iris tutored for two years, found Iris 'amazingly kind', very good to run ideas past: their discussions ranged beyond her dissertation topic of Women's Fashions. She was aware that Iris was researching her generation, and thought her too passionate and self-involved for sanctity, but a good person by whom she was not intimidated. The subsequently well-known painter Bill Jacklin's work was lastingly influenced by a comment Iris wrote at the bottom of his essay on Kant: 'What about love?'

The *Observer* wrongly ascribed to the RCA both Pop Art – in fact hatched by the ICA – and Op Art.[28] But paradoxically Robin Darwin's irascible leadership helped promote cultural innovation, partly by offering symbols of the English 'Establishment' for the students to attack; partly by supporting the experimental student magazine *ARK*, attributed with the development, in the 1950s, of a 'post-modern sensibility';[29] also by elevating the status of design for industry and breaking down the division between 'useful' applied arts and 'useless' fine arts.[30] The RCA invented the term 'graphic design',[31] and arguably also 'liberal studies'. That the college in the 1950s and 1960s produced so many good painters – Bridget Riley, Kitaj, David Hockney – and talented fashion designers – Zandra Rhodes, Ossie Clark, Janice Wainwright, Hylan Booker – is a tribute less to the teaching (where, outside General Studies, the great names ran from Ruskin Spear to Hugh Casson) than to the fact that the RCA was the only postgraduate art college in the world. It could pick the very best students.

Iris bought an abstract by Christopher Cornford, four Op Art Bridget Rileys and a Roger Hilton. Friendships she made with RCA students were lastingly important to her. She paid for Hylan Booker, ex-USAF, black, from Detroit, to make his first visit to Paris and see collections by Chanel, Balenciaga and Yves Saint-Laurent, helping launch him in a successful career as a fashion designer; when, later, he and A.J. Ayer's second wife Dee Wells fell in love, she and John stayed with them in New York. The sculptress Rachel Fenner, a rebellious, solitary, working-class 'good child' from North Yorkshire, wrote her dissertation under Iris's supervision on 'The Imagination as a Moral Tool', with references to Plato, Jakob Boehme and William Blake. Fenner and Iris's friendship was close until, in the 1970s, the birth of two sons increasingly preoccupied her. On 21 January 1966, a very cold day with an inch or more of snow with a 'damp furry texture', Iris went round to the Sculpture School on Queensgate, watched two students assembling a fibreglass sea serpent, and was impressed.

> I feel depressed and limp. Tuesday was good though . . .
> Rachel's whirling bulging Rodinesque Samuel Palmerly
> forms seemed much more coherent and significant than
> what I saw of her work last year . . . The atmosphere of the
> sculpture school, the very bright lights, the half-finished
> objects, the debris, the fibreglass on the floor, all this
> disturbs and moves me.

David Morgan was in his final year as a student of painting during Iris's first, seeing himself as a Birmingham rebel stuck among preciously genteel painter-tutors (apart from the genuinely eccentric Carel Weight and his protégé, the idiosyncratic Pop artist Peter Blake). He had not read Iris's books, but as he opened the door of her office with its Goya print, on the top floor of the JCR building at 23 Cromwell Road for a tutorial in April 1964, they 'recognised' each other – something clicked. She was pleased by the tough way he at once treated with her 'as one sovereign state treating with another'. An intense autodidact, Morgan had come through much, including breakdowns, to reach the RCA; Iris was, after years of secret reading, the first really intelligent person to befriend him, to see and speak to his intellectual hunger. The complications of his private life interested her – she was morally appalled and probably unconsciously excited by his treatment of girlfriends – as did the Dionysiac approach to art he shared with other students: a novelist's voyeuristic *frisson* was mixed up with the real help she gave. He saw her as 'feasting with panthers', and her letter referring to the 'paint so enchantingly entangled in [his] hair' links him to Will Boase in *Bruno's Dream*, while the subventions his situation then necessitated prefigure Marcus's to Leo in *The Time of the Angels*. She came to apprehend his dangerous wildness less as something 'charming', increasingly as confused, needing patient understanding. She assured him that their entirely platonic friendship was 'for life'.

Over successive decades their meetings declined, to his chag-
rin, from three times a year to a mere once per year. Iris was the
main civilising influence in Morgan's life – sometimes gentle; at
other times, when she feared that his 'delinquency', which she
partly loved, and which he partly acted out as an Iris Murdoch
'character' to keep her interested, might compromise her professional standing, very fierce indeed. She could, he felt, make
'time stand still'; she could also 'make things happen that only
happened when you were with her'. Her admonishing but loving
letters to him defend precisely that civility which the 1960s threatened, championing privacy, kindness, loyalty, mutual respect.
Soon he was a college lecturer living by some of these values: he
would tell her how his teaching was going, and she helped him
get it right.

For Iris's part, Morgan was one of the tiny band of human
beings with whom she could 'really talk'.[32] She commented that
RCA students were 'utterly different from Oxford students, they
don't accept anything on trust, they question everything. They're
instantly suspicious of any name you hold up for commendation,
religion means nothing to them ... they're *wild!*'[33] She wailed
when she felt she was not getting through to these students, and
tried anew.[34]

3

Paddy Kitchen's 1970 novel about the RCA, *A Fleshly School*, chronicles a 'breaking down of moral responsibility ... combined with
the supreme will to attainment'.[35] Iris's novels of the later 1960s
also employ the iconoclastic 'wildness' she encountered at the
college as part of their rhetoric. Leo Peshkov, the unlettered,
precocious delinquent of *The Time of the Angels*, actively trains
himself in immorality, in lying and stealing. He is a cultural symptom of the collapse of Christian belief, a collapse Iris saw as the
central drama of the age. How are we to keep our intellectual
and emotional connexion with two millennia of Western art when
we no longer understand the inner language from which they

were constructed? The disappearance of the age-old symbiosis between art and religion threatened, in her view, the future of both; and imperilled 'goodness'. Faith's 'long withdrawing roar' is the novel's topic. Those who cease to believe in God do not believe in nothing. As has been observed, they start to believe in *anything*. Carel Fisher, the Byronic priest who disbelieves in God, has driven his younger brother Julian to suicide, impregnating his wife from motives of revenge, and now commits incest with his own daughter. He argues that the 'single Good of the philosophers is a lie and a fake', and opposes his weak brother Marcus, whose Platonic treatise on 'Morality in a World Without God' – clearly echoing Iris's *The Sovereignty of Good* – comes to grief, being surreptitiously dependent, like hers, on the theology it is designed to supplant. There is authorial glee in the defeat of the three liberal do-gooders who cannot gain entry to the Rectory where Carel lives, or correct what is wrong within it. Carel, like all Iris's demons, is given the best tunes.

> Suppose the truth were awful, suppose it was just a black pit, or like birds huddled in the dust in a dark cupboard? Suppose only evil were real, only it was not evil since it had lost even its name? Who could face this? ... All philosophy has taught a facile optimism, even Plato did so ... There is only power and the marvel of power, there is only chance and the terror of chance ... All altruism feeds the fat ego ... People will endlessly conceal from themselves that good is only good if one is good for nothing.[36]

'It is always a significant question,' Iris remarked, 'to ask about any philosopher: what is he afraid of?'[37] What frightened her was the possibility that Carel, not Marcus, held the truth.[38] By giving Carel potent arguments, and also the most disturbing 'poetry', Iris partly confronts, even if she cannot outface, her own terror of the now unexplained multiplicity that survives.[39] But she also uses him to assert a spiritual vision of the universe willy-nilly, even in the absence of God. Carel's broodings on power recall Canetti's disquisitions, just as his 'dead birds in a cupboard' – a recurrent theme – recall the Underworld in the *Epic of Gilgamesh*, a book Canetti favoured.[40] Carel argues that 'there are principalities and powers. Angels are the thoughts of God. Now he has been dissolved into his thoughts which are beyond our conception in their nature and their multiplicity and their power.' The 'angels' of the title are the 'psychological forces' which, Iris commented, are now, in the absence of God, working loose, 'as if they were demons or spirits'.[41]

'Principalities and powers', a phrase borrowed from Romans 8: 38, reappear in *The Nice and the Good*, pointing to aspects of our apprehension of other people which are not, as in simple realism, 'inert' but full of ambiguous power. Iris's RCA years inspired the character of Jessica Bird, a primary-school English and painting teacher who started as a working-class art student as innocent of any knowledge of Christ as of Apollo, an 'untainted pagan' used to making love in the presence of third and fourth parties not out of perversity, but as a manifestation of freedom. This novel is a 'Song of Innocence' after *The Time of the Angels'* 'Song of Experience', set partly in endless summer sunshine, where the earlier book had only choking London winter fog, a summer's tale after a winter's tale. While *The Time of the Angels* was patronised as merely 'fairy-tale', *The Nice and the Good* was greeted as a 'true novel': Iris's quiet recovery of Gothic was unfashionably far ahead of its time, years before Angela Carter. It was mainly classified as a diseased attempt at Tolstoyan realism.

The Nice and the Good is also the first of Iris's novels to recall Shakespearian comedy, in its lyrical meditation, as in the late romances, on the themes of love, forgiveness and reconciliation. Its characters each wrestle with some unhappy past mistake. Paula has suffered the disfigurement of her husband by her lover; Mary Clothier the inadvertent death of her husband in a street accident after a furious row. Mary is given Iris's figure: 'Though not formally beautiful, Mary had as a physical endowment a strong confidence in her power to attract.'[42] She loves and tries to console the Central European Willy Kost, who may come from Prague. Willy is given Franz's slight build, his accent, and throughout the book the question Iris commemorated Franz with shortly after his death, '*What ees eet?*' His face is small and brown, his nose thin, his hands dainty and bony.

Willy nurtures extreme guilt about his betrayal, out of fear, of two people, leading to their deaths in Dachau, a dramatisation of Franz's self-reproach for abandoning his parents in 1938. Franz had *invented* the sociology of danger, and the reading of 'taboo' that relates it to the sacred. When his friends leave anxious gifts outside Willy's cottage-door, they are unconsciously appeasing a source of danger, propitiating an 'alien god'. Franz here is, in Willy, both sacred and taboo. Much about Willy and Mary's friendship recalls Franz and Iris. When Mary brings him a posy of sweet nettles and arranges them in a wine-glass, Willy comments that, if only he were a poet, he would write a poem about that – a direct reference to the gentians Iris bought for Franz and he arranged in a wine-glass on his return from Spain in 1952, and the poem with which he commemorated this. As Franz did Iris, Willy teaches Mary German, which they read together. He has one habit of Iris's RCA colleague Frederic Samson, that of jigging around the room to Mozart.[43]

All the characters are released into an Arcadian world in which love may have supernatural harmonising power, and the poignant mood, like that of Shakespeare's mature bitter-sweet comedies, is poised between joy and a sad complaisance. Ducane's expertise in Roman Law probably reflects Fraenkel's. 'By the way, since one or two people have asked,' Iris commented sternly, 'no one in the book is good,'[44] though she had a soft spot for the lively inquisitiveness of the twins Henrietta and Edward with their serendipitous researches – why cuckoos are silent in Africa, how large a breastbone a human being would need in order to fly (fourteen feet, apparently).[45] That we should need the novelist to pronounce on the goodness of her characters is remarkable. Why cannot her readers decide unprompted? This is the Iris whose end-of-term report on the human race appears to be 'Could try harder.' Sometimes she would announce that in her entire *oeuvre*, only Stuart in *The Good Apprentice* and Tallis in *A Fairly Honourable Defeat* are truly good, and even the latter's goodness was qualified by his being allegorical. At other times the cast of good characters is longer, but resembles Froebel's Knights and Ladies, an elect whose salvation is mysteriously earned, by grace rather than by works. The good done by the virtuous is magical overspill: Murdochian saints, like poems, need not *mean* so much as *be*. Their very mode of being is a rebuke to the error that surrounds them. Anne Peronett's virtue in *An Unofficial Rose* is, we are to understand, guaranteed by her passivity and formlessness; Denis Nolan's in *The Unicorn* by his remaining outside the action. The title of *The Nice and the Good* posed problems for translators (in France it mutated into *Les Demi-Justes*) and is glossed in the moving late vision of the sympathetic failed gay seeker Theo:

> Theo had begun to glimpse the distance which separates the nice from the good, and the vision of this gap had terrified his soul. He had seen, far off, what is perhaps the most dreadful thing in the world, the other face of love, its blank face. Everything that he was, even the best that he was, was connected with possessive self-filling human love.[46]

'Niceness', which thus defines the fallen world we share, is the quality exemplified by Theo's brother Octavian and his wife Kate, whose 'golden life-giving egoism and rich self-satisfaction' procure a measure of security and happiness for the denizens of their court. This echoes John Bayley's argument about the importance of physical self-satisfaction (*samodovolnost*) to Tolstoy in the prize-winning book he had just published on that author;[47] his argument influenced Iris profoundly, and complicated her rhetoric.[48]

Thus *Bruno's Dream* is happily even more clearly Janus-faced than its predecessor. Frank Kermode noted that Iris expressed herself not only in terms of an ascetic vocation but also, like some of her characters, in terms of a self-interested hedonism. Here the high-minded Gwen, jumping into the Thames in an attempt to save a girl who swims safely ashore, has a heart attack and drowns. The comedy of the novel is at the expense of the stern vision, rendering it complex and satisfying.[49] Written during 1967, the last of Iris's four RCA years, its character Will Boase comes from the same stable as Jessica Bird and Leo Peshkov – a tough, sexy, occasionally violent photographer and house-painter bravely claiming to be working-class when in fact a 'versatile Bohemianism had rendered him classless'. The book meditates on the Platonic Eros, and the consciousness of each major character is a 'dream', which is to say a state of Platonic illusion, not merely that of the eponymous Bruno. Since the novel debates the relations between Love and Death, it is bounded symbolically by Brompton Road cemetery and the Lots Road power station. Iris partly researched its city-scape with the help of Rachel Fenner and her car.

4

On 21 November 1964 Iris noted: 'I have got very fond of Frederic [Samson] but he is so melancholic and moody. Refuses to have lunch with me next week. Well, I shall take Rene to the Yardarm.' One year later she pondered, 'What is Frederic's trouble? I don't know. Perhaps just being Frederic.'[50] Soon Samson wrote to her that happy voices in the corridor filled him with anguish and horror. He was tubby, short, grey-haired, gnome-like, unattractive, dirty, a messy eater who took little care of himself, a most endearing loner. He taught European literature at the RCA, but at Cornford's behest after 1962 also lectured weekly on the History of Ideas to the entire first year, followed by numerous tutorials. Each year he pronounced Kant with a 'u', complaining furiously when students laughed. Cornford valued Samson's wit and wisdom, and published it.[51] People confided in him; unshockable, he was a good confessor, calm and wise as well as fussy and touchy. One student recalls his helping her through a depression.[52] Another refugee from Hitler's Germany suffering survivor-guilt, Samson would never discuss what became of his family.[53] (When informed of his death in 1981, Iris at once asked whether it had been suicide; possibly he had half-deliberately failed to take the medication for his heart condition.[54]) He was full of admiration for how he had been treated during wartime internment as an alien on the Isle of Man. On 15 January 1966 Iris wrote: 'I still find F "difficult" though he talks to me more frankly, talks almost too much, giving endless unclear mystifying panoramas of his past life.' She noted that he lived in her 'not with his own life only. He is the latest of my Jewish teachers, of whom the first was Fraenkel and the most beloved Franz.'

Humphrey Spender, tutoring in the Textile Department, observed that Iris and Samson's friendship thrived on acerbic argument and squabble. Samson liked to challenge and provoke, and could be hostile in disagreement. Iris, too, loved to be challenged. His attitude to women was said to be patriarchal. Certainly he criticised the 'modern' music composed by his partner Thea Musgrave. In his top-floor, mysteriously rent-free, Pembridge Villas flat, where his cooking-pans were black, filthily encrusted, he conducted Mozart on an old-fashioned gramophone with a knife and fork.

Much that was going on in the arts filled Samson with despair. The presentation by a third-year sculpture student (for example) of four six-foot plastic elephant turds enraged him, was 'symptomatic of the disintegration of modern society'. He saw the drooping, bulging, thin bookshelves in his room as another symptom of RCA decline: a student had designed them. During one such diatribe matters went awry with Iris. He had allowed her on 19 January 1966 to attend his class on *La Nausée* ('Very interesting and moving to see him in action'). During a pub-lunch afterwards at the bottom of Church Street he staggered her by saying – as she thought – quite casually and gratuitously that he thought her novels no good. The remark hit and hurt her much more in retrospect, seeming at moments unforgiveable: 'I live so near to despair about my work: why go on?' She wrote to him, and he explained, 'necessarily truthfully, since he is Frederic', that he had not said anything about her work specifically, and that she must have misunderstood – or misheard (she was partially deaf*) – some general remark about the unimportance of 'culture' and

---

* Iris had been diagnosed as partially deaf in March 1954. She wrote in her journal: 'It is "real" deafness, failure of reception. Likely to get worse, & no cure except amplifiers & lip-reading. I went for my first lip-reading lesson yesterday with a comic woman in the Radcliffe.'

so on: 'Any bus driver going about his work is of more importance than the whole work of Sartre etc. etc.' She had heard him in this vein before, and was relieved. Frederic was soon conducting piano concertos for Iris, 'flitting Puck-like about the room, his curious face all bright and jubilant'.

During the week before this reconciliation she found it hard to do anything but brood about Frederic.

> *23 January.* I feel a total loss of confidence. My present novel isn't yet strong enough to support me (though by the time it is it will be already 'spoilt'). Of course faith in my work will return. It goes away often enough anyway for no reason and comes back. But I hope that my friendship with F. is not damaged. I don't want to talk about my work to people & they don't have to like my books, but at least they can keep their mouths shut. I must try to be rational about this.
>
> *24 January.* I don't really think that all my stuff is worthless, but there's a large margin of possible error in my judgment of it. The thing I'm starting now will be long and take a lot of effort & thought. Why bother with it? A pain I am feeling I think is loneliness. Yet life here is happy and full of various joys & satisfactions. Puss fairly well at present I think. We have been on one or two good walks in the hard wintry sun, before the snow came.

If her confidence was fragile, her spirits still had resilience. She had told Frederic of the break in her friendship with Fraenkel after Fraenkel had criticised her work – conceivably *The Unicorn*, where he recognisably inspired Max Lejour. Frederic now suggested that she 'make peace with the great old man' – which after a humble letter asking to see him, she duly did. Fraenkel replied at once: 'Dearest Iris . . . I thought you had given me up . . . Friday Feb 4 at 8.30 will suit me ideally. I am looking forward to it as if I were 18 years old and not nearly 78. Yours ever, Edward.' This letter filled her with joy. The meeting, which she put to use when Gerard re-meets Levquist in *The Book and the Brotherhood*, happened in Fraenkel's room in Corpus, where she had, in June 1953, tried to console him after his daughter, during an unhappy love-affair, coolly and courageously planned her (successful) suicide. He had said then that he knew Iris better than many who saw her more, and knew what kind of wisdom it was that she lacked.

There were, as usual, burgundy and cigarettes. Iris wept and Fraenkel embraced her. They talked of Shakespeare, Sophocles, his work on the structure of Greek and Latin prose. He read Cicero. He confessed that, spotting a copy of one of her novels, warmly inscribed, on the table of the person he referred to only as 'the Regius Professor of Greek' – Hugh Lloyd-Jones – he had feared she had abandoned him. She had not sent him this novel as it post-dated their quarrel; he had felt slighted that another professor had been so favoured. She laughed about this afterwards. She walked back with him to his house on Museum Road, feeling 'great love for him, & shame and *surprise* at my senseless dereliction ... When I am with him knowledge & ideas seem to flow from him & into me quite automatically. Great teacher, great man ... I love him, & love him physically too. It was marvellous to touch him again.' She sent him copies of two novels, and dedicated *The Time of the Angels* to him later that year.

5

In September 1969 Iris noted a 'vacancy for a close woman-friend'. Neither Honor Tracy nor Esmé Ross Langley,[55] founder of the lesbian magazine *Arena 3* and for a while that autumn in love with Iris, fitted the bill. When Honor, eighteen months earlier, complained that Iris did not write her 'real letters', she replied with an enigmatic love-letter '(more than she bargained for?)', and awaited her reply 'with interest!'. There was 'eternally' Philippa, who, Iris rather earlier noted, represented 'a great reserve of good' on which Iris had 'never really called',[56] and who in December 1967 moved Iris by speaking of the importance to her of their friendship. Their relationship, Iris noted, had its own oddnesses. In May 1968: 'Saw Philippa Thursday & stayed night. Time and space problems. I am still a bit afraid of P, I think. She is numinous, taboo.' Iris long feared Philippa as a wise judge. There were 'people who, though much loved, remain[ed] sinister witnesses from the past'.[57] Their brief and tentative physical affaire in 1968 happened at Iris's insistence – it was, Philippa saw, somehow important for Iris, who felt that only thus could remaining barriers be conclusively removed. Iris found it hard to explain to Philippa that Philippa's 'compulsion to act the tyrannical princess child' where Iris was concerned satisfied her own 'rather specialized love for the tyrant': it was as if Philippa presented an immovable object, was the one person Iris could never entirely seduce. This was not, it appeared, the way that they could best express their love for each other.

Philippa, like other friends, would read each of Iris's novels once, fast, and with varying degrees of recognition. There was a passing resemblance between the predicament of the steel-corseted Elizabeth in *The Time of the Angels* enduring the incestuous visits of her father and her own distinctly more prosaic plight in 1942, corseted in plaster-of-Paris with suspected abdominal TB, having tutorials in her digs from Thomas Balogh and Donald MacKinnon. Paula in *The Nice and the Good* is a portrait of Philippa, divorced, foxy-faced, revered college friend of Mary/ Iris, an uncompromising person whom Mary experiences as an unconscious prig. The strength and clarity of Paula's being, her meticulous accuracy and truthfulness operate as a reproach to the mediocrity and muddle which Mary feels to be her own natural medium. (Verisimilitude is soon exhausted: details of Paula's marriage, divorce and remarriage do not correspond to Philippa's life.) The symmetrical exchange of lovers between Lisa and Diana at the end of *Bruno's Dream* has clear echoes of Seaforth: here was the dragon-myth eating its own tail whose compulsive takeover of her plots Iris would from time to time complain about. That Diana and Miles take the altruistic Lisa in as a 'bird with a broken wing' recalls Michael and Philippa's taking Iris in at 16 Park Town after the failure of the David Hicks engagement; Diana's pained witnessing of Lisa and Danby's final happiness echoes Iris watching Michael and Philippa's happiness in 1945. (This account presents Lisa/Diana as doubles: probably how Iris sometimes saw

Philippa.) Iris further noted to Philippa her own resemblance to Morgan, the 'swinish' emotionally obtuse heroine of *A Fairly Honourable Defeat*, of whose censorious elder sister Hilda Morgan is afraid.[58] After 1970 Philippa took visiting posts in the United States, at Cornell, MIT, Princeton and UCLA; Iris and John stayed with her twice. The friendship was sustained by meetings on Philippa's frequent return trips to Oxford, and by regular correspondence. There was no decade of her adult life in which this friendship was not important to Iris, or celebrated by her as such. Philippa, unlike some of her needier women-friends, 'never needs cheering up', and could give as well as take.

Iris's 'vacancy for a close woman-friend' had arisen when Brigid Brophy fell in love with the writer Maureen Duffy: drinking champagne in early May 1968 with Brigid and Maureen 'was like conversing with two amiable strangers'. Iris had met Brigid Brophy and her husband Michael Levey, then Assistant Keeper at the National Gallery, at the 1954 Cheltenham Literature Festival when *Under the Net* was runner-up to Brophy's novel *Hackenfeller's Ape*, which won the prize for a first novel. Brophy was Irish-descended, a brilliant, coolly witty novelist, typified by the *Observer* as a 1960s *enfant terrible*, a campaigner *against* marriage, the Vietnam war, factory farms, hunting and fishing, religious education in schools; and *for* Greek in schools, bisexuality, vegetarianism and *Fanny Hill*. She fought successfully with Maureen Duffy for a Public Lending Right, which would entitle authors to a payment each time one of their books was borrowed from a library.[59] With much of this (apart from religious education in schools, which she favoured), Iris would have concurred, especially the shared love of Greek; both supported Harold Wilson's Labour Party in the 1964 general election. This was, both intellectually and emotionally, an important relationship, complicated by Iris's skill at blurring the line between love and friendship. Not everyone could figure out exactly what it was that she wanted. Levey suspected that Brigid found Iris 'strangely secretive ... Whom she might be seeing later in the day, for instance, was often shrouded in mystery: "a person" was about all she vouchsafed. Such things made Brigid laugh a lot.'[60]

In November 1955 Brophy sent Iris ardent, witty letters and telegrams. Soon they exchanged verses pastiching Marvell's 'To his coy Mistress'. In 1956 Iris recorded calming Brophy's urgency, vividness, wildness with 'great generalities about love. There is a place for them here.' Brophy's gift that year of her novel *The Crown Princess* was inscribed 'For Iris with regret'. In 1962 Brophy made Iris dedicatee of her novel *Flesh*, making a collage of the cover of the copy she gave Iris so that it read, skittishly, '*Flash*, a navel by Brigid Bardot'. In 1964 Iris reviewed Brophy's *The Snow Ball*; she disliked reviewing, now did it rarely, and always as a favour to friends: 'There are novels one inhabits and others one picks up in one's hand. Perfection may belong to either. Miss Brophy's very beautiful new novel . . . belongs to the pick-able-up class'; she admired its 'sheer artistic insolence'.[61] Since her journals never normally record her well-attested pleasure in reading John Cowper Powys and Yukio Mishima, or mention contemporary fiction in general, a journal note praising Brophy's Firbankian *Finishing Touch* – described by its author as 'lesbian fantasy' – suggests real admiration, not propitiation.

On 8 July 1964 Brigid wrote: 'I am not determined to do anything except create that monument which our two extraordinarily opposing geniuses are designing. (It will be a regular baroque monster of the interpretation of opposites.)' In May 1965: 'I will bloody conduct the moon and stars in your praise!' Iris made a gift to her of the manuscript of *Under the Net*, which Brophy, with Iris's agreement, sold for the small sum of £500 to Iowa University in spring 1967.[62] Iris's later manuscripts were accordingly also sold to Iowa. When Brophy later succumbed to multiple sclerosis, Iris managed the tricky business of bedside visiting with 'instinctive tact'; Michael Levey could not forget his debt to Iris.[63] In 1985, not long before Brophy's death, Iris nominated her *Palace without Chairs* in the *TLS* as deserving to be better known,[64] and dedicated *The Good Apprentice* to her.

The friendship grew when Leveys visited Bayleys at Steeple Aston, and Iris saw both in London; for years Brigid and Iris would go away for a weekend break. Neither husband felt excluded. This friendship was neither without astringency nor without resilience.

'We writers are a strange crew', Iris wrote in *The Black Prince* – 'strange' meaning jealous, touchy, vain. Francis King met the Bayleys at parties given by Olivia Manning, who felt Iris to be overpraised, while she herself was underpraised. To King's pleas-antry 'In the house of literature are many mansions,' Manning retorted, 'But why do I have to be accommodated in an attic while Iris is always given the Royal Suite?'[65] Possibly resentment of 'overpraise' lay behind Brophy's 1958 letter accusing Iris of producing each year one more clay foot after another; also Bro-phy's 'very beastly' letter awaiting Iris in mid-April 1966 on return from a West Country visit with John, aborted by a blizzard. This was two months after the misunderstanding with Samson was resolved. If the pangs of disprized love also played their part, the immediate trigger was Iris's joking about Brigid's 'destructive' work-in-progress with Michael Levey and Charles Osborne – *Fifty Works of English and American Literature we Could do Without:*[66]

> *Pages* of violence in return accusing me of dishonesty etc. & having been a 'poor girl who just made it into a rich girls' school' and who consequently wants to, I forget what, conform or something.

Iris, who found such outbursts 'just vile, & terrifying', pondered whether 'real full-blooded hate' underlay Brophy's apparent devotion: 'I *dislike* her so much at the moments when she is malignant – & that dislike is depressing & awful.' The following day she felt rotten, shivery, as if with 'flu.

> Trying to work on philosophy. Feel sure it is all in Plato. Yet – Idiocy of my annoyance with BB. I recognize this as evil. My absolute Luciferian pride is hurt. That anyone cd call *ME* dishonest. Can one recognize the comparative (partial) injustice, & yet not resent at *all*? How is this done?

Nine days later, returned from Bristol with Brigid, she heard, in the early hours, the year's first cuckoo. On ringing Little Grange the housekeeper announced that BMB's life-companion Miss Rendall ('LJR') had just died. It had been absolutely sudden, a great shock. Iris went round the next morning to see BMB, who was approaching ninety. She was almost crippled with rheumatism but otherwise wonderfully herself, and very steady about LJR: 'such force and lucidity, such sheer *virtue* – a marvellous woman'. During this trip Brigid's eye was taken in the market of a West Country town by some small object, which Iris bought for her as a keepsake.[67]

6

The disjunction between the apparent aggression behind Brophy's letter[68] and the peaceable West Country visit is striking. Friendships have foundered on less, especially between writers, and Iris had then, not least where rudeness from a woman-admirer was concerned, a short fuse: her eyes would flash, her fists and teeth clench, even if there were no audible explosion. A propitiatory letter might follow. The friendship with a 'devoted' painter who portrayed Iris unflatteringly was said to have been damaged in this manner. Iris had wondered how to recognise the comparative (partial) injustice of Brophy's attack, and yet not resent it *at all.* How was this done? Unlike the many who make out of jealousy and hatred a career, Iris found the *experience* of dislike not just theoretically wrong, but also deeply disturbing and un-aesthetic. One's ego is often engaged, she accurately wrote, 'with *sorting and filing* damage done to its vanity';[69] she sought a way of not dwelling on grievance, indeed of transmuting it and finding a larger perspective. She had had a waking vision of 'the great void' of Kant's *Categorical Imperative**** while lying in bed the previous month on 13 March.

> One knows nothing except that the command is empty and yet absolute. An emptiness which lies beyond any-thing one knows of as love. Love as possessing, or grasping,

---

* 'The formal moral law in Kantian ethics, based on reason . . . opposed to hypotheti-cal imperatives, which depend upon desires.' *Oxford Companion to Philosophy*, ed. T. Honderich (Oxford, 1995), p.125.

489

or filling of self must be passed beyond. What lies beyond is scarcely recognizable as love. Yet love is the way & the only way.

The search for such self-transcendence is, in her fiction, philosophy and journals alike, a recurrent theme.[70] For those sceptical about – or repelled by – such high-minded rhetoric a 1983 novel offers alternative descriptions: 'Thus Tom enlarged his ego or (according to one's point of view) broke its barriers so as to unite himself with another in joint proprietorship of the world.'[71] Proust would habitually take out to dinner at the Ritz the hostile and uncooperative. It was his way of never relinquishing the upper hand. Iris, as we have seen, hated what she called 'mislaying' friends; and all release of spirit, she observed, is necessarily ambiguous.

In the summer of 1967 Brigid fell in love with Maureen Duffy, and talked of her and Iris's friendship in the past tense. Iris began to take in that she had really cut the painter. Brophy wrote, 'You and I are such a network; we're three-dimensional chess.' Iris had persuaded Brophy that a 'sufficiently diffused eroticism' might last forever. Brophy had now decided that biology was not to be cheated in this way. Iris felt 'a certain pain but mainly a kind of shock of relief, a sense of liberation & larger new possibility. The feathers are off Cherubino's hat.' She noted feeling 'rather lonely & full of hungry affections', relieved at the disappearance of a 'rather reluctant tied sense of responsibility I had about B – need to see her every week etc.'

7

Rummaging in an old chest in the autumn of 1968, Iris discovered a set of her diaries, running continuously, it seemed, from 1945 onward. As far as she could see she had kept up her journal-writing with remarkably few gaps. She hardly dared look at the references to Philippa, Elizabeth Anscombe, MacKinnon, Wallace Robson, etc. etc. 'Christ. Rather *awful* actually, this continuity of one's life. When seen all together, that business of falling in love with A, then with B, then with C (all madly) seems a bit sickening. The idea of being somehow "faithful" to it all seems a bit abstract – and thoroughly out of date!' November was a depressed time of year. 'The garden is dulled. First damp cold days.' The diary-discovery shook and saddened her.

> Why? Just passage of time, perhaps, sense of growing old, of being less beautiful than on the morning when Michael O[akeshott] kissed my feet. The passions which have just gone away and the things one has forgotten.

She remembered her 'world-renewing' struggles to free herself from obsession with Balogh in 1947, three years after that affair ended, and from 'the Chumman' in 1963. She did not feel too much identification with

> the ass that I was, yet this judgement is just as unimport-ant. How little work figures in this record – except for philosophy as I used to do it, and that very boring. The things which deeply sustain – puss, the novels – get little mention. Of course there is less obvious drama now & the tone has changed a bit.

Marriage and success had attenuated the drama. During 1966 – and what she later termed the summer of 'the three Ss' ('A warning: one is irrational in summer'[72]) – she underwent the revival of an old attachment to the philosopher Stuart Hampshire, and the inauguration of two newer ones, to the architectural critic Stephen Gardiner and to Scott Dunbar, Canadian and gay, writing his thesis at King's College on the philosophy of religion even though, like Iris, not a believer.[73] (Though so frequently in love, she tried to apply a 'strict set of rules' for putting on the brakes which John, 'the kindest man I've ever met', approved, never wanting to hear details; rules honoured in the observance as well as, sometimes, in the breach.) She noted that 'I think Stephen has his own troubles. Stuart prefers to remain an enigma.' Though all these friendships were durable, only Scott in 1967 looked then like proving 'something like a permanency, a real friend'. In December 1966: 'How lonely I was all those years [ago] ... Now, such good friendships: Frederic [Samson], Richard [Wollheim], Stephen [Gardiner], Dominic [de Grunne].'

8

Richard Wollheim invited Iris to give three lectures at University College London on 'good' and 'will' starting on 3 November 1966, surprising her 'pleasantly' by the schoolmasterly authority with which he dealt, after she had already agreed, with her subsequent 'craven indecision' and 'funk'. A characteristic card before the first lecture enquired 'where *exactly* I'm to be at 11 am. (it *is* 11 a.m.?) on Thursday (It *is* Thursday?) . . . Feel awfully nervous.' Though she wrote the lectures out and read them *verbatim* with her head down, they nonetheless went very well.

She was asked to Cambridge to give the Leslie Stephen lecture exactly one year later, in November 1967. The subject she chose was 'The Sovereignty of Good over other Concepts'. This was to form the third essay in a hundred-page monograph D.Z. Phillips commissioned for the series Studies in Ethics and Philosophy of Religion, which he edited for Routledge & Kegan Paul. He wanted her to include the essay 'Vision and Choice in Morality' from 1956, which he thought would make the book more various, but she refused. *The Sovereignty of Good*, as it was entitled, was never conceived of as a book, and such coherence as it has is fortunate, not designed. This may account for the fact that while it pleads for what has since been called 'Virtue Ethics', it pays no tribute to the pioneering work already done towards that end by Elizabeth Anscombe or Philippa Foot.[74] It is nonetheless rightly Iris's best-known work of philosophy, and its influence has grown since publication in 1970. It was fiercely original. To 'come out' then as a Platonist in morals seemed as bizarre as declaring oneself a Jacobite in politics.[75] The book was a passionately argued attack on both Anglo-Saxon and French orthodoxies, the fruit of a thorough professional involvement with the school of thought to which it was opposed. It also lucidly proposed a powerful and interesting 'rival soul-picture'.[76] *The Sovereignty of Good* was said to have returned moral philosophy to 'the people', those 'not corrupted' (*sic*) by academic philosophy: lay readers gained illumination from it, as well as philosophers. Like Iris's immature philosophies – Marxism, Existentialism, Anglo-Catholicism – it was a call to action, a programme for human change, this time by the lonely individual herself, with no help from party or priest. It located value, perhaps unusually for so passionate a Platonist, within attention to good things in *this* life, as well as in the spiritual quest itself.

9

To the biographer, one interest lies in how Freud is enlisted to deck out Plato's 'great Allegory' of the Cave and the Sun, which becomes in Iris's handling of it an account of how the lonely human soul struggles towards enlightenment. In this fable the unreconstructed human soul is imprisoned in a cave, deluded by the shadows dancing on the wall, shadows which are thrown by puppets manipulated between the prisoner's back and the fire. There are stages in the path to liberation.* Learning to turn around to see the fire, a first step, means – for Iris – discovering the ego. This casts its own heat and light, but by it she thought the 'moral pilgrim' might be detained on her ascent towards the sun – the ego being a false sun. Freud, whose demonstration that we are fundamentally un-free since enslaved to unconscious impulse she thought ignored by a facile liberalism, wanted to make men workable; Plato wanted to make men good. Hence Iris's growing antagonism towards psychoanalysis and psycho-therapy, which might delay the pilgrim. This hostility, David Pears believes, may have started when Harold Solomon, a post-graduate student at Oxford, gassed himself whilst in analysis, in 1959. Her journal entries before 1960 are sympathetic (in 1953

---

* 'The first reorientation is from pure fantasy to self-knowledge. The second (emergence from cave) from self-knowledge to a confused other-regard. In the cave, the shadows come to be seen as shadows, but without a sense of the outside world.' Journal, 1 October 1968.

the economist Paul Baran, 'since he is Jewish, ex-communist *and* has been psychoanalysed . . . can't but have *some* wisdom!'[77]).

Stuart Hampshire had a serious row with Iris at All Souls' around 1960 about the depth of her understanding of evil, at a time when he was entering psychoanalysis, of which she by then theoretically disapproved, a disapproval which gets into the novels. The psychoanalyst Palmer Anderson in *A Severed Head* is a demon; the psychotherapist Blaise in *The Sacred and Profane Love Machine* a temporiser, sexual cheat, and poor listener who reduces experience to formulae; while only Thomas McCaskerville in *The Good Apprentice*, having given up all faith in his subject as a 'science' and turned to Buddhism, is a good therapist. In *The Black Prince* Freudians are reducers, simplifiers, diminishers, and indeed the Freudian Francis Marlow's epilogue offers a fatuous reduction of the novel's events. At the Psychoanalytic Society in London around 1985 Iris duelled remorselessly with the writer and analyst Juliet Mitchell on this subject, and would allow analysis only demerits: the analyst had illicit power which he might abuse, and abuse sexually; only a 'saint' could be a therapist (and there are no good men or women). She felt that psychoanalysis generated self-concern, gave too abstract and crude a picture to account for human variousness, left the spiritual out of account. She disputed Hampshire's view that a 'perfect analysis' could ever make us wholly self-aware. Our energy should in any case be turned outwards in close loving attention of the quiddity of the world, not inwards, which tended to reinforce habitual pattern.

In practice Hampshire was one of many friends whose progress under analysis Iris took an interest in; nor was she so foolish as to fail to see that, when miserable, there are worse fates than employing a decent therapist. In an unpublished interview with David Pears[78] she got unconsciously close to another and interesting objection: analysis might 'solve' an artist's conflicts, without which she would lose the need to create. It is paradoxical that to a number of close friends Iris acted as mother-confessor or wise counsellor – which is to say roughly a therapist – making no objection to any love-'transference' entailed. It mattered to her that she be worthy of the role. Elsewhere, 'If you are a writer, you psychoanalyse yourself anyway.'[79]

10

Richard Wollheim, Frank Kermode and Iris agreed in May 1968 to express solidarity with the rebellious French students in a joint letter opposing '*Les Sclérotiques*'.[80] Francophilia presumably played a part here, for in Oxford two years later, shortly after a party at 10 Downing Street, John, Iris and lecturer in German David Luke went to a sit-in at the Clarendon Building. Students were occupying university buildings as an act of protest.[81] They were let in.

> (Cries of Yes! for puss. I think they didn't recognize me at first.) I talked briefly to the meeting but not eloquently. It felt frightening (mob-rule, however polite) & somehow nasty. Stupid people exercising power.

She put a student riot into her play *Joanna, Joanna*, written during 1969, and had surely been influenced in the interim by student treatment of Fraenkel, about whom she and Hampshire had a furious row. Hampshire saw Fraenkel as a frail human being, with ordinary imperfections (which he believed she overlooked), as well as a great scholar. She complained that the undergraduates did not 'respect' Fraenkel. Hampshire entirely saw why. For him, if you wanted a professorial adversary to challenge, you could not choose a better: 'pompous, Germanic, show-off, dominant, boastful, embarrassing, oppressive, humiliating those who were bad at writing Greek prose . . .'. He feared that Iris could not see the human being at all, just this 'golden figure'. (She had, it was said, nonetheless been affronted when Fraenkel harassed a student she sent to him.) There was an analogous row with John Simopoulos, who objected both to her piety about Ducane in *The Nice and the Good* merely because he was an All Souls' scholar, and to his anachronistic use of schoolboy slang. 'No one has said "What a terrific ass I am!", for forty years!' he objected. Iris was very angry. Both Hampshire and Simopoulos feared – as did

Samson – that she was growing reactionary.[82] Indeed, in *Sovereignty* she argued that 'we cannot be as democratic' about moral philosophy 'as some philosophers would like to think'.[83] While welcoming the liberalisation of the law against homosexuality, and (presumably) the abolition of hanging and the easing of the divorce laws, Iris feared the erosion of authority the 1960s represented.

Two weeks before the sit-in at the Clarendon Fraenkel's wife Ruth, who had more tact and a greater sense of humour than he did, died. He took a large overdose of barbiturates in order to follow her. He was eighty-one. 'There was no doubt about his intentions.'[84] Fraenkel's work always came first: indeed Ruth, despite having a Ph.D., had given up a promising academic career on marriage to act as his secretary and research assistant. Yet he would save up and list items for discussion with her, indicating love as well as pedantry. Maurice Bowra[85] wrote to Iris, 'How wise of Ed to follow his wife so soon. I saw him on Wednesday and he looked very old & shrunken.' She also had seen him, earlier that term, on the opposite side of the High. Fearing that he did not like sudden encounters in the street, she had not crossed. She felt so sad at this passing '– and sad for myself as one always does'.

18

Shakespeare and Friends
1970–1978

ritics had at first placed *Under the Net*, with its Dryden
epigraph (' 'Tis well an old-age is out/And time to begin
a new . . .') as the work of an 'Angry Young Man'. Iris
was neither a man, young, nor angry, and had not then read
Kingsley Amis's *Lucky Jim*. Yet – and despite the fact that the
relationship of her work with the political was not simple –
politics always interested her. In 1958 she wrote an essay
propagating Guild Socialism for a landmark collection of left-
wing political articles entitled *Convictions*;[1] in 1962 she campaigned for nuclear disarmament;[2] in 1964 she wrote a long
article for the magazine *Man and Society* arguing for the legalisa-
tion of homosexuality.[3] After homosexuality was decriminalised
in Britain in 1967 she lent her support to Senator David Norris's
campaign to legalise it in Ireland.[4] (Honor Tracy, who saw Iris
as a liberal intellectual who 'insists on feeling Responsible,
and – as far as she can – Guilty', joked heavy-handedly to Iris
that she was herself 'now working night and day to get bestiality
recognized'.[5]) Iris campaigned against the Vietnam war[6] and
rowed passionately with Leo Pliatzky, who contested her view that
American policy was wicked.[7] She wrote twice to *The Times* in
1968, first attacking the British government for keeping the
French student activist Daniel Cohn-Bendit out of the country
('What has happened to the nation in whose museum reading
room Karl Marx worked unmolested?'), later opposing the
Nigerian war against Biafra.[8] She went on demonstrations for

political prisoners in Russia* and helped agitate for, then delighted in the release of, the Soviet dissident Vladimir Bukovsky in 1976.

Bukovsky's bravery made him an iconic figure for Iris, one whose life showed, like Frank's, that 'history could be made to bow before the sheer stubbornness of a human conscience'.[9] Her friendship also mattered greatly to him. After smuggling to the West documented case histories of dissenters falsely classified as insane, he had himself been branded a mentally deranged criminal, spending fourteen years in Russian asylums and prison camps. He received a further twelve-year sentence in 1971, but was exchanged, after five years, for a Chilean Communist. Iris befriended him, noting how on his arrival in Britain he appeared, though only thirty-five, a pale and tense old man; he later regained his earlier beauty. In 1992 she wrote to her Member of Parliament requesting a copy of the Maastricht Treaty, of which, though broadly pro-European, she felt suspicious:[10] 'in France it was distributed to all electors'.[11] She was also an advocate of the sadly short-lived Irish Peace Movement.[12]

Education engaged her most: 'To stir people's imagination, to explode in their imagination – a good teacher can do this so that the pupils are never the same again.'[13] Such a teacher, she told a friend embarking on a teaching career, might utilise 'a certain sadism but ideally this should be entirely veiled'. In 1960 she entered a *Times* debate about offering women a 'softer' education, which struck her forcibly as the wrong way to protect them from their current position as 'second-class citizens'.[14] It was the emphasis on visiting schools and colleges that caused her to agree to accompany Julian Mitchell, Adrian Henri and John McGrath on the second Arts Council Writers' tour, to Lancashire, in March 1969. They made twenty-one such visits in a week.[15] The comprehensivisation of secondary schools provoked first a letter to *The Times* defending selective education in 1973;[16] then an article, 'Doing Down the Able Child: A Socialist's Case for Saving our

---

* See, e.g., journal entry, December 1976: 'Yesterday, at the Russian dissidents demo, and glad I went. Held poster for man I'd never heard of: Zshverdlin.'

Grammar Schools' in the *Sunday Telegraph*[17] (famously reprinted in *Black Paper 3 on Education*[18]); and helped trigger her voting Conservative in 1983 and 1987. She wrote a long article-review on education for the *New Statesman* in 1977.[19] The Tory attack on the independent funding of higher education prompted in 1988 a four-page letter expressing 'very strong feelings' to Kenneth Baker, then Secretary of State, and helped bring her back to Labour, for whom she voted in 1997. She drafted notes 'on the teaching of English in schools', probably for Baker, in 1988, and gave to the one 'saint' of her books, Stuart in *The Good Apprentice* (1985), the profession of schoolteacher.

In 1968 Iris remarked that she wanted to write a novel about either Vietnam or the colour bar.[20] Her *daemon*, however, had other plans. Politics were, she accurately saw, 'not in her blood'. She felt 'ordinary private things close, politics not'.[21] Her unpublished trades union novel 'Jerusalem' had been a failure, never bridging private and public worlds. Mor's pro-Labour views are unconnected to the life of *The Sandcastle*, a romance. *The Book and the Brotherhood* (1987), purporting to deal with the tensions between Marxism and liberal humanism, indeed gives us two 'casebook' welfare problems, in the chronic unemployment of Gulliver Ashe and the guilty misery of the potential single mother Tamar Hernshaw, who has her baby aborted. The first is cured by Ashe's kindness to a snail, the second by a magical ritual dreamt up by a priest. Possibly one reason for Iris's popular success lies in exactly this inaccessibility of the private to the public world. Post-war England increasingly rejected the good society in favour of the good relationship, isolating the self as the main site left for significant change. And criticisms here miss the point. Iris's gift is poetic, mythological, fabulous. It is not sociological – as, soberly, she acknowledged: the patterns holding up her work were 'sexual, mythological, psychological and not the great hub of society which a nineteenth century writer relied on'.[22] As Siegfried Sassoon said of Walter de la Mare: '(S)he makes you see the world with "re-christened eyes".'

George Orwell had pondered whether a 'merely moral' criticism of society might not be just as 'revolutionary' as 'politico-economic' criticism, the defects of society being the defects of the heart writ large.[23] But how to get society 'in'? The modern novel, Iris agreed with Canetti in 1953, having lost the structure given by 'society' in the nineteenth century, must create its own structure by the 'complete creation of a myth'. Her own rousing, brilliant early polemical essays – 'Against Dryness', 'The Sublime and the Beautiful Revisited' – pleaded none the less for a return to the strengths of nineteenth-century fiction, for a novel combining the social and the psychological, not separating the individual character and the type. These essays are a poor guide to her achievement. A.S. Byatt, impressed and puzzled by the singular 'forms' of the novels, found the essays while researching her pioneering study of Iris's first seven novels, *Degrees of Freedom* (1965). Byatt later blamed any astringency in her study, which partly demonstrated the shortfall between Iris's essays and her novels, on the influence of F.R. Leavis.[24] The critic Christopher Ricks endorsed Byatt the same year, arguing that Iris's novels 'exemplify what she most deplores . . . her beliefs and intentions [are] admirable, relevant, and almost completely unachieved'.[25] Iris condemned her inability to create memorable, free characters as a 'spiritual' failure.[26] Ricks, on the whole, agreed.

The number of persecuted maidens imprisoned in remote enclosures in Iris's work* presumably lay behind Malcolm Bradbury's perceptive argument (by contrast) that she had been wrongly taken for a 'realist' when she wished to explore romance-forms, and that her sense of the limitations to human freedom was far larger and more pessimistic than Byatt understood.[27] It is a tribute to the rhetorical force of Iris's essays that critics began by castigating her novels for their failure to live up to her own precepts: they trusted more the teller than the tale. To do so is to default on what Samuel Johnson argued was the primary duty of the critic: to 'exhibit his manner of being pleased'. As the novelist Paul Bailey astutely observed, if many of Iris's books

---

* From Annette in her cupboard in *The Flight from the Enchanter*, through Catherine in *The Bell* and Hannah in *The Unicorn*.

appeared to function with the mechanism commonly associated with bedroom farce, so then does a supreme work of art like *Cosi fan tutte*.[28]

A.S. Byatt's British Council pamphlet on Iris in 1976, by contrast, saw a conflict between her desire to have a strong 'apprehensible shape'[29] – leading to her writing 'closed' Gothic novels like *The Unicorn* – and an opposing desire to set her characters free – leading to novels like *The Bell*. Here Byatt suggests that the inspiration of Shakespeare helped Iris combine both satisfactions, learning to release her characters, but within plots as brazenly contrived as those of Shakespearian comedy itself. Byatt celebrated Iris as simultaneously bravely 'mandarin and sensational', implying that neither her seriousness ('mandarin') nor her popularity ('sensational') required apology. Iris Murdoch was that rare species, a serious novelist who was also genuinely popular. Like Shakespeare, she wanted, as John noted in 1955, 'something for everyone' in her novels.[30]

2

In 1968 Iris declared herself 'profoundly bored with my thoughts, notably with the whole long (ten years long at least) train which led up to "The Sovereignty of Good". Not that I think this is all "wrong" but I just sense it as fearfully *limited* and partial.' Christopher Cornford had written that her 'account of human nature & the good isn't apparently historical ... it treats the situation as perennial'. It left out of account the evolution of consciousness. Iris's journals explore her doubts throughout 1968, the year that she was writing *A Fairly Honourable Defeat*. She noted a number of friends, such as David Morgan and John Simopoulos, who lived 'right outside my comfortable Platonism. What about them? Have I come to the end of the path which started many years ago when I first read Simone Weil and saw a far off light in the forest? The woodcutter's house! Hardly an arrival.'

Although her 1982 Gifford lectures – published as *Metaphysics*

501

as a Guide to Morals – would still show the imprint of Plato and Simone Weil, her journals and fiction alike after 1968 criticise and test her own ideas. 6 January 1969: 'I used to think Good was more important than free because political freedom cd look after itself, theoretically at any rate. Now – perhaps it is goodness that can look after itself?' She wondered whether *Bruno's Dream* enacted the end of her subjection to Weil's puritanism; and of *A Fairly Honourable Defeat* she noted: 'Deplatonisation . . . running the whole machine into the ground.' She prayed to be able to 'stifle' her own high-mindedness.

Marcus, the Platonist of *The Time of the Angels*, lost his nerve and abandoned his monograph. *A Fairly Honourable Defeat* came out the same year as *The Sovereignty of Good*, and Rupert, its Platonist, has his work physically torn up by his son Peter together with the devilish Julius King. Rupert ends up drowned in his swimming-pool – dead, Julius comments, of vanity. Iris's sacrifice of Rupert could be seen as symbolic. Rather as Rupert and his wife Hilda make monthly payments to Oxfam as a talisman against loss of their super-abundant good fortune, so Iris sacrifices the character whose views most closely resemble her own, as a safeguard against the hubris of publicising her own philosophical views.

A Fairly Honourable Defeat, which rewrites *Much Ado About Nothing* in 1960s South Kensington, is one of her most satisfying, inaugurating a period of artistic maturity. Its painstakingly slow first half establishes the relationships within the small court with a cast of characters who are interesting, believable, even memorable. Its second half, through Julius's operatic plotting, blows these apart. (Detailed synopses of Iris's plots are as embarrassing as those of opera, and give as little idea of the experience of the work as a dramatic continuum.[31]) The novel's villain, Julius King, argues in front of the Turners in the Tate Gallery that:

> Human beings are roughly constructed entities full of indeterminacies and vaguenesses and empty spaces. Driven along by their private needs they latch blindly onto each other, then pull away, then clutch again. Their little sadisms and their little masochisms are surface

phenomena. Anyone will do to play the roles. *They never really see each other at all.* There is no relationship ... which cannot easily be broken and there is none the breaking of which is a matter of any genuine seriousness. Human beings are essentially finders of substitutes.[32]

So Julius preaches to the flighty intellectual Morgan, who left her Christ-like half-ineffectual husband Tallis Browne and fell in love with Julius. He then wagers Morgan ten guineas that he can break off Simon and Axel's happy homosexual partnership within ten days. This wager-scene also alludes distantly to Satan's disputation with God in the Book of Job about the existence of one righteous man.[33] The scene in which Julius and Simon spy, from behind a portico in a museum, upon the meeting of Rupert and Morgan borrows directly from the pleachèd bower of *Much Ado About Nothing*, Act III. Julius combines the roles of Don John – who tried to split up Claudio and Hero – and Don Pedro – who drew Beatrice and Benedick together. Julius steals letters to try to engineer an affair between the vain and foolish Rupert and Rupert's fickle sister-in-law Morgan, and nearly succeeds. Both the novel and the play explore what Benedick aptly terms the giddiness of the human heart.

3

Life, Iris (like Dostoevsky) believed, is so fantastic that we instinctively mix in a little fiction to render it plausible. Life feeds the novel as well as literature. Iris insisted in interviews that she had witnessed without naming him an 'alien god-figure' whose entry into situations, with the collusion of his slaves, caused trouble.[34] She further described Canetti as 'a good man who could have used his [intellectual] power[s], had he wished, for evil purposes'.[35] The satanic Julius in *A Fairly Honourable Defeat* is not Canetti (Iris's disdain at the suggestion is easy to imagine). But she could not have created Julius had she never known Canetti,[36] and she gave Julius some of his traits. Both Canetti and Julius are professional outsiders.* The trio of Julius and Tallis fighting for the soul of Tallis's wife Morgan belongs to Christian *psychomachia* – Christ and Satan struggling for the soul of the Common Man. It is also based on the battle between Canetti and John over Iris in 1953–56; John commented that he had 'wrestled spiritually' with his rivals.[37] Morgan's dislikeable, naïve belief that she can love everyone with impunity, that love conquers all, is partly that of the careless, vamp-like young Iris who had felt that she could love everyone without cost, and who would note, in the midst of multiple flirtations, 'Feel curiously detached, almost frivolous . . . as light as a feather, can't ever see myself as bloody or in danger or a menace to others.' Julius's parents changed their name from 'Kahn' to King. A small 'Kahn' is a Can-etti.

Tallis is partly inspired by Franz, grieving for a sister who died young, and symbolising the power of goodness.[38] Frequently Franz, interrupted when drafting a new lecture, would find in his typewriter only the words 'In my last lecture, I . . .' written there.† Tallis has the identical habit. The revelation that Tallis's sister was raped and killed by a sex maniac comes on the same page as the disclosure that Julius spent the war in Belsen, a symmetry, found sensational by some, meant to bear out Simone Weil's hard-nosed belief that affliction degrades all but the saintly. Tallis absorbs his own suffering: Julius, a scientist researching germ warfare, passes his pain on. Where Fox's evil in *The Flight from the Enchanter* is a 'given', never explored, his successor Julius's is a more detailed portrait, albeit, like Iago's, a mysterious one.

When the novel came out, the art historian John Golding, then teaching at the Courtauld Institute, was telephoned by friends who believed that his partnership with James Joll had inspired the depiction of Simon and Axel. Joll was eleven years older than Golding; Axel is older than Simon. This and his Courtauld

---

* Pamela Field, who met Canetti once (c1952), and never forgot it, recounted his comic alienation at the Athenaeum, where he compared the elderly clubmen behind their newspapers to crocodiles. English club life made him feel alien, an outsider; compare Julius's 'Clubs are not for such as me', *A Fairly Honourable Defeat*, p.80.
† See Iris's journal, 6 June 1977: 'Rainy for jubilee – so sad. Memory: Franz with his typewriter always stuck at "In my last lecture I . . ."'

background link Golding to Simon.[39] Golding and Joll never raised the matter with Iris. The resemblances were superficial, and what Iris made out of them was new and strange. Unlike Axel and Simon, dominated by Julius, neither Golding nor Joll was in thrall to Canetti. They knew him slightly, and thought him bogus.[40] Iris called the novel-in-progress the 'Simon-novel', and he is her most attractive gay character, with a promiscuous past, gentle, kindly, un-intellectual, and willing in the end to outface Julius.

Although some thought Julius's cruelty, boredom and Machiavellianism inspired, however distantly, by Kreisel,[41] he owes as much to the mythomaniac and manipulative Canetti, who in the words of Friedl's sister Susie, 'loved creating and undoing human relations and toying with people, watching their relations as a scientist might watch his white mice'.[42] Margaret Gardiner watched Canetti, on his return in 1948 from St Ives, talking into existence a relationship between her painter-friend Ben Nicolson and another friend, a woman-painter.[43] Canetti choreographed not merely Friedl's love-affairs but, after her death, that of her surviving partner Allan Forbes with Bernice Rubens, and then, for symmetry, that between Rubens's husband Rudi Nassauer and his mistress. Rubens, ringing frantically on the latter's door in the small hours in search of her husband, was distressed to uncover Canetti, masterminder of the affair, instead. Iris, a friend of both, would certainly have learnt of this. Nassauer, first in thrall to Canetti, later grew disenchanted. Julius is the erotic ringmaster, mischievous and malign, more than capable of the cruel practical joke Michael and Anne Hamburger saw Canetti play on Franz in 1952, of pretending that Franz's poems were now in print.[44] Susie, reading the novel in 1998, felt that Canetti's influence ran throughout, 'in particular in the long discussion about the fascination of evil and the boredom of good' in Chapter 18, and noted the echo of Canetti's fussy Jewish mother side when Julius cleans Tallis's kitchen at the end. She doubted that the real-life Canetti would have relinquished Morgan so easily.[45]

One of many surreal yet authoritatively 'seen' and evoked scenes involves Julius cutting up Morgan's dress and underwear in his Brook Street flat, then leaving her naked. The scene links variously to Canetti. His hero Kien in *Auto da Fé* dreamed of cutting up women's dresses;[46] and the theme ran through Canetti and Friedl's story. The painter-dwarf Endre Nemes had raped Friedl and torn her clothes to ribbons before slashing his own pictures. Nemes turned up when Friedl was with Canetti in Paris, having 'brought thirty dresses' from Sweden; Canetti kept making Friedl put one on, 'then tearing it off her and loving her, & making her put on another'.

Julius's spying – he enters others' flats and houses uninvited – is scarcely odder than Canetti's, who entered Friedl's house in Downshire Hill when she was out and read her private papers. Many recalled Canetti's habit of 'dropping by' – which some bluntly called spying; while Anne Wollheim recalled his being invited to lunch in 1947 and staying an extra twelve hours. Julius has both habits. Once Marie-Louise von Motesiczky disconcerted a friend walking with her in Holland Park by explaining persistent rustlings in the bushes, 'Oh, that's just Canetti; he's so jealous.'[47]

4

Iris gave the Satanic Julius the line, 'Few questions are more important than: "Who is the boss?"'[48] The Canetti of *Crowds and Power* underlay the question. But Julius, who, unlike Canetti, demeans both art and love and is wholly cold, is the *Geist der stets verneint* – the spirit that negates – alive only because Iris inhabits him *herself*, rendering him comical, fantastical and disturbing. Good fiction, against her tenets, is not made up out of 'high-mindedness', and she had succeeded in 'stifling' her own. Julius does to his puppets what Iris does to her characters: makes them fall in and out of love; and she here tests out the conventions on which her novels are based. She mentioned in a letter to Philippa that she was growing fond of her 'demon'.[49]

Canetti was circumspect with letters. Not all Iris's friends were so careful. One ex-lover acquired the reputation of giving readings from her letters to other girlfriends in California, and also to groups of interested listeners. Another kept Iris's letters in the glove-compartment of his Mini, where they led a semi-public life of their own. It is no accident that the purloining of letters plays a major role in the plot of *A Fairly Honourable Defeat*. The novel tests out the premises upon which the giddy emotional promiscuity of the average Murdoch plot is based: that 'Man is a giddy thing,' and most human beings 'never really see each other at all'. Here Julius is Iris-as-novelist, setting up a laboratory experiment on her own characters, and his manipulations are partly successful: Morgan and Rupert do start to fall in love, Hilda's marriage fails, Rupert drowns himself. Julius disturbs because he carries so much of the truth of the novel. But he does not have everything his own way. Axel and Simon's partnership survives and grows.

5

The Nice and the Good was dedicated to Lord David and Rachel Cecil, who lived, like the Grays in that novel, in Dorset, where 'everything is . . . *just the right size*'.[50] Although Cecil spoke of John as his best pupil,[51] he taught him for only a term.[52] But he would arrive unannounced at John's digs after he graduated in 1950 and say, 'Let's get up and wander around the garden a bit,' an Oxford habit of its period. John, like Isaiah Berlin, admired Cecil's clear, straightforward, unpretentious way of looking at things, shrewd and commonsensical, and inherited both his mantle as a critic unfussed by theory and his non-stop witty, agile speech-patterns, Cecil being articulate and audible, but speaking in such fast explosive bursts that not everyone caught what he said. This was contagious: Berlin copied Cecil to some degree. Rachel Cecil encouraged John to write his first novel, promising to do the same herself.[53] Both Cecils were devoted to John and Iris, hoped for their marriage and were glad when it happened. Both Bayleys shared the Cecils' benign and humorous interest in others.

The Cecils spent their weekends in an old pub, Red Lion House (to which they moved after David's retirement in 1969), a sociable house restlessly full of what Henry James called 'good talk', in Cranborne in Dorset, a village the Cecil family more or less owned. The Bayleys were frequent guests. An elder politician-brother known as Bobbity (Lord Salisbury) had a red-brick Georgian house; the handsome manor house belonged to his nephew Lord Cranborne. David's sister was Duchess of Devonshire. Cranborne, where the comfortable secure class-conscious civilisation of the past lay about,[54] probably introduced Iris to a more elevated social scene than either she or John had formerly known and helped prompt the difference of *milieu* in the novels of the 1960s. The title of *The Nice and the Good* echoes the cant phrase 'the Great and the Good' for the invisible decision-makers of the liberal English Establishment, and the novel's children go to Bedales, Bryanston, La Résidence; their parents are 'of course'[55] all Socialists. Only Casie the maid's Socialism, full of social envy, is comical or notable. Cecil cooking was famously bad, and Iris shared David's aristocratic indifference to such matters.

Rachel Cecil was the daughter of the literary critic Desmond MacCarthy, and Frances Partridge a great friend of both Cecils. Yet, while knowing many such Bloomsbury figures,[56] and with humorous tales to tell of Virginia Woolf, the Cecils found the Bloomsbury world mildly absurd: both were very religious as well as pleasure-loving. Iris, 'elemental and passionate and spiritual',[57] enjoyed working David up. He loved an argument – it was like sport, like fox-hunting. He once described to Frances Partridge himself and Iris shouting at each other, jumping up and down on the carpet.[58] Rachel would try to calm him down, but the arguments would go on and on, often about politics. In one David defended capital punishment, while Iris insisted that an ideal society would not need even imprisonment. In another Iris vigorously maintained that both Khrushchev and his wife were good-looking and/or sexually appealing. David's arguments were sometimes logic-chopping or for effect, Iris's more emotional. The rows were wholly without acrimony. David's son Hugh remembered his father stamping up and down the six feet between the sofa and the drawing-room fire, swigging quantities of watery whisky and choking angrily, Iris saying, 'Yes, but *dammit* David . . .' All four would go for walks together, David and John jabbering ahead about, for example, whether Tolstoy was really a hypocrite, Rachel and Iris bringing up the rear. Every so often David would pull up, like a cow or a horse, glued to the spot with excitement about the matter under discussion. Iris got him moving again by sheer force of will-power. More uproarious talk from 12 until 1 p.m., David's 'happy hour', his favourite drink a mixture of sweet and dry Vermouth.

Frances Partridge noted John and Iris's devotion to each other, and how his dryness, humour and effervescent vitality seasoned her charmingly unselfconscious solidity, good head, warm heart.[59] She recalled Iris's swift changes of mood: if told something sad, tears would stream down her face. Iris and John sang part-songs together in the middle of the night, and Iris was ready for any venture or outing.[60] Partridge liked Iris's high-mindedness. In a discussion about whether one would prefer to be executed in public or not, Iris put in a word for making an effective last speech.[61] Probably she had in mind the official version of Frank's death.

6

Janet and Reynolds Stone met the Bayleys in 1961 at a Cecil cocktail party,[62] after which[63] Iris wrote to 'Dear Mrs Stone' asking if they might call in. Soon they were *amis de famille* at the Old Rectory, the Stones' beautiful house at Litton Cheney in its magical nine acres of garden, hidden in a fold of chalk hill in far west Dorset. Iris drove part of the hundred-mile journey from Oxford. Reynolds, countryman, craftsman, engraver and painter, and Iris got on 'swimmingly'. Both were shy. John wrote a book on Hardy at Litton Cheney. There was a routine. Everyone worked in the first part of the morning. Reynolds then drove them the three miles down to the sea, perhaps showing them something he liked on the way. A quick swim, then lunch prepared by Winnie, who had been a Barnardo's girl: generally shepherd's pie and rice pudding. After a nap, and further work, Reynolds liked to read aloud around the hearth in the evenings – often Jane Austen. He read very well.

Janet, bishop's daughter, singer, photographer, liked knowing well-known people in the artistic world – not socially well-known, apart from Kenneth Clark, with whom she was very close. 'John Bayley,' she remarked in 1963, 'makes me laugh *desperately* long and *too*, too loud.' She called him 'the world's *most* amusing man', and loved the Bayleys' sense of humour, the peals of laughter that would come from their bedroom.[64] Reynolds would sit painting or engraving in one corner of the lovely drawing-room, inspired by looking out on one side onto the wooded garden where rushing streams fed a little lake, on the other to an unmown front lawn, full of daisies and buttercups. His work, descending from Thomas Bewick and Samuel Palmer, was 'precise, visionary and spiritual', and what Iris wrote of his art was also true of hers, that it 'proceeded unselfconsciously from an intensely personal privacy' to give that 'shock of beauty which shows how close, how in a sense ordinary, are the marvels of the world'.[65]

Much of Janet's energy went into creating an environment where a bewitched stream of summer guests, including many notable artists and writers, came to work and relax: L.P. Hartley, Leonard Woolf, Duncan Grant, Frances Partridge, Quentin Bell, Julian Huxley, Benjamin Britten, Henry Moore, Frances Cornford, the Day Lewises, John Piper, John Betjeman *e tutti quanti*. 'Janet's a real *artist* of life,' was often said of her; Hugh Cecil recalled that these gatherings represented 'a higher peak of English civilisation, despite their modesty, than most of the grand aristocratic establishments of the period'.[66] Iris dedicated *A Fairly Honourable Defeat* to Janet and Reynolds Stone, and noted that their hospitality kept alive the tradition of the reading-party.[67]

Despite Janet's extraordinary Edwardian outfits, some acquired through mail order – Dorchester High Street observed her more than once dressed from head to foot in mauve gingham with a parasol, a look Iris described as 'very summer-nymph'[68] – she was essentially unconfident, vulnerable, highly-wrought, full of fun, yet practical too. She brought up four quiet and talented children, each bedroom had a roaring fire in winter, cream was supplied and butter churned from milk from their own cow. There were picnics on deserted Chesil beach, where Iris once nearly drowned,[69] croquet, and a wild tennis-court – Iris and John would clap when the other contrived to hit the ball.[70] Janet taught Iris to sew *gros-point* needlework cushion-covers, one designed by Reynolds of a trout with 'JB' and 'IM' in the corners. Though this was partly a social device allowing Iris a refuge from conversation, she enjoyed the activity too, and made many designs. Janet protected Reynolds, whose gentleness made him easily upset by any violation of things, 'like a monk in the midst of worldly goings-on';[71] he in turn loved and supported her.

The Stones also visited Cedar Lodge, and Stones and Bayleys made expeditions together, staying in a cottage on the Pembrokeshire coast in 1972 and in the west of Ireland in 1975, where a horse attempted a bite out of John's appetising trousers with their exciting food-stains.[72] They visited the painter Derek Hill near Letterkenny, and Honor Tracy on Achill Island. In 1978 they went, more ambitiously, to Assisi, where Reynolds was unwell. A home-body like John, essentially not liking 'abroad', he once said he would be content to paint for the rest of his life within his own garden.[73] That year Iris completed twelve short bird-poems, one for each month, and Reynolds produced appropriate engravings: they were published as *A Year of Birds* in 1984. Reynolds died in 1979, after a massive stroke, at seventy. Iris missed 'his welcoming smile and open arms' and worried about Janet, who, devastated, lost the will to take her increasingly popular photographic portraits, whose publication in 1988 Iris encouraged and, indeed, helped oversee.[74] Those of Iris are notably successful, and were selected by her for a collected edition of her works. One of John shows him trying out a new discovery: he bought in Bicester some agricultural trousers of a tweed so stiff they stood up by themselves, cut out a superfluous section and glued the rest together with Copy-Dex, thereby acquiring what passed, to him, for a pair of stylish trousers for £2. He resembled, he remarked with satisfaction, a silly bear in a story.

7

As for Iris's dress-sense, after marriage she gave up feminine impersonation. Before then she could disconcert at dances, wearing a velvet dress and full make-up including mascara and lipstick.[75] John's old English teacher at Eton George Lyttelton, an important influence on him, called her in 1959 'a tousled, heelless, ladder-stockinged little lady – crackling with intelligence but nothing at all of a prig'.[76] 'I am very *fond* of clothes,' Iris remarked to Deirdre Connolly, who with her husband Cyril met the Bayleys after 1962 at the Stones', and with Elizabeth Bowen, and who was struck by her quietness. She appreciated the unique style Iris evolved – 'pie-crust frill shirt, dirndl-type skirt, or artist's smocks, but always nice colours & stuff & patterns'.[77] John's pupil Paul Binding, another Cecil and Stone guest, recalled Iris's 'Florentine hair-cut and *paysanne* skirts and (to an undergraduate) rather winning and subtly flirtatious manner'. Binding introduced the Bayleys to the novelist Barbara Pym, who recorded 'a rather dumpy woman wearing trousers and a sort of ethnic tunic', and was struck when Iris, much smaller than she had imagined, told her that she had to write things many times over, and that nothing came absolutely right first time.[78]

Iris visited Kingsley Amis and his second wife Elizabeth Jane Howard a few times at their house 'Lemmons' in Barnet – 'How are you, old chap?' she'd greet Amis, who despite doubts about the growing mandarin discursiveness of Iris's novels, always none the less deferred to her superior intellect.[79] Howard was always very shy and awkward with Iris, without understanding why. At a lunch *à deux* in Kensington, Iris said she was dining next week as guest of honour at an Oxford college, and felt unsure whether in her present clothes she would be suitably dressed. What did Howard think? Since Iris did not ask idle questions, Howard – appraising her black karate-like tunic and trousers lightly marked by what could very possibly have been scrambled egg – remarked that perhaps she would not. Iris nodded gravely and they discussed what she might buy. A week later a postscript arrived declaring, 'I didn't bother to change clothes and all was well.'

Although she could look bohemian or eccentric – as the tangerine-coloured plastic mac with purple outfit she wore in a filmed interview around 1970 suggests[80] – Iris could also be stylish. At a dinner Frances Partridge gave for her on 30 November 1966 she arrived in a splendid antique military coat made of the finest black cloth with gilt buttons. Partridge noted, too, 'her magnificent realism, her Joan-of-Arc-like quality, her way of attending to what everyone said, weighing it (to the accompaniment of a very Oxford "Yes, yes, yes") and then bringing out her response'.[81]

8

Iris assented when John called her 'not a boo-sayer':[82] both Bayleys liked to please. By 1964 Iris was answering ten letters a day.[83] A busy social life generated its own mythologies and household expressions: an '*Antrim Boat*' (borrowed from Rachel Cecil's family) described an arduous journey to a social occasion at which one's presence had been declared essential, only to find oneself invisible and unnoticed. A '*Gore*' (also Cecilian) occurred when two parties politely participated in an event neither wanted, each out of a mistaken desire to oblige the other. '*Shooting someone down*' happened when your invitation was declined: you gained all the merit for having offered, with none of the bother of fulfilment. '*Alibi cards*' were, by definition, sent when away as an apology for more general non-communication. '*Now we can be animals again,*' adapted from *The Wind in the Willows* (which John read aloud to Iris), was a formulaic utterance of relief at having survived a pretentious or otherwise disagreeable gathering. Such coolness Iris, who simultaneously wished to satisfy all requirements, could share, though she made no record of these usages. Social events are ranked, on Michelin principles, 'very good', 'good' or 'very OK', 'not good' and (more rarely) 'horrible'. Iris spoke of Shakespeare as a wordsmith trying to practise his craft while continually distracted by needing to bow and scrape and 'keep the grandees happy'.[84] She was proud of inventing the verb 'to porlock' to describe interruptions;[85] and learnt to hide her own fury when friends 'dropped by'.[86]

Some friends, they decided, were 'elephants', others 'angels'. John's brother Michael was Iris and John's premier example of the great category of elephants; later friends – Stephen Spender, George Clive who farmed and entertained in the Welsh Marches – were others. The defining characteristics of an elephant included quietness, secretiveness, impenetrability, small eyes, being kind and easy to be with, someone who might, in the pleasantest of ways, under an always polite exterior, be pursuing their own ends: kindness combining most happily with egoism. (John and Iris would frequently discuss whether there could be *female* elephants, and finally decided: definitely, no. How elephants propagate their species remains therefore a mystery.) 'Elephants' cannot be 'angels': angels have the wonderful capacity of never belonging entirely to themselves: there were not many angels. Elephants definitely do belong to themselves. They lead, however, unexamined lives, and don't desire self-knowledge.

9

'Parties and dinner parties. I always look forward to these, but often am disappointed,'[87] wrote Iris, not in her teens or her twenties, but shortly before her seventy-second birthday; a token of what made Victoria Glendinning memorably describe her as one who saw life, always, with the eyes of a 'wise child'. After a lunch party in 1987 Iris noted, 'Mysteriously, there is sometimes wonderful communication and camaraderie,' but 'sometimes social scenes are, for me at any rate, dead, I become speechless, utterly awkward, like I used to feel long ago'.[88] Her reserve was legendary. In 1969, after days at Litton Cheney and Cranborne, where she had recorded so much happiness, she wrote 'I am fond of these people but never quite communicate with them. Went to Dancing Ledge, to Reynolds's wonderful rock pool by the sea. I was afraid to go into the sea' – probably a reference to her near-drowning on an earlier visit.[89]

ABOVE Hochsteingasse displaced persons student camp, Graz, Austria, 21 July 1946. The three uniformed figures are John Corsellis, Margaret Jaboor and Group Captain Ryder Young (who flew Chamberlain to Munich), Director of UNRRA camp, Lienz. Looking over Corsellis' shoulder is Jože Jančar.

LEFT Officer Murdoch, UNRRA Grade 7, at Hochsteingasse, summer 1946.

ABOVE Marija and Jože Jančar, aged twenty-five and twenty-seven, on their last day in Hochsteingasse before leaving for England, Easter 1948.

ABOVE David Hicks.

BELOW 'Nadir': IM in Oxford Street, winter 1946–47.

BELOW RIGHT Wallace Robson.

ABOVE IM with Hal Lidderdale in London, *c.*1947.

RIGHT With Arnoldo Momigliano in Italy.

Three snapshots taken by Franz
Steiner in June 1952. The top
photograph was found in his
prayer book after his death.

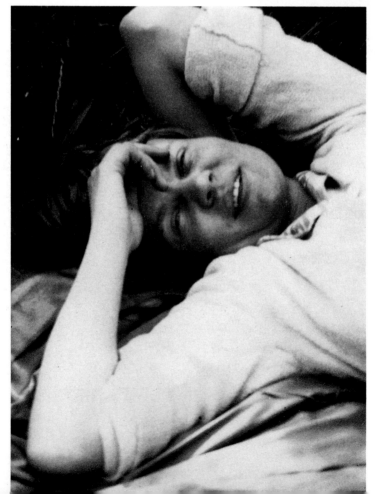

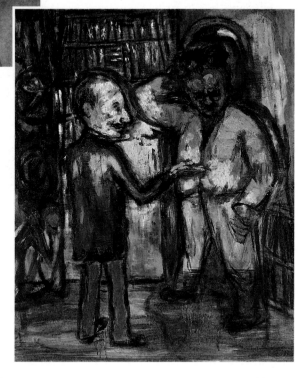

ABOVE With Franz in
London, August 1952.

RIGHT *Conversation in the
Library, 1950*: Steiner and
Canetti painted by Marie-
Louise von Motesiczky.

Elias Canetti, London, 1963.

ABOVE John Bayley
and IM, St Antony's, July
1954, shortly after the publication of *Under the Net*.
Bayley is concentrating on
pulling a string he has
arranged to take the shot.

RIGHT IM *c.*1954.

LEFT Eddy Sackville-West, Elizabeth Bowen and a watchful IM at Elizabeth Bowen's house in County Cork, Bowen's Court, July 1956.

BELOW Dinner at Bowen's Court. Left to right: Lady Ursula Vernon (daughter of Bend Or, second Duke of Westminster); Major Jim Egan (estate clerk); Mary, Lady Delamere; Elizabeth Bowen; Major Stephen Vernon; IM.

'We have bought a country house.' Cedar Lodge, Steeple Aston.

'August 14 [1956]. Married John.' Bayley and IM at Cedar Lodge.

'Report reading at St Anne's, 1958'. Clockwise, from the undergraduate at the head of the table: IM, Mrs Bednarowska, Miss Hubbard, Miss Bastock, Miss May, Lady Ogilvie, Miss Morrison, Mrs Barnes, Miss Reeves, Mrs Hart, Miss Griffiths.

ABOVE Yorick Smythies.

ABOVE RIGHT Peter Ady.

BELOW Lucy Klatschko (Sister Marian).

BELOW RIGHT David Morgan.

'It's like something she gives out.' A farouche study of IM which
startled John Bayley.

ABOVE IM with Reynolds Stone at Litton Cheney.

RIGHT John Bayley, Reynolds Stone and IM photographed by Janet Stone recumbent in dead leaves.

In Dorset, photographed by Janet Stone.

ABOVE Lanzarote, 1984.

RIGHT Agnes and David Bayley, Johnnie Stratton-Ferrier, IM, Gloria Richardson, Jackie Stratton-Ferrier, Michael Bayley and John Bayley in Berwickshire, 1991.

LEFT John Bayley prepares to try out the canal where Tim Reede swam in *Nuns and Soldiers*, 1998.

RIGHT In the downstairs study, Charlbury Road.

LEFT IM with the author's blue merle collie Cloudy, the model for Anax in *The Green Knight*, at Cascob, July 1996.

BELOW John Bayley and IM in Bath for the Café Philo, October 1998.

On 18 September 1969 she wrote: 'Happiness: to be utterly absorbed in at least six other human beings. (Provided these are not miserable or in some moral muddle involving oneself.)' Yet if she could sometimes feel awkward even among those she loved and in houses where she was secure, it is not surprising that others recorded her occasionally as being 'hard work'. Norway's best-known war hero, Max Manus (DSO, MC and bar for mining German warships in Oslo harbour), recounted that he found sitting next to Iris at dinner frightening: 'She looks so hard, and gives away so little.'[90] A.S. Byatt, 'frightened' at their first meeting, was still alarmed twenty-five years later, finding her 'very hard to talk to because she is always very scrupulous and just and is watching'.[91] Tony Quinton, who knew her for fifty years, described conversation with her as a 'pursuit of intimations', recalling Christmas 1914 when English and German soldiers played football in no-man's-land: 'armed truce' indeed. Iris never gossiped. Frank Kermode, who also knew her from 1947, noted that she could be both intellectually formidable and morally intimidating. Chitra Rudingerova, a friend from school and Oxford, and Mary Warnock, a friend after 1950, both used the same word of Iris – 'unearthly' – endorsed differently by Olivier Todd, who around 1947 had the sense of someone both present and elsewhere, and by Kreisel, who in 1968 wrote to her that such an impression (of being partly elsewhere, in the past and in the future, not here) 'produces a nervous & ... touching atmosphere';[92] a sense of presence-cum-absence the painter Tom Phillips would 'catch' in his official portrait in 1986.

Her journals suggest how hard it was for her to express a simple sense of need, partly because, as she pointedly expressed it, 'there are not many people whom one wants to know one!';[93] also because she liked to be one who looked after others.

> *19 September 1966.* Too anxious, not virtuous enough. The 'nobody understands me' feeling. *Nobody* understands me, *nobody*. This is idiotic, but I feel it dreadfully. Well, usually it doesn't matter. Pain & restless haunted yearning.
>
> *17 June 1967.* I feel I have been handing out a lot of

affection lately to a lot of people who don't really give a damn.

18 July 1969. Very *few* other people's happiness is an end to one.

11 October 1969. I am getting old and want real committed friends not people who blow hot and cold, & play hard to get & so on.

December 1969. We gave din[ner at] New Coll[ege] really for Janet [Stone] to meet Berlins [Isaiah and Aline] . . . R[eynolds] came. Din[ner] success, I think – the niceness of people one has known for *ages.*

17 October 1970. Further: I feel neglected and in need of love. (Maybe even in need of fun!) This is of course irrational, or largely so. I spend time and energy being a little ray of sunshine to many people but it occurs to nobody to spoil me . . . I saw Philippa, who never needs cheering up, & cd have talked to her about things, but she was (and why not) too full of her own adventures packing up the Old Hall . . . and we talked of that all the time.

June 1971. Uneasy relations with people I love, and feeling of there not being enough of them. (This is tosh, I am very lucky.) Desire to be spoilt, praised, sent thousands of flowers. (This ungrateful: Elliott [Kastner[94]] and Tessa sent huge bouquet recently.)

The October 1970 entry followed the failure of her play *The Servants and the Snow* (see Chapter 19), suggesting that an old link between desire for artistic success and for affection had not languished. A number of friends spoke 'only of their own affairs', or wrote 'plaintive letters'. Usually she was 'enough bucked by feeling [that others] are glad to see me – and they *are* glad, and I am lucky'. On 21 July 1971: 'A human being's craving for love is *infinite.* Most people realise this only in the context of being in love when the idea of the desire being fulfilled is present.' Like other writers she could best exercise her sense of self in the act of writing – letters, novels. Much loved by her friends, to whom she was unfailingly and fiercely loyal, and to whose tales she listened with seemingly endless patience, she remained a strangely isolated consciousness, whose genius for relationship – like a therapist – did not always involve mutual exchange: 'I find it rather hard to communicate with other members of the human race at the best of times.'[95] Perhaps her gift was to mirror each of her friends' different needs, and thus to differ herself within each friendship. She liked 'being told things'.[96] If she had simultaneously an only child's hunger for intimacy, she also understood, Proust-like, that intimacy is always partly illusory, solitude the common fate. 'Go alone, stay alone. Alone is good,'* she noted. She was also a passionate puritan who could lower her defences, chiefly when in love.

Despite a startling tendency – certainly out of shyness, and increasing with age – to begin conversations with total strangers, 'Do *you* believe in God?'[97] Iris was increasingly in demand. At a Royal Academy dinner in May 1968 she flirted with Yehudi Menuhin and had her hand kissed by Ralph Richardson. 'Do I now belong to the establishment?' she teased herself, and later Leo Pliatzky.[98] Lunching at the Connaught in 1971 she met Noël Coward, who announced, 'I'm a screaming Murdoch fan!' 'Unfortunately' this conversation was cut short by the arrival of Princess Margaret. Diffidence always accompanied Iris. In 1966 she sighted Samuel Beckett at a Bonnard exhibition but lacked the nerve to accost him.[99] Two years later she was thrilled to shake Hergé's hand in Hamley's toyshop – John Simopoulos had made her a Tintin fan. Lunch at Buckingham Palace provoked the single word 'Corgis'.[100]

Of her Jesuit student John Ashton she noted, 'Ultimately one loves unworldly people';[101] later, 'one likes people who are humble: and everyone has a reason to be'.[102] Conversely a gossipy

---

* Iris's journal, 12 September 1982. The quotation continues: 'Milarepa. (So I gather.)' After her marriage, her journals increasingly show her contemplating, rather than ways of escape, the necessity of solitude. e.g. 3 February 1968: '"Perhaps you are alone, my friend" is the message, & all my sense of company, the "transcendent scene" is utterly bogus?' 16 April 1971: 'You can't win. Either you live alone with your daemon – or you don't.' 8 October 1979: 'Thinking is done in solitude. When are women ever alone?'

1977 dinner depressed both Bayleys, and Iris more than John, who was lighter of touch:

> People who *shrink* other people . . . And some terrible loss of freedom, brought about by a forced complicity in malice. (Ubiquitous nature of malice.) It occurs to me in *this* context how much a sense of freedom is connected with fundamental shared moral attitudes . . . Freedom and goodness as *experienced* e.g. in David Cecil. Puss so evidently expresses this freedom in his *being* and I perceived this at the very start. Malice: a wrenching of everything into a belittled relationship to oneself.[103]

10

'Most friendship exists in a state of frozen and undeveloping semi-hostility,' says Arnold Baffin in *The Black Prince*,[104] a novel written in pain and about egotism. Like *Under the Net* it concerns relations between two writers. Jake's feelings about Breteuil in *Under the Net* are (very loosely) based on Iris's for Raymond Queneau. Translating Breteuil gives Jake the courage to publish his first novel – as translating *Pierrot mon ami* gave Iris the courage to publish *Under the Net*. In *The Black Prince* the blocked writer Pearson is the 'discoverer' of the facile best-seller Arnold Baffin. If Iris had a 'discoverer', A.S. Byatt might merit the title, having written the first academic monograph in 1965, after Iris had published nine novels, Byatt one. Byatt attested her indebtedness at the end of her 1994 reissue of this study, *Degrees of Freedom*, by including a critical essay proclaiming Iris as her 'literary mother'.[105] Byatt thought Iris the greatest living English novelist, and the person whose mind had done most for her own. In a 1970 journal entry Iris compared Byatt with Brigid Brophy, Esme Ross Langley and 'the Chumman' – whose relationships were important to her yet complex. By contrast with these, 'Toni [i.e. Byatt] has touches of greatness. Her tense tough intellectual fibre, fabric . . . This is just homage to Toni.'[106] Murdoch helped Byatt through a number of crises, coming to London in 1968 when

Byatt had a health-scare, breaking other arrangements in the autumn of 1972 to be with her after her young son was hit and killed by a car, listening weeping to the things Byatt could say to no one else, and, when able, helping over the years in many ways. Byatt noted that, though 'dailiness' – the things most of us struggle with and sink under – was an imaginative exercise for Iris, the 'big things, the best and the worst', she understood and looked steadily at.[107]

Iris understood how literary discipleship involves unique indebtedness. In 1945 she had noted that she sometimes wanted '*to be*' Queneau, sometimes Thomas Mann. After 1953 Canetti took Queneau's place as (literary) master. The 'discovery' of an older artist's talent or genius may give rise both to a sense of ownership of that artist's mind, and of having one's own 'stolen away'. To have one's talents unlocked by an older artist engendered special claims. Harold Bloom memorably pictured the literary master–disciple relation as an Oedipal – or cannibalistic, *à la* Canetti – drama: the jealous acolyte's secret wish, beneath public admiration, is for a diminution of the reputation of the older artist so that the younger can more effectively appropriate his '*mana*' – prestige or power. The older artist can then be turned into a John the Baptist heralding the significant arrival of the younger.[108] The creation of a Mischa Fox or a Julius King may be a secret act of revenge on or acquittal with Canetti. In any case *The Black Prince* concerns the jealous, implicitly murderous hostility that underlies the friendship between a facile artist-protégé and his serious-minded discoverer-patron. Both parties, Arnold Baffin and Bradley Pearson, are aspects of Iris herself.

11

Pearson, the blocked writer, represents that 'chaste and strict'[109] mind that produced the eloquent and compressed rhetoric of 'Against Dryness' and *A Severed Head*; Baffin the 'journalistic' discursive self that in the 1980s would churn out shapeless novels of over six hundred pages. The titles of Baffin's books – *Essays of a Seeker, Mysticism and Literature, The Maid and the Magus, Inside a Snow Crystal* (close to one working title for *The Time of the Angels*) – parody Iris's own, as does the sole account of a Baffin plot, with its ludicrous scenes of an abbot felled by an immense bronze crucifix and a Buddhist nun with a broken ankle rescued from an overflowing reservoir. Baffin's daughter Julian, another writer, describes him tellingly as living 'in a sort of rosy haze with Jesus and Mary and Buddha and Shiva and the Fisher King all chasing round and round dressed up as people in Chelsea' – satirising earlier Murdoch novels such as *Bruno's Dream* and *A Fairly Honourable Defeat*. Pearson typifies Baffin's novels as a congeries of amusing anecdotes loosely garbled into racy stories with the help of half-baked unmediated symbolism. He empties himself (memorably) 'like scented bath-water' over the world, seeing significance everywhere. Pearson, who hates his 'enthusiastic garrulous religiosity', his propensity for seeing life as 'simply one big gorgeous metaphor', physically tears up Baffin's books, and is falsely condemned as his murderer.

When Baffin answers these criticisms, Iris again speaks directly through his mask: 'Most artists understand their weaknesses far better than the critics do . . . Every book is the wreck of a perfect idea. The years pass and one only has one life . . . any artist has to *decide* how fast to work. I do not believe I would improve if I wrote less. The only result would be that there would be less of whatever there is . . . It would be unthinkable to run along beside it whimpering, "I know it's no good".' That the two writers are 'doubles' may be gleaned from the fact that Pearson's narrative suffers itself from Baffinesque frailties: solipsism, religiosity, allusiveness.

While his name came from a Bayley household joke – a typist had mistyped 'pearson' for 'reason' throughout one of Iris's essays – Pearson is given Iris's worst self too. She created him partly out of self-awareness, and the novel is one of her dark comedies of justified paranoia. Like many of her first-person narrators he is given both her humble social origins and her comic horror of contingency (which is to say a strong ego). Above all he is given Iris's puritanism – both her censorious recoil from certain situations, but also her Platonised belief in the possibility of transcendence; Iris elsewhere noted that 'Puritanism = Romanticism'.[110] Pearson finds trains (to take one instance) an object-lesson 'in the foul contingency of life: the talkative fellow-traveller, the possibility of children'. He is familiar with the unpleasant experience of arriving very early for a train, and finding himself comically catching its predecessor with only a minute to spare[111] (in August 1943 Iris and Philippa were split up while travelling to the latter's family home exactly because Iris's 'train-fever', as they joked about it, caused her to arrive just in time to take an earlier train than Philippa – who had the sandwiches*). In no other novel does Iris take such exquisite revenge on her own romantic puritanism.[112] The rush to indict her for over-plotting has obscured her own tolerant delight in the messy and contingent which, almost alone among critics, Lorna Sage always celebrated.[113]

12

Iris's essays defended a human 'difference' that her 1960s novels had not always implemented. She had, she would complain, only half a dozen recurrent types in her books, and could 'do' only two voices (educated English and Irish). *The Black Prince* explores why. 'The unconscious delights in identifying people with each other. It has only a few characters to play with,' Bradley instructs Julian.[114] The scholarly reference is to Ernest Jones's famous Freudian reading of *Hamlet* in which Hamlet identifies Ophelia with his mother and Claudius with his father. An intensely private reference is to Iris's own love for her father. During the composition of the novel she dreamt of telling Julian Chrysostomides that her father was dead, and wept about this, as if it had happened anew, not fifteen years before. Julian Baffin's love for Bradley Pearson, whom she late on discovers to be nearly forty

* According to Iris's memory they were separated within the same overcrowded train.

years her senior, has parallels in Iris's beloved father-figures: Fraenkel was born in 1888, Michael Oakeshott in 1901, Thomas Balogh and Canetti in 1905, Arnoldo Momigliano and Franz Steiner in 1908 and 1909 respectively. Julian substitutes Bradley for her own father. Iris had pleaded in her essays for 'the individual and the type', as in the best nineteenth-century fiction, to come together. In *The Black Prince* she succeeds. An illusion of depth and space results. These characters are 'alive'.

There are further complexities. Although she objected in public to John suggesting that she experienced herself as a man,[115] Iris told Rachel Fenner that she inwardly identified with male homosexuals, and one journal entry adds the adjective 'sadomasochistic'. 11 December 1966: 'Q. What am I? A. A male homosexual sado-masochist. (See *Bruno* passim.)' None of her novels is narrated in the first person by a woman. Those given to male first-person narrators are often her best. Apart from Mary Renault, few women novelists write with as much conviction from the point of view of male homosexuals, and no other woman writer so well impersonates men. Iris's love of male or androgyne names for young women characters was famous: Georgie Hands, Julian Baffin, Morgan Browne. One crisis in *The Black Prince* comes when Bradley is able to make love to Julian, whom he on first sighting mistook for a boy, only when she dresses as Hamlet. It would be perversity if literature alone aroused him: androgyny helps too. A girl hiding behind a man's name (based on the female mystic Julian of Norwich) dresses as a man and is made love to as a woman by a male narrator inhabited by his woman-creator. This recalls the erotic casuistry of *As You Like It* Act III, scene ii, where a boy-actor dressed as Rosalind, doubly *en travestie* first as a girl, then as a boy, shows Orlando how to woo. Small wonder that Iris called literature 'close dangerous play with unconscious forces'.[116] 'A lot of old nightmares have got inside this novel,' she commented.[117]

13

Iris wanted to create memorable characters, and in three 1970s novels – *A Fairly Honourable Defeat, The Black Prince* and *The Sea, The Sea* – she succeeded. All show the inspiration of Shakespeare, by whom she so longed to be touched. 'Any high theory about Shakespeare is no good, not because he is so divine but because he is so human. Even great art is jumble in the end. Should we grieve?' The sentiment recurs.[118] Shakespeare, called in her journals the 'cheerful nosepicking whoremaster', created not out of simple *high-mindedness* but, genius apart, out of an intimate and humble understanding of base emotions, of lust and rage, hatred, envy, jealousy and the will-to-power as well as astonishment at ordinariness. That we are all scandalously (and comically) emotional, no matter what we publicly pretend, is one secret Iris's novels joyously and painfully reveal. Neither sanctity nor high diction,[119] but intimate human-ness, makes these novels live. Here she defeats her own romanticism and puritanism, which she rightly equated.

That 'living personality' differs very widely from 'literary character' may be seen in the ways Canetti helped inspire types as radically different as Julius and the small-minded, self-absorbed and un-self-knowing tyrant Charles Arrowby in *The Sea, The Sea*, whose blind, paranoid, rapacious egoism is painfully real. Julius's manipulativeness was cool; Charles's will-to-power masquerades as sexual desire. Near the start of the novel we discover that Charles can never let go of an intimate. He tortures the gentle Lizzie Scherer by toying with her love for him, jealous of her platonic relationship with the effeminate old-stager Gilbert Opian, willing neither to release nor to satisfy her. In 1953 Canetti had told Iris of how Susie, his mistress Friedl's sister, had turned against him after he had spoken frankly about 'giving up' Friedl to Allan Forbes.[120] Susie reviled Canetti to Allan, telling him that 'Canetti never really let go of Friedl, wanting both Friedl and Allan within his power, to treat Allan like a little dog, etc – that Canetti was a demon-like destructive person.' Allan duly reported all this to Canetti, who told Iris, who noted it down. Just so Charles at one point nominally awards Lizzie to Gilbert, while willing both to remain his 'slaves'. The desire to let go – and the difficulty of doing so – are major themes in *The Sea, The Sea.*

Charles and Canetti share misogyny: 'How did I know so certainly that C[anetti] could never bear to spend a whole night with anybody?'[121] Charles cannot since 'in the morning she looks to me like a whore'.[122] Charles has been hurt by feminine rejection, Canetti by his tyrannical mother. Both Charles and Canetti take their revenge – for life – by punishing a masochistic female harem. Charles's fear of women singing – 'the wet white teeth, the red, moist interior'[123] – is textbook Freudian alarm at the *vagina dentata.* Canetti, in Forbes's view, for all his womanising, had – like Charles – low libido. Canetti haunts *The Sea, The Sea* variously: Iris's own lifelong meditation about him is echoed demonically in Charles's lifelong obsession with Hartley.

And Iris, like Canetti, was herself a 'mage' who attracted, fascinated and enchanted but expressed an 'anxious morality about not hurting'[124] acolytes and friends. She too called herself 'naturally a jealous person'.[125] The novel's strength is that Iris is everywhere and thus nowhere: in Charles's disgusting recipes ('But this is what John and I eat *all the time*,' Iris riposted to the psychologist Anthony Storr); in Charles's meditations on his father Adam Arrowby, a detailed portrait of Iris's father Hughes; in the gentle, beautifully-breasted, enslaved Lizzie, recalling the Iris of 1953; in the plump, elderly, drably be-mackintoshed Hartley whom the boy Charles loved, lost and now finds again; in the mysterious adept of white magic James Arrowby, a Tibetan Buddhist and Wykehamist soldier-saint distantly recalling Frank.

Charles, actor and theatre director, is imitating Prospero in *The Tempest,* Iris's favourite Shakespeare play,* in finally trying to give up power. Lizzie is Prospero's servant Ariel, a part she has

---

* In the draft of a list of works by which she had been influenced, it is the only Shakespeare mentioned. Journal, 4 July 1976: 'For B[ritish] C[ouncil] etc: a list with comments of books and authors that influenced me? . . . Iliad, Symposium, Tempest, Sir Gawain, Mansfield Park, Wuthering Heights, Our Mutual Friend, The Golden Bowl, Fear and Trembling, L'Attente de Dieu, Brothers Karamazov. Proust?'

successfully acted; Gilbert, still lustful for boys in his sixties, the earthbound Caliban. Both are Charles's half-willing slaves. But *The Sea, The Sea* can no more be resolved back into *The Tempest* than can *The Black Prince* into *Hamlet.* Just as *The Tempest* sets the good magician Prospero against his bad usurping brother Antonio, so *The Sea, The Sea* sets the questing James Arrowby against his egotistical cousin Charles. The magical aspects of Tibetan Buddhism interested Iris, and she commended a study emphasising these in 1981.[126] Charles has for forty years been obsessively in love with Hartley; James (though commentators missed this) has been all his life in love with his cousin Charles. Charles, when he rediscovers Hartley, kidnaps and coerces her; James by contrast returns to Charles to try to release them both from 'attachment'.

James's is 'the triumph of spiritual (free) power over magical (obsessional) power ... Power undoing itself in favour of love', and his, too, the lesson that 'Forgiveness, *inter alia,* is this' – lessons above Charles's moral level. His use of magic ('tricks') belongs inside the tale, reflecting as it does Shakespeare's Prospero as a Neoplatonic mage conjuring with spirits. James at one point practises levitation to save Charles from drowning; is recalled as having created a '*tulpa*' – Tibetan for a magically projected non-existent being paradoxically visible to others; and chooses the moment of his own death, finally released, Iris insisted, from the wheel of suffering. Some readers rightly intuited Iris's own interest in magic. She objected vehemently to the supernatural aspects of religion, feeling that the Virgin Birth and the Resurrection were not merely lies, but that insistence on their literal truth was helping to kill off Christianity, which needed to learn from Buddhism to demythologise itself. Yet, while denying the supernatural, the paranormal fascinated her. She had the rare power of 'lucid dreaming', the ability consciously to guide a dream.[127] She consulted a tarot pack in the 1950s and 1960s. Flying saucers in *The Nice and the Good* are succeeded by bi-location in *A Fairly Honourable Defeat,* there is further levitation in *The Good Apprentice,* and she attempted telekinesis while writing *The Green Knight.* Sternly sceptical in so many ways, for example about psychic research, which she deemed dangerous 'rubbish',[128] she was enthusiastically credulous in others. It seems apt that, when Stephen and Natasha Spender called on a water-diviner in Provence in the 1970s, the willow switch jumped violently out of Iris's hands at the very spot for a well. '*Madame a la fluide*,' observed the diviner reverently.[129]

The Sea, The Sea does not depend upon its paranormal elements. Iris noted in 1969 the paradox of 'Shakespeare's farewell to his art',[130] and the theatre in this novel stands in for the great world itself, 'with all its trickery'.[131] So the conjuring of spirits can also be taken as the novelist's rough magic, creating an intensely 'seen' imaginary world reflecting the one we share, but more memorably peopled. Creating magically projected non-existent beings paradoxically visible to others is, after all, what novelists attempt too.

The Sea, The Sea is diminished by synopsis. Not the least of its absurdities is that Charles has fortuitously retired to the exact spot where the woman he so obsessively loved now lives with a fire-extinguisher salesman. But it has also extraordinary strengths and felicities, patient powers of description of place – the sea of the title, in all its moods – of emotion, of character. Malcolm Bradbury praised it as 'merciless and painful' as well as poetic and truthful;[132] Gabriele Annan, always an astute Murdoch-critic, saw it as a 'comedy with portholes for looking out at the cosmos';[133] Francis King noted passages that 'simply take the breath away';[134] Susan Hill thought it 'among her best', intense and moving.[135] The novel's mixture of pain and comedy reaches some high point.

The Sea, The Sea was nominated for the 1978 Booker Prize, which had that year doubled in value to £10,000. A.J. Ayer chaired, without great diligence, a panel of judges including Derwent May, a strong enthusiast for the novel. The debate, after the usual liveliness, was resolved equably, and Iris was awarded the prize.[136] A.N. Wilson's picturesque claim that Ayer, crowing 'about not having read any of the novels . . . gave the prize to his old friend'[137] is poetic licence. As for Iris, she did not, unlike Prospero, abjure her magic. She wrote seven more novels after *The Sea, The Sea*. None sold as well, or arguably was as good.[138]

19

Discontinuities
1971–1978

'There was never any good biography of a good novelist. There couldn't be. He is too many people, if he is any good,' wrote Scott Fitzgerald.[1] Iris, named after the goddess of rainbows, has many colours. Travelling by train in summer 1981[2] she was accosted by a stranger in the train-bar, who greeted her enthusiastically as Margaret Drabble. 'How can you *tell*,' replied the philosopher thoughtfully, 'that I'm not Doris Lessing, Muriel Spark, or even Iris Murdoch?' The unperturbed admirer, putting a hand on Iris's sleeve, reassured her, 'Margaret, I'd know you anywhere.' Confusion about identity was sometimes shared by Iris herself. Eleven years before she had mused, 'I have very little sense of my own identity. Cd one gradually go mad by slowly slowly losing *all* one's sense of identity? I know there is a body that moves about and some thoughts, memories – but it's all scattered, & now more so.'[3] A discontinuous sense of being shows when she rediscovers her early journals, and is always surprised by the protean selves she finds therein: and discontinuity itself is a theme that needs exploring.

She often spoke of having no sense of identity,[4] partly subscribing to her own ideology, wherein virtue relates to 'lack of form (interior being)'.[5] Hence we are, in *An Unofficial Rose*, to prefer Anne Peronett, formless as a dog-rose, to her charming, rapacious husband Randall, an artist seeking self-definition. Iris was aloof and largely voiceless about her own life. Yet her 'case', unsimplified by belonging within a novel, is necessarily more complex: a good novelist escapes definition by shape-shifting, as Canetti knew. In her *Who's Who* entry she gave 'learning languages' as her only recreation, and her shelves held grammar books in many languages, including Esperanto, which she learnt sufficiently to be able to write in it to her old college friend and Esperanto expert Dr Marjorie Boulton.* Her journals abound in quotations from Latin, Greek, Russian, French. She gave a lecture in 1968 in Italian,[6] participated in a conference in French on the modern novel at the Centre Pompidou in October 1981,[7] and the following month gave a short morale-boosting BBC World Service broadcast in Russian,[8] a native-speaker translating and marking stresses for her. During the war she attempted Turkish, and for *The Red and the Green* she studied Gaelic. The inability to learn a language was for her the 'perfect image of spiritual limitation', and the Babel-like proliferation of languages on the planet God's jest to show that 'goodness is a foreign language'.[9]

Learning new languages is also a way of transforming or disguising oneself, of not being tied to a single identity. Perhaps being good – which shines through so much that Iris did and was – was a way of escaping definition too. 'The good are unimaginable,' James declared in *The Sea, The Sea*, and while none doubts the passion or urgency of Iris's quest, the artist in her wanted invisibility as much as the acolyte longed for perfection. Both the saint and the true artist were equally, in her coinage, 'unpersons'.[10] The idea of others imagining her did not appeal. In 1971 she jotted memorably, 'There are not many people whom one wants to know one!'[11] A 1959 entry indicted a novelist-friend who had written a *roman-à-clef*. Small wonder that Honor Tracy wrote to Sister Marian: 'there is little enough we can really know of any human being, however simple, let alone of a complex creature like I[ris].'[12] Iris found the idea of autobiography 'morally sicken-

---

* Her progress was slowed by the discovery that the Esperanto for 'mother' – *patrino* – was the diminutative of 'father'. Letters to Boulton for years stubbornly elaborated the 'staggering and (honestly, to me) offensive' insensitivity of using a diminutive suffix to designate the feminine: it recalled to her 'that male chauvinist book' the Bible, where Eve came only from Adam's rib. The point invaded *A Word Child.*

ing'* and applauded the bitingly satirical scene in Dostoevsky's *The Idiot* where Totsky invites his guests to disclose their worst fault. No one truly sees his own frailties. Under the guise of a pretended sincerity, each boasts competitively instead.

2

A friend noted in 1978 that in Iris 'a highly organised analytical mind [was] at war with her warm, irrational Irish heart'.[13] It is hard to relate the loving, practical common sense of her letters to the occasional emotionalism of her journals, the formidable energy and precision of her best philosophical essays, and the audacious inventiveness and power of the novels. Bradley Pearson in *The Black Prince* asserted that 'We are tissues and tissues of different *personae* and yet we are nothing at all.'[14]

Encouraged by Frank Thompson's enthusiasm, Iris wished, on 24 April 1942, to look for a volume by Bakhtin in the Bodleian Library.[15] The sole work of his in print was his 1929 *Problems of Dostoevsky's Poetics*, and it was available only in Russian. The book emphasises the 'unfinalisability' of Dostoevsky's portraits – a unifying topic in Iris's letters, novels, essays and journals. There is an unconscious echo between her January 1943 letter to David Hicks: 'Human lives are essentially not to be summed up, but to be known, as they are lived, in many curious partial & inarticulate ways,' and Charles Arrowby's wise pronouncement in *The Sea, The Sea* in 1978 that 'Judgements on people are never final, they emerge from summings up which at once suggest the need of a reconsideration.'[16] In 1956 her essay 'Vision and Choice in Morality' praised moral attitudes which

> emphasise the inexhaustible detail of the world, the end-lessness of the task of understanding, the importance of

---

* Journal, 13 May 1982: 'Autobiography: "to try to tell the truth about oneself" – why bother? So you are indifferent to truth? No – one struggles with truth versus falsehood all the time. But that effort would be pointless, one must just try to be good. Idea of autobiography is utterly unattractive to me as an art form – and also somehow morally sickening.'

not assuming that one has got individuals and situations 'taped', the connection of knowledge with love and of spiritual insight with apprehension of the unique.[17]

The same year she made the anti-art artist in *The Sandcastle*, Bledyard, ask: 'Who can look reverently enough upon another human face?'[18] In mid-February 1952 she attacked her quasi-fiancé Wallace Robson in the Mitre pub in Oxford for not reverencing people – 'meaning me'. She treated friends with sympathetic care, patient loving attention, imagination, generosity. She gave little appearance of noticing your frailties. She cared as passionately about the privacy of others as about her own. Her friendship ennobled you.

3

There was a discontinuity between the serene and Buddha-like stillness others increasingly saw in Iris, and the questing spirit within. 'Being is acting,' said Bradley Pearson, and it is not accidental that the young Iris was renowned at Oxford for her acting ability, nor that her tutor Mildred Hartley and her Dublin 'cousins' Eva and Billy Lee alike thought her often in fancy-dress. Her first novel, *Under the Net*, and her penultimate one, *The Green Knight*, enact key scenes within theatres, and *The Sea, The Sea* is narrated by a theatre director with a cast of actors, one of whom wished to play Honor Klein from J.B. Priestley's adaptation of *A Severed Head*, while another actor mentioned in *The Sea, The Sea* – 'that ass Will Boase' – returns from the cast of *Bruno's Dream*. 'Of course a novel is a drama,'[19] Iris remarked. The puritan who Priestley accurately noted did not really like the theatre, none the less craved theatrical success. She would say that a novelist's life is lonely, a playwright's sociable. She craved company, and liked actors, who resembled 'nice animals, or children'.[20]

While writing original plays she corresponded with the theatrical agent Peggy Ramsey,[21] who generously complimented her 'extraordinary talent' for the theatre, a compliment qualified by Ramsey's observations that the naturalism Iris had chosen for her play *Joanna, Joanna* made for complicated set changes; that representing a student riot by 'noises off' was a method not seen on stage for fifty years; and finally advising in exasperation that 'you should be able to see your plays, if necessary, out of town, and after seeing about two staged, and occasionally going to the theatre, you will very soon become a master.'[22]

Two of Iris's plays were performed – *The Servants and the Snow* in 1970 at the Greenwich Theatre and *The Three Arrows* in Cambridge in 1972. The failure of the first hit her hard. She saw it twice during its four-week run, the second time with 'extremely nice' Cecil Day Lewis. 'The play seemed terrible. It had been full of magic on the first night, for me anyway . . . It's clear the play won't go to the west end, after all those rotten notices.' She was grateful when the director Alun Vaughan Williams rescued her at Greenwich station after she dissolved into tears. She thought the play, which explored the relations between 'Eros' and political power, 'such a potent object . . . just not *seen*'. Its later adaptation by William Mathias as an opera called *The Servants*, staged in Cardiff in September 1980, consoled her. '*Wonderful.* The music moves inside me, moving and surging like sea among rocks.'

The love-hate affair with the theatre continued. Priestley had adapted *A Severed Head* in 1963, James Saunders *The Italian Girl* in 1967, when she noted that staging always revealed which were weak characters in a novel (in this case the Levkins). In 1975 she wished to canvas American managements to see whether they would put on *The Three Arrows*.[23] Two of her novels were adapted for television, one for radio.[24] Her radio-opera *The One Alone*, which concerned the spiritual struggles of a brave opponent of political tyranny subjected to solitary confinement, with music by Gary Carpenter, was broadcast on Radio 3 in 1986. Inspired by the novelist and impresario Josephine Hart, she adapted *The Black Prince* for the stage, and it premiered at the Aldwych Theatre in 1989: since its narrator Bradley Pearson survives (in the novel he dies), its blackly tragi-comic note was compromised. Iris had earlier adapted *The Sea, The Sea*, but found no one to stage it; she vigorously objected to Chatto including the adaptation in a collected edition of her plays, arguing that it should not be published before it had been performed. Possibly because she wrote reluctantly, or rebelliously, for the theatre[25] her efforts, she knew, had 'the formal stiffness of the juvenile work of a painter'.[26]

Theatrical success in 1970 would, she believed, have 'opened ways which now are much harder to enter upon' supposing, for example, her arthritis caused her in future to have to give up writing by hand and work with a tape recorder instead: arthritic pains in her right hand and arm that year were bad. On 20 April (writing with her left hand): 'I am not supposed to write with my right hand for a week. What a bore!' On 21 April (writing with her right hand again): 'Damn that.' The Bayleys even considered moving back to Oxford, to a house less damp (patches of green mould now adorned certain walls at Steeple Aston). Of course, at once the garden and countryside became 'bewitchingly beautiful ... golden leaves & apple trees out of Samuel Palmer'. They looked at a house in Davenant Road, but screaming children next door decided John against it. This Oxford prospect thoroughly unsettled them, Iris scorning her weakness of nerve: 'The thought of moving to Belbroughton Rd as a major crisis in one's life! God!' In due course a drug (Voltarol) helped her arthritis, and the move was postponed for fifteen years.

4

Iris's experience of the film world, whose comic, crass traducing of historical truth Jake acidly noted in *Under the Net*, was no happier than her theatrical ordeals. In 1962 a film company attempted unsuccessfully to shoot *Under the Net* in Earl's Court. The producer and director Tony Richardson bought an option on *The Unicorn* in 1964, but did not proceed. In 1968 the Swedish director Bo Widerberg showed interest in *The Sandcastle*, but once again it came to nothing. (Earlier, Iris had been advised that MGM's 1965 film *The Sandpiper* might have been plagiarised from *The Sandcastle*; after some confusion and depression she accepted an out-of-court settlement. She wondered whether this had scared Columbia off.) She wrote: 'There seems to be, for one reason or another, a persistent jinx on my cinema prospects.' The cinema, Peggy Ramsey replied, was indeed 'a nightmare of plots and counter-plots'.[27]

The only film to be made of one of Iris's novels to date is *A Severed Head*, directed in 1969 by Dick Clement. On 7 May she went to Paddington station to watch the shooting of the scene in which Honor arrives in London and is met by Martin: 'It was quite unexpectedly moving. As I came up the steps from the Underground I thought it's all a dream, there'll be no film unit really. But there they all were. I talked to Claire Bloom [who played Honor] later in her hotel room at the station. She was touchingly keen on the part.' Judging from her handwritten marginal addenda, Iris had reservations about Frederic Raphael's screenplay; and when she saw the film on its release a year later, in May 1970, she noted: 'Terrible'.

In 1971 Paul Newman and Joanne Woodward bought the rights to *A Fairly Honourable Defeat*, which Iris declared 'thrilling', but she and Ramsey disliked Peter Ustinov's script, and the project came to nothing. Ramsey, recognising Iris's hunger to be adequately filmed, recorded that Iris had (curiously) been unhappy with Priestley's adaptation of *A Severed Head*. Of an enquiry about the rights to *The Black Prince* in 1977 Iris wrote to Ramsey, 'I'd like to see a decent film of one of those books, in any language, before I die . . . tell them to do it.'[28] An option was sold on *The Flight from the Enchanter*, but no film was made. She wrote crossly to Ramsey after the latter had relayed Iris's unease about James Saunders writing a screenplay of *The Italian Girl* – 'please do not send my letters to you on to other people . . . my letters to you are *to you*'. She wanted Edward on film to be more serious than he had been in Saunders' stage adaptation. In 1978 she left Ramsey for another theatrical agent, Robin Dalton.

5

Iris signed her cheques and passport 'Iris Bayley'. Blessed by a happy marriage herself, she writes well of unhappy marriages – 'the bootless solitude of those . . . caged together – hell in a pure form';[29] 'every persisting marriage' in *The Sea, The Sea* is partly based on 'mean spiteful cruel self-regarding fear'.[30] With John – like her father 'a man entirely without the natural coarseness & selfishness of the male'[31] – she had freedom to explore the world as she would. Philippa Foot observed that this partnership was totally necessary for her, and John's memoirs of Iris well evoke its absolute mutual taken-for-grantedness. She burdened no one with her creative (and seasonal autumn) depressions. John periodically materialises in her journals – half-*puer aeternus*, half-friendly *Domovoy* or house-spirit, a vision of whom gladdens and touches – glimpsed as a separate being, acknowledged, loved, indispensable, mysterious. When he improvised a paragraph at her request about the capacity of Dora in *The Bell* to save herself by hiding, disappearing like some small animal into a hole, it was partly of Iris herself that he was thinking. The paragraph appears in the first chapter of the novel.

25 October 1969. Dear puss walking at the bottom of the garden looks so sad.

7 June 1970. Puss, with red braces, going down the centre path between tall grass. Very hot evening.

24 April 1971. Puss brought in one afternoon when I was sleeping a bunch of periwinkles in the pink & whiteish Venice glass vase. So pretty. I woke and found it just beside me. It made me so happy.

4 January 1978. Puss singing in kitchen below. He is a *good man*.

31 May 1979.

> Strindberg had a little skunk,
> Its coat was white as mink,
> And everywhere that Strindberg slunk
> That skunk was sure to slink.

... quoted by Puss. Of such is the kingdom of heaven.

She chronicles his serendipitous expertise ('Etruscans used false teeth'), his mowing in the vivid summer evenings, his surreally detailed and lengthy dreams – about a procession of cats, dowsing; about being with Pushkin, on whom he was writing a book, at a military college. Pushkin, in answer to a query about some dirty socks on the floor, replied coldly: 'Those are Bayley's socks.' Like the good Denis entertaining Marian in *The Unicorn* with rescued animals, John appears helping shrews ('little moles, short-sighted & long-nosed, with tiny hand-like paws'), toads and insects ('a very tiny red spider on his fingertip to shew me'). He sights birds, badgers, a silent vixen lying on the twilit scythed grass 'like Madame Recamier' while her four cubs play; is dashed when a favourite frog one night is not on duty. He paints her 'sea-lion' pool blue-green, is a 'sweet kind marvellous nurse' when she is ill, pours cooling water over her when she sunbathes, sings and dances with her on a Dorset beach.

Above all, he calms her down, and cheers her up.

> *12 February 1978.* Feeling depressed and very tired and in eclipse ... Puss, very very sweetly trying to cheer me up (and succeeding) says he will 'hop in my walks and gambol in my ways'.

She 'would despair' if anything happened to him.[32] On the rare occasions when illness depresses his effervescent high spirits or renders him irritable, she feels 'bottomless gloom'. 22 February 1968: 'Puss feeling ill & wretched. Says he hates life ... I feel so miserable & can't work, can't even write in this diary.' She heeded his comments on Shakespeare, on the necessary deviousness of the novel-form; included in her journal, at his request, the observation that their mulberry tree was on 29 May not yet in leaf;[33] noted his view about novels, 'Destroy the collusion [between writer and reader] which is all the more effective for being so efficiently disowned':[34] this affected *The Black Prince*. She pondered his advice, 'Write about conventional people, they are more interesting. Fanny Price is more convincing than Micawber & ultimately interests one far more'; stole his observation that 'We are tolerant and permissive because we don't take art seriously. In the USSR they pay it the compliment of censorship.' She recorded his views on artistic impersonality: 'Writers are invisible or intolerable.' While noting the phenomenon of John Berryman and Robert Lowell's confessional poetry, she favoured invisibility. Like Dostoevsky she wished to be able to say, 'I never showed my ugly mug'; or to resemble free Shakespeare, who in Matthew Arnold's words did not stay to 'abide our question', but escaped all definition.

John did not take Iris's (or anyone else's) ethical views seriously. On 30 September 1967 he remarked cheerfully at lunchtime, *à propos* nothing in particular, 'If I'd been the wolf of Gubbio I'd have *eaten* St Francis.' He none the less shared her special ability to lose himself in the act of looking – an ability about which she theorised. She was delighted to learn from a third party that, watching badgers, he had once been so absorbed he didn't notice a mouse run up his arm, along his collar and down the other arm. She captured him thus in her 1974 poem, 'John Sees a Stork at Zamorra':

> Walking among quiet people out from mass
> He saw a sudden stork
> Fly, from its nest upon a house.
> So blue the sky, the bird so white,
> For all these people an accustomed sight.
> He took his hat off in sheer surprise
> And stood and threw his arms out wide
> Letting the people pass
> Him by on either side
> Aware of nothing but the stork-arise.
>
> On a black tapestry now
> This gesture of joy
> So absolutely you.

In October 1979, when she visited China for three weeks without John, she kept a 10,000-word journal in which she noted that they had rarely been separated for more than two days since her month in Yale in 1959. On the morning of her departure John telephoned her in London from Steeple Aston. 'We are both tearful – He says, do you mind if I ring again?' During the trip she recorded 'terrible home-sickness and longing' for John, and on return she hurried to the baggage hall to ring Steeple Aston, anxious 'as phone rings 4–5 times. Then puss's voice.'

The Cultural Revolution had been even more terrible than she had imagined, but she observed that China, lacking religion, was able to feed its people: India, which retained religion, was not.[35]

6

Perhaps all persons are unfinalisable, but some more than others. Iris speaks audibly through Bradley Pearson in *The Black Prince* when he curses those who seek, like the Freudian hack Francis Marloe, to use Freud to diminish and 'place' him/her: her suspicion of psychoanalysis has already been noted.[36] She thought it added to Shakespeare's fascination 'that his character is unknown, except perhaps through his sonnets', adding, 'what a disaster it would be if a contemporary biography of him was unearthed',[37] a view suggesting artistic invisibility as sleight-of-hand. (Doubtless her letters after 1950 were undated in order to conduce to invisibility. Incoming letters, including her own when returned to her, she destroyed.) From 1970 she rented flat 4, 62 Cornwall Gardens, South Kensington, but within two years bought the top flat at number 29, on the opposite side of the square, a quiet modest flat, shaded by plane trees at the front, looking towards the Albert Memorial at the back. There was no lift: by the time most visitors had managed the six or so flights of stairs, before what resembled to some the final chicken-run up to the flat, they were breathless. While in Steeple Aston she worked in isolation, hardly emerging except to go to the village shop, in London she wrote of 'feeling ordinary & buying cigarettes & feeling a whole city, as it were, backing up one's incognito'.[38] The idea of an urban 'incognito' eloquently implied the twin, related pleasures of disguise and of moving unrecognised, 'invisible'. She loved London pubs all her life.

537

The character and history Iris presented to the world were not conscious artefacts, but resembled unconscious myths. She maintained the reputation of a recluse while giving numerous interviews, during which she often learnt more about the journalist than she revealed about herself. She was open-hearted yet reserved, put her intense inner life into the novels and was outwardly still, able to disappear under the surface. She attacked fantasy yet – 'philosophers attack their own faults' – came to believe that she and Frank Thompson had been engaged; they were not. She advocated a surrender to the contingent yet kept certain friends apart, and meetings could be preceded by a flurry of communications modulating the time of rendezvous by ten minutes.

She was all her life headstrong, yet in her philosophy attacked the will. The freest of spirits, she questioned freedom as a value in morals (never in politics). She praised monogamy – of which she indeed had a happy experience – attacking the promiscuity which she forgot had marked her own youth. Three years before homosexuality was decriminalised, she bravely argued in her *Man and Society* article that 'those who are homosexual should openly declare themselves to their friends',[39] yet, bisexual herself, rarely mentioned it ('There are not many people whom one wants to know one!'). She was a philo-Semite who admitted to her journal that the Jewishness of the odd friend could sometimes be boring, and who, on an official trip to Israel in 1977, wanted the Palestinian case advocated in the group's final press statement (she was furious when this was first diluted, then ignored). She wanted to be a painter, a Renaissance art historian, an engineer, an archaeologist,[40] a poet. The 'artist' in her wanted the intrigues of life to resemble those of Shakespearian drama, and she famously kept some relationships 'closed off', compartmentalised. The seeker in her admired simplicity. Like Rain Carter in *The Sandcastle* she had the twin faces of 'weeping ragamuffin' and 'authoritative artist'. She had a striking ability to be different with different friends.[41] She believed in 'unselfing' and had the extraordinary strength of a much-loved only child, attacked solipsism yet knew that the best art came from the truest self-involvement. She was fierce and gentle, vulnerable and tough, fastidious and energetic, English and Irish, defended tolerance and could be censorious, remonstrated with Hugh Cecil for catching a six-pound salmon at Lismore Castle in Ireland but noted (years later) 'the best fish meal ever' at the Fish Enterprise Co. Restaurant in Santa Barbara; probably it was blood-sports she hated. She also remonstrated with Hugh's brother Jonathan for his undergraduate acting, though long-remembered at Oxford for her own student acting career.

Iris admired the great Victorian novelists for creating free characters, but her novels show human beings as unfree, their behaviour capricious and identity precarious. A daughter of the impoverished middle class, insisting that her mother's family were 'minor gentry', she offered no objection to being taken as a 'grand bourgeois', yet detested social snobbery too. When Marjorie Boulton's tutor advised her in 1944 against seeking an academic post, Iris was furiously certain that the tutor under-estimated Boulton for this stupidest of reasons. She similarly longed for others from humble backgrounds, such as her RCA protégés, to succeed. She was an old-fashioned meritocrat: ability and intelligence must take precedence over privilege. Meanwhile one incidental charm of her novelistic world is that it is often profoundly bourgeois, the cushions made of toile de Jouy, '*Tiens!*' a common expostulation. Frances Stewart – Nickie Kaldor's eldest child – recalled Iris and John at the Kaldor house in the South of France, 'La Garde Freinet'. The house-party were invited to visit a neighbour, Tony Richardson. The invitation was issued because Richardson, with an option on filming *The Unicorn*, wanted to meet Iris; the Kaldors wanted to meet Richardson. All thought Iris 'serenely oblivious' of such considerations.[42]

She was in fact an acute observer. The working-class narrator of *A Word Child* notes that most cultured middle-class people are 'snobs ... quiet, intelligent, surreptitious beavering-away snobs, unless there is some positive quality of character ... to stop them'.[43] The expression 'beavering-away' is carefully chosen, graphic. Accompanying the indefatigable campaigner Lord Long-ford into a porn shop she noted dryly his unawareness that 'the real stuff was in the back'. 'Biting one's tongue. Let each man enjoy his own special form of meanness,' she alarmingly noted in 1969.[44] Her best fiction is part-fed by a species of cool rage which may relate to a radical *contemptus mundi et vitae*, but is sufficiently rooted in the world for it to live in the imagination of the reader. If her philosophy is lofty, her best novels are merciless and grim, as well as comical. There are writers – Conrad and Martin Amis spring to mind – who cannot bear to let you forget that they ceaselessly imagine the worst: where Iris's novels are dark, their author stays fiercely innocent.

Ibsen was inspired in Italy by watching a pet scorpion discharging its venom into an apple. Iris, too, had fiction as an 'escape-valve', and perhaps became good in life partly by being able to purge so much darkness into her best work. The novels, for all the pain, doubt, joy and terror involved in producing them, were an integral part of her psychic economy. She loved the actual writing so much when it was going well that she 'could not write fast enough',[45] rarely finding time to record the 'aura of creative aspiration and joy and clairvoyance'[46] that inspired her – the jokes emerging while writing *An Accidental Man* cheered her up. (Afterwards the light was withdrawn.) She wrote methodically, as if 'driven',[47] described by Francis Wyndham as like a Henry Moore statue seated between two massive piles of manuscript, moving only to write, one pile of empty paper, the other full,[48] her industry phenomenal. She was, she observed, '*devoured* by ambition', wishing 'always to write better'.[49] She often crashed into sleep 'as if diving into a deep sea'.[50]

7

Four lesser novels from the 1970s show the interplay within her of the social and the spiritual. *An Accidental Man* (1971) is fed by two kinds of symmetry. First there is a public one borrowing from the parable of the Good Samaritan: Matthew, a diplomat in Moscow, watches a passer-by coolly join a demonstration and instantly condemn himself to state persecution; Garth in New York witnesses a street-murder; Ludwig, in flight from the Vietnam war, passes by when depressed the guilt-ridden Dorina on her way to needless suicide. There is also, by way of private symmetry, a dance of lovers of the kind parodied by Malcolm Bradbury as 'Augustina is in love with Fred, Hugo is in love with Augustina, Flavia is in love with Hugo, Fred . . .'.[51] Entire chapters consist only of letters; others of unnamed voices overheard at a party. The final scene between upper-middle-class Charlotte and her overweight working-class ex-athlete lover Mitzi Ricardo, whose portrayal is a reminder that Iris's social range is larger than sometimes claimed, is Murdochian in a revealing way. The two women meet in a hospital ward, both unsuccessful suicides, fall in love, buy a cottage in the Surrey North Downs and set up house with a dog called Pyrrhus (which Mitzi mentally spells 'Pirrus'), who is frightened by their furious quarrels. The real-life dramas of 1963 may contribute to their convincing, sad, funny, fictional rows.

> Pyrrhus, a large black labrador, rescued, not for the first time, from the Battersea Dogs' Home, looked up anxiously from his place by the stove and wagged his tail. Pyrrhus's lot had always been cast with couples who fought and parted, abandoning him on motorways, on lonely moors, on city street corners. He had been called Sammy and then Raffles and then Bobo. He had only just learnt his new name. He had been happy for a little while in the snug cottage and the rabbity wood with his new humans. Now perhaps it was starting up all over again. He heard the familiar sounds of dispute, the cries, the tears, and he wagged his tail with entreaty. A virtuous affectionate nature and the generous nobility of his race had preserved him from neurosis despite all his sufferings. He had not a scrap of spite in his temperament. He thought of anger as a disease of the human race and as a dread sign for himself.[52]

Happily for Pyrrhus with his felicitous '*rabbity*' wood, Charlotte, her bags packed to leave, sheds defeated tears, 'like those of married people who love each other, cannot stand each other, and know that they can never now have any other destiny'.

Risking sentimentality, this passage becomes instead a species of Empsonian pastoral. Doggy simplicities oppose the neurotic human addiction to pain. Pyrrhus, like so many Murdoch dogs, is a crypto-Houyhnhnm looking in wonder at our 'fallen' human realm.

8

Such spiritual obsessions sometimes gave the appearance of sealing Iris's novelistic world off: A.N. Wilson in a memorial address believed that in her work 'there are no [Barbara] Pym-like evocations of office-life . . . No one comes home on the tube obsessed by envy or hatred of the boss.'[53] Hilary Burde, narrator of *A Word Child* (1975), lives on the Circle Line, obsessed by hatred and envy of his Civil Service boss Gunnar Jopling. Key scenes are set in the office. Yet Wilson is partly right: the Circle Line, its two erstwhile station-bars accurately observed, is a Dantesque circle of hell, an image as much of spiritual stasis as of locomotion. Burde is exactly the kind of brilliant working-class hero whom Iris's essays of the 1970s championed, whom she feared might have suffered under comprehensivisation. But the interest of the book is as much spiritual, even eschatological, as social. *A Word Child* continues Iris's stylised attack on the liberal fantasy of an unconditioned world, showing its protagonists enslaved to unconscious life-myths. In her novels human beings – even the so-called cultivated – repeat themselves irrationally. Most are dark to themselves. In *The Bell* Nick destroys Michael's career, then fourteen years later, his vocation. *An Accidental Man* (1971) explores Matthew's complicity in the death both of his brother Austin's first wife, then years later of his second, and, to underline the point, shows sibling rivalry poisoning the lives of Charlotte and her sister too. *A Word Child* also uses a repeating plot. Hilary had fallen in love with Jopling's first wife, who was killed in a car crash; in trying to put things right twenty years later he falls in love with Jopling's second wife, who also dies.

The Sacred and Profane Love Machine (a title posing translators interesting problems) (1974), winner of the Whitbread Prize, is a better novel than *A Word Child*.[54] Early in 1972 Iris twice noted that 'The same picture can represent Mary and Martha or Sacred & Profane Love. (Only of course the girls play different roles).' While it develops the usual mythic intensity, the novel has a social dimension whose bite and subtlety were underestimated. The 'bad' Emily's move from the role of mistress to wife improves her; the 'good' Harriet's demotion to rejected wife starts to render her feral and malign, before she is killed off with notable authorial coolness. Where one stands *vis-à-vis* society is not some airy irrelevance, but a leading determinant of 'character'. This makes *The Sacred and Profane Love Machine* a more disturbing and satisfying novel about a love-triangle than *The Sandcastle*. *Henry and Cato* (1976) contrasts Cato, another failed gay priest journeying into the demythologising landscape of Iris's Platonism, and Henry, trying to disburden himself of an imposing family house for 'political' reasons – in fact taking revenge on his dowager mother. The ending is a Whiggish compromise: Henry keeps the house, a new housing estate gaining some of its needed land. Each of Iris's convoluted plots fakes up a whole world, a society we enter and miss when we leave.

9

Both Henry and Cato have difficulties growing up. Good artists, however, in some sense stay childlike. Four of Iris's novels of the 1970s refer to 'the sinister boy' Peter Pan, J. M. Barrie's play being about 'one's relationship . . . to the subconscious mind'.[55] John had introduced her to Barrie's novel of the same title, which impressed her. She envisaged growing up as a gradual release from the cave (enslavement to one's unconscious – without which there was, however, no art), acknowledging that her philosophy, being in quest of 'salvation or enlightenment', was essentially religious. To be religious is to differ from oneself, to notice that everyone is (at least) two people, one worse or darker than the other, then to seek a means to privilege the better. She noted:

> When one is within the *small* net of irrationality one is
> mad and bad. *Just* outside it one feels rational and good
> again. *That* state then seems impossible! But the little
> net just does not communicate with the rest. Goodness
> (rationality) as making all such little enclaves connect
> with the open scene. (Pretty obvious! But sometimes one
> *feels* it in a sort of inner-spatial way.)[56]

The 'silly' overgrown child of June 1954 who, at nearly thirty-five, despaired because one of half a dozen suitors at a St Anne's ball flirted with someone else, was no more. In her 1970s journals Iris notes objectively in herself envy, jealousy, losses of nerve, depression, masochism, anger, anxiety, silliness, 'asininity', artistic vulgarity, surreptitious optimism. She observes good-humouredly that she is 'terribly sentimental. What is to be done about it?'[57] and is sometimes, usually through vanity, a bad judge of people. She enquires into how low, resentful states of being are to be expelled, transcended, 'seen through'. Such a movement from a closed-off obsessional enclave towards wonder at the more 'open scene' – what Zen calls little mind to big mind – marks her fictions, philosophy, and her private journey too. 'Amazement at the world', she observed, is something a novelist *and* philosopher might feel;[58] the novelist invites us to share it when, for example, Jake in *Under the Net* tells us, 'I had forgotten about rain.' Both the forgetting, then the recall, are necessary. The self-involvement of the journal-keeper, too, is repeatedly ambushed by amazement. She noted 'the extraordinary business of each night's sleep';[59] 'How extraordinary this moment to moment not-knowing-the-future way of existing!';[60] 'Looking down at one's body – so odd.'[61] Reynolds Stone's funeral was 'so *strange* . . .'[62]

If a technology existed to fuel this journey, Iris came to believe it might be found in Buddhism, whose truths she increasingly pondered. 'Sometimes, confronted with the religions of the east, one feels like the butcher's boy discovering the circulation of the blood,' she noted in 1971.[63] Buddhism offered a religion without belief in God or the supernatural, and confirmation of what she recognised about her own mind, and *ergo* about 'mind' as a factory of illusion in general. Both Japanese Zen Buddhism with its aes-

thetic puritanism, and the very different picturesque, superstitious and magical 'tantric' Buddhism of Tibet interested her
equally. Tantric Buddhism provided the backdrop to *The Sea, The
Sea*: unworthy emotions are not to be discarded but their energies
transmuted into wisdom, like a lotus growing in its necessary mud.
Tibet's favourite saint Milarepa, mentioned in *The Sea, The Sea*,
was a reformed murderer. 'The problem of the transformation
of energy is fundamental.'[64] She discussed this transformation
with Krishnamurti, the remarkable spiritual teacher who bravely
stood, as did she, outside all organised religions, when she was
invited to engage in dialogue with him in October 1984.[65]

It is striking that one Buddhist teacher with whom Iris herself
requested an interview came from the only tantric (Shingon)
tradition in the land of Zen. The Bayleys visited Japan three times,
in 1969, 1975 and 1993. On the 1975 trip they visited at Iris's
request the Daihonzan or temple of Ishiyamadera,[66] not far from
Kyoto, a venue associated with *The Tale of Genji*, an early Japanese
novel Iris loved and whose scene of cat-stealing she borrowed for
The Nice and the Good. Here they met the Abbot, Ryuko Washio.
After breakfast he performed the tea ceremony for them, with
strong green tea, each action having ritual and sacred significance. He resembled a tough Japanese colonel, asking searching
questions about how the American trappist monk, sometime her-
mit and prolific writer Thomas Merton had died: John told him
about Merton's heart attack triggered by electrocution from a
defective fan in Bangkok. The following day Iris and the Abbot
talked alone. No record of their conversation survives, but probably he gave her simple meditation instruction, which she also
sought from the Buddhist Society in London.[67]

A belief in goodness scarcely accords with the nihilism of the
age, which identifies the spiritual urge as pathological or self-
martyring, and argues that 'what goes up must come down'. Iris
believed, by contrast, that what is self-enclosed is disturbed, and
what is good, self-transcending. Attention – what she was to call
a 'passionate, stilled attention' – was the bridge. But she never
wholly abandoned 'original sin', or – with the notable exception
of some crucial passages in *The Nice and the Good, Bruno's Dream*

and *The Green Knight* – agreed with the Buddhist's certainties that evil is in a vital sense unreal, our original nature pure and awake. Goodness, for her as for Simone Weil, was by contrast essentially counter-natural.* She was obsessed by the religious life as something to be lived and experienced in every waking moment. She meditated, albeit irregularly, for much of her life thereafter.[68]

10

While reading about Buddhism in 1972, Iris asked herself, 'If art really thrives on . . . secret gratifications and its splendour is partly imagined, how does it relate to the spiritual quest at all?'[69] Dora in *The Bell* had had an epiphany in front of Gainsborough's picture of his two daughters in the National Gallery; while when demoralised by the devilish Julius, Morgan in *A Fairly Honourable Defeat* sees the Turners at the Tate as limited and amateurish. The painter Tim Reede's dream of hell in *Nuns and Soldiers* is of seeing the pictures in the National Gallery as trivial, valueless, inane. Perhaps, Iris pondered, all literature, all art misleads: the false unity of the art-work sanctioning an equally false sense of unity within its client. She satirised her own fiction in *The Black Prince* as 'a congeries of amusing anecdotes loosely garbled into racy stories with the help of half-baked unmediated symbolism'. This was partly protecting herself against criticism by getting a blow in first; yet also half-serious. She cared deeply about the novel-form, but, in a sceptical age, wished to strengthen it by radical criticism, as steel is the stronger for being tempered. She turned once more to Plato, who had put the case against art in terms so extreme that Iris could grant herself, and art, a final pyrrhic victory.

She gave the Romanes lecture in the Sheldonian Theatre on Plato on 13 February 1976,[70] and worked it up into a small book, *The Fire and the Sun: Why Plato Banished the Artists*. The book went

* See *The Sovereignty of Good, passim*, for Iris's exploration of how 'good' is both transcendent and immanent.

down better than the lecture, which lacked animation and pace, ran well over the statutory hour, tried too hard and got tangled, the audience becoming restless. The dinner that followed with Alastair Clayre at Brasenose College was uncomfortable. Clayre, a talented Wykehamist polymath – Fellow of All Souls', documentary film-maker, singer and songwriter – who never quite got his life 'together', committed suicide by throwing himself under an Underground train in January 1984. Iris liked his kindness and was fond of him; she hoped for responses to her talk, but got none.

If *The Sovereignty of Good* attempted to exorcise her fear that 'morality might turn out to be meaningless',[71] *The Fire and the Sun* addressed her ambivalence about art and the artist. In 1954 Canetti had confided his fear that even the 'innocent' power of creation was wicked. Iris reassured him, 'It is making more things possible for human beings.'[72] The challenge to prove this remained. Although *The Fire and the Sun* purports first to explicate Plato's case against art, then contest it, Iris's and Plato's voices increasingly become a single indistinguishable composite intellect. Her Plato, rumoured to have torn up his own poetry, felt within him, as did she, 'the peculiarly distressing struggle between the saint and the artist'.[73] Her identification with Plato was remarkable.

This Plato is also Simone Weil's, giving to love-experience a central place in ethics, yielding a whole metaphysic. For Weil the myth of the Fire and the Sun in *The Republic* provided half the story. Weil asked, 'What is the force that keeps the prisoners in the cave?' and 'What is the force that releases them?', finding the answer in Plato's two erotic dialogues, the *Phaedrus* and *Symposium*. The force that imprisons is low Eros – base, blind, obsessive desire; the force that releases high Eros – sublimated love, love of what is highest, desire educated and transformed, refined and dispassionate.[74] Falling in love played a role here. It was the only time you saw the world without yourself as the centre of significance, with someone else startlingly at its heart, a quasi-religious experience available to all. Falling in love made you discontinuous from yourself.

Here was one myth within which Iris moralised and made sense for herself of Canetti's idea of the self as discontinuous, prone to '*Verwandlung*', or transformation. Like Plato and Freud she gave to sexual love and to transformed sexual energy the central place in her thinking. This was the heart of her fiction, as of her philosophy. It was no accident that she used the difficulty of trying to 'check being in love' as an example of the primacy of 'attention' over 'will' in *The Sovereignty of Good*.[75] loving her many and varied friends dispassionately mattered too.

11

The theatre director Michael Kustow, excited by *The Fire and the Sun*, encouraged Iris to bring her philosophy closer to the interested lay reader. She accordingly wrote two Platonic dialogues, *Art and Eros: A Dialogue about Art* and *Above the Gods: A Dialogue about Religion* (published later as *Acastos*). The first made a well-received platform performance at the National Theatre in February 1980, with Andrew Cruikshank as Socrates and Greg Hicks as Plato. Nowhere else are her ideas brought so alive as in these two dialogues. Each, like the *Symposium*, contains a group of characters. Plato and Socrates here are two aspects of Iris herself, the former intensely puritanical and fanatical, the latter more relaxed, worldly-wise, pleasure-loving. Plato is an unbalanced twenty-year-old clicking his heels like a Prussian; his moral absolutism needs to be tempered by Socrates' quieter and more patient wisdom. Plato argues that 'Art is the final cunning of the human soul that would rather do anything than face the gods.' Socrates answers thus:

> You say art consoles us and prevents us from taking the final step ... It may be that human beings can only achieve a second best, that second best is our best ... Homer is imperfect. Science is imperfect ... our truth must include, must *embrace* the idea of the second-best, that all our thought will be incomplete and all our art tainted with selfishness. This doesn't mean there is no

difference between the good and the bad in what we achieve. And it doesn't mean not trying. It means trying in a humble modest truthful spirit. *This* is our truth . . .

It may even be that . . . good art tells us more truth about our lives and our world than any other kind of thinking or speculation – it certainly speaks to more people. And perhaps the language of art is the most universal and *enduring* kind of human thought . . . We are all artists, we are all story-tellers . . . And we should thank the gods for great artists who draw away the veil of anxiety and selfishness and show us, even for a moment, another world, a real world, and tell us a little bit of truth. And we should not be too hard on ourselves for being comforted.[76]

12

The understanding that Iris was Platonist inaugurated a second wave of criticism with Elizabeth Dipple's worthy but humourless *Work for the Spirit* in 1982. The characters in her novels were chastised for refusing to be saints; the pleasures of the text – details and their comedy, interiors, times of day, weather, seasons, parts of London, cars, dogs, *scènes-à-faire* – were neglected. If Plato can help the critic (as opposed to the novelist) it may be through his emphasis on the provisionality of all imagery. The pilgrimage towards the sun is a demythologisation, a progressive discarding of specious or illusory goods. It means seeing through one's own 'stories'.

In *Under the Net* Hugo argued that all stories are lies. *The Unicorn* too proposed that the spiritual life 'has no story' and so cannot be tragic. One reason Iris gave A.N. Wilson for destroying an early journal was that she 'did not want what it contained turned into a story'. Her work abounds in iconoclasm, books left incomplete, torn up, china or glass smashed. In 1961 she called her work 'an investigation that never ends, rather than a means of resolving anything'.[77] This strong playfulness and incompleteness can merge into a failure to be exact or demanding, where character is unfocused, depth of field facilely achieved, psychological inde-terminacies woolly: the novel being 'the most imperfect of art-forms'.[78] In the wilful obstinacy of her imperfection too – as in her refusal to be edited – she contrived to escape definition.

20

Icons and Patriarchs
1978–1994

Reading her journal in August 1969 it occurred to Iris to note, 'what an extraordinarily *silly* person I am in some ways. Silliness as a positive quality.'[1] The following month she woke in the middle of the night and wrote down in the dark the following: '"Staggering discovery – I now don't know anyone who is wiser than myself." (Well.) What on earth do I mean? Perhaps it's true? But then did I ever – or is it that I now feel my old gurus to be less than wise?' Not all dreams afforded equal insight. Waking in the night of 23 January 1970 she wrote down something extremely significant. The following morning, however, this turned out to read: 'Is ishood sufficient sufficiency?' She lacked self-conceit, indeed lacked a coherent self-image. 'We, the ungood', she wrote to a friend, and in an interview, praising Simone Weil's difficult idea that morality consists in 'decreating oneself', something she claimed was enormously difficult to do, went on to challenge the interviewer gloomily as to whether he knew anyone who had ever substantially changed himself.[2]

Iris certainly wished to leave the earth understanding more than when she arrived, and often felt she understood nothing. Yet an account of her good deeds would fill a weighty tome and make uncomfortable reading; she was, by any possible standard, a good person.* There is a moral charge in all she writes that is

---

* In 1961 Ved Mehta announced that she had the reputation of a saint, adding optimistically that she had no enemies. Certainly she early felt morality needed the concept of sanctity as an ideal limit. 'About saints I know nothing,' she wrote in her first *Adelphi* review in 1943. Mehta was echoed by, among others, the editor of the

often challenging, sometimes cosily familiar, occasionally repellent. Can we change ourselves? How is passion refined into compassion? The *allumeuse* or vamp orbited by admirers in 1953 had metamorphosed into what Martin Amis saw as a 'beautiful and benignant nun'[3] with a court of younger writers, painter-friends, seekers, relationships differently 'asymmetrical'. If her 1982 journal entry, 'To be a steady reliable (even if not very moved) recipient of love is to be a benefactor of the human race,'[4] is an unconscious yet vital transmutation of her 1945 'tendency to want to be loved, and not engage myself in return',[5] the self-worship and solipsism which endanger any spiritual path were not among her essential topics for nothing. That 'chaste love teaches' was the message of her 1982 Gifford lectures.

Andrew Harvey, ex-student of John's, in 1973 youngest Fellow of All Souls' and an author, spoke for many of Iris's friends in seeing her as a sage (no saint) who gave all her friends unstinting, patient and non-judgemental support, making them feel loved, blessed, accepted, unique. He noted the reserve which marked her natural dignity. She had no need to impress or prove anything, was an astonishing example of how to wear fame and assume the dignity of an elder, never for one second the *grande dame*. Her natural radiation stemmed from a powerful, peaceful, gentle wisdom, her journey an increasingly wide embrace from an increasingly private centre. She had '360° mindfulness-awareness'. He intuited the 'work' she had done on herself. She

---

Independent, who entitled an interview with her 'In the Presence of Perfect Goodness' (8 September 1992), and by Raymond Carr in his *Spectator* review of *Existentialists and Mystics,* where he mentions her reputation as 'a lay saint' (5 July 1997). A.N. Wilson suggested that not merely was she seen as a lay saint, but had perhaps started thus to perceive herself, in 'Iris Murdoch and the Characters of Love' (*News from the Royal Society of Literature,* 2000). The witness of Hilary Mantel, who saw her at parties but never spoke to her, was that 'Her presence was so powerful that it was the opposite of threatening, it was almost overwhelming ... She radiated a powerful benignity, a goodness that seemed to have little to do with "saintliness", but much to do with strength and *vertu;* there was a heartbreaking simplicity about her, like some simple comforting flower: a daisy. She seemed both aged and very young ... Her face ... had assumed lines of power and grace' (review of John Bayley's *Iris: A Memoir of Iris Murdoch,* in *Harvest: Journal for Jungian Studies,* vol. 45, no. 1, 1999).

helped him midwife his own mystical experiences, recorded a three-hour interview with him about Buddhism for the American journal *Tricycle*,[6] acted as guarantor of what he was coming to understand, showing him how to *be*. She appeared on a 1993 television programme about him, *The Making of a Mystic*,[7] was dedicatee of his excellent *Journey in Ladakh* which describes a spiritual quest, and went to Paris where in October 1990 Harvey introduced her to the Dalai Lama, who blessed her for some minutes in Tibetan. Iris and Harvey then wandered through the streets of Paris as if in a dream.

She bravely believed, against the temper of the times, that ordinary behaviour is mediocre, self-centred and neurotic, while good is un-neurotic. If the philosopher Martha Nussbaum was right to argue that her attitude to her own characters was one of 'disdain',[8] that may be truer of some of her later novels – for example *The Philosopher's Pupil* (1983). After 1980 she sometimes became, like the ageing Tolstoy whose spiritual obsessions hurt his later work, too 'good' to be novelistically true. Her best work came out of struggle, discontinuity and self-division.

2

Such self-division marks her early journals, full of the dissolving vapour-trails of her search. The journey itself – the spiritual work entailed in what she termed 'decreating oneself'[9] – is now invisible, untraceable. On 25 April 1965: 'Saw Wasfi Hijab, lunch at Mitre. I had the impression we had both *improved* since our last meeting. Is that possible?' She had, all her life, dreams of holiness which she recounts with the same cool objectivity she gives to recording watching four grisly operations under acupuncture as anaesthesia in China in 1979. Sometimes in these dreams she is back at school. There are comical or ludicrous tests and ordeals, which she occasionally passes, more often fails, as well as wise counsel. In April 1982 she dreamt of a 'rather ridiculous-looking' yet beautiful Tibetan wearing a sort of dhoti with European coat and bowler hat. Unsure if she was allowed to speak to him, she felt healed and thrilled when he touched her back, experiencing strong desire when she leant her face gently against his and he advised her not to kiss him. After darkness and sleep she 'awoke' in Oxford High Street, where she invited the holy man to drink in a pub: 'a mistake'. The very rude landlord would not serve drinks. There were now eight or twelve people, 'very upset', who ate a meal together. A woman sitting beside Iris said, 'He pardoned you.' Iris replied, 'Yes,' but was sorry that he had evidently spoken about her to a third party. After some confusion and 'a sort of pink substance smeared on my face (some ritual)', she felt excluded and that she must go away.

At this point she awoke (about 6.30 a.m.) and tried to continue the dream in drowsy waking thoughts. It went on as a conversation. She wanted to find out 'what he said to me', which turned out to be: 'Give up drinking. Live a quiet orderly life. Bring *peace* and *order* into your life. Give up certain thoughts, send them quietly away. When you feel your clutching craving hands holding onto something, gently detach them. Sit, kneel, or sometimes lie on your face in a quiet room. Have flowers in the room. Love the visible world.' She asked him about penance. 'Penance? Think in that way if you like, but not with intensity.' 'Can I see you sometimes?' 'I am nobody, you must give me up too.' A feeling of grace, of a door opening, accompanied these half-waking thoughts.

Sometimes she allotted such dreams to her characters, as when Monty in *The Sacred and Profane Love Machine* was given her dream of failing a spiritual test by scooping up imaginary water at the 'wrong' level. 'A most strange & vivid dream' she had on the night of 20 January 1947 waited thirty years to be used. She saw in a garden two allegorical figures of birds of prey who transmuted into angels, be-winged and with golden hair. They came down from their pillars, passing her by.

> I follow them, a little afraid, & call after them. 'Can I ask you one question: Is there a God?' They reply 'Yes', & disappear round a corner. I follow them and find myself alone in a gravel walk by the side of a building. Then I hear the footsteps approaching of someone

whom I know to be the Christ. Filled with an indescribable terror & sense of abasement I fall on my face. The footsteps pass me & I hear a voice say: '*Ite*' – which I take in the dream to mean 'Come' in Greek. I dare not look up.

She heard another person approaching with a rustling dress. This person – the Virgin Mary – stopped beside her and put her hand on Iris's shoulder: 'The burden of terror is lifted a little and I say "Forgive me."' She replies to the effect that 'Your sins are forgiven.' The Virgin passed on, Iris keeping her face hidden.

The dream had other sequences, some terrifying, two blissful: the first in which Donald MacKinnon made a careful plaster-cast of her, then kissed her; and another in which the family reassured Hughes, unexpectedly home after having gone missing on a secret service job in which he had to make himself 'look like a German', and was afraid he still did. There were 'very vivid colours throughout . . . – & a certainty, especially in the gravel walk scene, that this is not a dream – it is a vision'. Thirty years later she gave the first half of this waking vision to the ex-nun Anne Cavidge in *Nuns and Soldiers* (1980), married to Dame Julian of Norwich's well-known dream of meeting Christ[10] and being handed by him a hazelnut, the universe in microcosm. Christ mysteriously reassured Julian, in answer to her question about how fatally flawed Creation is by sin and suffering, that 'All will be well, and all will be well, and all manner of thing shall be well; and sin is behovely.' To Cavidge, Christ, in whom she no longer in the ordinary sense believes, provides different assurances, a pebble substituting for the hazelnut, and her finger burns when she tries to touch him; the burn survives into waking life as an ambiguous sign.

3

In these dreams, as in her schooldays, Iris is partly cast as a lonely child longing for approval; and just as Froebel schoolchildren accumulated within their desks their growing collection of red stars, so she privately recorded a lifelong love of praise. The Iris who in 1938 was instantly enslaved when Ruth Kingsbury praised her *Cherwell* poems was in evidence when she noted in May 1967 her old friend Tino de Marchi's letter thanking her for a meeting: 'It was like reviving after the torture chamber. And your marvellous note! The power of your words! There are people who are mean with them. You are not one. I wish I were like you – as strong, as human, as generous as you are.' In January 1972 she found 'very cheering . . . dear Cecil Beaton' wishing to photograph her impromptu outside the Victoria and Albert Museum. The next month David Hicks wrote after a lunch, 'By God, that was the happiest meeting with you I have had for years, and I wept with pleasure in the tube going back to my office. What an absolute darling you are!' In November 1981 the French critic Jean-Louis Chevalier after a conference at the Centre Pompidou wrote, '*Le mélange de modestie et de conscience de sa juste valeur chez I.M. m'a énormément séduit.*'* The following year a letter praising her Gifford lectures, which had profoundly dispirited her, was 'one she hoped for'.

Against such a background her hope for 'change' must be read. Certain themes recur. She noted in 1949 her deep desire to please others, a willingness which is 'on my face like a birthmark'.[11] She thought this weak. In July 1980: ' "Weakness of will" is not a unitary phenomenon. I am very strong willed in some ways, absurdly weak in others. (E.g. strong in my work; weak in pleasing others, sometimes anyway) I suppose this is obvious.' That this is not the only possible reading of the instinct to propitiate and confirm others is suggested by her quoting Traherne's *Meditations*: 'Never is anything in this world too much loved, but is loved in a false way and in too short a measure.'[12] Love of her friends, of her characters, of the visual world, marks her too.

She accordingly praised a passage from Auden's 'The Horatians' that runs: 'Look at/This world with a happy eye'. She thought Auden's love of what we see before us is preferable to Shake-

---

* 'I was enormously taken by the mixture of modesty and of awareness of her true worth in I.M.'

speare's emphasis on music ('The man that hath no music in himself/Nor is not moved with concord of sweet sounds/Is fit for treasons, stratagems and spoils'*). Iris preferred to say that 'the man who does not love the visual world, who does not *see* what is before him', is in poor case. Her friendships with painters – Canadian Alex Colville, Harry Weinberger – were very important to her. She spent much of her Booker Prize money acquiring Weinberger's paintings, and wrote introductions to two of his catalogues.[13] They met often, at his studio in Leamington and touring the National Gallery in London, and her four hundred or so letters to him show how zealously she tried to find him a good dealer and to explore with his help, *inter alia*, her liking for Francis Bacon, Egon Schiele and Titian, and her doubts about Lucian Freud, Giacometti or Picasso – 'Great painter but the personality shows too much.'[14]

Her journals abound in deft evocations of ordinary magic making what is strange familiar, and what is familiar, strange.

> *13 October 1968.* Very engaging gentle tapir in Harrods zoo ... trudging around ... sniffing the other cages, pushing past a dust bin, sniffing at it with his long sensitive proboscis-like nose. Wonderful round intelligent eyes and strange hoofed feet with divided toes which folded up when he lifted them, and splayed out as he set them down ... when he came near we stroked his soft naked warm nose. He had strong back legs, a tiny tail. Puss offered him a peppermint which he accepted with dignity.
>
> *13 May 1981.* Yesterday we found a *queen hornet* which had crawled out of the woodpile by the kitchen door. We took her outside on a piece of cardboard and looked at her closely. She stared back with her huge eyes, waving her feelers. We put her on the ground and she crawled away among the plants. I hope she is all right.
>
> *25 May 1984.* Last night a strange scene in the garden. Just before twilight, very vivid darkish evening light (after a sunny day), we saw from the window [a] deer ...

---

* *Merchant of Venice*, V.i.

daintily walking and feeding in the longer grass of the lawn. Such a pretty graceful brown animal. We watched for a while, the deer lifted her head, then there appeared, like an entry of dandyish quarrelsome youths in a theatre, three large fox cubs, who stood insolently displaying the tawny frills of fur round their necks, just under the yew trees by the new lawn. They approached the deer, who lowered her head menacingly, ran at a cub who approached her and drove him away. Then the three began to run round, one always appearing behind her, while she kept turning aggressively. This game, I think the cubs just playing, went on for some time, until the deer suddenly raced away. The fox cubs stayed and played on the lawn where we watched them for a long time till it got dark. It was like something out of a Book of Hours, the colours were so vivid.

A sense for what Gabriele Annan, reviewing *The Book and the Brotherhood*,[15] called *lacrymae rerum*,* was always with her. James Scott noted in 1937 that she had, even as a teenager, a feeling for 'something sad and deep that belonged to the very structure of the universe'. Leo Pliatzky wrote to Frank Thompson in September 1942, 'She finds the world tragic and moving, but that is not unusual.'[16] She was easily moved, struck by the fact that 'many men cannot weep';[17] noted that 'A very acute realisation that people are suffering elsewhere in the world is a very precious thing to have.'[18] On the one hand, 'the planet is *crawling* with misery'; on the other, she made a strong case for the quest for happiness and pleasure.[19] As for goodness, she noted in her journal, perhaps no discussion or portrayal of it can, in the end, evade sentimentality. Early in *Nuns and Soldiers* Anna Cavidge and the dying Guy Openshaw have a critical discussion, at the end of which they agree that goodness is a 'conjecture'.

---

* 'The tears of things'; from Virgil's *Aeneid*, where Aeneas in the temple of Juno at Carthage sees a picture of fighting in the Trojan War: 'there are tears in the very nature of things and men's affairs touch the heart'.

4

The characters in *Nuns and Soldiers*, Martin Amis observed, inhabit a 'suspended and eroticised world, removed from the anxieties of health and money and the half-made feelings on which most of us subsist'.[20] The questioning of her old gurus lies behind this last phase of Iris's novel-writing, the seven novels starting with *Nuns and Soldiers* in 1980, which begins with the death of a wise older man, Guy Openshaw. Each succeeding novel chronicles the death of a patriarch, whose wisdom often resembles madness. The modern world, it sometimes seems, has been too much for them. Rozanov in *The Philosopher's Pupil* and Vallar in *The Message to the Planet*, like Iris with *Metaphysics as a Guide to Morals*, are struggling to write their 'great books'. Many are pursued by needy younger disciples or son-figures: the anxiety of influence a common topic. *The Philosopher's Pupil* chronicles the death in a bath-house of the cruel Rozanov, and supposed redemption of his nasty epigone George, resenting his enslavement. *The Good Apprentice* has the death of a crazed artist-mage who lusts after his own daughter, Jesse Baltram; in *The Book and the Brotherhood* the old classicist Levquist and Gerard's father die. *The Message to the Planet* concerns the demise of the Holocaust-maddened Jewish mathematician Marcus Vallar; *The Green Knight* the mission, the life after death, and then the real expiry of the Buddhist-Russian-Jew Peter Mir.

Rozanov has been compared to a menacing side of Donald MacKinnon. Levquist is based on Fraenkel, Gerard's father's death on Hughes's, and Gerard's last meeting with Levquist inspired by Iris's meeting with Fraenkel in 1965. Baltram, like the earlier priapic Otto in *The Italian Girl*, owes something to Iris's readings of Eric Gill's life;[21] she claimed Vallar was based on Kreisel,[22] who, however, compared the Holocaust to a mere act of nature.[23] It is partly Kreisel's profession as mathematical logician that she exploits – the working title of *The Message to the Planet* was 'The Language of the Planet', mathematics being construed, since Pythagoras, as a universal language – and partly his unpredictable relations with his friends. Vallar's spiritual struggle derives both from Franz and from Arnoldo Momigliano,[24] and apparently predicted the writer and Auschwitz survivor Primo Levi's suicide in April 1987.*

Iris wondered in 1990 whether her writer's guardian angel had been 'assigned to somebody else?' She used a fountain pen for two drafts – 'One should love one's handwriting' – then personally brought her novels, swollen now with superfluous ideas and characters, to Chatto in a plastic bag or two. None after 1971 had chapter divisions. Chatto was frustrated that she magisterially refused editorial guidance, and sensitive about it too: Norah Smallwood wrote to Sebastian Faulks, then editing *New Fiction*, that his suggestion that Chatto was pusillanimous over editing Iris's books, were it true, was 'an impertinence, if not libellous'.[25] Norah Smallwood's successor Carmen Callil, newly arrived, and attempting to have *The Philosopher's Pupil* copy-edited,[26] received a careful letter from Iris requesting her, at some expense, to please 'put it all back'. She would rather, she said, be read by fewer readers who were more intelligent. On the one hand she now required to approve every comma change;† on the other, as Chatto's Editorial Director Andrew Motion noted with despairing good humour, 'she's a self-confessed bad speller and checker of detail, so the common or garden copy editing has to be done carefully. Heigh ho.'[27]

A note from Norah Smallwood in 1982 tells Iris that the sum of £200,000 awaited her instructions. Her novels were selling 25,000 copies in hardback. Norah Smallwood retired, and in 1984 bequeathed Iris to the good offices of the literary agent Ed Victor. The old-fashioned contract – an advance of £10,000 per novel and a 50:50 royalty split – was succeeded, thanks to Victor,

---

* Iris wrote to Sister Marian from 30 Charlbury Road, undated: 'I too read Primo Levi's book – and before his death, wrote in one of my books about such a death of someone, years later, who had been haunted by the Holocaust.'
† Jane Turner, who helped edit Iris's novels from roughly 1969 onwards, recalled Norah Smallwood's strong sense that, so valued was Iris as a writer and a friend, nothing must be cut – particularly, perhaps, by an editor unknown to Iris. However, as friendship and trust grew, Turner observed that Iris would agree to occasional changes and small cuts.

by more advantageous terms, and much larger advances: £50,000 for *The Book and the Brotherhood* in the UK alone. Soon Callil referred to Iris as 'Queen of Chatto';[28] to herself as 'putty in [Iris's] hands'.[29]

Iris vigorously defended in *The Good Apprentice* both her invention 'oblivescent',[30] meaning 'in the process of being forgotten', and her resurrection of the archaic 'to cote'.[31] Each novel now grew fifty or so pages longer than its predecessor. Her characters, older than her when she began, were now often younger. Instead of having them educated at Oxbridge, she was increasingly likely to send them to polytechnics. The map of modern living criticised in the opening Fulham dinner party of *The Good Apprentice* (1985) is sobering. The old liberal values Iris treasured were threatened by nuclear war, computers and pornography, while a sterile scientistic rationalism promises the decay of faith in the significance of the individual, and of any vision of human destiny that might be termed spiritual. In her Gifford lectures in November 1982 she remarked that the world needs 'fewer prophets and more saints'. The prophetic note came easily, none the less. Her Platonic dialogues of 1986, which she noted could be staged in modern dress, see the present as a period of critical breakdown of old values, while *The Book and the Brotherhood* (1987) threatens a future that is bookless, technocratic, soulless and violent, mankind living on the brink of the fastest change in the history of the planet. Honor Tracy had told her humorously that the Days of Mercy were ending as the Days of Wrath drew nigh; in her next hurried scrawl Iris wrote, 'Thanks inform. Days Wrath.'[32] Her dislike of television as 'frenetic shadows' that destroy exactly that sense of reality which novels supply perhaps belongs to the early 1950s, when the contempt of intellectuals for television was at its height, and did not prevent her occasional appearances on it.[33]

Unlike E.M. Forster after the Great War, Iris did not lose the ability either to think about, or to fear, the contemporary world. Fear gave her vision edge. There were also new refuges from modern vulgarity and domestic chaos. From around 1985 the Bayleys stayed with Diana, Lady Avebury, who had a small literary agency, in the top flat at Lepe, looking out over the Solent in Hampshire.[34] Diana's step-brother Bill Pease, owner of Lepe House, had been (though younger) at Eton with John, and his wife Lizzie was a niece of Lord David Cecil's; there were eleven acres of garden. There were regular visits, too, to George Clive and his mother Lady Mary, sister-in-law of Anthony Powell, friends of the Stones, at their eighteenth-century red-brick house and splendid grounds, Whitfield, in Herefordshire.

5

Summers were enlivened by friendship. On 30 July 1977 Iris noted: 'Back from France. A very good time with Stephen and Natasha [Spender]. I begin to feel at home in that countryside, so that I cd write about it. Swam in magic aquaduct, and in pool under rock.' The Bayleys' first stay at the Spenders' Mas Saint-Jerôme, near Maussane in the Alpilles, was in August 1973. When Natasha Spender met them at Marignane airport, Iris and John were convulsed in helpless laughter at some private joke. The Spenders were 'doing up' the old farmhouse in its great natural limestone amphitheatre, within which Natasha was creating a large and notably beautiful garden. There were Cézanne pine trees in the foreground, 'frilly' rocks at the horizon on which windswept smaller trees took on the look of a Chinese painting. This became an annual pilgrimage, in the *grand chaleur* succeeding exams, both John and Stephen being university professors. The Spenders enjoyed Stuart Hampshire's description of the Bayleys as Hansel and Gretel. John and Iris bought zinc-capped cheap supermarket wine in three-starred bottles which the Spenders nicknamed 'child-wine' – playing surrogate children was a role to which they were used. The Bayleys relaxed Spender in a way that some of his worldlier friends did not. Douglas Cooper,[35] art historian, critic and collector, kept the château de Castille at Argilliers near Tarascon and wrote reviews intended to cause 'unassuageable anguish'. Spender found him spiteful and destructive.[36] With this gay *'Monstre'*, as he was nicknamed,

Iris was completely self-possessed, calming, dominant. Like the Virgin with the Unicorn, she was the one who, to the astonishment of onlookers, 'led' and tamed the Beast. Cooper adored Iris; with her his character changed for the better. Travel writer Rory Cameron, who built a palatial house for his mother Lady Kenmare at Cap Ferrat, gave Iris the phrase '*une vie de baton de chaise*' for *The Green Knight*. Referring to sedan chairs, it betokened a rackety life at a high social level. Scrabble was sometimes played in the evenings. The Bayleys enjoyed watching the competitive edge with which the Spenders played – Stephen's face wore a delightfully cunning look – and liked it when the Spenders won (which was often).

Gardening early one morning, Natasha was excited to hear a woodpecker towards the end of her lilac-walk. Closer inspection showed this to be John tapping out a book on his portable type-writer, getting up and humming a little song as he walked about, then sitting down and woodpeckering away again. Iris would come out and, without ado, help with whatever gardening chore needed finishing, sometimes in silence. She knew the names of moths, and loved to rescue small creatures – for example ants – from humans teetering down the steps. 'I say, old thing, do be careful . . .'. The cat Daisy favoured her. Iris wrote in the small room next to the Bayleys' bedroom in the 'Bergerie'.

Around 11.30 the Bayleys would disappear for a swim. Iris told her fellow-guests the Rodrigo Moynihans and the Noel Annans in July 1975, 'I'm going to let you into a secret.' They trooped down in a crocodile to reach an ever-changing, rapidly flowing winding strip, the sixteenth-century *canal de Craponne*, which brought fertility and brilliantly coloured dragonflies to an arid land, at a point where it is bridged and easy to enter from a parapet. 'Splendid, splendid,' said Noel Annan, watching from the bridge Iris float on her back in the *eau agricole* in her mother's ancient skirted bathing-suit, noting her resemblance to one of the beautiful mauve jellyfish that proliferate in the Mediterranean in summer.[37] The party cheered as they raced each other towards a short but alarming downhill chute, down which the Moynihan boys dared to plunge. By 1977 Iris was trying to work out whether it might be possible for her hero Tim Reede in *Nuns and Soldiers* to go through the hundred-yard tunnel ingeniously scooped through a limestone hill, obscured by brambles at each end, through which the canal later flowed. Natasha naughtily said, 'Only one thing for it, John has got to try it.' John declined. After the book came out – to 'screams of rage and hate' from critics, Iris untypically lamented[38] – a fire cleared both ends and John and Iris swam through the tunnel, emerging looking regal and exhilarated, only their torch lost. Natasha was relieved to see them. Ten years later another adventurous soul was killed trying this feat, concussed against the roof and then drowned. Tim's feat was plausible: the tunnel was dangerous, but sometimes survivable. The novel anticipated the journey.

The vividly memorable landscape in *Nuns and Soldiers* is a *collage* and shows something of the workings of Iris's imagination. The scale of the canal is magnified; a significant local pool, given by Iris a grander valley background from Caisse de Servannes, a Celtic-Ligurian sanctuary, is brought together with a rocky fountain from Salon-de-Provence twenty kilometres off. Just before lunch Stephen and Iris liked to sit on the stone seat below a flower-filled sarcophagus for a pre-lunch drink – talk would centre on whatever each was writing – the Gifford lectures for Iris around 1977–82. Visits to the Camargue to see the flamingos took place after tea. Once they saw bee-eaters. Iris would plunge into almost any available water. Such sights and experiences were precious, both to her and for her art.

6

Nuns and Soldiers was dedicated to Stephen and Natasha Spender, and prompted in Stephen the nightmare that he had unexpectedly been made Pope, and had to deliver a sermon to waiting millions (the election of John-Paul II figures at the end of the book). He noted that Iris, though extremely gifted, 'doesn't seem quite a novelist'. The lack of surface realism, and the inclusion of a big green and gold lizard which he had never observed, bothered him.[39] Iris and John had watched it lying motionless in the dense creepers on the outside wall. The novel is fed by Henry James's *The Wings of the Dove*, whose story of two impoverished outsiders plotting an opportunistic marriage it plays with and alters, and whose famous final line ('We shall never be again as we were') it twice echoes. The dying Guy is one of those Murdochian characters whose mere existence acts as a guarantee of meaning, continuity, stability, in a frightening world. He represses his own cruelty and is generous financially, morally and emotionally, expecting a calm dignity in those to whose problems he patiently listens. In Iris's godless universe such people shine out with the force that once accrued to the Church. For Tim and the Count, as for his widow Gertrude whom both love, Guy's Ebury Street flat is an 'abode of value', providing some sense of family.[40]

While Iris agreed with Guy's argument that the possibility of the Good is only 'a conjecture'* – he himself is none the less what she termed an 'icon' to his world. On 16 April 1966 she noted that an *Iris stylosa* whose bud she had picked in the snow had blossomed unexpectedly indoors. Its silky sky-blue flower prompted the thought: 'Completely pure things as starting-points.' This rhetoric about icons she developed in the third of her ten Gifford lectures in Edinburgh in 1982. Positive icons – like objects of prayer – were objects, persons, events whose contemplation brought an access of good spiritual energy. In *Metaphysics as a Guide to Morals*, which wrote up the Giffords and was received with a certain baffled respect in 1992, she noted that we often keep such icons private.[41] Negative icons degrade and demoralise.

Iris wrote and rewrote the Gifford lectures repeatedly, but found it hard to bring her thoughts together, and the audience, partly of good ladies from Morningside, shrank during the fortnight it took to deliver them. There were moments of involuntary comedy, as when one lecture was introduced in error as concern-

---

* 'Everybody except a few saints (and how much close examination wd they stand?) is very selectively kind and good, if they are kind and good at all.' Journal, 7 November 1976.

ing the Ontological Proof of God, rather than of Good. Iris crossly cited the fact that swallows are obliged by their supposed Designer to migrate 12,000 miles each year of their brief lives: 'The arrangement is both *wasteful* and *immoral*.' She urged that our task is to love other people 'and perhaps dogs'. She used to consider the image of the mother as the paradigm good person, but had come to see mothers as complicit with power. The good man, she augustly announced, *should behave like an aunt*. A promised lecture on the 'Return to the Cave' and the uses of Good in politics and in the marketplace was postponed and never happened. The official historian of the Gifford lectures wrote a sceptical report on Iris's performance.[42]

The rhetoric about icons gets into *The Good Apprentice*, one of two marvellous late novels (the other is *The Green Knight*). These are saved from shapelessness by cannibalising and reworking earlier myths. *The Good Apprentice* recycles the parable of the Prodigal Son, *The Green Knight* the myth of Sir Gawain. *The Good Apprentice* (1985) is based on the premise that most lives go terribly wrong at some point. Its hero Edward inadvertently kills his friend Mark in the electrifying opening sequence, then maps a comic journey out of modern London into the mysterious counter-pastoral world of Seegard, from guilt, via ordeals, to self-renewal. Seeking saviours, he finally has to learn self-forgiveness. Stuart, his foster-brother, and the saint of the book, finds spiritual help from watching mice living on the Underground tracks, an image of the power of meekness in a dangerous world (Iris was then re-reading Dostoevsky's *The Idiot* every year, with its own rhetoric about meekness). Conversely, the image of shorn-off plaits of girls' hair at Auschwitz, which the Bayleys visited in 1974, haunts Stuart as an emblem of the horrors of the age. Stuart, whose white grub-like face links him to Anne Cavidge's vision of Christ in *Nuns and Soldiers*, is the single non-allegorical good figure in Iris's work. It is observed of him that, while preaching selflessness, he has a strong ego. Stephen Medcalf in the *TLS* was typical of many reviewers in finding Stuart's style of chastity self-deceived and inhumane, his interventions disastrous, his refusal to believe in God incomprehensible.[43] Myshkin, too, was controversial in his time.

The Green Knight (1993) merits comparison with the late romances of Shakespeare: poised and fantastical, with its quasi-divine intervention, it is a myth about redemption which is none the less full of actuality, and an extraordinarily achieved mixture of joy and pain. Iris noted that she wanted this novel to 'fight back against philosophy'. Her characters usually arrived in a small group 'carrying a box which contains the plot. Not this time.' Peter Mir in *The Green Knight* is more clearly allegorical than Stuart; he is a figure from elsewhere, possibly raised from the dead, his Russian Jewishness a token only of otherness. He links interestingly with Hugo in *Under the Net*. Both are non-English, and spiritual aliens. Hugo startles us by becoming an apprentice watchmaker in Nottingham; Mir reveals he was formerly a butcher. The ordinariness of their trades is a token of authenticity. Both come to redeem the social worlds they find themselves in. Neither is properly apprehended or understood. Both, again, owe something to Myshkin. Mir is as interesting as Hugo, but more integrated with the life of the novel, as well as with its ideas.

Two episodes in *The Green Knight* stemmed from a holiday with Borys and Audi Villers, friends of the Bayleys for thirty years and travelling companions in the 1980s: the evening parade through the piazza, which they experienced together at the little town of Ascoli Piceno, where they went to look at the Crivellis in September 1988; and the tense bridge scenes, which were inspired in Spoleto. The bridge so frightened Iris that she refused to cross. Her fear informs the novel as the ordeal Harvey twice has to suffer. John and Iris first went to stay with the Villerses, dedicatees of *The Message to the Planet,* on Lanzarote in the Canary Islands in 1983. Many trips abroad followed: the Villerses and Bayleys had in common the love of painting, books and music, and mutual friends in Oxford and London. Borys, who started, then sold, a profitable firm manufacturing electric blankets, had been born Emil Chwoles in Vilnius in 1923, converted from Judaism to Catholicism, and anglicised himself at school in England and at Christ Church. The Villerses' London flat, where Borys died in 1992, was, like the dying Anglo-Jewish Guy's in *Nuns and Soldiers*, in Ebury Street, near Victoria station. When Iris invented

567

Guy's death in Ebury Street in 1978, however, the Villers had not dreamt of moving to that address. Her art anticipated life.

7

Iris once watched a boy on the Oxford train devouring a novel of hers, wholly unaware of its inventor sitting opposite, eyeing him quizzically throughout. On alighting she reflected, 'Say what they like: at least I can tell a story . . .'. Such narrative skills apart, she strove to get out of what she saw as the second division into the first. Since her first contains Homer, Shakespeare, James, Proust, Tolstoy, Dostoevsky, Dickens and Austen, a place just below these is not dishonourable.

Guy Openshaw and Peter Mir in *The Green Knight* resemble Charles Dickens's lonely altruists Jarndyce and the Cheeryble brothers. Each offers the material and spiritual help that society no longer provides. They are suitable angels in a Thatcherite state. Iris believed in such beings. She wrote to a friend, ill and contemplating suicide, that she wished the friend might find someone who could really help: 'Sometimes such persons can appear.' The friend decided against drastic action. For a number of her now worldwide collection of pen-friends Iris was such an iconic being herself. For some their only friend. The 'feeling you're not understood, that nobody cares what happens to you' was, she believed, a prime cause of unhappiness.[44] There were 'many lonely folk who are desperately waiting for attention'.[45] Friendship mattered more than such public duties as being an honorary member of the Friends of the Classics and of the Tyndale Society,[46] or Trustee of the Jan Hus Foundation, to which she made a generous donation[47] – all gained from her name – proposing a statue of Proust for the empty plinth in Trafalgar Square[48] or agitating unsuccessfully to keep Somerville for women only. The joke about the socialite with 'a hundred close friends' was no joke in Iris's case. Unlike the socialite, she knew each of them. Yet Sir Leo (as he now was) Pliatzky was not alone among her older friends in minding the perhaps understandable alternation in her, now, of peremptory invitations and silence.

Iris began her epistolary career, pre-war, with letters to pen-friends such as James Scott. Answering such correspondents could now take four hours a day. She always answered rapidly, in her own hand, without secretarial help ('I could not *bear* a secretary'), on J.R.R. Tolkien's rolltop desk, which she and John had bought in the 1970s, apologising when absence delayed her reply. She met everyone at their own level, addressing their troubles and happinesses alike. Her answers made her friends more interesting to themselves, each uniquely apprehended. Many of her letter-runs have more than a hundred letters in them; some more than three hundred. This energetic expenditure of sympathetic warmth, intelligence and encouragement is, surely, quite remarkable: such unpaid authorship brought comfort and down-to-earth advice. One Belgian correspondent displayed interest in the market value of his collection of her letters. Though in *The Black Prince* Iris had described letter-writing as a 'complex warding-off process', keeping the world at bay, David Hicks was not alone in avowing a shock of delight when a letter with her handwriting came through the door. Her complaints of tiredness became more frequent. When it was suggested in 1992 that the penalty for virtue was a steadily increasing burden,[49] she replied with mordant humour, 'Yes! *Pals for life!*' After a short absence in September 1993 she found seventy letters awaiting her. Christmas brought two hundred. She had an educated heart, imagination, and fearsome industry. Her letters, friendship and visits lightened dark places. That she was there mattered. Yeats told us that 'The intellect of man is forced to choose/Perfection of the life, or of the work,'[50] Auden retorting that perfection was attainable in neither. Would Iris's later work have been better had she allowed herself to be a less 'perfect' correspondent? But the work and the life were the same project. Walking with her friend David Luke outside St Aldate's one day in the 1960s, she interrupted a violent altercation between an unknown young couple, saying 'Stop that! Stop it at once! Don't do that.' Luke found this both naive and warm-hearted. It also presaged Tallis in *A Fairly*

Honourable Defeat, who memorably knocked out an unknown thug intimidating a black diner in a restaurant.

Honor Tracy noted to Sister Marian: 'She is so very famous . . . Perhaps she feels that, wherever she goes, a kind of other imaginary distorted self has got there ahead of her and put obstacles in her way.' Tracy thought she had no enemies, 'except among the envious and less successful'. It is not clear that Iris wholly understood her own celebrity, nor how the age had made out of fame itself its secret religion. Simplicity did not make her less of an icon. A journalist wrote that Iris's entire career was familiar to educated persons, like national folklore. A television advertisement for British Rail showed a contented passenger reading *Henry and Cato*. A.S. Byatt on Iris's seventieth birthday argued, 'She's not a minor writer. She's at the centre of our culture.'[51] ('Everyone *very kind*,' Iris noted, in Queen Victoria mode, of the messages she received.) Owing to her friendship with Iris, Byatt announced, it was no longer possible for her to tell a lie. The artist Tom Phillips spent years painting her portrait, pale, still and mystical, a light shining in darkness, for the National Portrait Gallery, in front of her own favourite Titian's late *The Flaying of Marsyas*.* This portrait, on permanent display in the gallery, was also made into a postcard. Iris did not mind being a postcard. On a BBC TV *Bookmark* programme about her in 1989 she praised the separateness and coolness of Phillips's portrait, adding that she did not think she had any very strong sense of her identity: 'I don't think of myself as existing much, somehow.'[52]

The Bayleys went more frequently now on the British Council lecture tours that had begun in the 1960s, performing an unscripted double-act all over the world, ambassadors for liberal British culture and the traditional novel alike. One advantage of such travel was visiting art galleries, and she remarked to the noted critic of her work Richard Todd in 1986 of the three Vermeers, including the *View of Delft*, at the Mauritshuis in The Hague: 'I'm sorry, but if we don't manage to see those pictures

---

* The agonising removal of Marsyas' skin was, for Renaissance painters as for Iris, a central religious image of the loss of ego; it recurs in her fiction.

I'm afraid I shall go mad.' (On the flight back, so as not to have to check any baggage, she wore four cardigans one on top of the other. To Todd's enquiry, 'Iris, aren't you going to be incredibly warm?' she replied, 'No, we shall make a quick getaway at Heathrow.') In Malcolm Bradbury's good-natured parody of a Murdoch novel there are characters called Moira LeBenedictus, Hugo Occam, Sir Alex Montaubon.[53] There were plenty of names as odd in real life: in Japan in 1975 she met Endymion Porter Wilkinson and read about Tabitha Powledge.

Iris was made a Dame of the British Empire in 1987 – 'There is nothing like a Dame,' friends predictably quipped – and wore to her investiture at Buckingham Palace black plimsolls that allowed the natural expansion her painfully crippled hammertoes required. In 1993 alone she was awarded four honorary doctorates – from Alcalar de Henares (in Spain), Cambridge, Ulster and Kingston. She was disconcerted to find she had to give the speech at the Barbican for Kingston, finding it hard to plan the jokes, rewriting many times. Although her best novels are comedies, she was never an entertainer. Kingston's Vice-Chancellor suggested she curtail her speech; dismayed, she cut out a section on the necessity of Christ in the twenty-first century.[54] She vowed to accept thereafter no more doctorates.

8

On Saturday, 10 January 1987 Iris sat next to E.P. Thompson on an Air India jet,[55] both flying first class to a New Delhi conference commemorating the recently assassinated Indira Gandhi, Iris's contemporary at Badminton.[56] Thompson had never travelled first class before, and noted that 'young Dame Iris' took all – including champagne, cocktails, caviar, lobster – as her customary due. However fast asleep she seemed to be, she had a preternatural seventh sense to catch the wine waiter passing by. His father had been a friend of Indira Gandhi's father Jawaharlal Nehru, family tradition maintaining that Indira was married at Somerville before the war in a sari borrowed from E.P. and Frank's mother

Theo. He used the occasion to brood upon political change. In 1941–45, 'that half-democratic, half anti-Fascist' time, the chances of life were shared, the young gave priority to the injured, the sick, children and the old, and the pursuit of private privilege was deemed contemptible. He neglected to congratulate 'the young Dame Iris' on the title she had accepted from a mean and malevolently philistine government: 'How could Iris Murdoch have forgotten the oaths of yesteryear?'[57]

Despite saying of the miners during the 1981 strike, 'they should be put up against the wall and shot,'[58] and approving the Falklands war, Iris's own perception was not that she had moved to the right, but that the Labour Party had been taken over by left-wing extremism. The formation of the moderate Social Democratic Party by four ex-Labour Cabinet Ministers in 1981 was (at first) splendid news: 'I am on the whole very glad about this development.' It reminded her of February 1940 and the splitting of Oxford University Labour Club, when Roy Jenkins, now a member of the 'Gang of Four' founders of the SDP, abandoned the extremist left, led by her. 'How right he was,' she wrote, 'on both occasions.'[59] Iris was a nominator for Jenkins in 1987 as Chancellor of Oxford, he soon nominating her for an honorary doctorate in his inaugural – hence personally chosen – list.[60] She deplored Labour's policies in the early 1980s of leaving the Common Market and NATO, of doing without the House of Lords and abolishing private schooling. Of the extremists whom Labour failed to purge she felt particular venom towards the miners' leader Arthur Scargill, whom she blamed for the fact she was 'now rather a floating voter', although she maintained in 1991 that she 'continued to believe in socialism as represented by the Labour Party'.[61] She accepted an invitation from Margaret Thatcher to a reception at 10 Downing Street also attended by Sir Raymond Carr – with whom, fifty years before in 1938, she had canvassed in the 'Munich' by-election – now a distinguished historian and Warden of St Antony's College. She recorded in her journal 'Margaret Thatcher as will-to-power'.[62] Before the June 1983 general election she wrote to Philippa Foot that she did not much like the Tories what with unemployment and no incomes policy, but what are the alternatives? I might vote Liberal if they were an independent body, but the SDP business seems very shadowy, & SDP is (they keep it dark) deeply divided left & right . . . the whole party seems unreal. And wd Michael Foot* make a good PM? . . . (If Denis Healey not so bad, but it wouldn't be him). Anyway the Labour Party is deeply, by now, contaminated by the extreme left who want to abolish parliamentary democracy in favour of some sort of party government by 'activists'. On things I really know about, such as education and Ireland, I agree with the Tories, and very much not with the Labour Left. It's all very depressing. Some sort of reform or control of the unions is very important but even the Tories' feeble attempts have got nowhere (their little law is ignored!) – and anyway they ought to *talk* to the Unions. (The LP wd just be run by them.) Enough of politics.[63]

In 1988 she wrote at length to Kenneth Baker, then Secretary of State for Education and Science, registering 'acute anxiety'.[64] The Tories were attacking the independence of universities, and thus of the 'old liberal intelligentsia' in general. The proposed abolition of the University Grants Commission[65] ceded control over higher education to the government. She defended Mods and Greats as training students in 'independent' thought, against the demand for more vocational courses. She grieved over the decline of Latin and Greek. The new pressure on academics to publish worried her. The current watchwords of relevance and manpower planning were wholly alien, the notion that British universities should be geared to increasing national productivity loathsome: hers was a meritocracy in the old sense, hostile to the new managerial Thatcherite ethos. Accordingly: 'I send very best wishes for yr plans for better, more selective school education which will change the fates of clever children from poor bookless homes.' Baker replied, and proposed that Iris become a member of his committee on the English Language Curriculum.[66] She

* Leader of the Labour Party 1980–83; unrelated to M.R.D. Foot.

declined, but wrote out six further pages of suggestions, defending selection and exams, requesting more money for schools, more prestige for teachers and for training colleges. She again waxed indignant on the injustices perpetrated by the current system on 'poor children from bookless homes'. Her fury and misery over those denied higher education is also expressed in her journals.*

9

While Iris and E.P. Thompson were flying to India (they later made up their differences) *The Book and the Brotherhood,* a favourite novel of hers, was being readied for publication. A group of Oxford friends – once Marxist like Iris and both Thompson brothers – agree to fund one of their number, Crimond, to write his great work. He has stayed Marxist; they have tired into liberalism. Crimond resembles Frank, in that both stay true to the ideals of their youth; and Gerard's blond brother who died young yet still haunts the survivors may recall Frank too. Gulliver Ashe cannot get a job and fears he is ceasing to be a person; Tamar expects a baby she does not want. She is the unwanted daughter of spiteful, resentful Violet, herself an unwanted illegitimate daughter. In the hands of a lesser novelist Tamar's story might have made a whole novel. Unemployment and Tamar's problems are solved alike in ways that appear fey, although Tamar is the best thing in this big, rambling, confused book. If there are absurdities in the plot, there is also wealth in the book's margins, in its profligate details.

---

* As, also, her anger at the plight of the homeless in interviews: 'I take it as a shocking thing that there are such poor people in this country.' Y. Muroya and P. Hullah (eds), *Occasional Essays by Iris Murdoch* (Okayama, 1998), p.65.

10

Iris's mother's health had started a ten-year decline in the summer of 1975. Rene was becoming irrational. She often stayed at Cedar Lodge, where she would summon Iris to help her from the lavatory by calling for her dead sister, Gertie. 'How odd these identifications are in a family,' Iris wrote.[67] The Bayleys had taken Rene to France and Spain and to Italy and Yugoslavia, and when apart Iris wrote to her each day, even if only a postcard. There would be fewer journeys abroad now. Iris wrote to Philippa, 'How awful the loss of the person can be in old age – there is a sort of ghostly likeness, often a *caricature.*' When, in 1976, Iris was made a CBE,[68] she wanted only Rene to accompany her to Buckingham Palace. The following year Rene's presence tired and saddened her deeply: 'The complacent slowness and helplessness of old age is terribly wearing and it is hard to be absolutely patient. Yet she is *so good.*' In 1978 Rene was admitted to Charing Cross Hospital after falling downstairs: 'vague and helpless and seems to get no better . . . The burden of worry and incurable sadness about Rene is with me all the time.' Iris noted how important it was to understand Rene's ramblings about the past. A coherent sentence was now an event: by the first autumn frosts, when John was saying he'd 'had a nice day' in Oxford, Rene suddenly said, '*We've* had a lovely day!' Iris noted in her journal that her mother was 'so stoical and kind even in this utterly reduced state'. She added an upper-case 'N', signifying 'of possible use for a future novel', notating the poetry of Rene's nonsense talk. 'N: Where are the children? The little boy. Have they had their tea? Who is that man there? Oh, he has gone away to his own room.' Presumably putting her mother's dementia into a novel might have been one way of negotiating the pain. The process by which one gets used to someone's senility, 'laughs at simple jokes etc', struck Iris as good. One's smile, she observed, despite feeling the same inside, was as one aged less charming to others.

By 1983 there was serious trouble. Holidays in Provence and in Spain were cancelled. Iris was angelically kind and also ruthlessly practical. In July Rene appeared finally to Iris to be mad, crying to her over the telephone, 'Gertie, Gertie, take me home!': '*Misery of this.*' She came to stay for weeks, taking pleasure in the tumbler of mimulus Iris had put in her room, but one nightmare day she became very violent, screaming, beating on the door, wanting to rush down the street, calling for the police, throwing things about and, when Iris and John tried to restrain her, attacking them with tremendous strength. She waved her stick, said she would break all the windows unless they took her back to her flat, called a solicitor, accused Iris of cheating her out of her home. Iris could not recall crying so continually for a long time. They got her into St Andrew's Hospital, Northampton, where Rene had a stroke. Iris sat a lot with her in the big ward, trying in vain to wake her, talking to her, touching her face and hands. When Rene woke she held her hand and spoke to her and smiled a dim sweet smile, then began to look upset and anxious and tried to say something but failed, falling asleep again.

Soon she was talking a little, not very coherently, in a low voice, sitting up in the television room, not watching TV. She and another old lady sat side by side in the otherwise empty room. Her face expressed self-enclosed grief and a sort of annoyance. She smiled at Iris once. An effort of politeness in greeting John made her look more alert.

The nightmare summer continued. Rene made a good recovery in hospital, walking well, her talk sane and cheerful, but memory all blurred. They moved her to Marelia Lodge nursing home in Northampton, and then to an old people's home in Oxford at 111 Woodstock Road, a friendly place, with a lovely room looking out on the church, and a little path to North Parade where Iris imagined herself coming through and waving to her. Iris brought books, clothes and thought how she would decorate her room. Then, on 15 September 1983 the telephone rang. Rene had become 'quite mad' in the night, rushed about 'all over the house etc etc, and could I please remove her *at once*'. Iris rang her London GP, who was away. Another doctor arranged for Rene to go straight to a mental hospital in Banstead, Surrey. John and Iris took her and her belongings away in their Volvo. She was sweet and cheerful on the journey, her 'best dearest self'. They even stopped at the Bull pub at Bisham – and Rene was reminded of Bispham, where she and Hughes had lived during the war, at Blackpool, where Hughes's ministry was evacuated. They talked of that.

After getting lost near Epsom they eventually found the hospital and Ward E1; Iris knocked and went in and saw 'a *terrible* scene of mad old women'. Rene said she wouldn't go in, stamped and shouted, threatened never to speak to Iris again. At last forms were filled in and Iris left her, very angry, asking why she couldn't go back and live in her flat, saying she wouldn't need looking after, just someone to do her shopping and so on. Iris tried to explain that she was *ill* and couldn't just be left alone. She would not believe this. Iris cried driving home.

In mid-October Iris took Rene out of Banstead, trying her in a small Oxford nursing home: 'No end to the problems.' They invented a solution, putting her in a small home in Fulham they effectively subsidised, where Rene was looked after by a district nurse who had visited and bathed her in her flat in Barons Court. Her old friend Jack Sing, who had before retirement worked in a car factory, lived nearby, in her flat. He had known her for fifteen years, had driven her to and from Steeple Aston, and taken her to her choir for singing practice. Now he visited each day, taking her to the pub for a drink or two. Previously teetotal, Rene overdid matters after Hughes's death.[69] On the night of Friday, 30 August 1985 she had another and massive stroke. Iris saw her the next day, her eyes occasionally opening, without recognition or response. She died at four minutes past ten on the night of Thursday, 5 September, never regaining consciousness. Iris had sat with her earlier in the day, and now felt 'absolutely desolated by her *absence*'.

Rene was cremated at Mortlake, on a very sunny hot day, with an Anglican burial service. John, Iris, Jack Sing and three other carers were the only mourners. Many blue irises adorned the coffin. Iris asked for Rene's ashes to be scattered between two conifers. The previous evening, miraculously warm and still, she and John had walked in Kensington Gardens. The Albert

Memorial against the blue sky reminded her of Orvieto cathedral.
People were going into a Prom, some picnicking on the grass
with wine. Everything was green and warm, there were the big
quiet trees: 'The beautiful sun and quiet was anguish.' In her
journal Iris had sketched dogs which she had intended to copy
onto cards to cheer up her mother. They would not be needed
now.

11

The Bayleys were growing older too. Cedar Lodge had become
too much for them. On 1 December 1985 Iris noted, 'We have
bought a house in Oxford, 68 Hamilton Road, OX2 7QA.' They
sold Cedar Lodge for £225,000. Hamilton Road, much smaller,
cost £90,000. Departure the following 2 March was '*terrible*. For
30 years kings of infinite space, now to live in a nutshell.' She
and John walked together in the garden of Cedar Lodge, she
crying a lot. Meanwhile the necessity of clearing out thirty years
of papers became urgent, and by January she was destroying letters. It was psychologically as well as physically exhausting.[70] She
found a postcard from Fraenkel dated 29 September 1952, and
a letter from Canetti describing Friedl's death.

At first they were tearful after the move, and kept referring to
Cedar Lodge as 'home'; but soon number 68 was home, Cedar
Lodge 'the outpost'. Four further years of sorting and destroying
old letters and papers followed. 1 May 1986: Sunny weather.
Old letters. Many cards from Fraenkel from all over Europe ...
D[onald MacKinnon] on corkscrew turning of spirit ... My
friends, the apple tree and the birch tree, are at last a little hazy
with green.' The following day she witnessed 'Interesting scene
of dustman collecting my discarded letters from bin!' On 21
December 1988: 'I have torn up some early diaries (about 1943)
and also what looks like a novel. Looking at the fragments they
seem rather interesting.' The destruction of letters, with their
cargo of dead passions, gave her the idea for a novel – 'That such
a storm of feeling could simply be annihilated by time.'[71] On 15

July 1990 she noted, 'Am 71 today. Looking at old diaries and destroying much. Entry for 10 October 1970: "I feel bloody bored by my novel." *Plus ça change.*' Two weeks later: 'I have been tearing up some old diaries – sad in a way. So much silliness etc. – but strange meetings with my former self which I might well record or reflect upon. Perhaps I should resurrect some events and thoughts. A lot of self-examination went on in those days!'

Iris destroyed her war journals, a journal starting autumn 1972, and excised probably 5 per cent of her remaining journals with a razor-blade, though the proportion varies from volume to volume. Where an excision on the recto causes loss of something valuable on the verso, she writes in the missing words in the hand of c1990. It is impossible to know what has been removed, but it is likely that survivors, including John, are protected, while her own story is streamlined and sanitised. Occasionally words are crossed out and written over. When Iris dedicated *Under the Net* to Raymond Queneau and received what she regarded as an insufficiently fulsome letter of thanks,[72] she wrote in 1953 – deletions italicised within square brackets – 'This caused me [*anger and*] distress . . . I felt upset [replacing '*almost contempt for him*'] at his inability to respond properly.' Queneau died in 1976. The Iris of 1990 did not approve the Iris of 1953 experiencing 'anger and contempt' for others. Such sanitising recalls those Beerbohm cartoons in which a successful public figure confronts her own juvenile *persona.*

There were further such confrontations. In 1965 Iris praised Honor Klein in *A Severed Head* as a conqueror of self-deception. By 1983 Honor was a demon.[73] In 1963, 'because I had a feeling of mortality', she had deposited with Norah Smallwood a cycle of a hundred poems entitled 'Conversations with a Prince': 'I would like one or two of these poems to have a chance of surviving.'[74] It was now that she deposited with Ed Victor her family tree, a copy of the short story 'Something Special' and a copy of John's Newdigate Prize-winning poem 'Eldorado'. She did not want these mislaid. In 1989, just before her seventieth birthday, she asked Chatto for the poems back. Probably she now saw herself more as a versifier than a poet.

When, in a 1985 interview, she pontificated on the joys of monogamy and severely censored promiscuity to the writer Adam Mars-Jones, she was not being consciously hypocritical.[75] She had no memory of her own bohemianism. In August 1993 she commented, 'I have been looking over my old diaries from 1945 to 1954 circa and am *absolutely amazed* to find how very many people I was in love with, also dear friends with!' In 1987 she wrote to monitor Chatto's use of photographs of her for a collected edition. Often the photographs she objected to were those she had requested, now commending previously censored ones. Small wonder a Chatto editor wrote, 'I will try very hard not to swear about the attached' memo concerning this; or that Iris coined 'oblivescent' in three different books.[76]

12

Three years after their move to North Oxford, the Bayleys moved again. John had bought Hamilton Road on the spur of the moment without exploring much inside, or enquiring about the neighbourhood. Iris was 'good about it'. Anthony Powell noted that a mutual friend had dined with the Bayleys. Iris, expressing a deep philosophic truth, removed the casserole from the oven, upsetting it over a beaded cushion. Without pausing in her talk she reversed the cushion over a serving-dish, gave it a brisk wipe, and dinner proceeded.[77] They were moving, Powell wrote, to get away from the noisy children who pervaded the surrounding houses. They bought 30 Charlbury Road, not far off, but quieter.[78] It was also bigger, pebble-dashed, a Betjeman villa soon, after John retired, bulging at the seams with books. Domestic arrangements remained idiosyncratic. The journalist Kate Kellaway's hilarious, tender interview for the *Observer* painted an unforgettable picture of benign chaos, the recklessly squalid kitchen doubling as John's wardrobe, objects breeding out of their normal habitats in the zestful, prolific space. 'Would you like to see what is going on in the cupboards?' asks Iris. What is going on? 'We don't really know,' she says. Iris pointed at one point to the pretty blue-and-white mugs in the top cupboard. 'They are all together,' she says, as though this were an unusual and significant point.[79] In 1953 she had contrasted 'the terrible untidiness of E[lizabeth Anscombe]'s house' with the equal and opposite 'tidiness of the J[oneses, John and Jean]. I love what lies between.' Terrible tidiness had ceased to be a serious danger. In Mary Killen's 'Your Problems Solved' column of the *Spectator* appeared a letter from Oxford, name withheld, asking advice about a guest, the male member of an elderly literary couple, who loaded his pockets as well as his plate with items from the serving dishes, to fry up his booty later at home. Killen suggested that the host in future serve only soup, soft roes, creamed spinach, vegetable curries and syllabubs.[80] Iris was especially fond of potatoes, which John, a top-of-the-stove cook, could not bake. Hot baked potatoes were frequent plunder, and tasted good unless pocketed together with chocolate biscuits.

The 1980s saw a renewal of Bayley family holidays, lapsed since the war. From 1982 Gloria Richardson, an old Bayley family friend keen to keep them together, borrowed her cousin's Dumfriesshire house, set in wild country. Iris and John occasionally swam in the big loch nearby, which had the disconcerting habit of going violently up and down when used for hydro-electric power. John's brothers Michael and David played golf nearby. David's wife Agnes cooked, John and Gloria helped. There were walks and sightseeing. Then from 1986 until 1994 they rented houses in Cornwall, north Wales, Shropshire and Suffolk. Iris loved being in the bosom of a family, and felt sadness when these outings came to an end.

13

There are scattered signs over the years that Canetti's friendship continued to matter to Iris. Her letters to him are loving and respectful. One, probably in 1966, acknowledges that there are things she can only say – or best say – to him. He inscribed that year in the copy he gave her of his *Aufzeichnungen 1942–8*, '*In*

*Alter Liebe und Freundschaft von EC'.** In 1976 she put his observation that Czech is unique in having so strange a word for music – *hudba* – into *A Word Child*, where she misspellt it *hutba*.[81] On 18 May 1978 she was reading from *The Black Prince* at the *Gesellschaft für Literatur* in Vienna. She had never read from her works before: 'It wasn't bad.' Tea at the British Embassy with Canetti, also in town, was arranged. They had not met since Canetti moved his principal residence to Zürich early in the 1970s. Meanwhile she went to the Kunsthistorisches Museum, to see the collection she had first visited early in 1946, much struck by the Rembrandts, 'especially the long mid-period one of the gazing romantic R which I so much identified with when I saw the collection when I was young and did not know my life'. At the Breughels she '*met Canetti*' (underlined). They exchanged simple news. '6 years no see.' This accidental meeting was so perfect, they cancelled the Embassy tea party. She flew to Zürich to see him in 1990, just after the revolutions in Eastern Europe, which had thrilled her. In October that year she pondered whether her relationship with religions, 'which is by no means clear', was 'just making me feeble and soft? Canetti's advice from long ago. "The way of brokenness"?' In August 1992 a flight to Zürich to see him was cancelled after he rang saying he was unwell. In March 1993 she re-read her diaries from January 1953 onward and commented, 'About Franz. Also Canetti, Friedl. Amazing stuff. The depth of deep emotions.' (But *The Sea, The Sea* showed their tragi-comical emptiness, too.)

Canetti spent some days in February 1993 recording memories of Iris and others in England, passing sentence.[82] He chronicled their affair, inaccurately, and insinuating that Iris had not been slow to instigate it. He was not confused[83] – he lists, correctly, the professions of those Iris loved (ancient historian, economist, theologian etc.), and adds insightfully that these represented her 'alter egos' (*Verwandlungen*), whom she absorbed during 'endless' conversations. Thus her male characters were conceived. He noted critically her aptitude for intent listening and patient cross-

---

* *Notes, 1942-8*: 'From EC in [remembrance of] old love and friendship'.

questioning – capacities, after all, which he shared. She collected hungrily, he tells us, usable confidences, 'like a housewife doing her shopping'. (This 'housewife' sounds suspiciously like Canetti himself. It is doubtful that – to take one instance – Peter Ady, who turned to Iris for support after the death of two nieces, would have recognised Canetti's chill account.)

Canetti had lived in England for nearly forty years, hating it.* He blames Iris for its faults.[84] Having watched her 'assemble' herself before his eyes four decades before as a 'complete Oxford parasite', he could not take her seriously. He notes her lack of dress-sense, bad figure, promiscuity, bisexuality and religiosity, her '*vulgar*' success, the mixture in her of eternal schoolgirl and headmistress which hurts her fiction, her '*scheming*' opportunism and essential toughness, the meticulous schedule governing her love-life. Her novels are too Oxonian, her characters simply her pupils and friends, all 'physically conceived and born in Oxford', a city for which he expresses withering contempt. He spends some hundreds of words on a revealing silk blouse which she demeaned herself by wearing at Hampton Court in 1955, to attract Sir Aymer Maxwell,† because Maxwell, though homosexual, was grandson to a Duke of Northumberland; although it was nearly forty years before, Canetti can neither forget nor forgive this episode. When she lied to him, 'You are beautiful,' this meant no more than 'I am hungry. Come!' Calling each of her victims 'beautiful' was a way of glossing over unpleasantness. He often got himself into a fury simply thinking about her. He considered her to be – unlike him – what he termed a '*sozusagen "illegitimin" Dichter*': a so to say illegitimate Poet or Master of Transformations. *Real* Masters of Transformations, it appears, may blithely traduce old friends.

Canetti's attack is one-sided. If Iris was indeed an adventuress – 'Mem: *to make my mark*', Philippa jested in 1943 that Iris wrote in her diary – her schemes were often upset by unpredictable attacks of soft-heartedness. Canetti claimed that she 'shrank' from

---

* Probably retrospective wisdom. Allan Forbes, who was close to Canetti from 1951 to 1959, does not recall any anglophobia then.
† Canetti implies that Iris and Maxwell had never met before this 1955 outing. Her journal shows that she knew him by July 1953.

what is truly frightening, so that 'always self-interested, never having to suffer as a writer, she was unable truly to lose herself'. Real terror, he argues, she knew only from literature. This last is a curious charge, coming from someone who went to Amersham to escape the Blitz. While Iris was undergoing what she called the 'utter break-down of human society'[85] in the Austrian refugee camps in 1945–46, Canetti's boast that he had visited Auschwitz was by contrast mendacious. His claim that she was ignorant of 'real terror' is flatly *wrong*. She dramatised such emotions, certainly; yet struggled to understand and command them objectively too: part of the greatness of *The Black Prince* lies in its meditation on the horrors of life, and on our squeamish strategies of avoidance. It is impossible to imagine Canetti conveying, as did Iris, Gertrude's grief in *Nuns and Soldiers*; and no accident that, in sixty years, he never finished another novel after *Auto da Fé* in 1935. She had the toughness that permits vulnerability – he, the very different toughness that conceals it. She certainly enjoyed the company of the grand and exotic, as of the unknown or unremarkable. She agreed when Philippa remarked, 'You find *no one* boring, do you?'

It is possible that, after decades of mystification, Canetti has unwittingly vouchsafed an accurate self-portrait. In a late novel Iris followed the well-known French maxim that 'Jealousy is born with love but does not die with it' with her own black and mordant observation, '*Bad news for the young.*' It is hard to see what, apart from jealousy, informs Canetti's portrait of Iris. He appears still jealous of her breaking free of him in 1956, jealous of her fame and, an *arriviste* himself, of her artistic and social success. 'A woman, write poetry!' he had joked in 1953. She represented something unforgivable, blasphemous: *an independent and successful woman*. He overlooks the extraordinary closeness in the 1950s and 1960s of Oxford and London.* Perhaps he hated Oxford because its rejection of him stung – his play *The Numbered* flopped

---

* 'Senior members of the University were supremely confident ... wooed by the BBC and at home there, as well as in the "corridors of power" ... Oxford left-wing dons seemed to take it for granted that they would advise Labour, and seriously influence policy.' Mary Warnock, *A Memoir: People and Places* (London, 2000), p.156.

there in 1956. He certainly minded never being introduced to Oxford's leading mage, Isaiah Berlin, who was not difficult to meet. It is noteworthy that Canetti overlooked Iris having given one of only two glowing reviews of *Crowds and Power* confirming his genius, which she always proclaimed. More seriously, he is blind to the role of London, rather than Oxford, as the city her fictional world is in love with: no earlier novelists apart from Dickens and Virginia Woolf loved London so well, or celebrated it so memorably as she.

He acknowledged that she 'researched' him, then put him into her work, affecting a mixture of Olympian forgetfulness and shame about the details. Perhaps, for all that he made her suffer from 1952 to 1956, she never really understood evil. Her novels do. Where *he* can be felt behind a novel of hers, the sense of danger is unavoidable, disturbing. Knowing Canetti gave her portraits of the enchanter Mischa Fox, the jealous, paranoid, rapacious tyrant Charles Arrowby, the wickedly manipulative Julius King some of their weight and authority. Iris's own darkness moves in each of these characters too. Perhaps she had heeded his 1959 advice to try to 'draw blood'; and he resented her accuracy.

Canetti had maundered obsessively to the last about it being his destiny to defeat death. It was through a pen-friend[86] that Iris learnt that, on 19 August 1994, he had died notwithstanding. She had just written to him for his eighty-ninth birthday.[87] When Jeremy Adler telephoned she was upset. He had to explain more than once that Canetti was being buried next to James Joyce in Zürich. She wrote to Adler that she was glad Canetti went quietly, expressing concern for his daughter Johanna, whose education she and Canetti had discussed. One year earlier, on 23 September 1993, she had noted, 'Find difficulty in thinking and writing.' And added characteristically, 'Be brave.'

21

'Past speaking of'
1994-1999

In November 1993 proofs of *Heidegger*, to be dedicated to Stanley Rosen,[1] arrived. After attempting to edit them, Iris decided that this book, on which she had been working for six years,[2] was no good and should be abandoned. It argued that the two thinkers who most deeply disturbed philosophical thinking in the twentieth century were Wittgenstein and Heidegger – the latter the most influential, if not the greatest, philosopher of the century – and bemoaned the fact that so few were interested in both. The world of philosophy was divided into two kingdoms, each either unaware, or actively contemptuous, of the other. Iris liked the openness of the early Heidegger to the idea of the Holy, and feared the obfuscations of the later Heidegger. He lacked the concept of goodness, his philosophy remote from the concerns of common life. She continued to call for a new theology: 'The sun of Good is darkened, our life has no horizon, the great multifarious ocean of world-being has gone, the waters are dried up.' She noted the paradox that our world is terrible, also sacred and that 'the "simplicity" of mystics, or of, in some instances, great artists, is an achievement related to a comprehensible visible human road which begins on our doorstep.'

Her theory of two kingdoms was soon validated. Philippa Foot, deputed to ask Iris for a contribution to a *Festschrift* in Phillipa's honour, declined Iris's offer of the script of a lecture on the Ontological Argument for the Existence of Good with the excuse that – even though Iris addressed Good (rather than God) – the flavour was too theological. No clearer instance of how far Iris had drifted from the Oxford analytic school could be desired. Nor could such a reminder be pain-free. At the University of Chicago in May 1994, by contrast, a conference was held on her philosophy: although the theologians publicly rebuked her for her atheism, such notable philosophers as Charles Taylor, Martha Nussbaum and Cora Diamond honoured her achievement.[3] Another conference on her thinking would be held at the Philosophy Department at Brown University, Rhode Island in 2001.[4]

Iris had helped restore moral philosophy to the people, showing its importance as something other than a remote, enclosed speciality, an arcane ritual conducted by an elite within the academy. She wrote a recommendation for the cover of Mary Midgley's *Beast and Man* (1979), which explores the continuities between humans and other animals.[5] The influential psychoanalyst Nina Coltart wrote in *Slouching Towards Bethlehem* (1993) that rarely had she seen the inner nature of human consciousness so well evoked as in *The Black Prince*.[6] Monthly public discussions on diverse issues held at the Café Philo in the Francis Hotel in Bath are based on principles derived from Iris's philosophy. In 1996 a Benedictine monk from Glenstal Abbey in County Limerick wrote to Chatto to say, 'I would like to speak with her. More than that, I feel I *should* speak with her': the monks at Glenstal felt inspired by their understanding of some of her 1980s novels to reorganise their abbey.

2

Iris believed in a timeless human nature, and a perennial philosophy that might address it. Subversively unfashionable, this lends her best comedies their sense of the mythic. Yet of course all her thinking came out of a precise historical moment: the 'Existentialist' moment when God the Father departed the scene. She thought the disappearance or weakening of religion the most important thing that has happened to us over the past hundred years.[7] Plato, who preceded Christ, succeeds him also for her.

587

She wanted the idea of the holy to survive in a partly terrible world.

It is her strength that all her life she was alive to the world's uncanny beauty too. In 1935, a schoolgirl, she had noted, 'If a visitor from Mars were to see this free land . . .'. This interplanetary note, which showed her at a remarkable distance from the world we share, yet perceiving it with a surreal immediacy, marked her always. In *A Fairly Honourable Defeat* Morgan comments, 'People from a planet without flowers would think we must be mad with joy the whole time to have such things about us: white campion, self-heal, bryony, vetch.'[8] To a television interviewer, on the importance of her sense of the comic, she said that a visitor from another planet should be told that 'this is the planet where we make jokes all the time, and in terrible situations, in prison and so on, we make jokes.'[9] To John Haffenden: 'I want there to be religion on this planet.' To Harry Weinberger, of his gift to her of a Tibetan ritual dagger: 'How nice objects are – I'm glad we live in a thingy world.'[10]

3

Iris Murdoch was diagnosed with Alzheimer's Disease in 1997: the simplicity of the child soon augmented the simplicity of the mystic. She copied out in a faltering hand many times, on lined paper, letter after unfinished and undated letter, beginning, 'My dear, I am now going away for some time. I hope you will be well . . .'. At a party of Beryl Bainbridge's in 1996 Iris put her arms around Bernice Rubens and said, 'I used to write novels.' ('Why weep for the end of life?' Seneca is said to have asked: 'The whole of it deserves our tears.')

Her journal entries reduce to a heart-rending simplicity.

> *1 August 1993.* My friends, my friends, I say to the teacups and spoons. Such intense love for Puss – more and more.
> *1 July 1995, of a peaceful Thames swim.* Indescribable. Holiness. Only one yacht quietly passed.

October 1995. The Cloud of Unknowing in the which [*sic*] a soul is oned with God.

November 1995. Dorothy Thompson writes, Edward has died. (And Frank –)

February 1996. At last, and continuously, snow. Poor little birdies. *Astonishing.*

Among her final entries, on 8 June 1996. We swam in the Thames, in our usual secret place, for the first time this year. Ducks, geese, swans – a delightful man comes swimming in – we talked – no one else in the whole huge area. He swimmed by, swimmed off, conversation, beautiful. The area: immense field, river, another immense field, no one, no sign of the road on other side, cows wander. Poor cows!

She had always lived among and through her characters. Like the dying Balzac summoning Doctor Bianchon whom he had invented in the *Comédie Humaine*, she started to address her own creations. Her character Moy in *The Green Knight* had fretted over the fate of the rare black-footed ferret. When a friend wrote to say that it was alive and well in North Dakota, she noted, 'I must tell Moy.'[11] In June 1996 she wrote, 'How I wish I could talk to Jackson' – the hero of her confused final novel *Jackson's Dilemma*, over-respectfully received the previous year. One of the stories Eva Lee had entranced young Iris with, sitting on the rocks in Dun Laoghaire harbour in the 1920s, went: 'They went on and on and on, and then they came to a dark place. And then they went on and on again, and they came to another dark place' – repeated *ad infinitum.* Iris liked this simple tale. The metaphor returned in December 1997 when she mentioned, with grim exactitude, a friend she had heard nothing from 'since I began sailing away into the darkness'.

4

John was not ready until late to have 'respite care'. From each part of Iris's life friends rallied, gaining him brief intervals of relief. Julian Chrysostomides would drive from Reading to walk with her. Marjorie Boulton helped. Philippa gave her lunch every Friday: she observed how Iris brightened after a photographer arrived to take her picture. Frances Lloyd-Jones, John's ex-pupil George Haines, Penny Levi, Audi Villers, among many, lent support. In May 1995 John and Iris came to stay with me and my partner Jim O'Neill in Cascob, Radnorshire, where I had a birthday party. The following summer they came for a week. It was the first of many visits. We all four went abroad, to stay in Philip and Psiche Hughes's house in Provence in 1997, with Audi Villers on Lanzarote, and with Natasha Spender at Mas Saint-Jerôme in 1998. Philippa joined us twice in Wales.

Iris was in 1996 intensely depressed, lamenting her inability to write. 'I don't have a world,' she said. Cascob offered distractions and a sense of family. She loved Radnorshire, hated leaving, swam often in our small lake, walked on the hills, watched birds, gardened, tended our dog. When she got anxious, we sang – Anglican hymns, Irish airs, folk-songs, ballads, French *chansons*, songs from the 1930s. 'Singing *rescues* me,' she remarked. Among the many gifts she loved John for – such as patient good humour, and courage – practicality did not rank high. She herself when well had planned ahead, organised trips, bought tickets. Cascob offered what Gloria Richardson aptly called 'boy-scout' help. She would kneel each visit on a meditation-cushion ('Just like Lady Jane Grey getting ready for execution,' John encouraged her) to have her hair washed, purring with pleasure when it was blow-dried. When, once, she screamed on being bathed, Jim screamed too, and got her to admit that she enjoyed screaming, at which point she laughed. He bought her, on two occasions, multiple sets of clothes from the British Legion shop in Knighton. She was thrilled. A fashion parade ensued.

'How did this anguish *start?*' she one day reasonably enquired.

If her affliction has the effect of unmasking one, then gentleness and kindness were her kernel. Deserted by language, she found other ways of communicating love or gratitude: through physical affection – she would kiss the hands of friends – or by bowing with her hands together in prayer. Beauty of mind gone, that of spirit remained. The last visit happened when Michael Bayley drove Iris and John down after Christmas 1998, weeks before her death. Michael, John and I walked through the sessile oak-woods of Litton Hill, in hail, while Jim washed and tended to Iris and read to her from the newspapers. She said gently, in what was perhaps her last coherent sentence: '*I wrote.*' Jim agreed. 'Yes darling, you did.'

John was writing too, his 'beautiful and terrible'[12] *Iris: A Memoir of Iris Murdoch.* Those closest understood that this helped him, hurting no one. Shantideva's *Bodhicaryavatara* sees the Bodhisattva as willing to be, according to the various needs of the Other, like a bridge, a boat, or a road – whatever the situation requires: hundreds of letters from carers of Alzheimer's victims (of whom there are 750,000 at the time of writing) showed appreciation for John's breaking of a taboo. Others felt Iris was cast in this very public role of quixotic benefactress without her consent. Like the gentleman witnessing Lear's madness, it was a 'sight most pitiful in the meanest wretch/Past speaking of in a king!'

5

The old schoolhouse at Cascob abuts a graveyard. Iris had asked happily in 1995: 'Do you *know* many of the dead people in your cemetery?' Although she had in interview expressed a fear of death, she also maintained that dying should ideally be, not the significant Wagnerian last moment that Christianity can make of it, but an aspect of the daily attempt to perceive less selfishly, which she tied, in a godless world, to mysticism.[13] What we term mystical experience is incommunicable. Here one kingdom is indeed deaf to the other. Mysticism has been called an experimental science of self-transformation codified only in the East, an inward Path towards direct cognition. The dictionary tells us that the mystic is the person who, believing in the apprehension of truths beyond understanding, seeks, by contemplation or self-surrender, identity with or absorption into the deity or Ultimate Reality. The mystic has opened her heart to find beyond words a direct way of knowing. Cousin Cleaver wrote from Belfast in 1997 encouraging Iris to return to Christ.[14] But the goodness of the mystic, she believed, though often connected to the life of one of the great world religions, goes beyond it.* She thought this vision lacking in the West, and needed for its wholeness, and her Plato is a visionary, educated by wonder. A key moment in her *oeuvre* comes when the fool Effingham in *The Unicorn*, sinking in the bog, comes to understand that 'with the death of the self a perfect love is born'. Mystic: one who has died and therefore fallen in love with the whole world.

6

Gloria Richardson researched and found a nursing home, The Vale in Oxford, where Iris, with a teddy-bear she named Jimbo,[15] felt at home, and where she died on Monday, 8 February 1999, at four in the afternoon. On television that night news of her death preceded that of King Hussein of Jordan and the latest difficulties of President Clinton. Like many in the last stages of her affliction, she had declined food and drink for some time. Her brain was donated to Optima.† At her own request, none attended her cremation; nor the scattering of her ashes 'North of J8 flower-bed', as the undertakers vouchsafed, at Oxford Crematorium; and no memorial service followed. You could sense in the public tributes 'a rather stunned realisation of her original-ity and energy and daring'.[16] Philippa, whom Iris recognised days before her death, remarked, stricken, 'She was the light of my

---

* Iris's second cousin Max Wright succinctly distinguishes between the expectations he felt a Brethren childhood inculcated, and the very different freedom from hope and fear for which Simone Weil's mysticism stands (*Told in Gath*, pp.37–8).
† At the Radcliffe Hospital, Oxford, specialising in Alzheimer's research.

life,' adding, typically and judiciously: 'A good number of people will feel this.' Iris was – always – quite simply the best human being Philippa knew, free from malice, pettiness or self-absorption. The deceptively large sum (£1,803,491) the newspapers cited as Iris Murdoch's estate included the values of the London flat and Oxford house, both in her name. She had never had much grip on her finances, giving plenty away, but much had accrued. Among thirty-two friends remembered in her will were four writers: Josephine Hart, Andrew Harvey, Peter J. Conradi, A.N. Wilson. By surviving one month, John became sole heir.

7

Clare Campbell once asked, 'Do you really think that if you die on Sunday, the whole of reality goes on into Monday without you?' Iris replied very consideringly and slowly, 'Yes – I think – I – do.' With that a shutter came down, and she wouldn't go on.

Her fiction remained. 'Once I've finished a novel IT, not I is telling its story, and one hopes that it will – like some space-probe – go on beaming its message, its light, for some time . . .'[17]

AFTERWORD

When Iris was asked which contemporary writers she thought would be read in fifty years, she would wisely answer that we cannot know: during the 1930s everyone had thought Charles Morgan a major writer and Evelyn Waugh minor. Time upset both judgements. The philosopher Charles Taylor similarly wrote of Iris that 'summing up her contribution is impossible. Her achievement is much too rich, and we are much too close to it.'[1] What is sure is that she is read in Japanese and Russian and French, and belongs to her worldwide readership as much as she does to the British, who notoriously underestimate their major artists. We see them as smaller than they are, needing to have them explained to us from outside; this is one true measure of our provincialism. The American critic Harold Bloom wrote that there were now, after Iris's death 'no first-rate writers left in Britain'.[2] He praised her Shakespearian facility for intricate double plots and ranked her only below Proust and Freud as a major student of Eros, an original and endlessly provocative theorist of the tragi-comedy of sexual love.[3] Lorna Sage in the *TLS* saw her influence in the work of A.S. Byatt, A.N. Wilson, Candia McWilliam, Alan Hollinghurst and Marina Warner. Her writing, argued Sage, would survive because it spanned an extraordinary range, including high seriousness.[4] Malcolm Bradbury noted: 'In a day when fiction has grown more commercial, sensational and morally empty, it is a joy to return to her work – with its sensuous pleasures, fantastic invention, high intelligence and moral dignity.'[5] Of all the post-war English novelists she has the greatest intellectual range, the deepest rigour.

Iris studied power as deeply as love, and wrote well on both. She had important things to say about desire in human life and its relationship with goodness. She explored the rivalry between men, and the Oedipal conflict between strong-willed mothers and their Nietzschean offspring. She could capture those moments of startled vision when we see our world without preconception, could describe the ordinary and make it magical. Above all, she kept the traditional novel alive, and in so doing, changed what it is capable of. She made out of a mixture of love-romance and spiritual adventure-story a vehicle capable of commenting on modern society. She was not the heir – as she early and wrongly imagined – to George Eliot, but to Dostoevsky,[6] with his fantastic realism, his hectically compressed time-schemes, his obsessions with sado-masochism and with incipient moral anarchy. Her best novels combine Dostoevsky with Shakespearian romance and love-comedy: combining myth with realism, these will last. Like all major writers Iris Murdoch invented a unique yet recognisable world, with its own logic and its own poetry.

Plotting in Dickens and Henry James is largely a matter of sentimental and melodramatic contrivance: Iris's life seems more improbably packed with strange coincidence than her own plots, and one aim of this biography has been to suggest how intensely she lived, felt and engaged with the pressures of her age. She wrote Gothic twenty years before Angela Carter, and romance years before David Lodge. She helped pioneer a writing about homosexuality as merely one part of human life. It is typical of her quiet subversiveness that only the gay partnership survives in *A Fairly Honourable Defeat* – the heterosexual relationships all fall apart under the strain of the plot. Few women novelists write with as much conviction from the point of view of male homosexuals, and no other woman writer so well impersonates men.

The posthumous inclusion of one of her poems in an anthology of Irish women poets would have given Iris pleasure.[7] Perhaps the twin and opposed veins of fantasy and of puritanism in her owe something to her Irishness. Being Irish – moreover *Protestant* Irish and relatively poor – made of her an outsider. Her novels often picture refugees, and meditate on displacement and uprooting. What are good and evil? What is courage? How is it that a few fanatics – Nazis in Weimar Germany, Communists in post-war Europe, the IRA – can drive their cultures mad? Like

William Golding, and perhaps Muriel Spark, the Second World War made Iris think anew about human wickedness and irrationality. If there is a common influence on both her philosophy and her fiction, it is surely Hitler. Some feeling about homelessness and exile came out of the war and its aftermath in the camps, so that the enchanters and maguses of her fiction belong on an international stage, and have always a political dimension.

Iris kept a debate about human difference alive, through the bad years when fools pretended that it did not matter, or even did not exist. Human difference also meant moral difference. How is it that some human beings are morally better than others? What is it that might make a man good – Frank Thompson, or Franz Steiner – even in extreme situations? How did it come about that in the epoch of greatest political evil, the century of Stalin and Hitler, moral terms had simultaneously been evacuated of any absolute significance by philosophers?

Her vision of the world as sacred looks forward to ecology and the Green movement. *The Sovereignty of Good* (1970), *The Fire and the Sun* (1976) and *Metaphysics as a Guide to Morals* (1992) have been important to theologians, to aestheticians and moral philosophers, and seem likely to remain so. She could not believe in a personal God demonic enough to have created the world whose sufferings are clear, yet she wanted religion to survive, too. She wanted Buddhism to educate Christianity, to create a non-supernatural religion. God and the afterlife were essentially anti-religious bribes to her. She breathed new life into the oldest philosophical puzzle – 'What is a good life?'; and did so by living one herself.

Philippa Foot's obituary notice for Somerville College spoke of Iris's 'magical goodness', and linked this with the way she combined 'passion and spontaneity with reserve'. Though living so deeply within herself, Iris was 'completely present' also.[8] She indeed connected goodness, against the temper of the times, not with the quest for an authentic identity, so much as with the happiness that can come about when that quest can be relaxed. We are lucky to have shared an appalling century with her.

NOTES

ABBREVIATIONS

CWA   Conversation with Author
DH   David Hicks
DM   David Morgan
EC   Elias Canetti
EM   Iris Murdoch, ed. Peter J.
　　Conradi, *Existentialists and Mystics:*
　　Writings on Philosophy and
　　Literature (London, 1997)
FBS   Franz Baermann Steiner
FT   Frank Thompson
IM   Iris Murdoch

J   IM's journal
JB   John Bayley
LP   Leo Pliatzky
LTA   Letter to Author
MB   Marjorie Boulton
MM   Mary Midgley
MRDF   Michael R.D. Foot
PF   Philippa Foot
RQ   Raymond Queneau
RW   Richard Wollheim

INTRODUCTION

1 To Norah Smallwood, January
  1963. One hundred pages of
  poems, entitled 'Conversations with
  a Prince', are at the Brotherton
  Library, Leeds University. Other
  versions survive in IM's estate.
2 Richard Cohen, 'Iris Murdoch:
  Half-Believer', *The Tablet*, 13
  February 1999, p.208.
3 First broadcast on Radio 3 in 1986.
4 4 March 1946.
5 Undated, but address indicates
  between 1979 and 1991.
6 22 October 1948.
7 Anita Brookner's description, cited
  by Allan Massie reviewing Judith
  Thurman, *Secrets of the Flesh: A Life
  of Colette, New York Review of Books*,
  10 February 2000, p.33.
8 CWA.
9 Anthony Powell's description in
  Hearing Secret Harmonies (London,
  1975), p.76.

CHAPTER 1

1 So his marriage certificate
  affirms. According to the dates on
  his gravestone, he was thirty-
  one.
2 Marriage certificate shows Louisa
  Shaw, daughter of John Shaw,
  farmer, and Elizabeth, *née*
  Holdsworth, born and living in
  Ararium, married Wills John
  Murdoch, farmer, son of Richard
  Murdoch, farmer, and Sarah, *née*
  Hughes, born 'Cown', resident
  Bombay (New Zealand).
3 For Irish emigration to the
  Antipodes see David Fitzpatrick,
  Oceans of Consolation (Melbourne,
  1994).
4 Their great-grandfather did have
  one surviving son, to whom he left
  only £10, while his sisters were
  more richly endowed with various
  properties and/or rentals.
  Conceivably this son had made a
  marriage of which his father could
  not approve.

5 Doris Sloan, Ballymullan owner and no relation to the Murdochs, to IM's genealogist, Arthur Green, 1990.

6 As thirty years earlier in 1917, when a letter to her from Hughes bears that address.

7 Her husband had three further sisters-in-law: another Margaret, Charlotte and Isabella.

8 The Bayleys visited de Grunne's château in the Auvergne a number of times. He taught at the Royal College of Art immediately after IM left in 1968.

9 Sybil Livingston, CWA, 10 December 2000.

10 For example during the Famine, when so-called 'soupers' of different denominations, especially Non-Conformist, would compete to gain souls in exchange for sustenance.

11 F.S.L. Lyons, *Ireland Since the Famine* (London, 1973), p.24.

12 IM, letter to DH, 29 April 1940.

13 Jean-Louis Chevalier, '*Rencontres avec Iris Murdoch*' (Centre de recherches de littérature et linguistique des pays de langue anglaise, Université de Caen, 1978), p.93.

14 The shops kept the name of Murdoch into the 1980s, long after the family connexion had gone, but are now closed.

15 IM believed he joined up in August 1914, with a commission deriving from his having been in the Territorial Army (see letter to Harry Weinberger, 4 October 1985). No evidence to support this has come to light.

16 CWA, June 1997.

17 Sybil Livingston, CWA, March 1998. IM, contemplating incorporating her father's war experiences into a novel, comments (5 November 1991): 'Trench warfare. Goya. Barbed wire. Grunewald. (What did my

father see.) Rescue from continually unexpected cruelty?'

18 A point I owe to Professor Roy Foster.

19 Lionel James, *The History of King Edward's Horse* (London, 1921), p.205. Hughes gives second lieutenant as his rank on the back of a photograph from June 1918, and no rank on the back of the 1916 photographs. A surviving document shows his discharge as a result of commission on 22 February 1918. That he spent the period between April 1917 and February 1918 in cadet school does not seem probable, and no explanation is as yet forthcoming.

20 A letter survives from Hughes to his mother giving this date.

21 Aunt Ella kept them. Cousin Sybil rescued them when Ella went into a home. Like his daughter's journal, it had been cut: discretion was a family trait.

22 J: 5 November 1991.

23 Sources for Hughes's betting: MM and JB.

24 A photograph of him in his regimentals, dated June 1918, taken in Dublin, shows him proudly astride a beautiful bay with a white blaze.

25 Source: Billy Lee, widower of Eva, August 1998. The church is now done up in post-modern style inside: Penco Insurance Co., and other smaller companies, work from there.

26 IM's mother spells her name in the French style, 'Renée'. IM uses both Renée and Rene, but more often the latter, which this text follows.

27 Don Douglas's vicarious recall that Rene lodged during the marriage 'at a shop' (letter to Arthur Green, 31 January 1990) endorses this; 'the marriage was a hurried affair', he added. For an 'unhurried' wedding Rene would

presumably have stayed at Blessington Street. Douglas's first cousin, Professor Brian Murdoch, vouched in July 1999 for the reliability of his now deceased cousin (CWA).

28 Max Wright; see p.10.

29 Arthur Green, 'The Worlds of Iris Murdoch', *Iris Murdoch Newsletter*, no. 10, 1996.

30 Professor Roy Foster, LTA.

31 IM's terms: 'A Certain Lady', *Bookmark*, BBC TV, 29 December 1989.

32 IM writing to her editor at Chatto & Windus, Jane Turner, 1993.

33 Chatto sent the piece on to the *Iris Murdoch Newsletter* which, under my co-editorship, published it, to the understandable vexation of Mr Green, in shortened form – see n29 above.

34 Letter to Arthur Green, dated 9 August 1990. IM possibly meant *O'Hart's Irish Pedigrees* (1884).

35 Tullinisken Notebook V, compiled by the Rev. Henry Gordon Waller Scott, MA, LDS film 1279325. Presented to Armagh County Museum, The Mall East, Armagh, by Mrs Gordon Scott. For the Rev. Scott see Leslie's *Armagh Clergy and Parishes* (Dundalk, 1911), under 'Creggan, Tullinisken and Clonfeacle'. These Tyrone Richardsons who stem from Scotland differ from those of Rossford and Rich Hill (who come from Worcestershire); from the Richardsons of Eagerlougher, Loughall, County Armagh (from Warwickshire); and from the Richardsons of Polar Vale, County Monaghan (from Norfolk). IM's second cousin Canon John Crawford unearthed this.

36 In this following O'Day's *Irish Pedigrees*.

37 See A. Rowan, *Pevsner's Guide to North-West Ulster* (London, 1979), where it is misspelt 'Furlough'.

38 Walter Lindesay was a younger son of Alexander Richardson, eldest son of John Richardson of Farlough.

39 As Arthur Green observes.

40 H. Staples (ed.), *The Ireland of Sir Jonah Barrington: Selections from his Personal Sketches* (London, 1968), pp.31–3.

41 E.L. Richardson's first marriage occurred, curiously, in the same parish church of St George's, Dublin (Church of Ireland), and on the same day, as his own father's second marriage, in 1889. E.L.R.'s elder brother R.L. Richardson acted as witness both to his brother's and to his father's second marriage.

42 Billy Lee has provided a Registry of Assignment for a grave at Dean's Grange Cemetery for a Mrs Gertrude Bell, widow of Thomas Bell, 15 Bishop Street, Dublin, died 7 February 1957, aged sixty – in fact she would have been at least sixty-five. Eva Lee seems to have dealt with the burial; Rene at that time was dealing with Hughes's last illness.

43 JB, CWA.

44 Y. Muroya and P. Hullah (eds), *Occasional Essays by Iris Murdoch* (Okayama, 1998), p.84.

45 Where E.L. Richardson (1) was a law assistant, E.L. Richardson (2) was a JP and manager of the Board of Trade at the Dublin Labour Exchange. E.L.R.(2)'s second name was Lindesay; on marriage and baptism into the Roman Catholic Church he took the name Patrick.

46 *The Red and the Green*, p.44. IM believes the street to have somewhat grander architectural features – 'graceful' fanlights, 'ornate' porticos – than is the case. The street is minimally decorated Georgian, though not jerry-built.

47 1901 census return.

48 See Jacinta Prunty, *Dublin Slums, 1800–1935: A Study in Urban Geography* (Dublin, 1998).

49 A point I owe to Professor Roy Foster.Of some seventy-odd households in the street, at least twelve were members of St Mary's (Church of Ireland), now closed. Their occupations included clerks, fitter, wagon-builder, ex-soldiers, compositor, policemen etc., as noted in the church register.

50 Douglas to Arthur Green, 23 January 1990. The accuracy of Douglas's recall needs one qualification: rather than a trainee singer, he thought that Rene, whom he never met, was a ballet dancer.

51 CWA, March 1998.

52 IM's adjective; J: 15 October 1976.

53 30 Glengariff Parade, where Patrick Effingham Richardson (2) lived at the time of his 1883 Catholic wedding; 2 Melrose Avenue, where he lived with wife, six children, niece and mother-in-law at the time of the 1901 and 1911 censuses; 28 Portland Place, where Rene's grandfather lived at the time of his first, 1881, wedding; 126 North Strand Road, where her father lived at the time of his 1889 wedding: all were in North Dublin.

54 CWA, 1996.

55 e.g. Harriet in *The Sacred and Profane Love Machine*; Hilda in *A Fairly Honourable Defeat*.

56 Author of *Mind You I've Said Nothing* (1953) and *The Straight and Narrow Path* (1956). Her friend Barbara Pym lampooned her as the vividly brusque and mannish Edith Liversidge in her novel *Some Tame Gazelle* (1950).

57 Maurice Harmon's biography *Sean O'Faolain: A Critical Introduction* (Notre Dame, 1966) details

Tracy's long, passionate affair with him.

58 The letters are to Sister Marian – a friend of IM since 1938 at Somerville, and from 1954 a nun. This letter is undated, but written in the year IM published a novel of 391 pages, a length Tracy mentions as grimly comical; this is *A Word Child*, hence 1975.

59 Also: in possible recognisance of the as yet unidentified Iris Richardson whose signature is in the book of prayer *The Christian Year* given 'After Church' in Christmas 1887 and in IM's London library.

60 So-called because of their tendency in times of trouble to support the viceregal line at Dublin Castle.

61 Nonetheless IM was awarded honorary doctorates by Queen's University, Belfast (1977), Trinity College, Dublin (1985) and Ulster University (1993).

62 *The Red and the Green*, p.10.

63 Undated letter from IM, c1940.

64 Eighteenth-century Ireland in its cultural pluralism has been compared to eighteenth-century America, with the significant difference that the English migrating to Ireland did not, unlike those entering America, liquidate the original inhabitants.

65 Letter from IM to Ann Leech from 15 Mellifont Avenue, Dublin, 11 August 1934.

66 A June 1967 journal entry compares Stuart Hampshire's first wife Rene with herself: 'Struck by Rene's resemblance to me – blonde roundfaced slightly awkward serious-minded Anglo-Irish only child! *Tiens!*'

67 Billy Lee, CWA, August 1998.

68 Gertie is not present in any surviving Murdoch family holiday snapshot. Her son Victor has been crudely cut off the edge of an

early 1930s photograph showing Rene, IM and Victor; he survives on another copy of the same photo, and is identifiable through wartime photos of him in Irish Army uniform. What caused his extirpation from the snap? Tidiness? Some misdemeanour? He is looking pleased with himself, and IM, looking past her mother and towards him, wary.

69 Patrick West, 'When the IRA's Alarm Clock Struck', *Spectator*, 16 January 1999, p.12.

70 Churchill, angered by Irish neutrality, and hoping to persuade Dublin to change policy, embargoed shipping into Eire, thus causing many shortages.

71 Letters to Paddy O'Regan.

72 David Lee reports that IM paid a genealogist to prepare a three-page Richardson family tree, which has not as yet materialised. He recalls as a small child in the late 1940s visiting a mysterious Colonel Berry in a grand house with suits of armour, maids, two staircases and ghost (which he sighted), not far from Belfast. He took it that his mother was a by-blow of the Colonel's. A letter dated 1984 from his mother Eva Lee, answering a query of IM's about O'Hart's *Old Irish Families*, survives, in which she appears to point to Anna Nolan, IM's step-great-grandmother, as her own grandmother – see footnote, p.49.

73 As Roy Foster observes: *W.B. Yeats: A Life, Vol. 1, The Apprentice Mage* (Oxford, 1997), p.29.

74 Unpublished interview with RW, 17 July 1991.

75 R.B. McDowell, *Crisis and Decline: The Fate of the Southern Unionists* (Dublin, 1997), p.168.

76 Later claimed as family by IM, as a (regrettably incomplete) letter she lodged with Ed Victor, from a Bell relative (Jack MacMenamin, who married Connie Bell's sister Phyllis), makes clear. Also mentioned in draft (only) of Jeffrey Meyers' 1990 *Paris Review* interview, where he is associated with the Second World War.

77 MM, CWA.

78 The testimony of Muriel Chapman, the cousin closest to IM, would have been valuable, but she died before this biography was started.

79 On 'A Certain Lady', *Bookmark*, BBC TV, 29 December 1989, IM mentioned a single year.

80 'A Certain Lady', *Bookmark*, BBC TV, 29 December 1989.

81 Chevalier, '*Rencontres avec Iris Murdoch*', op. cit., p.93.

82 Roy Foster's eloquent phrase; *Paddy and Mr Punch*, (London, 1993), p.220.

83 See above (Shena Mackay interviews in Muroya and Hullah, *Occasional Essays by Iris Murdoch*, op. cit., p.84).

84 Muroya and Hullah, *Occasional Essays by Iris Murdoch*, op. cit., p.29.

85 Those who recall how passionately she felt in the 1950s include Rosemary Cramp and Julian Chrysostomides.

86 *The Red and the Green*, p.191.

87 A. Rowan, in *Pevsner's Guide to North-West Ulster*, op. cit., recounts some family history and the fact that the house is now a 'picturesque shell'. The demesne is now owned by the Forestry Commission.

88 See Foster, *Paddy and Mr Punch*, op. cit., Chapter 11, 'Protestant Magic'.

89 Ibid, p.232.

90 Ibid, p.221.

91 Ibid, p.214.

92 IM, CWA, 1997.

93 Eva Lee's memory, recalled by Billy Lee, August 1998: probably

one *donnée* for *The Red and the Green*.

94 Billy Lee, CWA. Since the Lees married in 1941, Billy Lee's direct recall belongs to the last fifteen or so years of Hughes's life.

95 J: 14 December 1994.

96 Now (1998) closed, they were at the bottom of Mellifont Avenue, where Eva Lee lived with Mrs Walton at number 16, or possibly 15. Two letters from IM at number 15 to her schoolfriend Ann Leech survive from August 1934.

97 Postcards were kept in the Murdoch family album, and prove a resource to the biographer. This card is dated 18 August 1949.

98 She also taught IM a Sunday school song: 'Jesus bids us shine/ With a pure clear light,/Like a little candle/Burning in the night./In this world is darkness,/ So let us shine,/You in your small corner,/and I in mine.' Cousin Sybil knew this also. It seems possible IM might have heard it at the Revivalist meetings she went to with Eva Robinson (later Lee) and Mrs Walton, meetings with the Crusaders at the Mariner's Church in Dun Laoghaire; Professor Roy Foster believes that it may well be in the Church of Ireland hymnal.

99 Canon Crawford, CWA.

100 J: 31 December 1969.

101 IM later recalled the cats as her mother's – J: 17 March 1986: 'simple love of parents healing. My mother's cats.' Billy Lee and others recall them as her father's. Presumably they belonged, like most cats, to all.

102 17 August 1996.

CHAPTER 2

1 From IM's contribution, written in 1992, to 'The Early Childhood Collection', held at Froebel College, Roehampton Institute Library. JB used the same word – docile – of IM as a child; LTA, September 1997.

2 To PF, undated.

3 Heinz Cassirer's daughter Irene in 1942, Tommy Balogh's stepdaughter Tiril in the 1950s, Vera Crane's daughter Frances.

4 John Haffenden, 'John Haffenden Talks to Iris Murdoch', *Literary Review*, lviii, April 1983, pp.31–5.

5 EC recalled the Charing Cross Road.

6 Source: JB.

7 J: 1981–92.

8 J: 1 December 1984: 'I recall my father reading Ernst Jünger's novel about the war when I was a child.'

9 Interview with Susan Hill, *Bookshelf*, BBC Radio 4, 30 April 1982.

10 Elizabeth Bowen's *Bowen's Court* (London, 1942) makes clear how popular an author, perhaps unexpectedly, Kipling was in Ireland: when the IRA occupied the house during the serious Troubles, she was much struck that they spent all day reading Kipling in the library.

11 J: 30 May 1971: This is inference, not fact. On recording that the first thing in literature that made Clare Campbell cry was her mother reading this quarrel between two men, IM writes, 'Yes, yes.'

12 *The Sea, The Sea*, p.28 (my emphasis). The same remark, about how no one ever knew her father's goodness, occurs in IM's journals on his death in 1958. And, later: 'My father: a marvellous man, known to very few people. A good man' (12 September 1981).

13 Sybil, despite being Protestant and Loyalist, feared being treated as a pariah.

14 J: 14 January 1992.

15 Barbara Denny, whose mother found Rene's 'dishiness' (Denny's word) intimidating.

16 Miriam Allott, LTA, June 1998.

17 Miriam Allott did not share IM's view that Froebel instilled a love of learning – that, for her, came later. She is nonetheless grateful to the school for teaching her a lot about the pagan Greeks and Romans, and especially about the betrayal of Rome. She also feels indebted to it for the fact that she can, to this day, recognise many constellations in the night sky, and some families of plants.

18 Hughes took Billy Lee to Lord's cricket ground to watch Middlesex play Gloucestershire. It was on their return from this outing that Billy watched Hughes make notes of small expenditures in his pocket-notebook. Hughes was generous as well as meticulous.

19 Margaret Gardiner, *A Scatter of Memories* (Free Association Press, 1988), p.40.

20 Barbara Denny, *The Play-Master of Blankenburg: The Story of Friedrich Froebel, 1782–1852* (Autolycus, 1982).

21 Miriam Allott's recollection.

22 Recalled by Miriam Allott, seven decades later.

23 C.H.K. Marten and E.H. Carter, published between 1925 and 1927 (with Blackwell) a series of four history books: Elementary Histories: *Our Heritage from the Beginning of the Normans* and *The Middle Ages*; and Histories: *New Worlds 1485–1688* and *The Latest Age*.

24 Gardiner, *A Scatter of Memories*, op. cit., p.56.

25 Barbara Denny in 'The Early Childhood Collection', op. cit.

26 Gardiner, *A Scatter of Memories*, op. cit., p.55.

27 Denny, CWA.

28 *Kensington News*, 1 December 1978: 'Headboy was Tom Wilson'.

29 J: 14 May 1972.

30 Miss Bain in *Old Froebelian's News Letter*, 1936, p.1.

31 J: 30 May 1975.

32 On one occasion, having been repeatedly scolded for talking in class, Denny was sent 'down' to the Kindergarten for the day, sitting on a tiny chair amongst the babies since she was 'obviously a baby if she could not stop talking when told'. She did not talk out of turn again.

33 Letter from IM to Barbara Denny.

34 Probably *Observer*, 17 June 1962, p.23, where IM's Hammersmith and Chiswick background and Anglo-Irish parentage are mentioned, though not Froebel.

35 In the early 1980s Professor Allott first told me of IM's imaginary brother. Allott's Froebel reminiscence: 'She would at times refer to her brother, and the references always seemed to me to express special feeling for him. I seem to recall too that she confirmed this in her answering letter, now lost I fear.'

36 Interview with Susan Hill, *Bookshelf*, BBC Radio 4, 30 April 1982.

37 To DH, 11 November 1945.

38 William Eastcote in *The Philosopher's Pupil.*

39 Compare Gardiner, *A Scatter of Memories*, op. cit., p.56: 'We were a snobbish lot, our clique: we felt snootily superior to the "common" girls who came from a lower social rung.' Gardiner was fifteen years Allott and IM's senior, and indeed may have taught them.

40 Shena Mackay, interview with IM, in Muroya and Hullah, *Occasional Essays by Iris Murdoch*, op. cit., p.84.

41 Sybil Livingston, CWA.

42 J: April 1956 (p.4). These 'anxieties' refer to his lung cancer.

43 Billy Lee from Dublin, who stayed at Chiswick a number of times without his wife Eva, remembers Hughes as more active around the house than many husbands, but

recalls no dereliction of duties on Rene's part.

44 J: 18 March 1971.

45 IM gave Rene's antique red leather card-carrying case to her godson Ben Macintyre when at the age of ten he decided, after much reflection and watching the film *The Sting*, that he wished to pursue an adult career as a gambler.

46 Sybil Livingston, March 1998.

47 MM, CWA.

48 '*Nachdenklicher, ungemein anziehender*', EC's unpublished 1993 reminiscences.

49 Sir Lawrence Airey, CWA, 11 December 1997.

50 Sir Peter Baldwin, CWA, 7 January 1998.

51 Cleaver Chapman: Hughes went to the canteen at work and was mortified when, having made an incision into his meat pie, the gravy spurted onto his work colleague seated opposite him, not once, but on the second incision also. This should not make him sound like that other clerk, Mr Pooter in *The Diary of a Nobody*: Hughes must have told this story against himself.

52 Chevalier, '*Rencontres avec Iris Murdoch*', op. cit., p.93.

53 *The Red and the Green*, p.10.

54 Billy Lee, CWA.

55 See Chapter 16.

56 Recalled by IM during her speech when accepting an honorary doctorate at Coleraine University, c1992.

57 To Ann Leech.

58 Letter from Rae Hammond, child of Richard, but present on the 1936 crossing, to IM, 3 January 1987.

CHAPTER 3

1 Badminton was possibly so-named to recall the name of the estate of the Dukes of Beaufort.

2 A fictionalised but accurate, critical and humorous account of the school at a slightly later date (as 'Greenslades') appears in Anne Valery's autobiography *The Edge of a Smile* (London, 1977).

3 July 1936 to March 1937, preparing for Oxford entrance. The story remembered by a much later friend that IM and Gandhi had 'enjoyable pillow-fights' does not perhaps strike the tone of their acquaintanceship, given the shyness and reserve of both girls, Gandhi's unhappiness – her mother died early in 1936 – and her age (nineteen in November 1936). See Katherine Frank, *Indira: The Life of Indira Gandhi* (London, 2001).

4 'Indira at School, and After' – IM's obituary remarks probably delivered January 1987, New Delhi conference. See also G. Parthasarthi and H.Y. Sharada (eds), *Indira Gandhi: Statesmen, Scholars, Scientists and Friends Remember* (Delhi, 1985), p.308.

5 *At Badminton with BMB, by Those who were There*, compiled and edited by Jean Storry (Badminton School, Bristol, 1982), a major source for this chapter. All unascribed quotations hereon come from it.

6 IM and JB, CWA, 1997.

7 Alas, the stoicism she so vehemently preached all her life deserted her in her last, sad years, when she exemplified much that, as a pedagogue, she had disapproved of.

8 IM's speech for the official opening of Badminton School's new swimming pool, c1992.

9 This was Professor Dennis Nineham, who demurred on the reasonable grounds that it might seem odd for them to be found in a girls' boarding school in the middle of the night; but 'she almost dragged me out of the car'. IM's subsequent attempts to find her way into the Roman Catholic cathedral at Clifton – of which every door was

locked – were, to his immense relief, vain.

10 David Thomson, *Europe Since Napoleon* (London, 1957), p.758.

11 Letter from Brigid Brophy quoted in J: 12 April 1966.

12 Margaret Rake, CWA, February 1998.

13 Undated letter to DM.

14 Basic fees c1936 were forty-five guineas per year for girls entering under fourteen years of age. No note of the value of IM's scholarship has come to light.

15 Margaret (also known as 'Penny') Orpen, later Lady Lintott,.

16 Rosemary Cramp, CWA, 13 February 1998.

17 Information from Vera Crane. IM visited Badminton when Vera's daughter Frances was confirmed there c1968.

18 Margaret Orpen, CWA, July 1998.

19 Dulcibel MacKenzie, *Steps to the Bar* (Greengate Press, 1989), p.31.

20 'A Certain Lady', *Bookmark*, BBC TV, 29 December 1989.

21 Unfortunately lost when her parents moved house.

22 Margaret Orpen, CWA, January 1999.

23 Margaret Rake, CWA.

24 MacKenzie, *Steps to the Bar*, op. cit.

25 *Badminton School Magazine*, issue 61.

26 IM in 'The Early Childhood Collection', op. cit.

27 *A Word Child*; *The Sea, The Sea*.

28 Stuart in *The Good Apprentice*.

29 Letter to DM, undated, 1966.

30 5 November 1990.

31 Born Hereford, 4 May 1876.

32 Source: Margaret Rake.

33 It became so only up to Junior School, as Joseph Cooper recalls in his *Facing the Music* (London, 1979).

34 J: February 1978.

35 The Monday-morning prayer horrified Margaret Orpen, who could recite it in 1999. It included the words: 'Help us this week to do our work well/To seek knowledge for its own sake and not for mere reward/To show our gratitude for our opportunities by good and honest work/Done in the spirit of the artist with pride/And not like the drudge with fear.' The penultimate line seemed peculiarly officious.

36 Margaret Orpen recalls Congregationalism; Ann Leech Anglicanism.

37 Letter to JB from Ms Sychrava, *née* Cassirer, 4 August 1999. She was sent to Badminton in 1942, IM being instrumental in this.

38 Priscilla Hughes's and JB's belief. Ann Leech identified the church. In *Revelations: Glimpses of Reality*, ed. R. Lello (London, 1985), IM claimed to have been confirmed at fifteen – which would make the year 1934 or 1935.

39 This was Margaret Rake's view. Not all agreed. Dulcibel MacKenzie recalls them as 'most peculiar clothes'; Indira Gandhi thought the outfits capable of improvement, and resented – possibly for religious reasons – having to wear a hat. 'Consider the featureless and irrational way in which one had to dress,' commented IM in an unpublished draft for a journalistic piece, 'Iris Murdoch Regrets she was Never a Teenager' (in Muroya and Hullah, *Occasional Essays by Iris Murdoch*, op. cit., pp.27–31). Her teacher Leila Eveleigh, at Badminton from 1921 to 1968, recorded that 'more freely expressed feelings of the girls themselves resulted in some modifications. Grey/blue replaced navy, and a loose, pleatless design replaced the pleats.' LTA, 8 August 1998.

40 Dulcibel MacKenzie, CWA, 12 July 1998.

41 MacKenzie, *Steps to the Bar*, op. cit.

42 It featured in *Ideal Home and*

Gardening, August 1945, pp.89 *et seq.* The architect was Eustace Button RWA, FRIBA.

43 Margaret Orpen, CWA July 1998.

44 On her application to join UNRRA in June 1944 she recalled this trip as of three weeks' duration. The contemporary account in the *Badminton School Magazine*, issue 68 (autumn term 1935), by her schoolmistress Miss Feaver gives ten days. One contemporary believes they hiked for a second ten days, making three weeks in all.

45 Margaret Orpen recalls that French teaching was not always rigorous. Mlle Marie du Verduzan, a humorous French Royalist, taught them French, but not very much, as she also liked to tell jokes: 'If you learn these French verbs, I'll tell you what are the names of two French towns that describe an article of clothing.' Answer: Toulon and Toulouse (too long and too loose). Leila Eveleigh points out Mlle du Verduzan's great wartime courage, working in the French Resistance, smuggling messages concealed in her umbrella.

46 See Frank, *Indira*, op. cit., *passim*.

47 Interview with Susan Hill, *Bookshelf*, BBC Radio 4, 30 April 1982.

48 Leila Eveleigh, letter to John Fletcher, 1982.

49 Ibid.

50 Margaret Rake, CWA.

51 Jennifer Hart, CWA.

52 Katie Bazell (later Lourie), CWA, July 1999. She was at both Froebel and Badminton with IM: 'Though at English IM was in a quite different league she was otherwise simply a quiet, ordinary girl.'

53 Letter to John Fletcher, 22 February 1981.

54 See Woolf's essay 'Middlebrow', republished in *The Death of the Moth* (London, 1942).

55 Address to Kingston graduates, 1993. See *Occasional Essays*, op. cit.

In *The Green Knight*, 'sentimental thirties songs' are deemed worthy of the tears of the three Anderson girls.

56 Draft for 'Iris Murdoch Regrets she was Never a Teenager', op. cit.

57 JB, *Iris: A Memoir of Iris Murdoch* (London, 1998; US title *Elegy for Iris*), p.25.

58 Robert Conquest, *Reflections on a Ravished Century* (London, 1999).

59 George Orwell, 'Inside the Whale'.

60 Unpublished interview with RW, 17 July 1991.

61 e.g. John Grigg.

62 Unpublished interview with RW, 17 July 1991.

63 'Indira at School, and After', op. cit.

64 'Come Pale Feet', and the untitled 'Power is a beautiful thing'.

65 She sang also in the chorus of *The Yeomen of the Guard* – so she wrote to Clare Campbell, not vouchsafing when ('I can vividly recall the tall booted girl who played Fairfax').

66 Letter to DM, 1964.

67 Badminton get-together at Lynmouth, August 1941, described by IM in *Badminton School Magazine*.

68 Ann Leech did not in the end accompany IM to Oxford.

69 Born Dundalk, 8 November 1913, married Olive Marron 1945, he won the Symington Prize for anatomy at Queen's University and raised the profile of dental students.

70 IM in E. Whitley (ed.), *The Graduates* (London, 1986), p.63.

CHAPTER 4

1 Draft for 'Iris Murdoch Regrets she was Never a Teenager', op. cit.; but compare 1945 J: 'Or the pale tragic adolescents of Mauriac. Not all adolescents are tragic. I wasn't. I enjoyed myself. Oh how I have enjoyed myself!'

2 IM to Vera Hoar, whom she encouraged to join her in learning Russian with Steen during the war – see Chapter 5.

3 One exception: Lilian Eldridge, meeting IM in March 1939 (see Chapter 5), thought her very unconfident about exams. Those who found her assured did not dispute that she was shy also. Compare Miriam Allott's perceptive comment ten years before: that IM's firm clear voice possibly countered shyness. Ken Kirk, co-Treasurer of the OULC with IM, writes that 'her reserve was a function not of shyness but of self-confidence' (LTA, 7 September 1998).

4 LTA, 6 December 1998.

5 Undated letter to Paddy O'Regan, probably 1940.

6 *Badminton School Magazine*, no. 79, spring and summer 1939.

7 IM in Whitley, *The Graduates*, op. cit.

8 On 'A Certain Lady', *Bookmark*, BBC TV, 29 December 1989, IM named Carol Stewart; Lucy Klatschko was a particular friend but is sure she was not the third student; Carol Graham-Harrison (January 1999) does not recall the incident: 'We went there often.'

9 Muroya and Hullah, *Occasional Essays by Iris Murdoch*, op. cit., pp.16–20.

10 Ibid, p.85.

11 Letter to DH, 20 November 1938.

12 Her immediate neighbour, who recalls this room, was Margaret Stanier.

13 FT's unpublished 'Snapshots from Oxford'. IM four years later called Leonie 'still the same charming, aggressive, nervy individualist. Definitely three dimensional. A person. I enjoyed her company enormously.' Letter to FT, 11 June 1943.

14 Muroya and Hullah, *Occasional Essays by Iris Murdoch*, op. cit., p.50. And, to E. Whitley, editor of *The Graduates*, op. cit., p.73: 'Of course this is a time when you will be acquiring friends for ever.' Pre-war Oxford numbered 6,742 students compared to 10,788 in 1998; many recall that it was then possible to know, if not everyone, at least most prominent peers.

15 Janet Vaughan, later Principal of Somerville, destroyed many papers. This account of IM's entrance comes from conversations in 1998 with Isobel Henderson's surviving sister Katherine McDonald; with Jennifer Hart who co-set the General Paper, and who was also told that Lascelles had turned IM down; and with IM's contemporary MM, with help from the Somerville archivist Ms Pauline Adams. Somerville College Education Committee Minute Book vol. V, p.153, reads: 'Miss J.I. Murdoch (English, merit in the examination).' PF points out that 'merit' refers always to the General Paper. 'I very nearly decided to read English instead of Greats, but I'm very glad I read Greats, but I was very attached to English Literature, and very keen on poetry, and very keen on modern poetry so I read all the writers, you know, Eliot, Auden, Day-Lewis, Spender' (unpublished interview with RW, 17 July 1991). IM was strongly political at once, as soon as she arrived. Possibly, MM speculated, IM wrote politicised essays on libertarian writers such as Shelley or Milton, which Mary Lascelles did not care for. In the Bodleian UNRRA interview (MSS.Eng.c.4718, fols.132–62; c 4733, item 16) IM recalls that she was interviewed before going up to Oxford.

16 See T.J. and E.P. Thompson (eds), *There is a Spirit in Europe: A Memoir*

of Frank Thompson (London, 1947), p.12.

17 An ex-Classics mistress, a Mrs Mott (*née* Ruth Harder), married to a well-known nuclear physicist, had helped IM in the summer of 1938. (See Mrs Jeffery's 1981 letter to John Fletcher). MM was coached by Diana Svegintsov, an ex-Somerville Classicist living in Chiswick quite near IM, and believes Svegintsov also coached IM.

18 Source: Professor Sally Humphreys.

19 Anne Elliott, at St Hugh's reading Mods and Greats 1938–42; also PF.

20 Barbara Craig (later a Principal of Somerville), LTA.

21 Source: Anne Elliott.

22 Charlotte Wallace, *née* Williams-Ellis, LTA, 9 April 1998.

23 Three undated letters to Paddy O'Regan, summer 1940. In a LTA, 13 January 1992, IM wrote that 'there was no wide consideration of Plato, he was simply misunderstood. I learnt nothing of value about him as an undergraduate (he was regarded as literature!) ... Reading Weil [later] helped me very much.' In fact IM's Marxism rendered her deaf to Plato.

24 In Mark Amory's *Lord Berners* (London, 1998) he is found sharing an interest in 'improper French novels': p.187.

25 'Somerville has always had a reputation for intense seriousness', Benjamin Thompson, review of Pauline Adams's *Somerville for Women: An Oxford College* (Oxford, 1996) in Somerville College Report 1996, pp.99–100.

26 *Badminton School Magazine*, no. 82, 1941–42.

27 Denis Healey, *The Time of my Life* (London, 1989), p.35; and FT's unpublished 'Snapshots of Oxford', from which all unascribed quotations in this chapter are taken.

28 IM denied authorship to LP. He

recalled the opening lines accurately in 1998. Margaret Stanier, fellow-Somervillian, who collected some of IM's Oxford poems, believes it may have been inspired by an exhibition entitled 'Guernica', of pictures and sketches from the Spanish Civil War. IM's verse-journal shows that she wrote it on 4 February 1939, at 1 a.m.

29 So, for example, MM feared. She researched this and the demotic 'Link' while waiting to come up to Somerville, like IM, in September 1938.

30 E.P. Thompson, *Beyond the Frontier* (Stanford, 1997), p.54. Hogg was, of course, later Lord Hailsham.

31 Slavcho Trunski, *Grateful Bulgaria* (Sofia Press, 1979), p.14. Here IM believes both that 'The very first thing I did when I arrived at Oxford was join the CP,' and accounts herself a member by November 1938. In Whitley, *The Graduates*, op. cit., she mentions her second term as the time that she joined. She told Margaret Stanier that she went first to the nearest Catholic church, St Aloysius, but finding it closed, took this as some sort of sign. Earlier this church visit was recalled as June 1941, when IM was troubled by the CPGB's change of line on the war effort. This is a more probable date, given Donald MacKinnon's influence after 1940. (Mary Douglas, two years younger than IM, believes, though this is as yet uncorroborated, that IM gained some reputation in debate as a formidable opponent of religion.)

32 Unpublished interview with RW, 17 July 1991.

33 Compare the following year: Ken Kirk, nominated OULC co-Treasurer with IM for a term in 1940, wrote (LTA, 23 June 1998) that he was 'a fresher in 1939, while she was in her fourth year'. He felt 'in awe of her' – a *leitmotiv*

of IM's story, from Barbara Denny in 1925–32, through Hugh Lloyd-Jones and Kirk (1940) onwards.

34 Reading PPE, 1938–41. She never spoke at OULC meetings, says LP (CWA, 22 October 1998). Soon Mrs Teddy Jackson, she went into the Board of Trade in 1941, where she worked with Frances Meynell, who wrote of her: '[Her] eyes were as bright as her mind, with her gypsy-like hair falling over her lovely small face, which would still look fashionable today.' Frances Meynell, *My Lives* (London, 1971), p.273. She died in 1992.

35 From FT's 'Snapshots of Oxford'.

36 Born 17 August 1920, Darjeeling.

37 T.J. and E.P. Thompson, *There is a Spirit in Europe*, op. cit., p.47.

38 In 1937.

39 These may flatter him: Tony Forster and MRDF spoke of him as ungainly – as did LP – and did not recall his beauty.

40 Letter, 1945–46, to E.P. Thompson, from Innsbruck.

41 Trunski, *Grateful Bulgaria*, op. cit., p.15.

42 6, 7 and 8 June 1940. Hugh Lloyd-Jones, coming up later that year, was in awe of IM: 'She was already famous in the University for having been Leader of the Chorus in a very successful production in Christ Church of *Murder in the Cathedral*. It was her existentialist period, and she seemed very serious' (LTA, 15 January 1998). Milein Cosman, who saw the production, especially recalls IM also.

43 IM gave 'a superb talk' as an undergraduate, just before her Finals in 1942, on 'Poets of the 1930s'. MB, letter to Jonathan Auburn, Friends of OULC, November 1997. IM praises 'A Summer Night' in *Lifelines* (an anthology of poems chosen by celebrated persons), ed. Niall MacMonagle (London, 1993).

44 LP, to protect his father who was a 'stateless alien', never became card-carrying, but was a Communist and did believe that all in the USSR was perfect, until June 1941.

45 Letter to FT, August 1943.

46 Nominally as a clerk. His duties included sweeping the floors, however.

47 It is almost certainly 'delightful' Doug Lowe from Ruskin whom FT recorded as saying, not *à propos* any named girl, 'Oi never tike a girl to the pichers, unless it's definitely understood that she wants penis afterwards and Oi said to mself, there's a short trip for the SS penis there.'

48 IM, letter to E.P. Thompson from Innsbruck, 1945–46.

49 Antony Forster.

50 Not good poems. e.g. 'Himeros': 'Putting down my pen, I looked out into the garden/At the chestnuts thoughtfully budding; the tired wall/Exulting silently in the evening; the grass/Still like a pool beneath a waterfall./A white cat ambled along the wall and vanished;/In the quadrangle someone was laughing; once again/ It hopped up to bask in the sunlight. Nothing would answer/ The scum of anger simmering in my brain./Then suddenly something cracked. My heart went numb./My rage, frustration and hate all droped asleep./I thought of you. I knew that you would not come./And I longed to lie with my head on your knees and weep.'

51 FT's version in 'Snapshots of Oxford' makes the digging up of the irises his mother's idea, presumably as therapy, and omits mention of the Doug Lowe 'trigger', recalled independently by LP, who did not believe that IM and Doug Lowe were lovers.

52 IM to E.P. Thompson, 1945–46.

53 Recalled by PF.

54 To FT, in a letter dated 13 April 1942.

55 LTA, April 1998.

56 MRDF met IM on 4 March 1939, the same day he joined the TA, and two days before *It Can Happen Here*. Quotation from Sue Summers, 'The Lost Loves of Iris Murdoch', *Mail on Sunday*, 5 June 1988, p.17.

57 CWA; Herbert Reiss's jokey description to IM, a little later. He accompanied Noel Martin and LP on their summer 1939 European journey, and was also in the OULC.

58 Possibly 19 November, when he returned for the conferral of his degree. He and IM had CP friends in common.

59 Source: Kenneth Dover to Simon Kusseff.

60 To DH, 13 May 1945.

61 His gift arrived in July 1940. FT's posthumous sister-in-law Dorothy Thompson, who knew nothing of this, met IM not long after the war. She was struck by IM's being 'white-blonde and very beautiful' and by her artificially 'plummy' voice, a voice IM later lost. For her, IM's attractive appearance 'called to mind C.S. Lewis's *Allegory of Love*'; CWA.

62 A letter to DH, early 1939, speaks of a 'mad Irishman who writes me verse'; while an undated letter to Paddy O'Regan describes his Irishness. The Irishman referred to was not O'Regan, since he came up to Merton College only in 1939. Margaret Stanier recalled IM's (undated) attachment to the Irish actor Cyril Cusack, who was in Oxford acting for one term.

63 IM's good friend Dorothy Thom (later Kent) was recalled by Vera Hoar (31 October 1998) as saying, 'It's not Iris's attractiveness that people fall for but her beauty of character.'

64 Born December 1919; at Liverpool Grammar School as LP had been at Manchester Grammar. Both got firsts in Mods. Neither continued to Greats: NM dropped out; LP changed after the war to PPE.

65 Tony Forster's adjective; CWA, 4 May 2000.

66 NM does not remember FT being in the *Agamemnon* class (any more than did Kenneth Dover, Clare Campbell, MM or LP), but then he was distracted by IM. He has vivid recall of FT, a charming man whom he still misses, as did LP.

67 J: October 1958.

68 October–November 1939.

69 Hilary term, 1940. Whether this production took place is in doubt. Same-sex plays (see footnote p.91) were going out of fashion.

70 1939: 4 and 18 May, pp.572, 627; 1 and 15 June, pp.681, 741. Lynda Patterson, *née* Lynch, who shared digs with IM from 1940 at 43 Park Town, passed on this task to IM. Though anonymous, they bear the hallmark of IM's lively style. Lynch accurately recalled one piece on a visit by Dorothy L. Sayers.

71 Eric Hobsbawm, CWA, 16 August 1999. IM associated with Ulster grandees' daughters such as the Craig daughter of Lord Craigavon, then Prime Minister of Ulster. (Deirdre Levi, granddaughter of Lord Craigavon, says there was no such CP daughter, or CP relative, apart from one male cousin called Nares.)

72 To DH, 8 March 1945.

73 Eric Hobsbawm (16 August 1999) does not recall FT's presence at the Surrey summer school he and IM attended: these may have been different events.

74 Set by Geoffrey Bush and Jonathan Mayne. See Geoffrey Bush, *An Unsentimental Education* (London, 1990), pp.111, 127.

75 Fletcher wrote of his plan to create

the Magpie Players in *Cherwell*, LVI, no. 3, 13 May 1939, pp.50–1. As evidence of public fascination with Oxford he cites the film *I was a Yank at Oxford* and the popularity of the Boat Race.

76 *Cherwell*, LVI, no. 6, 3 June 1939, pp.112–14, collected in Muroya and Hullah, *Occasional Essays by Iris Murdoch*, op. cit. The title refers to Emil Renier's book *The English – Are they Human?*, published a few years before. On 17 June Denis Brooman answered her with another light-hearted and more effective polemic, 'Scot-free, or a true way with Traitors', one of whose claims is that IM is Scottish.

77 To FT, 30 December 1941. Patricia Shaw (later Lady Trend), at the Treasury with IM in 1942, similarly believed, until 1998, that IM's father was then still working in Dublin.

78 IM in a postcard to Rene and Hughes, 30 August 1939, mentions the silver plate and that Lady Bicester was 'particularly taken with my acting'.

79 Moira Dunbar agreed about IM's characterisations: 'One always felt [Denys] needed a nanny.' LTA, 14 September 1998.

80 CWA, 20 May 1999. IM's J continues: 'He is so exceedingly young & spontaneous & so completely the artist. He seems moreover to be devoid of vices. In "Tam Lin" he embraces and kisses me without the least embarrassment, which is good. I was afraid he might be shy. But of course he has done a great deal of acting before.'

81 Joanne Yexley. Second name supplied by Moira Dunbar.

82 This episode is recalled by Moira Dunbar – IM has torn a page out of the journal. IM confirmed she had met the Brüderhof in a letter to Harry Weinberger.

83 Fletcher turned up in Oxford shortly before his death, around 1991, ebullient as ever, after a life spent teaching abroad. JB secured him St Catherine's college theatre for the night, since he wished to put on a one-man performance of the eighteenth-century Swedish Bellman's *Ballads*. Apart from IM and JB and the then Master (Brian Smith) and his wife, no one came. Fletcher, unperturbed, sang the ballads to his guitar quite happily.

84 Letter from Moira Dunbar confirms 3 September as the date, which is unclear from the journal.

85 The page is torn out, so exactly how she got there is unclear.

86 IM to FT, 12 November 1943.

CHAPTER 5

1 April/May 1942, to FT, now stationed in Lebanon/Syria. IM's meeting John Willett prompted this fond recall.

2 FT, letter to Desiree Cumberlege. True, he was acquainted with other Oxford 'Bolshevickas', notably Leonie Marsh, but the repetition of the epithet 'Bolshevicka' in the title of his poem 'Madonna Bolshevicka' also suggests IM, who was his 'muse', in poem after poem, over a period of four years. Desiree was pacifist, IM the Communist. See n9 below.

3 *Spectator*, 5 January 1940.

4 Graham Lehmann, CWA.

5 See Trunski, *Grateful Bulgaria*, op. cit., p.16.

6 MRDF, LTA, 31 August 1998. Two dozen of them went by bus: 'I took part ... [&] had a long, fairly useful chat with A.P. Herbert, then member for Oxford University ... I believe (though I am not quite sure) [FT] took part.' MRDF, like about half of FT's contemporaries at New College, belonged to what the Habsburg monarchy called

'*Kaderfamilie*', families of the old officer class who, like MRDF's grandfather, and then Brigadier father in 1912, and himself early in 1939, foreseeing a great European war, joined a Territorial unit.

7 A friend since childhood days, Andrew Ensor, had severely shaken FT's confidence in the inevitable and absolute purity of Soviet intentions, *vis-à-vis* the USSR–Germany non-aggression pact, as Ensor recounts persuasively and at length in a letter to Simon Kusseff.

8 While Raymond Carr, whose acceptance into the Party by Peter Shinney at Queen's College partook of a religious ceremony, with candles and oaths, felt bullied by both these doctrines, the entry of others – e.g. Patrick Denby – was less dramatic. Nonetheless Vera Hoar was present when John ['Jack'] Terraine was, at Hythe Bridge Street, informally tried, then summarily drummed out of the Party for some such error.

9 He wrote in praise of the Madonna as a feminine stereotype – a Wykehamist loyalty too – and Apollo as a male one, in a later letter, and also addressed Desiree Cumberlege (see n2, above) as 'madonna'.

10 Lord Healey recalls Professor D.W. Brogan using this phrase when answering IM's 'defence of the Party line' in the *Spectator*, 1939–40. Although the correspondence has so far proven elusive, the phrase rings true.

11 Lionel Hale in the *Oxford News Chronicle*, quoted by FT in a letter to Desiree Cumberlege.

12 To Paddy O'Regan, no date, probably June 1940.

13 To DH, 21 March 1941.

14 To Paddy O'Regan, undated, c1940. In unpublished interview with RW, 17 July 1991, IM dated Austin's lectures to March 1940.

15 Lindsey Lynch, LTA, 8 April 1999.

16 Wartime letters to both Paddy O'Regan and DH mention coltsfoot growing near the house in Blackpool where IM's parents spent the war, and mention IM painting and framing there also.

17 *Cherwell*, LVI, no. 3, 11 November 1939, p.63.

18 Eliot's name is repeatedly invoked in IM's poetry journals of the time.

19 Peter Conrad, *Observer* Books section, 14 February 1999, p.16.

20 Whether or not IM skated no one recalls, but 'most of Somerville' did. Eight miles of the Thames was frozen solid. A pair of IM's skates from Steeple Aston days survived: white leather, scarcely used, made by Lilywhites c1963.

21 Undated, but must refer to April or so, as she mentions 'next term'.

22 Letter to FT, 24 December 1941.

23 She helped her friend Janet Vaughan to become college Principal. Isobel Henderson's 1934 cartoon of Helen Darbyshire, with Somerville motto, as a spoof of the Winged Victory (used by Pauline Adams as cover for her college history) shows both her understanding of the absurdity of women's colleges and her great love of them.

24 Sally Humphreys, eulogy for Isobel Henderson, *Somerville Report*, 1967.

25 See Chapter 3.

26 JB's recollection: see *Iris*, op. cit. Mildred Hartley also told IM and MM about the class. She said it was a 'most distinguished affair and the condition of entry was that they should undertake never to miss it – if ill, or dying, we must tell Prof Fraenkel in advance and in writing'. When MM did indeed have to miss a class because of a broken leg, Fraenkel answered her

letter of apology by sending her a small book as a gift. She thinks she and IM would have checked their plans for Mods with Isobel Henderson in their first year, which would have been when Henderson made the quoted remark.

27 David Pears, CWA.

28 Fraenkel, for example, 'once put out feelers that he could do with [Clare Campbell] as secretary/ paramour; nothing doing'. Clare Campbell, LTA, 23 February 1998.

29 Mary Warnock, *A Memoir: People and Places* (London, 2000). She notes that Fraenkel's behaviour disgusted a friend of hers (Imogen Wrong), and had a lasting and bad effect on her attitide to sex.

30 MM, LTA.

31 MM, LTA, 25 August 1998. She was in love with Nick Crosbie, killed in the war. Noel, FT and LP were variously in love with IM.

32 Hugh Lloyd-Jones, LTA, 3 February 1998.

33 Kenneth Dover, *Marginal Comment* (London, 1994), p.39. Dover attended the class 1938–40.

34 J: 1964–70, p.8.

35 IM, undated, to Tony Forster, probably 1967: 'So you were at that terrifying class of Fraenkel's – it was the most frightening part of my university education.'

36 Gordon Williams, 'Eulogy of Eduard Fraenkel', *Proceedings of the British Academy*, LVI, 1970 (OUP, 1972), p.438. My account of Professor Fraenkel is throughout deeply indebted to Williams's vivid, scholarly and detailed eulogy.

37 From IM's notes of Fraenkel's and Beazley's classes.

38 Hugh Lloyd-Jones, LTA, 3 February 1998.

39 Letter to DM, 17 July 1966.

40 Kenneth Dover, LTA, 27 February 1998.

41 Williams, 'Eulogy', op. cit., p.438.

42 One well-known brief account is Perry Anderson's 'Components of the National Culture', in A. Cockburn and R. Blackburn (eds), *Student Power* (London, 1969), pp.214–84.

43 To DH, 21 March 1941.

44 Mark Amory, *Lord Berners*, op. cit., p.179.

45 See G. Hirschfeld, 'Durchgangsland England? Die Britische "Academic Community" und die wissenschafltliche Emigration aus Deutschland', in *England? aber wo liegt es? Deutsche und Österreichische Emigranten in Grossbritannien 1933–45*, C. Brunson et al (eds) (Munich, 1996), pp.59–70.

46 In the 1920s a light was always visible through the night in Fraenkel's study in Kiel: physical hardship was of little account compared with scholarship. What religion is to some, work was to him – it gave shape, purpose and meaning to his life. His first major work, on Plautus, was written between 10 p.m. and 3 a.m. after his day's work was over.

47 Fraenkel dedicated his study of the *Agamemnon* to his wife Ruth and to Professor Sir John Beazley.

48 *Sunday Times*, 23 December 1934.

49 Williams, 'Eulogy', op. cit.; see p.435, n24.

50 *The Unicorn*, p.80.

51 An idea repeated in *Nuns and Soldiers*.

52 J: 1945, undated.

53 Williams, 'Eulogy', op. cit., p.429; Fraenkel on the Hymn to Zeus (pp.16off of Fraenkel's study). My emphasis.

54 See Toynbee, *Friends Apart*, op. cit., p.67. Toynbee, like IM, read Greats at Oxford, though a few years before.

55 Williams, 'Eulogy', op. cit., p.440.

56 Ibid, pp.431–3.

57 J: 1975–78, p.38.

58 Letter home, 15 May 1943.

59 FT, letter to Desiree Cumberlege, June 1940 (i.e. after Dunkirk). He also jokily proposed that she acquire a 'good translation of the famous chorus from *Agamemnon*', to strengthen her pacifism.

60 17 April 1941, on board ship.

61 Respectively 30 December 1941 and 29 January 1942.

62 She read PPE at Somerville 1940–43.

63 David Pears, CWA.

64 George Steiner, unpublished eulogy of Donald MacKinnon, 20 May 1994, Corpus, Cambridge.

65 MRDF, CWA.

66 J: 15 May 1971. IM is describing the anthropologist Evans-Pritchard's voice, which recalled MacKinnon's clearly to her.

67 George Steiner, eulogy of Donald MacKinnon, op. cit.

68 Dennis Nineham, CWA.

69 David Pears, CWA.

70 'Evil and Personal Responsibility' and 'The Crux of Morality', both from *Listener*, 18 March 1948, pp.457–9 and 16 December 1948, pp.926–7. 'Things and Persons' from *Proceedings of the Aristotelian Society*, Supplementary Vol. XXII, 1948, pp.179–89.

71 Vera Crane's recollection.

72 Preface to EM, p.x.

73 PF has an identical recollection. These short wartime courses, incidentally, IM refers to as 'dismal' (7 April 1942, to DH).

74 Nicholas Lash, obituary of Donald MacKinnon, *Guardian*, 5 March 1994.

75 IM to Rosalind Hursthouse, undated, c1994.

76 IM wrote (from Seaforth, undated, but probably summer 1943 since there is as yet no kitchen) inviting PF to stay with her in London: 'Yes, please come & stay – if you don't mind no cooking & a shortage of furniture & blackout (there is however an extra campbed & blankets so you will at least be comfortable at night). I've been feeling intensely lonely on and off lately – do come Pip. Let me know when.'

77 Surmise of various friends, including MM, Vera Crane, Margaret Lintott. See Chapter 6, n37 below.

78 'Students cut down on social activities and dig potatoes in the parks – joining some society such as the Cosmos, all of which gives them a vague sensation of social betterment without confronting them at any point with a realistic picture of the world. Oxford does its best to dream even now.' *Badminton School Magazine*, 82, 1941–2. The Cosmos was recalled by Marjorie Reeves as a predecessor to the Socratic Club, hence Christian.

79 Undated letter referred to in n76, probably summer 1943, since the occasion of the letter is PF's arrival in London.

80 See Whitley, *The Graduates*, op. cit.

81 Toynbee, *Friends Apart*, op. cit., p.61. Compare also Toynbee's depiction of the disagreeable attempt to convert Jasper Ridley; and Jennifer Hart on love as bourgeois fiction in *Ask me no More* (London, 1998).

82 Healey, *The Time of my Life*, op. cit., p.36.

83 Toynbee, *Friends Apart*, op. cit., p.18.

84 See *Spectator*, 12 January 1940.

85 Jenkins, in *A Life at the Centre* (London, 1992), says Crosland, Ian Durham and he were the only three not on the CP line (a phrase that might or might not indicate membership). Robert Conquest (LTA) says Christopher Mayhew was the only notable OULC person not in the CP.

86 Robert Conquest, LTA, April 1998. Also LP, CWA, February 1998.

87 Dennis Healey, CWA.

88 In none of her longish letters to the *Badminton School Magazine*, recounting the doings of Old Girls, does IM mention this. Her Communism had less shock value at Badminton.

89 This was the only time he and IM ever met after 1932. He has cause to recall the month: having been called up to the Royal Engineers, he was trying to buy Schlomann's *Technical French Dictionary* for use in France, whither his unit was being sent.

90 The minute book for the OULC for 1940–41 recently came to light: Herbert Reiss found it in his Cambridge attic in December 1997.

91 To take place on 15 May 1940.

92 November 1941: 'The only useful lesson I learnt was the cunning . . . with which Communists infiltrate other groups, non-political (religious, for instance), as well as political.' Kingsley Amis, *Memoirs* (Penguin, 1991), p.37. But *The Letters of Kingsley Amis*, ed. Z. Leader (London, 2000), suggest his commitment went at least a little deeper: see pp.1–5.

93 Jenkins, *A Life at the Centre*, op. cit., p.36. The Labour Party had just disaffiliated itself from the ULF.

94 Roy Jenkins, LTA, June 1998.

95 Ibid.

96 Susan Crosland, *Tony Crosland* (London, 1982), p.11.

97 *New Statesman*, 11 May 1940, p.610. MM believes this was a rump OULC meeting.

98 Susan Crosland, *Tony Crosland*, op. cit., p.12.

99 *Badminton School Magazine*, 81.

100 Unpublished minutes of OULC, 22 February 1942: 'It was unanimously decided to approach the Senior ex-Chairman from Somerville [sic] . . . to take Comrade Terraine's [i.e. the future military historian] place . . . in the debate against the OUDSC.' No one else appeared willing.

101 IM to FT, 17 February 1943: 'I don't know if it will mean much to you after these years & years . . . but the two clubs, who were always at each others' throats, have now amicably amalgamated & all is unity & progress. This is a fine thing & a real tonic to me. Leo's heart will leap slightly.' FT was interested in the news and passed it on in a letter to his brother E.P. No history of the OULC after 1934, when M.P. Asley and C.T. Saunders's *Red Oxford* came out, has yet been written.

102 They did not meet until long after the war, when both were established writers.

103 Two vivas. In the morning viva MM froze, and was hospitably invited back that afternoon by the examiners. IM wrongly feared that the fact that she herself was not to be viva'd meant she had done less well. Her philosophy papers, if not her history papers, were outstanding.

104 MM, LTA, January 1998.

105 Compare 'John Haffenden Talks to Iris Murdoch', op. cit.: 'The good man creates space; the bad eats it up.'

106 Recalled by A.L. Rowse around 1980 at an All Souls' dinner, at which recollection IM then smiled.

107 To FT, 16 September 1941, from 9 Waller Avenue, Bispham, Blackpool, whither her parents had moved for the war with Hughes's civil service department, and an airgraph from Somerville dated 24 April 1942. IM's first

cousin Muriel Chapman was teaching at Reigate during these years and spent one summer with the Murdoch family – probably 1940 – after discovering, too late, that she could make only one annual trip home to Belfast in wartime.

108 To DH, 7 April 1942.

109 IM records that she was interviewed for the Treasury in her recollections of UNRRA in the Bodleian Library (op. cit.). MM: 'Somerville had been advised to let us know that they would be glad if we went into the Civil Service rather than the forces, because the Civil Service was very short of people.' It was to MM that IM communicated her fears about her CP membership prejudicing her chances of a job.

110 *Badminton School Magazine*, 82, pp.41–2.

111 J: 17 February 1978.

112 IM calls herself 'temporary Assistant Principal' in *Badminton School Magazine*, 1942, on her UNRRA application in June 1944, on the backs of her novels, and in *Who's Who*. FT used the same term to describe her grade when writing to his family. Sylvia Raphael, a Treasury colleague of IM's, pointed out that it was only the Treasury that, true to its sense of being different, did not in fact use the term '[Temporary] Assistant Principal', but called its young women graduate recruits 'Temporary Administrative Officers', the title IM is allotted in the *British Imperial Calendar* for 1943 – none being produced in 1942 or 1944 (or, for that matter, 1941).

CHAPTER 6

1 Iris wrote from 55 Barrowgate Road, Chiswick, a street away from her parents' house, which had suffered bomb damage a year or more before.

2 Vera Hoar, at the Ministry of Supply in Carlton House Terrace from 1943, later at the Shell-Mex Building in the Strand, recalls that many if not all APs used the office telephones for social calls as well as business ones.

3 IM to DH, January 20 1943.

4 The door onto the street now (1998) closed.

5 Letter to FT, 31 May 1943.

6 IM gives her Principal on her UNRRA application form as A.H.M. Hillis, but most worked to two different Principals; Vera Crane thought Hilary Sinclair (a man) her Principal. Peggy Pyke-Lees thought it B.D. Fraser; John C. Robinson is a name crossed out on IM's 1944 UNRRA application.

7 Olive Pound was also there.

8 Peggy Pyke-Lees, and also Professor Raphael, Sylvia's widower, CWA, 5 June 2000.

9 Also known as E/G.

10 Peggy was in 'SS', or Social Services. Her husband Walter dealt with some of the same tasks as Iris before 1944.

11 On IM's UNNRA application, June 1944.

12 19 October 1942. To DH she wrote on 20 January 1943 that 'urgent letters sojourn neglected at the bottom of my tray, & the notes of important telephone calls which I write on the back of OHMS envelopes get lost somehow. I get a kick out of it all though . . .'.

13 IM to DH, 20 January 1943.

14 MRDF to FT, 24 August 1942.

15 FT to IM, 7 June 1942.

16 Letter to FT, 22 October 1943.

17 This is inevitably based on a

straw-poll among survivors. At least neither Peggy Pyke-Lees nor Lady Trend visited the flat, though the latter recalled its reputation as legendarily 'modern'. Sylvia Daiches Raphael was once invited to a supper, probably in 1943 – to help keep Iris safe, she felt, from the advances of Nickie Kaldor and Tommy Balogh.

18 Letter to DH, 8 March 1945.

19 Every tenth night they had to fire-watch or perform other duties. One stayed up the whole night, often in the company of the Great and Good. Peggy Pyke-Lees believes that sleeping took place, if at all, on bunk-beds in concrete bunkers in the basement.

20 Peggy Pyke-Lees's mother's wisdom.

21 MRDF, CWA.

22 To MB, undated: 'I rarely escape from the office now before 7 or later.'

23 J: 10 September 1971.

24 IM to Rosalind Hursthouse, undated, c1994.

25 A postcard from IM at the Shakespeare Festival in Stratford dated 28 July 1940 shows Rene and Hughes living at 196 Cavendish Road, Bispham, Blackpool, where they moved at the outbreak of war. A letter to DH shows the move from Cavendish to Waller Avenue was complete by 21 March 1941.

26 After the Blitz, property was scarce and hence costly, so Rent Acts were passed to protect tenants against unjust rent rises, tying rents to earlier rateable values. IM and PF thus acquired a protected tenancy, which Marion Bosanquet (later Daniel) inherited. The rent stayed at sixty guineas a year for decades.

27 Letter to MB dated 16 August 1942: 'I move in in September' – on a three-year lease.

28 To MB, 16 August 1942.

29 Called PRHA (People's Rest-House Association).

30 IM downplays its unusualness when writing to DH, 20 January 1943: 'a long & erratic studio on top of an empty warehouse down a rather dark alleyway'. Her letters to DH are more worldly, less lyrical than those to FT. To Clare Campbell in late 1942 she also writes of living above a mouse-ridden warehouse.

31 Probably after 'Killycoonagh', the modern but grand house of Paddy O'Regan's family near Marlborough, which IM visited and recalled later. It also boasted an 'atrium'.

32 Not necessarily so designated at first, since a letter to PF warns of 'no cooking'. There was mains gas laid on, and IM must have acquired the ancient stove, probably second hand.

33 Now a canteen for Scotland Yard.

34 All unascribed quotations come from PF's record; see *Iris Murdoch Newsletter*, no. 13, 1999, pp.1–2.

35 22 January 1943.

36 The coach-houses in the corner off Spencer Street, where a linden tree now flourishes, waited a little longer.

37 This was the view of her closest schoolfriend Margaret Lintott, who was told during the war that IM was a CP member while at the Treasury, and of MM and of Vera Crane, who was also involved with the CP.

38 Letter from MRDF to FT, dated 15 and 23 July 1943.

39 MB recalled how IM always loathed jokes about the purges.

40 CP archives (1943–92) at the Labour History Archive and Study Centre, 103 Princess Street, Manchester.

41 By Ruth Kingsbury.

42 In September 1945 doodles were drawn low down on the wall, possibly by bored Party members during such meetings.

43 As Dorothy Thompson pointed out,

'The loan of a flat by an absent owner/tenant happened regularly at CP meetings.'

44 Source: Thomas Balogh's son Steve, December 1999. Paul Streeten, Balogh's student and friend from 1944, points out (e-mail, 31 December 2000) that Balogh moved from far right, supporting Horthy and working with Hjalmar Schacht, to far left, overestimating the USSR's economic strength and therefore opposed to provoking the Russians.

45 *Née* Towers, then Sale.

46 Clare Campbell, LTA.

47 This sleeping in the bath was something PF had not, in 1998, known or recalled that IM also did.

48 Marion recalls that MM was a little indignant when it was returned after the war, somewhat the worse for wear.

49 Letter to MB dated 16 August 1942.

50 In a closed Bodleian collection. IM lent some of FT's letters to E.P. Thompson in 1946 when the latter was co-editing the commemorative *There is a Spirit in Europe*, op. cit.

51 J: 7 August 1991. This comment is *à propos* the letters she wrote to Paddy O'Regan c1940.

52 Anne Valery, then a pupil at Badminton, vividly recalls IM, on a trip to the school c1941, enquiring as to which house Valery was in and, with a joky peremptoriness criticising her 'back bent like a hoop!' Badminton girls who developed early were embarrassed by and wished to conceal the fact that they now had breasts. Until 1999 Valery assumed that IM was then still a prefect, although it was in fact three years after IM had left.

53 IM to FT, 20 March 1943.

54 FT to IM, 17 October 1942.

55 IM to FT, 22 January 1943.

56 FT, letter home, 17 September 1943.

57 Probably summer 1942. Compare MRDF to FT, 2 April 1943: 'Shocked to see how nakedly and crudely we put our intimate selves into our typewriters.'

58 Compare also FT to E.P. Thompson, 21 April 1942: 'You & my old friend IM are the only 2 of my contemporaries in England with whom I correspond regularly.'

59 FT consoled Desiree Cumberlege, one of whose suitors was killed in November 1941: 'next to my parents', your letters are the best I get'. In spring 1942 Desiree got engaged, though she never married; her surviving brother believes she was in love with FT. FT wrote also to Catherine Nicholson, daughter of Robert Graves, whom his mother favoured, and to his cousin, young 'Tubsie' Pilkington-Rogers, now Mrs Barbara Sloman.

60 C/o an aunt, Margaret Levitt, in Beirut.

61 FT had jaundice at the time of writing, late 1942.

62 This was probably in summer 1944, in the UNRRA offices in Portland Place. See IM's UNRRA reminiscences, Bodleian Library, op. cit.

63 Dated 14 March 1944, a Tuesday. Thomas Balogh used Kaldor's flat in Chelsea Cloisters each Wednesday.

64 See e.g. EM, pp.112, 124, 160, and *The Sea, The Sea, passim.* IM's journal references to Lawrence continue until late. JB teased her about this: see *Iris*, op. cit., p.72. Aldous Huxley in *The Perennial Philosophy* and William James in *Varieties of Religious Experience* both predicate the saint on the model of the soldier – a moral conscript, as it were.

65 Born 2 February 1920, he started as a pacifist at Merton in 1939, enlisted in the RAMC in 1940, then

SOE in Italy in 1944, where he won the MC and bar. He died aged forty-one on 9 March 1961 after a career in the Diplomatic Service. His surviving elder brother John says how much he owed to IM for giving him the courage and determination to fight.

66 LTA from MRDF, expert on SOE, and himself ex-SAS. See also *Nuremberg Trials*, vol. 15, p.297 (HMSO, 1948).

67 IM to FT, 17 February 1943: 'Yet you are a Romantic too.'

68 IM to FT, November 1943.

69 Compare FT to IM, April 1944: 'I know forgiveness is one of your chief virtues.'

70 IM to FT, 16 September 1941.

71 IM to FT, 24 April 1942.

72 FT to IM, 29 January 1942.

73 FT to IM, 12 November 1943.

74 Ibid.

75 Ibid.

76 Such was the general belief of acquaintances such as Anne Elliott, reading Mods and Greats at the same time as IM, though at a different college, St Hugh's.

77 Lilian was sceptical about Noel and IM having been lovers without her having caught wind of it, as she and Noel were close, but also commented: 'It could conceivably be hard for a nicely-brought-up young girl to say "no" – especially in wartime – precisely because they had been brought up to oblige.'

78 CWA, 15 October 1998; LP strongly implied that the relationship had not been 'fully' sexual at that stage. A 1940 letter from IM to Paddy O'Regan, agreeing in principle to a camping holiday with him, in which she wonders whether she has the courage to lie to her parents about the sex of her companion, opens the field to another contender. No evidence survives about whether or not the expedition took place, but in August 1991 IM wrote to O'Regan's surviving brother John an affectionate letter in which she vouchsafes that the relationship had been 'distinctly passionate'. IM told MRDF, with whom she had an affair starting in July 1943, that her first lover had been at Queen's. Noel Eldridge was at Balliol, LP at Corpus. A lover at Queen's would fit Denis Healey's recollection that IM had been briefly 'lined up' with his fellow-ex-Bradford Grammar School acquaintance Derrick Brooman, who entered Queen's in 1937 to study PPE but left in 1939 to join up, then went to Bristol University and Oxford, and died in June 1979. Though no one else recalls Brooman, IM pasted a snap of him in an early photograph album. She told Vera Crane, Clare Campbell, DH and FT that she had lost her virginity by early 1943. To DM she remarked much later that she was anxious to get rid of her virginity as soon as she could.

79 For example, she at some point told her Belfast cousins that her only lover before JB was Noel Eldridge. She wrote to DH (20 January 1943) that she had relinquished her 'quaint virginity cult' some time ago. A poem would seem to date this to April 1943 (in Redhill), however.

80 Margaret Stanier was by no means alone in recalling IM at Oxford as very promiscuous: CWA, 8 March 2000 and LTA, 10 March 2000.

81 Margaret Stanier, LTA.

82 See e.g. Toynbee, *Friends Apart*, op. cit., or Pat Sloan (ed.) *John Cornford: A Memoir* (London, 1938)

83 To PF, c July 1942.

84 J: 1992–96. Susie Williams-Ellis did not, in 1998, share this recollection.

85 Source: her stepson Julian Jackson.

86 FT to E.P. Thompson, March 1940.

87 When he describes a visit to a brothel, he finds himself without any money. LP, meeting FT in 1943, thought his new confidence and physical coordination might have come from his having had an affair. His biographer Simon Kusseff believes that, on the contrary, it was the result of intense physical training that preceded the Sicilian landings, and that he died a virgin.

88 Robert Graves's daughter Catherine Nicholson recalls a visit by E.P. Thompson around 1946 to check that she was financially secure. Her understanding was that FT's first will was in her favour, and was changed only after her marriage in the summer of 1942.

89 A point I owe to Simon Kusseff.

90 For his part Hal Lidderdale spoke to Christopher Seton-Watson of FT's 'wide interests, appetite for experience and good humour'. The Lidderdale house was in Woodstock.

91 15 September 1942.

92 She believes autumn 1942 (CWA, 1 August 2000).

93 Dr Ken Roberts (son of W.C. Roberts), LTA, 14 January 2001.

94 Anecdote told to Richard Lyne in 1954 by Dr Ken Roberts; also told to Margaret Bastock, later a colleague of IM at St Anne's, and her husband Aubrey Manning. The two versions differ somewhat – Lyne has the bus into work on which IM usually sat at the front on the left, Roberts at the back, normally only a formal greeting passing between them. Manning has the bus home. But the two accounts overlap significantly.

CHAPTER 7

1 Not sentiments that he shared directly with IM.

2 J: 11 December 1977.

3 J comment by IM on re-reading her 1943 diaries, on 21 December 1988.

4 IM wrote to MB in 1967 of Seaforth as a 'real Naboth's vineyard' – i.e. a possession coveted by its legal owner – and spoke wistfully of the flat during the war (CWA, September 1994). She paid an unheralded visit to Seaforth one evening in the early 1970s. Marion and Peter Daniel were delighted to see her and opened some hock, but such an impromptu call was very out of character, and a token of her strength of feeling: unsolicited visits IM deplored in principle.

5 She worked under Rosenstein Rodan, preparing plans for the Balkans and Central Europe.

6 Unpublished interview with RW, 17 July 1991.

7 IM to Rosalind Hursthouse, c1994.

8 J: May 1959: 'Or was that at Oxford?' IM lodged at PF's at 16 Park Town in 1948–49.

9 An American told MRDF that IM put an empty hock bottle on her mantelpiece each time she turned down a proposal. (Liebfraumilch, Noel Martin recounts, was the drink of the time if you wished to try to get your girlfriend tipsy and amorous.)

10 David Worswick, with whom Balogh worked at Balliol, doubts that Balogh would have been permitted, as an alien, to do such hush-hush work, though noting too Balogh's skill at getting to know the 'right people'.

11 Confirmed by Ruth Kingsbury: IM got cross if her books were borrowed and not returned to their correct spot.

12 Published 1943, so presumably bought back from Paris after the Liberation; see Chapter 8.

13 Undated letter to MB. She utilised a substance called 'Liverpool virus'.

14 CWA, 1993. A letter inviting Clare

Campbell to the ballet survives. JB believes IM especially liked the adaptation of Tchaikovsky's *Pathetique* Symphony as music for a ballet of *Hamlet*, and that she went to see Stravinsky's *Petroushka*.

15 J: 4 April 1948.

16 PF, LTA, June 2000. They would not necessarily go to the same parties. Vera Hoar recalls that one brought a bottle to Seaforth parties.

17 Saunders not merely worked at the Treasury, but appeared to his friend Mervyn James even to sleep there.

18 To DH, 4 October 1945.

19 See Jane Williams (ed.), *Tambimuttu: Bridge Between Two Worlds* (London, 1989), esp. pp.278–9. Eliot supported 'Tambi' both financially and by commissioning him to edit poetry anthologies for Faber, *Poetry in Wartime* appearing in August 1942. Such, at least, were the myths. See Julian Maclaren-Ross, *Memoirs of the Forties* (London, 1965), pp.137ff, and Gavin Ewart, 'Tambi the Great', *London Magazine*, December 1965, p.60, for their debunking. IM wrote 'Poem and Egg' for Tambimuttu in 1977, and attended the relaunch of *Poetry London/Apple Magazine* in October 1979.

20 It is hard to date the beginning of IM's friendships with other denizens of the Swiss and the Wellington – i.e. of artistic and literary London – such as Audrey Beecham, Dan Davin, Gerald Wilde, Mulk Raj Anand and Paul Potts – but the last two of these certainly started in the war. Ralph Larmour, Les Epstein, Keidrych Rhys and Olivier Wormser, all represented in IM's photograph album, were, JB believes, among her other wartime beaux, and Wormser and Rhys wished to marry her.

21 J: 27 January 1967.

22 MM. Ruth Kingsbury believes Potts may have been in the CP. Dorothy Thompson recalls Potts as having written 'My name is Paul Potts/And I've holes in my socks'.

23 Unpublished interview with RW, 17 July 1991.

24 IM to FT, 24 December 1941.

25 'Some of it looked rather good,' she dispassionately noted in her journal of the fragments in her waste-bin.

26 MM and Jewel Smith.

27 On 21 September 1947 she wrote to RQ that this manuscript greeted a return of hers to London.

28 IM told Ruth Kingsbury she was writing a novel about a professor.

29 *Spectator*, 18–25 December 1999.

30 Standard biography F.A. Lea, *The Life of John Middleton Murry* (London, 1959). Lois MacKinnon doubted that Donald MacKinnon and Murry were acquainted.

31 *Adelphi* reviews of Nicodemus's *Midnight Hour*, January–March 1943, pp.61–2; of S. Cook's *Rebirth of Christianity* and K. Ingram's *Taken at the Flood*, July–September 1943, pp.125–7; and E. Hayman's *Worship and Common Life*, July–September 1944, pp.134–5.

32 FT to Desiree Cumberlege, c1940. Simon Kusseff dates 'Pollicita Meliora' to around 1940–41.

33 MRDF to FT, July 1943.

34 In July 1990 she noted that her publisher Carmen Callil and agent Ed Victor took her out to the restaurant Nico's, then at this address.

35 According to FT's reminiscences of Winchester.

36 This was one of at least three occasions on which PF borrowed Balogh's Dorchester cottage.

37 Michael Hamburger's translation, as IM wrote to him fifty years later. Her copy is inscribed 'IM Oxford Sep 1943', with 'HMT' underneath.

38 Whose 'perfect beauty was marred

only by a receding hairline', as Ruth Kingsbury recalls IM saying (May 2000).

39 Lady (Catherine) Balogh, CWA, 15 February 1999.

40 Not recalled by MRDF, December 2000.

41 Lady Balogh, CWA, 15 February 1999.

42 When IM feared, falsely, that she might be pregnant by Balogh, he was willing if necessary to marry her. Many expressed their sense of ill-omen about this affair: Balogh was considered egotistical.

43 13 April 1942.

44 5 July 1943.

45 Thompson, *Beyond the Frontier*, op. cit.

46 Ibid, p.42.

47 Major, later Lord, Henikker calls them a compound of 'bombastic deserters and inexperienced Communists' (*Beyond the Frontier*, op. cit., pp.79–80).

48 Thompson, *Beyond the Frontier*, op. cit., p.23.

49 So, at least, claims Stowers Johnson, whose study *Agents Extraordinary* (London, 1975) is notoriously ill-documented.

50 Sharova came to England as a delegate to a World Trades Union Congress in 1945, and so was probably a CP member. She is the sole source both for the story of the trial and for FT's avowal of Communism thereat. See *News Chronicle*, 8 March 1945. The story was recycled in T.J. and E.P. Thompson, *There is a Spirit in Europe*, op. cit.; by Trunski in *Grateful Bulgaria*, op. cit., who did not believe it but who had himself been tortured c1947 as a 'British spy'; by Stowers Johnson in *Agents Extraordinary*, op. cit. ('slowly & quietly, [FT] declar[ed] boldly he was a Communist', p.166); finally in Thompson, *Beyond the Frontier*, op. cit.

51 FT's sister-in-law Dorothy Thompson recalls (15 February 1999) the film-maker Tony Simmons at an unspecified later date uncovering some of FT's clothes, the condition of which strongly suggested torture. In October 1999 Dorothy, on being told the story of the execution, pointed out that the blood could also have been a product of the shooting.

52 Ken Scott, speaking on the Bulgarian television film entitled *Major Frank Thompson*, 1977, now in the British Film Institute.

53 Trunski, *Grateful Bulgaria*, op. cit., p.66.

54 Slavcho Trunski, who saw FT on and off for four months in 1944, says his Bulgarian was by no means fluent.

55 Simon Kusseff: the date is uncertain, but between 7 and 10 June.

56 T.J. and E.P. Thompson, *There is a Spirit in Europe*, op. cit., pp.10–11.

57 IM's journals at different times mention her ownership of both.

58 So Dimitri Markov, prize CP writer, told Robert Conquest. Discovering this when researching a play about the partisans helped make Markov decide to defect.

59 Source: *Major Frank Thompson*, Bulgarian television, 1977.

60 To the Algerian Ambassador. See also Arnold Rattenbury, review of Thompson, *Beyond the Frontier*, op. cit., 'Convenient Death of a Hero', *London Review of Books*, 8 May 1997, pp.12–13.

61 Trunski, *Grateful Bulgaria*, op. cit., p.52; Rattenbury, a family friend but not an eye-witness, believed that FT's Communism would have survived into peacetime: see 'Convenient Death of a Hero', op. cit.

62 FT, letter home, 18 December 1942.

63 To Catherine Nicholson.

64 One example: FT gave brilliant 'mess'-talks in 1943 on the history of the Balkans, on Beveridge, on the make-up of the German army, astonishing in their range and their grasp of detail. He knew of the liquidation of a million Jews also. When the 1940 Katyn massacre of Poles by Soviets was discovered in 1943, however, he refused to believe that this was not a Nazi crime.

65 Fellow-Wykehamist Tony Forster (telephone CWA, May 2000), who last saw him in Egypt in 1943, where Forster joined Phantom, never took him for a dogmatic Communist at all.

66 As Luisa Passerini has excellently observed, in *Europe in Love, Love in Europe* (London, 1999), p.314.

67 As the post-war show trials were to demonstrate.

68 Thompson, *Beyond the Frontier*, op. cit.

69 Rattenbury, 'Convenient Death of a Hero', op. cit. See also Trunski, *Grateful Bulgaria*, op. cit., p.50: the British feared arming a left-wing regime and so did not rush to aid the guerrillas. Basil Davidson (*Major Frank Thompson*, Bulgarian television, 1977), with SOE in Yugoslavia, also believed British support for SOE in Bulgaria equivocal, as Britain feared a non-bourgeois post-war government.

70 LTA, 2 February 1999: 'Of about a hundred SAS men taken prisoner in 1944, only six (of whom by a blind stroke of fortune I was one) ever returned.' See Chapter 8.

71 IM and PF probably did not regularly read the papers; PF believes they could not afford them. From IM's letters to DH it is clear that she learnt of FT's death shortly after 10 October.

72 Since the same source – Summers in 'The Lost Loves of Iris Murdoch', op. cit. – claims that IM 'lived for three years' with FBS, it cannot be accounted reliable. In October 1996 IM said to the author, 'I adored FT; we were to have been married.' She described him as burly and 'one who laughed a lot'.

73 Summers, 'The Lost Loves of Iris Murdoch', op. cit.

74 Misrecall: FT sighted IM in the autumn of 1938, but first spoke to her on 6 March 1939.

75 This was his name 'in the family'. He was Edward to non-family. IM put the name to use in *A Severed Head*, where Palmer Anderson is the villain, a borrowing E.P. took in good part.

76 Dorothy Thompson's recollection, December 1999.

77 To FT's biographer, Simon Kusseff.

78 And, around 1980, a fourth was mooted, by E.P. Thompson, MRDF and Anthony Forster together. This came to nothing.

79 IM to *The Times*, 27 August 1975.

80 To Sue Summers, 1993.

81 IM to *The Times*, 27 August 1975.

CHAPTER 8

1 E.P. Thompson, *Persons and Polemics* (London, 1994), pp.2–9.

2 J: 9 July 1976.

3 IM to LP, 16 May 1945.

4 Two weeks before his death Slavcho Trunski said the entry was made strictly 'under orders; they were partisans, and their job to fight'. FT's biographer Simon Kusseff points out that Apostolski, a leading Serbian partisan, was among those specifically warning FT against this move.

5 J: '. . . Burning-eyed, his torrent of restless talk, his undergraduate room, the way he rushed away suddenly nervously to get cigarettes, the way he made tea,

his pictures. A sort of resemblance in him to Frank.' Isaiah Berlin later recommended Kullman to the Royal College of Art.

6 Peter Wiles.

7 IM to Tony Forster.

8 IM to DH, September 1944.

9 JB, *Iris*, op. cit., p.24.

10 IM to RQ, 6 November 1947.

11 As, for example the revelation at the end of *An Unofficial Rose* that Miranda always loved Felix.

12 See Chapter 3.

13 To DH.

14 As Jenny Hartley points out in *Hearts Undefeated: Women's Writing of the Second World War* (London, 1994), p.2.

15 IM visited Hal Lidderdale's and John Willett's mothers – almost certainly others too, now lost to view.

16 To DH, 5 January 1946.

17 To DH, 20 May 1944.

18 Ken Kirk, active in the OULC with IM, LTA, 7 September 1998.

19 To DH, 12 December 1944.

20 'Wild' is JB's vicarious recall; 'adorable' IM's, in a letter to DH.

21 To DH, May 44.

22 Sister Marian, LTA, 18 January 1999: 'He pursued me relentlessly from 1936 when I came up until into the war.'

23 Ibid.

24 Written after DH's death on 5 November 1991 for a *Times* obituary, but never used, since Hal died two months later, on 20 January 1992.

25 Sixty years later David's sister Barbara Robbins had a dim recall of a girl with long, straight blonde hair.

26 IM, airgraph to LP, 8 February 1943.

27 To DH, 10 February 1945.

28 IM noted to DH on 4 February 1946: 'I get hypersensitive & worry if I'm "left out" of anything, just like I did at school – all very

infantile & interesting to observe.'

29 Ann Toulmin, CWA, 2 March 2000.

30 Hilda Foster in *A Fairly Honourable Defeat*, p.22.

31 28 February 1943.

32 Two letters, 16 and 24 September 1945.

33 'Being determined that immediately upon the liberation by the armed forces of the United Nations or as a consequence of retreat of the enemy, the population thereof shall receive aid and relief from their sufferings, food, clothing and shelter' (pamphlet published for the whole UN Information Organisation by HMSO, London, 1944).

34 Jo Grimond, *Memoirs* (London, 1979), pp.133–40.

35 The separation happened 'shortly after I wrote to you last', IM says in a letter dated 24 September 1944. The previous letter was started on 20 May and finished on 7 June.

36 Olivier Wormser, whom JB recalls as wanting to marry IM. When Wormser and his wife later visited Steeple Aston IM and JB were amused by Madame Wormser's question on seeing foxes in the garden: '*Est ce qu'ils sont dangereux?*' PF was asked out to Dorchester to meet Wormser in 1942–43: Wormser was a friend of Thomas Balogh's.

37 IM remarked to Ruth Kingsbury, 'He hurt me; I hurt him.'

38 Simon Kusseff dates this to between 7 and 10 June – see Chapter 7.

39 To Paddy O'Regan, undated, summer 1940.

40 To LP, 4 April 1945.

41 Date deduced from letter to DH. IM's UNRRA application form, held at the UN in New York, gives

June, but no date. She speaks of 'wangling' a job at UNRRA in earlier letters to DH.

42 An inability a later letter shows her as having rectified while staying in 1951 in Devon, too late for the post in question.

43 IM's account of UNRRA in the Bodleian Library, op. cit., is of interest despite occasional inaccuracies regarding dates and times. Her misrecall that she worked for UNRRA in London for only 'a few months' – it was fifteen – may relate to the fact that her time abroad was more rewarding. She further misremembers that she came back from Austria to go directly to Cambridge. This elides an entire year of depression and inactivity – 1946–47 – during which she was refused an American visa.

44 Letter to Noel Eldridge's twin sister Lilian, 1 December 1944. They had re-established contact through attending classes with the same Russian teacher.

45 17 June 1945.

46 Letter to Lilian Eldridge, 1 December 1944.

47 Three letters to DH: April 1942, January 1944, December 1944.

48 See Peter Davison (ed.), *The Complete Works of George Orwell* (London, 1998), 20 vols, item 2620: 'I am leaving . . . for Paris' (15 February 1945). Probably IM's friend John Fulton, then also with UNRRA, went to Paris; and it is possible that in this way she obtained RQ's *Pierrot mon ami*, to which she introduced PF.

49 Letter to DH, 10 February 1945.

50 The Nonsuch Bookshop in Cambridge has IM's copy, dated 19 January 1945, with some underlinings, of *An Introduction to Dilthey* by H.A. Hodges.

51 Partly to learn Greek on what might now be called a philosophy junior research fellowship, though teaching philosophy began soon after. 'Can you teach economics as well?' asked Janet Vaughan. 'No!' said PF. IM, from her letter to DH, appears wrongly to have thought that PF's post was publicly advertised.

52 To DH.

53 To DH.

54 IM to DH, 11 November 1945 (i.e. Pen Tower, then Gatty, later Balogh).

55 To DH, 8 March 1945.

56 She had been staying the previous weekend with Vera Crane in Leighton Buzzard. They came down to London for the celebrations of Tuesday, 8 May.

57 PF recalls that a single picture only in the whole gallery would be on show for weeks. She and one Goya got to know each other well.

58 1 June 1945.

59 MM hazards the guess that this may have been late in the war, perhaps after IM had learnt more at UNRRA about the 1940 Soviet acquisition of the Baltic states, IM's irritation with an anti-Yalta Pole in March 1945 notwithstanding. IM mentions the shift in a letter to E.P. Thompson, c December 1945.

60 To LP, 16 June 1945.

61 Arthur Koestler, *The Yogi and the Commissar* (London, 1945), p.7.

62 To DH, 1 June 1945.

63 Frances Stewart, LTA, 6 January 2000.

64 IM, *Sartre: Romantic Rationalist* (Cambridge, 1953), p.76.

65 To DH, 24 September 1944.

66 To E.P. Thompson, November 1945.

67 To DH, 27 July 1945.

68 J: 5 August 1945.

69 Marion Bosanquet believes she moved into Seaforth in August 1945.

70 To LP, 4 September 1945.

71 6 November 1945.

72 CWA. She kept a key and even used the flat occasionally, e.g. on Hijab's last night before his sailing to Port Said in the summer of 1948, when it seems the flat was sub-let to Ruth Kingsbury and her future husband William Mills.

73 To DH, January 1944. Also to Jeffrey Meyers, 'The Art of Fiction cxvii: Iris Murdoch', *Paris Review* 115, 1990, p.209.

74 IM to Hal Lidderdale, 6 November 1945: 'It was so very good to see you in Brussels.' To LP she wrote of the meeting with Hal as recent on 30 October 1945. An Italian song copied into the end of a poetry journal is inscribed 'Haaltert [a town near Brussels] Hal & Marie Sep 8 1945', the probable date of that meeting.

75 *The Sea, The Sea*, p.64.

76 Doris Lessing, *Walking in the Shade* (London, 1997). The passage continues: 'And there was another emotion, too, among women. Frenchmen loved women and showed it . . . adorable France, which loves its women and gives them confidence in their feminity.'

77 To DH, March 1945.

78 16 September 1945.

79 13 May 1945.

80 4 October 1945.

81 4 December 1945.

82 10 October 1945.

83 16 September 1945.

84 10 October 1945.

85 'He was rather standoffish': Bodleian Library, op. cit., p.13. Since DH was 'crazy about the Marx brothers', according to his son Tom, IM's meeting Chico would presumably have given him pleasure.

86 Unpublished interview with RW, 17 July 1991.

87 6 November 1945.

88 3 November 1945.

89 To LP, 30 October 1945.

90 Letter to Mrs Theo (short for Theodosia) Thompson, 21 November 1945.

91 Letter to Paddy O'Regan from Cavendish Road, c1940.

92 Letter to MB from 9 Waller Avenue, 13 November 1943.

93 Bernanos, *Journal d'un curé de campagne* (1936, translated 1954); 'through his self-sacrifice [he] brings Christ's redemption to enslaved souls'. Bernanos's theme is 'the strife between good and evil, fought in the souls of a saintly elect'. *Penguin Dictionary of European Writers* (1969), pp.106–7.

94 PF asked IM one afternoon why she did not approach Donald MacKinnon with some problem. IM silently changed the subject: 'Look at that aeroplane up there!' PF dates this to before September 1943. In her letter to DH, 11 November 1945, IM reports that she has not seen MacKinnon 'for 2 years', but that MacKinnon must know the 'outline of the events that followed' through, for example, MRDF. To RQ, 21 April 1946: 'I have not seen [MacKinnon] for 2 years.'

95 In *The Sovereignty of Good*.

96 IM interview with Laura Cecil, 'How to write a Novel', *Cover* magazine, Oxford, issue 4, March 1968, pp.9–10.

97 Pat and Andrew in *The Red and the Green*; Pip and Max in *The Unicorn*.

98 LTA, 8 February 2000.

99 To DH, 11 November 1945.

100 5 December 1945 and 13 January 1946.

101 7 January 1944.

102 1 December 1945.

103 5 January 1946.

104 To Harry Weinberger, 9 June 1992.

105 The postcard of Berchtesgaden she sent home on 22 December

1945 bears only the legend, 'And I have been here too!'

106 To Harry Weinberger, 3 December 1981.

107 Interview in *The Radical Imagination and the Liberal Tradition: Interviews with English and American Novelists*, ed. H. Ziegler and C.W.E. Bigsby (London, 1982), pp.209–30.

108 Anne Valery, ex-Badmintonian, was around 1944 a co-denizen of Fitzrovia, and saw IM looking both 'very glamorous' with her long blonde hair, and very well-turned out, in a French restaurant in London.

109 Diary reference of Harry Brumfitt, fellow-OULC campaigner, then at Queen's reading French, 1942.

110 Undated, probably c1950; and 24 June 1952.

111 She wrote that she had known quite well three young people who became seriously 'depressed ['that mysterious soul-ailment so many seem to have now'] and killed themselves – one was Caspar, son of Ian Fleming, handsome, rich, clever &tc &tc but just did not want to live. The determination to go was in all the three cases, very very deep.'

112 Letter to IM, 12 April 1977.

113 Inferences: she had two catalogues for 'An Illustrated Souvenir of the Exhibition of Persian Art', one probably given her by MRDF, whose first initial she wrote into it, together with 'London February 4th 1944'. Her Russian notebooks survive and are dated.

114 20 May 1944.

115 February 1945.

116 31 December 1945.

CHAPTER 9

1 28 February 1946.

2 Copied into a 1994 journal, ascribed an original date of 25 April 1946 (but 1947 is more likely, since it was originally written in Paris).

3 See Chapter 8, n48.

4 On 11 April 1946 IM wrote to RQ: '*J'ai fait une traduction quelconque des premières 25 pages de Pierrot. Beaucoup de lacunes: et je dois réviser la chose deux, trois, dix fois. Je vous l'enverrai en quinze jours peut-être. Je ne m'presse pas (et je manque de temps d'ailleurs). Mélange de joie et de désespoir. Le premier provient de votre style, et son reflet (même pauvre) en anglais (oui, c'est un travail passionnant que la traduction). En effet, c'est pas facile . . . C'est des choses très simples, des riens d'argot, que je trouve difficile.*'

5 *New York Times*, Living Arts section, 22 February 1990, p.B2: 'He would never speak English with me.'

6 Olivier Todd, CWA, 26 October 1999: 'an awful accent!' Kreisel and Harry Weinberger believed her spoken German poor.

7 He translated into French Amos Tutuola's *The Palm-Wine Drinkard* [*sic*].

8 See *New York Times*, Living Arts section, 22 February 1990.

9 e.g. Henri Calet (1904–56).

10 *The Quest for Queneau*, BBC Radio 3, 11 October 1985.

11 Asa Briggs, CWA, March 1998: 'They were friends, not lovers.' RQ's biographer Michel Lecureur's view also.

12 J: 12 July 1947: IM admires 'that vertiginous heart-breaking absurdity which Queneau achieves by his ambiguous serio-comic play. Oh oh I wish I could write like that.'

13 Letter to Walter Redfern, 14 March 1979.

14 28 February 1946.

15 14 January 1954.

16 To DH, 25 January 1946.

17 G. Woodbridge (ed.), *The History*

of UNRRA (New York, 1950), vol. II, p.320.

18 To LP, 4 March 1946.

19 'John Haffenden Talks to Iris Murdoch', op. cit.

20 She was giving him help in collecting material for the commemorative *There is a Spirit in Europe*, op. cit.

21 Undated, but probably late February 1946.

22 Possibly after Klagenfurt; IM's letter to PF in late March makes no mention of Puch. The exact sequence is unclear.

23 Richard Symonds, 'Amiable Despair: UNRRA in Austria', Bodleian MSS.Eng 4703, UN Careers Records Project, Chapter 2.

24 Woodbridge, *The History of UNRRA*, op. cit., p.306.

25 To LP, 4 March 1946.

26 Woodbridge, *The History of UNRRA*, op. cit., vol. 2, p.504.

27 Her position there is given in the 'UNRRA Austrian Mission Directory of Personnel' as 'Registrar'.

28 To MB, 17 April 1946.

29 Symonds, 'Amiable Despair', op. cit., *passim*.

30 J: 20 May 1978.

31 *The Sandcastle*, p.251.

32 J: 23 May 1978.

33 Her time there was further shortened by a brief period of leave in mid-May in Venice and Florence. Source: postcard home. John Corsellis recalls that UNRRA personnel such as IM were sometimes given a vehicle and driver when on leave.

34 BBC European Productions, *Meeting Writers*, no. 5, ref. no. 4222, 4 February 1957.

35 Interview with Susan Hill, *Bookshelf*, BBC Radio 4, 30 April 1982.

36 Michael Ignatieff on M. Djilas, *Fall of the New Class, New York Review of Books*, 4 March 1999, p.29.

37 Nigel Nicolson, *Long Life: A Memoir* (London, 1997), p.116.

38 Documented in John Corsellis, *Slovenian Phoenix* (forthcoming). See also Nikolai Tolstoi, *The Minister and the Massacres* (London, 1986; subsequently withdrawn from circulation after legal proceedings); and Nicolson, *Long Life*, op. cit., Chapter 5, 'The Witness'.

39 See Gitta Sereny, *The German Trauma* (London, 2000), p.359.

40 Carinthia had been claimed in 1945 as sovereign territory by Tito's partisans, who posted proclamations on public buildings; after the repatriations such claims seem to have been dropped.

41 Nicolson, *Long Life*, op. cit., p.123.

42 The exception was Hochsteingasse, reserved for students at Graz University.

43 See Corsellis, *Slovenian Phoenix*, op. cit, Introduction.

44 J: 1947.

45 See e.g. Nikolai Tolstoi, *Victims of Yalta* (London, 1977), p.468n, dealing with the Kempten incident in Bavaria, in the American Zone.

46 To MB, 17 April 1946.

47 Dr Edgar Chandler, *The High Tower of Refuge: The Inspiring Story of Refugee Relief Throughout the World* (London, 1959), Acknowledgements.

48 See Bodleian Library, op. cit., for IM's recall. In interview with John Corsellis c 1979 Jaboor said 'emphatically that Iris's role . . . was a very junior one'. Her grade on her letter of resignation is Grade 7, her position Admin Assistant.

49 On 28 June 1946.

50 From FBS's journal.

51 To LP, 17 June 1945, from Seaforth.

52 To PF, 27 March 1946.

53 5 September 1946.

54 Letter to RQ.

55 'It's still there. I have to ask for a waiver if I want to come to the United States,' Meyers, 'The Art of Fiction, op. cit.; see also unpublished interview with RW, 17 July 1991. IM spoke resentfully of the ban in 1997. Source for Gaitskell's involvement: Denis Healey.

56 IM to Hal Lidderdale, 6 September 1946.

57 To PF, 30 May 1947.

58 Cheryl Bove, 'America and Americans in Iris Murdoch's Novels', in R. Todd (ed.), *Encounters with Iris Murdoch* (Amsterdam, 1988), pp.69–78, a paper to which IM responded, 'I love America . . .'.

59 *A Fairly Honourable Defeat* and *Nuns and Soldiers*.

60 For example Henry in *Henry and Cato*, or Christian in *The Black Prince*.

61 Two letters to Harry Weinberger, 2 May 1978 and 26 March 1984.

62 J: 19 November 1989.

63 Letter to RQ, 20 July 1948.

64 Undated letter to PF, but before September 1947.

65 Both Jančar and Kenneth Robinson thought IM in this decade torn between ancient CP sympathies and Anglo-Catholicism, though Robinson is unaware of the latter.

66 15 September 1946.

67 His letters are mentioned in Dame Magdalen Mary's day-books first in 1946, again in 1947, and several times in 1948. He wrote in 1946, probably to ask for the nuns' prayers, and Dame Magdalen Mary's warm personality led to a continuance of the correspondence.

68 Lois MacKinnon, LTA, 24 September 1999.

69 Around 1980.

70 Not always at the same house: they rented more than one.

71 Sybil Livingston, LTA. Sybil herself does not recall this.

72 J: 10 June 1985.

73 Thus IM wrote to her second cousin Max Wright, ex-Brethren, in 1990.

74 Sybil Livingston dates this possibly to before the war, which Margaret Lintott finds inconceivable: when Margaret left Badminton, a year before IM did, IM was non-religious. If the episode was indeed in 1938–39, then James Scott's influence may lie behind it – he was in the process of moving towards Catholicism. Margaret Stanier's story of IM knocking on the door of St Aloysius in 1938–39 and finding it closed also suggests a mind not entirely closed to religion.

75 Undated, but from 1940.

76 CWA, from a conference on Literature and Theology at Durham University, autumn 1984.

77 Letters 9 January 1998, 18 February 1999.

78 EM, p.153.

79 J: 5 April 1947.

80 September 1946.

81 As her 11 November 1945 letter to DH makes plain.

82 Undated but probably c15–20 October 1946.

83 Undated letter to Paddy O'Regan, probably summer 1940.

84 Undated, but probably January 1947.

85 To RQ, 7 August 1946.

86 To DH, 16 September 1946.

87 To PF. It is cold and end of term, so either December 1946 or March 1947.

88 To DH, September 1946.

89 Unpublished interview with RW, 17 July 1991.

90 Postcard in album dated 18 February 1947.

91 Evidence: correspondence with RQ.

92 She told DM that RQ – 'the bloody fool' – had given her a small scar when opening the boot of his car to insert her luggage and colliding the boot and her forehead.

93 Letter to DM, June 1964, in which she claimed not to know Soho striptease, though LP had taken her, at her request, to one 'joint' c1946. Probably she had forgotten this when she wrote in 1964.

94 Letter to DM, June 1964.

95 (1922–1994). Also actor, composer, singer, painter.

96 Jonathan Cecil, CWA.

97 JB, CWA.

98 J: 23 September 1947.

99 Although their reading knowledge was good, Lois taught Heinz Cassirer and Friedrich Waissman spoken English.

100 J: 28 February 1947.

101 See, for example, his strange observations in 'Moral Objections', from *Objections to Christian Belief* (London, 1963), introduction by A.R. Vidler, on the 'woman of affairs who eggs on a tired middle-aged husband to rejuvenate himself by sexual adventure', pp.11–34.

102 Lois MacKinnon, LTA.

103 Mark, xvi, 9.

104 Letter to DH, November 1945.

105 To Vera Crane.

106 In 'Intercommunion: A Comment', collected in Donald MacKinnon, *The Stripping of the Altars* (London, 1969), he makes clear his move away from the Anglo-Catholicism that marked him in the 1930s.

107 Interview in Ziegler and Bigsby (eds), *The Radical Imagination and the Liberal Tradition*, op. cit.

108 *The Sandcastle*, p.77.

109 15 April 1947.

110 6 May 1947.

111 Donald MacKinnon to PF, 30 December 1948.

112 J: 12 June 1947. IM also used the identical phrase to PF: see p.269.

113 J: 15 August 1947.

114 J: 15 April 1947.

115 IM to PF, c13 September 1947.

116 J: 31 July 1947; also undated letter to PF.

117 To PF, August 1947.

118 E.P. Thompson had stayed in the Balkans with his future wife Dorothy Sale, helping the Yugoslavs build the Samac–Sarajevo railway.

119 J: 13 August 1947 mentions the Bledlow visit. Evidence for disapproval: Dorothy Thompson's reminiscence. Theo, a 'Daughter of the American Revolution', was socially ambitious for her sons, and hoped they would marry 'up'. Dorothy says she was, towards her, like the mother-in-law in *The Sovereignty of Good*.

120 *Major Frank Thompson*, Bulgarian television, 1977. The inspiration for the ceremony came from Robert Conquest, press attaché to the Allied Control Commission in Bulgaria, 1944–47.

121 A J reference of IM's states that the volume of Catullus from which she has quoted bears FT's name.

122 J suggests 4–8 October as the date of her arrival in Cambridge.

123 IM's copy, in French, of Simone Weil's *The Need for Roots* bears the publication date 1949.

124 For a discussion of this indebtedness see Peter J. Conradi, *The Saint and the Artist: A Study of the Fiction of Iris Murdoch* (third edition, London, 2001).

125 23 September 1951.

126 Simone Weil, *Intuitions Pré-Chrétiennes* (Paris, 1951), p.21.

CHAPTER 10

1 Women were first permitted to graduate from Cambridge only in 1948.

2 LTA, 9 January 1999.

3 He returned to act as clerk to a refugee council in Nablus; then, once Nablus was absorbed into Jordan, taught in Syria and, after gaining a Ph.D. in Mathematics from Gainesville, Florida, the American University in Beirut; then worked for Unesco, emigrating to the USA c1981.

4 'Her attention moved during the year from Hijab to Shah.' Hijab, CWA, February 2000.

5 Peter Geach (ed.), *Wittgenstein's Lectures on Philosophical Psychology*, (London and New York, 1988).

6 J: 29 April 1968.

7 In her unpublished Heidegger book (1993) IM claimed that Wisdom (not Broad) was her supervisor. Broad was later attacked by Donald MacKinnon for believing that moral philosophy could be studied 'in gentlemanly detachment from the agonising choices and dilemmas of the practical moralist': Christopher Stead, obituary of Donald MacKinnon, *Guardian*, 5 March 1994. This suggests one motive for IM's move. Another was Wisdom's greater closeness to Wittgenstein.

8 Letter to RQ, 14 October 1947.

9 Letter to PF, 24 April 1948.

10 Wasfi Hijab, CWA, 13 February 2000.

11 'Some Hitherto Unpublished Letters from Ludwig Wittgenstein to Georg Henrik von Wright', *Cambridge Review*, vol. 104, no. 2273, 28 February 1983, p.57.

12 CWA.

13 Unpublished interview with RW, 17 July 1991.

14 Stephen Toulmin, LTA, February

2000; and interview with Wasfi Hijab, 13 February 2000.

15 Wasfi Hijab, e-mail to author, 9 March 2000.

16 Wasfi Hijab, e-mail to author, March 2000.

17 Ludwig Wittgenstein, ed. B. McGuinness and G.H. von Wright, *Cambridge Letters* (Oxford, 1995), p.305.

18 6 November 1947.

19 So she told Sir John Vinelott in 1993. See also Jeffrey Meyers, *Privileged Moments: Encounters with Writers* (Wisconsin, 2000).

20 29 January 1968.

21 In April 1948.

22 A holiday during which they were obliged once, for want of better accommodation, to spend the night in a ruined Wessex cottage; they were mainly friends, not lovers.

23 25 March 1977.

24 3 November 1947.

25 See P. Odifreddi's celebratory *Kreiseliana: About and Around Georg Kreisel* (Wellesley, 1996), *passim*.

26 See JB, *Iris*, op. cit.

27 Odifreddi, *Kreiseliana*, op. cit., pp.12, 20.

28 Wasfi Hijab, CWA, 13 February 2000.

29 Kreisel, CWA, 4 March 1998.

30 So she vouchsafed to Sir John Vinelott when she gave a talk in 1993 at Gray's Inn, of which he was then Treasurer.

31 B. MacGuiness, *Wittgenstein, A Life: Young Ludwig (1889–1921)* (London, 1988), p.131.

32 Kreisel, CWA, 4 March 1998.

33 Ved Mehta, *The Fly and the Flybottle* (Harmondsworth, 1963), p.52.

34 J: 25 July 1947.

35 Peter Strawson, CWA, 11 March 1999. That IM continued in this belief, found strange by PF, is shown by Chapter 9 of *Metaphysics as a Guide to Morals* (London, 1992), entitled 'Wittgenstein and the Inner Life'. See also Fergus

Kerr in *Iris Murdoch Newsletter*, no. 14, autumn 2000, *passim*.

36 J: 10 November 1947.

37 J: 4 November 1947.

38 J: 17 November 1947.

39 A letter to Michael Hamburger (at the Brotherton Library, Leeds University) makes this clear. On a draft for Book 2, Chapter 10 of *A Fairly Honourable Defeat*, IM wrote in the margin: 'make more Kafkaesque'.

40 *Sartre*, pp.48–9.

41 J: 6 March 1948.

42 Wasfi Hijab in February 2000 remembered only IM's excellent literary style, and had no recall of having walked out, an idea the cruelty of which distressed him.

43 J: 19 October 1947.

44 To PF, June 1947.

45 To PF, July 1947.

46 When IM was writing her monograph, Olivier Todd, who knew Sartre well through his first father-in-law Paul Nizan, asked Sartre – not known for anglophilia – whether he wished to meet IM. 'No,' he replied

47 *Sartre* (second edition, London, 1987), Chapter 1.

48 To RQ, 5 October 1947.

49 J: 1 March 1948. IM notes an asymmetry between first and third persons in both Sartre's and Wittgenstein's treatment of emotions.

50 *Sartre* (second edition), Introduction.

51 Hence her re-interpretation of *Angst*: the fear, not of freedom, but of unfreedom. See EM, *passim*.

52 See 'Existentialists and Mystics', EM, pp.221–34. The fact that the 'mystical' heroine Simone Weil is also a heroine to Existentialists, as IM notes (p.157), complicates the dualism.

53 15 and 22 October. The venue is not named in IM's journal notes. Milein Cosman attended a talk given by her in that church at around this time.

54 To RQ, 9 July 1946.

55 J: 1947, no further date.

56 *Sartre*, pp.78–9.

57 Warnock, *A Memoir*, op. cit., p.93.

58 EM, p.59 *et seq*.

59 22 March 1950, in Reading archive. Senhouse wrote, as a translator of de Beauvoir, to thank IM for her broadcast *The Existentialist Hero*.

60 To RQ, 27 February 1949.

61 23 March 1954.

62 25 July 1947.

63 13 May 1953.

64 e.g. to DH, October 1945.

65 J: 17 October 1947.

66 J: 24 October 1947.

67 'Communism': an address given at a Conference of Clergy and Youth Leaders in Carmarthen, 18 April 1950, under the auspices of the Provincial Youth Council of the Church of Wales.

68 Letter to PF, 24 April 1948.

69 Adam Phillips, *On Flirtation* (London, 1994), p.xvii.

70 Letter to LP, August 1946.

71 Todd read Moral Sciences at Corpus, Cambridge, 1947–49.

72 19 April 1956.

73 Foster, *W.B. Yeats, Vol. 1*, op. cit., p.27.

74 Letter to DM, May 1964.

75 J: 12 December 1948.

76 J: 26 November 1958.

77 Daphne Williamson, a student of Anscombe's, quoted Mrs Tinckham as sitting like a serene Buddha, wreathed in tobacco smoke and surrounded by cats: Anscombe didn't have cats, but did have lots of children, went in for long silences, had a serene face, and sat in tutorials wreathed in smoke. Williamson had mentioned the resemblance to a fellow-student who shared the recognition.

78 Chapter 5.

79 Yorick's wife Polly Smythies believed that Anscombe, devoutly

Catholic, had fallen in love with IM.

80 Elizabeth Anscombe, CWA, 17 April 1998.

81 Undated letter, 'August', probably 1959.

82 For a fuller account of such figures within the novels see Peter J. Conradi, 'The Metaphysical Hostess', *English Literary History*, xlviii, summer 1981, pp.427–53.

83 *Nuns and Soldiers*, pp.60–1.

84 *The Good Apprentice*, p.50 (my emphasis).

85 Harriet in *The Sacred and Profane Love Machine*, p.228.

86 Stuart in *The Good Apprentice*; interview with Pamela Callaghan, *Weekend*, BBC Radio 4, 18 April 1982; interview with Susan Hill, *Bookshelf*, BBC Radio 4, 30 April 1982.

87 Letter to DM.

CHAPTER 11

1 To RQ, 22 October 1948.

2 As a flurry of anxious letters from IM shows.

3 On 22 July she writes, protesting too much, apologising for her 'nerves of the day before. It will be pure joy to be so near to you. I feel less & less fear & more & more joy.'

4 MRDF, CWA, 9 February 1998.

5 Humphrey Carpenter, *The Envy of the World: Fifty Years of the BBC Third Programme and Radio 3, 1946–96* (London, 1996), p.111 *et seq.*

6 See EM, pp.108–15.

7 Ibid, pp.151–3.

8 Ibid, p.115.

9 Anne Robson, LTA, June 1999.

10 Hart, *Ask me no More*, op. cit., Chapter 9.

11 Marjorie Reeves, CWA.

12 'Just to ask my eternally recurring question, whether you would like to be Principal of St Anne's?' IM, letter-card to Jane Lidderdale, date unreadable, but the stamp bears

the head of Elizabeth II, hence 1953.

13 On 27 January 1953.

14 Janet Adam Smith, telephone CWA, January 1998.

15 This view was shared by JB and Marjorie Reeves – that Plumer was strict, disliking all liaisons, while Lady Ogilvie was more liberal.

16 Active in education, wife to Vice Chancellor of Belfast University and to Principal of Jesus College. Widowed c1948.

17 See JB, *Iris*, op. cit., *passim*. Also Mary Warnock, LTA, 4 July 1999, confirming this adoration, which Jennifer Hart and Rachel Trickett attested.

18 e.g. Anne Brumfitt.

19 IM changed Ann Venables's life in 1948. Rejected by Lady Margaret Hall for medicine, and wanting to be a psychologist, IM took her in to do PPE, changing to PPP in her second year. IM started probing, wanting to know what made her 'tick'. Venables remembers IM as an excellent moral tutor, and very easy to talk to. IM went to her wedding.

20 Learning of this, IM invited Levinson for a drink; friendship followed.

21 Anne Robson, CWA. Robson's friend Josephine Boulding crossed the Parks in Trinity term 1952, so the lover was almost certainly FBS.

22 Julian Chrysostomides.

23 From 58 Park Town (end of 1951 to 1952), King Edward Street, June 1953. A letter of 10 January 1950 to MB mentions another 'impending *crise de logement*'. And to RQ, 20 January 1950: address given as Musgrave House, St Anne's, as 'I'll be leaving Museum Rd.'.

24 Katrin Fitzherbert, *True to Both my Selves* (London, 1997), p.281.

25 Other 'Dancing Economist' parties were given by Teddy Hall,

subsequently Professor of Archaeology who studied the Turin shroud; by Dick Sargent, wealthy Worcester economist; and by Nicholas (finance correspondent of *Spectator*) and Audrey Davenport. Asa Briggs, CWA.

26 Hart, *Ask me no More*, op. cit., p.147.

27 Ian Little, CWA, 27 April 1998.

28 Warnock, *A Memoir*, op. cit., p.159.

29 Asa Briggs, CWA, 13 March 1998.

30 Dan Davin, *Closing Times* (London, 1975), p.108.

31 The two had not met in 1944 when the novel appeared. See Maclaren-Ross, *Memoirs of the Forties*, op. cit., p.191.

32 Wendy Campbell-Purdie and Fenner Brockway, *Women Against the Desert*, with Forewords by IM and Lord Boyd Orr (London, 1967), pp.11–13.

33 For reading Starkie's *Rimbaud*; see J: 10 November 1947.

34 Davin, *Closing Times*, op. cit., p.65.

35 Rosemary Cramp (who did wear gloves), CWA.

36 Mary Douglas saw her thus in about 1948. CWA, 11 February 2000

37 Mehta, *The Fly and the Flybottle*, op. cit., p.50.

38 *Potnia dendropuleia, potnia theeron.*

39 So Elizabeth Sewell recalls IM telling her; the Greek wording suggests Artemis.

40 22 October 1948.

41 IM to RQ, 27 February 1949.

42 e.g to Betsy Barnard, Rosemary Warhurst, Mother Grant.

43 Jennifer Dawson, obituary in *The Ship* (year-book of the St Anne's College Association of Senior Members), 1999.

44 Lively was interviewed by IM, who asked, 'What were you reading on the train here?' ('Hemingway, fortunately!') but was never taught by her.

45 See also discussion between IM and Mother Grant written into J 1992–

96, p.9, dated 30 November, probably 1948.

46 Thus her 1993 journal, p.11. And Mother Grant, telephone CWA, 21 June 1999.

47 Mother Grant, LTA, 1998.

48 Echoed by Harry Weinberger, May 2000.

49 Letter to JB, 20 July 1999.

50 Warnock, *A Memoir*, op cit., p.19.

51 Ibid, Chapter 2.

52 In *The Sovereignty of Good.*

53 Stuart Hampshire, CWA, 18 March 1998.

54 IM reviewed Gellner's *Words and Things* in the *Observer*, 29 November 1959. See Mehta, *The Fly and the Flybottle*, op. cit., Chapter 1.

55 Ryle in 1948 had instituted a popular and important new postgraduate degree in philosophy, the B. Phil.

56 Williams acknowledges IM as a Wittgensteinian influence in *Ethics and the Limits of Philosophy* (Collins, 1985), Chapter 8, n5.

57 Cora Diamond, *The Realistic Spirit: Wittgenstein, Philosophy, and the Mind* (Boston, 1991), Chapter 11.

58 Mark Platts, *Ways of Meaning* (London, 1979), p.262, n6.

59 John McDowell, LTA, and *Mind, Value and Reality* (Harvard, 1999).

60 Michael Dummett felt Ryle would speak dismissively and was a source of narrowness, a view with which not all concur.

61 Ryle, interested in German phenomenology in the 1920s, had reviewed it when it first appeared.

62 S. Aldwinckle, *Christ's Shadow in Plato's Cave: A Meditation on the Substance of Love* (Amate Press, Oxford, 1990), Foreword by IM.

63 On 17 November 1950. IM's paper does not appear to have survived.

64 To David Pears, CWA, 8 July 1998.

65 Rev. Professor Christopher Stead, LTA, 11 March 1999.

66 David Pears, CWA, 8 July 1998. Compare IM's journal reference:

'At a wonderful St. Antony's ox-roasting in June 1953, [Ayer] was short and rude to me as usual. Then stared at me a lot as we danced. I felt his great sexual magnetism.'

67 See also her essays 'Thinking and Language', 'Metaphysics and Ethics' and 'Vision and Choice in Morality' (EM, pp.31–76).

68 David Pears, CWA, 8 July 1998.

69 Dennis Nineham, CWA.

70 Ibid.

71 To Dennis Nineham.

72 Basil Mitchell, in *Philosophers who Believe: The Spiritual Journeys of Eleven Leading Thinkers*, ed. J.K. Clark (Intervarsity Press, 1993), recalled her presence: p.42.

73 Basil Mitchell confirms that this was a meeting of the Metaphysicals, these being all core members; CWA, 23 June 1999.

74 The group went on until Basil Mitchell's retirement in 1984. John Lucas, visiting Mitchell in June 1999, came up in Michaelmas 1953 to a Fellowship at Merton and confirms that IM was present at at least one meeting – so it was probably in late 1953 or early 1954 that she left.

75 Clark, *Philosophers who Believe*, op. cit., p.43.

76 Robin Waterfield, in an introduction to the Delos Press's 1989 edition of IM's 'The Existentialist Political Myth', says that this was the talk IM gave for the Socratic Club during Hilary term 1952, her respondent being Dr Eric Mascall.

77 Aldwinckle, *Christ's Shadow in Plato's Cave*, op. cit., p.10.

78 In *Metaphysics and the Philosophy of Mind* (Minneapolis, 1981), p.x, Anscombe gives a milder account of this famous confrontation.

79 As Ryle pointed out; see Mitchell in Clark, *Philosophers who Believe*, op. cit., p.2.

80 November 1942.

81 Compare Julian Chrysostomides's Professor Joan Hussey, who spoke around 1956 of IM's simplicity and unspoiltness, and how rare both are, observing something IM was never to lose.

82 Frances Partridge, *Memories* (London, 1981), p.87.

83 To RQ, 17 November 1949.

84 Sources: John Simopoulos, CWA; and J.

85 Jean Floud, CWA, 16 March 1999: Lichtheim (c1913–73) killed himself 'after feeling inferior to Habermas with whom he had been staying'.

86 Later married to the philosopher Sarah Waterlow, he recalled IM with great affection in two telephone calls in 1999.

87 LP recalled that IM and Hal were at some point engaged.

88 J: 30 June 1954: 'I am terribly to blame for all this duplicity. (I feel this when it is being unsuccessful.)'

89 Hart, *Ask me no More*, op. cit., p.126; and CWA.

90 Jennifer Dawson's recollection of tutorials in *The Ship*, op. cit.

91 Anthony Quinton, CWA.

92 Robson's future wife Anne Moses, approaching his room in the back quad at Lincoln when he had just received IM's letter breaking off the relationship, heard what she thought was quarrelling and shouting. Passionately angry, Robson explained to her that he and IM had been seriously committed to each other, but that IM had been unfaithful to him with 'a Hungarian' who had just died (see Chapter 12). He had written asking her to return to him, but had been refused.

93 *A Severed Head*, Chapter 19.

94 J: November 1953.

95 Momigliano's diary notes, in Italian, were returned to IM after his death by his wife.

96 J: 18 January 1953.
97 Possible misrecall: DH's letter jilting her arrived on 18 February 1946.
98 See Graham Lord, *Just the One: The Wives and Times of Jeffrey Bernard, 1932–97* (London, 1997), pp.86, 329.

CHAPTER 12

1 Postcard to her parents, probably 20 September 1951.
2 Letter to DH; and letter from Arnoldo Momigliano.
3 Oddly enough Milein Cosman, who drew IM c1940, believes she may have sketched FBS at Somerville on some open occasion in 1941, only later learning his identity.
4 He wrote to Isabella von Miller-Aichholz on 11 February 1951, and to EC on 2 December 1951, that he still lived in 'enforced, degrading solitude'.
5 Copied by IM into J, January 1994, with no indication when this letter was written to her.
6 Possibly he and IM had been introduced through the anthropologist Godfrey Lienhardt, who had also studied English under Leavis and who certainly by 1966, if not before, knew Wallace Robson (both are shown serving on the board of the *Oxford Review* in that year). See also Srinivas in *Orientpolitik, Value, and Civilisation: Franz Baermann Steiner, Selected Writings, Vol. II*, ed. Jeremy Adler and Richard Fardon (Oxford and New York, 1999).
7 Summers, 'The Lost Loves of Iris Murdoch', op. cit.
8 *Taboo, Truth and Religion: Franz Baermann Steiner, Selected Writings Vol. I*, ed. Jeremy Adler and Richard Fardon (Oxford and New York, 1999), p.40.
9 As Adler saw.
10 Peter Rickman of City University,

who knew FBS's parents in Prague, the father with a limp and a dry sardonic wit, recalled that FBS before 1943 was sexually highly promiscuous. CWA, 11 February 2000.
11 David Wright, 'Franz Steiner Remembered'.
12 Mary Douglas, CWA, 11 February 2000. Leach's tale is told in his preface to *Political Systems of Highland Burma* (Athlone, 1971).
13 Srinivas's journal, 15 June 1945.
14 Michael Hamburger, *A Mug's Game: Intermittent Memoirs* (London, 1975), p.187.
15 *Taboo* (London, 1956), with a preface by E.E. Evans-Pritchard.
16 Helga Mackie, CWA.
17 Mary Douglas, in 'Franz Baermann Steiner Celebrated: From Prague Poet to Oxford Anthropologist, a Workshop', at the Institute of Germanic Studies, London, 11 February 2000.
18 On 19 March 1939.
19 The friend was Anne Hamburger, wife of the poet Michael.
20 A later journal vouchsafes this. Also Momigliano's diary for August 1952 where he is jealous when IM, in Rome with him, writes to FBS in Spain.
21 See Chapter 11.
22 They were walking also with the psychiatrist Paul Senft, who later worked with R.D. Laing and with Foucault.
23 This must be a first draft, since the second was started only on 18 July 1952, three months before FBS's return.
24 This was also six days after his birthday.
25 From 18 October until 18 November 1952.
26 FBS regarded the picture of Balogh as an ill omen. IM's journal, by contrast, makes her sound somewhat recovered. Sitting with Nickie Kaldor at the Mill pub in

Cambridge and looking at the ducks in October 1947, she recorded a sudden liberation. On 11 February 1952, a day full of activity, 'in a crazy state of mind' IM had gone 'chez the Alohgs (why have I forgotten how to spell Thomas's name?)' to pick his wife Pen up to go to a psychoanalytic group. 'It was off – stayed & talked with Pen and Thomas till 9.30, indifferently. T. took me back in the car. No communication. Sad. I took his hand as I got out. No response.'

27 Jeremy Adler however, in 'Franz Baermann Steiner Celebrated', op. cit., reported a letter from FBS to EC envisaging in detail the consequences of FBS's marrying 'out'.

28 '*Junges Weib in Spiegel*' and FBS's '*Bild einer Heimkehr*'.

29 Jeremy Adler, CWA, 11 September 1997.

30 In London, two hours before his departure from England, they had bought a delightful rattle on which little birds were moving to and fro. The toy rattled away as they walked to a restaurant, *en route* to the station. 'It was if there were three of us, also as if we had been given an omen and a fertility symbol. Our present to this Spanish child, which was a stranger to us, made us feel married, as we had never felt before. And now the child is dead' (FBS's journal, 11 November 1952).

31 Also: 'What is Canetti-like in me, is how again and again, he transforms himself into the beloved. As with Canetti, no love without transformation' (FBS's journal, 12 November 1952).

32 Compare 'A highly interesting conversation [not with IM] about Jewish mysticism and Chassiduth [and the] absolute necessity of bringing together non-gnostic

elements of Jewish mysticism . . .' (FBS's journal).

33 One Dr Braun.

34 Wilfred Evill's paintings at 39 Eton Avenue, Swiss Cottage, London.

35 J: 1994. See also letter to Gunther Adler: 'I did not think he would die, I could not believe it.'

36 So Heinz Schenk, who was present, recalled her to his wife Hazel.

37 David Pocock to Jeremy Adler, 13 June 1997.

38 16 December 1952.

39 John Jones, LTA, 8 July 1999.

40 See footnote, p.280.

41 FBS's name, like FT's, recurs in her journals. She noted in June 1953 how he had stowed notes of facts in piles of cigarette boxes. Around 1985 she transcribed and wrote his name on a story from Scholem's *Major Trends in Jewish Mysticism* (p.350).

42 About a hundred unpublished typewritten poems dating from around 1959 bear the inscription in IM's hand: 'To those for whom these poems were written they are now dedicated'. Only on 'Invocation' – i.e. a poem to commemorate the dead – are any initials inscribed in pen by IM, to indicate identity: WFT [William Frank Thompson] and FBS. 'The cenotaph of ceremonious death/ With images of tenderness I'll strew'.

43 FBS, *Fluchtvergnüglichkeit: feststellungen und versuche, eine Auswahl von M.Hermann-Röttgen* (Stuttgart, 1988), pp.129–38. A *propos* solipsism, EC complained that FBS cared more about the publication of his poetry than about the dead and dying in the Blitz.

44 IM travelled from London to Oxford to see Waissman, who spoke precisely and volubly of the Vienna circle, then showed her Tommy's room, his yacht, and

photographs. She stayed with him
till Karl Popper came later.

45 Byron, *Don Juan* III, stanza viii.

46 p.51.

47 IM, letter to Sue Summers, 12 April
1988.

48 In *The Flight from the Enchanter, The
Nice and the Good, A Fairly
Honourable Defeat.* Jeremy Adler
argues that Ludens in *The Message
to the Planet* also owes something to
FBS: *Taboo, Truth and Religion,*
op. cit., pp.49, 90.

49 'A Certain Lady', *Bookmark*, BBC
TV, 29 December 1989.

50 Mary Douglas, in 'Franz Baermann
Steiner Celebrated', op. cit.

51 *FBS: Orientpolitik*, op. cit., p.74.

CHAPTER 13

1 IM to Michael Hamburger, c1993–
94. EC invited FBS on 5 July 1952
to greet Iris specially on his behalf
(Deutsches Literaturarchiv Schiller
Nationalmuseum, Marbach). IM
wrote formally to EC – signing both
her names – proposing a meeting
in Paris, undated but possibly
August/September 1952, when her
journals circumstantially suggest she
may have been there. On 4 June
1952 she wrote to RQ, who became
a friend of EC, mentioning her
interest in the thinking of 'Canetti,
Kojève, Hegel'.

2 EC's 1993 account (see Chapter
20) differs: he saw her to Finchley
Road Underground station; a long,
poetical and probably partly
fictitious account follows.

3 IM acknowledged to JB having been
EC's lover until late 1955.

4 His name was excised by IM c1990.

5 JB, 'Canetti and Power', *London
Review of Books*, 17 December 1981–
20 January 1982, pp.65–7.

6 Jeremy Adler, CWA, 11 September
1997.

7 Kathleen Raine, *Autobiographies*
(London, 1991), p.297.

8 Kathleen Raine, CWA, 1 January
1998.

9 Honor Frost, CWA, 16 February
1998.

10 See Jeremy Adler on her novel *Die
Gelbestrasse*, in the *European*, 22–24
June 1990, pp.4–5; and Julian
Preece, 'The Rediscovered Writings
of Veza Magd-Canetti: On the
Psychology of Subservience', in
Modern Austrian Literature, vol. 28,
no. 2, 1995, pp.53–70.

11 Born 3 November 1916, in a taxi:
Susie Ovadia (*née* Benedikt), LTA,
19 February 1998.

12 Benedikt (1882–1973) was the son
of Moriz.

13 To her parents from Downshire
Hill, November 29, no year but
probably 1943.

14 The Centre Pompidou catalogue
for its exhibition on EC gives the
date of that affair as 1933; friends
recall that it was 'passionate'.

15 Judging from testimony from
Marie-Louise's close friend Milein
Cosman, and from Friedl's sister
Susie. EC, however, learnt the news
of Friedl's death from phoning
Marie-Louise: IM's J, 12 April 1953:
'He learned the news at Monveith,
phoning Marie Louise'.

16 Gardiner had gone to Fingest to
give birth to her son by J.D. Bernal.

17 Allan Forbes, telephone CWA, 21
September 1999; LTA, 23
December 1999.

18 Anne Hamburger, CWA.

19 Veza Canetti to Gwenda David and
Kathleen Raine; and probably to
others.

20 Published in America as *Tower of
Babel.*

21 Sontag was told by two people in
Stockholm, one a publisher, the
second a writer who went on to
become a member of the Swedish
Academy, that her essay 'Mind as
Passion' (*New York Review of Books*,
25 September 1980, pp.47–52) was
'most influential' in putting EC at

the top of the list for the 1981 Nobel Prize (fax to author, dated December 1998, from Sontag's assistant Benedict Yeoman). Sontag and EC never met.

22 See EC, *The Play of the Eyes*, trans. Ralph Mannheim (New York, 1986), p.228.

23 EC, *Memoirs* (New York, 1999), p.744.

24 Ibid.

25 e.g. John Simoupolos, Pierre Riches (who thought him a 'terrible man, very very very difficult . . . very violent'), Julian Chrysostomides. EC's was, in December 1998, the last name IM recognised.

26 So Jeremy Adler attests he said in his Büchner Prize speech. The theme runs throughout his writings.

27 Secretary of the Anthropological institute, Phyllis Puckle, Institute Secretary to Professor Srinivas. See *FBS: Orientpolitik*, op. cit., p.10.

28 In his final book, *Aufzeichnungen* (Munich, 1992–93), pp.17–24.

29 Among others Hans Keller and Milein Cosman-Keller in the 1950s, and his publisher Michael Krüger as recently as the 1990s. Krüger, LTA, 19 September 1997: 'Whenever I talked to [EC] he came back to IM, and especially the love-affair between IM and Franz Steiner was a subject that interested him until his last days.'

30 IM's journals give, by contrast, a day-by-day account of how, after 28 November, she and EC became close over a fortnight.

31 Summers, 'The Lost Loves of Iris Murdoch', op. cit., passim.

32 Louis Dumont, letter to Richard Fardon, 9 May 1997.

33 *The Times*, 6 December 1952.

34 *Secret History: Killer Fog*, Channel 4 TV, September 1999.

35 Carol Graham-Harrison, CWA.

36 These are inferences based on the initials IM uses (consistently) in her journals.

37 EC, *Aufzeichnungen*, op. cit., *passim*.

38 'A Certain Lady', *Bookmark*, BBC TV, 29 December 1989.

39 M. Atze (ed.), *Ortlose Botschaft: Der Freundekreis H.G. Adler, Elias Canetti und Franz Baermann Steiner im englischen exil, Marbacher Magazin*, no. 84, 1998, p.15, for the exhibition in the Schiller Nationalmuseum, Marbach, September–November 1988.

40 Jeremy Adler, John Simopoulos, Allan Forbes, CWA, LTA.

41 Pamela Myers, CWA, 11 May 1998; Wilhelmina Barnes-Graham, LTA, January 1998.

42 EC, *Notes from Hampstead, 1954–71* (New York, 1998), p.8.

43 See Atze, *Ortlose Botschaft*, op. cit. EC replied to only one in three of FBS's letters, Veza sometimes writing in his stead.

44 Raine, *Autobiographies*, op. cit. Also letters from Raine and CWA, 1 January 1998.

45 Her husband Constant Huntingdon was head of the publishing company Putnams. EC flirted with their daughter Alfreda Urquhart by moving his sponge closer to hers in the bathroom each day. He was angered when Rudi Nassauer used the story in his novel containing a portrait of EC, *The Cuckoo*.

46 Allan Forbes, LTA, 23 December 1999.

47 Graham-Harrisons, CWA, 31 December 1997.

48 See Raine, *Autobiographies*, op. cit., and Douglas Botting, *Gavin Maxwell: A Life* (London, 1993).

49 Raine, *Autobiographies*, op. cit., p.298.

50 Gwenda David, CWA.

51 Susie Ovadia, LTA, 11 February 1998.

52 See Botting, *Gavin Maxwell*, op. cit., *passim*.

53 To Milein Cosman he spoke insultingly of his patron-mistress of fifty years Marie-Louise von

Motesiczky and of his neighbour Gwenda David.

54 To Michael Hamburger, c1994: 'I am sad to hear of Canetti being unpleasant to him (hurtful jokes).'

55 See also Chapter 18.

56 During her 1982 Gifford lectures IM named the ancient Greeks as the only people free from sado-masochism.

57 Like a character in Henry James. JB, 'Canetti and Power', op. cit., pp.5–7.

58 Atze, *Ortlose Botschaft*, op. cit.

59 Hymning EC's warm heart, nobility, and humanity: see Chapter 12.

60 Sebastian Haffner, *New York Review of Books*, 20 November 1997, p.20.

61 Completed 1948, published 1955.

62 See *FBS: Taboo, Truth and Religion*, op. cit.

63 Carol Graham-Harrison, English translator of *Crowds and Power*, CWA, 31 December 1997.

64 Mary Douglas, LTA; and Sontag, 'Mind as Passion', op. cit.

65 As Friedl's sister pointed out, CWA, April 1998.

66 Source: Honor Frost. Carol Graham-Harrison says (CWA, 6 July 1999) this is almost certainly apocryphal: EC didn't like to travel, and they would certainly have heard via either EC or Veza. Milein Cosman (CWA, 8 July 1999), who met EC only in 1950, says it is 'certainly a fantasy'. EC spoke much to Cosman's husband Hans Keller, who had so terrible a time after the *Anschluss*. Given that EC told them the story of his Nobel Prize three times, he would certainly have mentioned the Auschwitz trip to them.

67 EC, *Notes from Hampstead*, op. cit., pp.8–9.

68 Saul Bellow, *Herzog* (New York, 1961), p.316.

69 John Carey, *The Intellectuals and the Masses, 1880–1939* (London, 1992), pp.29–31.

70 Susie Ovadia, CWA: 'Perhaps the strict, severe, ridiculous order of this flat evidenced disorder elsewhere.'

71 e.g. Bernice Rubens, Susie Ovadia.

72 Frances Spalding, *Stevie Smith* (London, 1988), pp.172–3, points out Friedl's likeness to the young Simone Signoret, whom IM also resembled.

73 3 May 1953.

74 'I have still not conquered death,' EC remarked to Jeremy Adler in the 1990s, his eyes bright with insanity.

75 Both Allan Forbes and Susie Ovadia confirm that neither island was within their gift.

76 Susie kept a journal in 1953.

77 See e.g. review of Friedl's *The Dreams, Listener*, 9 February 1950.

78 Gotheburg diary, dated 8 May only, probably 1951.

79 To Gwenda David, walking in Well Walk one day; also to Margaret Gardiner. Susie does not recall Friedl or anyone else mentioning EC's physical or verbal brutality: LTA, 27 August 1998.

80 Evidence for the termination of her pregnancy by Goldman at EC's behest comes independently from three different sources: Friedl's first cousin Margaret Gardiner, living in London; Friedl's sister Susie in Paris; and Friedl's ex-lover Allan Forbes in Boston.

81 Allan Forbes, LTA, November 1998.

82 To Bernice Rubens. EC boasted to Forbes that he had never slept with Veza since they married. This boast was probably false – and Veza, though in love with EC's brother Georges, would not, Rubens believed, have 'wandered'. Forbes did not think the story that EC ordained Veza's abortions improbable.

83 Conceivably based on the strongly

left-wing and feminist weekly review *Time and Tide* (1920–77).

84 *The Flight from the Enchanter*, p.173.

85 Allan Forbes, LTA, 23 December 1999; EC was 'no Andre Gide'.

86 EC, *Aufzeichnungen*, op. cit., p.20.

87 J: February 1953.

88 One sole exception: when she thought she had lost her purse and borrowed £10 from Norah Smallwood in January 1968.

89 He also admitted that he stole his brother Georges's letters to Veza to see what they were 'plotting' about his visit to Paris.

90 A view of EC with which Adler's son Jeremy concurred.

91 W.H. Auden, '1 September 1939'.

92 Hartley, *Hearts Undefeated*, op. cit., p.82.

93 J: 6 October 1953.

94 Olivier Todd, CWA, 13 September 2000.

95 *Under the Net*, p.31 (my emphasis).

96 Susan Gardiner, CWA, 31 January 1999.

97 EM, p.21.

98 The portrait now hangs in the Principal's dining-room.

99 John Wain the novelist; Lyne was Assistant Secretary to the Delegacy for Extra-Mural Studies and had arranged a day-school on the contemporary literary scene.

100 Letter from R. Lyne to JB, 20 September 1998.

101 JB, *Iris and the Friends: A Year of Memories* (London, 1999), p.194.

CHAPTER 14

1 Summers, 'The Lost Loves of Iris Murdoch', op. cit.; also JB, *Iris*, op. cit., *passim*.

2 J: 12 November 1952.

3 J: 27 January 1990; the date of Noel Martin's letter is 27 October 1942.

4 A character in Simone de Beauvoir's *She Came to Stay*.

5 See Warnock, *A Memoir*, op. cit., p.60.

6 Peter Strawson, CWA.

7 Barry Pink, a friend from Cambridge in c1934, CWA, 10 August 1998; also Peter Daniel, CWA, March 1998.

8 Polly Smythies, CWA, January 1998; Peter Daniel explains that they asked him trick questions.

9 Reading University archive, 1 December 1977.

10 *The Changing World*, no. 1, summer 1947, pp.72–81. Yorick's lecture-notes, together with those of Rush Rhees and James Taylor, were used in L. Wittgenstein, *Lectures and Conversations on Aesthetics, Psychology and Religious Beliefs* (1970) and in Wittgenstein's *Foundations of Mathematics* (1970).

11 Clive Donner, 'I once met Iris Murdoch', *The Oldie*, September 1999, p.15.

12 See Conradi, *The Saint and the Artist*, op. cit., *passim*.

13 e.g. CWA, 1983.

14 IM so identified the black jazz-singer in her unpublished *Heidegger*.

15 To RQ, 28 June 1954.

16 J: 12 July 1947.

17 *Under the Net*, Chapter 2.

18 Source: Arnoldo Momigliano, letter to IM.

19 To RQ, 28 June 1954.

20 Thus Chatto's records assert, though it is always possible an error has crept in.

21 *The Flight from the Enchanter*, p.221.

22 Ibid, p.242.

23 In his doctorate, extracts from which are published in *FBS: Orientpolitik*, op. cit.

24 e.g. IM to Michael Hamburger, 1993–94: 'Canetti is not anywhere in my novels by the way! I would not want to "copy" people, I invent them.' Brotherton Library, Leeds University.

25 EC, *The Human Province* (London, 1986) pp.32 *et seq.*

26 Graham-Harrisons, CWA, 31 December 1998.
27 Allan Forbes ate two meals a day during this Moroccan trip with EC, and finds it unimaginable that EC would not have mentioned this episode. He now wonders whether it was an invention, albeit a brilliant and suggestive one.
28 EC, *Memoirs*, op. cit., pp.551–77.
29 As all three Cecil children recall, CWA, 20 March 2000.
30 To DM, probably mid–1960s.
31 Kenneth Robinson, CWA.
32 IM, 'What I See in Cinema', British *Vogue*, 112.8, August 1956, pp.98–9; reprinted in *Vogue Bedside Book*, II (London, 1986), pp.186–7.
33 JB, CWA, 1996.
34 As David Cecil pointed out to Paul Binding.
35 *Under the Net*, p.157.
36 Earlier JB wondered whether Iris had bought at Elliston & Clavell on the Cornmarket a bright-blue fine linen top. The dress fits the recollections of others.
37 Later Robinson, reading French at St Anne's 1952–55.
38 *Daily Telegraph*, 25 July 1998, p.16.
39 Ibid.
40 From a letter by Keats.
41 *Daily Telegraph*, 25 July 1998, p.16.
42 These funded his late novel *George's Lair*.
43 A.N. Wilson, review of JB, *Iris*, op. cit., 'The True Story of how He Finally Captured Her', *Literary Review*, September 1998.
44 Despite JB's later jest (in *Iris and the Friends*, op. cit.) that he had lived for forty-three years with the most intelligent woman in England and never had a serious conversation with her. See also Conradi, *The Saint and the Artist*, op. cit., *passim*.
45 JB, 'Character and Consciousness', *New Literary History*, v, winter 1974, pp.225–35.
46 John Goode, 'Character and Henry James', *New Left Review*, 40, 1966, pp.55–75.
47 W.H. Auden, *Poems 1930* (London, 1930).
48 JB, *The Romantic Survival: A Study in Poetic Evolution* (London, 1956), p.69.

CHAPTER 15

1 To DM, undated, 1964.
2 To Vera Crane, 23 November 1957.
3 In March 1958 IM inherited £3,374 in shares from a wealthy great-uncle, William Hughes Murdoch, a Liverpool doctor.
4 JB disputes whether the electric fire was there for long. It was independently spoken of by the present owners of Cedar Lodge, July 1999, and by others.
5 To e.g. Vera Crane in June 1971, a six-page letter about nurseries and plants; as to others.
6 *Sunday Times*, 5 May 1957.
7 Derwent May, 'Iris Murdoch's Best Seller in the Swim', *Observer*, 26 November 1978.
8 See Jeremy Lewis, *Kindred Spirits: Adrift in Literary London* (London, 1995), Chapter 7, 'King William IV Street'.
9 Norah Smallwood to IM, 6 March 1975.
10 R. Todd, *Encounters with Iris Murdoch*, op. cit., p.17.
11 Gwenda David to Marshall Best, 19 January 1954 (Viking New York archives).
12 IM to Marshall Best, 27 September 1956.
13 IM to Norah Smallwood, 2 December 1963.
14 They were helped by the Novice Mistress of the Community of the Epiphany in Truro, the Anglican sisterhood where they sometimes stayed; the name they chose to go by – Epiphany Philosophers – derived from the name of the sisterhood. At the time *The Bell* was

being written they met in a lovely tower-mill off the Norfolk coast (with which Iris had nothing to do), discussing, sharing chores, following the Offices. The young physicist Ted Bastian, Richard Braithwaite and Dorothy Emmet lived together with some students from 1966. Dorothy Emmet, CWA.

15 Iris's undated letter could also conceivably refer to Sister Marian's acceptance into the Catholic faith in 1952.

16 Her journal makes no reference to staying, but Sister Marian points out that the Mass Iris attended was in the small hours: LTA.

17 EM, pp.171–86.

18 *The Bell*, p.99.

19 *New Statesman*, 15 November 1958; *Spectator*, 7 November 1958; *The Times*, 6 November 1958; *TLS*, 7 November 1958.

20 Letters to MB and to DM, 1964. Also John Grigg, CWA.

21 To Vera Crane, 23 November 1957.

22 Meyers, *Privileged Moments*, op. cit.

23 His salary in 1950 a 'personal scale' of £1,200–£1,500.

24 Sir Lawrence Airey, CWA, 11 December 1997.

25 See Chapter 1.

26 Gill Davie, 'I Should Hate to be Alive and not Writing a Novel: Iris Murdoch on her Work', *Woman's Journal*, October 1975, pp.64–5.

27 May, 'Iris Murdoch's Best Seller in the Swim', op. cit.

28 Held at Iowa University.

29 See Frank Baldanza, 'The Manuscript of Iris Murdoch's *A Severed Head*', in *Journal of Modern Literature*, February 1973, pp.75–90 for an excellent account of her working methods.

30 JB, *Iris*, op. cit., p.38. His passage appears on p.10 of *The Bell*.

31 *A Severed Head*, p.14.

32 To Norah Smallwood, c1964. She contrasts it with *An Unofficial Rose*,

'a public object in the traditional sense'.

33 Peter Green, 'Bomb in a Bloomsbury Eden', *Daily Telegraph*, 16 June 1961; and Ronald Bryden, 'marvellously and seriously funny', in 'Phenomenon', *Spectator*, 16 June 1961.

34 Dan Jacobson, 'Farce, Totem and Taboo', *New Statesman*, 16 June 1961; Anonymous, 'Leisured Philanderings', *TLS*, 16 June 1961; Philip Toynbee, 'Too Fruity to be True', *Observer*, 18 June 1961; Barbara Everett, *Critical Quarterly*, autumn 1961, pp.270–1; Rebecca West, review of *An Unofficial Rose*, *Sunday Telegraph*, 10 June 1962.

CHAPTER 16

1 He took her round a Dorset printing works for *Bruno's Dream*; IM to Rachel Fenner, 3 September 1967.

2 To LP, 6 October 1968.

3 1887–1974.

4 1889–1974.

5 Interview with Susan Hill, *Bookshelf*, BBC Radio 4, 30 April 1982.

6 Meyers, *Privileged Moments*, op. cit., p.62.

7 See Victoria Glendinning, *Rebecca West: A Life* (London, 1987), pp.116–17.

8 e.g. Dennis Nineham, Vera Crane.

9 A point I owe to Victoria Glendinning, CWA, 31 September 2000.

10 To Norah Smallwood, c1964, she also wrote of her earlier fear that the 'personal' nature of *A Severed Head* might surprise and displease readers. See Chapter 15.

11 EM, p.283.

12 Ibid, pp.271–2.

13 IM, 'Notes on my relations with my characters', unpublished, c1967.

14 11 February 1954.

15 Susan Sontag saw Fox, by contrast, as merely 'effortlessly superior' to

the English. See Sontag, 'Mind as Passion', op. cit.

16 EC, *The Human Province*, op. cit., p.75.

17 Marjorie Locke (Sister Ann Teresa), CWA, June 1998.

18 An estimate: Locke had burnt them. CWA, June 1998

19 Angus Wilson, 'Who Cares?', *Guardian*, 8 June 1962, p.5. 'The strange things that happen in Pelham Crescent!' wrote IM in RW's copy of *A Severed Head*: the Wollheims then lived in that street, where Palmer has incestuous relations with his sister. Chapter 18, below, suggests Wilson was partly right that IM now moved in new social worlds.

20 Dan Davin, *Closing Times*, op. cit., p.61.

21 A Chatto & Windus letter from the early 1970s showing IM's total sales figures – i.e. including hardbacks, paperbacks and book clubs – up to 31 March 1972 gives: *Under the Net* 242,945; *The Flight from the Enchanter* 148,116; *The Sandcastle* (oddly – this may be an error) 29,346; *The Bell* 56,042; *A Severed Head* 58,367; *An Unofficial Rose* 223,471; *The Unicorn* 108,352; *The Italian Girl* 124,796; *The Red and the Green* 136,564; *The Time of the Angels* 82,960; *The Nice and the Good* 131,508; *Bruno's Dream* 104,963; *A Fairly Honourable Defeat* 52,959; *An Accidental Man* 86,039.

22 Arthur Green, 'The Worlds of Iris Murdoch', op. cit.; and A.N. Wilson, 'Iris Murdoch and the Characters of Love', in *News from the Royal Society of Literature*, 2000, pp.56–65.

23 Jeremy Trafford said he was upper-middle class; Anne Wignall claimed to be 'Aristocratic, darling, what else?'

24 Letter to DM, 20 June 1964.

25 The story – undated – is written into the manuscript of the first draft of *The Sandcastle*, a draft begun on 29 August and finished on 18 September 1955. Perhaps 'Aunt Noonie' was Eva's foster-mother Mrs Walton. Billy Lee, who knew Mrs Walton from 1939 until her death in 1944, did not recall this (CWA, 12 February 2001).

26 Inaccurately 'puffed' on its republication in 1999 as hitherto unknown. Its reputation is clarified in 'The Problem of Gender in Iris Murdoch's "Something Special" ', in *Journal of the Short Story in English* (University of D'Angers Press), no. 21, autumn 1993, pp.19–27.

27 Eva's widower Billy Lee, CWA, December 1999.

28 Billy Lee, however, points out that Mrs Walton's shop had a single, not a double, counter, and so was not large (CWA, 12 February 2001).

29 In 1944 and 1941 respectively. See Chapter 1.

30 See Foster, *Paddy and Mr Punch*, op. cit., p.305.

31 To DH, 12 June 1945.

32 To DM, undated.

33 J: 1 November 1964.

34 IM to Viking, 17 March 1956.

35 See footnote, p.49.

36 Points for which I am indebted to Professor Roy Foster and Victoria Glendinning.

37 Peter Somerville-Large, *The Irish Country House: A Social History* (London, 1995), p.141; Valerie Pakenham, *The Big House in Ireland* (London, 2000), p.79; guidebook to Belvedere House, County Westmeath; J.S. Lyons, *The Grand Juries of Westmeath* (privately printed, c1840); *The Autobiography and Correspondence of Lady Granville, Mrs Delany* (1861–62, six volumes). Frances Gerard gives a notable account in *Some Celebrated Irish Beauties of the Last Century* (London, 1895).

38 *The Unicorn*, p.60.

39 As Malcolm Bradbury noted: 'Under the Symbol', *Spectator*, 210, 6 September 1963, p.295.

40 *The Unicorn*, p.92.

41 In fogbound 'Jerusalem' in 1958, moreover, both a Thames barrage and a primitive answer-machine are projected, decades before either would exist in real life.

42 *The Unicorn*, p.43.

43 Robert Scholes, *The Fabulators* (New York and Oxford, 1967); in an interview with Laura Cecil IM derided this.

44 Phrase used of the tarot pack, with which she entertained herself in the 1950s; one card in particular ('La Papessa') struck her as herself. J: 15 June 1952.

45 See Harold Hobson, 'Lunch with Iris Murdoch', *Sunday Times*, 11 March 1962, p.28.

46 *The Unicorn*, p.54.

47 Stuart Hampshire and Raymond Carr, CWA; IM, CWA.

48 *The Sacred and Profane Love Machine*, p.325.

49 In, respectively, *Under the Net, The Bell, A Fairly Honourable Defeat, The Philosopher's Pupil.*

50 See Chapter 11.

51 Letter to DM.

52 Letter to DM.

53 12 February 1971.

54 The other, recalled by Carol Graham-Harrison, was by Philip Toynbee, presumably in the *Observer.*

55 27 March 1963.

56 *The Unicorn, The Time of the Angels, The Nice and the Good.*

57 Two letters from Steeple Aston, October/November 1963 and December 1967.

58 *The Ship* (year-book of the St Anne's College Association of Senior Members), no. 53, 1962–63, p.4.

59 IM wrote to the Principal on 21 December 1962, resigning with effect from the end of March 1963,

since it had already been agreed that she was on sabbatical for her final term (summer 1963).

60 J: 8 September 1963.

61 Letter series 30 December 1963 to 31 January 1964.

62 In Anthony Burgess, *Ninety-Nine Novels: The Best in English Since 1939* (London, 1984).

63 P.N. Furbank, 'Gowned Morality', *Encounter*, 23, November 1964, pp.88, 90.

64 Sister Marian, LTA.

65 J: 13 February 1970.

66 David Lee (Eva's eldest son), CWA.

67 A point I owe to Professor Roy Foster (LTA, 31 July 2000).

68 Arthur Green, 'The Worlds of Iris Murdoch', op. cit.

69 *Guardian*, 16 October 1965.

70 Chevalier, '*Rencontres avec Iris Murdoch*', op. cit. p.92. Thus Christopher Bellman is shot by a sniper's bullet, 'no one knew from which side'; Perry Arbelow in *The Sea, The Sea*, having acquired 'a darling little theatre in Londonderry that's only a tiny bit bombed', is also shot during the Troubles by an unidentified terrorist.

71 Muroya and Hullah, *Occasional Essays by Iris Murdoch*, op. cit., p.84.

72 F.S.L. Lyons, *Ireland Since the Famine*, op. cit., p.377.

73 Curiously, E.P. Thompson in *Beyond the Frontier*, op. cit., would, independently, describe FT's death as having the same symbolic value as that of Irish Nationalists in the Easter Rising.

74 *The Red and the Green*, p.235.

75 Sean Lucy, *Irish Independent*, 24 December 1965; Joy McCormick on *Bruno's Dream*, *Hibernia*, 28 February 1969; Sean O'Faolain, *Irish Times*, 16 October 1965.

76 For example, Lady Millie: 'It's not your freedom or your youth I'm after envying at the moment'; Pat: 'And don't be after touching that.'

Dictionaries of Hibernian English indicate the Gaelic 'after' approximates to the English perfect tense. Professor Roy Foster agrees that Lady Millie would not affect a brogue unless deliberately guying the natives (as does, for example, Charlotte Mullen in Somerville and Ross's *The Real Charlotte*) or indicating non-Britishness (like the two Anglo-Irish *grandes dames* towards the end of Elizabeth Bowen's *The Last September*). IM's usage lacks subtlety (Professor Roy Foster, LTA, 31 July 2000). See Foster, *Paddy and Mr Punch*, op. cit., p.106.

77 So Roy Foster has argued: *Modern Ireland 1600–1972* (London, 1988), p.492.

78 Canon Crawford, IM's second cousin, and amateur Richardson genealogist, CWA.

79 To A.N. Wilson – see his 'Iris Murdoch and the Characters of Love', op. cit. However, at Caen in 1978 she championed the book.

80 The author's Royal Society of Literature obituary of IM, *News from the Royal Society of Literature*, 2000, pp.86–91.

81 Honor Tracy to IM, October 1979. The letter continues: 'They have nothing to grumble about. Nothing prevents them from moving down if they wish but they don't, knowing well how much better off they are up there. And no one down here wants them either, whatever they may say. The amount of sheer humbug is breathtaking, and when you think what it has lost in lives and cripplings and blindings. But you know all this.'

82 To the author, 1982.

83 To MB, July 1985.

84 To MB, 11 March 1983.

85 IM, CWA, c1985.

CHAPTER 17

1 J: 19 March 1969.

2 J: 26 April 1969.

3 IM, interview with Ronald Bryden, *Lively Arts*, Radio 3, 14 February 1968.

4 Letters to LP make clear that by November 1963 she is settling into both job and flat.

5 In spring 1967 she was granted a sabbatical to visit Australia, and recommended Graham Martin to replace her.

6 Official letter, 21 June 1963.

7 He was, Humphrey Spender recalled, looking for moral principles and structure outside himself, an ex-Marxist, now Roman Catholic, with a flat in South Kensington but a main home in Cambridge.

8 *The Black Prince* (1973), *The Three Arrows* (1973), *A Word Child* (1974).

9 J: 7 January 1965.

10 DM, LTA, 13 February 2000.

11 Rachel Fenner, CWA.

12 IM, letter to RW, 17 July 1991: 'Steeple Aston is best address except for letters arriving Tues to Thursday first post.' Confirmed by Rachel Fenner.

13 IM to LP.

14 IM to LP, 15 March 1959.

15 JB, CWA.

16 She kept exam papers in Cornwall Gardens.

17 Source: Jenny Sharp, RCA 1964–7, fashion designer.

18 Gadney and she discussed the RCA in 1979.

19 In the words of one of IM's RCA colleagues.

20 Christopher Frayling, *The Royal College of Art: 150 Years of Art and Design* (London, 1987), p.190.

21 DM, LTA, 29 February 2000.

22 Inference: her exam papers are addressed to second-year students in tutorial groups G, H, J, K.

23 Letter to RW, undated, 1967.

24 David Hockney (ed. N. Stangos), *David Hockney* (London, 1977), p.42.

25 Frayling, *The Royal College of Art*, op. cit., *passim*.

26 Christopher Frayling was appointed.

27 Some books in the series, such as Freud's *The Psychopathology of Everyday Life*, sold more copies than many best-selling novels.

28 Frayling, *The Royal College of Art*, op. cit., p.164; Riley when an RCA student in 1952–55 had not yet experimented with this form.

29 Alex Seago, *Burning the Box of Beautiful Things* (Oxford, 1995).

30 Ibid, p.212.

31 Ibid, p.26.

32 Letter to DM.

33 Ronald Bryden (with A.S. Byatt), 'Talking to Iris Murdoch', *Listener*, 4 April 1968, pp.433–4.

34 Letter to DM, summer 1964.

35 Paddy Kitchen, *A Fleshly School* (London, 1970), p.62.

36 *The Time of the Angels*, pp.163–5.

37 *The Sovereignty of Good*, p.72; collected in EM, p.359.

38 As she acknowledged in 'John Haffenden Talks to Iris Murdoch', op. cit.

39 See W.K. Rose, 'An Interview with Iris Murdoch', *Shenandoah*, xix, winter 1968, pp.3–22.

40 An e-mail from Canetti scholar Michael Mack confirms that this was a favourite book.

41 IM, interview with Ronald Bryden, *Lively Arts*, BBC Radio 3, 14 February 1968.

42 *The Nice and the Good*, p.96.

43 Mary Douglas (CWA, 11 February 2000) believes FBS might have shared such a habit.

44 'Premium Books', in *New Fiction Society*, 1, October 1974, p.8.

45 A discussion, the MS of the novel held at Iowa University shows, given to Jake and Hugo in an early draft of *Under the Net*, later cut out.

46 *The Nice and the Good*, p.350.

47 *Tolstoi and the Novel* (London, 1966), winner of the 1967 W.H. Heinemann Award.

48 See Conradi, *The Saint and the Artist*, op. cit., *passim*, for extended discussion of this point.

49 A point developed in *The Saint and the Artist*.

50 19 December 1965.

51 Frederic Samson, *Concepts of Man* (RCA, 1979), with a foreword by Christopher Cornford; and *Dotes and Antidotes* (RCA, 1979).

52 Fashion student Jenny Sharp.

53 Jenny Sharp however recalls his description of the death of his mother, not in the Holocaust, and the problems of being 'with' her at her deathbed.

54 Humphrey Spender's hypothesis.

55 Iris wrote to the *Guardian*, adding a short tribute to Eve Watt's obituary of Esme Ross Langley; *Guardian*, 25 August 1992, p.35.

56 J: 1 February 1964.

57 28 August 1975.

58 Undated, summer 1968.

59 *Dictionary of Literary Biography*, Vol. 14, *British Novelists Since 1960, Part I, A–G*, ed. J. Halio (Detroit, 1983): S.J. Newman on Brigid Brophy, pp.137–46.

60 Michael Levey, LTA, 9 January 1998.

61 'A Jewelled Occasion', *Sunday Times*, 19 January 1964, p.37.

62 Bertram Rota Booksellers, item 80, catalogue 150, spring 1967, p.3.

63 Michael Levey, LTA, 9 January 1998.

64 'Neglected Fictions', *TLS*, 18 October 1985, pp.1179–88. IM also nominated Honor Tracy's *The Straight and Narrow Path*.

65 Francis King, LTA, 29 December 1998.

66 (London, 1967).

67 Michael Levey, LTA, 6 February 1998.

68 This does not survive.

69 *The Black Prince*, p.191.
70 For example, J: 12 August 1951: 'A day and a half of weak-kneed misery. Wisdom and courage – names for love . . . summoning my forces and the great positive of loving. Yes.'
71 *The Philosopher's Pupil*, p.121 (my emphasis).
72 J: 26 June 1971.
73 Letter to RW, c1966.
74 See e.g. *Virtue Ethics*, ed. R. Crisp and M. Slote (Oxford, 1997).
75 As Anthony Kenny observed: 'Notes and Queries', *New Statesman*, 18 October 1971, pp.389–90; see also *Listener*, 7 January 1971, p.23.
76 As Anthony Quinton remarked: 'Proper Study of Mankind', *Sunday Telegraph*, 29 November 1970.
77 J: 17 November 1953.
78 'The Idea of Freedom', IM in conversation with David Pears, Logic Lane/Oxford Philosophy series, Chanan Films Ltd, 1971.
79 Michael Bellamy, 'An Interview with Iris Murdoch', *Contemporary Literature*, xviii, 1977, pp.129–40.
80 RW, CWA.
81 28 February 1970: the reason for this sit-in is not identified.
82 So Samson would complain to Humphrey Spender. IM to Rachel Fenner, undated internal memo on RCA paper, 1966: 'I am an old traditionalist.'
83 To Rachel Fenner, 16 August 1964: 'Might Plato be right about mediocre art that it veils reality? As in fact very few people are made for sanctity this fact need not be important to the majority.'
84 *The Times*, 10 February 1970.
85 This Maurice is unidentified by surname; Noel Annan in *The Dons* (London, 1999) confirms how important IM's friendship was for Bowra.

CHAPTER 18

1 *Convictions*, edited by Norman Mackenzie (London, 1958), included essays by, among others, Peter Shore, Raymond Williams, Richard Hoggart, Hugh Thomas and Paul Johnson. 'A House of Theory' appeared on pp.158–62; reprinted in *Partisan Review*, 26.1, winter 1959, pp.17–31 and in *Power and Civilization: Political Thought in the Twentieth Century*, ed. D. Cooperman and E. Victor (New York, 1962), pp.442–55.
2 'Morality and the Bomb' in *Women Ask Why: An Intelligent Woman's Guide to Nuclear Disarmament* (CND, London, 1962) pp.1–6.
3 'The Moral Decision About Homosexuality', *Man and Society*, 7, summer 1964, pp.3–6; reprinted in *The Humanist*, 80.3, March 1965, pp.70–3.
4 The Irish law was liberalised in 1993.
5 '. . . provided of course that the animals are consulted and their consent obtained. Iris's worst enemy, if she has an enemy at all except among the envious and less successful, would have to admit that she always joins in a laugh against herself.' Two undated letters to Sister Marian, probably c1976 and 1977, the date of vol. 2 of Michael MacLiammoir's memoirs, referred to by Honor Tracy.
6 'Political Morality', *Listener*, 21 September 1967, pp.353–4; reprinted in *Authors Take Sides on Vietnam*, ed. C. Woolf and J. Bagguley (London and New York, 1967), pp.56–7.
7 Sir John and Sally Vinelott (he read Moral Sciences at Queen's, Cambridge, 1947–50 and met IM then) were fellow-guests at a dinner IM gave at Harcourt Terrace, and witnessed the row. The flat was tidy, IM a competent cook.

8 18 June 1968, p.9; 31 August 1968, p.7.

9 The phrase is Michael Ignatieff's on Anna Akhmatova, in *Isaiah Berlin: A Life* (London, 1999), p.168.

10 Muroya and Hullah, *Occasional Essays by Iris Murdoch*, op. cit. pp.56, 86.

11 *Independent*, 24 March 2000, p.7. He replied that she could acquire one from H.M. Stationery Office.

12 Muroya and Hullah, *Occasional Essays by Iris Murdoch*, op. cit., p.56.

13 Letter to DM, c1966.

14 *The Times*, 16 January 1960, p.9.

15 For Julian Mitchell's diary see *Guardian*, 5 April 1969; for Adrian Henri's, *TLS*, 10 April 1969.

16 2 July 1973, p.15.

17 13 April 1975, p.8.

18 With a distinctly different title: 'Socialism and Selection'; both in 1975.

19 Tim Devlin and Mary Warnock, 'The Blackboard Jungle', article-review of *What Must We Teach?*, *New Statesman*, 21 October 1977, pp.546–8.

20 W.K. Rose, 'An Interview with Iris Murdoch', *Shenandoah*, xix, winter 1968, pp.3–22.

21 J: 7 September 1969.

22 Interview with Ronald Bryden, *Listener*, 4 April 1968, pp.432–6.

23 In his essay 'Charles Dickens'.

24 A.S. Byatt, *Degrees of Freedom* (second edition, London, 1994), p.ix. Byatt declares herself 'sometimes dismayed by its solemn, almost Leavisite insistence on making severe judgements'.

25 'A Sort of Mystery Novel', *New Statesman*, 22 October 1965, p.604.

26 EM, pp.283–4.

27 *Spectator*, 3 September 1965, p.293.

28 Paul Bailey, 'Naming Love', review of *The Sacred and Profane Love Machine*, *Guardian*, 21 March 1974.

29 IM's phrase in interview with

Ronald Bryden, *Listener*, 4 April 1968.

30 See JB, *Iris*, op. cit.

31 As Stephen Wall pointed out *à propos A Word Child* in the *TLS*, 18 April 1975. Martin Amis's blow-by-blow account of the plot of *Nuns and Soldiers* in his review in the *Observer*, 7 October 1980, is hilarious and unfair in exactly this way.

32 *A Fairly Honourable Defeat*, p.233 (my emphasis).

33 See Chapter 13: Kathleen Raine accurately observed that EC's quarrel with God was in the ancient Jewish tradition stemming from Job.

34 e.g. interviews with Heyd (*University of Windsor Review*, 1965), Rose (*Shenandoah*, 1968), Bellamy (*Contemporary Literature*, 1976).

35 See Meyers, *Privileged Moments*, op. cit., p.67.

36 In Morgan acting as destructive henchperson to Julius there may also be an unconscious echo of IM acting as cruel sidekick to Thomas Balogh in 1943–44.

37 *The Times*, Weekend section, 12 September 1998, p.2.

38 Like Saward in *The Flight from the Enchanter*: both Saward and Tallis lost a sister when young.

39 Though Axel, unlike Joll, is a civil servant rather than politics don at St Antony's.

40 Frank Hauser, who directed EC's unsuccessful play *The Numbered* in Oxford in 1956, asked Joll to arrange a gathering afterwards at St Antony's. EC arrived with 'entourage'. Golding and Joll also met him for dinner at the Graham-Harrisons.

41 R. Parikh found Kreisel both 'bored' and 'Machiavellian': Odifreddi, *Kreiseliana*, op. cit., p.95. See Chapter 10.

42 LTA, 11 February 1998, before she had read *A Fairly Honourable Defeat*.

43 The artist Wilhelmina Barnes-Graham believed that the painters of St Ives were well able to make mischief by themselves. She recalled EC with affection. Clement Glock had been his driver-lieutenant on that visit.

44 See Chapter 13.

45 LTA, 27 August 1998: 'He was quite unable to let go completely of an intimate.'

46 EC, *Auto da Fé*, p.155.

47 Curiously enough Susie Ovadia knew of the same tale, though set on the north side of Hyde Park, and told of Friedl rather than of Marie-Louise. CWA.

48 *A Fairly Honourable Defeat*, p.225.

49 Letter to PF, undated, 1968.

50 *The Nice and the Good*, p.47.

51 *The Lyttelton/Hart-Davis Letters*, vols 3, 4, 1958–9 (London, 1978–79), p.21. Rachel Trickett and Wallace Robson were sometimes said to have made up, with John Bayley, Cecil's trio of best students.

52 Following which Cecil became a professor.

53 Rachel Cecil, *Teresa's Choice* (London, 1958).

54 Frances Partridge, *Hanging On: Diaries 1960–63* (London, 1998), p.52.

55 *The Nice and the Good*, p.15.

56 See e.g. David Cecil's introduction to *Lady Ottoline* [Morell]*'s Album* (New York, 1976) pp.3–14.

57 Hugh Cecil, LTA, 27 October 1999.

58 Partridge, *Hanging On*, op. cit., p.75.

59 Frances Partridge, *Other People: Diaries 1963–66* (London, 1993), p.67.

60 CWA, 13 January 2000.

61 Frances Partridge, *Good Company: Diaries 1967–70* (London, 1994), p.148.

62 Janet Stone, *Thinking Faces 1953–79* (London, 1988), p.18.

63 9 August 1961.

64 'A Certain Lady', *Bookmark*, BBC TV, 29 December 1989.

65 From IM's eulogy, St James's, Piccadilly, 20 July 1979 (published by Warren Editions, 1981).

66 Obituary, *Guardian*, 2 February 1998, p.16.

67 Stone, *Thinking Faces*, op. cit., pp.7–8.

68 16 July 1969.

69 See JB, *Iris*, op. cit., pp.35–6.

70 Stone, *Thinking Faces*, op. cit., p.28.

71 JB, CWA, April 1998.

72 Emma Stone's recollection. IM wrote her a poem about a horse on that holiday.

73 From IM's eulogy, St James's, Piccadilly, 20 July 1979.

74 Stone, *Thinking Faces*, op. cit.

75 Sources: John Vinelott, who saw her thus attired at the Cambridge University Vacation Club around 1950. And JB, who recounted IM similarly prepared with Rene's help at the party for *The Flight from the Enchanter* in March 1956.

76 *The Lyttelton/Hart-Davis Letters*, op. cit., p.256.

77 LTA, 25 November 1999.

78 *A Very Private Eye: The Diaries, Letters and Notebooks of Barbara Pym*, ed. H. Holt and H. Pym (London, 1984), p.308.

79 See *The Letters of Kingsley Amis*, op. cit., *passim*; and Martin Amis, *Experience* (London, 2000), p.357n.

80 'The Idea of Freedom', IM in conversation with David Pears, Logic Lane/Oxford Philosophy series, Chanan Films Ltd, 1971.

81 Partridge, *Other People*, op. cit., p.282.

82 J: 6 December 1968.

83 Letter to MB.

84 DM, LTA, 13 February 2000.

85 This new verb, borrowed from the person from Porlock who interrupted Coleridge's 'Kubla Khan', occurs in *Bruno's Dream*, though in a letter to Chatto, 11 February 1985, IM misremembers

the novel as *The Time of the Angels*, which contains the different coinage 'oblivescent'.

86 For example, J: May 1966: '[x] called unannounced yesterday! Furious, but calmed down and took them to lunch in Woodstock & then into Oxford.'

87 J: 31 May 1991.

88 J: 21 December 1987; compare J: 1 March 1981: 'I feel I am becoming more silent and awkward, as I was when I was young.'

89 J: 26 September 1969.

90 Audi Villers, CWA.

91 'A Certain Lady', *Bookmark*, BBC TV, 29 December 1989.

92 J: 23 June 1968.

93 J: 12 August 1971.

94 Film producer associated (Peters, Fraser & Dunlop believed) with *A Severed Head*.

95 Letter to DM.

96 Letter to DM, 1964.

97 e.g. to Barbara Craig, Principal of Somerville, at a college dinner, and to Audi Villers on first meeting in 1967.

98 Letter to LP, January 1970.

99 In January 1966.

100 J: 15 December 1976.

101 J: 10 June 1969.

102 J: 3 October 1969.

103 J: 16 January 1977.

104 *The Black Prince*, p.173.

105 Byatt, *Degrees of Freedom*, second edition, op. cit., p.338. In a LTA, December 2000, Byatt indicated a strong dislike for the phrase 'literary mother'.

106 23 May 1970.

107 LTA, 10 July 1995.

108 Harold Bloom, *The Anxiety of Influence* (New York and Oxford, 1973).

109 Gabriel Pearson, review of *The Black Prince*, *Guardian*, 22 January 1973.

110 Found among IM's papers; but also referred to in *The Sovereignty of Good*, where she speaks of puritanism and romanticism as 'natural partners and we are living with their partnership still', EM, p.366.

111 *The Black Prince*, pp.66–7.

112 See Conradi, *The Saint and the Artist*, op. cit., for a fuller development of this idea.

113 See Lorna Sage, 'Female Fictions', in *The Contemporary English Novel*, ed. M. Bradbury and D. Palmer (London, 1979), pp.67–87; 'No Trespassers' (review of *The Fire and the Sun*), *New Review*, September 1977, pp.49–50; 'The Pursuit of Imperfection', *Critical Quarterly*, xix, no. 2, summer 1977, pp.67–87; *Women in the House of Fiction* (London, 1992), pp.72–83; 'In Praise of Mess: Iris Murdoch 1919–1999', *TLS*, 19 February 1999, p.12.

114 And IM dreamt of her friends 'doubling' – J: 17 February 1969: 'Dream other night, about DH. Later saw it was "really" A[lasdair] C[layre] not DH. Never thought of these two doubling before.'

115 The author twice witnessed IM contradict JB when he spoke of this identification: in Amsterdam in October 1986, and at Alcala de Henares in 1992.

116 EM, p.195.

117 J: 27 June 1971.

118 Both in her journals, 1970–72, and also in *The Black Prince*.

119 Philip Larkin's playful traducings of the text of *The Flight from the Enchanter* (see Andrew Motion, *Philip Larkin: A Writer's Life* (London, 1993), pp.318–19) read as reactions against high-mindedness and 'high diction' alike.

120 J: 31 December 1953. See also n45, above: 'He was quite unable to let go completely of an intimate.'

121 J: 13 January 1953.

122 *The Sea, The Sea*, p.52.
123 Ibid, p.60.
124 e.g. J: 19 July 1970.
125 Letter to DM, undated, 1964.
126 IM commended John Blofield's
*The Way of Power: A Practical Guide
to the Tantric Mysticism of Tibet*
(London, 1970) to the author.
127 'John Haffenden Talks to Iris
Murdoch', op. cit.
128 DM, LTA.
129 Natasha Spender, LTA.
130 J: entries March/April 1969.
131 Interview with Jackie Gillott,
Kaleidoscope, BBC Radio 4, 22
November 1978.
132 *New Statesman*, 25 August 1978.
133 *Listener*, 24 August 1978, p.250.
134 *Spectator*, 26 August 1978.
135 *The Times*, 24 August 1978.
136 IM spent much of the prize
money on paintings by her friend
Harry Weinberger.
137 A.N. Wilson, review of Ben
Rogers, *A.J. Ayer: A Life, Guardian*,
19 June 1999. Besides Ayer and
May, the other Booker judges in
1978 were Angela Huth, P.H.
Newby and Clare Boylan. The
other shortlisted novels were
Kingsley Amis, *Jake's Thing*; Andre
Brink, *Rumours of Rain*; Penelope
Fitzgerald, *The Bookshop*; Jane
Gardam, *God on the Rocks*; Bernice
Rubens, *A Five-Year Sentence*. Ayer
praised *The Sea, The Sea* for 'the
force of its imagery, its delineation
of character, and its descriptive
power', *Tablet*, 2 December 1978.
138 An internal Chatto memo dated 4
December 1984 gives hardback
sales to that date of 37,264 for
The Sea, The Sea; 23,799 for *Nuns
and Soldiers*; 16,277 for *The
Philosopher's Pupil*. There was also a
'dramatic dropping-away of sales
of translation rights'.

CHAPTER 19

1 In his notebooks; quoted *New York
Review of Books*, 4 February 1999,
p.3.
2 *En route* to Norwich, where she was
to be awarded an honorary
doctorate by the University of East
Anglia.
3 J: 26 July 1970.
4 To JB; to the author.
5 J: 6 April 1978.
6 IM to Rachel Fenner, 23 March
1968: 'Have lectured in Italian &
impressed myself.' But also 9 April
1968: 'My Italian absurdly simple
for speaking purposes.' See 'The
Response of Italian Critics', *Iris
Murdoch Newsletter*, no. 14, autumn
2000, for further details of this
lecture.
7 Letter to Harry Weinberger, 18
January 1982.
8 November 1981.
9 *A Word Child*, p.98.
10 Of Tallis in *A Fairly Honourable
Defeat*, p.145.
11 J: 12 August 1971.
12 Undated.
13 Peter Lennon, *Sunday Times*, 26
November 1978.
14 *The Black Prince*, p.200.
15 Mikhail Bakhtin's brother Nikolai
had arrived in England in the
1930s and moved to Birmingham
University around 1946. It is more
probable that FT was referring to
Mikhail.
16 *The Sea, The Sea*, p.477.
17 EM, p.87.
18 *The Sandcastle*, p.77.
19 'John Haffenden Talks to Iris
Murdoch', op. cit. See also Hilda
Spears's study, *Iris Murdoch*
(Basingstoke, 1995), *passim*, for
discussion of the point.
20 J: 19 January 1980.
21 British Library, Modern
Manuscripts, Peggy Ramsey archive
deposit number 9625.
22 Peggy Ramsey to IM, 8 August

1969. The play referred to was *Joanna, Joanna*.

23 IM to Peggy Ramsey, 17 January 1975.

24 *An Unofficial Rose* in 1975 by Simon Raven; *The Bell* by Reg Gadney in 1982 for television; *The Sea, The Sea* for BBC Radio 4 by Richard Crane in 1993.

25 See John Fletcher, 'A Novelist's Plays: Iris Murdoch and the Theatre', in *Essays in Theatre*, vol. 4, no.1, November 1985, pp.3–20.

26 J: 12 February 1971.

27 Peggy Ramsey to IM, 23 February 1968.

28 IM to Peggy Ramsey, 12 May 1977.

29 *The Black Prince*, p.91.

30 *The Sea, The Sea*, p.160.

31 J: 31 August 1970.

32 See e.g. interview with Susan Hill, *Bookshelf*, BBC Radio 4, 30 April 1982; and with Pamela Callaghan, *Weekend*, BBC Radio 4, 18 April 1982.

33 In 1969.

34 J: 16 February 1970.

35 IM to PF, 31 May 1982.

36 See Chapter 17, *passim*.

37 'An Evening with Iris Murdoch', *Bristol Medical-Chirurgical Journal*, August 1986, p.91.

38 Letter to DM.

39 'The Moral Decision About Homosexuality', op. cit.

40 Interview in Ziegler and Bigsby (eds), *The Radical Imagination and the Liberal Tradition*, op. cit.

41 MM, CWA and LTA, 22 June 2000.

42 Frances Stewart, LTA, 6 January 2000.

43 *A Word Child*, p.6.

44 J: 7 September 1969.

45 Interview with Susan Hill, *Bookshelf*, BBC Radio 4, 30 April 1982.

46 To RQ, 11 August 1947.

47 John Grigg, CWA.

48 Peter Levi, LTA, 25 November 1999.

49 *Weekend*, BBC Radio 4, 18 April 1982.

50 DM's recollection.

51 Malcolm Bradbury, *Who do you Think you Are?* (London, 1976), pp.166–71.

52 *An Accidental Man*, p.405.

53 'In Memory of Iris Murdoch', *Spectator*, 18–25 December 1999, pp.79–81.

54 Iris dreamt its opening conceit, of a child's face glimpsed in a tree, just as she dreamt of the swimming girls David spies upon.

55 *An Accidental Man, A Word Child, The Black Prince, The Sea, The Sea*. See Chevalier, '*Rencontres avec Iris Murdoch*', op. cit., for IM's comments on the play.

56 J: August 1971.

57 J: 12 May 1969.

58 Interview with Pamela Callaghan, *Weekend*, BBC Radio 4, 18 April 1982.

59 J: 12 March 1971.

60 J: 22 May 1971.

61 J: 21 November 1971.

62 J: 14 July 1979.

63 J: 12 August 1971.

64 J: 5 February 1972.

65 'Who is the Experiencer?', *Questioning Krishnamurti* (London, 1996), pp.99–128.

66 Ishiyamadera belongs to the esoteric Shingon sect (the word '*shingon*' meaning 'mantra'), the sole sect to keep alive the tradition of the Mahavairocana Sutra, brought from China by a towering figure of Japanese religious history in 804–5. *The Encyclopedia of Religion*, ed. M. Eliade, vol. 13 (New York, 1987), pp.272–7.

67 At an unknown time (CWA, 1989). Don Cupitt believes it was in the 1970s.

68 Though JB takes another view in *Iris*, op. cit., IM mentioned her meditative practice to the author, to PF and to John Simopoulos.

69 J: 14 January 1972.

70 IM hoped that keeping philosophy going alongside her fiction

'somehow fed my whole mind and made everything better . . . [But] maybe it has stolen from the novels some greater intellectual strength?' J: 20 February 1969.

71 'John Haffenden Talks to Iris Murdoch', op. cit.

72 J: 4 February 1954.

73 EM, p.372.

74 Simone Weil, *Notebooks*, vol. 2, trans. A. Wills (London, 1956), pp.383–4.

75 EM, p.345.

76 Ibid, pp.492–3.

77 Interview with John Barrows, 'Living Writers – 7', *John o' London's*, 4 May 1961, p.495.

78 IM, 'Force Fields', review of A.S. Byatt's *The Virgin in the Garden*, *New Statesman*, 3 November 1978, p.586.

CHAPTER 20

1 J: 14 August 1969.

2 'John Haffenden Talks to Iris Murdoch', op. cit.

3 W (formerly *Women's Wear Daily*), 18–25 October 1985, p.54 *et seq.*

4 J: 30 May 1982.

5 Letter to DH, 11 November 1945.

6 March 1991, unpublished. *Tricycle* no longer has it.

7 *The Making of a Mystic*, Channel 4 TV, 1993.

8 'Love and Vision: Iris Murdoch on Eros and the Individual', in M. Antonaccio and W. Schweiker (eds), *Iris Murdoch and the Search for Human Goodness* (Chicago, 1996), pp.29–53.

9 'John Haffenden Talks to Iris Murdoch', op. cit.

10 IM recycled this dream in *The Green Knight*, pp.366–7, where it is given to Bellamy James.

11 30 January 1949.

12 J: 12 July 1983.

13 Herbert Art Gallery, Jordan Well, Coventry, 26 March–24 April 1983; and Duncan Campbell

Contemporary Art (undated, but autumn 1994).

14 23 July 1988.

15 Gabriele Annan, 'Murdoch at the Gallop', *Sunday Telegraph*, 13 September 1987, p.16.

16 15 September 1942.

17 IM, CWA, c1985.

18 BBC Radio 4, April 1982.

19 Interview with Pamela Callaghan, *Weekend*, BBC Radio 4, 18 April 1982.

20 Martin Amis, review of *Nuns and Soldiers*, 'Let's Fall in Love', *Observer*, 7 September 1980.

21 For *The Italian Girl* she read and annotated D. Attwater's *Eric Gill: Workman* (London, undated).

22 To Sir John Vinelott, 1993.

23 Kreisel, CWA, 4 March 1998.

24 He was devastated by the loss of his parents and requested that the fact of their murder by the Nazis be engraved on his tombstone in Cuneo.

25 2 November 1978. Faulks replied with great courtesy, but without giving any ground.

26 By Jeremy Lewis; (Carmen Callil, telephone CWA, July 2000).

27 To Allegra Huston, undated, but c1986.

28 Roger Lewis, 'A Dangerous Dame', *Telegraph Weekend Magazine*, 8 July 1989, pp.16–19.

29 Carmen Callil to Ed Victor, 22 December 1988.

30 Before *The Good Apprentice* she had used 'oblivescent' in *The Time of the Angels* and *A Word Child*.

31 IM to Jeremy Lewis, 11 February 1985.

32 Honor Tracy to Sister Marian, 6 February 1977.

33 A letter (undated) to Harry Weinberger reassures him about how easy a TV appearance is – there are 'so many cameras one ceases to notice them'.

34 They met Avebury through their Oxfordshire neighbours Michael

Campbell (brother of Lord Patrick, the stammering broadcaster) and his Canadian friend Bill Holden.

35 1911–1984.

36 Stephen Spender, *Journals 1939–83*, ed. J. Goldsmith (London, 1985), p.305.

37 Noel Annan, LTA, 14 October 1999.

38 IM to Norah Smallwood, 23 September 1980, *à propos Nuns and Soldiers* and her opera *The Servants*.

39 Spender, *Journals 1939–83*, op. cit., pp.409–10.

40 To what degree such values are a function of money is discussed in Conradi, *The Saint and the Artist*, op. cit.

41 *Metaphysics as a Guide to Morals*, p.496.

42 S.L. Jaki, *Lord Gifford and his Lectures: A Centenary Retrospect* (Edinbugh, 1995), p.42.

43 *TLS*, 27 September 1985, pp.1047–8.

44 Interview with Pamela Callaghan, *Weekend*, BBC Radio 4, 18 April 1982.

45 Meyers, *Privileged Moments*, op. cit., p.72.

46 Where she appeared unexpectedly at St Brides crypt, Fleet Street, c1992 – David Daniels, ex-UCL and Fellow of Hertford College.

47 Roger Scruton, *Velvet Revolution*, Appendix 1. Kathleen Wilkes e-mailed that IM came to one AGM and made a generous donation.

48 Anthony Powell, *Journals 1987–89* (London, 1996), p.97.

49 CWA, February 1992.

50 W.B. Yeats, 'The Choice', *Collected Poems* (London, 1960), p.278.

51 R. Lewis, 'A Dangerous Dame', op. cit.

52 'A Certain Lady', *Bookmark*, BBC TV, 29 December 1989.

53 Bradbury, *Who do you Think you Are?*, op. cit.

54 It was published in full in Muroya

and Hullah, *Occasional Essays by Iris Murdoch*, op. cit., pp.49–53.

55 The party included the politician Michael Foot, Jean Floud, William Radice, Sir Richard Attenborough. Other conference participants were Bella Akhmadulina, Chinua Achebe, Régis Debray, Mulk Raj Anand, Yuri Zhukov, Simone Weil, Germaine Greer.

56 Indira Gandhi was shot by one of her bodyguards on 21 October 1984.

57 *London Review of Books*, 7 May 1987, pp.20–1.

58 *London Review of Books*, letters, 17 February 2000.

59 Letter to PF, dated 'St Valentine's Day'. Since the SDP was formed in March 1981, the year is probably 1982.

60 Michael Brock, official historian of Oxford University (who shared at Corpus with Pat Denby), LTA, 22 June 1999.

61 Unpublished interview with RW, 17 July 1991.

62 J: 5 March 1989.

63 Letter to PF, late 1982.

64 Letter to Kenneth Baker, 25 April 1988. Baker was Secretary of State 1986–89.

65 It was replaced by the University Funding Council (UFC).

66 Kenneth Baker, LTA, 17 November 1999.

67 To PF, undated but probably 1975.

68 The photograph of Rene at Buckingham Palace in JB, *Iris*, op. cit., described as taken on the occasion of IM's DBE, is in fact on the awarding of her CBE. Rene had died two years before Iris was awarded the DBE.

69 In this she followed, reputedly, her father as well as, by common consent, her elder sister Gertie.

70 Letter to Harry Weinberger, 28 April 1986.

71 J: 14 March 1989.

72 J: 'His letter is very brief: nothing

but "Thank you very much – I look forward to reading your novel. It is for me a double joy. As I expect you know I've been two or three times to London, always on the spur of the moment, etc." Very brief.'

73 See Conradi, *The Saint and the Artist*, op. cit.

74 To Norah Smallwood, January 1963. One hundred pages of poems, entitled 'Conversations with a Prince', are at the Brotherton Library, Leeds University.

75 Adam Mars-Jones, 'Conversation with a Mastermind', *Sunday Times*, 29 September 1995.

76 See n30 above.

77 Powell, *Journals 1987–89*, op. cit., p.186.

78 In April 1989.

79 Kate Kellaway, 'Pile High Club', *Observer*, Life section, 24 September 1995, pp.68–9.

80 *Spectator*, 27 May 1995, p.63.

81 EC, *Memoirs*, op. cit., p.825; *A Word Child* p.80. A Czech friend or her trip to Prague in 1969 might also, of course, have taught her this.

82 EC's publishers plan a collection which is likely to include this.

83 Jeremy Adler confirmed that Canetti was entirely *compos mentis* to the end. CWA, 8 May, 2001.

84 IM's Englishness, which A.S. Byatt had praised in 1989, was apparently now a liability. Byatt too admitted 'to a certain curiosity as to what she would have been like if he [JB] hadn't made her as English as she has become'. Ian Hamilton, 'An Oxford Union', *New Yorker*, 19 February 1996.

85 'John Haffenden Talks to Iris Murdoch', op. cit..

86 Rosemary Varty.

87 25 July 1994.

CHAPTER 21

1 To Rosen's delight, IM wrote him a 'fan letter' (her expression) some time in the late 1980s, *à propos* his collection of essays *The Quarrel Between Philosophy and Poetry*. He then sent her a copy of his *Plato's Symposium*, which she received with great generosity. A friendship developed, based on a shared love of writing and reading poetry, and frustration with 'analytical' philosophy. IM read his manuscript *The Question of Being*, a very extensive criticism of Heidegger, for Yale University Press and cited him admiringly in *Metaphysics as a Guide to Morals* as the philosopher who best understood the contemporary scene.

2 J: 20 April 1987: 'I am spending a lot of time trying at last to understand Heidegger – all his ideas, and his development. Wish I had thought of this earlier!'

3 The conference's proceedings were published as *Iris Murdoch and the Search for Human Goodness*, op. cit.

4 Papers included Maria Antonaccio, 'The Virtues of Metaphysics: A Review of Iris Murdoch's Philosophical Writings'; Richard Moran, 'Vision, Choice and Existentialism'; Roger Crisp, 'Moral Value: Iris Murdoch and the Benefits of Stopping to Look'; Martha Nussbaum, 'Love, Perception and Illusion in *The Black Prince*'; and Peter J. Conradi, 'Holy Fool and Magus: The Uses of Biography in *Under the Net* and *The Flight from the Enchanter*'.

5 MM's *Heart and Mind, Beast and Man, Wisdom, Interest and Wonder, Utopias, Dolphins and Computers* all cite IM.

6 Nina Coltart, *Slouching Towards Bethlehem* (London, 1993), pp.186–7.

7 EM, p.27.

8 *A Fairly Honourable Defeat*, p.186.
9 Interview on Icelandic TV, shown on *Bookmark*, BBC TV, 4 September 1981.
10 4 April 1982.
11 J: 18 January 1994.
12 A phrase used by a friend in letter to JB.
13 See e.g. 'John Haffenden Talks to Iris Murdoch', op. cit.; or *The Good Apprentice, passim.*
14 Canon Brian Mountford recalls how IM, in the early 1990s, would occasionally be seen standing in the back of Oxford's University Church of St Mary the Virgin, and gave one talk there, in the library: so many came to hear her that the doors had to be closed once the room was filled, to the vexation of those excluded. But she could never entirely leave Christianity, she could never embrace its myths of Virgin Birth and Resurrection either; and God (see Afterword) remained to her an anti-religious bribe, like the idea of an afterlife.
15 Our 1998 Christmas gift. IM divined his name.
16 Lorna Sage to JB, 22 March 1999.

17 Interview with Susan Hill, *Bookshelf,* BBC Radio 4, 30 April 1982.

AFTERWORD

1 Antonaccio and Schweiker, *Iris Murdoch and the Search for Human Goodness*, op. cit., p.3.
2 *The Times*, 28 November 2000.
3 Harold Bloom, 'A Comedy of Worldly Salvation', *New York Times Book Review*, 12 January 1986, pp.30–1.
4 Sage, 'In Praise of Mess', op. cit.
5 *Time*, 22 February 1999.
6 For a further exploration see Peter J. Conradi, 'Iris Murdoch and Dostoevsky', in R. Todd, *Encounters with Iris Murdoch*, op. cit.; reprinted in *Dostoevski and Britain*, ed. William Leatherbarrow (Oxford and New York, 1995), pp.277–91.
7 Joan McBreen (ed.), *The White Page (An Bhilog Bhan): Twentieth Century Irish Women Poets* (Dublin, 1999). IM's 'Motorist and Dead Bird' is on p.174.
8 *Somerville College Report,* 1998, pp.135–9.

SELECT BIBLIOGRAPHY

See also the bibliography in Peter J. Conradi, *The Saint and the Artist: A Study of the Fiction of Iris Murdoch* (3rd edition, London, 2001), and John Fletcher and Cheryl Bove, *Iris Murdoch: A Primary and Secondary Annotated Bibliography* (London and New York, 1995; new edition forthcoming).

CHAPTER 1

Elizabeth Bowen, *Bowen's Court* (London, 1942)

David Fitzpatrick, *Oceans of Consolation* (Melbourne, 1994)

Roy Foster, *Paddy and Mr Punch: Connections in Irish and English History* (London, 1993), Chapter 11, 'Protestant Magic', pp.215ff

Roy Foster, *W.B. Yeats: A Life, Vol. 1* (Oxford, 1997)

Arthur Green: 'The Worlds of Iris Murdoch', *Iris Murdoch Newsletter*, no. 10, 1996

Lionel James, *The History of King Edward's Horse* (London, 1921)

F.S.L. Lyons, *Ireland Since the Famine* (London, 1973)

R.B. McDowell, *Crisis and Decline: The Fate of the Southern Unionists* (Dublin, 1997)

John O'Hart's Irish Pedigrees (Dublin, 1884)

Douglas Pike (ed.), *Australian Dictionary of National Biography* (Melbourne, 1968)

Meg Probyn (ed.), *Marriage Lines: The Richardson Family Letters* (Melbourne, 2000)

Jacinta Prunty, *Dublin Slums, 1800–1935: A Study in Urban Geography* (Dublin, 1998)

A. Rowan, *Pevsner's Guide to North-West Ulster* (London, 1979)

H. Staples (ed.), *The Ireland of Sir Jonah Barrington: Selections from his Personal Sketches* (London, 1968)

Tullinisken Notebook V, LDS film 1279325, compiled by the

Rev. Henry Gordon Waller Scott. Presented to Armagh
County Museum, The Mall, East Armagh, by Mrs Gordon
Scott
Patrick West, 'When the IRA's Alarm Clock Struck', *Spectator*, 16
January 1999, p.12
Max Wright, *Told in Gath* (Belfast, 1990)

CHAPTER 2

Barbara Denny, *The Play-Master of Blankenburg: The Story of
Friedrich Froebel, 1782–1852* (London, 1982)
Margaret Gardiner, *A Scatter of Memories* (London, 1988)
Iris Murdoch, Barbara Denny and others, contributions to 'The
Early Childhood Collection' held at Froebel College,
Roehampton
Old Froebelian Newsletter, 1934 and 1936
Peter Weston, *Friedrich Froebel: His Life, Times and Significance*
(Roehampton, 2000)

CHAPTER 3

Badminton School Magazine
Robert Conquest, *Reflections on a Ravished Century* (London,
1999)
Joseph Cooper, *Facing the Music* (London, 1979)
Katherine Frank, *Indira: The Life of Indira Gandhi* (London,
2001)
Ideal Home and Gardening, August 1945, p.89 *et seq*
Dulcibel MacKenzie, *Steps to the Bar* (Greengate Press,
1988)
J. Storry (ed.), *At Badminton with BMB, by Those who were There*
(Badminton School, Bristol, 1982)
Anne Valery, *The Edge of a Smile* (London, 1977)

CHAPTER 4

Pauline Adams, *Somerville for Women: An Oxford College* (Oxford,
1996)
G. Bush, *An Unsentimental Education* (London, 1990), pp.111–12
Cherwell, LVI, no.3, 13 May 1939, pp.50–1

Vera Farnell, *A Somervillian Looks Back* (Oxford, 1948)
E. Whitley (ed.), *The Graduates* (London, 1986), pp.73ff

CHAPTER 5

Kingsley Amis, *Memoirs* (Penguin, 1991)
Perry Anderson, 'Components of the National Scene', in Robin
    Blackburn and Alexander Cockburn (eds), *Student Power*
    (London, 1970)
M.P. Ashley and C.T. Saunders, *Red Oxford* (Oxford, 1934)
Susan Crosland, *Tony Crosland* (London, 1982)
Kenneth Dover, *Marginal Comment* (London, 1994)
Denis Healey, *Time of my Life* (London, 1989)
G. Hirschfeld, '*Durchgangsland England? Die Britische "Academic
    Community" und die wissenschaftliche Emigration aus Deutschland*',
    in *England? Aber wo liegt es? Deutsche und österreichische
    Emigranten in Grossbritannien 1933–45*, ed. C. Brunson *et al*
    (Munich, 1996), pp.59–70
Sally Humphreys, eulogy of Isobel Henderson, *Somerville Report*,
    1967
Roy Jenkins, *A Life at the Centre* (London, 1992)
Nicholas Lash, obituary of Donald MacKinnon, *Guardian*, 5
    March 1994
Donald MacKinnon, 'Evil and Personal Responsibility', *Listener*,
    18 March 1948, pp.457–9
Donald MacKinnon, 'The Crux of Morality', *Listener*, 16
    December 1948, pp.926–7
Donald MacKinnon, 'Things and Persons', from *Proceedings of the
    Aristotelian Society*, Supplementary Vol. XXII, 1948, pp.179–89
Arnoldo Momigliano, *Quinto contributo all storia degli studi classici e
    mondo antico* (Rome, 1977), pp.1026–9
Philip Toynbee, *Friends Apart* (London, 1954)
Mary Warnock, *A Memoir: People and Places* (London, 2000)
Gordon Williams, 'Eulogy of Eduard Fraenkel', *Proceedings of the
    British Association*, LVI, 1970 (Oxford, 1972), p.438

CHAPTER 6

Jane Williams (ed.), *Tambimuttu: Bridge Between Two Worlds*
    (London, 1989)

CHAPTER 7

Stowers Johnson, *Agents Extraordinary* (London, 1975)

Major Frank Thompson, Bulgarian TV film, 1977, now held in
British Film Institute, London

Luisa Passerini, *Europe in Love, Love in Europe: Imagination
and Politics in Britain Between the Wars* (London,1999),
pp.307–17

Arnold Rattenbury, 'Convenient Death of a Hero', review of E.P.
Thompson, *Beyond the Frontier, London Review of Books*, 8 May
1997, pp.12–13

Raina Sharova, in *News Chronicle*, 8 March 1945

State archives in Vielki Tarnovo (Bulgaria), letter N-4454/19–20
December 1945

E.P. Thompson, *Beyond the Frontier* (Stanford, 1997)

T.J. and E.P. Thompson (eds), *There is a Spirit in Europe: A
Memoir of Frank Thompson* (London, 1947)

Slavcho Trunski, *Grateful Bulgaria* (Sofia, 1979)

CHAPTER 8

Jo Grimond, *Memoirs* (London, 1979), pp.133–40

D. Johnson on J. Bennett's *Aragon, Londres et la France libre*, in
TLS, 10 December 1999, p.28

CHAPTER 9

Dr Edgar Chandler, *The High Tower of Refuge: The Inspiring Story of
Refugee Relief Throughout the World* (London, 1959)

John Corsellis, *Slovenian Phoenix* (forthcoming)

Donald MacKinnon, ed. A.R. Vidler, *Objections to Christian Belief*
(London, 1963), pp.11ff

Donald MacKinnon, 'Intercommunion: A Comment', in D.
MacKinnon, *The Stripping of the Altars* (London, 1969)

Meeting Writers No 5, BBC European Productions, ref. no. 4222, 4
February 1957

Iris Murdoch, UNRRA reminiscences, Bodleian MSS.Eng.c.4718,
fols.132–62; c4733, item 16

New York Times, Living Arts section, 22 February 1990,
p.B2

Nigel Nicolson, *Long Life: Memoirs* (London, 1997), Chapter 5, 'The Witness'

Raymond Queneau, *Journeaux 1914–1965* (Paris, 1966)

The Quest for Queneau, BBC Radio 3, 11 October 1985

Roger Shattuck, 'Farce and Philosophy' (article-review of Queneau's *Stories and Remarks*), *New York Review of Books*, 22 February 2001, pp.22–5

Richard Symonds, 'Amiable Despair – UNRRA in Austria', Bodleian MSS.Eng 4703, UN Careers Records Project

Nicolai Tolstoi, *Victims of Yalta* (London, 1977)

Nikolai Tolstoi, *The Minister and the Massacres* (London, 1986)

G. Woodbridge (ed.), *The History of UNRRA* (New York, 1950), 2 vols

CHAPTER 10

Peter Geach (ed.), *Wittgenstein's Lectures on Philosophical Psychology in 1946–7* (London and New York, 1988)

Brian McGuinness, *Wittgenstein, A Life: Young Ludwig (1889–1921)* (London, 1988)

Ved Mehta, *The Fly and the Flybottle* (Harmondsworth, 1963)

Jeffrey Meyers, *Privileged Moments: Encounters with Writers* (Wisconsin, 2000)

P. Odifreddi, *Kreiseliana: About and Around Georg Kreisel* (Wellesley, 1996)

Adam Phillips, *On Flirtation* (London, 1994)

'Some Hitherto Unpublished Letters from Ludwig Wittgenstein to Georg Henrik von Wright', *Cambridge Review*, vol. 104, no. 2273, 28 February 1983, p.57

Ludwig Wittgenstein, ed. B. McGuinness and G.H. von Wright, *Cambridge Letters* (Oxford, 1995), p.305

CHAPTER 11

S. Aldwinckle, *Christ's Shadow in Plato's Cave: A Meditation on the Substance of Love*, foreword by Iris Murdoch (Amate Press, Oxford, 1990)

Wendy Campbell-Purdie and Fenner Brockway, *Women Against the Desert*, with forewords by Iris Murdoch and Lord Boyd Orr (London, 1967), pp.11–13

Humphrey Carpenter, *The Envy of the World: Fifty Years of the BBC Third Programme and Radio 3, 1946–96* (London, 1996), p.111 *et seq*

Dan Davin, *Closing Times* (London, 1975)

Katrin Fitzherbert, *True to Both My Selves* (London, 1997), p.281

Jennifer Hart, *Ask me no More* (London, 1998), Chapter 9

Graham Lord, *Just the One: The Wives and Times of Jeffrey Bernard, 1932–97* (London, 1997)

Basil Mitchell (ed.), *Faith and Logic: Oxford Essays in Philosophical Theology* (London, 1957)

Basil Mitchell, in *Philosophers who Believe: The Spiritual Journeys of Eleven Leading Thinkers*, ed. J.K. Clark (Intervarsity Press, 1993)

Frances Partridge, *Memories* (London, 1981)

Marjorie Reeves, *St Anne's College: An Informal History 1879–1979* (Abingdon, 1979)

Robin Waterfield, introduction to Iris Murdoch, *The Existentialist Political Myth* (Delos Press, 1989)

CHAPTER 12

Jeremy Adler, 'An Oriental in the West: The Originality of Franz Baermann Steiner as Poet and Anthropologist', *TLS*, 7 October 1994, pp.16–17

Jeremy Adler, 'The One who Got Away: H.G. Adler and Theodor Adorno: Two Approaches to Culture After Auschwitz', *TLS*, 4 October 1996, pp.18–19

M. Atze (ed.), '*Ortlose Botschaft: Der Freundekreis H.G. Adler, Elias Canetti und Franz Baermann Steiner im englischen exil*', *Marbacher Magazin*, 84, 1998 for the exhibition in the Schiller Nationalmuseum, Marbach, September–November 1998

Michael Hamburger, *A Mug's Game: Intermittent Memoirs* (London, 1975)

Franz Baermann Steiner, *Fluchtvergnüglichkeit: Feststellungen und Versuche, eine Auswahl von M. Hermann-Röttgen* (Flugasche Verlag, Stuttgart, 1988)

Franz Baermann Steiner: Modern Poetry in Translation, new series, no. 2, autumn 1992, with translations and an introduction by Michael Hamburger (King's College, London, 1992)

Franz Baermann Steiner, ed. Jeremy Adler and Richard Fardon, *Selected Writings Vol. I: Taboo, Truth and Religion* (Oxford and New York, 1999)

Franz Baermann Steiner, ed. Jeremy Adler and Richard Fardon, *Selected Writings Vol. II: Orientpolitik, Value and Civilisation* (Oxford and New York, 1999)

'Franz Baermann Steiner Celebrated: From Prague Poet to Oxford Anthropologist, a Workshop' at the Institute of Germanic Studies, London, 11 February 2000

Franz Baermann Steiner papers in Deutsches Literaturarchiv, Schiller Nationalmuseum, Marbach, Germany

CHAPTER 13

Jeremy Adler on Veza Canetti's novel *Die Gelbestrasse*, in *European*, 22–24 June 1990

John Bayley, 'Canetti and Power', *London Review of Books*, 17 December 1981–20 January 1982, pp.65–7

Saul Bellow, *Herzog* (New York, 1961), p.316

Douglas Botting, *Gavin Maxwell: A Life* (London, 1993)

Elias Canetti, *Auto da Fé*, trans. Veronica Wedgwood (London, 1946; US title *Tower of Babel*)

Elias Canetti, *Crowds and Power*, trans. Carol Stewart (London, 1962)

Elias Canetti, *Aufzeichnungen* (Munich, 1992–93)

Elias Canetti, *Notes from Hampstead, 1954–71* (New York, 1998)

Elias Canetti, *Memoirs* (New York, 1999)

John Carey, *The Intellectuals and the Masses, 1880–1939* (London, 1992), pp.29–31

Centre Georges Pompidou catalogue for the exhibition 'Elias Canetti', 1995

Rudi Nassauer, *The Cuckoo* (London, 1962)

Julian Preece, 'The Rediscovered Writings of Veza Magd-Canetti: On the Psychology of Subservience', in *Modern Austrian Literature*, vol. 28, no.2, 1995, pp.53–70

Kathleen Raine, *Autobiographies* (London, 1991)

Anna Sebastian, *The Monster* (London, 1944)

Anna Sebastian, *The Dreams* (London, 1950)

Secret History: Killer Fog, Channel 4 TV, September 1999

Susan Sontag, 'Mind as Passion', *New York Review of Books*, 25 September 1980, pp.47–52

Frances Spalding, *Stevie Smith* (London, 1988)

CHAPTER 14

John Bayley, *Iris: A Memoir of Iris Murdoch* (London, 1998; US
 title *Elegy for Iris*)
John Bayley, *Iris and the Friends: A Year of Memories* (London,
 1999; US title *Iris and her Friends*)
John Bayley, *Widower's House* (London, 2001)
Elias Canetti, *The Human Province*, trans. J. Neugroschel
 (London, 1985)
Clive Donner, 'I Once Met Iris Murdoch', *The Oldie*, September
 1999, p.15
Yorick Smythies, *The Changing World*, no. 1, summer 1947,
 pp.72–81
A.N. Wilson, review of John Bayley, *Iris: A Memoir of Iris Murdoch*,
 Literary Review, September 1998, p.18

CHAPTER 15

Frank Baldanza, 'The Manuscript of Iris Murdoch's *A Severed
 Head*', in *Journal of Modern Literature*, February 1973, pp.75–90
Jeremy Lewis, *Kindred Spirits: Adrift in Literary London* (London,
 1995) Chapter 7, 'King William IV Street'
Raymond Mortimer, in *Sunday Times*, 5 May 1957

CHAPTER 16

The Autobiography and Correspondence of Mary Granville, Mrs Delaney,
 vol. 2 (London, 1861)
Roy Foster, *Modern Ireland 1600–1972* (London, 1988)
Frances Gerard, *Some Celebrated Irish Beauties of the Last Century*
 (London, 1895)
Victoria Glendinning, *Rebecca West: A Life* (London, 1987),
 pp.116–17
The Grand Juries of Westmeath (privately printed, c1840; held at
 Westmeath County Library, Mullingar, County Westmeath)
Manuscripts of the Earl of Egmont: Vol. 3, 1739–1747 (HMSO,
 London, 1923)
Gearoid O'Brien, *Belvedere: House, Gardens and Park* (Mullingar,
 2000)
Peter Somerville-Large, *The Irish Country House* (London, 1995)

CHAPTER 17

Noel Annan, *The Dons* (London, 1999)
Christopher Frayling, *The Royal College of Art: 150 Years of Art and Design* (London, 1987)
Paddy Kitchen, *A Fleshly School* (London, 1970)
Iris Murdoch, short tribute added to Eve Watt's obituary of Esme Ross Langley, *Guardian*, 25 July 1992, p.35
Frederic Samson, *Concepts of Man*, foreword by Christopher Cornford (RCA, 1979)
Frederic Samson, *Dotes and Antidotes* (RCA, 1979)
Alex Seago, *Burning the Box of Beautiful Things* (OUP, 1995)

CHAPTER 18

John Bayley, *Tolstoi and the Novel* (London, 1966)
Vladimir Bukovsky, *To Build a Castle: My Life as a Dissenter* (London, 1978)
Tim Devlin and Mary Warnock, 'The Blackboard Jungle', article-review of *What Must We Teach?*, *New Statesman*, 21 October 1977, pp.546–8
Andrew Motion, *Philip Larkin: A Writer's Life* (London, 1993), pp.318–19
Janet Stone, *Thinking Faces 1953–79* (London, 1988)

CHAPTER 19

Malcolm Bradbury, *Who do you Think you Are?* (London, 1976), pp.166–71
British Library, Modern Manuscripts, Peggy Ramsey archive, deposit number 9625
John Fletcher, 'A Novelist's Plays: Iris Murdoch and the Theatre', in *Essays in Theatre*, vol. 4, no.1, November 1985, pp.3–20
A.N. Wilson, 'In Memory of Iris Murdoch', *Spectator*, 18–25 December 1999, pp.79–81
A.N. Wilson, 'Iris Murdoch and the Characters of Love', in *News from the Royal Society of Literature*, 2000, pp.56–65

CHAPTER 20

Elias Canetti, unpublished reminiscences
Andrew Harvey, *The Making of a Mystic*, Channel 4 TV, 1993
S.L. Jaki, *Lord Gifford and his Lectures: A Centenary Retrospect*
  (Edinburgh, 1995), p.42
Kate Kellaway, 'Pile High Club', *Observer* Life, 24 September
  1995, pp.68–9
Iris Murdoch on Harry Weinberger in brochures for Herbert Art
  Gallery, Jordan Well, Coventry, 26 March–24 April 1983; and
  Duncan Campbell Contemporary Art (undated, but autumn
  1994)
Martha Nussbaum, 'Love and Vision: Iris Murdoch on Eros and
  the Individual', in *Iris Murdoch and the Search for Human
  Goodness*, ed. M. Antonaccio and W. Schweiker (Chicago,
  1996)
Anthony Powell, *Journals 1987–89* (London, 1996), p.186
Stephen Spender, ed. J. Goldsmith, *Journals 1939–83* (London,
  1985), pp.409–10
E.P. Thompson, 'Diary', in *London Review of Books*, 7 May 1987,
  pp.20–1
W (formerly *Women's Wear Daily*), 18–25 October 1985, p.54 *et
  seq*

NOVELS BY IRIS MURDOCH

Under the Net (London, 1954)
The Flight from the Enchanter (London, 1956)
The Sandcastle (London, 1957)
The Bell (London, 1958)
A Severed Head (London, 1961)
An Unofficial Rose (London, 1962)
The Unicorn (London, 1963)
The Italian Girl (London, 1964)
The Red and the Green (London, 1965)
The Time of the Angels (London, 1966)
The Nice and the Good (London, 1968)
Bruno's Dream (London, 1969)
A Fairly Honourable Defeat (London, 1970)

An Accidental Man (London, 1971)
The Black Prince (London, 1973)
The Sacred and Profane Love Machine (London, 1974)
A Word Child (London, 1975)
Henry and Cato (London, 1976)
The Sea, The Sea (London, 1978)
Nuns and Soldiers (London, 1980)
The Philosopher's Pupil (London, 1983)
The Good Apprentice (London, 1985)
The Book and the Brotherhood (London, 1987)
The Message to the Planet (London, 1989)
The Green Knight (London, 1993)
Jackson's Dilemma (London, 1995)

PHILOSOPHY BY IRIS MURDOCH

Sartre: Romantic Rationalist (second edition, London, 1987)
The Sovereignty of Good (London, 1970)
The Fire and the Sun: Why Plato Banished the Artists (London, 1977)
Acastos: Two Platonic Dialogues (London, 1986)
Metaphysics as a Guide to Morals (London, 1992)
Existentialists and Mystics: Writings on Philosophy and Literature, ed. Peter J. Conradi (London, 1997)

PLAYS BY IRIS MURDOCH

A Severed Head (with J.B. Priestley) (London, 1964)
The Three Arrows with *The Servants and the Snow* (London, 1973)
Joanna, Joanna (London, 1994)
The One Alone (a radio play broadcast on BBC Radio 3, 13 February 1987) (London, 1995)

POETRY BY IRIS MURDOCH

A Year of Birds (with wood engravings by Reynolds Stone)
(London, 1984)
Poems by Iris Murdoch, ed. Yozo Muroya and Paul Hullah (Japan,
1997)

SELECTED INTERVIEWS

See also Gillian Dooley, *Conversations with Iris Murdoch* (University
of South Carolina, forthcoming)

1950s

BBC European Productions, *Meeting Writers*, no. 5, ref. no. 4222,
4 February 1957
Anon, 'Mainly about Authors', *Bookman*, 26 November 1958
Anon, 'Portrait Gallery', *Sunday Times*, 17 May 1959, p.5

1960s

Dilys Rowe, 'Sympathetic Fellow', *Guardian*, 1 February 1960, p.6
John Barrows, 'Living Writers – 7', *John o' London's*, 4 May 1961,
p.495
Ved Mehta, 'Onward and Upward with the Arts: A Battle Against
the Bewitchment of our Intelligence', *New Yorker*, 9 December
1961, pp.59–159
Harold Hobson, 'Lunch with Iris Murdoch', *Sunday Times*, 11
March 1962, p.28
Frank Kermode, 'Myth, Reality, and Fiction', *Listener*, 30 August
1962, p.311
Frank Kermode, 'The House of Fiction: Interviews with Seven
English Novelists', *Partisan Review*, xxx, 1963, pp.61–82
Anon, *The Times*, 13 February 1964, p.15
Ruth Heyd, 'An Interview with Iris Murdoch', *University of
Windsor Review*, spring 1965, pp.138–43
F. Dillistone, 'Christ and Myth', *Frontier*, August 1965, pp.219–21
Stephanie Nettell, 'An Exclusive Interview', *Books and Bookmen*,
September 1966, pp.14, 15, 66
David McGill, 'Talking with a Traditionalist', *New Zealand
Listener*, 28 April 1967, p.7

Peter Lewis, 'Crying Blue Murdoch', *Daily Mail*, 30 January
1968

Laura Cecil, 'How to Write a Novel', *Cover*, no. 4, March 1968,
pp.9–10

Ronald Bryden (with A.S. Byatt), 'Talking to Iris Murdoch',
Listener, 4 April 1968, pp.433–4

W.K. Rose, 'An Interview with Iris Murdoch', *Shenandoah*, xix,
winter 1968, pp.3–22

M. Jarrett-Kerr, 'Good, Evil and Morality', *CR: Quarterly Review of
the Community of the Resurrection*, no. 266, Michaelmas 1969,
pp.17–23

1970s

Ronald Hayman, 'Out of the Tutorial', *The Times*, 30 September
1970, p.13

Jane Taylor, 'Iris Murdoch Talks to Jane Taylor', *Books and
Bookmen*, April 1971, pp.26–7

A.S. Byatt, 'Now Read On', BBC Radio 4, 27 October
1971

David Pears, 'The Idea of Freedom', Logic Lane/Oxford
Philosophy series, Chanan Films Ltd, 1971

Hugh Hebert, 'The Iris Problem', *Guardian*, 24 October 1972,
p.10

Gill Davie, 'I Should Hate to be Alive and not Writing a Novel:
Iris Murdoch on her Work', *Woman's Journal*, October 1975,
pp.64–5

Malcolm Bradbury, 'Iris Murdoch in conversation, 27 February
1976', British Council tape no. RI 2001

Simon Blow, 'An Interview with Iris Murdoch', *Spectator*, 25
September 1976, pp.24–5

Malcolm Bradbury and Lorna Sage, Interview, A-V Centre, 20
October 1976

Stephen Glover, 'Iris Murdoch Talks to Stephen Glover, *New
Review*, iii, November 1976, pp.56–9

Michael Bellamy, 'An Interview with Iris Murdoch', *Contemporary
Literature*, xviii, 1977, pp.129–40

Valentina Ivasheva, 'Epistolatory Dialogue', *Soviet Literature*, xi,
1977, pp.48–61

H.D. Purcell, 'Faust Lives OK', *Books and Bookmen*, November
1977, p.52

Bryan Magee, *Men of Ideas: Some Creators of Contemporary Philosophy* (London, 1978), pp. 264–84

Jack Biles, 'An Interview with Iris Murdoch', *Studies in the Literary Imagination*, xi, fall 1978, pp.115–25

Peter Lewis, 'On the Crest of a Wave', *Daily Mail*, 23 November 1978

Peter Lennon, 'The Odd (but Triumphant) World of Iris Murdoch', *Sunday Times*, 26 November 1978

Derwent May, 'Iris Murdoch's Best Seller in the Swim', *Observer*, 26 November 1978

Jean-Louis Chevalier, '*Rencontres avec Iris Murdoch*' (Centre de recherches de littérature et linguistique des pays de langue anglaise, Université de Caen, 1978)

1980s

Tom Sutcliffe, 'Interview with Iris Murdoch', *Guardian*, 15 September 1980

Anon, 'An Interview with Iris Murdoch', American *Vogue*, March 1981, pp.329, 367

Antony Curtis, 'Novels up to Now: Programme 3 – Ordeals and Fake Ordeals', radio interview, tape no.TLN22/207Y861, 1 August 1981

Anon, interview on Icelandic TV, shown on *Bookmark*, BBC TV, 4 September 1981

C.W.E. Bigsby, in H. Ziegler and C.W.E. Bigsby (eds), *The Radical Imagination and the Liberal Tradition: Interviews with English and American Novelists* (London, 1982), pp.209–30

Pamela Callaghan, 'Interview with Iris Murdoch', *Weekend*, BBC Radio 4, 18 April 1982

Susan Hill, 'Interview with Iris Murdoch', *Bookshelf*, BBC Radio 4, 30 April 1982

John Haffenden, 'John Haffenden Talks to Iris Murdoch', *Literary Review*, lviii, April 1983, pp.31–5

Rachel Billington, 'Crusading in a Fantasy World', *The Times*, 25 April 1983, p.9

Peter J. Conradi, unpublished interview, September 1983

Simon Price, 'Iris Murdoch: An Interview with Simon Price', *Omnibus*, March 1984, pp.1–4

William Slaymaker, 'An Interview with Iris Murdoch', *Papers on Language and Literature*, 21 April 1985, pp.425–32

Niall MacMonagle, 'Murdoch Magic', *Irish Times*, 22 July 1985

Adam Mars-Jones, 'Conversation with a Mastermind', *Sunday Times*, 29 September 1985

Edward Whitley, 'Iris Murdoch', in E. Whitley (ed.), *The Graduates* (London, 1986), pp.63–74

Anon, 'An Evening with Iris Murdoch', *Bristol Medical-Chirurgical Journal*, August 1986, p.91

Eric Robson, in *Revelations: Glimpses of Reality*, ed. R. Lello (London, 1985), pp.82–90

Niall MacMonagle, 'A Fairly Honourable Success', *Dublin Sunday Tribune*, 6 September 1987

Bryan Appleyard, 'Iris Murdoch as she is Writ', *The Times*, 23 January 1988

Barbara S. Heusel, 'A Dialogue with Iris Murdoch', *University of Windsor Review*, xxi (1), 1988, pp.1–13

Jonathan Miller, *My God*, Granada TV, 3 April 1988

Sue Summers, 'The Lost Loves of Iris Murdoch', *Mail on Sunday*, 5 June 1988, p.17

David Gerard, 'Iris Murdoch', in *Women Writers Talk: Interviews with Ten Women Writers*, ed. O. Kenyon, (Allen & Unwin, Sydney, 1989), pp.134–47

Nigella Lawson, 'The Warm-Hearted Crusader for Good', *Sunday Times*, 16 April 1989, p.C7

Ed Vulliamy, 'The Murdoch Dialogues', *Guardian*, 22–23 April 1989, p.19

Anon, 'A Believer in the Triumph of Good', *Independent*, 29 April 1989

Roger Lewis, 'A Dangerous Dame', *Telegraph Weekend Magazine*, 8 July 1989, pp.16–19

Bookmark, 'A Certain Lady', BBC TV, 29 December 1989

1990s

Jeffrey Meyers, 'The Art Of Fiction: cxvii – Iris Murdoch', *Paris Review*, 115, 1990, pp.207–25

Richard Wollheim, unpublished interview with Iris Murdoch in California, 17 July 1991

Jeffrey Meyers, 'An Interview with Iris Murdoch', *Denver Quarterly*, xxvi, 1992

Angela Lambert, 'In the Presence of Great Goodness', *Independent*, 8 September 1992

Bryan Appleyard, 'Paradox of All the Virtues', *The Times*, 3
    October 1992, pp.4–5
Michael Kustow, 'Boundary Breaker and Moral Maker', *Guardian*,
    8 October 1992, p.23
Shena Mackay, 'When Shena Met Iris', *Independent*, 11
    September 1993, pp.40–3
David Blow, 'The Unofficial Wandering Angel', *Waterstone's
    Christmas Catalogue*, 1993, p.5
'Who is the Experiencer?', Iris Murdoch in conversation with
    Krishnamurti, in *Questioning Krishnamurti* (London, 1996),
    pp.99–128   *

For the *Iris Murdoch Newsletter* contact Dr Anne Rowe, 21 Upper
Park Road, Kingston-on-Thames, KT2 5LB, in the UK; or Tony
Bove, 5400 W. Autumn Springs Court, Muncie, Indiana 47304,
in the the USA

INDEX

Works by Iris Murdoch appear under title; works by others under author's name